Scots Commercial Law

CW01066965

Scots Commercial Law

Edited by

A D M Forte MA, LLB
Professor of Commercial Law, University of Aberdeen

Edinburgh
Butterworths
1997

United Kingdom	Butterworths, a Division of Reed Elsevier (UK) Ltd, 4 Hill Street, EDINBURGH EH2 3JZ and Halsbury House, 35 Chancery Lane, LONDON WC2A 1EL
Australia	Butterworths, SYDNEY, MELBOURNE, BRISBANE, ADELAIDE, PERTH, CANBERRA and HOBART
Canada	Butterworths Canada Ltd, TORONTO and VANCOUVER
Ireland	Butterworth (Ireland) Ltd, DUBLIN
Malaysia	Malayan Law Journal Sdn Bhd, KUALA LUMPUR
New Zealand	Butterworths of New Zealand Ltd, WELLINGTON and AUCKLAND
Singapore	Reed Elsevier (Singapore) Pte Ltd, SINGAPORE
South Africa	Butterworth Publishers (Pty) Ltd, DURBAN
USA	Michie, CHARLOTTESVILLE, VIRGINIA

All rights reserved. No part of this publication may be reproduced in any material form (including photocopying or storing it in any medium by electronic means and whether or not transiently or incidentally to some other use of this publication) without the written permission of the copyright owner except in accordance with the provisions of the Copyright, Design and Patents Act 1988 or under the terms of a licence issued by the Copyright Licensing Agency Ltd, 90 Tottenham Court Road, London, England W1P 9HE. Applications for the copyright owner's written permission to reproduce any part of this publication should be addressed to the publisher.

Warning: The doing of an unauthorised act in relation to a copyright work may result in both civil claim for damages and criminal prosecution.

© Reed Elsvier (UK) Ltd 1997

The moral right of the author has been asserted. A CIP Catalogue record for this book is available from the British Library.

ISBN 0 406 891 648

Typeset by Phoenix Photosetting, Chatham, Kent
Printed and bound in Great Britain by Redwood Books, Trowbridge, Wiltshire

Preface

Commercial law now moves at such a pace that both academic and practising commercial lawyers are fast developing specialisms. This book reflects the divergent interests of the commercial lawyers in the Faculty of Law in the University of Aberdeen and also, of course, the subjects which are taught in the general course on commercial law in the second year of study in this faculty. Many, if not all, of these topics are also taught to students in the same year in the other law faculties of the Scottish universities and we hope that they too will find this book of interest and value. Should it also find a place in the commercial law courses undertaken in the newer Scottish universities or, indeed, in the busy practitioner's library, that would be a bonus. No two commercial lawyers today are likely to agree on what constitutes commercial law, let alone agree on what the contents of a book on the subject might be. I hope, however, that this work covers most of the topics which all would agree are part of the commercial law of Scotland.

I am grateful to the many people who helped this book on its way. To Butterworths, for suggesting that the time was right for such a work, and to each of my colleagues (not even the *Emeritus* was spared) who contributed to it, for their willingness to do so and for their forbearance in the face of my importunate demands on their time and patience. Other colleagues in the Faculty of Law are due thanks for reading and commenting on earlier drafts, and the staff of the Taylor Law Library are thanked for the service they supply without complaint and all too frequently without praise. Ray Coyle provided entertaining diversions from editorial pressures and Lucy helped me to keep a sense of proportion.

We have tried to state the law as at the end of June 1997.

A D M Forte
Aberdeen
5 August 1997

Authorship of this work

Resolution of commercial disputes
    Margaret L Ross LLB, NP, Solicitor
    Senior Lecturer in Law, University of Aberdeen

Sale and supply of goods
    Keith R Wotherspoon LLB, Dip LP
    Lecturer in Law, University of Aberdeen

Carriage of goods by road and sea
    Professor A D M Forte

    Michael C Meston MA, LLB, JD, NP
    Emeritus Professor of Law, University of Aberdeen

Insurance
    Iain MacNeil LLB, PhD
    Lecturer in Law, University of Aberdeen

Commercial paper – negotiable instruments
    Professor A D M Forte

Rights in security
    Scott C Styles MA, LLB, Dip LP
    Lecturer in Law, University of Aberdeen

Bankruptcy
    Donna McKenzie-Skene LLB, Dip LP, NP
    Lecturer in Law, University of Aberdeen

Agency
    Judith J H Pearson LLB, LLM
    Senior Lecturer in Law, University of Aberdeen

Partnership
    Judith J H Pearson

Intellectual property
    Keith R Wotherspoon

Contents

Table of statutes

Table of orders, rules and regulations

Table of cases

List of abbreviations

AC	Law Reports, Appeal Cases (House of Lords and Privy Council) 1890–
ALR	Argus Law Reports (Australia) 1895– and Australian Law Reports 1973–
All ER	All England Law Reports 1936–
App Cas	Law Reports, Appeal Cases (House of Lords) 1875–90
B & C	Barnewall and Cresswell's Reports (King's Bench) (England) 1822–30
BCC	British Company Cases 1983–
BIE	Reports of Benelux Court of Justice
Beav	Beavan's Reports (Rolls Court) (England) 1838–66
Bell App	S S Bell's Scotch Appeals (House of Lords) 1842–50
Bos & PNR	Bosanquet and Puller's New Reports (Common Pleas) (England) 1804–07
Burr	Burrow's Reports, King's Bench, 5 vols, 1756–72
CA	Court of Appeal
CB	Common Bench (England) 1845–56
CBNS	Common Bench, New Series (England) 1856–65
CCLR	Consumer Credit Law Reports
CIPA	Journal of Chartered Institute of Patent Agents
CLR	Commonwealth Law Reports (Australia) 1903–
CMLR	Common Market Law Reports 1962–
CPD	Cape Provincial Division Reports, 1910–46
Ch	Law Reports, Chancery Division (England) 1890–
Ch App	Law Reports, Chancery Appeals (England) 1865–75
Ch D	Law Reports, Chancery Division (England) 1875–90
Cl & Fin	Clark and Finnelly's Reports (House of Lords) 1831–46
Cowp	Cowper's King's Bench Reports 1774–78
D	Dunlop's Session Cases 1838–62
De GM & G	De Gex, Macnaghten and Gordon's Reports (Chancery) (England) 1851–57
Deac	Deacon's Reports, Bankruptcy, 4 vols, 1834–40
E & B	Ellis and Blackburn's Reports (Queen's Bench) (England) 1852–58
EB & E	Ellis, Blackburn and Ellis's Reports (Queen's Bench) (England) 1858–60
ECR	European Court of Justice Reports 1954–
EIPR	European Intellectual Property Review
EMLR	Entertainment and Media Law Reports
EPOR	European Patent Office Reports

ER	English Reports 1220–1865
Exch	Exchequer Reports (England) 1847–56
F	Fraser's Session Cases 1898–1906
FC	Faculty Collection (Court of Session) 1752–1825
FSR	Fleet Street Reports
GWD	Green's Weekly Digest 1986–
H & C	Hurlstone and Coltman's Reports (Exchequer) (England) 1862–66
HL	House of Lords
HL Cas	House of Lords Cases 1847–66
Hare	Hare's Reports, Chancery (England), 11 vols, 1841–53
Hume	Hume's Decisions (Court of Session) 1781–1822
ICR	Industrial Case Reports (England) 1972–
IH	Inner House
IPR	Institute of Public Relations Intellectual Property Reports (Australia)
JC	Justiciary Cases 1917–
JLSS	Journal of the Law Society of Scotland 1956–
JR	Juridical Review 1889–
KB	Law Reports, King's Bench Division (England) 1900–52
LJ Ex	Law Journal, Exchequer (England) 1831–75
LJ Ch	Law Journal, Chancery (England) 1831–1946
LJQB	Law Journal, Queen's Bench (England) 1831–1900
LR A & E	Law Reports, Amiralty and Ecclesiastical (England) 1865–75
LR CP	Law Reports, Common Pleas (England) 1865–75
LR Eq	Law Reports, Equity (England) 1865–75
LR Exch	Law Reports, Exchequer (England) 1865–75
LR HL	Law Reports, House of Lords (England and Ireland) 1866–75
LR PC	Law Reports, Privy Council 1865–75
LR QB	Law Reports, Queen's Bench (England) 1865–75
LT	Law Times Reports (England) 1859–1947
Ll L Rep	Lloyd's List Law Reports 1919–50
Lloyd's Rep	Lloyd's List Law Reports 1951–67; Lloyd's Law Reports 1968–
M	Macpherson's Session Cases 1862–73
M & S	Maule and Selwyn's Reports (King's Bench) (England) 1813–17
M & W	Meeson and Welsby's Reports (England) 1836–73
MacG Cop Cas	MacGillivray's Copyright Cases, 9 vols, 1901–49
Macq	Macqueen's House of Lords Reports 1851–65
Mer	Merivale's Reports (Chancery) (England) 1815–17

Moo PCC	Moore's Privy Council Cases1836–63
Mor	Morison's Dictionary of Decisions (Court of Session) 1540–1808
Morr	Morrell's Reports, Bankruptcy, 10 vols, 1884–93
NE	New edition
NJ	Nederlandse Jurisprudentie (Netherlands law reports)
NLJ	New Law Journal, 1965–
OH	Outer House
OJEPO	Official Journal of the European Patent Office
P	Law Reports, Probate, Divorce and Admiralty Division (England) 1890–1971
PC	Privy Council
PD	Law Reports, Probate, Divorce and Admiralty Division (England) 1875–90
QB	Law Reports, Queen's Bench Division (England) 1891–1901, 1952–
QBD	Law Reports, Queen's Bench Division (England) 1875–1890
R	Rettie's Session Cases 1873–98
RPC	Reports of Patents, Designs and Trade Marks Cases 1884–
RTR	Road Traffic Reports 1970–
S	P Shaw's Session Cases 1821–38
SC	Session Cases 1907–
SCLR	Scottish Civil Law Reports 1987–
SLR	Scottish Law Reporter 1865–1925
SLT	Scots Law Times
SN	Session Notes 1925–48
Sh Ct	Sheriff Court
Sh Ct Rep	Sheriff Court Reports in Scottish Law Review 1885–1963
TLR	Times Law Reports
TS	Reports of the Supreme Court of the Transvaal, 1902–09
Term Rep	Term Reports (England) 1785–1800
USPQ	United States Patent Quarterly
WLR	Weekly Law Reports 1953

1 Resolution of commercial disputes

INTRODUCTION

In any commercial relationship there is scope for dispute between the parties either about the implementation or non-implementation of an obligation or about interpretation of the extent of the parties' obligations. Such disputes require to be resolved, and in the commercial setting it is important to the completion of the commercial transaction, as well as to preservation of the parties' commercial relationship, present and future, that the dispute is settled quickly and effectively. Methods of resolution fall into two main categories, adjudicated and consensual, and within each category there are options open to the parties. Which option is selected will depend upon the needs of the parties, and the nature of the dispute. Parties may provide that different types of dispute will be dealt with in different ways.

In this chapter the particular characteristics of different forms of commercial dispute resolution will be considered, together with restrictions or limitations on their use, and factors influencing the choice of one method of dispute resolution over another. Primarily the study is limited to resolution of domestic commercial disputes, ie those arising between parties in Scotland, but some reference is made to cross-border or international commercial relationships. The main dispute resolution processes to be considered are as follows.

Adjudication

Generally parties have a right to submit a dispute arising from or about their commercial relationship to adjudication, ie the imposition of a resolution by a third party who has been apprised of the relevant facts and law relating to the dispute. The most widely known form of adjudication is civil litigation and in certain circumstances commercial actions raised in the Court of Session can be processed according to specially adapted rules. However, particularly in commercial matters, the parties may agree that the adjudication will take the form of arbitration, ie the adjudication will be carried out by an individual or tribunal of individuals chosen by the parties for their technical expertise and knowledge, rather than litigation. A binding agreement to submit a dispute to arbitration will oust the jurisdiction of the court in relation to the merits of that dispute, so that any party attempting to litigate the issue will face a plea in bar of litigation. Such agreement to submit disputes to arbitration may have been built into the contract which created the commercial relationship between the parties ('the principal contract') or may be reached by separate agreement after the dispute has arisen. The parties may specify their own terms for the conduct of the arbitration, or may submit to a process of arbitration defined by a convention or legislation or by the arbiter[1].

Consensual resolution

Parties will achieve consensual resolution if the dispute can be dealt with by agreement between the parties following discussion and *negotiation*. This discussion and negotiation may take place between the parties them-selves, or between their respective advisers. These advisers may be lawyers or any professional or technical person employed by either party to facilitate the discussion and negotiation. For example, negotiation of a dispute arising in the course of a building contract may involve engineers or surveyors employed by each party. Alternatively, the parties may engage a neutral person to facilitate a consensual resolution of the dispute. The neutral person will conduct *mediation* between the parties, and a mediator may be chosen because of underlying knowledge of or expertise in a particular area of commerce and because of training and skill in mediation. It is open to the parties to agree that consensual resolution will be attempted before the dispute is submitted to adjudication, but the enforcement of such a term is in itself open to adjudication.

ADJUDICATION BY LITIGATION

Judicial remedies

In civil litigation the parties can seek enforcement or implement of commercial obligations. Payment may be sought as an alternative to or in addition to implement. A defender can counterclaim[2] for related obligations allegedly due by the pursuer to the defender, and can bring into the proceedings a third party whom the defender considers to be the true obligant. Protective orders can also be sought such as interdict against use of commercial 'knowhow', arrestment of the defender's funds in security for the sum claimed (ie arrestment on the dependence) and inhibition of the defender's right to alienate heritable property[3]. The court cannot grant a remedy which goes beyond that specifically sought by a party, and must conduct the litigation within the procedural framework set out in the relevant rules of court. In addition to the pursuer's principal claims the court can determine liability for the expenses of the case and interest on any sums found due by one party to the other. Expenses are normally awarded to the party who succeeds in the litigation. If no interest is specifically claimed by a party the court will award interest on the sum for

1 The person chosen to conduct the arbitration is generally known in Scotland as the 'arbiter' but in England and Wales as the 'arbitrator'. The former term will be used throughout this chapter except in relation to the Arbitration (Scotland) Bill which uses the term 'arbitrator'. The terms are now synonymous but, historically, were distinct: see Hunter *The Law of Arbitration in Scotland* (1987) paras 1.3–1.4.
2 Except in sheriff court small claim actions where counterclaim procedure is not competent.
3 Inhibition is available by petition to the Court of Session only.

which the other party has been found liable and on the expenses from the date of granting decree[1], which interest will be at the judicial rate applying when the decree is granted. That rate of interest is fixed from time to time by statutory instrument[2]. If the parties' contract which gave rise to the litigation provides for interest at a different rate or to be calculated in a particular manner, such as interest on a bank loan running at a prescribed percentage above base rate[3] that can be claimed as an alternative to the judicial rate of interest. In certain circumstances the court can award interest to run on the principal sum awarded from a date before the granting of decree, namely, from the date of citation[4] or the date when the payment was wrongfully withheld[5].

Jurisdiction

Jurisdiction: general

Litigation of a commercial dispute in Scotland proceeds in the civil courts, ie the sheriff court or the Court of Session. To entertain the litigation the court must have first have jurisdiction over the dispute. The jurisdiction of a particular court depends upon the value of the claim, the nature of the remedy sought, and whether the parties or the subject matter have a connection with the geographical area over which that court has jurisdiction. In relation to the Court of Session this means a connection with Scotland, while in relation to the sheriff court this means connection with that sheriff court's district.

Jurisdiction: value and nature of remedy

If the financial value of the claim excluding interest and expenses does not exceed £1,500 the claim may only be raised in the sheriff court[6] under the summary cause procedure[7], and if the value does not exceed £750 the small claim version of summary cause procedure is used[8]. Summary cause procedure is also used for claims *ad factum praestandum* (eg delivery or implement) and for sequestration for rent or furthcoming, provided that any additional or alternative claims for payment do not exceed the £1,500 limit.

---

1 *Dalmahoy and Wood v Brechin Magistrates* (1859) 21 D 210.
2 Currently 8 per cent: Act of Sederunt (Rules of the Court of Session 1994) 1994 (as amended by SI 1994/2310, 1996/1756 and 1996/2168), (hereafter RCS) r 7.7; Act of Sederunt (Interest in Sheriff Court Decrees or Extracts) 1975, SI 1975/948 (as amended by SI 1993/769).
3 *Bank of Scotland v Forsyth* 1969 SLT (Sh Ct) 15.
4 *Blair's Trs v Payne* (1884) 12 R 104.
5 For a recent discussion of interest, see annotations to RCS r 7.7 in Parliament House Book Division C.
6 Sheriff Courts (Scotland) Act 1907, s 7 (as amended by SI 1988/1993).
7 Sheriff Courts (Scotland) Act 1971, s 35 (as amended by SI 1988/1993). Summary cause procedure will not be considered in detail, but see Mays *Summary Cause Procedure in the Sheriff Court* (1995).
8 Sheriff Courts (Scotland) Act 1971, s 35(2)–(4) and Small Claims (Scotland) Order 1988, SI 1988/1999. Small claims procedure will not be considered in detail here, but see Kelbie *Small Claims Procedure in the Sheriff Court* (1994).

For financial craves and related orders where the value is above £1,500 (with no upper limit), parties normally have the option of litigating in the sheriff court using the ordinary cause procedure[1] or in the Court of Session. In the Court of Session, summons procedure[2] is used if there is an existing obligation between the parties in respect of which the court is asked to make and order, and petition procedure[3] is used if the pursuer has no existing obligation to enforce but seeks a remedy which it is just and equitable for the court to award under common law or statute. Special procedures can be invoked for commercial actions commenced by summons. Certain remedies, such as reduction of a deed[4], can only be awarded by the Court of Session, forcing the party who seeks such a remedy to litigate there. Otherwise the choice between litigating in the sheriff court or in the Court of Session may be dictated by the complexity of the issues in the case, logistical convenience for the parties or their agents, desirability of involving counsel or a solicitor advocate, access to the commercial cause procedure, and cost.

Jurisdiction: Civil Jurisdiction and Judgments Act 1982

Litigation will only be entertained by a court which has a connection with the parties or their dispute. Jurisdiction in commercial litigation in Scotland is governed by the Civil Jurisdiction and Judgments Act 1982, s 20 and Sch 8[5]. The main basis for establishing jurisdiction under Sch 8 is the domicile of the defender[6]. Domicile in respect of an individual is determined by the place of the defender's residence. Jurisdiction under this ground exists if and only if the defender is resident in a place in Scotland and the nature and circumstances of the residence indicate a substantial connection with that place, three months residence being classed as substantial[7]. In respect of a corporation or association, domicile is determined by the seat of the corporation or association ie the place of registered office or other official address or where central management or control is exercised[8].

---

1   Sheriff Courts (Scotland) Act 1907, s 39 and Sch 1 (substituted by SI 1993/1956 as amended by SI 1996/2167, SI 1996/2445 and SI 1996/2586, for actions commenced on or after 1 January 1994). The rules contained in Sch 1 are known as the Ordinary Cause Rules 1993 (hereinafter OCR).
2   RCS ch 13.
3   RCS ch 14.
4   Other than reduction *ope exceptionis* (by exception).
5   The Act, as amended by the Civil Jurisdiction and Judgments Act 1991, also regulates jurisdiction in commercial civil litigation within and outwith the UK by giving effect to the European Convention on Jurisdiction and Enforcement of Judgements in Civil and Commercial Matters 1968 ('the Brussels Convention') as extended by the Lugano Convention of 1988. The Scottish provisions apply to establish jurisdiction in Scotland, unless they are in conflict with the terms of the Brussels Convention rules or the UK rules. Generally the Scottish rules do not so conflict but a discussion of the detail is outwith the scope of this text. For a summary, see Gloag and Henderson (eds Wilson and Forte) *The Law of Scotland* (10th edn, 1995) paras 2.12-2.17 and for full consideration, see Anton and Beaumont *Civil Jurisdiction in Scotland* (2nd edn, 1995).
6   Civil Jurisdiction and Judgments Act 1982, Sch 8, r 1.
7   1982 Act, s 41.
8   1982 Act, s 42.

However, in addition to jurisdiction based upon the defender's domicile, other grounds of jurisdiction are set down in the 1982 Act[1], and the following are some examples which are particularly useful in commercial litigation[2].

(1) *Place of performance of the contract.* A contract may specify the place of its performance, but, if it does not, then the place of performance is deemed to be the residence or place of business of the creditor[3]. However, this ground of jurisdiction does not apply to consumer contracts, which are subject to special grounds[4].

(2) *Interdict where the wrong is likely to be committed in Scotland.* If one party wishes to prevent the other from committing an anticipated civil wrong, such as fraud or breach of contract, the court of the place in which the wrong is likely to be committed will have jurisdiction[5].

(3) *Multiple defenders.* A court will have jurisdiction over all defenders if it has jurisdiction over one of them and there is a connection between the claims against the various defenders which renders it expedient for the claims to be litigated together[6].

The 1982 Act acknowledges the parties' rights to prorogate jurisdiction to any nominated court[7] (ie to reach agreement affording jurisdiction to a court which would not otherwise have jurisdiction). The parties may agree this in their principal contract or when the dispute arises. Determining the jurisdiction of a court to entertain a dispute is a separate matter from selecting the law which the court should apply to that agreement. It is open to the parties to any contract to specify which law will apply to the construction of that contract. If they have not specified which law will apply this will be determined in accordance with the Contracts (Applicable Law) Act 1990 which, in giving force to international conventions on conflict of laws[8], provides that the contract will be governed by the law of the country with which it has the closest connection, which is normally determined by the habitual residence of the person due to effect performance.

Commercial litigation

Background

Most commercial disputes are litigated before the same judges and sheriffs, and under the same procedures, as all civil cases. Decree may be

---

1 1982 Act, Sch 8, r 2. But in many respects these reflect grounds which already existed at common law.
2 Further possible grounds for jurisdiction in commercial causes are to be found in Sch 8, r 2(6) and (9) of the 1982 Act.
3 1982 Act, Sch 8, r 2(2). *Bank of Scotland v Seitz* 1990 SLT 584 also confirms that if the creditor has more than one place of business, any one of these at which he or she could insist upon performance can be used to establish jurisdiction.
4 1982 Act, Sch 8, r 3(3). For the grounds of jurisdiction and definition of a 'consumer contract', see r 3.
5 This ground is contained in Sch 8, r 2(10) of the 1982 Act but was also a ground of jurisdiction at common law: *Toni Tyres Ltd v Palmer Tyre Ltd* (1905) 7 F 477.
6 1982 Act, Sch 8, r 2(15).
7 1982 Act, Sch 8, r 5.
8 The Rome Convention, Luxembourg Convention, Brussels Protocol and Funchal Convention.

granted without enquiry into the facts if the action is not defended provided that the action is, on the face of it, competent and within the court's jurisdiction. If the action is defended the case proceeds through adjustment of written pleadings[1] to identify legal issues upon which the parties will proceed to debate and factual issues in repect of which they will lead evidence at a proof[2]. Expert witnesses may be led by the parties. Experts can give an opinion upon facts in the case which are outwith the general interpretative powers of the court[3], but are not permitted to usurp the function of the court by giving an opinion on the ultimate issues in the case[4].

Court of session procedure for commercial actions

In the Court of Session, special procedures for commercial actions were introduced in 1934 and, although updated over the years, were subject to a recent major overhaul after the Working Party on Commercial Causes chaired by Lord Coulsfield reported in 1993 and recommended changes to facilitate the speedy and efficacious determination of commercial litigation[5]. These changes involved increasing procedural flexibility, more extensive and effective disclosure requirements, and generating judicial expertise and proactivity in commercial actions. Judicial expertise is ensured by the appointment of a full-time commercial judge[6].

The new rules are found in ch 47 of the Rules of the Court of Session 1994 as amended[7], which should be read with Court of Session Practice Note No 12 of 1994 (Commercial Actions). In r 47.1(2) a commercial action is defined as any action arising out of or concerned with any relationship of a commercial or business nature. In the practice note this is expanded to clarify that the relationship may be contractual or not, and a non-restrictive list of examples is given, namely: actions relating to the construction of a commercial or mercantile document; the sale or hire purchase of goods; the export or import of merchandise; the carriage of goods by land, air or sea[8], insurance; banking; financial services; mercantile agency; mercantile usage or custom of trade; a building engineering or construction contract; a commercial lease. The special procedures will apply only if the

---

1 Except in claims of not more than £1,500 in value which are subject to restricted pleading and procedure: Summary Cause Rules, Sheriff Court 1976, SI 1976/476 (as amended) and Small Claims Rules 1988, SI 1988/1976 (as amended).

2 In the sheriff court under OCR ch 9 in order to expedite the resolution of a civil case the sheriff determines the disputed issues after a fixed period of adjustment and may refuse to allow debate or restrict issues for proof. In the Court of Session when a petition is lodged it is up to the court to decide what orders are necessary for intimation and written defences, and to determine what further procedure is necessary to deal with disputed issues of fact and law. For further detail on petition procedure, see McBryde and Dowie *Petition Procedure in the Court of Session* (2nd edn, 1988).

3 *Davie v Edinburgh Magistrates* 1953 SC 34 at 40, per Lord President Cooper.

4 *Morrison v Maclean's Trs* (1862) 24 D 625 at 631, per Lord Justice-Clerk Inglis.

5 Morrison 'Scotland's New Commercial Court' (1994) JLSS 354.

6 Ie Lord Penrose. Lord Coulsfield and Lord Cameron of Lochbroom are also designated commercial judges.

7 By SI 1994/2310.

8 Other than an action which meets the definition of an admiralty action found in RCS r 46.1, and for which the special procedures in RCS ch 46 are to be needed.

pursuer has elected to adopt them by marking 'commercial action' on the summons[1]. The summons need not be in traditional form so long as it clearly identifies the orders sought, the parties, transaction and circumstances giving rise to the dispute and the grounds of action and is accompanied by the 'core' documents relating to the case[2].

In an action which is not marked as commercial at the outset either party may thereafter apply by motion for the cause to be so treated[3]. While the right of the pursuer to elect for commercial procedure appears to be absolute, the case may be withdrawn from the commercial roll. Withdrawal can be applied for only at or before the preliminary hearing, and if the parties consent the court must transfer the action to the ordinary summons roll. If the application is not consented to the court has to consider whether, having regard to the need for detailed pleadings, the requirement for lengthy preparation, or other relevant circumstances the speedy and efficient determination of the case would not be best served by keeping it on the commercial roll[4]. It appears that the commercial court will not entertain cases involving consumers[5], and those concerning intellectual property[6]. While the former is understandable, since the procedure is geared towards use by litigants who are in business, the reason for the latter is unclear. One possibility is that many disputes concerning intellectual property involve a remedy under statute[7] which must, in terms of that statute, be sought by petition procedure. The commercial roll procedure is an offshoot from summons procedure only and is not therefore available in proceedings which must be commenced by petition[8].

Instead of the ordinary process of written pleadings and structured procedure, in a commercial action the case will have a preliminary hearing, one or more procedural hearings, and, if still then required, a hearing for final disposal of fact or law or both. A defender must lodge answers to the summons, including a statement of the legal and factual basis for the defence, and any documents founded upon, but the answers need not be in the traditional form of defences[9]. The case first calls on the commercial roll for preliminary hearing fourteen days after defences are lodged. The case can only be heard by a commercial judge, but every effort is made to ensure that the same commercial judges conducts the case throughout[10]. At this hearing the commercial judge will already be familiar with the summons, defences and documents lodged and in a position to take a proactive role regarding the identification and disposal of the issues[11]. The hearing takes the form of a meeting chaired by the judge with no gowns or wigs worn[12]. The parties' representatives are expected to be well prepared

1 RCS r 47.3.
2 RCS r 47.3(2) and (3) and PN No 12 of 1994, para 3.
3 RCS r 47.10(1).
4 RCS r 47.9(1).
5 Morrison (1994) 39 JLSS 354.
6 According to research findings of Clancy, Murray and Wadia, set out in 'The New Commercial Cause Rules' 1997 SLT (News) 45 and 53; see at 47.
7 Insolvency and remedies under companies legislation are in a similar situation.
8 Similarly a remedy available only on petition could not be introduced in the commercial action: *Ross v Davy* 1996 SCLR 369.
9 RCS r 47.6 and PN No 12 of 1994, para 6.
10 PN No 12 of 1994, para 17(1).
11 PN No 12 of 1994, para 5.
12 PN No 12 of 1994, para 11(3).

and informed in relation to their client's positions[1] and the judge has extensive powers to order further specification of the issues in the form of statements, documents or pleadings, disclosure of lists of witnesses and production of evidence in the form of expert reports and affidavits[2]. Timescales which are short but realistic will be set for the fulfilment of such orders[3] and at the end of the preliminary hearing a procedural hearing will be fixed. At least three days in advance of the procedural hearing each party must lodge a written statement of proposals for further procedure, together with details of witnesses (including what the witnesses will testify about), copies of expert reports, and, if a debate on legal issues is to be sought, a note of the legal propositions upon which that debate would concentrate[4]. The procedural hearing is also informal and the judge at this stage can determine whether debate or proof is necessary and order such further disclosure, discussion or analysis of evidence as is appropriate[5].

The common law right of parties to withhold from the other party reports or other evidence obtained *post litem motam*[6] (ie after litigation is in progress), appears to be overtaken by the disclosure requirements and by the proactive procedural powers of the judge. The court may even appoint its own expert to examine evidence, including expert evidence, disclosed by the parties[7]. The parties are encouraged to expose and agree evidence, leaving only the disputed facts and law for determination at a proof or debate. The court is not obliged to fix a proof or a debate if that type of hearing is not considered appropriate for determination of the issues, and the refusal to fix such a hearing will only be reviewed if no reasonable Outer House judge would have reached the decision taken by the commercial judge[8]. At proof or debate the parties may be allowed to address issues not covered in the written pleadings if those issues are identified in summaries produced for the procedural hearing[9].

ADJUDICATION BY ARBITRATION

Nature of arbitration and its sources

Arbitration is the process by which a dispute between parties may be adjudicated upon by an arbiter, or tribunal of arbiters, chosen by the parties rather than by the courts[10]. While civil courts have an inherent juris-

---

1 PN No 12 of 1994, para 11(1) and see Clancy, Murray and Wadia 1997 SLT (News) at 53–54.
2 RCS r 47.11(1).
3 PN No 12 of 1994, para 11(2).
4 RCS r 47.12.
5 For examples, see Clancy, Murray and Wadia 1997 SLT (News) at 53–56.
6 *Anderson v St Andrews Ambulance Association* 1942 SC 555.
7 RCS r 47.12(2)(f).
8 *Highland & Universal Properties Ltd v Safeway Properties Ltd* 1996 GWD 27-1628.
9 *Highland & Universal Properties Ltd* above and Clancy, Murray and Wadia 1997 SLT (News) 53 at 57.
10 For detailed studies of the common law of arbitration, see Bell *The Law of Arbitration in Scotland* (2nd edn, 1877); Irons and Melville *Law of Arbitration in Scotland* (1903). More recent studies are Hunter *The Law of Arbitration in Scotland* (1987) and 2 *Stair Memorial Encyclopaedia* 'Arbitration' at paras 401ff.

diction to adjudicate upon commercial disputes raised before them and parties to a commercial transaction have an inherent right to take any dispute to litigation, that jurisdiction and those rights can be supplanted by the parties' agreement to arbitrate. The parties are free to agree whether to submit the dispute to arbitration and to agree upon all other aspects of the conduct of an arbitration, such as the selection of the arbiter, any time limits for the conclusion of the arbitration, and whether the arbitration is for the purpose of determining all disputes between them or only those specified by the parties. Only a private dispute can be submitted to arbitration, so if a dispute involves a matter or public interest or policy it cannot be arbitrated[1]. The arbiter has been described as a private judge[2]. Arbitration is essentially a voluntary matter and arbitration operating by agreement in Scotland can be traced to the twelfth century[3].

Some arbitrations are a requirement of statute, such as those concerning agricultural leases under the Agricultural Holdings (Scotland) Act 1991, or those set up under industrial relations legislation[4], but these lack the voluntary nature of true arbitration. Historically the general law of arbitration in Scotland has had little statutory regulation, a situation entirely compatible with its voluntary nature. By comparison in England and Wales since 1889, arbitration in general has been subject to statutory control, most recently in the form of the Arbitration Act 1996[5]. In Scotland the limited statutory involvement with arbitration can be summarised as follows: Articles of Regulation of 1695 controlled some aspects of arbitration and still regulate the grounds for reduction of an arbiter's decision; the Arbitration (Scotland) Act 1894 made some minor amendments to the common law concerning the naming and selection of arbiters; the Arbitration Act 1950[6] and the Arbitration Act 1975 respectively give effect in Scotland to the Geneva Convention and the New York Convention (both on the enforcement of awards made in foreign arbitrations); the Administration of Justice (Scotland) Act 1972[7] enables parties to an arbitration to request an arbiter to state a case on a point of law for determination by the Court of Session; and the Law Reform Miscellaneous Provisions (Scotland) Act 1990[8] adopts into the law of Scotland the model law on international commercial arbitrations approved by the United Nations Commission on International Trade Law ('UNCITRAL').

For some time the Scottish law of arbitration has been under consideration by an advisory committee chaired by Lord Dervaird[9] which, in order to 'consolidate[e] existing enactments' and 'render the arbitration process

1 *Bell* paras 216–227. Throughout this chapter only, *'Bell'* refers to *The Law of Arbitration in Scotland* above.
2 *Bell* para 13.
3 For a history of arbitration in Scotland, see *Hunter* ch 2.
4 Statutory arbitrations and arbitrations in industrial relations disputes are outwith the scope of this chapter.
5 Arbitration Act 1996, ss 89–91 concerning unfair terms in consumer arbitration agreements apply to Scotland. Consumer arbitrations agreements, which are also regulated in Scotland by the Consumer Arbitration Agreements Act 1988, ss 6, 7, are outwith the scope of this chapter.
6 1950 Act, Pt II and Sch 1.
7 1972 Act, s 3.
8 1990 Act, s 66 and Sch 7.
9 Scottish Advisory Committee on Arbitration ('SACAL'), also known as 'the Dervaird Committee'.

speedier and more effective'[1], has made recommendations leading to the publication of a draft Arbitration (Scotland) Bill for consultation. However, the Advisory Committee stresses[2] that the Bill is not intended to enact a complete code for arbitration. The terms of the draft bill are summarised below after examination of the law of arbitration as it stands at present.

The binding nature of arbitration

Arbitration agreements

In Scotland the courts have bluntly confirmed that '[i]f parties have contracted to arbitrate, to arbitration they must go'[3]. If one party to an arbitration agreement attempts to litigate while a valid contract to arbitrate exists, the other party can plead that the court has no jurisdiction to hear the case until the arbitration has been completed. This plea must be upheld in respect of the merits of the case[4] unless the court is satisfied that the arbitration agreement is void or does not apply to the issue which is being litigated. The court must sist (ie suspend consideration of) the case pending the completion of the arbitration[5], and when the arbitration is completed the parties may have the case dismissed or seek a decree from the court in the same terms as the arbiter's award[6]. It is not appropriate to award expenses to either party at the time when a case is sisted for arbitration, since the issue of which party succeeds in the claim can only be determined in the arbitration[7]. The only exception to the suspension of the court's jurisdiction while a valid arbitration agreement exists, arises where the defender participates in the litigation to such an extent that the right to insist upon the arbitration clause is impliedly waived[8]. This may occur if the defender fails to state a preliminary plea of no jurisdiction[9], or, having stated such a plea, fails to insist upon it while the litigation continues, and generally acts in a manner inconsistent with an intention to exercise the right to go to arbitration[10].

It has been a strength of arbitration in Scotland that an arbitration agreement effectively and conclusively replaces the jurisdiction of the court[11]. This has not been the case in England and Wales where until recently the

---

1 SACAL *Consultation Paper on Legislation for Domestic Arbitration in Scotland* (1997, Scottish Courts Administration), para 1.1. Note the similarity with the rationale behind the new Commercial Court rules.
2 Ibid, para 1.2.
3 *A Sanderson & Son v Armour & Co Ltd* 1922 SC (HL) 117 at 126, per Lord Dunedin.
4 *Hamlyn & Co v Talisker Distillery* (1894) 21 R (HL) 21.
5 (1894) 21 R (HL) 21 at 25, per Lord Watson, and *Motordrift A/S v Trachem Co Ltd* 1982 SLT 127.
6 *Svenska Petroleum AB v HOR Ltd* 1986 SLT 513; *Mendok BV v Cumberland Maritime Corpn* 1989 SLT 192.
7 *Presslie v Cochrane McGregor Ltd (No 2)* 1997 GWD 14-617.
8 *Dundee Provident Property Investment Co v Macdonald* (1884) 11 R 537.
9 *Motordrift A/S v Trachem Co Ltd* above; *Halliburton Manufacturing and Service Ltd v Bingham Blades & Partners* 1984 SLT 388; *Presslie v Cochrane McGregor Group Ltd* 1996 SLT 988.
10 *Inverclyde (Mearns) Housing Society Ltd v Lawrence Construction Co Ltd* 1989 SLT 815.
11 For a discussion of modern challenges to that strength, see Murray 'Letting arbiters get on with the job' 1997 SLT (News) 64.

court had discretion to entertain the litigation despite the existence of an arbitration agreement[1]. Even now, the court in these countries may find that there are sufficient grounds not to require the parties to abide by an arbitration agreement[2].

Arbiter's decision

The decision (usually termed the 'award') of the arbiter is binding upon the parties. The arbiter cannot order enforcement but either the court may be asked to grant a decree in terms of the arbiter's award or the award may contain a clause stating that the parties consent to its registration in the Books of Council and Session or in the Sheriff Court Books for preservation and execution. The award is indeed more binding than a court decree because it is not open to review or rehearing by the courts. It cannot be appealed on its merits or on a point of law. It will bind the parties unless the court sets the decision aside in proceedings for reduction but such proceedings can succeed only if the process of arbitration itself was fundamentally flawed: eg by the arbiter exceeding his or her powers, acting improperly or contrary to the natural justice[3] or having been misled by the parties to such an extent that his or her award is held to be procured by improper means or obtained by fraud[4].

If litigation is commenced after an arbitration has taken place it may be defended on the basis that the issues which have been arbitrated are *res judicata*[5], ie they have already been adjudicated upon and cannot be re-opened. A plea of *res judicata* will bring the proceedings to an end with a decree of absolvitor in favour of the defender if the litigation concerns the same parties or their successors in title to sue, the same cause of action, and the same remedy as the arbitration. Any issues raised in the litigation which were outwith the scope of the arbiter's decision can still be litigated.

Submission to arbitration

The parties' agreement to use arbitration for adjudication of a dispute is sometimes termed the submission or the reference. These terms normally describe the stage at which the arbiter is brought in after a dispute has arisen. However, the agreement to submit any dispute to arbitration may be made earlier, when the parties are entering into their principal contract, and in that situation is normally found in a clause of that contract. The agreement to submit to arbitration is a governed by the law of contract and is normally in writing but does not have to be[6]. It is for the parties to agree upon and specify the terms of that contract and to prove the contract if a dispute arises about its existence or its terms. Formal arbitration clauses in self-proving contracts are the norm, but arbitration can be agreed informally in the course of normal commercial dealings.

1 Arbitration Act 1950, s 4(1).
2 Arbitration Act 1996, s 86(2) and (3).
3 As in *Fountain Forestry Holdings Ltd v Sparkes* 1989 SLT 853.
4 See 2 *Stair Memorial Encyclopaedia* para 484.
5 *Bell* para 5.
6 *Irons and Melville* p 51.

The submission may be general or special or general-special, ie a mixture of both. General arbitration clauses state that any dispute arising between the parties in relation to obligations under a principal contract or commercial relationship shall be referred to arbitration. The special submission limits the reference to the arbiter to the specific issue stated in the submission (eg questions of value of certain services provided by one party to another) and the arbiter cannot exceed the scope of the special submission. A mixed (or general-special) submission is one which contains a clause agreeing to arbitrate all disputes between the parties coupled with a reference to a specific dispute or class of disputes. In this situation the reference to specific disputes limits the scope of the general reference to those disputes which are *ejusdem generis* with (ie of the same kind as) those specified[1].

General arbitration clauses do not specify the exact dispute to be referred, simply because it is impossible or undesirable to attempt to predict what disputes will arise. However, in order that the arbiter is clear as to the terms of his or her remit, it is desirable to focus the dispute at some stage, and this is usually in the notice to the arbiter requesting that he or she commence the arbitration process. Evidence of the nature and scope of the submission may, therefore, be found not only in the arbitration clause or agreement, but in subsequent writings. It has been held competent to narrow the scope of the original clause in these subsequent submission documents[2]. If the original agreement is in formal self-proving form, later writings intended to vary the scope of the original agreement should be in similar form.

Even in a general submission to arbitration, the parties can agree issues of process or procedure: such as the way in which the arbitration will be conducted and the powers of the arbiter. They may do this by setting out at length in the arbitration agreement agreed procedures for the arbitration, or they may refer to standard terms for arbitration such as those devised by the building[3] and civil engineering[4] industries, or those recommended by the Law Society of Scotland[5]. The UNCITRAL Model Law on Arbitration adopted for Scotland by s 66 of the Law Reform (Miscellaneous Provisions) (Scotland) Act 1990 in relation to international commercial arbitrations, may be incorporated as appropriate by agreement of parties in domestic arbitrations. If the contract is not specific or is silent there are certain powers implied at common law, including the arbiter's power to regulate procedure. However, the common law is itself unpredictable at times, providing simply that the arbiter has such powers as are reasonable to enable his or her function to be carried out[6]. It is undesirable that the parties should have to rely upon implied powers and pro-

1   Erskine *Institute* III, 4, 9.
2   *Whatlings (Foundations) Ltd v Shanks & MacEwan (Contractors) Ltd* 1989 SLT 857.
3   The Scottish Building Contract Committee and the Joint Contracts Tribunal produce forms of standard contracts for building works which include arbitration clauses with some rules of procedure.
4   The Institute of Civil Engineering produces standard conditions of contract which include arbitration clauses, and a separate statement of arbitration rules for Scotland.
5   For which, see 2 *Stair Memorial Encyclopaedia* para 508.
6   *Macintyre Bros v Smith* 1913 SC 129.

cedures when they have the opportunity to dictate the terms upon which an arbitration should proceed.

The arbiter and oversman

The parties are free to choose the identity of an arbiter. They may do this when contracting originally or when the dispute arises. They may name a specific arbiter or may identify the qualifications which the arbiter should hold, leaving the identity to be determined when the arbitration is to commence. They may name a body of persons from whom the arbiter is to be chosen, such as a relevant professional body, or they may name a firm or association. If in so doing the parties do not name the arbiter personally, they will be deemed to accept the judgement of the firm or association concerned as to which of their number will conduct the arbitration[1]. The parties may agree to appoint one arbiter or to appoint an arbitral tribunal of two or more members. It is often the case that in a dispute involving two parties each may select an arbiter to sit on a tribunal of two.

If a tribunal of two is to be appointed then it is normal and prudent to provide also for the appointment of an oversman, who, in the event of the two arbiters failing to agree, will take over the determination of the dispute: ie the arbitration will devolve to the oversman[2]. If the arbitration agreement does not expressly provide for the appointment of an oversman and does not expressly prohibit the arbiters from appointing an oversman, under statute[3] the arbiters are deemed to be entitled to appoint an oversman if they fail to agree on the outcome of the arbitration or any part of it in respect of which they have not made a partial award. In the event that they have made a partial award only the remainder of the dispute not covered by the partial award will devolve to the oversman. Devolution to the oversman renders the arbiters *functus officio* (ie discharged from the duties of the office).

An arbitration clause is valid even if no arbiter is named[4], but the clause may be unenforceable if it is impossible to determine whether the parties wanted one arbiter or a tribunal of more than one[5]. The Arbitration (Scotland) Act 1894 empowers the court to appoint an arbiter if (1) in the case of a single arbiter one party refuses to concur in the nomination of the arbiter[6], and (2) in the case of two arbiters, of whom one is to be appointed by each party, one party refuses to name an arbiter[7]. These provisions apply only if no provision exists in the arbitration agreement for dealing with such refusal.

Arbiters may be chosen for their skill or knowledge in a particular sphere. They may be legally qualified, and commonly arbiters are chosen from the memberships of local or national bodies of solicitors, or from the

1 *William Dixon Ltd v Jones, Heard and Ingram* (1884) 11 R 739.
2 *Bell* para 344, the oversman is sometimes (usually in England and Wales) called the umpire.
3 Arbitration (Scotland) Act 1894, s 4.
4 1894 Act, s 1.
5 *Archibald McMillan & Son v David Rowan & Co* (1903) 5 F 317.
6 1894 Act, s 2.
7 1894 Act, s 3.

Faculty of Advocates. Judges of the Court of Session may accept nomination as arbiters in commercial matters[1]. However, a major attraction of arbitration procedure is the scope to nominate non-legally qualified persons to adjudicate in areas within their specialist knowledge or skill. Commonly architects or engineers are appointed whether as individuals or from the membership of a relevant professional body. But, no requirement of professional qualification on the part of an arbiter is necessary. The parties have complete freedom of choice in appointing an arbiter and, provided that no question of bias or bad faith on the part of the arbiter arises, they cannot challenge an award which exhausts the submission merely because it appears to have been poorly handled by the arbiter. Generally, to avoid such concerns, arbiters are chosen for their experience not only in a particular field of business, but in the process of arbitration itself. Arbitration is a recognised specialism, and those who are suitably trained and experienced can become associates or fellows of the Institute of Chartered Arbitrators.

It is implicit in the arbitration process that the arbiter will be impartial, independent of both parties, and have no interest in the dispute[2]. Generally, if this condition is breached the arbiter is disqualified and any award which has already been issued is open to reduction on the grounds of the arbiter's bias or interest. However, if the parties, with the knowledge of the arbiter's interest or connection, nevertheless appoint that arbiter, they are deemed to have waived the right to challenge the appointment or award on that basis[3].

Stages in the arbitration

Having agreed that arbitration is their chosen method of adjudication, when a dispute arises the parties initiate the procedure by notice to the arbiter, who at that stage indicates whether he or she accepts or declines the submission. The proposed arbiter should accept unless excluded in some way. For example: the proposed arbiter may have a conflicting interest in the matter under dispute or may no longer hold the office (such as sheriff principal, president of a professional body) upon which the appointment was based. He or she may appoint a clerk to assist with the processing of the arbitration[4]. It is common for an arbiter who is not a lawyer to appoint as a clerk a lawyer who has knowledge of the process of arbitration, and the clerk may provide assistance of an administrative, clerical and procedural nature.

The arbiter then invites the parties to state specifically the matters in dispute between them. It has become common for the arbiter to receive these statements in the form of written pleadings similar to the averments in civil litigation. However, there is no requirement to proceed in this way, and using written pleadings in arbitration recently attracted disap-

1 Law Reform (Miscellaneous Provisions) (Scotland) Act 1980, s 17.
2 *Bell* para 20.
3 *Bell* paras 241–242, but see *Hunter* paras 10.37–10.39 regarding the undesirability of such an appointment.
4 *Irons and Melville* p 239. But appointment is not essential: *Mowbray v Dickson* (1848) 10 D 1102.

proval from the First Division of the Court of Session which noted that it is quite sufficient for the parties to write to the arbiter setting out the position[1]. It would be competent for the parties to state their positions orally, although it would then be prudent for the arbiter to record this in writing and have the parties endorse the record of what had been said. Apart from being good practice, this ensures that all parties understand the extent of the arbiter's remit, and can assess whether the award exhausts or exceeds the remit.

If the dispute is on a point of law only the arbitration may proceed without the need for evidence but normally there will be issues of fact and law to determine and the arbiter will need to consider evidence on the factual issues. The parties may in the arbitration agreement or submission documents agree a restricted process for assessment of the facts, such as presentation of the evidence in documentary form only. If they have not so agreed the arbiter controls the process for ascertaining the facts and law behind the dispute, subject to certain implied duties described below. The arbiter will generally require to hear oral evidence on the disputed facts.

Powers and duties of the arbiter

The powers and duties of the arbiter are again essentially a matter of contract, but at common law certain powers of the arbiter are implied. Implied powers and duties have been acknowledged which are 'manifestly essential to the execution of the office of arbiter'[2]. Since the arbiter is a privately appointed judge much of what is implied derives from proper execution of any judicial function such as appointing a clerk, requiring the parties to specify adequately the nature of the dispute, to receive evidence from the parties concerning the dispute, and to hear their submissions about that evidence and about any points of law[3]. The existence of these powers and duties is clear, but questions often arise as to the extent of the arbiter's functions in their implementation.

It is clear that unless the parties prescribe in the arbitration agreement that the arbiter will conduct the proceedings in a particular way, the arbiter is free to adopt his or her own approach to procedure provided that he or she observes the rules of natural justice, namely, openness, fairness and impartiality[4]. The arbiter may call upon his or her own knowledge in addition to the evidence brought to his or her attention by the parties, and, indeed, an arbiter is often chosen for his or her specialist knowledge in a particular area. However, if the arbiter is to call upon his or her own knowledge to add to, rather than merely to interpret, the evidence of the dispute, he or she must bring this to the parties' attention and allow them the opportunity to address him or her on the matter[5]. The arbiter may seek expert advice before reaching a conclusion upon a mat-

---

1 *ERDC Construction Ltd v HM Love & Co (No 2)* 1997 SLT 175 at 180, per Lord Prosser.
2 *Bell* paras 251–322.
3 *Bell* para 253.
4 *Bell* para 313.
5 *Fountain Forestry Holdings Ltd v Sparkes* 1989 SLT 853, following *Fox v PG Wellfair Ltd* [1981] 2 Lloyd's Rep 514.

ter outwith his or her own field, but must come to his or her own conclusion on the submission which is referred for his or her judgment alone[1]. This may include taking an opinion from counsel or an academic expert on a point of law, particularly if the arbiter is not legally qualified. The arbiter is empowered by statute[2] to state a case to the Court of Session on a point of law, unless the parties have expressly agreed that the statutory provision will not apply in their arbitration[3]. Stated case procedure is described below.

The arbiter's award

Scope of award

If there is a question raised by a party about the arbiter's jurisdiction to deal with the dispute, this is a matter upon which the arbiter can make a ruling: ie the arbiter is deemed competent to consider the extent of his or her own jurisdiction or competence. However, at common law the arbiter's ruling on his or her own competence is not binding upon the parties and they would have the right to litigate that issue if they did not agree with the arbiter's conclusion. The arbiter otherwise has the power to address only the dispute brought to him or her by the parties. If the dispute is one which on determination could entitle a party to an award of damages, the arbiter has no power to assess and award damages unless that is expressly provided for in the arbitration submission[4]. The arbiter has an implied power to award liability for expenses of the proceedings as between the parties, including a claim for his or her own fees and the expenses of conducting the arbitration[5]. The arbiter also has an implied power to award interest to run from the date of any award of a financial nature, but not to award interest from an earlier date unless this is expressly provided for in the arbitration agreement[6]. If there is an ongoing contract between the parties which provides for payment of interest the arbiter has no implied power to override that by awarding interest on different terms.

Interim and part awards

The arbiter may have the power to make an interim award if the parties have expressly provided for this[7]. An interim award is a provisional one which subsists for temporary purposes only until recalled or replaced by a final award. The final award should mention that an interim award was made but the final award may be entirely different from the interim award. The arbiter may make a partial award, which is a final determina-

---

1 *Irons and Melville* p 165.
2 Administration of Justice (Scotland) Act 1972, s 3.
3 1972 Act, s 3(3).
4 *Aberdeen Rly Co v Blaikie Bros* (1853) 15 D (HL) 20.
5 *Macintyre Bros v Smith* 1913 SC 129.
6 *John G McGregor (Contractors) Ltd v Grampian Regional Council* 1991 SLT 136; *Farrans Construction v Dunfermline District Council* 1988 SCLR 272.
7 *Lyle v Falconer* (1842) 5 D 236; *Irons and Melville* p 185.

tion on a part of the issue submitted to him or her. The arbiter may make more than one partial award but ultimately requires to produce a final award which together with the partial awards exhausts the issues presented to him in the arbitration submission.

Final award

A final award in an arbitration has the effect of rendering the arbiter *functus officio* and thus unable to amend his or her award or adjust any point made in that award. Since the arbiter's award is not open to review or appeal it is important that it is carefully written and records all relevant issues of fact and law considered by the arbiter. It is common practice for the arbiter to provide a draft of his or her award to the parties for examination and comment before the award is issued, so that any omissions or misconceptions can be identified and, subject to the limits of the arbiter's overall jurisdiction, dealt with before the award is issued. This may also prompt a party or parties to request the arbiter to state a case on a point of law to the Court of Session, since a stated case cannot be taken after the award is issued. The arbiter has an implied power to reveal to the parties his or her proposed findings or a draft award, but, although this is desirable, there is no corresponding implied duty to do so. The parties could of course expressly provide in the arbitration agreement that the arbiter must produce findings in draft for their consideration.

Set aside of the arbitration award

The arbitration award is not open to review or appeal. However a party may apply to the court for the arbitration award to be set aside at common law or under the 25th Act of the Articles of Regulation 1695. At common law the grounds relate to breach of the submission: eg the award does not fulfil the submission, or it exceeds the submission, or a party has materially misled the arbiter, or the arbiter has acted improperly to such an extent that the award is compromised[1]. Under the 1695 provisions the propriety of the arbiter's conduct is the test: ie has there been corruption, bribery or falsehood?[2] If the award exceeds the terms of the arbiter's remit the court can grant partial set aside, preserving such parts of the arbitral award that do deal with the submitted dispute.

Powers of the courts in an ongoing arbitration

Protective orders and recovery

As a private judge the arbiter does not possess powers to secure the preservation of any fund or property of the parties, nor to order the attendance of witnesses, nor to recover evidence. These powers often do

---

1 For an excellent recent discussion of the grounds for reduction, see 2 *Stair Memorial Encyclopaedia* paras 472–491.
2 2 *Stair Memorial Encyclopaedia* para 473.

require to be exercised in an arbitration, just as they do in civil litigation, and the court has jurisdiction to grant or refuse such orders to facilitate the conduct of the arbitration and to secure the interests of the parties by arrestment or inhibition pending the completion of the arbitration. If there is civil litigation in the Court of Session or sheriff court which has been suspended until the completion of the arbitration, an application for arrestment on the dependence[1], preservation of documents or property under s 1 of the Administration of Justice (Scotland) Act 1972, or commission and diligence for the recovery of evidence, can be made in those proceedings. Otherwise they are sought by application to the Court of Session or the sheriff court.

Stated case

Although there is no right of appeal or review of any awards or procedural rulings made by the arbiter, the courts can become involved if the arbiter of his or her own accord or on the application of a party states a case to the Court of Session on a point of law. The provision for a stated case is to be found in s 3 of the Administration of Justice (Scotland) Act 1972, but it applies only if the parties have not expressly agreed otherwise in the arbitration submission[2]. In terms of s 3 an arbiter or oversman may, of his or her own accord, apply to the Court of Session by stated case for the opinion of the court on a question of law arising in the arbitration. A party may ask the arbiter to state a case on legal questions proposed by the party. If the arbiter refuses to submit all or some of those questions to the court, a party may ask the Court of Session to order that the arbiter states the case for the court's opinion[3]. If the arbiter agrees to state a case the court has no power to order alteration of the questions contained in it[4]. The opinion of the court on the stated case is not open to appeal[4] and the arbiter is obliged to follow that opinion in making the award. An opinion of the Court of Session may be sought at any time in the arbitration process[5] prior to issue of the final award, since at that point the arbiter is *functus* and has no jurisdiction to state a case.

Arbitration (Scotland) Bill

A draft Arbitration (Scotland) Bill was circulated in January 1997 by Scottish Courts Administration following recommendations by the Dervaird Committee. At the time of writing, consultation with interested parties has taken place but a Bill has not yet been presented to Parliament. Accordingly the following account of the approach taken in the Bill is sub-

1 *Mendok BV v Cumberland Maritime Corpn* 1989 SLT 192. An order for inhibition on the dependence can only be granted by the Court of Session.
2 1972 Act, s 3(1) and see *Whatlings (Foundations) Ltd v Shanks & MacEwan (Contractors) Ltd* 1989 SLT 857.
3 RCS rr 41.7(3) and 41.8.
4 *John G McGregor (Contractors) Ltd v Grampian Regional Council* 1990 SLT 365.
5 But see *ERDC Construction Ltd v HM Love & Co (No 2)* 1997 SLT 175 at 178, per Lord President Hope.

ject to the proviso that if a new Arbitration (Scotland) Act is enacted its terms may differ from those in the draft Bill. The Bill does not attempt to codify the law of arbitration in Scotland and leaves some areas of the common law unaffected. However, it does seek to produce a statutory framework for arbitration and to introduce powers to ensure fairness and completion of the arbitration whilst complementing rather than overriding the agreed arbitration terms[1]. Throughout the Bill the term 'arbitrator' is used instead of 'arbiter', to bring Scottish terminology in line with that of the UK and international arbitration.

The Bill has four themes[2], namely:

(1) to address common problems preventing the commencement of the arbitration, such as problems with specifying the number and identity of arbitrators and questions concerning the arbiter's competence[3];
(2) to make provisions regarding practical difficulties with the exercise of the arbiter's powers and duties, such as early disclosure of circumstances which might give rise to justifiable concern about the arbiter's impartiality[4], resignation or removal of the arbiter[5], power to award interest and damages[6], and power to make interim and partial awards[7],
(3) to introduce measures to protect the parties' interests such as time limits for completion of procedural steps[8] and powers to proceed to a determination even if a party is in default[9]; and
(4) to define the relationship between the courts and arbitration[10], including power to terminate arbiters' appointments[11], and the repeal of s 3 of the Administration of Justice (Scotland) Act 1972 so that the power to state a case to the Court of Session on a point of law would be removed[12].

The Bill carries forward the UNCITRAL Model Law on International Commercial Arbitration on the same terms as apply at present[13]. The combination of these themes and the proposed provisions for their implementation appears to make arbitration procedure less fluid than it can be at present and to distance it from the court on matters of legal merit, but to increase the court's power to provide procedural support for speedy conclusion of the arbitration against delay or default by the parties or the arbiter.

---

1 SACAL *Consultation Paper on Legislation for Domestic Arbitration in Scotland* (1997, Scottish Courts Administration), para 2.1–2.2.
2 Set out at ibid, para 2.4.
3 Addressed in cls 2(5) and 4.
4 Cl 6.
5 Cls 11 and 7.
6 Cls 22 and 24.
7 Cl 23.
8 Cls 8(4) and (8), 9(1) and 15(6).
9 Cl 19(1) and (6).
10 Cl 17.
11 Cl 10.
12 Cl 29.
13 Cl 31.

CONSENSUAL RESOLUTION OF DISPUTES

Introduction

When a dispute arises in a commercial matter, although it may involve only the parties to the transaction, it will often impinge upon the interests of other persons. Those others may be closely related to one of the parties, such as employees, customers, suppliers or investors; or may be the general public if the matter, eg, concerns completion of public works such as water or road schemes. These extrinsic interests often make it unwise or ineffective for parties to submit the dispute to litigation, a process which is adversarial, public, limited to a fixed range of remedies, potentially expensive in terms of court and legal fees and time, and generally destructive of future commercial trading between the parties. In comparison, consensual methods of dispute resolution are private, flexible in approach to outcomes, speedy, limited in cost to the value of the time of the persons involved, and capable of preserving ongoing or future commercial relationships between the parties.

Negotiation

Parties always have the option of negotiating a resolution of a particular dispute. However, whether the dispute is the symptom or the cause, cordial relations between the parties may well have broken down and conditions are no longer prime for negotiation. There may also be an uneven bargaining situation between the parties which militates against direct negotiation, or differences in negotiating goals and strategies which inhibit settlement of the dispute. Negotiation through advisers has the benefit of distancing the parties from each other whilst drawing upon the advisers' expertise in legal, technical or negotiating terms. There are acknowledged strategies and styles for effective negotiation in which many advisers are skilled but with which most disputing parties will not be familiar[1]. However, the negotiator is always limited by the party's instructions and is tied to one side of the dispute.

Mediation

Background

Through the 1980s concern about the disadvantages of delay and cost in civil litigation led to increased interest in alternative methods of dispute resolution (ie alternatives to adjudication) and in the commercial area this has taken the form of mediation or conciliation. While the terms are interchangeable conciliation is more commonly associated with assisted negotiation of consumer disputes or complaints; the assistance being provided

---

1   For negotiation strategies, see Fisher and Ury *Getting to Yes* (2nd edn, 1991); Ury *Getting Past No* (1991).

under the auspices of a trade association or professional regulatory body such as the Law Society of Scotland's complaints conciliation procedure[1].

Mediation is a method of dispute resolution which pre-dates litigation in many parts of the world, having been the 'rational' method of dispute resolution in simple societies[2]. In some countries, such as Japan, consensual dispute resolution is still the norm, particularly in commercial disputes, and resorting to adjudication is considered a failure for all concerned. While adjudication does not carry the same stigma in Scotland, mediation is perceived to have commercial benefit for the parties over direct negotiation or adjudication; although to date there has been a comparatively small take up rate for the mediation services available in the UK[3]. Commercial enterprises[4] and professional bodies[5] train or accredit mediators and arbiters and those who are members of a professional body are subject to the regulation and indemnities required by that body. There is no national process for the training or regulation of mediators and a mediation service may be provided by anyone who chooses to offer the service. Mediators charge a fee for their services, which is met by the parties in proportions agreed by them. It is open to the parties to agree whether the mediator will be facilitative or investigative. In the former, the mediator offers a personal evaluation of the parties' stances. But in the latter, the mediator merely assists the parties to evaluate their own stances and options.

The mediation process

Mediation is a process whereby a neutral person (the mediator) is appointed to participate in the negotiation between the parties. The mediator has no power to impose a solution on the parties[6] but can identify possible solutions and facilitate agreement between the parties. If the parties are to submit to mediation they must first agree upon the terms on which they are to submit. This agreement to mediate may be built into the principal contract, or may be reached after the dispute has arisen. Such agreement would include eg the identity, or at least the desired expertise, of the mediator, the extent of the issues to be mediated, a timescale for the mediation if the parties wished to restrict that in advance and to prevent litigation about the dispute during that period, arrangements for meeting the costs of the mediation, provision for confidentiality by the parties and

---

1 See Yelland and Davies 'Conciliating complaints' (1997) 42 JLSS 151.
2 MacCormack 'Procedures for the resolution of disputes in simple societies' (1976) XI Irish Jurist 175.
3 For a discussion of the practice of commercial mediation in Scotland, see Hollerin 'Alternative Dispute Resolution in Scottish Commercial Disputes' in Moody and MacKay (eds) *Alternative Dispute Resolution in Scotland* (1995) at p 73; and for a detailed examination of the process in commercial mediation, see Brown and Marriott *ADR Principles and Practice* (1993) ch 8.
4 Such as Centre for Dispute Resolution ('CEDR') and International Dispute Resolution Ltd ('IDR').
5 Such as the Law Society of Scotland whose accredited mediators promote mediation through the 'ACCORD' service.
6 Unless the parties have submitted to a 'med-arb' agreement described below.

the mediator and any other matters relevant to the conduct of the process. Generally the mediator is bound to neutrality and confidentiality by the contract to enter into mediation[1], and only after that contract is completed will the mediation proceed.

Commercial mediation will normally commence with each side making an opening statement about the dispute and their desired outcomes. Then the process moves through stages which can be a mixture of direct mediation, when both parties are in the room in the presence of the mediator (and may be accompanied by advisers if this has been agreed in advance); caucuses in which each party retires to discuss with advisers and/or the mediator proposals received or to be made; and shuttle mediation in which the mediator conveys from one party to the other proposals or responses to proposals. If agreement is achieved as a result of the mediation this will be summarised by the mediator in the presence of the parties and then recorded in contractually binding form.

Nature of mediation

Neither party is bound to reach agreement through the mediation process. If an agreement made in mediation is breached this may give rise to another dispute which the parties may refer to mediation or adjudication as they have agreed or as they see fit. Mediation in commercial disputes is governed wholly by agreement of the parties, and it may be that the wariness which one party feels about the other in the event of a dispute arising militates against reaching agreement to submit to mediation. Parties are more likely to appreciate the scope for mediation as a means of dealing with commercial disputes when they are entering into their principal contract and clauses providing for submission of disputes to mediation are often to be found in styles for commercial contracts. Mediation does not *per se* prevent litigation of a dispute, but an agreement to mediate could justify a plea of personal bar to litigation raised before mediation had at least been attempted. However, the fact that parties can walk away from the mediation without reaching agreement and with no apparent sanction may discourage them from attempting it in the fear that time will be wasted during which adjudication could have been proceeding.

Other methods of alternative dispute resolution

Some variations upon the pure adjudication or consensual methods have been developed in the United States in order to extend the options of parties wishing to effectively resolve a dispute without litigation and the following are options to consider for disputes arising in Scotland.

---

1 There is an argument that what occurs during mediation would attract the privilege attaching to communications with a view to settling litigation. Such communications cannot be founded upon in subsequent proceedings between the parties in so far as they are concessions made purely for the purposes of settling the dispute, but unequivocal admissions made within such communications are not privileged: *Daks Simpson Group plc v Kuiper* 1994 SLT 689.

Med-arb

'Med-arb' involves both mediation and arbitration. A person is appointed to act as mediator but if the mediation process fails, the mediator assumes the role of arbiter and adjudicates on the dispute. The main benefit of such an arrangement is that if the mediation fails the mediator possesses information which makes it possible to reach an arbitrated outcome more speedily and cost-effectively than if a separate arbiter had to be appointed. If the med-arb process is to be entered into the neutral person should be carefully chosen for possession of skills in both mediation and arbitration. However, med-arb carries the risk that the parties and the mediator will not give full commitment to the mediation process because they know that the in the event of failure to agree arbitration will take over.

Mini-trial and neutral evaluation

Mini-trial involves presentation of a potted version of the case in dispute to a privately chosen judge (usually an experienced commercial lawyer or retired judge) through a small number of witnesses: usually one factual witness and one expert witness. Sometimes the judge sits with a technical expert to assist in the evaluation of expert evidence. The process may be purely advisory, in which the judge's evaluation of the issues is sought to assist the parties in deciding how to negotiate a settlement or approach subsequent litigation. However, sometimes the neutral 'judge' will form a tribunal with executives of the parties involved in the dispute, and after hearing evidence the executives negotiate an outcome with the assistance of the neutral. The latter process is sometimes termed 'executive tribunal'. The terminology used to describe these processes is less important than the processes themselves, which are adaptable to suit the needs of the parties and the nature of the dispute.

PRESCRIPTION AND DISPUTE RESOLUTION

An obligation for payment which has subsisted for a continuous period of five years without any relevant claim having been made or without the subsistence of any claim having been relevantly acknowledged, prescribes and is extinguished from the expiration of the five-year period[1]. A claim may be made by commencing litigation for enforcement of the obligation, including recovery of the debt, or by commencing arbitration in respect of the obligation. Litigation is commenced when an action in which the claimant's case is relevantly made out (ie stated in sufficient detail) is served upon the defender, and arbitration is commenced when one party serves notice upon the other of the nature of the dispute and the intention to refer it to arbitration. The existence of an arbitration clause does not interfere with the normal operation of the five year prescriptive

---

1 Prescription and Limitation (Scotland) Act 1973, s 6(1).

period[1] and parties must, in the absence of acknowledgment of the claim, ensure that one or other method of adjudication has been validly commenced to preserve the claim from prescription. This applies even if the parties have commenced mediation within the five-year period, since submission to mediation does not *per se* constitute an acknowledgement of the claim.

CHOOSING A METHOD OF DISPUTE RESOLUTION

The methods of dispute resolution examined above are varied in terms of accessibility, flexibility, privacy, and enforceability. The following table identifies factors relevant to the method chosen. It must be borne in mind that only litigation can be commenced without any agreement of the other party. Arbitration is available only if the parties at some stage agree that the dispute will be adjudicated by arbitration, although once that is agreed the arbitration can be insisted upon in the face of opposition. Mediation and negotiation are entirely dependent upon agreement to enter into the process and to complete it.

Relevant factors	Litigation	Arbitration	Mediation
Privacy	Court documents and proceedings are open to the public.	No public access, although the existence of an arbitration may become known to eg subcontractor; stated case on point of law is public.	Private to parties and mediator. Mediator bound by duty of confidentiality to parties.
Cost	Court dues for initiating proceedings, lodging items of process, court dates assigned to case; fees of solicitors (and counsel, if used); witnesses' expenses in attending court; possible liability for opponent's expenses; same range of costs for appeal if taken.	Fees and expenses of arbiter(s), and if needed oversman and arbiter's clerk; fees of solicitors (and counsel, if used); hiring premises for arbitration hearing; witnesses expenses in attending arbitration; possible liability for opponent's expenses.	Mediator's fee.

1 *Rippin Group Ltd v ITP Interpipe SA* 1995 SLT 831; *Lowland Glazing Co Ltd (in receivership) v GA Group Ltd* 1997 SLT 257. Unusually the obligation itself, as distinct from the value or extent of the obligation, is contingent upon the outcome of the arbitration as in *Caledonian Insurance Co v Gilmour* (1892) 20 R (HL) 13, and in that event the prescriptive period would not begin until the arbitration was concluded.

Relevant factors	Litigation	Arbitration	Mediation
Flexibility	Limited to claims made by parties within traditional judicial remedies and procedures; unpredictable timespan and scope for delay; special commercial procedure flexible and less wasteful of time.	Subject to the terms of the arbitration agreement, but potentially flexible; over-reliance on quasi-judicial written pleadings undesirable; bound to observe natural justice and act within terms of arbitration agreement: can be very lengthy, particularly if cases are stated for the court's opinion.	Subject to parties' agreement unlimited range of outcomes; scope to negotiate future or contingent agreements, or amendments to existing agreement.
Enforceability	Judgment in form of decree; enforceable by all lawful means; procedure fixed and enforceable; judgment open to appeal.	Judgment in form of partial and final awards; enforceable by all lawful means if contains agreement for registration for execution; can be given the force of decree by application to the court; not open to review or appeal; may be set aside in limited circumstances.	Cannot insist upon mediation, although can provide for in principal contract; cannot insist on agreement being reached in mediation; if agreement reached, record in contractual form with consent to registration for execution; that agreement enforceable by litigation or arbitration.
Accessibility	Open access subject to ability to meet the expenses involved.	Accessible if other parties agree to arbitrate rather than litigate.	Accessible only if both parties agree, subject to finding suitably trained mediator.
Accountability	Bound to adhere to law and procedures; exercise discretion fairly and openly; open to appeal.	Failure to act impartially or in bad faith can lead to set aside of award and damages for breach of contractual duties; must exhaust but not exceed the submission, must follow any opinion of the court, otherwise wide discretion and not open to review.	If mediator shows bias mediation may fail. Liability for breach of contractual duties. No requirement for mediator to be registered or regulated. If mediator accredited by commercial or professional organisation may be subject to quality control.

2 Sale and supply of goods

This chapter examines Scots law in relation to three of the most common forms of commercial transaction: sale, hire and hire-purchase. Each of these contracts is governed not only by the general law of contract (eg on formation or breach of contract) but also by separate sets of statutory and common law rules which regulate the rights and duties of the parties depending on the particular type of contract involved. In addition, since many transactions depend on the customer's use of credit facilities, the complex provisions of the Consumer Credit Act 1974 will frequently apply. Statutory controls on the use of exclusion clauses are also important in all three types of contract, particularly as each contract involves the incorporation of a set of statutory implied terms which are specifically designed to protect the customer.

The scheme of treatment which follows considers the three contracts separately, starting with contracts of sale. In the case of hire and hire-purchase agreements, specific reference is made to detailed provisions in the Consumer Credit Act. Thereafter the chapter concludes by outlining some of the more important general features of the Consumer Credit Act.

Sale of goods

GENERAL

The sale of goods is undoubtedly the most common form of commercial transaction and covers contracts ranging from the sale of a daily newspaper to the sale of an aeroplane or an ocean-going yacht. Apart from the general law of contract, the relationship between the seller and buyer is mainly governed by the Sale of Goods Act 1979 (as amended)[1]. This Act repealed and replaced the Sale of Goods Act 1893 which was a codifying statute drafted to provide business throughout the UK with a comprehensive code on the law of sale. Much of the case-law decided under the original legislation is still valid today since the 1979 Act merely consolidated the amendments which had been made over the years to the 1893 Act.

Since the 1979 Act was passed, however, Parliament has made a number of important amendments, notably via the Sale and Supply of Goods Act 1994. The basic purpose of the legislation remains, however, unaltered and that is to protect the buyer's position by incorporating a series of implied terms into the contract of sale. To add to the protection provided by statutory implied terms, attempts by the seller to avoid liability under these terms through the use of exclusion clauses or notices are controlled by the Unfair Contract Terms Act 1977 and the Unfair Terms in Consumer Contracts Regulations 1994.

1 Referred to hereinafter simply as 'the 1979 Act'.

The nature and consequences of the contract of sale are now considered under three broad headings: the contractual liability of seller and buyer; delictual liability for defective goods; and, more briefly, criminal liability for misdescribing goods.

CONTRACTUAL LIABILITY

Formation of contract

Capacity

The Sale of Goods Act 1979 provides that the legal capacity to enter into a contract of sale is determined by the general law on contractual capacity[1]. Thus, eg, the contractual capacity of children and young adults is governed by the Age of Legal Capacity (Scotland) Act 1991. Individuals below the age of 16 generally have no capacity to enter contracts[2] and depend on their guardians – usually their parents – to transact on their behalf[3]. Hence contracts made by those under the age of 16 are void[4]. However, the 1991 Act recognises that many under 16s are active consumers who would be greatly inconvenienced if they did not enjoy some contractual capacity before their sixteenth birthday. Under 16s can therefore validly enter contracts of the kind which are 'commonly entered' by others of the same age and circumstances. The proviso to this limited form of capacity is that the particular contract is entered into 'on terms which are not unreasonable'[5].

The effect of this relaxation of the general rule is that many under 16s will be able to conclude valid contracts to buy food as well as (say) some kinds of clothes or sports equipment. However, other contracts involving, perhaps, the purchase of a CD player or a set of computer games might be set aside by the court, depending on the buyer's age and circumstances.

Individuals aged 16 and over enjoy full contractual capacity to enter into any contract of sale[6]. The legislation does, however, contain a safeguard where a contract proves to be 'prejudicial' and it was made when the buyer was 16 or 17. The affected individual can apply to the sheriff court or the Court of Session before the age of 21 to have the contract set aside on the basis that an adult exercising reasonable prudence would not have entered the contract given the same circumstances as the applicant faced. The applicant must convince the court that the contract has caused or is likely to cause him or her substantial prejudice[7]. The benefit of the right to have the transaction set aside will be lost if the applicant fraudulently misrepresented his or her age when he or she entered the contract[8].

1 1979 Act, s 3(1).
2 Age of Legal Capacity (Scotland) Act 1991, s 1(1)(a) (hereinafter referred to as 'the 1991 Act').
3 1991 Act, s 5.
4 1991 Act, s 2(5).
5 1991 Act, s 2(1).
6 1991 Act, s 1(1)(b).
7 1991 Act, ss 3 and 4.
8 1991 Act, s 3(3)(g).

Formalities

No formalities need be observed in forming or concluding a contract of sale; it can be done verbally or in writing or be partly verbal and partly written[1]. The actual terms of the contract may also be inferred from a regular course of dealing between the contracting parties or the established custom in a particular trade.

Consensus

Before an enforceable contract exists, the seller and buyer must have reached agreement or consensus on the goods which are being sold and the price for those goods.

Goods

The 1979 Act defines 'goods' in terms of all corporeal moveables or things except money. The exclusion of money is generally thought to refer only to current legal tender so that the sale of antique coins and notes would fall within the ambit of the Act[2]. The interpretation provision goes on to state that the term 'goods' includes industrial growing crops and things attached to the land which are agreed to be severed before sale or under the contract of sale[3]. Gow[4] suggests that a sale will fall within the Act when the contract relates (eg) to the sale of water, minerals, stone and buildings 'lying on top of the ground, or attached to thereto, or forming part of the subjacent strata'.

After more than a century, there appears to be little in the way of reported litigation on whether particular subject-matter qualifies as 'goods' for the purposes of the 1979 Act. In one Scottish case, the court swiftly disposed of the argument that unit trusts, as intangible forms of investment, could be regarded as 'goods'[5]. More controversially, however, the issue has been raised whether a sale of computer software is a sale of goods. There seems little doubt that the disks on which software is stored are goods so that the buyer of faulty or defective disks has a statutory remedy against the seller under the 1979 Act.

The more problematic question is whether defective software (eg infected by a virus) also gives rise to a claim under the Act. The recent obiter view of a judge sitting in the Queen's Bench Division is that 'software probably is goods within the [Sale of Goods] Act' because computer programs are 'of necessity contained in some physical medium, otherwise they are useless'[6]. However, in a later Scottish case, Lord Penrose held that a contract for the supply of software is not a contract of sale but a *sui*

---

1 1979 Act, s 4(1).
2 See eg Gow *Mercantile and Industrial Law of Scotland* (1964) p 81.
3 1979 Act, s 61(1).
4 Gow p 81.
5 See *Waverly Asset Management Ltd v Saha* 1989 GWD 8-346.
6 See Scott Baker J in *St Albans City and District Council v International Computers Ltd* [1995] FSR 686.

generis contract 'which may involve elements of nominate contracts such as sale, but would be inadequately understood if expressed wholly in terms of any of the nominate contracts'[1].

The American experience[2] in software disputes suggests that the UK courts could usefully draw a distinction between 'off the shelf' software and 'customised' software which is tailor-made to the buyer's requirements. If the software is bought 'off the shelf', the software should be regarded as goods bought under a contract of sale of goods. This would reflect the fact that the relationship between the parties is a limited one, leaving the dissatisfied customer with an immediate remedy against the seller who in turn could seek to hold the software manufacturer liable under the Act. The commercial reality is different, however, in the case of 'customised' software packages because the relationship between the parties is an on-going one which endures as the software is modified or tested in the light of the customer's experience. In other words, the customer who buys a tailor-made software package is not simply entering an agreement to purchase a product; he or she is also entering a contract which entitles him or her to call on the programming skills of the software designer after the package has been installed. Given the commercial importance of computer software in commercial life and the current uncertainty, an appellate decision on this aspect of the 1979 Act is awaited with considerable interest.

Types of goods

The 1979 Act recognises that things which fall within the definition of 'goods' can be either existing goods or unascertained goods. Existing goods are those which the buyer actually sees and selects at the time of purchase, such as the tin of beans sitting on the supermarket shelf or the secondhand car parked on the forecourt of the local garage. In other words, the parties know which particular goods are being sold and bought – or, as the 1979 Act puts it, the goods have been 'identified and agreed upon' at the time of sale[3].

In contrast, goods which are not specific goods are known as unascertained goods. Basically, goods are unascertained if they cannot be pointed to at the time the contract is made. For example, if a trader orders two tons of Jersey Royal potatoes, the goods will only become specific or ascertained goods when they are specifically set aside for that particular buyer. However, for the purposes of the 1979 Act, the contract is deemed to be one for the sale of unascertained goods because the goods were in an unascertained state when agreement was reached between the parties.

The categorisation of the type of goods sold under a particular contract is not merely of academic interest; it has important consequences for the parties as regards the passing of property and risk in the subject-matter of the contract (see below).

---

1 *Beta Computers (Europe) Ltd v Adobe Systems (Europe) Ltd* 1996 SLT 604 at 609.
2 See Atiyah and Adams *The Sale of Goods* (9th edn, 1995), pp 47–48.
3 1979 Act, s 61(1).

Price

Apart from the subject matter being sold, the parties must have agreed on the price to be paid before the contract of sale is enforceable. The price may be a specific figure or they may choose instead to settle it by agreeing on a price-fixing formula or method[1]. Examples of the latter include an agreement to pay the price determined by a mutually-chosen valuer or perhaps an undertaking to abide by the market price for a certain commodity on a particular day.

Seller's title

General rule

The buyer in a contract of sale enters into the agreement expecting to receive an unchallengeable legal title to the goods he or she has bought. Section 12(1) of the Sale of Goods Act 1979 stipulates that every contract of sale contains an implied condition that the seller 'has the right to sell the goods', either because he or she owns them or has the owner's authority to sell. Any attempt by the seller or supplier to contract out of this provision is automatically void under s 20(1) of the Unfair Contract Terms Act 1977. What happens, then, if the seller did not have the right to sell? The answer is given in s 21(1) of the 1979 Act, which sets out the general rule in such cases: 'where the goods are sold by a person who is not their owner, and who does not sell them under the authority or with the consent of the owner, the buyer acquires no better title than the seller had'. The rule is sometimes expressed in the time-honoured Latin phrase *nemo dat quod non habet*.

The effect of the *nemo dat* rule is that goods sold by a seller who lacked title or authority to sell are tainted by inherent fault and can be recovered from the buyer even though he or she bought in good faith. The buyer's only remedy in such cases is to seek return of the price by bringing a damages claim against the seller under s 12(2). This assumes, however, that the seller can still be located and is solvent.

Exceptions to the nemo dat *rule*

Parliament recognised that a strict application of the *nemo dat* rule would result in unfairness and so the general rule in s 21(1) has been relaxed in certain circumstances so as to protect the buyer's title to the goods he or she has bought. Where the circumstances indicate that the owner is personally barred from the 'denying the seller's authority to sell', the buyer will receive a good title. Also, if the goods were bought under a statutory power of sale, as often happens with lost property sold by the police or the railway authorities, the previous owner cannot challenge the buyer's title[2].

---

1 1979 Act, s 8(1). In the absence of the price being fixed in this way, the buyer must pay a reasonable price: s 8(2).
2 1979 Act, s 21(2)(b).

The owner is also barred from challenging the buyer's title under s 23 where the owner has taken insufficient steps to cancel or rescind the original contract of sale and the goods have since been sold to another buyer. This bar applies in cases where the first buyer's title was voidable because he or she acquired the goods from the owner by fraudulent means. As *MacLeod v Kerr* indicates, the owner must take sufficient steps to bring the rescission to the notice of the other party before the goods are re-sold. The facts in this case were as follows: Kerr sold his car to Galloway, who paid using a stolen cheque book. As soon as Kerr discovered that he had been defrauded, he informed the police but a day later, Galloway sold the car to a buyer who acted in good faith. The Inner House held that 'by no stretch of the imagination could we treat an intimation to the police as of any materiality to found a plea of rescission of the contract'. Kerr was therefore barred under s 23 from challenging the buyer's title; he should have raised a court action against Galloway or notified the buyer of the fraud before the car was re-sold[1].

'Mercantile agents' are deemed under the 1979 Act to have authority to sell goods on the owner's behalf so that they pass on a good title to the buyer who is innocent of the fact that the owner had removed his or her authority at the time of the sale. Auctioneers and brokers are covered by the term 'mercantile agent'[2].

Part III of the Hire Purchase Act 1964 safeguards the buyer's title where he or she has purchased a motor vehicle[3] in good faith when the vehicle is still subject to a hire-purchase agreement. In other words, the finance house which owned the vehicle which the buyer has bought will not be able to recover it from the buyer provided he or she acted in good faith[4]. The protection extends to private purchasers only and not to 'trade or finance purchasers'[5] for the reason that the latter are better able to protect themselves[6]. Anyone who 'carries on a business' trading in vehicles which are acquired for re-sale purposes will not be protected if they acquired the relevant vehicle for purely personal use[7]. Another limitation on the 1964 Act's protection is the fact that it only relates to undisclosed hire-purchase agreements and not to leasing or hire agreements. If the buyer falls outside the protection of the 1964 Act, he or she must return the vehicle to the finance house as owner. The buyer's remedy is to claim damages from the seller under s 12 of the 1979 Act assuming the latter can be traced and is worth suing.

---

1 1965 SC 253 at 257, per Lord President Clyde.
2 See definition of 'mercantile agent' in Factors Act 1889, s 1.
3 Defined in the Hire Purchase Act 1964, s 29(1) as a 'mechanically propelled vehicle intended or adapted for use on the roads to which the public has access'.
4 Hire Purchase Act 1964, ss 27(1) and (2).
5 Hire Purchase Act 1964, s 27(3) .
6 Trade or finance purchasers can check the central register of hire-purchase agreements kept by Hire Purchase Information (HPI). The system is not, however, totally foolproof: see *Moorgate Mercantile Co Ltd v Twitchings* [1977] AC 890 and criticism of this decision of the House of Lords in Ervine *Consumer Law in Scotland* (1995) p 64.
7 See *Stevenson v Beverley Bentinck Ltd* [1976] 2 All ER 606.

Transfer of property and risk

The object of every contract of sale is to transfer legal ownership or 'property' in the goods to the buyer. The Sale of Goods Act 1979 draws an important distinction between the physical delivery of goods and the transfer of property in the same goods. Property or ownership can pass independently of delivery. Depending on the circumstances, therefore, it is possible for a buyer to have become the legal owner of goods which he or she has still to receive or, conversely, for the buyer to have taken delivery of goods over which the seller retains ownership.

The distinction drawn above is of practical importance for several reasons. If the buyer is deemed to have acquired the property or ownership in the goods, he or she becomes liable for the price at the time when he or she becomes owner (unless the parties have agreed a different time for payment). Should the buyer become bankrupt when ownership of the goods has already passed to him or her, the goods will belong to the buyer's estate even if they were not in the buyer's possession when he or she became bankrupt.

Another reason why the distinction between ownership and possession is important concerns the risk that the goods are damaged or stolen. Under s 20(1) of the 1979 Act, the risk normally lies with the owner of the goods at the time of damage or loss *unless the parties have agreed otherwise*. Thus the risk falls on the buyer who has acquired the property in goods which are damaged while still on the seller's premises. The buyer will therefore be obliged to pay for the goods provided there was no question of negligence on the seller's part. Should, however, the seller have delivered the goods to the buyer but retained ownership under the contract (eg pending full payment), the risk of loss or damage remains with the seller until the property passes to the buyer.

Passing of property in specific goods

Given the importance of determining whether property has passed under a particular contract, the 1979 Act contains a series of rules in s 18 which are to be followed in settling any disputes that might arise. The detailed 'intention' rules in s 18 are subject to the overriding general rule in s 17(1) which states that property in specific or ascertained goods passes to the buyer when the parties intend it to pass. So the starting point in any dispute or uncertainty about transfer of property in goods is to examine the terms of the contract itself. The courts will also look at the conduct of the parties and the entire circumstances of the case[1]. Only if the parties' intention still remains unclear can the courts then resort to the rules in s 18 as 'a guide to the intention of the parties'[2].

A common element in the s 18 rules is the fact that they apply irrespective of delivery or possession of the goods. The intention rules also deliberately disregard whether payment for the goods has already been made

---

1   1979 Act, s 17(2).
2   See *Woodburn v Andrew Motherwell Ltd* 1917 SC 533 at 538, per Lord President Strathclyde.

or not. Delivery and payment are therefore totally irrelevant to the question of whether the buyer has acquired the property in the goods supplied under the contract. In all, there are four separate intention rules which apply to sales of specific or ascertained goods.

RULE 1

Rule 1 of s 18 applies to the simplest scenario, where the dispute involves the sale of specific goods 'in a deliverable state'. Goods are in a 'deliverable state' when they are ready in their contractually-agreed state and the buyer would be bound to take delivery[1]. In such cases, the property passes to the buyer when the contract is made. This outcome is not altered by the fact that the time of payment or the time of delivery or both were postponed by agreement. The decision in *Tarling v Baxter*[2] is an early instance of the immediate passing of property in specific goods which were in a deliverable state. Baxter bought Tarling's haystack but it was destroyed by fire before it could be collected. The court held that Baxter acquired ownership of the haystack as soon as the contract was made and so he had to pay for it (the risk of destruction having passed at the same time as ownership). In other words, Baxter was liable for the price even though he had not paid for the goods or taken delivery of them.

The first intention rule, like all the other intention rules in s 18, is subject to evidence that the parties had a contrary intention. This has led one court to hold that, in shop and supermarket sales, 'the intention of the parties quite clearly is that the property shall not pass until the price is paid'[3]. Also in this connection, it has been stated[4] that in sales to consumers 'very little is needed to give rise to the inference that the property in specific goods is only to pass on delivery or payment'. In other words, there is an arguable case that rule 1 is disapplied in a retail sale until the parties have at least agreed on the method of payment[5].

RULE 2

The second intention rule relates to specific goods which the seller is contractually bound to alter in some way so as to put them into a deliverable state. Until the alteration is carried out and the buyer has notice of the fact that the goods are now in a deliverable state, the property in the goods remains with the seller. For example, in *Brown Bros v Carron Co*[6], the defenders bought the pursuers' steam crane, which was to be modified and installed by the pursuers. The pursuers did not complete the modifications but tried to sue for the price when the defenders changed their minds about buying the crane. The court held that it was incompetent to sue for the price when the modifications had still to take place; the only remedy for the defenders' breach of contract was to sue for damages.

1 1979 Act, s 61(5).
2 (1827) 6 B & C 360.
3 *Lacis v Cashmarts* [1969] 2 QB 400 at 407, per Lord Parker.
4 *R V Ward Ltd v Bignall* [1967] 1 QB 534 at 545, per Diplock LJ.
5 See eg Carey Miller *Corporeal Moveables in Scots Law* (1991) p 150.
6 (1898) 6 SLT 231.

In contrast, in *Cockburn's Tr v Bowe & Sons*[1], the defenders agreed to buy an entire crop of potatoes from a farmer, on condition that the farmer lifted, stored and eventually transported the crop to the harbour. The farmer became bankrupt and the trustee in bankruptcy claimed that the potatoes, which had been lifted and stored by this time, still remained part of the farmer's estate. The court held that the goods were in a deliverable state at the time of bankruptcy; transporting them to the harbour was 'only a facility for their removal' and not necessary to make the goods deliverable. The crop of lifted potatoes therefore belonged to the defenders, who were obliged to pay the trustee the price which had earlier been agreed.

An interesting but apparently untested question under rule 2 – and also rule 3 below – is whether the requirement that the buyer 'has notice' means that only actual notice to the buyer is sufficient to transfer property. The common view[2] seems to be that constructive notice is not sufficient for title to pass to the buyer. On the other hand, property would probably transfer to the buyer if actual notice to him did not come directly from the seller[3].

RULE 3

This intention rule applies to the sale of specific goods where the seller 'is bound to weigh, test or measure, or do some other act or thing with reference to the goods for the purpose of ascertaining the price'. The property in such cases only passes to the buyer when the price-determining act has been carried out and the buyer has been informed of the price. It would seem that rule 3 applies only where duty is on the seller to do the weighing or measuring. Thus if the contract states that the relevant act is to be carried out by a sub-purchaser who has agreed to buy the goods from the original buyer, property will pass in accordance with rule 1 or 2 unless the parties have otherwise agreed[4].

RULE 4

The final rule on passing of property in specific goods deals with cases where the goods have been supplied on approval or on a 'sale or return' basis. The property in goods delivered on approval passes to the buyer when he signifies acceptance of the goods 'or does any other act adopting the transaction'. The latter phrase in rule 4 refers to what the courts used to term as 'an act of disposition' by the buyer. Lord Justice-Clerk Moncreiff in *Brown v Marr* referred to the need for evidence that the buyer had given up the right to return the goods. Evidence of deemed acceptance would come from the fact that the buyer 'exercises any right of property in the subject of the sale, as by selling, lending, hiring or pledging [pawning] the property'[5]. Thus, for instance, a retailer choosing to pawn items of jewellery which were delivered by a wholesaler on a sale or

1 1910 2 SLT 17.
2 See eg *Carey Miller* p 153.
3 *Gow* pp 126–127.
4 See *Nanka-Bruce v Commonwealth Trust Ltd* [1926] AC 77, PC.
5 (1880) 7 R 427 at 435.

return basis has been held to signify approval of the items pawned[1]. Other instances of adoption would include using or gifting the goods.

Rule 4 also provides that property in the goods is deemed to have passed when the buyer has retained the goods beyond the fixed period for approval stipulated under the contract without giving the seller notice of rejection. If the contract fails to mention a specific period for approval, the buyer becomes the owner of the goods after a 'reasonable period' has expired. In *Poole v Smith's Car Sales (Balham) Ltd*[2], the Court of Appeal held that a period of three months was more than a reasonable period for a dealer in secondhand cars to indicate rejection of cars supplied on a sale or return basis. The dealer was held to have accepted the cars and was thus liable for the price.

Passing of property in unascertained goods

The rules on passing of property in unascertained goods are different from those which apply to the sale of specific or ascertained goods. The term 'unascertained goods' is not defined in the Sale of Goods Act 1979 but the implication of s 61(1) is that term covers goods which have not been individually identified and agreed on. As Gow[3] notes, the essence of unascertained goods is that 'the buyer cannot point to any particular and individualised entity and say "*that* is what I have agreed to buy"'.

Contracts for the supply of unascertained goods are commercially important transactions, frequently involving the sale of commodities[4]. As a general proposition, unascertained goods fall into one of three categories[5]:

(1) 'future goods'[6] which have to be grown, manufactured or acquired by the seller so as to give effect to the contract (eg 50 bicycles to be made to the buyer's specification or a set of Georgian candlesticks to be acquired from a third party);
(2) 'generic goods' which have been agreed upon by reference to an accepted description of kind and quantity where the seller is free to supply the goods from any source (eg 20 tons of Western White Wheat); and
(3) 'goods forming part of an identified bulk' where the order is for a specified quantity which is to be supplied out of a larger, undivided bulk. An example of the latter category would be a contract to sell 100 tons of coffee stored as part of a larger cargo of coffee held on board the SS Bon Accord.

According to s 16 of the 1979 Act, the overriding principle in all contracts involving the sale of unascertained goods is that the property only passes to the buyer when the goods are specifically ascertained. As the

---

1 See *Bryce v Ehrmann* (1904) 7 F 5.
2 [1962] 2 All ER 482, CA.
3 *Gow* p 129.
4 See eg Burns 'The Reform of the Law on the Sale of Goods Forming Part of a Bulk' (1996) 59 MLR 260.
5 See eg *Carey Miller* pp 162–166.
6 The term is defined in the 1979 Act, s 61(1).

Law Commissions[1] have recently noted, s 16 is mandatory; the buyer and seller cannot contract out of it. Once the goods have been ascertained, the intention of the parties in relation to passing of property determines when the buyer acquires ownership[2]. Thus, for instance, if the contract appears to provide that the goods were to remain at all material times at the seller's risk, the court will conclude – on the basis that risk normally follows ownership[3] – that the property in the goods was prima facie intended to remain with the seller[4]. If the intention is not apparent from the terms or nature of the contract or the conduct of the parties[5], the courts are then free to use rule 5 of s 18 to determine when property passes to the buyer.

Rule 5(1) stipulates that goods of the required description must be 'unconditionally appropriated' to the contract. The act of appropriation also requires the assent of the non-appropriating party before the property in the goods transfers to the buyer.

APPROPRIATION

The need for appropriation means that the goods must be overtly marked or identified in some way as being the buyer's goods. The simplest act of unconditional appropriation is to deliver goods answering the contractual description to the buyer or the buyer's carrier 'in pursuance of the contract'[6]. In the absence of delivery, appropriation depends on goods of the stipulated quantity or weight having been 'individualised as a distinct entity'[7]. It would not be enough, however, for the seller merely to set goods apart which he might use in performance of the contract; there also needs to be evidence of an intention to commit these goods irrevocably to the contract with the buyer[8].

The leading Scottish case on the need for specific appropriation to a particular buyer is *Hayman & Son v McLintock*[9], where the buyer contracted to buy 250 sacks of flour stored in the seller's warehouse. The order was noted in the warehouse records but the sacks were never set aside or specifically labelled for the buyer. When the seller became bankrupt and the buyer tried to claim the goods, it was held that the property passed to the seller's trustee in bankruptcy under s 16. However, the fact that the goods have been set aside and clearly marked with the buyer's name will not itself be sufficient for property to pass if the contract requires the seller to do something further (eg arrange for the goods to be shipped to the buyer)[10].

1 *Report on the Sale of Goods forming part of a Bulk* (Law Com no. 215, Scot Law Com no. 145) (1993), para 2.3.
2 1979 Act, s 17; and *Karlshamns Oljefabriker v Eastport Navigation Corpn* [1982] 1 All ER 208 at 212, per Mustill J.
3 1979 Act, s 20(1).
4 *Carlos Federspiel & Co SA v Charles Twigg & Co Ltd* [1957] 1 Lloyd's Rep 240 at 256, per Pearson J.
5 1979 Act, s 17(2).
6 See 1979 Act, s 18, r 5(2). The delivered goods must be unmixed with other goods before appropriation takes place : see *Healey v Howlett & Sons* [1917] 1 KB 337 at 345, per Avory J.
7 See *Gow* p 130.
8 *Carlos Federspiel & Co SA v Charles Twigg & Co Ltd* [1957] 1 Lloyd's Rep 240 at 255, per Pearson J.
9 1907 SC 936.
10 *Carlos Federspiel & Co SA v Charles Twigg & Co Ltd* [1957] 1 Lloyd's Rep 240.

Where the goods are held by a third party, it would seem that the necessary appropriation takes place when the goods are identified and the third party acknowledges that he or she now holds the goods for a particular buyer. In *Wardars (Import and Export) Co Ltd v W Norwood & Sons Ltd*[1], the contract concerned a bulk order for frozen kidneys which were stored for the seller at a cold store. The haulage firm acting for the buyer called at the store with a delivery note and found that cartons had been set aside to await collection. The Court of Appeal held that the goods had been appropriated when the delivery order was accepted by an employee supervising the operation of the cold store.

ASSENT

Appropriation necessarily involves a mental element in addition to the physical act of earmarking or appropriation. The fact that goods have been physically set aside is not enough since the seller may change his mind; the act of appropriation therefore also needs to be supported by the intention of the parties that 'those goods and no others are the subject of the sale and become the property of the buyer'[2]. Thus rule 5(1) of s 18 states that the buyer needs to give his or her express or implied assent to the seller's act of appropriation before property passes[3]. For instance, in *Pignataro v Gilroy*[4], the sellers sent the buyer a delivery order informing him that the goods were in deliverable state and ready for collection. The buyer's assent to the appropriation was implied from his failure to collect the goods for over a month.

Rule 5(1) also states that assent can be given before or after appropriation takes place. In one old English case[5], the property in a quantity of barley was held to have passed to the buyer when the seller filled bags which the buyer had specifically provided for this purpose.

GOODS AS PART OF A BULK

The passing of property in goods which have been sold as part of an undivided bulk (eg 10 tons of tea out of the cargo on board a named ship) caused particular problems under the 1979 Act before it was amended by the Sale of Goods (Amendment) Act 1995. Prior to these amendments, the Law Commissions[6] published a joint report which found that 85 per cent of traders in commodities (tea, coffee, oil, grain etc) bought goods while they were still part of a larger bulk. As already noted, under the mandatory rule in s 16 the property in such goods could only pass when the part sold had been ascertained. There was evidence that the application of s 16 could result in injustice where the buyer had not received the goods out of bulk because the seller had gone bankrupt after the price had been paid

1 [1968] 2 QB 663, CA.
2 *Carlos Federspiel & Co SA v Charles Twigg & Co Ltd* [1957] 1 Lloyd's Rep 240 at 255, per Pearson J.
3 The converse situation, with the seller assenting to the buyer's act of appropriation, is also possible under r 5(1) but less likely.
4 [1919] 1 KB 459.
5 See *Aldridge v Johnson* (1857) 26 LJQB 296.
6 *Report on the Sale of Goods forming part of a Bulk* para 1.3.

but before delivery had taken place. For example, in *Re Wait*[1], the buyer contracted to buy 500 tons of wheat out of a ship's cargo of 1,000 tons and paid for the goods in advance. The seller became bankrupt before the order was separated from the bulk cargo. The court held that the property in the goods had not passed to the buyer since the goods remained unascertained. The buyer therefore lost the goods and had to rank as an unsecured creditor for return of the price.

The full rigour of s 16 had been partly mitigated by the courts which were prepared to recognise that the buyer's goods could become ascertained by a process of exhaustion where other orders were removed from the bulk leaving only the part destined for the buyer[2]. However as Burns[3] notes, case law produced other uncertainties for buyers of commodities which latterly resulted in some traders considering changing the applicable law of their contracts to avoid the application of the 1979 Act altogether.

Part of the effect of the 1995 amendments[4] is to put the ascertainment by exhaustion rule on to a statutory footing[5]. Thus, where the buyer has contracted to buy a specified quantity of unascertained goods forming part of a bulk, the property passes to the buyer if the bulk is reduced by deliveries so that it contains only the quantity sold to the buyer. The passing of property depends on the source of the bulk being identified either at the time the contract was made or subsequently by agreement between the parties.

Retention of title

The Sale of Goods Act 1979 allows an unpaid seller to deliver goods on credit to a buyer while retaining ownership or title over the goods[6]. As a result, many commercial contracts of sale include a 'retention of title' clause which expressly reserves property in delivered goods to the seller until the goods have been paid for. In *Archivent Sales and Development Ltd v Strathclyde Regional Council*[7], the sellers stipulated that 'until payment of the price in full is received by [the sellers] the property in the goods supplied by [the sellers] shall not pass to the customer'. Since the House of Lords endorsed the validity of the 'all debts owed' retention of title used in *Armour v Thyssen*[8], 'all sums' clauses are increasingly employed in commercial contracts to protect the seller's position where he regularly supplies goods on credit to the same buyer. Should the buyer become

1   [1927] 1 Ch 606.
2   See eg *Karlshamns Oljefabriker v Eastport Navigation Corpn* [1982] 1 All ER 208, where a Swedish buyer agreed to buy 6,000 tons of copra stored on a ship carrying 22,000 tons. After calling at Rotterdam and Hamburg to offload 16,000 tons for other buyers, it was held that the Swedish buyer's goods were ascertained when the discharge was completed in Hamburg.
3   Burns (1996) 59 MLR 260 at 266–267.
4   For the impact of the other amendments which resulted in the common ownership provisions found in the 1979 Act, ss 20A and 20B, see Burns (1996) 59 MLR 260 at 268–269.
5   See 1979 Act, s 18, r 5(3) and (4).
6   1979 Act, s 19.
7   1985 SLT 154.
8   1990 SLT 891, HL.

bankrupt without having paid for the goods, the seller can rely on the retention clause to reclaim the goods from the buyer's trustee in bankruptcy.

Sub-buyers are protected under s 25(1) if they buy goods in good faith which are still subject to a retention of title clause in the contract between the original seller and buyer. If the sub-buyer purchases the goods without notice of the earlier retention of title, he obtains a good title to the goods and can fend off any claim brought by the original seller. The application of s 25(1) was illustrated in *Archivent Sales and Development Ltd v Strathclyde Regional Council*[1]. Building contractors purchased ventilators on credit from suppliers who stipulated in the contract that the property in the goods was not to pass to the buyers until the price had been settled in full. The ventilators were fitted into a new school building but the buyers became insolvent before settling the invoice. The court held that the property in the goods had passed to the defenders who had taken over the new school from the buyers without notice of suppliers' reservation of title.

Risk and frustration

Transfer of risk

If the goods are damaged or stolen after the contract is made, who bears the risk (or cost) of the resultant loss – the seller or the buyer? Section 20(1) of the 1979 Act establishes the general rule in such cases: risk follows ownership of the goods unless the parties have 'otherwise agreed'. The parties are therefore free to separate ownership and risk. The contract could, for instance, require the buyer to insure the goods as soon as the contract is made even though property or ownership is not due to pass until a later stage. Assuming the parties have not made some other arrangement, the buyer takes on the risk of loss or damage at the point when the property in the goods passes to him under the contract 'whether delivery has been made or not'[2]. For instance, in *Pignataro v Gilroy*[3] the buyer owned various bags of rice which he failed to collect from the seller's warehouse. The bags were stolen and the court found that the buyer had to bear the loss because the property had passed to him before the goods were stolen.

The general rule in s 20(1) is subject to two important exceptions. If delivery of the goods has been delayed through the fault of either buyer or seller, the party at fault bears the risk of 'any loss which might not have occurred but for such fault'[4]. The term 'fault' is defined in s 61(1) as meaning wrongful act or default. The buyer had to bear the loss in *Demby Hamilton & Co Ltd v Barden*[5] when a quantity of apple juice had to be destroyed because he delayed in taking delivery of his regular order. The

---

1 1985 SLT 154.
2 1979 Act, s 20(1). If the goods unavoidably deteriorate in transit, the buyer must bear this risk unless the parties have agreed otherwise: 1979 Act, s 33.
3 [1919] 1 KB 459.
4 1979 Act, s 20(2).
5 [1949] 1 All ER 435.

sellers were therefore entitled to the price for the juice which went bad. The other exception relates to liability as custodier or temporary keeper of the other party's goods[1]. The custodier is under a duty to take reasonable care of the property in his or her possession and will be liable for any loss or damage sustained as a result of a failure to exercise such care. According to Bell[2], the place chosen to store the goods 'must be secure against the ordinary accidents incident to the property to be preserved'.

Frustration

The general law of contract recognises the principle of *rei interitus* by which a contract is dissolved if the subject-matter of the contract is totally destroyed and neither party is at fault[3]. The same principle is reflected in s 6 of the 1979 Act. Thus if the seller concludes a contract for the sale of specific goods which unknown to him or her have perished, the contract is void. Similarly, under s 7, where there is an agreement to sell specific goods and these goods are subsequently destroyed without the fault of either party, the contract is dissolved if the risk remained with the seller at the time of destruction. In other words, the buyer is not liable for the price and the seller is not liable in damages for non-delivery.

However, the 1979 Act only deals with specific goods which 'perish'. Nothing is said nothing about the destruction of unascertained goods or the effect of events apart from destruction which make the contract impossible to perform (eg refusal of an export licence). These matters are, therefore, left to the common law or any *force majeure* clause which parties in a commercial sale might have prudently included in the contract[4]. At common law, for instance, an agreement to sell generic goods would not be frustrated merely because the seller's 'only source has dried up'; the seller would still be liable in damages for non-delivery[5]. However, where the agreement is to sell future goods which the seller has undertaken to grow, manufacture or acquire to meet the buyer's order, the contract is frustrated if the goods are destroyed or lost through no fault of the seller[6].

Description of goods

The seller is under an implied duty under s 13 of the Sale of Goods Act 1979 to ensure that, where the goods are sold '*by* description', the goods supplied correspond with that description. The obligation applies to specific and ascertained goods and to private and business sellers alike. Goods can, of course, be described in terms of size, weight, colour, com-

---

1 1979 Act, s 20(3).
2 *Commentaries* I, 488.
3 On frustration generally, see McBryde *The Law of Contract in Scotland* (1987) ch 15.
4 *Force majeure* clauses can deal with a whole range of unforeseen events (eg strikes, bad weather, embargoes, refusal of import or export licences) which render the contract practically impossible to perform. See eg *McBryde* paras 15.45–15.48.
5 *Monkland v Jack Barclay Ltd* [1951] 2 KB 252 at 258, per Asquith LJ.
6 See eg *Howell v Coupland* (1876) 1 QBD 258 (potato blight); *H R & S Sainsbury Ltd v Street* [1972] 3 All ER 1127 (poor harvest).

position and many other characteristics[1]. The essence of a sale *by* description is that the buyer has relied on the seller's description when contracting to buy.

Sales by description most obviously take place when someone orders through a mail order catalogue or responds to a newspaper advert; the customer clearly has not seen the goods and is therefore relying on the description alone when agreeing to buy[2]. Section 13 also applies where the goods are packed in such a way that the buyer effectively relies on the description found on the packaging or labelling before contracting with the seller. Moreover, the Act specifically provides that a sale is not prevented from being a sale by description merely because the buyer has actually seen and selected the goods[3]. Thus in *Grant v Australian Knitting Mills Ltd*[4], the Privy Council held that the sale of woollen underpants sold across the shop counter was a sale by description because the goods were sold 'not merely as the specific thing but as a thing corresponding to a description'.

The courts have held that a buyer who examines the goods in some detail may still be able to hold the seller liable for a breach of s 13. In *Beale v Taylor*[5], eg, the buyer responded to a newspaper advert for a car which was described as a 'Herald, convertible, white, 1961'. After inspecting the car he bought it, only to discover later that the car in fact consisted of two welded parts, only one of which dated from 1961. The Court of Appeal held that the seller was in material breach of s 13 because the buyer placed considerable reliance on the '1961 Herald' description in the seller's advert.

A sale by sample constitutes another form of sale by description. The goods ultimately supplied to the buyer must not only correspond with the sample shown earlier; they must also comply with the description applied to the goods at the time the contract was made[6].

The Court of Appeal emphasised in *Harlingdon & Leinster Enterprises Ltd v Hull Fine Art Ltd*[7] that the buyer can only succeed under s 13 by showing that he relied on the seller's description of the goods. In this case, the buyer bought a painting from a private gallery which the gallery described as being the work of a particular German expressionist artist. The gallery owner disclaimed any expertise in German art and the buyer bought the painting for £6,000 relying on his own expertise. When the painting proved to be the work of another artist and worth only £100, the court held by a 2:1 majority that there was no breach of s 13 because the seller's description was not influential in securing the sale. The buyer had chosen to rely on his own expertise and judgment so that there was no sale '*by* description' as such.

Case law indicates that s 13 is not appropriate where the buyer's complaint has to do with the quality rather than the identity of the goods sup-

1 Eg indications as to age, origin or approval by official bodies.
2 See *Varley v Whipp* [1900] 1 QB 513 (secondhand machine bought purely on the basis of seller's written description).
3 1979 Act, s 13(3).
4 [1936] AC 85 at 100, per Lord Wright.
5 [1967] 3 All ER 253, CA.
6 See 1979 Act, s 13(2).
7 [1990] 1 All ER 737, CA.

plied. Questions to do with product quality or performance are properly raised under the satisfactory quality provision in s 14. Thus in *British Steamship Co Ltd v Lithgows Ltd*[1], the buyers placed an order for a bulk carrying vessel and precise engine power requirements were specified in the contract. The buyers later alleged a breach of s 13 when there were repeated problems with part of the main engine. The court held that the question of the engine's performance or reliability was a complaint about the quality of the goods which should have been brought under s 14; the description provision in s 13 was only relevant to the engine's technical capacity (which was not an issue in the case).

Quality of goods

General issues

The seller is under an implied duty under s 14 to supply goods of 'satisfactory quality'. This duty only applies where the seller 'sells goods in the course of a business'. The term 'business' includes a profession and the activities of any local authority or government department[2]. Thus, for instance, when the Ministry of Defence sells off surplus clothing, it is bound to supply goods of satisfactory quality. The Act does not require the seller to be a regular supplier of the goods which he or she has sold or, indeed, to be someone who regularly sells goods of any kind. It is arguable, eg, that the vet who sells his or her firm's Range Rover every two years is within the scope of s 14 because he or she is still selling the vehicle 'in the course of a business'. In the only reported case on this point under the 1979 Act, the Court of Session has held that the final sale in the life of a business is covered by s 14. In *Buchanan-Jardine v Hamilink*[3], a farmer who was retiring held a closing down sale. Lord Cameron held that this was still a sale in the course of a business since the proceeds should properly be entered in the business accounts.

To ensure that buyers are not duped into thinking that advertised goods are being sold by a private seller (against whom they have no remedy under s 14), advertisements must indicate that the seller is selling in the course of a business. Thus, eg, the symbol 'T' (for trader) frequently appears in small advertisements for second-hand cars. Failure to carry an indication of the seller's status is a criminal offence[4].

Liability under s 14 extends to cases where a private seller (or principal) employs a trader to act as his or her agent when dealing with the buyer[5]. In such cases, the disappointed buyer can sue either the principal or the agent[6]. The principal can only avoid liability if reasonable steps were taken before the contract was made to bring the buyer's attention to the fact that the principal was not selling the goods in the course of a business.

---

1 1975 SLT (Notes) 20 at 21, per Lord Maxwell.
2 1979 Act, s 61(1).
3 1983 SLT 149 at 153.
4 See Business Advertisements (Disclosure) Order 1977, SI 1977/1918.
5 1979 Act, s 14(5).
6 See *Boyter v Thomson* 1995 SLT 875, HL.

The duty to supply goods of satisfactory quality applies to the goods actually supplied under the contract, so that the presence of foreign material accidentally supplied along with the order will determine whether the goods supplied are of satisfactory quality. Thus in *Wilson v Rickett, Cockerell & Co Ltd*[1], the pursuer unexpectedly received a detonator in the bag of coal which he had ordered. Not surprisingly, the hidden detonator exploded when the contents of the bag were put on his living room fire. The Court of Appeal held that the duty under s 14 applied to all the goods delivered in pursuance of the contract, including any extraneous or offending material. The courts will consider not only the goods themselves as physical items but also the packaging and the instructions which accompany the goods to determine whether s 14 has been breached. Thus failure to supply adequate instructions on how to use a particular product or to package the goods properly is relevant in deciding whether s 14(2) has been breached.

The need for goods to be of satisfactory quality replaces the merchantable quality test which applied to contracts made before January 1995. The old test was removed on the recommendation of both Law Commissions, partly because it did not seem particularly appropriate to consumer transactions. The new test is considerably more expansive than its predecessor, though in many respects it simply puts onto the statute book factors which the courts were already beginning to regard as being relevant to the seller's liability under s 14. Two aspects of liability under s 14 remain, however, unaltered since the satisfactory quality standard was introduced. The seller is not liable for defects which were specifically drawn to the buyer's attention before the contract was made. Also, where the buyer chooses to examine the goods before purchasing, the seller is not liable for defects which the buyer's examination ought to have revealed[2].

Satisfactory quality

The 1979 Act establishes an objective standard for satisfactory quality. According to s 14(2A), the goods must meet the standard 'that a reasonable person would regard as satisfactory, taking account of any description of the goods, the price (if relevant) and all the other relevant circumstances'. It will be relevant, for instance, that the goods have been described as 'seconds' or 'smoke-damaged', or that the buyer negotiated a reduction in the price because of some defect or blemish in the goods.

In addition to the basic definition of satisfactory quality, s 14(2B) lists a series of specific aspects of product quality which may be taken into account in appropriate cases in determining whether the seller has met the required standard. The list is not exhaustive and other factors may be considered by the court if they are relevant to the standard of quality which a reasonable person would expect.

1 [1954] 1 QB 598.
2 1979 Act, s 14(2C).

Fitness for purpose

The first aspect of quality mentioned in s 14(2B) states that the goods supplied must be fit for *all* their common purposes. This reverses the decision in *Aswan Engineering Establishment Co (M/S) v Lupdine Ltd*[1] that goods were of merchantable quality even if they were only fit for one purpose. This aspect of product quality only relates to common or usual purposes; goods used for unusual purposes will not be supplied in breach of s 14(2) unless the buyer made his or her particular purpose known to the seller at the time the contract was made[2].

Appearance and freedom from minor defects

The Law Commissions recognised in their joint report[3] that consumers derive satisfaction from the way goods are finished, particularly in the case of expensive or luxury items. It is not enough, for instance, that a new car is delivered in a roadworthy condition and can be driven safely from A to B; the buyer is also looking for an 'appropriate degree of comfort, ease of handling and reliability and of pride in the vehicle's outward and interior appearance'[4]. Section 14(2B) therefore recognises that 'appearance and finish' and 'freedom from minor defects' will be relevant factors in many cases in judging satisfactory quality[5]. To quote from the Law Commissions' report, this means that 'dents, scratches, minor blemishes and discolourations, and small malfunctions' will in 'appropriate cases' be breaches of s 14 provided the defects are not 'so trifling' as not to be breaches of contract.

The effect of s 14(2B) is to overturn the decision in *Millars of Falkirk Ltd v Turpie*[6], where the Inner House held that an oil leak in the power steering system of a new car, which would have cost only £25 to repair, did not amount to a breach of s 14. Lord President Emslie did not regard the presence of 'some defects' in new cars as in any way 'exceptional'[7]. The Law Commissions' report is, however, at pains to point out that not every minor defect will necessarily amount to a breach of s 14[8]. Ultimately, each case will depends on its own facts and requires the courts to conduct an objective comparison of the condition of the goods supplied with the standard which a reasonable person would find satisfactory.

Safety

The safety of the goods is another factor which s 14(2B) explicitly allows the courts to consider in appropriate cases, although unsafe goods had

1 [1987] 1 All ER 135, CA.
2 See 1979 Act, s 14(3).
3 *Report on Sale and Supply of Goods* (Law Com no. 160; Scot Law Com no. 104) (1987) para 3.31.
4 See *Rogers v Parish (Scarborough) Ltd* [1987] 2 All ER 232 at 237 per Mustill LJ.
5 Contrast Rougier J's obiter comments in *Bernstein v Pamson Motors (Golders Green) Ltd* [1987] 2 All ER 220 at 229 to the effect that 'even the buyer of a new car must put up with a certain amount of teething troubles'.
6 1976 SLT (Notes) 66.
7 1976 SLT (Notes) 66 at 68.
8 *Report on Sale and Supply of Goods* para 3.40.

been held to be of unmerchantable quality before the Act was amended[1]. The fact, for instance, that potentially hazardous or dangerous goods are sold with inadequate instructions or warnings may amount to a breach of s 14(2)[2].

Durability

The final factor which can be relevant to satisfactory quality is the durability of the goods supplied. As far back as 1981, the Scottish Consumer Council had recommended that the Sale of Goods Act should be amended to include a specific reference to durability. This view found judicial support in the House of Lords, where Lord Diplock expressed the view that goods ought to be reasonably durable from the time of delivery[3]. However, the Law Commissions[4] found that very few cases on durability were ever reaching the higher courts and 'that judicial attitudes expressed in some of the lower courts on the question of durability make it hard for consumers to achieve a satisfactory settlement'. The amended legislation means that goods must be durable, a matter which is to be judged at the time the goods were delivered.

The fact that goods break down or no longer function properly following a short period of normal use will be prima facie evidence that the goods were not of satisfactory quality at the time they were delivered. However, the court's overall judgment on durability will also depend on how the goods were described at the time of sale, the price and the type and frequency of use to which the goods were put before the problems emerged. In other words, goods must last for a reasonable period but that assessment will depend, in part, on whether the goods have, for instance, been heavily used or badly treated.

However, the buyer loses the statutory right to reject undurable goods if he or she has retained them long enough for acceptance to be deemed to have taken place. Buyers therefore enjoy only a short-term period of rejection during which they can reject the goods and reclaim the price: after the right to reject has been lost, the only remedy is to seek damages from the seller based on the loss 'directly and naturally' arising from the breach of contract. The buyer's loss will prima facie amount to the difference between the value of the goods at the time of delivery and the value which the goods would have had if they had been durable[5].

Fitness for particular purpose

In addition to the need to supply goods of satisfactory quality, the seller comes under a further obligation to the buyer under s 14(3) if the buyer expressly or impliedly makes known to the seller that the buyer requires the goods to fulfil a purpose. Where a particular purpose is conveyed to

1 See eg *Lambert v Lewis* [1982] AC 255.
2 See eg *Wormell v RHM Agricultural (East) Ltd* [1986] 1 All ER 769; reversed on appeal, though not doubting that instructions have to be taken into account: [1987] 3 All ER 75, CA.
3 See *Lambert v Lewis* [1982] AC 255 at 276.
4 *Report on Sale and Supply of Goods* para 2.15.
5 1979 Act, s 53A.

the seller, there is an implied term in the contract that the goods supplied are 'reasonably fit' for that purpose. The buyer can rely on s 14(3) if the purpose of the goods is normal or obvious. In *Priest v Last*[1], the buyer relied on the seller's selection of a hot water bottle which burst on the fifth time it was used. The court held that there had been a breach of what was now s 14(3).

However, where the buyer has some special or unusual purpose or need in mind, this must be expressly communicated to the seller if the buyer is going to rely on s 14(3). Thus in *Griffiths v Peter Conway*[2], the buyer of a Harris Tweed coat had unusually sensitive skin. Her dermatitis was aggravated when she wore the coat but the court found that the cloth would not have affected a normal person's skin. The claim under s 14(3) failed because the buyer did not disclose her dermatitis at the time of purchase. Again, in *Flynn v Scott*[3], the buyer's claim under s 14(3) was rejected because he failed to inform the seller that he was purchasing a lorry which he intended to use to transport livestock and furniture. More recently, the House of Lords has held that there is no breach of s 14(3) where the seller is not informed of an abnormal feature or idiosyncrasy 'in the circumstances of the use of the goods by the buyer. That is the case whether or not the buyer is himself aware of the abnormal feature or idiosyncrasy'[4].

Liability under s 14(3) is avoided if the buyer did not rely on the seller's skill or judgment in selecting the goods for a particular purpose, or it was unreasonable for him or her to rely on the seller's choice.

Sale by sample

Where goods are sold by sample, s 15 implies a term in the contract that the bulk will correspond with the sample in quality. The implied term also gives the buyer a 'reasonable opportunity' to compare the bulk delivered with the sample shown earlier. The goods must be free of any defect rendering them of unsatisfactory quality which would not be apparent on reasonable examination of the sample. The best known application of s 15 is the case of *Godley v Perry*[5]. The plaintiff was blinded in one eye after using a toy catapult which broke. He sued the seller who had bought the catapult by sample from a wholesaler. A sample catapult had been tried but no defect was apparent from the examination. The evidence in the case was that poor quality plastic has been used in making the goods which left them unsuitable for the purpose of being used as catapults. The seller was found liable for breach of s 14 but was held entitled to recover from the wholesaler under s 15.

Exclusion of implied terms

Sellers frequently attempt to rely on an exemption clause or notice to avoid liability to the buyer for breach of implied terms under the Sale of

1   [1903] 2 KB 148.
2   [1939] 1 All ER 685.
3   1949 SC 442.
4   *Slater v Finning Ltd* 1996 SLT 912 at 916, per Lord Keith.
5   [1960] 1 All ER 36.

Goods Act 1979. The discussion below proceeds on the assumption that the relevant term has been incorporated into the contract and can be construed to cover the buyer's complaint – something which the common law rules on incorporation and construction of terms determine[1].

The Unfair Contract Terms Act 1977

If the seller attempts to exclude the implied term as to title to the goods, the clause or notice is void under the Unfair Contract Terms Act 1977[2]. Should the seller attempt to exclude or limit his liability to the buyer for breach of ss 13 to 15 of the Sale of Goods Act 1979, the clause or notice is void in a consumer contract and is subjected to a 'fair and reasonable' test in all other cases[3]. A consumer contract under the Unfair Contract Terms Act 1977 is one where the buyer ('the consumer') does not deal in the course of a business but the seller does. The goods supplied to the consumer must be of a type 'ordinarily supplied for private use or consumption'. The seller has the onus of showing that the contract was not a consumer contract[4].

If the 'fair and reasonable' test applies, the onus is on the seller to show that it was reasonable to incorporate the term in the contract[5]. In resolving the matter, the court will consider the Sch 2 guidelines in the 1977 Act. Several factors may need to be considered, including the relative bargaining strengths of the parties, whether the term was customary in the trade and whether there were alternative means of meeting the buyer's requirements. The Court of Session has held that the 'very width' of the matters listed in Sch 2 requires the court 'to look critically at any provision which is wholly conceived in the interests of the author' and at the expense of the other party's statutory rights. A term which is drafted in this way will only pass the reasonableness test if the meaning of the exclusion is 'clear and unambiguous'[6].

In a case dealing with alleged inequality of bargaining power between buyers and sellers at Peterhead fish market, the sheriff principal held that a term was not unreasonable merely because it was part of a set of non-negotiable terms tendered by the seller. The situation would be different if buyers were forced to buy from the same seller but that was not the case in this instance. Moreover, the buyers were a substantial organisation which employed skilled and experienced staff who were capable of looking after their own interests[7].

The Unfair Terms in Consumer Contracts Regulations 1994

In addition to the Unfair Contract Terms Act, further controls on the seller's exclusion of liability are contained in the Unfair Terms in

---

1 On which, see *McBryde* ch 13.
2 Unfair Contract Terms Act 1977, s 20(1)(a) (hereinafter referred to as 'the 1977 Act').
3 1977 Act, s 20(2).
4 1977 Act, s 25(1).
5 1977 Act, s 24(4).
6 *Knight Machinery (Holdings) Ltd v Rennie* 1995 SLT 166 at 170, per Lord McCluskey.
7 *Denholm Fishselling Ltd v Anderson* 1991 SLT (Sh Ct) 24 at 25.

Consumer Contracts Regulations 1994[1]. The Unfair Terms Regulations implement the UK's obligations under a Directive[2] of the same name and came into force on 1 July 1995[3]. The Regulations apply to a term which has not been individually negotiated in the sense that the term was drafted in advance and the 'consumer' has not been able to influence the substance of the term[4]. Arguably, the Regulations apply to the unnegotiated part of a term where the rest of that term was individually negotiated[5]. The term 'consumer' refers to an individual 'who is acting for purposes outside his business'[6]. The seller is someone who sells goods for purposes related to his or her business. The onus is on the seller to show that the relevant term was individually negotiated[7].

Assuming the term has not been individually negotiated, it will be subject to a test of 'fairness'. The consumer is not bound by a term which is deemed to be unfair[8]. The fairness test consists of three distinct requirements: the term must (1) be contrary to the requirements of good faith; (2) cause a significant imbalance in the parties' rights and obligations under the contract; and (3) be detrimental to the consumer[9]. The unfair nature of the particular term must take into account the nature of the goods, all circumstances attending the conclusion of the contract and all the other terms of the contract[10]. The core principle of 'good faith' requires consideration of the respective bargaining positions of the parties, whether the consumer had an inducement to agree to the term and the extent to which seller has dealt 'fairly and equitably' with the consumer[11]. To assist the courts, an 'indicative and non-exhaustive' list of terms which 'may be regarded as unfair' is annexed to the Regulations[12]. However, the Regulations are silent on where the burden of proof lies in relation to proving or disproving unfairness. The assumption must be that the onus lies with the consumer to show that a particular term is unfair.

Buyer's remedies

The buyer has remedies against the seller under the Sale of Goods Act 1979 where the express or implied terms of the contract have been

---

1 SI 1994/3159.
2 EC Council Directive 93/13 (OJ L95, 21.4.93, p 29).
3 For an excellent critique of the Regulations, see Brownsword and Howells 'The Implementation of the EC Directive on Unfair Terms in Consumer Contracts' (1995) JBL 243.
4 1994 Regulations, reg 3(1) and (3).
5 See 1994 Regulations, reg 3(4); but some doubt must remain about this proposition until the European Court of Justice provides a definitive interpretation.
6 1994 Regulations, reg 2.
7 1994 Regulations, reg 3(5).
8 1994 Regulations, reg 5(1).
9 1994 Regulations, reg 4(1). It could be argued that a term causing a significant imbalance to the detriment of the consumer is simply a definition of good faith itself but this is not apparently what the DTI had in mind: see DTI 'Implementation of the EC Directive on Unfair Terms in Consumer Contracts 93/13/EEC: A Further Consultation Document' (September 1994), p 3, quoted in Brownsword and Howells (1995) JBL 243 at 254.
10 1994 Regulations, reg 4(2).
11 1994 Regulations, reg 4(3) and Sch 2.
12 1994 Regulations, reg 4(4) and Sch 3.

breached. Remedies are also specifically provided where the seller has delivered the wrong quantity of goods or has failed to deliver the goods altogether.

Breach of express or implied terms

The disappointed buyer is entitled under s 15B of the 1979 Act to claim damages from the seller where the seller is in breach of any express or implied term of the contract. If the seller's breach is material, the buyer can reject the goods and treat the contract as repudiated by the seller's failure to perform. Consumer purchasers are given additional protection by the recent insertion of s 15B(2) into the 1979 Act. They can treat any breach of ss 13 to 15 of the Act (or any express term dealing with the same matters) as a material breach on the seller's part and so reject the goods and rescind the contract. The buyer qualifies as a 'consumer' purchaser if he or she did not deal or hold himself or herself out as dealing in the course of a business. Thus private buyers now enjoy a right of rejection as the standard remedy for any breach of contract[1]. On the other hand, commercial buyers will only be able to reject goods if they can show that the seller's breach was a material breach.

Right to reject goods

Rejection is effectively exercised as a remedy only if the buyer has unequivocally indicated that he or she has not accepted the goods. Intimation of refusal to accept the goods is sufficient; it is then the seller's responsibility to collect the goods from the buyer who is entitled to claim reasonable storage costs to cover the period after rejection has been intimated[2].

The buyer's right to reject is lost if he or she is deemed to have 'accepted' the goods in one of three cases mentioned in s 35 of the 1979 Act. The first case concerns express intimation of acceptance to the seller. The Law Commissions' report[3] noted the problem of so-called 'acceptance notes' which the buyer may be asked to sign before he or she has had an opportunity to examine the goods. In the past, signature of the seller's acceptance note on taking delivery of the goods was regarded as a form of express intimation of acceptance barring the buyer from subsequently rejecting the goods[4]. Following the Law Commissions' recommendations, the position has now been altered so that, under s 35(2), the buyer's express intimation of acceptance (written or verbal) does not bar subsequent rejection if that intimation was given before he or she had a reasonable opportunity to examine the goods.

In addition to the right to examine under s 35(2), buyers in consumer

---

1 The position was previously in some doubt following Lord President Emslie's obiter suggestion in *Millars of Falkirk Ltd v Turpie* 1976 SLT (Notes) 66 at 68 that 'minor and readily remediable' breaches of implied terms did not justify rescission of the contract.
2 1979 Act, s 36.
3 *Report on Sale and Supply of Goods* para 5.20.
4 See *Mechans Ltd v Highland Marine Charters Ltd* 1964 SC 48.

contracts are given special protection against the impact of signing acceptance notes. Consumer contracts arise whenever the seller deals in the
course of a business and the buyer does not so deal. Section 35(3) guarantees that the consumer buyer's right to examine the goods cannot be lost
'by agreement, waiver or otherwise'. This protection deliberately does not
extend to commercial buyers who may be deemed to have waived the
right of examination by virtue of one of the express terms in the contract.
In other words, it is possible for the parties in a commercial transaction to
contract out of the reasonable opportunity to examine delivered goods.
The wording of s 35 indicates, however, that while the consumer buyer's
right of examination cannot be lost, the buyer can still lose the right to
reject by agreement or waiver once the right to examine has been exercised[1]. Thus the consumer buyer who examines the goods and decides to
keep them but later changes his or her mind will be barred from rejecting
the goods.

The second case of deemed acceptance under s 35 arises where the
buyer is barred from rejecting the goods because he or she has done something in relation to them which is inconsistent with the seller's continued
ownership[2]. Selling the goods to third parties would be an obvious form
of 'inconsistent act' barring a right of rejection. The Law Commissions[3]
also identified cases where the buyer has 'destroyed, damaged or used the
goods or incorporated them into another product, so that they cannot be
returned to the seller in good order'. Again, this form of deemed acceptance is now subject to the buyer's overriding right under s 35(2) to have a
reasonable opportunity to examine the delivered goods in order to ascertain whether they are in conformity with the contract.

To take an example: a wholesaler sells goods to a retailer who has no
opportunity to examine the goods before selling them to a customer. The
customer later rejects the goods. The fact that the retailer sold and delivered the goods to the customer is not a bar to the retailer rejecting the
goods against the wholesaler. The amended Act also makes it clear that
agreeing to have the goods repaired does not bar rejection after the repair
has been attempted.[4] The fact, too, that the goods have been given to
someone else as a gift is not of itself sufficient to bar rejection[5].

The third case where deemed acceptance occurs under the Sale of
Goods Act 1979 is where a reasonable time has elapsed since delivery and
the buyer has failed to intimate rejection[6]. Lapse of a reasonable time now
includes the buyer's reasonable opportunity to examine the goods to
ascertain whether they conform to the contract[7]. Before the Act was
amended the right to have an opportunity to examine the goods was not a
factor in determining whether the right to reject had been lost after the
expiry of a reasonable period. Thus in *Bernstein v Pamsons Motors (Golders
Green) Ltd*, the court held that buyer of a new car was barred from reject-

1 See Furmston *Sale & Supply of Goods* (2nd edn, 1995) p 51.
2 1979 Act, s 35(1).
3 *Report on Sale and Supply of Goods* para 5.34.
4 See 1979 Act, s 35(6).
5 1979 Act, s 35(6); and *Report on Sale and Supply of Goods* para 5.38.
6 1979 Act, s 35(1).
7 1979 Act, s 35(5).

ing the vehicle three weeks after purchase when the engine seized up after only 140 miles. Rougier J held that that the buyer was only entitled to 'a reasonable time to inspect and try out the car generally rather than with an eye to any specific defect'[1].

This right to a reasonable opportunity to examine delivered goods is particularly valuable to buyers purchasing goods which, for various reasons, they do not actually use or try out for some time. As the Minister of State confirmed during debate in the House of Lords, where the buyer's personal circumstances mean that he or she would not have examined the goods the buyer is not deemed to have accepted them. The fact, for instance, that goods were initially put in storage after purchase or that the buyer was ill just after making the purchase will be relevant to the question of reasonable time. The legislative intention is to allow the buyer a reasonable opportunity to see if the goods are in conformity with the express and implied terms of the contract. According to the Minister, the buyer's right of examination was now 'more than just an examination in general terms'. It encompassed 'the type of examination which it is necessary to conduct in order to ensure that the goods in question are in conformity with the contract'[2].

The Minister of State insisted at second reading that the amended version of s 35 was 'designed to remove the ambiguity which many feel led to the *Bernstein* judgment'. Doubts must remain, however, whether the decision has been reversed in the case of latent defects which no kind of examination could have discovered. The internal defects in the engine of the new car in that case could only have been discovered when the engine itself seized up. Despite lobbying by the Consumers' Association, s 35 is clearly not drafted in such a way as to give buyers an open-ended or long-term right of rejection; acceptance is still deemed to take place after the lapse of reasonable time. It remains to be seen whether future cases involving latent defects will attract greater latitude in the calculation of reasonable time than the judge was prepared to concede in *Bernstein*.

Partial rejection

Section 35A was inserted into the Sale of Goods Act 1979 to give disappointed buyers the right of partial rejection where some, but not all, of the goods delivered are defective. The effect of the new remedy is to replace the old 'all or nothing' rule which forced the buyer to accept or reject the entire order[3]. The new remedy also brings the law into line with other jurisdictions[4]. The buyer who receives a consignment of goods where some of the goods do not correspond to the contract description or are of unsatisfactory quality has two options: he or she can either reject the entire order or, alternatively, reject only those goods which do not conform. The right of partial rejection is available if the order comes in a single delivery or over a series of instalments. The fact, therefore, that the

---

1 [1987] 2 All ER 220 at 230.
2 Earl Ferrers in 557 HL Official Report (5th series), cols 479–480 (22 July 1994).
3 See *Report on Sale and Supply of Goods* paras 6.6–6.7.
4 Eg US Uniform Commercial Code (UCC), s 2-601.

buyer has chosen to accept one instalment does not prejudice his or her right to reject another instalment.

The right of partial rejection is lost if the goods have been 'accepted' or the contract expressly or impliedly removes the right[1]. The Law Commissions also felt that partial rejection was not appropriate in some cases; eg, they thought that the buyer of a defective motor car should not be able to remove the parts which were in good working order and reject the rest. To tackle this concern, the Law Commissions were attracted by the concept of the 'commercial unit' which is used in the United States Uniform Commercial Code[2] and this has found its way into the revised legislation. As a result, where the buyer accepts only part of a 'commercial unit' he or she is deemed to have accepted the remainder of that unit[3]. A 'commercial unit' is a unit the division of which would materially impair the value of the goods or the character of the unit. Thus the buyer who orders a set of encyclopaedias will normally be deemed to have accepted the whole set if he or she accepts a single volume. The buyer is, of course, entitled to a reasonable opportunity to examine the goods forming part of a 'commercial unit' before being deemed to have accepted them[4].

Rejection of wrong quantity

The buyer's rights are slightly different where the seller delivers the wrong quantity. If the seller errs on the side of generosity and delivers too much (as often happens with everyday commodities), the buyer can reject the excess[5]. However, if the delivery is materially larger than the quantity agreed in the contract, the buyer is entitled to reject the entire delivery[6]. Where the buyer receives slightly less than he ordered, he or she cannot reject the goods delivered but must pay for them at the contract rate and then seek damages for non-performance[7]. If the shortfall is material, however, the buyer is entitled to reject the goods[8]. The 'materiality' test for rejection was introduced because the Law Commissions[9] recognised that it was extremely difficult to deliver the exact amount ordered where commodities were involved and it would be potentially unfair to allow a buyer an unqualified right to reject the whole of the goods because of a trifling excess or shortfall.

Damages

Damages are the appropriate remedy for the disappointed buyer in several situations. As already noted, damages can be claimed where the seller is in non-material breach of contract. Damages are also available where

1 1979 Act, s 35A(4).
2 UCC, s 2-105(6).
3 1979 Act, s 35(6).
4 1979 Act, s 35(2).
5 1979 Act, s 30(2).
6 1979 Act, s 30(2D).
7 1979 Act, ss 30(1) and (2D).
8 1979 Act, s 30(2D).
9 *Report on Sale and Supply of Goods* para 6.21.

the buyer has accepted the goods and has thereby become personally barred from rejecting the goods and rescinding the contract. Moreover, the buyer who decides to keep the goods despite the seller's material breach is also entitled to damages. The Sale of Goods Act 1979 expresses the normal principle of contract law that damages are designed to be restorative rather than punitive. Thus the amount of damages which can be awarded is the sum which compensates the buyer for the loss 'directly and naturally resulting, in the ordinary course of events, from the seller's breach'[1].

If, for instance, the buyer has decided to keep defective goods, the amount of damages awarded will reflect the difference between the value of the goods at the time of delivery and the value they would have had if they had fulfilled the contract[2]. In addition, the buyer can claim consequential losses where defective goods have caused bodily injury or damage to property. Claims have been allowed for pain and suffering and the loss of an eye due to a faulty catapult[3] and damage to a dining room and furniture caused by the explosion of defective coalite[4]. Following the general law of contract, damages for trouble and inconvenience or disappointed expectations may also be possible[5].

Where the seller fails to deliver the goods, damages for non-delivery can be claimed under s 51 of the 1979 Act. Again, the measure of damages is the loss directly and naturally arising, in the ordinary course of events, from the seller's breach of contract[6]. Thus in *Allen v W Burns (Tractors) Ltd*[7], the supplier failed to deliver five new combine harvesters and the buyer was forced to obtain the same model from other sources. The Lord Ordinary held that the buyer was not under a duty to accept the suppliers' offer of an alternative make and model when he had specifically contracted to buy only one particular model. The buyer was therefore awarded damages under s 51 to reflect both the higher price paid to an alternative supplier and the additional interest charges incurred as a result of paying more for the same model.

The Consumer Credit Act 1974

The buyer who has purchased faulty or defective goods on credit may be able to hold the credit-provider and the seller jointly and severally liable in damages under s 75 of the Consumer Credit Act 1974[8].

Specific implement

Where the buyer is ready to pay for the goods but the seller refuses to deliver, the buyer can sue for specific implement requiring delivery of the

---

1 1979 Act, s 53A(1).
2 1979 Act, s 53A(2).
3 *Godley v Perry* [1960] 1 All ER 36.
4 *Wilson v Rickett, Cockerell & Co Ltd* [1954] 1 QB 598.
5 See *Jarvis v Swans Tours Ltd* [1973] QB 233.
6 1979 Act, s 51(2).
7 1985 SLT 252.
8 Discussed in more detail below.

goods which he or she contracted to buy[1]. Given the nature of an action for delivery, specific implement is only available where there has been breach of contract to deliver specific or ascertained goods. While specific implement should in theory be available to the buyer 'as of right'[2], the remedy is rarely granted in practice because the court retains the discretion 'to say whether the remedy of specific implement or one of damages is the proper and suitable remedy in the circumstances'[3]. If the buyer can obtain the goods by going back into the market, the court will award damages for the seller's failure to deliver.

Specific implement is therefore restricted to cases where the buyer can show some special reason (or *pretium affectionis*) for requiring delivery of the particular goods which the seller undertook to supply[4]. Thus in an old English case[5], the Vice-Chancellor ordered delivery where the contract was for the purchase 'of articles of unusual beauty, rarity and distinction so that damages would not be adequate compensation'. More recently, the court[6] was only prepared to award damages where the undelivered goods were 'ordinary articles of commerce and of no special value or interest'.

Seller's remedies

If the buyer refuses to accept and pay for the goods, the seller's remedies depend on the express and implied terms of the contract (eg in a commercial contract which contains an arbitration clause, any dispute will go to an independent arbiter whose decision is binding on both parties). The seller's options also depend on the circumstances which existed at the time of non-payment (eg where the goods are in transit to the buyer).

The seller's remedies fall into two basic categories: (1) personal remedies which are enforced by taking court action against the buyer; and (2) various 'self help' remedies which can be exercised against the goods themselves without going to court.

Personal remedies

The seller can either sue for the price or raise an action claiming damages for non-acceptance. An action for the price is competent if the property or ownership in the goods has passed to the buyer[7]. The question of ownership is determined by the terms of the contract; otherwise the intention rules in s 18 of the 1979 Act will resolve any dispute about the passing of property. In cases where the property has yet to pass to the buyer, the seller can still sue for the price if the agreed date for payment has already passed[8].

---

1 1979 Act, s 52.
2 See *Gow* p 219.
3 *Moore v Paterson* (1881) 9 R 337 at 351, per Lord Shand.
4 *Union Electric Co Ltd v Holman & Co* 1913 SC 954 at 958.
5 *Falcke v Gray* (1859) 62 ER 250 at 252.
6 *Cohen v Roche* [1927] 1 KB 169 at 181, per McCardie J.
7 1979 Act, s 49(1).
8 1979 Act, s 49(2). This also applies if the seller has not appropriated the goods to the contract.

Damages for non-acceptance can be sought in cases where an action for the price is incompetent and the buyer has refused to accept the goods. The amount awarded will reflect the loss directly and naturally arising from the buyer's breach[1]. The usual measure of damages is going to be the difference in price between the contract price and the market price at the time of the buyer's refusal to accept the goods[2].

Remedies against the goods

The unpaid seller[3] has a right of lien or retention over the goods until he or she is paid. The Sale of Goods Act 1979 assumes that payment and delivery are concurrent unless a contrary agreement is apparent from the terms of the contract or the conduct of the parties[4]. Thus if the seller has agreed to give the buyer a certain period of credit, the seller is bound by that undertaking and can only exercise his or her lien once the agreed period has expired. The circumstances in which the seller can exercise his or her lien depend on the goods being in his or her possession when the buyer fails to pay or becomes insolvent[5]. The seller also has a lien in respect of the undelivered part of the buyer's order where the rest of the order has already been supplied[6]. The seller's lien is lost as soon as the goods are released from his or her possession; eg, allowing a carrier to collect the buyer's order will normally terminate the lien[7].

The seller's right of lien depends on maintaining possession of the goods. If the goods are sent by carrier to the buyer and the unpaid seller then discovers that the buyer has become insolvent, the seller can stop the goods while they are in transit. The carrier who is stopped must be independent of either party[8] and stoppage must be effected in the proper manner before the course of transit has ended[9]. The seller can personally intercept the carrier and take the goods back or he or she can give notice of his or her claim to the carrier[10]. The carrier (eg ScotRail or Express Parcels) must comply with the instructions in the stop notice regarding redelivery of the goods. Failure to comply with a stop notice renders the carrier liable in damages to the seller[11]. The expenses of re-delivering the stopped goods must be met by the seller[12].

1 1979 Act, s 50(2).
2 1979 Act, s 50(3).
3 Eg where the seller has accepted the buyer's cheque which is later dishonoured: 1979 Act, s 38(1)(b).
4 1979 Act, s 28.
5 1979 Act, s 41.
6 1979 Act, s 42. The right of lien in such circumstances assumes that the contract does not require separate payment for each instalment which is delivered.
7 1979 Act, s 43(1); but stoppage in transit may still be available under the 1979 Act, s 44.
8 Stoppage in transit is not available if the goods have already been collected by the buyer or his agent: 1979 Act, s 45(1).
9 1979 Act, s 44.
10 1979 Act, s 46(1). The notice can be given to the person in actual possession of the goods or to his principal provided the latter receives adequate time to communicate the seller's instructions to his or her employees or agents.
11 *Mechan & Sons Ltd v North Eastern Rly Co* 1911 SC 1348. For the effect of the exercise by the seller of the right of stoppage on the carrier's lien, see Carriage of Goods by Road, ch 3 below.
12 1979 Act, s 46(4).

The unpaid seller's final remedy is to re-sell the goods, though this right is strictly limited by the terms of the Sale of Goods Act 1979[1]. Where the seller retains possession of perishable goods, he or she can re-sell these goods without giving notice to the buyer so long as he or she gave the buyer a reasonable time in which to pay the price[2]. Once perishable goods have been re-sold, the seller is entitled to recover any loss resulting from the original buyer's breach of contract. Normally the amount is going to be the difference between the contract price and the re-sale price but it could also include the seller's reasonable storage and advertising costs[3]. In the case of non-perishable goods, the seller must give the buyer notice of his or her intention to re-sell so as to allow the buyer a reasonable opportunity to pay the agreed price. Failure to pay within a reasonable period entitles the seller to rescind the contract, re-sell the goods and then claim damages for the loss sustained as a result. The buyer who acquires goods which have been re-sold obtains a good title against any claim brought by the original buyer[4].

Unsolicited goods

'Inertia selling' of goods was a particularly prevalent problem in the 1960s. Unscrupulous suppliers would send out unsolicited goods, perhaps along with items which the customer had already ordered, in the hope that the recipient would agree to pay for them. The recipient would then face increasingly hostile demands for payment. Faced with such pressure, the recipient would often simply pay for the goods even though no contract existed. If the recipient refused to buy the goods, the problem remained that he or she was in possession of items which belonged to the supplier. Was the recipient obliged to send the unwanted goods back or did he or she at least have to store them until the supplier arranged for collection? And what happened if the supplier failed to collect the goods after a certain period?

In response to these difficulties, the Unsolicited Goods and Services Act 1971 deems unsolicited goods to be an unconditional gift to the recipient if the goods are not reclaimed within six months of the date of receipt[5]. The recipient can short-circuit the six-month period by giving the supplier 30 days' notice in writing of the fact that he or she has received unsolicited goods and that they may be collected from a certain place at specified times. The recipient is entitled to keep the goods as his or her own property if the sender fails to respond within the required period. The 1971 Act also makes it a criminal offence to demand payment for goods where the supplier lacks reasonable cause to believe that there is a right to payment[6].

---

1 See 1979 Act, s 39(1)(c).
2 1979 Act, s 48(3).
3 See *Ward v Bignall* [1967] 2 All ER 449 (damages included a sum for reasonable expenses incurred in advertising re-sale).
4 See 1979 Act, s 48(2) and the conditions mentioned therein. Good faith on the new buyer's part is not required should the seller have re-sold without having the right to do so.
5 Unsolicited Goods and Services Act 1971, s 1.
6 1971 Act, s 2.

DELICTUAL LIABILITY

Introduction

The fact that someone suffers loss or harm caused by defective goods prima facie gives rise to a claim under s 14 of the Sale of Goods Act 1979. At first sight, s 14 is an attractive remedy: the seller who supplies goods of unsatisfactory quality incurs strict liability regardless of any negligence on his or her part. Moreover, the seller is liable not only for the loss directly arising under the contract itself[1] but also for any consequential losses caused by the defective goods such as personal injury to the buyer[2] or damage to the buyer's property[3].

However, s 14 suffers from two drawbacks. First, as a general rule[4], only the buyer can sue for breach. Injured third parties – such as members of the buyer's family, a donee who received the goods as a gift, employees of the buyer and bystanders – cannot bring a claim. Secondly, the 1979 Act confines the buyer's remedy to suing the actual seller who may have little or no money to meet the claim; in contrast, the manufacturer, who is better able to afford insurance cover, has no liability whatsoever under s 14.

The restricted scope of the 1979 Act leaves injured parties (particularly non-buyers) with the option of bringing a delictual action at common law based on the manufacturer's breach of duty of care. The classic statement of the manufacturer's duty to take reasonable care is found in Lord Atkin's speech in *Donoghue v Stevenson*[5]:

> '... a manufacturer of products, which he sells in such form as to show that he intends them to reach the ultimate consumer in the form in which they left him, with no reasonable possibility of intermediate examination, and with the knowledge that the absence of reasonable care in the preparation or putting up of the products will result in an injury to the consumer's life or property, owes a duty to the consumer to take that reasonable care'.

The principle enunciated in *Donoghue* has been applied in many later cases to hold manufacturers liable to injured parties where goods have been negligently made. Thus, for instance, in *Grant v Australian Knitting Mills*[6], the Privy Council held that the manufacturers of woollen underpants were liable to the consumer who developed a severe skin rash after wearing the item. The difficulty with the common law is the need to show that the manufacturer has breached a duty of care. For instance, in *Daniels v R White & Sons Ltd*[7], the plaintiff's husband bought a bottle of White's lemonade containing carbolic acid which injured them both when they drank some of the contents of the bottle. The husband was held entitled to

---

1 1979 Act, s 53A.
2 See *Godley v Perry* [1960] 1 All ER 36 (loss of eye).
3 See *Wilson v Rickett, Cockerell & Co* [1954] 1 QB 598 (damage to dining room due to explosion).
4 Exceptions exist if the buyer assigns his or her rights or the buyer purchased the goods as agent for the injured party.
5 1932 SC (HL) 31 at 57.
6 [1936] AC 85.
7 [1938] 4 All ER 258.

damages from the retailer under the Sale of Goods Act but the plaintiff failed in her claim against the manufacturer because she had failed to prove negligence.

Another area of difficulty presented by the common law concerns faulty components in manufactured goods. If the components have been made by different manufacturers, the pursuer may find it impossible to identify which manufacturer was at fault. The problem was highlighted in *Evans v Triplex Safety Glass Co Ltd*[1] where the court found no evidence of fault on the part of the manufacturer of a car windscreen which shattered injuring the plaintiff; the fault possibly lay with the car manufacturer who had fitted the windscreen. Other hurdles may prevent a successful claim against a manufacturer. A pursuer who has failed to follow a manufacturer's warning or instructions on use will not be awarded damages because his or her failure will have broken the chain of causation between the defender's breach of duty and the harm complained of. Moreover, the common law only allows claims for personal injury and damage to the pursuer's property; damages are not available for pure economic loss where the only property damaged is the defective product itself.

Some of these difficulties in the law of delict have been addressed since the EC adopted the Product Liability Directive in July 1985[2]. Article 1 of the Directive required member states to make producers strictly liable for defective products. As a result, Part 1 of the Consumer Protection Act 1987 introduced strict liability for defective products[3]. The effect of the 1987 Act is that anybody who suffers 'damage' caused by a 'product' which was 'defective' can hold the 'producer' and various non-producers liable in damages without having to prove fault or negligence.

Before examining the statutory scheme in detail, several general points should be made about Part 1 of the 1987 Act. First, s 1(1) provides that the legislation has to be construed by the courts in such a way that it complies with the wording of the Directive. Secondly, liability under the Act only arises where the defective products were supplied by their producers after 1 March 1988[4]. Thirdly, rights given under the Act are in addition to the pursuer's existing contractual and delictual rights[5].

What is a 'product'?

The pursuer has to show that he or she has suffered loss or damage which has been caused by a defective product. The term 'product' is defined in s 1(2) of the 1987 Act as 'any goods or electricity'. The definition expressly includes components and raw materials incorporated into finished products. The term 'goods' includes 'substances, growing crops and things comprised in land by virtue of being attached to it and any ship, aircraft or vehicle'[6]. The reference to 'substances' is thought to include contaminated

1 [1936] 1 All ER 283.
2 EC Council Directive 85/374 (OJ L210, 7.8.85, p 29) ('the Product Liability Directive').
3 The Consumer Protection Act 1987 is hereinafter referred to as 'the 1987 Act'.
4 1987 Act, s 50(7).
5 1987 Act, s 2(6).
6 1987 Act, s 45(1); and also s 45(5) which refers to moveables becoming heritable by accession to heritable property.

blood supplied by transfusion but this is not entirely certain. Inclusion of things 'attached' to land would allow liability for such things as faulty central heating systems or shower units.

Buildings are not products under the Act[1]. Thus no claim can be made if a new house collapses due to a design fault or poor construction methods. However, s 46(3) preserves the right to seek damages where defective goods are incorporated into a building and these goods cause personal injury or damage to property. Thus, for instance, the person who is injured by a defective shower unit which he or she has had installed in his house is entitled to compensation.

There is no liability under the Act for agricultural produce[2] or game unless it has 'undergone an industrial process'[3]. The aim is to remove liability from those who supply, for instance, fresh meat, fish or vegetables. The question is: when is agricultural produce subjected to an 'industrial process'? Speaking in the House of Lords on the Government's intention in this respect, Lord Lucas[4] indicated that 'some essential characteristic of the product must have been altered' by an industrial process which was 'carried on on a large and continuing scale and with the intervention of machinery'. As examples, he thought that freezing fresh peas or turning potatoes into frozen chips would involve an industrial process, but cutting sprouts or harvesting potatoes would not.

What is a 'defect'?

Liability under the 1987 Act depends on proof that the product was defective; there is no need to prove negligence in the process of manufacture or production. 'Defect' is defined in s 3(1) in terms of an expected level of safety: a product is defective if its safety is 'not such as persons generally are entitled to expect'. The meaning of 'safety' includes safety in the context of risk of damage to property as well as risk of death and personal injury; it also refers to safety in respect of component parts comprised in a product. In applying the expected level of safety test, the court is obliged under s 3(2) to take 'all the circumstances into account' when determining whether a particular product possessed the degree of safety which consumers are 'generally entitled to expect'.

The expected level of safety test requires relative, not absolute, safety from products. Manufacturers are not expected to make completely safe, totally risk-free products; their products need only possess the level of safety which consumers are '*generally* entitled to expect'. This point is reinforced by s 3(2) which lists various specific circumstances which the court must take into account in assessing safety expectations. The way in which the goods were marketed or advertised has to be considered: eg, it may be significant to a particular claim for damages that the allegedly defective

---

1 See 1987 Act, s 46(4).
2 Which is defined in s 1(2) as 'any produce of the soil, of stock-farming or of fisheries'. Hence injury caused by vegetables which have been hydroponically grown in a soil-free culture cannot give rise to a claim under the Act.
3 1987 Act, s 2(4).
4 483 HL Official Report (5th series), col 737 (19 January 1987).

product was aimed at children of a certain age. The safety of packaging and the provision of adequate warnings and instructions for proper use must also be considered by the court. The 'reasonably expected' use of the product is another factor which the court will take into consideration. The upshot is that, apart from the normal uses to which a product may be put, manufacturers are also expected to take into account reasonably foreseeable misuses and issue appropriate warnings or instructions.

What is 'damage'?

Damage in relation to defective products means death, personal injury or damage to any property (including land)[1]. Personal injury is defined in s 45(1) as including 'any disease and any other impairment of a person's physical or mental condition'. Article 9 of the Directive ensures that damages for pain and suffering can be claimed as part of any award of damages sought for personal injury. The reference in s 5(1) to damage to 'any property (including land)' clearly covers corporeal and incorporeal property, including (presumably) intellectual property. So, if a computer program is bought which contains a virus, the pursuer could sue under the Act for damage done to other software or the loss of any data caused by the infected program[2].

Claims for property damage are, however, subject to a number of restrictions. To prevent small claims being pursued, the minimum level of liability for damage to property is £275; damages below that figure cannot be awarded under the Act[3]. Section 5(2) also bars claims for pure economic loss – as the common law does – where the claim relates to loss or damage to the defective product itself. This exclusion extends to a finished product which is damaged by faulty components 'comprised in' the product *when it was supplied*. Thus if a washing machine overheats because of a faulty part which was supplied with the machine, no claim is allowed for damage or loss of the part or the machine. The position is different if a faulty part was fitted separately after the machine was supplied: the pursuer can then claim for damage to the machine but not for loss of the part itself. It should be stressed that the bar on claims for pure economic loss does not prevent the pursuer claiming for personal injury or damage to other property.

Section 5(3) contains another important restriction on claims for damage to property. The Act only allows claims in respect of damage to private or consumer-type property; compensation is not available for loss or damage to public or business property[4]. Thus, eg, if a television set explodes in the pursuer's living room, he or she can claim for the loss or

---

1 1987 Act, s 5(1).
2 See *Atiyah and Adams* p 233. This assumes that software, as a series of encoded electrical impulses, falls within the definition of 'product' in s 1(2) of the 1987 Act which refers to 'any goods or electricity'.
3 1987 Act, s 5(4). The figure relates to the amount actually awarded by the court and not the original claim entered.
4 1987 Act, s 5(3).

damage caused to other property in the room, but no such claim could be made if the faulty television blew up in a hotel bedroom or a dentist's waiting room.

Who is liable?

Producers

No-fault liability under the 1987 Act falls on the producer of the defective product or on various non-producer suppliers. Three categories of 'producer' are listed in s 1(2). The first and obvious category of producer covers the person who manufactured the product which has caused injury or damage. The scope of the manufacturer category of producer is confirmed by article 9 of the Directive which refers to 'producer' in terms of the manufacturer of a finished product, the producer of any raw material or the manufacturer of a component part. Thus liability[1] falls on both the manufacturer of a finished product and the producer of a component or raw material where the finished product is defective due to a defect in the raw material or the component[2].

The second category of producer covers parties who have 'won or abstracted' a substance which has not been manufactured[3]. Thus, for instance, those who produce minerals or natural gas may incur strict liability under the Act. The final category of producer covers products which have not been 'manufactured' in the traditional sense. If the 'essential characteristics' of the defective product 'are attributable to an industrial or other process', the producer who carried out that process is liable[4]. This third category is intended to cover parties such as food producers and those who refine petroleum products.

Own-branders

In addition to the above categories of producer, the 1987 Act holds the producers of 'own-brand' products strictly liable because they are deemed to have held themselves to be the producer[5]. Supermarkets which market their own brands will therefore be potentially liable to injured consumers. The 'own-brander' will only escape liability as a producer if the product was labelled so as to reveal the name of the actual manufacturer[6].

---

1 Which is on a joint and several basis, with a right to contribution among joint wrongdoers under the Law Reform (Miscellaneous Provisions) (Scotland) Act 1940, s 3: 1987 Act, ss 2(5) and 6(1).
2 But see the important proviso in the 1987 Act, s 1(3) and the explanation therefor in Blaikie ' Product Liability: The Consumer Protection Act 1987, Part I' (1987) 32 JLSS 325 at 326.
3 1987 Act, s 1(2)(b).
4 1987 Act, s 1(2)(c).
5 1987 Act, s 2(2)(b).
6 Such identification would also exempt the own-brander from liability as a supplier under the 1987 Act, s 2(3).

Importers

Importers who bring products into the European Union are also treated as constructive producers under the Act[1]. Thus, for instance, if a child in the UK is injured by an electronic toy which was made in Japan and then imported into the UK via Germany, the German importer will incur strict liability for the injuries.

Suppliers

Where the actual manufacturer or importer of a defective product cannot be readily identified, s 2(3) provides that 'any person who supplied the product' is strictly liable. Supplier liability is intended to be a liability of last resort which aims to encourage suppliers (eg a retailer or wholesaler) to divulge the identity of those further up the chain of distribution who supplied the product to them. The supplier becomes liable only if he or she fails to respond within a reasonable time to a request from the injured party for the identity of his or her suppliers or manufacturers[2]. The term 'supplier' is very widely defined in s 46 to include anyone selling, hiring or lending the defective product or even giving it away as a gift or prize. However, the potential for supplier liability is qualified by the fact that private transactions, where the goods were supplied 'otherwise than in the course of a business', fall outside the ambit of the Act[3].

What defences are available?

Clearly the defender is not going to be liable in the absence of 'damage' which has been 'caused' by a 'product' which contained a 'defect'. Assuming these general conditions of liability are satisfied under the Act, s 4 avails the defender of a number of specific defences. The onus is on the defender to establish the defence which is raised.

Compliance

In a few cases, the producer may be able to rely on the 'compliance defence' in s 4(1)(a) by showing that the defect was attributable to compliance with statutory safety requirements[4] or a Community obligation. Clearly the defence would not cover compliance with a voluntary set of standards set by an association of manufacturers.

---

1 1987 Act, s 2(2)(c).
2 1987 Act, s 2(3).
3 See the defence in 1987 Act, s 4(1)(c).
4 Eg safety regulations made by the Secretary of State for Trade and Industry under the 1987 Act, s 11.

Non-supply

This defence allows the defender to show that he or she did not in fact 'supply' the products to another party[1]. Thus, for instance, the manufacturer who finds that some of his or her products are stolen from the warehouse will not be liable if the products are subsequently sold or distributed and cause damage. Similarly, a manufacturer will not be liable to an injured employee who is harmed by a defective product before it leaves the factory.

Non-commercial transactions

The defender escapes liability if the goods were not supplied commercially: eg, defective goods sold at a school fête would not be covered by the Act[2].

Relevant time

There is no liability if the product was safe when it left the defender's hands but subsequently became unsafe[3]. The intention is not to hold the defender liable for defects which are attributable to others further down the chain of distribution. Examples covered by the defence would include the removal of warning labels; improper use of the product; failure to service the product regularly or properly; and selling processed food after its shelf-life has expired.

State of the art

The most controversial defence in the 1987 Act excludes liability for so-called 'development risks'[4]. The 'state of the art' defence was included in the Product Liability Directive at the UK's insistence. The European Court of Justice (ECJ) has recently rejected arguments by the European Commission that the Act fails to implement the defence properly[5].

In terms of the Act, a producer escapes liability if the defect in his or her own product was not a defect that other producers of a similar product 'might be expected to have discovered' given the state of scientific and technical knowledge at the time when the defender's product was supplied. As the ECJ's recent judgment confirms, the state of the art defence is not based on 'the subjective knowledge of a producer taking reasonable care in the light of the standard precautions taken in the industrial sector in question'[6]. Instead the defence requires proof of the 'objective state of

---

1 1987 Act, s 4(1)(b).
2 1987 Act, s 4(1)(c).
3 1987 Act, s 4(1)(d).
4 1987 Act, s 4(1)(e).
5 See Case C-300/95 *EC Commission v United Kingdom* (Judgment of 30 May 1997). The author is grateful to his colleague Dr Angus Campbell for providing a copy of the judgment.
6 *EC Commission v United Kingdom* para 36.

scientific and technical knowledge of which the producer is presumed to have been informed'[1]. Thus the resources and technical expertise of the defender are not relevant to the defence. Nor can the defender rely on the standard tests and safety trials followed by fellow producers if the state of scientific and technical knowledge requires further tests to be made. The ECJ's judgment confirms that the defender's presumed level of scientific and technical knowledge includes 'the most advanced level of such knowledge at the time when the product in question was put in circulation'[2]. Such knowledge will, however, only be relevant if it was accessible at the material time[3]. The increasing availability of on-line technical databases means that a good deal of up-to-date scientific and technical knowledge can be ascertained by producers with relative ease[4].

Component producer

The 'component producer' defence is intended to protect manufacturers of component parts or raw materials whose products are incorporated into other products. The component producer has a defence if the defect was wholly attributable to the design of the finished product or he produced the component parts in compliance with instructions given by the producer of the finished product[5]. For instance, if a car manufacturer asks a component supplier to make certain parts to a particular specification, the supplier has a defence if he or she followed the specifications and the parts later cause injury because they prove to be unsuitable. If the defence is not made out, both the producer of the finished product and the component producer are jointly and severally liable to the pursuer[6].

Contributory negligence

Where the damage is caused partly by the defect and partly by the fault of the victim, the normal rules on contributory negligence apply[7]. Thus apportionment of liability will take place under the Law Reform (Contributory Negligence) Act 1945 so as to reduce the amount of damages awarded.

Exclusion of liability

Contracting out of strict liability under Part I of the Consumer Protection Act is prohibited by s 7.

---

1 *EC Commission v United Kingdom* para 27.
2 *EC Commission v United Kingdom* para 26.
3 *EC Commission v United Kingdom* para 28.
4 On this point, see *Atiyah and Adams* pp 238–239.
5 1987 Act, s 4(1)(f).
6 1987 Act, s 2(5).
7 1987 Act, s 6(4).

CRIMINAL LIABILITY

A large number of consumer protection statutes[1] contain criminal sanctions which apply where goods are sold in breach of statutory requirements. These statutes are policed by trading standards officers who are employed by local authorities. While officials will act in response to specific complaints, a good deal of the trading standard department's caseload will come from making test purchases and entering premises to inspect and seize goods[2]. After evidence is gathered, a report is sent to the local procurator fiscal who will make the final decision on whether to prosecute a particular trader.

If a trader is successfully prosecuted, the fiscal can ask the court to grant a compensation order against the accused requiring him or her to pay compensation to his or her victims. Payment of compensation orders take precedence over fines due to the court[3]. However, as one commentator[4] has observed, the victim of a criminal offence has no standing to make an application for compensation 'and much depends on the procurator fiscal raising the matter and having some evidence on which the sheriff [or justice of the peace in the district court] can base a compensation order'[5].

The Trade Descriptions Act 1968

The Trade Descriptions Act 1968 is the best-known and most frequently used consumer protection statute backed by the threat of criminal sanctions. Indeed the Act has proved to be a model for later statutes which use the criminal law to protect the consumer[6]. Under s 1 of the 1968 Act, it is an offence to apply a 'false trade description' to any goods which are being sold in the course of a business. It is also an offence for a trader to supply or to offer to supply goods which carry a false description. Both offences are strict liability offences which do not require proof of intention to deceive or wilful recklessness. Section 2 defines a 'trade description' in terms of direct or indirect indications given to the consumer on the following matters: quantity and size; method of manufacture or processing (eg 'hand-crafted'); composition (eg 'pure new wool'); fitness for purpose; strength, performance or accuracy; other history, including previous ownership or use (eg car sold with 'only 24,000 miles' on the clock).

---

1 Eg Trade Descriptions Act 1968, s 1 (false trade description of goods); Consumer Protection Act 1987, s 20 (misleading price indications); Food Safety Act 1990, s 8 (selling food in breach of safety requirements).
2 On these powers, see Trade Descriptions Act 1968, ss 27–29. Another example of the same powers can be found in the Trade Marks Act 1994, ss 92–93, where the offence relates to the counterfeit use of trade marks.
3 See Criminal Justice (Scotland) Act 1980, ss 61 and 62.
4 See *Ervine* p 317.
5 See eg the doubts expressed by *Atiyah and Adams* p 258 on the possibility of establishing loss where the accused is convicted of giving a misleading price indication contrary to the Consumer Protection Act 1987, s 20.
6 See eg Cartwright 'Defendants in Consumer Protection Statutes' (1996) 59 MLR 225 at 228.

Not surprisingly, the adjustment of the mileage shown on secondhand cars provides trading standards officers with the most frequent form of false trade description. In the year to 31 December 1995, over 500 cases of this kind were prosecuted by the authorities throughout the UK, resulting in fines totalling £340,000 and compensation orders of nearly £150,000[1]. However, the Scottish Consumer Council has expressed concern that the number of prosecutions brought in Scotland under the 1968 Act as a whole has been significantly lower than the rest of the UK[2].

Due diligence defence

The potential harshness of strict liability under the 1968 Act is mitigated by the due diligence defence in s 24. There are two elements or limbs to the defence and both must be established to avoid conviction. Under the first limb in s 24, the accused must show that the offence was committed 'due to a mistake or to reliance on information supplied to him or to the act or default of another person'. This part of the defence allows the accused to name 'another person' whose 'act or default' caused the accused to commit the offence. Usually an employee in the accused's business will be named as 'another person'. In one case, a company avoided conviction by naming a shop manager who had failed to comply with instructions from head office[3]. Similarly, the House of Lords held in the *Tesco* case that a national supermarket chain was entitled to name a local store manager as 'another person' for the purposes of the 1968 Act[4].

The effect of *Tesco* is to draw a distinction between different categories of employee. Those employees who form part of the accused company's 'directing mind and will' cannot be named as 'another person' because they are too closely identified with the company itself. Thus the company cannot avoid conviction by seeking to blame senior managers for what has happened because they 'carry out the functions of management and speak and act as the company'[5]. On the other hand, the conduct of other employees in the company can properly be used as a defence if they are 'subordinates [who] carry out orders from above'[5].

The second limb in s 24 requires the accused to satisfy the court that, despite the act or default of another person, he or she took 'all reasonable precautions and exercised all due diligence' to avoid the offence being committed. The accused will have taken 'reasonable precautions' if he or she has set up a system within the business to avoid offences being committed. In an early case under the 1968 Act, the High Court of Justiciary held that the sales manager in a firm of car dealers had failed to take reasonable precautions when he took no positive steps to check that the mileometer on a secondhand car displayed the correct reading[6]. The

---

1 See OFT *Annual Report of the Director General of Fair Trading 1995*, App G. These figures probably understate the position because information is only supplied to the OFT on a voluntary basis by trading standards departments.
2 See *Ervine* p 273.
3 See *Beckett v Kingston Bros (Butchers) Ltd* [1970] 1 All ER 715.
4 *Tesco Supermarkets v Nattrass* [1972] AC 153.
5 [1972] AC 153 at 171, per Lord Reid.
6 *Macnab v Alexanders of Greenock Ltd* 1971 SLT 121.

manager's omission was compounded by the fact that he had failed to check the office records which were available to him when he knew that the car had been serviced by the firm six months earlier.

The 'due diligence' part of the defence requires the accused to show that he or she adequately trained or supervised employees to ensure that instructions and control systems were properly adhered to within the business. In the latter connection, it has been held that the managing director's failure to see that his explicit instructions were carried out by a clerkess in a firm of auctioneers was a failure in due diligence[1].

Hire of goods

INTRODUCTION

Unlike the contract of sale, which contemplates the transfer of ownership, the purpose of the contract of hire is merely to transfer possession of goods to the hirer[2]. Bell[3] gives the classic definition of hire: 'By this contract, one party [the lessor] in consideration for a certain hire, which the other [the hirer] agrees to pay, agrees to give, during a certain time the temporary use of a certain subject'. Hiring in Scots law involves the temporary letting for hire of moveable property or things rather than the letting of heritable property or the hire of someone's services. Contracts of hire also differ from contracts of hire purchase because under the latter the customer has entered an agreement which gives him or her the option of buying the article. In contrast, the sole object of hire is to permit temporary use of the thing hired; the contract does not envisage the customer having a right to convert possession into ownership at some point[4].

Hire contracts are governed by a mixture of statute and common law rules. The main statutory controls are to be found in the Consumer Credit Act 1974, the Supply of Goods and Services Act 1982[5], the Unfair Contract Terms Act 1977 and the Unfair Terms in Consumer Contracts Regulations 1994[6].

FORMATION OF CONTRACT

Entry into most contracts of hire is governed by the provisions of the Consumer Credit Act 1974[7]. These statutory controls cannot be contracted out of[8] but they apply only where the proposed contract is a regulated

1 See *Aitchison v Reith and Anderson (Dingwall and Tain) Ltd* 1974 JC 12.
2 See *Gow* p 241.
3 Bell *Principles* s 133.
4 Bell *Commentaries* I, 482.
5 As amended by the Sale and Supply of Goods Act 1994, s 6 and Sch 1.
6 SI 1994/3159.
7 Hereinafter referred to as 'the 1974 Act'.
8 1974 Act, s 173.

'consumer hire agreement'. A regulated hire agreement under the 1974 Act is a proposed agreement 'capable of subsisting for more than three months' which does not require the hirer to make payments in excess of £15,000[1]. For the avoidance of doubt, the 1974 Act also defines a 'consumer hire agreement' as one which does not involve hire purchase of the goods involved. Unfortunately, use of the term 'consumer' would lead one to think that the statutory controls only protect private hirers. In fact, the 1974 Act also applies to some business hirers – sole traders and partnerships are covered but limited companies are not[2].

If the hire agreement is regulated by the 1974 Act, the hirer becomes entitled to various forms of protection. Adverts[3] and quotations[4] must disclose the 'true cost' of the hire facilities on offer to the potential hirer. Detailed regulations made by the Secretary of State for Trade and Industry specify the form and content of adverts and written quotations. The hirer is also entitled to receive certain specific information before he or she signs the hire agreement. If this information is not disclosed, the hire agreement is deemed to be improperly executed[5]. This means that the agreement which has been signed can be enforced against the hirer only if the lessor applies to the sheriff for a court order (eg to take repossession of the goods)[6].

The 1974 Act requires the contract to be in writing. The document which the hirer is asked to sign must include specific information about his or her rights and duties under the hire agreement. It must also inform the hirer what protection and remedies he or she enjoys under the 1974 Act[7]. The hire agreement must be signed by both parties and the hirer is then entitled to a copy[8]. If the lessor fails to observe these formalities, the agreement is improperly executed and it can be enforced against the hirer only by obtaining an order from the sheriff court[9].

The hirer is also entitled to cancel the signed agreement during a 'cooling off' period. Two conditions have to be met before cancellation is possible: the agreement must have been preceded by face-to-face negotiations; and the hirer must have signed the agreement away from the lessor's trade premises. The period of cooling off is relatively short; the hirer has five clear days from receipt of a copy of the agreement in which to serve a written notice of cancellation. The effect of serving the notice on time is to free the hirer from any further obligations under the cancelled agreement. The hired goods must be returned and the hirer is entitled to the return of any payments already made[10].

1 1974 Act , s 15(1). The financial limit is uprated from time to time by statutory instrument.
2 See 1974 Act, s 189(1).
3 1974 Act, s 44.
4 1974 Act, s 52.
5 1974 Act, s 55(2).
6 1974 Act, ss 65 and 189(1).
7 1974 Act, s 60 and Consumer Credit (Agreements) Regulations 1983, SI 1983/1553.
8 1974 Act, ss 62–64.
9 1974 Act, ss 65 and 189(1). The sheriff's discretion to dismiss the lessor's application altogether is limited by the 1974 Act, s 127.
10 See 1974 Act, ss 67–73.

LESSOR'S DUTIES

Implied terms

The Supply of Goods and Services Act 1982 incorporates various implied terms into contracts of hire. Thus the lessor is obliged to ensure that the hirer enjoys undisturbed possession of the goods throughout the period of hire[1]. This right is, of course, subject to the lessor's right to recover possession under the express or implied terms of the contract (eg where hire charges are paid late). The goods supplied to the hirer must correspond with their description[2] and be of satisfactory quality[3]. Goods meet the required standard if a reasonable person would regard them as satisfactory, taking into account how the goods were described, the level of hire charges and all other relevant circumstances. No claim can be made if the hirer inspected the goods and the examination which he or she actually made ought to have revealed the defects which later emerge. If the hirer expressly or by implication makes the particular purpose of his or her hire known, the lessor must supply goods which are reasonably fit for that purpose[4]. The lessor's duty is removed, however, if the lessor can show either that the hirer did not rely on the lessor's skill and judgment or that it was unreasonable for the hirer so to rely.

Other forms of liability

The lessor is liable at common law to ensure that the thing hired is maintained in sufficiently good order to enable the hirer to continue to use it throughout the period of hire[5]. If the hirer incurs repair or maintenance costs, these expenses can be recovered from the lessor provided the hirer was not at fault and the repairs were necessary. The lessor incurs strict liability as a supplier[6] under the Consumer Protection Act 1987 if the thing hired proves to be defective[7] and the defect causes personal injury or damage to private, non-business property[8]. The lessor would need to identify the manufacturer or the party who imported the goods into the UK to avoid statutory liability to pay damages[9]. Part II of the same Act allows the Secretary of State to adopt safety regulations in relation to goods. If the lessor supplies goods which breach the safety regulations, he or she is liable to be prosecuted for committing an offence under s 12 of the 1987 Act. In addition, breach of the safety regulations gives rise to civil liability for breach of statutory duty under s 41.

1 Supply of Goods and Services Act 1982, s 11H.
2 1982 Act, s 11I.
3 1982 Act, s 11J(2)–(4).
4 1982 Act, s 11J(5)–(7).
5 Bell *Commentaries* I, 482.
6 Consumer Protection Act 1987, ss 2(3) and 46(1)(a).
7 As defined in the 1987 Act, s 3.
8 1987 Act, s 2(1) and 5.
9 1987 Act, s 2(3).

HIRER'S DUTIES

The hirer or lessee is bound at common law to pay the agreed hire charge or, if agreement has not been reached, a reasonable charge. Subject to the terms of the contract or custom to the contrary, hire charges are payable in arrears[1]. However, as Bell recognised, the obligation to pay is subject to the hirer's right to deduct reasonable sums from the hire charge to reflect the fact that he or she has been temporarily deprived of the use of the goods because they have proved to be faulty[2]. If the goods are accidentally destroyed, the doctrine of frustration of contract applies so that the hire contract is automatically terminated along with the hirer's obligation to make any further payments to the lessor. The hirer is expected to take reasonable care of the hired goods. The standard of care imposed on the hirer is the degree of care which a diligent and prudent person would exercise over their own property[3]. Thus the hirer would not be liable for fair wear and tear but would be at fault for overworking the hired thing[4] or not taking reasonable precautions against the risk of fire or theft. It is no defence for the hirer to argue that he or she treated his or her own property with the same lack of care as appears to have been shown in relation to the lessor's property[5].

EXCLUSION CLAUSES

Contracts of hire fall within Part II of the Unfair Contract Terms Act 1977[6]. Thus any clause or notice which seeks to exclude or limit the lessor's liability for death or personal injury will automatically be void[7]. Clauses or notices which seek to restrict or exclude the lessor's liability for breach of duty are enforceable only if the lessor can show that it was 'fair and reasonable' to incorporate them in the contract[8]. So far as the implied terms found in the Supply of Goods and Services Act 1982 are concerned, the parties are free to negative or vary their statutory rights and duties by inserting appropriate clauses in the contract. A course of dealing between the parties may also give rise to an inference that certain statutory rights and duties under the 1982 Act have been waived or altered[9].

An additional control on the use of exclusion clauses is found in the Unfair Terms in Consumer Contracts Regulations 1994[10]. As we have

1 See 14 *Stair Memorial Encyclopaedia* para 1045.
2 See Bell *Principles* s 143.
3 Stair *Institutions* I, 15, 5.
4 See eg *Seton v Paterson* (1880) 8 R 236, where the Inner House held, by a 2:1 majority, that the hirer was at fault for 'recklessly galloping' a horse in a field where the contract only contemplated the horse being taken on the road at ordinary pace.
5 *Raes v Meeks* (1889) 16 R (HL) 31. See also *McLean v Warnock* (1883) 10 R 1052 at 1055, per Lord Shand.
6 Unfair Contract Terms Act 1977, s 15(2)(a).
7 1977 Act, s 16(1)(a).
8 1977 Act, s 16(1)(b).
9 Supply of Goods and Services Act 1982, s 11L.
10 SI 1994/3159.

already seen, the Regulations apply a test of fairness to terms in consumer contracts which have not been individually negotiated[1]. The fact that a specific term (eg duration of hire) has been individually negotiated does not prevent the Regulations applying to the rest of the contract if an over-all assessment of the contract would indicate that it is a pre-formulated standard contract[2]. For the purpose of the Regulations, a 'consumer' is an individual who enters the hire contract for purposes outside his or her business[3]. A term is deemed unfair if 'contrary to the requirement of good faith [it] causes a significant imbalance in the parties' rights and obliga-tions under the contract to the detriment of the consumer'[4]. The court is obliged to consider various factors when assessing good faith[5]. It can also draw on a long illustrative list of terms which may be regarded as unfair[6]. Should the court conclude that the term is unfair, that term will not bind the consumer[7].

TERMINATION OF CONTRACT

By hirer

At common law, the contract of hire may be terminated by the hirer giv-ing the lessor the period of notice stipulated in the contract. Should the contract fail to provide for notice, a reasonable period of notice has to be given. If the contract is regulated by the Consumer Credit Act 1974, the process of termination is determined by legislation. The hirer has the right to terminate the agreement ahead of time by giving notice under s 101 of the 1974 Act. The right is subject to several significant conditions. Early termination is only possible if the first 18 months of the agreement have already elapsed unless the contract permits the hirer to give notice after a shorter period. The minimum period of notice which must be given will usually be equal to the interval falling between regular hire payments; eg, if payments are made monthly, the hirer need only give one month's notice of termination. If more than three months elapses between pay-ments, the period of notice is three months. In any event, the hirer's right to terminate early is excluded altogether under s 101(7) if the hire pay-ments exceed £900 in any year or the goods were hired for business pur-poses (eg sub-leasing). These exceptions are aimed particularly at preventing the early termination of contracts involving the hire of motor vehicles or equipment for use in a business.

---

1 A term has not been 'individually negotiated' if it has been drafted in advance and the consumer has not been able to influence the substance of the term: 1994 Regulations, reg 3(3). The onus is on the lessor to show that a term dealing with exclusion of liability was individually negotiated: reg 3(5).
2 1994 Regulations, reg 3(4).
3 1994 Regulations, reg 2(1).
4 1994 Regulations, reg 4(1).
5 1994 Regulations, reg 4(3) and Sch 2.
6 1994 Regulations, reg 4(4) and Sch 3.
7 1994 Regulations, reg 5(1).

By lessor

If the lessor wishes to terminate the hire agreement because the hirer is in breach of contract, the 1974 Act requires the lessor to serve a default notice on the hirer[1]. The notice must be in the form prescribed by statutory instrument and it must allow the hirer at least seven days to remedy the default. If the hirer complies with the default notice before the date specified in the notice, the breach is cured. The hirer does have the right to ask the sheriff to extend the seven-day period by granting a time order[2]. The sheriff will only extend the statutory period for compliance if it appears just to do so. Assuming that the hirer does not comply with a default notice, the lessor is entitled to take steps to repossess the goods as soon as the default notice expires. While the lessor can attempt to seize physical possession, he or she is not allowed to enter premises without the occupier's permission. This means that the lessor could be liable in damages for breach of statutory duty if he or she enters premises without obtaining consent or a court order[3].

Where the lessor recovers possession of the goods, the hirer can apply to the sheriff court for financial relief under s 132. The purpose of this provision is to protect the hirer against having to pay more than he or she should when the agreement is terminated[4]. In particular, the court can require sums to be repaid or cancel sums due if this appears to be just. The only specific factor which the sheriff is obliged to consider is the extent of the hirer's enjoyment of the goods but the weight to be attached to this fact is left to the court's discretion. In the only reported case on s 132, Sheriff Principal Ireland emphasised that what 'appears just' will depend on a consideration of the interests of both the lessor and the hirer[5].

Hire-purchase

INTRODUCTION

Hire-purchase contracts involve the hire of goods with the option of buying if certain conditions are met[6]. The contract has been described as 'a device for financing what in the end will amount to a sale' and it can arise in one of two ways[7]. The customer visits a retailer and agrees to take cer-

---

1 1974 Act, ss 87–89.
2 1974 Act, s 129(1)(b)(i).
3 1974 Act, s 92.
4 This protection for the hirer assumes particular significance in view of the fact that consumer hire agreements are excluded from the court's discretionary power to re-open 'extortionate' credit bargains: see 1974 Act, ss 137–140.
5 *Automative Financial Services Ltd v Henderson* 1992 SLT (Sh Ct) 63 at 64.
6 For a trenchant criticism of the juridical concept of hire purchase, see *Gow* pp 249–251.
7 *Report on Sale and Supply of Goods* (Law Com no. 160; Scot Law Com no. 104) (1987) para 5.46.

tain goods on hire-purchase. The contract can either be made directly between the retailer and the customer or, more usually, the retailer will first sell the goods to a finance company which then enters a hire purchase agreement with the customer. The contract allows the customer or hirer to use the goods in return for regular hire payments. During the currency of the agreement, the creditor retains ownership but the hirer has the contractual right to buy the goods. The option to buy will depend on the terms of the particular contract but it can usually only be exercised after all the hire or rental payments have been made and the hirer is prepared to pay an additional sum to purchase the goods.

In commercial contracts where both parties are in business, it can sometimes be difficult to determine the true legal nature of the agreement which the parties have reached. For instance, the contract may refer to a 'period of hire' and 'hire payments' when the reality is that the parties intend the agreement to be of one conditional sale. As a consequence, the courts will pay less attention to the actual words appearing in the contract than they will to the underlying intention of the parties. Thus on the facts in *John G Murdoch & Co Ltd v Greig*, a contract which referred to 'hire' payments was nevertheless found to be a contract of sale subject to a suspensive condition in which each so-called 'hire' was merely an instalment of the purchase price. Lord President Inglis emphasised that the court had to consider the 'substance and effect' of the contract before deciding whether it was truly a contract of sale or hire-purchase or possibly one of hire[1].

ENTRY INTO CONTRACT

Most contracts of hire purchase fall within the ambit of the Consumer Credit Act 1974. The broad definition of consumer credit agreement is wide enough to cover hire-purchase agreements[2]. Basically, the hire-purchase agreement will be regulated under the Act if the hire payments do not exceed £15,000 and the hirer is not a limited company – individuals, partnerships, clubs, societies and charities are all considered to be consumers for the purposes of the Act[3]. If the agreement is regulated, the hirer is entitled to receive certain information in adverts and quotations[4]. The same obligation of disclosure is carried through into terms of the hire-purchase agreement itself[5]. Failure to comply with the obligation of disclosure means that the agreement is improperly executed. Such an agreement can be enforced against the hirer only if the sheriff court grants an appropriate order[6].

---

1 (1889) 16 R 396 at 400.
2 See 1974 Act, ss 9(3), 15(1)(a) and 189(1).
3 1974 Act, ss 8 and 189(1).
4 1974 Act, Pt IV.
5 1974 Act, Pt V.
6 1974 Act, s 65.

IMPLIED TERMS

Nature of implied terms

As with contracts of sale and hire, Parliament has ensured that hire-purchase contracts carry certain implied terms designed to protect the customer or hirer. Thus it is an implied term of every hire-purchase contract that the hirer will enjoy quiet possession of the goods. It is also implied that the creditor will have a right to sell the goods at the time when the conditions in the contract are fulfilled[1]. If the goods were hired by description, the goods must correspond with that description[2]. It is also an implied term of the contract that the goods will be of satisfactory quality[3].

Exclusion clauses

Any attempt to contract out of the implied terms dealing with description or quality of the goods is void in the case of a consumer contract[4] and subjected to a 'fair and reasonable test' in all other cases[5]. The Unfair Terms in Consumer Contracts Regulations 1994 also apply if the hirer was an individual who entered the contract other than for the purposes of his business[6]. If the exclusion clause in the contract was not individually negotiated[7], it is subject to a test of fairness which depends on an assessment of good faith[8]. A term which is found to be unfair does not bind the consumer[9].

Breach of implied terms

If the creditor is in material breach of any express or implied term of the contract, the hirer is entitled to reject any goods which have been delivered and also to claim damages[10]. In the case of a consumer contract of hire-purchase[11], the hirer is entitled to treat any breach of the implied terms relating to description or satisfactory quality as a material breach.[12] The right of rejection can be lost at common law through the operation of personal bar or waiver but it is not clear when the hirer would lose the right. As the Law Commissions[13] have observed, the nature of the action

1 Supply of Goods (Implied Terms) Act 1973, s 8.
2 1973 Act, s 9.
3 1973 Act, s 10.
4 Ie a contract in which one party deals in the course of a business and the other does not *and* the goods supplied are of a type ordinarily supplied for private use: Unfair Contract Terms Act 1977, s 25(1).
5 1977 Act, s 20.
6 1994 Regulations, reg 2(1)(definition of 'consumer').
7 As defined in 1994 Regulations, reg 3(3).
8 See 1994 Regulations, reg 4 and Schs 2 and 3.
9 1994 Regulations, reg 5(1).
10 1973 Act, s 12A.
11 As defined in the 1977 Act, s 25(1).
12 Supply of Goods (Implied Terms) Act 1973, s 12A(2)–(3).
13 *Report on Sale and Supply of Goods* paras 2.53–2.54.

taken when a defect comes to light and the continuing relationship between the parties will be relevant factors. Should the creditor commit only a minor breach of contract, the hirer's remedy is to seek damages[1].

TERMINATION

By hirer

If the contract is regulated by the Consumer Credit Act 1974, the hirer may terminate the contract at any time before the final payment falls due by giving notice to the creditor under s 99. No special form of words is required and it would appear that verbal notice may be sufficient (though not advisable). Any outstanding payments which were due before the date of termination must be settled[2]. If the hirer has paid less than half of the total price, he or she is also liable under s 100 for the amount necessary to bring payments up to 50 per cent of the total price. A smaller payment may be due if the hire-purchase agreement provides for this. The sheriff court also has the discretion to order payment of a lesser sum if that amount would compensate the creditor for the loss he or she has sustained by early termination of the agreement[3]. If, however, the hirer has failed to take reasonable care of the goods, the creditor is entitled to compensation over and above any other payments due by the hirer[4].

By creditor

Where the hirer is in breach of the contract (eg by falling behind with payments), the creditor must serve a default notice before he or she can terminate the agreement and recover possession of the goods. The notice must take a prescribed form and give the hirer seven days in which to remedy the breach[5]. The hirer is also protected against the possibility of the creditor attempting to 'snatch back' the goods without a court order. The hirer's protection applies where he or she has already paid one-third or more of the total price. In that situation, the goods become 'protected goods' under s 90 and the creditor must obtain an order from the sheriff court before he or she can retake possession. Should the creditor recover the goods without a court order or the hirer's genuine consent[6], the hirer is released from all liability under the hire-purchase agreement. In addition, the hirer can recover all the sums which he or she has previously paid to the creditor[7].

---

1 1973 Act, s 12A(1)(a).
2 1974 Act, s 99(2).
3 1974 Act, s 100(3).
4 1974 Act, s 100(4).
5 1974 Act, ss 87 and 88.
6 On the issue of consent, see further *Ervine* pp 214–215.
7 1974 Act, s 91.

Time orders

Where the creditor has applied to the court to recover possession of the goods or has served a default notice, the hirer can apply to the court for a time order under s 129 of the 1974 Act. This provision gives the sheriff wide discretionary powers to achieve a 'just' solution in a particular case. The interests of both parties will be considered and the court may decide that it is appropriate to reschedule payments. In particular, the sheriff has the specific power to make an order dealing with the making of payments which will become payable subsequently under the agreement[1].

Return and transfer orders

The 1974 Act contains special provisions in relation to hire-purchase agreements which allow the courts the discretion to make a 'return order' or a 'transfer order' if it appears just to do so[2]. The orders are available where the creditor has already applied to the court for recovery of possession of the goods or for an enforcement order. They are also available where the debtor has applied for a time order under s 129. As the name suggests, a 'return order' is simply an order requiring the goods to be returned to the creditor. A 'transfer order' is an alternative form of 'return order' which is available where a number of different goods are the subject of the hire-purchase agreement and the debtor has paid part of the total price. In that situation, the court can make a transfer order splitting the goods delivered under the agreement so as to transfer the creditor's title to some goods to the hirer while requiring the other goods to be returned to the creditor. The effect of a transfer order is to allow the hirer to keep the goods which have been transferred without making any further payment.

The court has the discretion in deciding which goods will be transferred. However the sheriff can only consider making a transfer order if the hirer has already paid a minimum amount. This amount is calculated by adding (a) the part of the total price which is attributable to the transferred goods to (b) one-third of the unpaid balance of the total price. For example, if the total price is £2,600 and the transferred goods are worth £800, the hirer will need to have paid £1,400 [£800 + (£1,800 x 1/3)] before the transfer order can be made.

Even after a return order or transfer order has been made, the hirer who can find the necessary money is entitled under s 133(4) to pay the balance of the total price and claim the goods which were originally ordered to be returned to the creditor. The right to claim the goods by paying the full price is available only if the creditor has not retaken actual possession.

1 1974 Act, s 130(2).
2 1974 Act, s 133.

The Consumer Credit Act 1974

The purpose of this section is to provide a brief overview of the overall operation of the Consumer Credit Act 1974 as it affects contracts for the sale or supply of goods. Some general features of the scheme of the Act will be outlined before consideration is given to the important detailed provisions dealing with connected lender liability and the sheriff's power to re-open extortionate credit bargains.

OVERVIEW

The policy of the 1974 Act is to ensure a reasonable level of protection for consumers who obtain almost any form of credit. Three general features stand out in the legislative scheme: (1) a comprehensive system for licensing credit and hire businesses; (2) strict controls on seeking new credit business from customers; and (3) regulation of the respective rights and duties of the parties when a contract is entered with a consumer. Since many of the detailed provisions affecting the parties in hire and hire-purchase agreements have already been considered, the opportunity is taken below to outline how the licensing system operates and what controls are placed on the seeking of credit business.

Before turning to these issues, however, it is worth observing that use of the term 'consumer' in the Act is slightly misleading because it suggests that the legislation protects only private individuals or consumers. The reality is that partnerships, clubs, societies and charities all fall within the definition of consumer[1]. Only limited companies stand outside the scheme of protection. The importance of the consumer's statutory rights under the Act is underlined by the fact that any attempt to contract out of the legislation is void[2]. The overall operation and enforcement of the legislation is overseen by the Director General of Fair Trading (DGFT) but, at local level, this responsibility is exercised by trading standards officers employed by local authorities.

LICENSING

Need for a licence

Any business which offers credit or hire facilities to consumers will require a licence from the DGFT. Only two kinds of business can avoid the need to apply for a licence: those whose customers consist entirely of limited companies; and those who offer credit or hire facilities where the cost to the consumer will always exceed the current limit of £15,000[3]. The

---

1 See the extended definition of 'individual' in the 1974 Act, s 189(1).
2 1974 Act, s 173.
3 The financial limit can be varied by statutory instrument made under the 1974 Act, s 181.

licensing provisions also extend to so-called 'ancillary credit businesses'[1]. Credit brokers fall within this category so that any business (eg a retailer) which introduces customers to a potential source of finance (eg a finance house) requires a licence. Debt counsellors (eg Citizens Advice Bureau) who give advice on how debts can be re-negotiated also require a licence, as do debt collectors and credit reference agencies.

Types of licence

The DGFT grants licences for five years. Most licences are 'standard licences' which are issued to individual businesses; in the period 1976 to 1995, 387,000 standard licences had been issued. A few 'group licences' are issued to organisations where the DGFT believes this to be in the public interest. At present, 16 group licences are in force, covering such organisations as the Law Society of Scotland (1,200 member firms); the Institute of Chartered Accountants of Scotland (1,300 member firms); and Citizens Advice Scotland (64 advice bureaux)[2].

Obtaining a licence

The applicant must convince the DGFT that he or she is a 'fit person to engage in the activities covered by the licence'[3]. The 1974 Act requires the DGFT to consider various factors, including any convictions for fraud or dishonesty and any previous contraventions of the Act itself. The DGFT will also consider whether the applicant's business practices are unfair or improper (though not necessarily illegal)[4]. It is an offence to give false or misleading information when applying for a licence[5]. If the DGFT is minded to refuse the application, the applicant must be given the opportunity of making written representations[6]. Should the application ultimately be refused, the applicant has a right of appeal to the Secretary of State for Trade and Industry[7].

Revocation or suspension

Once granted, licences can be suspended or revoked if the DGFT 'is of the opinion that if the licence had expired at that time he would not have been minded to renew it'[8]. It seems that motor traders account for the largest number of revocations or suspensions, mainly because of a history of 'clocking' mileometers[9].

1   1974 Act, s 21.
2   See OFT *Annual Report of the Director General of Fair Trading 1995,* App C.
3   1974 Act, s 25(1).
4   1974 Act, s 25(2).
5   1974 Act, s 7.
6   1974 Act, ss 27 and 34.
7   1974 Act, s 41.
8   1974 Act, s 32.
9   See OFT *Annual Report 1995* p 25 and *Ervine* p 189.

Unlicensed businesses

Credit or hire businesses which do not possess a DGFT licence commit a criminal offence[1]. More importantly, perhaps, any agreement made by an unlicensed business which falls within the 1974 Act cannot be enforced through the courts against the consumer unless the business persuades the DGFT to 'cure' the problem by issuing a validation order. The factors which the DGFT is obliged to consider when exercising his discretion include the extent to which other consumers were prejudiced by the trader's conduct; the trader's degree of culpability in failing to obtain a licence in the first place; and whether it was likely that a licence covering the relevant period would have been issued had it been sought at the appropriate time[2]. Again, an appeal lies to the Secretary of State against the refusal of a validation order[3].

CONTROLS ON SEEKING BUSINESS

General policy

The 1974 Act controls the way in which credit business is sought. The basic policy is to promote 'truth in lending' by ensuring that consumers have detailed and accurate information about what they are undertaking if they agree to take credit facilities. Perhaps the best example of the 'truth in lending' policy is the need for traders to state compound interest rates as an APR (or Annual Percentage Rate) figure in adverts and quotations. The object of this kind of information is to allow consumers to make an informed choice about the different credit facilities which are on offer from competing traders.

Adverts

The 1974 Act controls the form and content of adverts where the advertiser is offering credit or hire facilities and the amount of credit does not exceed £15,000[4]. Regulations issued by the Secretary of State specify in considerable detail how an advertiser is to convey 'a fair and reasonably comprehensive indication of the nature of the credit or hire facilities offered' and 'of their true cost to persons using them'[5]. The advertiser commits an offence by breaching the regulations or by publishing materially false or misleading information[6].

1 1974 Act, s 39.
2 1974 Act, s 40.
3 1974 Act, s 41.
4 1974 Act, s 43.
5 1974 Act, s 44(1) and Consumer Credit (Advertisements) Regulations 1989, SI 1989/1125.
6 1974 Act, s 47.

Quotations

Regulations issued under s 52 of the 1974 Act control the form and content of written quotations given to potential customers and these basically require the disclosure of the same information as an advertiser would need to disclose[1].

Canvassing customers

Another control on the seeking of business relates to the canvassing of agreements away from trade premises (eg at the customer's home). It is an offence to canvass in this way unless the customer had previously invited the canvasser to visit[2].

Agreements

The form and content of the agreement which the customer signs is covered by regulations made under s 60 of the 1974 Act[3]. The documentation concluding an agreement must inform the customer of his or her rights and liabilities under the agreement; the cost of the credit the customer is obtaining expressed as both a specific sum and an APR figure; and the cancellation and other remedies available to the customer under the Act.

CONNECTED LENDER LIABILITY

The consumer has certain rights during the currency of a regulated agreement and one of the most important of these rights is found in the 'connected lender liability' provision in s 75 of the 1974 Act. This covers cases where goods or services are supplied by one party (eg a shop or restaurant) and the customer is given credit facilities by a creditor (normally a finance house or credit card company) with whom the supplier has a pre-existing arrangement. The important point is that the supplier and creditor must be different parties. Assuming this is the case, the customer can hold the supplier and the creditor jointly and severally liable for any misrepresentation or breach of contract. For instance, shops and stores which accept credit cards (eg Visa, Access) will have a pre-existing arrangement with the credit card issuer. Thus if the customer uses his or her credit card to buy goods which prove to be faulty, he or she has a remedy under s 75 against both the retailer and the credit card company. On the other hand, the customer using a store card (eg issued by Marks & Spencer) cannot rely on s 75 as the store is acting as both supplier and creditor.

It is not possible to claim under s 75 if the cash price for the goods or services was £100 or less, or above £30,000. Claims by a disappointed hirer under a hire agreement (eg car rental or hire of a suit) are also outside the

---

1 See Consumer Credit (Quotations) Regulations 1989.
2 1974 Act, ss 48 and 49.
3 See Consumer Credit (Agreements) Regulations 1983, SI 1983/1553.

scope of s 75[1]. Consumers who have entered a hire-purchase agreement similarly do not fall within s 75.

EXTORTIONATE CREDIT BARGAINS

The sheriff court has the discretionary power to re-open any extortionate credit bargain 'so as to do justice between the parties'[2]. This power relates to any credit bargain and not just to those which fall within the £15,000 credit limit generally recognised under the 1974 Act. However, the provision is not open to debtors who are limited companies[3] or in cases where the bargain involves a contract of hire. The bargain is 'extortionate' if it requires the debtor to make 'grossly exorbitant' payments or the agreement 'otherwise grossly contravenes ordinary principles of fair dealing'[4]. The sheriff is bound to consider several factors in determining whether the bargain is extortionate, including the prevailing level of interest rates when the bargain was entered into; the debtor's age, experience and business capacity; and the degree of financial pressure the debtor faced. From the creditor's standpoint, the court has to consider the creditor's relationship to the debtor; and the degree of risk the creditor undertook by entering the bargain, having regard to any security offered as part of the deal[5].

If the debtor alleges that the credit bargain he or she has made is extortionate, the onus is put on the creditor to prove the contrary[6]. Should the sheriff decide to reopen the agreement, he or she can order the debtor to be relieved from making any payment 'in excess of that fairly due and reasonable'. The creditor can be ordered to repay sums already paid by the debtor. The court also has the power to set aside all or part of the bargain or order the return of property given as security[7].

The draftsman of the 1974 Act predicted that the courts would be sparing in granting relief under these provisions and so it has proved in practice in the few reported cases on the subject[8]. One successful case is that of *Prestonwell Ltd v Capon*[9], where Corby County Court halved the flat rate of interest from 42 per cent to 21 per cent. There was evidence that the agreement had been made by debtors who were under financial pressure and had little business experience. The court also considered comparative interest rates and the fact that the debtors lacked proper legal advice as relevant factors. Similarly, in another case[10], the county court held that the

1 This is because s 75(1) of the 1974 Act refers to 'debtor' and not hirer.
2 1974 Act, s 137(1).
3 But see the broadly similar provision under the Insolvency Act 1986, s 244 where an extortionate credit transaction has been entered into by a company in the three years before an administration order was made or the company went into liquidation.
4 1974 Act, s 138(1).
5 1974 Act, s 138(2)–(4).
6 1974 Act, s 171(7).
7 1974 Act, s 139.
8 See Bennion 'Implementing the Consumer Credit Act' (1977) 121 Sol Jo 484 at 485 where he points out that 'the bargain must after all be *grossly* exorbitant or unfair'.
9 (1988, unreported), Corby County Court, discussed by Harvey and Parry *The Law of Consumer Protection and Fair Trading* (5th edn, 1996) pp 310–311.
10 *Castle Phillips Co Ltd v Wilkinson* [1992] CCLR 83, discussed in *Harvey and Parry* p 311.

bargain was extortionate where a bridging loan was lent at over three times the building society rate and security was given in excess of the amount borrowed.

On the other hand, in *A Ketley Ltd v Scott*[1], the court refused to reopen a bridging loan to buy a flat where the interest worked out at 48 per cent per annum. It was held that the interest rate was not unduly high. The creditor had lent 82 per cent of the value of the flat at short notice and therefore the risk undertaken was highly speculative. It was also relevant that the debtor had failed to disclose his substantial bank overdraft and the guarantees that he had given to third parties.

---

1 [1981] ICR 241, discussed in *Harvey and Parry* pp 309–310.

3 Carriage of goods by road and sea

Carriage by road

CARRIAGE GENERALLY

Once goods have been sold the matter of their delivery to the purchaser may arise. In many instances, where goods are too bulky for the purchaser to uplift, a contract for their carriage from the seller's place of business to the residence or place of business of the purchaser will have to be made with someone who specialises in the transportation of goods. By far the greatest proportion of goods carried in the UK goes by road and, in the case of goods sold for export, the largest proportion travels by sea. Multimodal transport (ie combined transport) by road and sea, is now common in the case of containerised goods. In this chapter we will look at the principal features of the law relating to carriage of goods by road and by sea.

CLASSIFICATION – COMMON AND PRIVATE CARRIERS

A contract of carriage, whether by road, rail, air, or sea, is a contract for the hire of work and services (*locatio operis faciendi*). Carriers by road fall into one of two categories, either common or private: the rights and obligations of the former being regulated by the common law and by the Carriers Act 1830 and of the latter by the contract of carriage. Today most carriers contract out of the status of common carrier and in some instances status as a private carrier is already fixed by law[1].

'A common carrier', wrote Bell, 'is one who, for hire, undertakes the carriage of goods generally, or of certain classes of goods, for any of the public indiscriminately from and to a place'[2]. Having regard to this definition, it is, nonetheless, a question of fact whether or not a carrier is common or private. Where, for instance, a carrier's promotional material (eg advertisements, calendars and circulars) professed that goods would be transported at standard rates, regardless of the attractiveness of an offer of business, it was held that the carrier was a common carrier[3].

A carrier who limits the types of goods to be carried[3], or who restricts the destinations to which the goods will be carried[4], is still a common carrier so long as he or she holds himself or herself out as willing to carry

---

1 The Post Office is not a common carrier: Post Office Act 1969, ss 29, 30 (as amended by the British Telecommunications Act 1981, Schs 3 and 6, and the Telecommunications Act 1984, s 99 and Sch 7). Note also *Harold Stephen & Co Ltd v Post Office* [1977] 1 WLR 1172 at 1177, CA, per Lord Denning MR.
2 Bell *Principles* s 160; *Barr & Sons v Caledonian Rly Co* (1890) 18 R 139.
3 *A Siohn & Co v RH Hagland & Son (Transport) Ltd* [1976] 2 Lloyd's Rep 428.
4 *Johnson v Midland Rly Co* (1849) 4 Exch 367.

goods of that type, or to those particular destinations, for anyone who asks him or her to do so. In contrast, a carrier who offers to carry goods only after their prior inspection by him or her, in order to determine their suitability for carriage and the rate at which they will be carried, is not a common carrier[1]. Whether the type of goods to be carried or the routes travelled be restricted or not, a common carrier is one who makes a standing offer to the public to carry. A private carrier, in contradistinction, makes no such offer[2]. In order to avoid confusion, most road haulage contractors expressly declare in their contracts of carriage that they are not common carriers and that goods are accepted for carriage on that basis only. Thus the most recent version of the Road Haulage Association's Conditions of Carriage (1991) reads: 'the carrier is not a common carrier and accepts goods for carriage only upon that condition and the Conditions set out below'.

REFUSAL TO CARRY

While a private carrier is free to refuse business, refusal to carry goods renders a common carrier liable in damages unless it is justified[3]. Refusal is justified in the following circumstances[3]: (1) where goods are not of the type which the carrier professes to carry; (2) where the carrier does not carry to the destination for which the goods are intended; (3) where no space is available on the vehicle; (4) where the consignor refuses to pay the freight charge; (5) where there exists a 'popular tumult' in an area through which the vehicle carrying goods must pass; (6) where the goods are of a dangerous nature or are not properly packed.

EDICTAL LIABILITY

'The rule is that common carriers . . . are responsible for the loss of things committed to their charge, although no neglect can be proved'[4]. The liability of a common carrier for loss of or damage to goods while in transit is, therefore, strict and does not depend upon proof of fault on the carrier's part. In sharp contrast, the liability of a private carrier depends upon proof of negligence on the part of the carrier or of his or her employees[5]. However, both common and private carriers are strictly liable for loss or damage to goods caused by accidental fire[6]. In the case of the private car-

---

1 *Watkins v Cottell* [1916] 1 KB 10.
2 *Belfast Ropework Co Ltd v Bushell* [1918] 1 KB 210.
3 Bell *Principles* s 159.
4 Stair *Institutions* I, 13, 3; Bell *Principles* s 235. This liability derives from the praetorian edict *nautae caupones stabularii*: *Digest* IV, 9, 1. In England, where the position is the same, the rule is based on custom of the realm.
5 This duty of care may be broken down into several components: provision of suitable vehicle; proper packing of goods; taking ordinary care of the goods; no deviation from the normal route of travel. See Bell *Principles* s 164.
6 Mercantile Law Amendment (Scotland) Act 1856, s 17. See also *James Kemp (Leslie) Ltd v Robertson* 1967 SC 229, OH; *Anderson v Jenkins Express Removals Ltd* 1967 SC 231, OH; *Graham v Shore Porters Society* 1979 SLT 119, OH; *Boomsma v Clark and Rose Ltd* 1983 SLT (Sh Ct) 67.

rier, therefore, it can be seen that strict liability for loss or damage caused by fire is superimposed upon liability based on negligence. The same is true for common carriers, whose strict liability is superimposed upon an underlying obligation to take reasonable care of goods entrusted to them. Multi-layered liability can be an issue where a carrier relies on a contract term purporting to exclude liability.

There are exceptions to the rule that a common carrier is strictly liable for loss of or damage to goods being carried. There are also limitations to this rule and strict liability can be excluded.

Exceptions

There are four situations in which a common carrier will not be liable for loss of or damage to goods entrusted to his or her care. These are where the loss was caused by act of God; by acts of the Queen's enemies; through inherent vice in the goods; and as a result of the consignor's fault. An act of God (*damnum fatale*) is an occurrence which cannot be reasonably foreseen and provided for: eg an unexpected heart attack which strikes down an unsuspecting victim[1]; or severe and unexpected rain in mid-July in Moray which causes rivers to flood and roads to be submerged. Civil riots are not treated as acts of the Queen's enemies[2], but, possibly, the acts of participants in an armed rebellion may be so included[3]. Where goods possess a defect which is not apparent to the carrier and which causes them to be damaged, the carrier cannot be held liable for loss arising from that defect since there is nothing he or she could do to guard against its occurrence[4]. So while, eg, a carrier might be liable for damage to fruit or meat which are spoiled because they were not carried in a refrigerated van[5], he or she would not be liable if unpacked fruit were damaged by a combination of its own weight and the normal movement of the van[6]. If the consignor of goods is at fault, eg by providing the wrong address for delivery of the goods, then the carrier can not be held liable for their loss[7].

While the perils just described 'except' strict liability[8], they do not exclude the common carrier's basic duty to take reasonable care of goods entrusted for carriage. As a result, although the immediate cause of loss may be an expected peril, if the real or true cause of loss was the carrier's failure to take reasonable care, then, the carrier remains liable[9]. Unjustifiable deviation also precludes reliance on the excepted perils unless it can be shown that the loss which occurred was unavoidable[10].

The Road Haulage Association's Conditions of Carriage 1991 are broadly similar to, though in some instances more extensive than, the

1 *Ryan v Youngs* [1938] 1 All ER 522, CA.
2 *Curtis & Sons v Matthews* [1919] 1 KB 425, CA.
3 *Curtis & Sons v Matthews* above; *Secretary of State for War v Midland Great Western Rly Co of Ireland* [1923] 2 IR 102. In both cases the court considered a state of war to exist.
4 *Ralston v Caledonian Rly Co* (1878) 5 R 671.
5 *Blower v Great Western Rly Co* (1872) LR 7 Exch 373.
6 *Kendall v London and South Western Rly Co* (1872) LR 7 Exch 373.
7 *Caledonian Rly Co v W Hunter & Co* (1858) 20 D 1097.
8 These are sometimes described as 'excepted perils'.
9 *Blower v Great Western Rly Co* (1872) LR 7CP 655.
10 *James Morrison & Co Ltd v Shaw, Savill and Albion Co Ltd* [1916] 2 KB 783, CA.

exceptions to the common carrier's liability just described. Provided that he or she has taken reasonable care to minimise their effect, a private carrier, transporting goods under a contract to which the 1991 Conditions apply, is not liable for loss or misdelivery of or damage to those goods where this is due, inter alia, to act of God, latent and inherent defects in goods, insufficient or improper packing, labelling or addressing, acts of foreign enemies, hostilities, rebellions, riots and civil commotion[1].

A common carrier is not liable for delay which occurs through no fault on his or her part. The carrier's obligation is to deliver goods within a reasonable time having regard to circumstances. So, where the cause of the delay is the carrier's unjustified deviation, he or she will be liable for loss or damage to the goods carried[2]. But where the delay is caused by an unexpected blockage on the carrier's usual route (eg a motorway pile-up), he or she will not be liable[3]. Should unexpected delay threaten the spoilation of perishable goods, the carrier should contact the owner for instructions where this is reasonably practicable. If contact cannot be made, then the carrier, acting as a *negotiorum gestor*, may sell the goods[4]. The position is much the same in the case of private carriage under a contract to which the Road Haulage Association's Conditions of Carriage 1991 apply. Here the carrier is entitled to sell the goods and remit payment, under deduction of any costs incurred in so doing, provided that: (1) the carrier has taken reasonable steps to ensure that payment should reflect the value of the goods he or she is forced to sell and (2) he or she has done what is reasonable to ensure that the consignor, or consignee, is notified that the goods are to be sold and given an opportunity either to collect these or provide instructions for their disposal[5].

Limitations

The contents of a small package may be of great value: eg where it contains jewellery, securities, gold or silver. Consequently, unless the consignor of such a package declares the nature and value of the items contained therein when it is entrusted to the common carrier, and pays any increased freight charge, the latter will escape liability for its loss or damage where the value of its contents exceeds £10[6], except where loss was caused by an employee's dishonesty[7]. Where the nature and value of goods are declared and any increased charge paid, the owner may recover up to the declared value of the goods plus the increased freight charge[8]. It is open to the carrier to show that lost goods were worth less than their

---

1 Condition 9(2)(b).
2 *Mallet v Great Eastern Rly Co* [1899] 1 QB 309.
3 *Anderson v North British Rly Co* (1875) 2 R 443.
4 *Springer v Great Western Rly Co* [1921] 1 KB 257; *China Pacific SA v Food Corpn of India* [1982] AC 939, HL; *Forth Tugs Ltd v Wilmington Trust Co* (28 December 1984, unreported), OH; affd 1985 SC 317.
5 Condition 7.
6 Carriers Act 1830, s 1. See also *Rusk v North British Rly Co* 1920 2 SLT 139. The 1830 Act lists goods whose nature and value must be declared.
7 *Shaw v Great Western Rly Co* [1894] 1 QB 373.
8 1830 Act, s 7.

declared value but their owner cannot plead the converse[1]. The common carrier's right to demand payment of increased freight charges should be displayed on a conspicuous notice in his or her office[2]. Failure to do so probably means only that the carrier's right to claim an increased charge is lost but not his immunity under the 1830 Act[3]. A common carrier is free to vary the terms of the 1830 Act or to limit his liability to the owners of goods carried[4].

Exclusion

A common carrier cannot exclude liability by means of a public notice but only by contract[5]. However, a contract may incorporate, by reference, terms found in such a notice[6]. Furthermore, exclusion of his or her strict liability for loss of or damage to goods by a common carrier is not subject to the Unfair Contracts Terms Act 1977. The 1977 Act applies, amongst other things, to contract terms which exclude liability for breach of a duty to take reasonable care[7]. While, therefore, exclusion and limitation clauses in the contracts of private carriers (who are obliged to take reasonable care of goods entrusted to them) fall within the ambit of the legislation[8], the edictal liability of the common carrier, which imposes a higher duty than that of reasonable care, is not covered by the 1977 Act. Where, however, the contract of carriage is in standard form, and where also the consignor acts privately and not in the course of his or her business (ie acts as a consumer), a contract term which excludes edictal liability may be treated as being unfair and not binding on the consignor of the goods[9].

It has already been noted that a carrier may be liable for loss of or damage to goods under more than one head. This can cause problems where the carrier attempts to rely on a term in the contract of carriage which purports to exclude his liability. In *Graham v Shore Porters Society*[10], one term in the contract purported to exclude liability for loss or damage 'caused by or incidental to' fire. The pursuer's furniture perished as a result of a fire which occurred during its carriage by the defenders. Since the wording of this clause did not make clear whether it was intended to exclude the carrier's strict liability under s 17 of the Mercantile Law Amendment (Scotland) Act 1856 and also liability for breach of contract or negligence, there was doubt as to its meaning and it had to be construed *contra proferentem* It was decided that the only reasonable construction of the wording of the clause was that it was intended to exclude only the carrier's strict liability, leaving intact liability for breach of contract or negligence.

1 1830 Act, s 9; *McCance v London and North Western Rly Co* (1864) 3 H & C 343.
2 1830 Act, s 2.
3 *Rusk v North British Rly Co* 1920 2 SLT 139.
4 1830 Act, s 6.
5 1830 Act, s 4.
6 1830 Act, s 6.
7 Unfair Contract Terms Act 1977, ss 16(1)(b) and 25(1).
8 Where the contract is either a consumer or standard form contract: 1977 Act, ss 15(2)(c), 17, 25(1). See also *Boomsma v Clark and Rose Ltd* 1983 SLT (Sh Ct) 67.
9 Unfair Terms in Consumer Contracts Regulations 1994, SI 1994/3159. Note in particular regs 2(1), 5 and Sch 3, para 1(b).
10 1979 SLT 119, OH.

CARRIER'S LIEN

A carrier has a special lien over the goods he or she carries for payment of the freight charges incurred in transporting them. A carrier has no general lien, however, over such goods in respect of moneys owned to him or her by a customer under earlier, unpaid, contracts of carriage[1]. It is quite legitimate for a contract of carriage to create, expressly, a general lien[2]. Where, however, the unpaid seller of goods currently in the course of being carried exercises his or her right of stoppage in transit[3], this has priority over any general lien created by the contract under which those goods are carried[4]. A carrier who fails to comply with a stop notice will be liable in damages to the seller[5].

DURATION OF CARRIAGE

Carriage begins when the carrier or his agent accepts delivery of the goods[6]. It ends on their delivery to the consignee at the address stipulated for their delivery[7]. Where that address is not the consignee's premises, the latter must be notified of the arrival of the goods and allowed a reasonable time within which to collect them[8]. Should the consignee prove non-existent, or refuse or delay to take the goods, the carrier is then treated as a depositary and obliged only to take due care for their safety until their redelivery to the consignor[9]. In the case of the common carrier, the net effect of all of this is that from the moment when he or she receives goods for carriage, even though actual transit may not commence at that time, he or she is under edictal liability in respect of those goods. That edictal liability subsists either until the consignee takes delivery of the goods from the carrier or until the consignee refuses to do so. The Road Haulage Association's Conditions of Carriage 1991 stipulate that carriage ends when goods are delivered at the consignee's address and if delivery there is prevented by the absence of safe and adequate access to that address, or through the absence of adequate unloading facilities there, then transit ends on the expiry of one clear day after the carrier has given notice to the consignee that the goods are now at the carrier's premises[10]. If goods

1 *Peebles & Son v Caledonian Rly Co* (1875) 2 R 346.
2 *Great Eastern Rly Co v Lord's Tr* [1909] AC 109, HL. Note also the Road Haulage Association's Conditions of Carriage 1991, condition 15: 'The Carrier shall have a general lien against the Customer, where the Customer is the owner of the goods, for any moneys whatever due from the Customer to the Carrier'.
3 Sale of Goods Act 1979, ss 44–46.
4 *United States Steel Products Co v Great Western Rly Co* [1916] 1 AC 189, HL.
5 *Mechan & Sons Ltd v North Eastern Rly Co* 1911 SC 1348.
6 Bell *Principles* s 162. The Road Haulage Association's Conditions of Carriage 1991, condition 6(1) provides: 'Transit shall commence when the Carrier takes possession of the Consignment whether at the point of collection or at the Carrier's premises'.
7 Bell *Principles* s 235.
8 *Chapman v Great Western Rly Co* (1880) 5 QBD 278 at 281, per Cockburn CJ.
9 Bell *Principles* s 235.
10 Condition 6(2) and proviso (a).

cannot be delivered for some other reason, or where these are held by the carrier 'to await order', or 'to be kept till called for', transit ends after the expiry of a reasonable time without the goods having been collected[1].

INTERNATIONAL CARRIAGE OF GOODS BY ROAD

The 1956 Geneva Convention on the Contract for the International Carriage of Goods by Road is given force in the UK by the Carriage of Goods by Road Act 1965[2]. International carriage occurs where the contract of carriage indicates that the place where goods are collected and the place of delivery are in different states and where either or both of these places is located in a state which is party to the Convention[3]. Although an oral contract of carriage may be made, this must be confirmed by a written consignment note, in triplicate, which is signed by both carrier and consignor of the goods[4]. The consignment note is prima facie evidence of the making of a contract of carriage, the conditions of the contract, and of receipt of the goods by the carrier[5]. Amongst other things, the consignment note must declare that the contract of carriage is governed by the Convention[6]. If the carrier has reservations about the condition of goods entrusted to his or her care, these should be written on the consignment note and failure to do so raises a rebuttable presumption that the goods were in good condition when the carrier received them[7]. The carrier is liable for loss of or damage to goods and also for delay in their delivery[8]. Where, however, loss, damage, or delay is not attributable to wilful misconduct or default on the part of the carrier[9], then the carrier's liability is modified as follows: (1) in the case of loss, to 8.33 units of account per kilogram of gross weight of the goods[10]; (2) in the case of damage, to the amount by which the goods have diminished in value provided that this does not exceed the amount payable in respect of their loss[11]; and (3) in the case of delay, to the carriage charges[12]. Where loss, damage, or delay is attributable to the claimant's instructions to the carrier, or to the claimant's negligence or wrongful act, or to some inherent vice of the

1 Condition 6(2) proviso (b).
2 A Protocol to this Convention is given force by the Carriage by Air and Road Act 1979.
3 Carriage of Goods by Road Act 1965, Schedule, art 1(1).
4 1965 Act, Schedule, arts 4 and 5. Both carrier and consignor retain a copy each and the third copy accompanies the goods.
5 1965 Act, Schedule, art 9(2); *Texas Instruments Ltd v Nason (Europe) Ltd* [1991] 1 Lloyd's Rep 146.
6 1965 Act, Schedule, art 6(1)(k).
7 1965 Act, Schedule, art 9(2); *SA de Zeven Provincien v SPRL Ultra Rapid Wagner Freers* 123 ETL 776 (1977).
8 1965 Act, Schedule, art 17(1).
9 1965 Act, Schedule, art 29. On what constitutes 'wilful misconduct', see *National Semiconductors (UK) Ltd v UPS Ltd and Inter City Trucks Ltd* [1996] 2 Lloyd's Rep 212.
10 1965 Act, Schedule, art 23(3). It is left to a national court dealing with a case involving limitation of liability to convert the unit of account into the national currency.
11 1965 Act, Schedule, art 25; *William Tatton & Co Ltd v Ferrymasters Ltd* [1974] 1 Lloyd's Rep 203.
12 1965 Act, Schedule, art 23(5).

goods carried[1], or to some unavoidable occurrence[2], then the carrier escapes liability completely[3]. However, the burden of proving that the loss, damage or delay was attributable to one of these causes rests on the carrier[4]. Except where more than one carrier will be used, in which case they are free to allocate amongst themselves rights of contribution should liability be incurred, any contract term which 'directly or indirectly derogate[s]' from the Convention's provisions is null and void[5].

Carriage by sea

INTRODUCTION

The contract of affreightment for the carriage of goods by sea has long been a vitally important part of the commerce of Scotland. When roads were poor, even where they existed, goods mostly had to be carried by sea. The long-standing importance of sea-borne commerce is well demonstrated by the maritime styles in the Aberdeen Stylebook of 1722[6]. The styles display a well-developed maritime commerce as actually practised in Aberdeen at the beginning of the eighteenth century.

In so far as they are common carriers, shipowners would be under strict liability to the persons shipping the goods. If the shipowner were to be treated as a common carrier, the shipowner would for, all practical purposes, be an insurer of the goods, liable for their safety irrespective of any question of negligence, apart from the exceptions already mentioned in connection with the common carrier by road. In *Nugent v Smith*[7], eg, both act of God and inherent vice of the goods were proved, thus exempting the carrier from liability. Proof of a true general average sacrifice would also serve to exempt the carrier from liability for lost goods.

Few shipowners do nowadays qualify as common carriers, for virtually none purport to carry the goods of anyone offering them for shipment. The right to reject any item of cargo is usually reserved, thereby making the carrier a private carrier liable only on proof of negligence.

It may seem odd, in view of the stringency with which hotel keepers are prevented from contracting out of liability to their guests[8], that at common law the courts were fairly ready to permit shipowners, even those who were common carriers, to contract out of their strict liability, and some very wide disclaimers of liability began to appear. However, the Carriage

---

1 On what constitutes 'inherent vice', see *Ulster-Swift Ltd and Pig Marketing Board (Northern Ireland) v Taunton Meat Haulage Ltd* [1975] 2 Lloyd's Rep 502.
2 Unavoidable in the sense that even the taking of utmost care would not have prevented the occurrence: *JJ Silber Ltd v Islander Trucking Ltd* [1985] 2 Lloyd's Rep 243.
3 1965 Act, Schedule, art 17(2).
4 1965 Act, Schedule, art 18(1).
5 1965 Act, Schedule, art 41(1).
6 To be published by the Stair Society.
7 (1876) CPD 423, CA.
8 Under the Hotel Proprietors Act 1956: Gloag and Henderson *The Law of Scotland* (10th edn, 1995) (eds Wilson, Forte et al) pp 431–432.

of Goods by Sea Act 1971 now prevents any shipowner from purporting to reduce his liability beyond that permitted by the Rules in the Schedule[1] (ie the Hague-Visby Rules).

The contract of carriage by sea is likely to take one of two main forms, bills of lading or charterparties.

BILLS OF LADING

The simplest transaction is the carriage by sea of goods in lots of less than a full shipload. These will be carried by a general ship offering to take mixed cargoes, and are carried under a bill of lading. After booking space on a vessel, and after receiving instructions as to the time and place of loading, it is up to the shipper to get his or her goods to the port of loading and alongside the ship, At this point the shipper (ie the person sending the goods) gets a 'dock receipt'. The carrier (ie the shipping company) then takes over and loads the goods aboard its ship: in practice it will normally employ a firm of stevedores to perform the loading. Once the goods are loaded, the carrier then issues, in place of the dock receipt, the bill of lading. Although negotiation on its terms is theoretically competent, the bill of lading is in practice a classic example of the standard-form contract.

A bill of lading has three main functions. First, It serves as a written embodiment of the terms of the contract for the carriage of the goods. Secondly, it is a receipt for the goods on board the ship, and, in this capacity, it notes the condition of the goods on receipt and any distinguishing marks on their containers. Thirdly, it is a negotiable document of title to the goods mentioned in it, and it is in this capacity that it is used in the financing of the purchase of the goods. The bill is usually forwarded through a bank to the buyer, together with a bill of exchange for the price, an insurance policy and sundry other documents. On paying or accepting the bill of exchange the buyer gets the bill of lading, and with it can claim delivery of the goods from the master of the ship when it arrives at its destination. It is essential to remember these three separate functions which such a bill performs in order to understand the case law.

The bill of lading as the contract of carriage

A bill of lading certainly purports to be the contract between the shipper and the carrier for the carriage of goods in question. It specifies in some detail the ports of loading and discharge, the dates, rate of freight and detailed conditions of the contract, and for most purposes it certainly is the contract which has been entered into between the parties.

However, questions sometimes arise as to whether the bill is the contract or is merely evidence of the contract of carriage. In other words, whether a statement of terms appearing in the bill can be contradicted by evidence that the parties to it concluded a different agreement. The point could be of some importance, since if it actually is the contract, fraud or at

1 Carriage of Goods by Sea Act 1971, Schedule, art III.

least error would presumably have to be shown in order to alter it. If it is merely evidence, other evidence may contradict the terms apparently shown. This type of problem is particularly liable to arise in the case of a standard printed form contract such as the bill of lading. The shipper may have made some stipulation, agreed to by the carrier or vice versa, but when the master of the ship comes to sign the bill of lading simply the top copy of the file of blank bills is used, and the special stipulation is not inserted. In *Phillips v Edwards*[1], casks of brandy were shipped with carriers whose printed schedules of sailings (referred to as time bills) included the stipulation that they received goods only on condition that they were not to be responsible for any loss or damage however arising sustained on the voyage. One of these time bills had been delivered to the shipper, and he was apparently held to have had sufficient notice of the terms excluding liability. After the casks were put on board, however, a document, which appears to have been a bill of lading, though it was termed a 'freight note', was delivered to the shippers by the carriers. The terms of this document were not the same as those on the printed bills, and in particular the clause of exemption was such that the carriers were responsible for faulty stowage of the goods carried. The stowage did in fact turn out to be faulty and the casks were stove in during the voyage. The question then arose as to whether the carriers were exempt from liability by virtue of the printed time bills or were liable for damages in respect of faulty stowage under the bill of lading. It was held that the carriers were completely exempt from liability, the time bills representing the true contract between the parties. The issue of a bill of lading (probably old stock used by mistake) was a matter occurring after the contract of carriage had been formed.

This will, one imagines, normally be the result in such a case. If the parties have concluded a particular contract, the subsequent issue of a bill of lading with different terms should not normally override it. It is not necessary for the shipper even to see the bill of lading until the goods are on board and often only after the ship has sailed. The shipper certainly does not sign it, and its binding quality may arise only by his or her acceptance of it without protest. Thus if a specific stipulation has been made and agreed to between the parties it is difficult to see how a bill of lading subsequently (and effectively unilaterally) issued can alter the terms of a contract already concluded.

But there appears to be still some dubiety in cases where no specific stipulations have been made by either side. Is the bill of lading in these circumstances conclusive evidence of the terms of the contract of carriage? If the shipper accepts it without protest (and even more clearly if the agreement to carry the goods was made by reference to the 'ordinary form'of bill of lading) it is difficult to imagine that the bill does not contain all the terms of the contract. There have however been dicta, in cases where protest was made, suggesting that one can, on occasion, look beyond the bill for other terms. In *The Ardennes*[2], eg, Lord Goddard said: 'It is, I think, well settled that a bill of lading is not in itself the contract between the shipowner and the shipper of goods, though it has been said to be excel-

---

1   (1858) 28 LJ Ex 52.
2   [1950] 2 All ER 517 at 519–520.

lent evidence of its terms … The contract has come into existence before the bill of lading is signed, the latter is signed by one party only and handed by him to the shipper usually after the goods have been put on board. [The shipper] is no party to the preparation of the bill of lading, nor does he sign it'.

The answer would seem to be that in the usual case where the bill of lading is signed by the master of the ship, the master, as such, cannot have authority to vary the terms of a contract already entered into between the shipowners and the persons shipping the goods. And so a bill of lading issued in these circumstances would not prevail over the terms already agreed between the parties. In *The Ardennes*[1] the situation was that the ship's agent had orally promised that the ship would not deviate from the agreed route. But the bill of lading subsequently issued by the master contained a clause permitting deviation. In reliance on the promise of no deviation and in the belief that the ship would arrive by 30 November at latest, the shipper shipped 3,000 cases of mandarines for sale in the London market. Import duty was to be increased on 1 December and he was anxious to get them in before the rise. There was also an issue of better prices. The earlier they arrived, the higher the price. The carriers knew all this. The ship in fact deviated to Antwerp and did not arrive in London until 4 December, a substantial loss was incurred, and the shipper claimed damages. The carrier attempted to rely on the deviation clause in the bill of lading, but the court held that the bill was not of itself the contract, and that evidence was admissible of the terms of the prior contract between the shipper and the carrier. Only in a case where there is no prior contract between the parties can the bill of lading signed by the master be the contract of carriage as opposed to evidence of its terms.

Goods are sometimes shipped without any bill of lading or other document. In the coasting trade around the UK or crossing to Ireland, bills of lading are not particularly common. In such situations it is an ordinary case of establishing the terms of the contract of carriage from the negotiations of the parties and any announcements or notices issued by the shipping company which have been incorporated into the contract[2].

McCutcheon v David MacBrayne Ltd[3], involved the shipment of a car on a ferry from the island of Islay to the Scottish mainland. Bills of lading are not issued in such circumstances. The car was lost when the ferry sank, and it then became necessary to establish the terms of the contract between the car owner and the ferry company. Various documents were considered in an attempt to establish what the parties had agreed. A receipt for freight (ie the receipt for the cost of the ferry crossing) was held not to be part of the contract but merely a receipt for the money paid. The company's normal practice was to include in the contractual documents what they called a 'risk note' exempting themselves from liability, but they had not done so on this occasion, although the car owner had signed such risk notes on several occasions in the past. At the point of embarkation there were various posters which included a reference to a limitation

1 [1950] 2 All ER 517.
2 *McCutcheon v David MacBrayne Ltd* 1964 SC (HL) 28, 1964 SLT 66; *Harland and Wolff Ltd v Burns and Laird Lines Ltd* 1931 SC 722, 1931 SLT 572.
3 1964 SC (HL) 28, 1964 SLT 66.

of the company's liability, but it was held that these had not sufficiently been brought to the car owner's attention to be incorporated into the contract. Hence MacBrayne's (who admitted that the loss of the ship was due to negligent navigation for which they were answerable) were therefore liable for loss of the car.

Although it had long been recognised that one of the functions of a bill of lading was to act as a negotiable document of title to the goods, negotiation and transfer of the bill did not transfer the contract of carriage of the goods. Under the English doctrine of privity of contract, the transferee did not acquire any right to sue for a breach of the contract of carriage in his or her own name, nor was he or she liable to be sued on the contract.

To circumvent this difficulty, the first provision of the Bills of Lading Act 1855[1] transferred to the new owner of the goods any right of action against the carrier in respect of those liabilities which were not excluded by the bill of lading: eg damage by negligent stowage. Equally the new owner was liable for any payments of freight or other charges due on completion of the voyage, with the intention that the whole incidents of the contract of carriage would pass along with the goods themselves.

However, the 1855 Act still did not cover some regularly occurring situations, particularly when property in the goods had not passed even although the buyer was on risk. This problem is now resolved by the Carriage of Goods by Sea Act 1992, which removes the link between title to sue and the passing of ownership. Section 2 of the 1992 Act permits a contractual action against the carrier by the 'lawful holder' of a bill of lading, and, in addition, by the consignee in a sea waybill or the person entitled to delivery as set out in a ship's delivery order.

Bill of lading as a receipt

The bill of lading as a receipt is a very important aspect of its functions, in as much as it acknowledges the quantity and the condition of the goods when put on board. This receipt function was the original purpose of the bill, the custom of including the terms of the contract of carriage and of using the bill as a negotiable document of title having developed later.

Mate's receipt

The bill of lading is now a somewhat complex document, the issue of which may take some days. Thus a common practice developed of giving the shipper an informal and temporary receipt, known as a 'mate's receipt', to be superseded by, and usually exchanged for, the formal bill of lading. This mate's receipt is not a negotiable document of title and mere indorsement or transference of it without notice to the carrier does not pass the property in the goods being shipped. In *Hathesing v Laing*[2], **A**, acting as agent for the purchaser **B**, bought goods and shipped them in a vessel chartered to **B**, obtaining a mate's receipt for the goods. The purchaser then indorsed the mate's receipts to his agent **A**, who kept them in secu-

---

1 1855 Act, s 1 (repealed by the Carriage of Goods by Sea Act 1992, s 6).
2 (1873) LR 17 Eq 92.

rity of payments due to him by **B**. The agent to whom the receipts had been indorsed did not, however, give notice to the captain. In the meantime, **B** obtained formal bills of lading from the ship's captain. Ignoring the transfer of the mate's receipts to his agent, **B** indorsed the bills of lading to a bank. A conflict arose when both the agent and the bank claimed the goods, the agent founding on a custom of the port in question that mate's receipts were negotiable instruments. The court apparently held that even if such a custom existed, it was not effective. The captain, having no notice of any other claims, was justified in issuing bills of lading to **B**, and the bank, as holder of the bills of lading (true negotiable documents) had precedence over the agent as holder only of mate's receipts.

The main purpose of the mate's receipt is as evidence that the goods are now in the carrier's possession and, apart from any special contractual arrangement, at his risk. Normally, if a mate's receipt has been issued, it is the person to whom it has been issued who is entitled to receive the bills of lading. The receipt should normally be given up when bills are issued, but the master is justified in issuing bills to a person proven to be the owner of goods, even without production of any mate's receipt previously issued, so long as the master has no notice of other claims[1].

However, apart from the special situation when a mate's receipt is also issued, the bill of lading performs the function of a receipt for the goods on board the ship. As such, in addition to acknowledging the existence of the goods on board, it normally also contains statements of the condition of the goods on their receipt on board. Two opposing interests are involved here. The carrier has an interest to note on the bill of lading any doubts as to the quantity shipped and any possible defects in the goods, in order to protect himself against claims that they were damaged in transit. The shipper, on the other hand,does not want any qualifications to appear on the bill of lading. It is not easy to sell goods if the document of title says the packing cases are damaged or that the goods are mouldy. Equally banks will be chary of lending on security of such a bill in the financing of the transaction. And where a banker's documentary credit calls for 'clean' bills of lading, payment will not be made to the seller if the bills are 'claused'. A bill of lading with no rude remarks about the goods and no reservations as to the quantity etc shipped is termed a 'clean' bill, but it has been said that a technically clean bill is as common as a white blackbird or a pink elephant. A bill of lading bearing some such qualifications is a 'qualified' bill or, more picturesquely, a 'foul' bill. The duller description now more commonly used is that the bill is 'claused'.

A rare example of a bill of lading which was not qualified by the master of the ship, when he should have commented on the condition of the goods, is *Naviera Mogor v Société Metallurgique de Normandie*[2]. A consignment of coils of wire had been stored for some time in the open and had become rusty, but when put on board the master signed the bills of lading presented by the charterers describing the wire as 'clean on board' without any qualification. The shipowners, who had accepted liability to the consignees for delivery of faulty goods, sought repayment from the

1 *Hathesing v Laing* (1873) LR 17 Eq 92.
2 [1988] 1 Lloyd's Rep 412.

charterers for presenting inaccurate bills. The master had had the opportunity to 'clause' the bill of lading, but did not take it and it was held that
even if the charterers might have been in breach of contract, the master's
negligence broke the chain of causation so that the shipowners could not
recover.

The bill of lading as evidence of quantity

If the question arises of whether the goods listed in the bill have in fact
been shipped, the real point at issue is the burden of proof. Obviously the
carrier's obligation is to deliver what he or she receives, but who has to
prove what was or was not received? A receipt being prima facie evidence
of the statements contained in it, if the person who issued a bill of lading
seeks to deny its accuracy, the burden of proof is on him or her to prove
that it was wrong. Thus if the carrier has acknowledged receipt of 100
sacks of cement and delivers only 90, he or she will find it very difficult to
avoid having to pay damages. The inference would be that the missing 10
sacks were lost in the carrier's hands and it would not be easy for the carrier in the face of the receipt embodied in the bill of lading to show that
only 90 were in fact delivered to him or her for shipment. This might be
possible if, eg, evidence could be produced of an obvious arithmetical
error in counting the sacks as they were loaded. However, the evidence
required to displace the presumption that goods acknowledged in the
receipt were in fact shipped must be very cogent[1]. Even evidence that it is
extremely improbable that any removal occurred during transit is
unlikely to be sufficient to displace the presumption that the quantity
mentioned in the bill of lading was in fact put on board.

However, if the carrier can show that the goods were not shipped, it
used to be that he or she escaped liability, despite the bill of lading. The
leading case here was *Grant v Norway*[2]. There a bill of lading for 12 bales of
silk was signed by the master. None of the silk was in fact shipped, and
the shipowner was able to prove this. Having done so, the shipowner, as
carrier, was under no liability when the silk was not delivered, despite the
fact that the bill had been indorsed to a third party as security for a debt in
good faith and for value. The decision was based upon the law of agency.
The master signs bills of lading as agent for the owners and, as such, his
authority extends only to acts usual in the employment of ships. Signing
bills for items not put on board is not within the usual scope of his duties.
Hence he had no authority to issue a bill of lading for goods not shipped,
and the shipowners were not liable.

However, the Carriage of Goods by Sea Act 1992[3] now provides that a
bill of lading which represents that goods have been shipped, or have
been received for shipment, and which has been signed by the master, or
other authorised person, is conclusive evidence against the carrier that the
goods have been shipped or received. The difficulty, however, is that this
does not apply to cases where the Hague-Visby Rules apply.

1 *Hain SS Co v Herdman and McDougal* (1922) 11 Ll L Rep 58.
2 (1851) 10 CB 665.
3 1992 Act, s 4.

The master or other persons signing the bill may be personally liable if there are errors, but this is not often of much value to the pursuer. However, in *Rasnoimport V/O v Guthrie & Co*[1] (a case under the Bills of Lading Act 1855) the amount actually shipped was 90 bales of rubber, although the bill of lading issued by Guthries as agents for the owners stated that 225 bales had been shipped. Guthries counted as 'other persons signing' the bill within the meaning of the 1855 Act and hence the bill was conclusive evidence against them, even if it did not give a remedy against the shipowners. The result was that contractual damages were awarded against Guthries to represent the value of the bales not delivered.

'Weight and quantity unknown' clauses

There can be problems, especially for third parties relying on a bill of lading as title to the goods referred to in it, in the practice of qualifying the bill on the question of quantity. Because of the danger of being held responsible for goods not in fact received for shipment, owners now in practice almost invariably include in bills of lading a stipulation such as 'weight and quantity unknown'. One typical bill reads 'measurement, weight, quantity, brand, contents, condition, quality and value as declared by the Shipper but unknown to the Carrier'.

Courts do take account of these stipulations, but construe them strictly according to their terms. The general effect of one such as the above is to destroy almost completely the value of the bill of lading as a receipt, for it shifts the onus of proof back to the shipper. If short delivery is made, it is then up to the shipper to prove that the quantity mentioned in the bill of lading was in fact put on board, not up to the carrier to disprove it. The carrier has not admitted receiving the quantity mentioned. All the carrier has done is to admit that something was shipped, said by the shipper for the purposes of computation of the freight, to come to a given amount. In *New Chinese Antimony Co v Ocean SS Co*[2] a bill of lading specified that 937 tons of antimony oxide had been shipped on board, but the exclusion clause read 'weight, measurement, contents and value (except for purpose of estimating freight) unknown'. It was held that this did not give even prima facie evidence of quantity as against the shipowners, and when less than 937 tons was delivered, it was up to the shipper to prove that what had been put on board amounted to that weight.

Strict interpretation would, however, have the effect that if the bill mentions a specific number of bags as having been shipped, 'weight and contents unknown', the number of bags is prima facie evidence against the shipowner, even if their weight and contents are not[3]. There is now a statutory modification to prevent the worst abuses in cases falling under the Carriage of Goods by Sea Act 1971[4]. Briefly, the Act applies only to outward shipments from British ports under bills of lading. It does not therefore apply to homeward shipments, nor to charterparties, nor to the coasting trade where bills of lading are not issued, but it does none the less

1 [1966] 1 Lloyd's Rep 1.
2 [1917] 2 KB 664.
3 *Hogarth Shipping Co v Blyth, Green Jourdain & Co Ltd* [1917] 2 KB 534, CA.
4 1971 Act, Schedule, art III, rr 3(b), 4 and 5.

include a large proportion of the contracts for the carriage of goods by sea. A bill which expressly includes the Hague-Visby Rules is also included. In these cases, the 1971 Act provides that a shipper can demand that a bill of lading be issued to him or her showing either the number of packages or pieces, or the quantity or weight, as the case may be, as furnished in writing by the shipper. Such a bill of lading is prima facie evidence of the receipt of goods as therein described, the main purpose being the protection of third parties who take the bill of lading by indorsement for value (eg banks lending on the security of the bills of lading). The carrier is therefore liable to them for short delivery[1]. The carrier may have a right of recourse against the shipper, who is deemed to guarantee the weights and measurements supplied by him or her, but the primary responsibility to third parties is the carrier's.

The bill of lading as evidence of the condition of goods

Another aspect of the bill's function as a receipt, is the extent to which it is evidence of the condition of the goods when shipped. Similar questions arise here, but they are complicated by the fact that almost every bill of lading commences with the words 'Shipped in apparent good order and condition'. In the absence of any qualification of this statement elsewhere in the bill, it amounts to an admission that so far as carrier and master could judge the goods were in good condition. The statement would normally be understood as referring to obvious external condition only, for carrier and master would have no means of establishing internal quality of goods. If the goods are externally damaged on arrival, an unqualified bill of lading would put the onus on the carrier to prove that they were in fact shipped in bad condition externally. If the carrier cannot do this, the inference would be that the goods were damaged in carrier's possession.

Furthermore, if there is no qualification of the statement 'shipped in good order and condition' the carrier will normally be treated as personally barred from denying that they were shipped in good condition in a question with an indorsee of the bill who has relied on that admission as to the condition of the goods. The leading case is *Compania Naviera Vasconzada v Churchill and Sim*[2]. Timber was seen to have been badly marked and stained by oil before shipment, but the master made no comment on this in the bill of lading, which read 'shipped in good order and condition' and 'to be delivered in like good order and condition'. The bills were indorsed to Churchill and Sim, who gave value in reliance on the condition as stated. In fact the timber was of much lower value because of the staining and they claimed damages representing the reduction in value of the timber. The shipowner was held liable, and was barred from denying the accuracy of the representations in the bill that the timber was shipped in good condition.

There is, therefore, considerable doubt as to how far a 'condition unknown' clause will protect the carrier. The situation is rather different from the quantity cases, where there is no mutual representation of accu-

1 1971 Act, Schedule, art III, r 4.
2 [1906] 1 KB 237.

racy to correspond to the initial statement of good condition in the condition cases. It seems likely that a disclaimer of knowledge of the condition
of the goods will not be sufficient to exempt the carrier from liability[1].

One might wonder, then, why carriers do not omit the 'good order and
condition' clause or at least limit its extent. It is true that the 1971 Act, in
any case to which it applies, gives a shipper a right to insist on the bill of
lading incorporating a statement as to apparent order and condition but
this does not of course require a statement that the apparent condition is
good. It may be thought to be easier to treat good condition as the normal
situation and to qualify that statement as necessary.

Bills of lading as documents of title

The third function of a bill of lading, ie as a document of title, is particularly important in commerce and is a very special feature of bills of lading.

In some respects a bill of lading is like a bill of exchange. And as a document of title, possession of the bill is equivalent in law to possession of
the goods. Bills have been described as the 'key of the warehouse' entitling the consignee to take delivery. Like bills of exchange, bills of lading
may be order or bearer bills. Order bills require indorsement, bearer bills
can be transferred by mere delivery. Much (but not all) of the law can be
treated as an application of the law of bills of exchange. However, it is
important to remember one major difference. A bill of lading is not 'negotiable' in the strict sense of giving an indorsee a better title than the transferor had. In the case of bills of lading, one can transfer only as good a title
as one has.

None the less, transfer of a bill of lading with the consent of the owner
may possibly transfer sufficient title to permit fraud. In *The Argentina*[2] the
seller of goods had arranged with his agent at the port of delivery that the
buyer was not to get the bill of lading until actual payment had been
made. The agent was offered a bill of exchange by the buyer and treated
that as sufficient to count as actual payment. The agent handed over the
bill of lading to the buyer, who promptly then indorsed it to a bona fide
third party for value. Thereafter the buyer went bankrupt. In the competition between the original seller and the bona fide third party over title to
the bill of lading (and to the goods) it was held that the buyer had
obtained the bill of lading with the consent of the seller's agent. Hence the
buyer had a good title and could therefore transfer a good title to the third
party endorsee.

Sets of bills

Complications might obviously arise, but in fact rarely do, over the practice of drawing bills of lading in 'sets'. Frequently three copies of a bill are
issued, although more or fewer may be used. Each is signed and each is a
principal. Together they form a set of bills, one being usually kept by the
master of the ship for his own information, one being kept by the shipper,

1 *The Skarp* [1935] P 134; cf *Canadian and Dominion Sugar Co v Canadian National (West Indies)
   Steamships* [1947] AC 46, PC.
2 (1867) LR 1 A & E 370.

and the third sent to the consignee. The origin of the practice was that different copies would be sent by different routes to avoid the danger of loss through the perils of the sea. Even today similar considerations apply. One 'part' or copy of the bill will frequently be sent by air, any others following by sea mail. Air mail also has the advantage of getting the bill to the consignee at the other end before the ship in question arrives, so that the consignee can produce it to claim delivery.

Each of the parts is an original, transferable, document of title and the carrier is under a duty to deliver against whichever part is first presented. To meet the obvious danger that the carrier will be called upon to deliver the goods more than once by different people holding different parts of the set of bills, the clause is usually inserted that 'one of these bills of lading being accomplished, the others shall stand void'. Having once delivered, the carrier thus discharges all liability on the other bills. Hence, in *Sanders v Maclean*[1], it was held that tender to the buyer of one bill of lading was sufficient. The buyer (no doubt for quite different commercial reasons) had refused to pay on the ground that only two out of the three bills in the set had been tendered to him.

However, although this protects the carrier, it does not prevent fraud on indorsees. One person holding two parts of a bill of lading could indorse one to one party and the second to another. This problem does not, however, appear to arise very often, although there have been comments on the undesirability of the practice. In *Glyn Mills, Currie & Co v East and West India Dock Co*[2] Lord Blackburn said: 'I have never been able to learn why merchants and shipowners continue the practice of making out bills of lading in parts'.

The American Bills of Lading Acts, in an attempt to meet this problem at least partially, prohibit the issue of domestic bills of lading in sets of parts, leaving this possible only in foreign oceanic commerce where the danger of fraud is outweighed by the need for safe communications. In this country, however, nothing of this nature has been done, probably because this type of fraudulent double indorsement has not arisen frequently. There is also the point, of course, that bills of lading are rare in the domestic coasting trade around Britain.

CHARTERPARTIES

General

The other main form of contract for the carriage of goods by sea is the charterparty, often referred to simply as a charter. An exporter who has large bulk consignments to make will usually find it economically advantageous to charter the whole, or a defined part, of the carrying capacity of a ship. The contract which will be concluded in these circumstances is the charterparty. It is possible to have a charter of less than the entire ship, but this is very rare, and will not be further considered. Charterparties are

---

1 (1883) 11 QB 327, CA.
2 (1882) 7 App Cas 591 at 605, HL.

good examples of standard form contracts, and one of a small number of existing forms of charter will almost invariably be used in any particular case.

The three main types of charterparty are as follows:

(1) *Voyage charters.* These are used when the vessel is required for a single voyage, irrespective of the time involved, normally using the shipowner's crew. The charterer wishes to move a cargo from one point to another. This is probably the commonest form of charter, and the form used will usually be the Uniform General Charter – otherwise known as Gencon.

(2) *Time charters.* These are used when the vessel is chartered for a fixed time, also normally using the shipowner's crew. The charterer acquires the use of the ship's capacity for the carriage of goods anywhere within such geographical limits (if any) as may be specified in the charter and on as many different voyages as will with reasonable latitude fit within the charter period. A typical example is the Baltime charter.

(3) *Demise (or bareboat) charters.* These are outright leases of the vessel, for which the charterer provides his own crew and undertakes complete responsibility for running and navigating the ship. The master of a demised ship is the agent of the charterer, not of the owner and this is probably the main test of the existence of a demise charter[1]. Demise charters are less common than voyage or time charters, but may have good commercial justification in the oil industry. They were in the past used for the pirate radio stations which operated in the North Sea and appear also to be the preferred form of acquiring ship capacity when major cargoes of illegal drugs are being smuggled into this country.

Voyage charters

A firm seeking to send a bulk cargo overseas will normally use the services of a broker to find a ship with the required capacity which will be available at the appropriate port to carry it. The use of a standard form of charter, such as Gencon, means that only a few points, in particular the cost, need to be negotiated. Although the 1971 Act regulates the terms of most bills of lading there is no corresponding legislation affecting the form of charterparties, possibly because the bargaining power of the parties to a charter are more likely to be equal.

The express terms of the charter include the shipowner's obligation to provide a ship that will proceed with reasonable despatch on its preliminary voyage to the port where the cargo is to be loaded. There will usually be an express representation that the ship is fully seaworthy for the voyage concerned, although this will always be implied in any event. An important clause for the shipowner is the obligation on the charterer to load 'a full and complete cargo' and pay freight on it. The cost of a voyage charter is commonly fixed by reference to the quantity shipped, and there would be a dramatic loss to the shipowner if the charterer were to ship only one ton in a ship with a capacity of one thousand tons. Hence there

1 *Page v Admiralty Comrs* [1921] 1 AC 137, HL.

will invariably be an obligation to provide a full cargo. The charter will also spell out some specific exemptions from liability, and very important provisions for the time to be allowed for loading and unloading the ship. Demurrage[1] – at very high rates – will be specified if the time allowed is exceeded. An arbitration clause will require disputes to be settled by arbitration rather than by normal court action, but this does not always prevent disputes over precisely what issues must be referred to arbitration[2].

Various terms will also be implied in the charter. The courts say that they are not making a contract for the parties, but their efforts to give the transaction the business efficacy which the parties are presumed to have intended may sometimes seem like making a new contract. However, the implied terms are now well known and are relied upon by all parties. The three main implied undertakings by the shipowner in a voyage charter are: (1) to provide a seaworthy ship; (2) to proceed on the voyage with reasonable despatch; and (3) to proceed on that voyage without any unjustifiable deviation.

Seaworthiness

There is no absolute standard of seaworthiness, and the owner's undertaking is measured against the standard of what is necessary for that particular voyage with that particular cargo. A ship which might be perfectly seaworthy for a summer coastal delivery in sheltered waters might not be seaworthy for a winter voyage across the North Atlantic. A ship required for a cargo of meat would be unseaworthy if its refrigeration plant is inoperative, even although it might be suitable for other cargoes[3].

The seaworthiness requirement is a very stringent one. It is a guarantee that the ship is seaworthy, and not merely a requirement that the owner has taken all reasonable steps to make it seaworthy[4]. However, being seaworthy does not necessarily mean that the ship must be capable of withstanding anything that may happen in the course of a voyage. If a ship is swamped by a tidal wave following on an earthquake, that would not indicate unseaworthiness. The standard of seaworthiness is therefore that the ship is reasonably fit to meet the ordinary perils which it is likely to encounter. If a prudent owner, had he or she known of a defect, would have had it repaired before the ship put to sea, that defect is one making the ship unseaworthy – even although the owner did not in fact know of it[5].

The first element of the warranty of seaworthiness is that the ship must be fit to receive the particular cargo at the time of loading, and must be so loaded that it is safe to go on the voyage. Thus if heavy cargo is insufficiently secured and causes damage when it breaks loose, or if the ship's

1 A chartered ship will be given a stipulated period for loading and discharging her cargo known as 'lay-days'. Demurrage is the sum payable for a stipulated period after the expiry of the lay-days. Demurrage, therefore, is not dissimilar to an agreed damages clause: *Suisse Atlantique Société d'Armement Maritime SA v NV Rotterdamsche Kolen Centrale* [1967] 1 AC 361, HL. The issue is explored more fully below.
2 *The Ioanna* [1978] 1 Lloyd's Rep 238, CA.
3 *Maori King (Cargo Owners) v Hughes* [1895] 2 QB 550.
4 *The Glenfruin* (1885) 10 PD 103.
5 *McFadden v Blue Star Line* [1905] 1 KB 697 at 706.

pumps are insufficiently powerful to cope with a wet cargo, the ship is unseaworthy[1].

The second element is that the ship itself, or its management and equipment, must be seaworthy at the time of sailing. Faults such as the ship sailing with a hole in its hull, or without navigation equipment, obviously amount to unseaworthiness, but so also would be setting out with insufficient bunker fuel[2] or with an unqualified engineer in charge[3].

It is possible to contract out of the implied undertaking of seaworthiness, but any such exemption clause would have to be very clearly expressed[4].

Reasonable despatch

The shipowner impliedly undertakes that his or her vessel will be ready to commence the voyage agreed upon, to load cargo and to complete the voyage with reasonable despatch.

If there is seriously excessive delay, such as to deprive the charterer of the whole benefit of the contract, the charterer (but not the shipowner) may rescind the contract. Note that this is not therefore a case of true frustration of contract. If the delay does not reach that standard of seriousness, the charterer's only remedy will be a claim for damages, in answer to which the carrier may be able to prove that the delay arose from a peril in respect of which the contract includes an exemption from liability[5].

No deviation

In every voyage charterparty there is an implied undertaking that the ship will proceed by the usual, and reasonable, route without unjustifiable deviation. In the unlikely event of a different route being prescribed in the contract, that route would have to be followed. If deviation is found it can have very serious consequences for the shipowner, and charterers, in attempting to avoid their own liabilities under the contract, can sometimes be very ingenious in spotting a deviation. Prima facie, the proper route is the shortest route between the two ports concerned, or at least the shortest route that it is possible for that ship to take. A supertanker, eg, is unlikely to be able to pass through the Panama Canal. There may be more than one usual route, in which case any of them would be acceptable[6].

Deviation is always justifiable if it is to save life or to go to the aid of a ship in distress when there is danger to life[7]. This implied authority does not, however, extend to deviation to save property. Thus towing a disabled ship to port in an attempt to earn salvage would be a deviation, even if taking off the crew in danger would not be.

---

1 *Kopitoff v Wilson* (1876) 1 QBD 377; *Stanton v Richardson* (1875) LR 9 CP 390.
2 Bunker fuel is used to propel the ship. In *The Vortigern* [1899] P 140, some of the cargo had to be used for fuel.
3 *The Roberta* (1938) 60 Ll L Rep 84, CA.
4 *Itoh & Co v Atlanska Plovidba, The Gundulic* [1981] 2 Lloyd's Rep 418.
5 *Barker v McAndrew* (1865) 18 CB 759.
6 *Reardon Smith Line Ltd v Black Sea and Baltic General Insurance Co* [1939] AC 562, HL.
7 *Scaramanga v Stamp* (1880) 42 LT 840.

Deviation which is not voluntary on the part of the master of the ship will probably be justified. If a storm causes damage requiring immediate repair, it is a justifiable deviation to go to the nearest port where such repairs can be effected – assuming that the need for repairs does not indicate unseaworthiness at the commencement of the voyage. Again exemption clauses may have to be taken into account, but any clauses will be strictly construed *contra proferentem*[1].

An owner whose ship is held to have deviated has committed a fundamental breach of the contract of carriage, giving the charterer the option either of repudiating the whole contract or of waiving the repudiation and reserving a right to damages for the loss arising from the deviation[2]. If only damages are claimed, the contract remains in force – along with any exemption clauses in it. If the contract is repudiated, the charterer is still entitled to delivery of his or her goods, and would have to pay freight (although not necessarily at the contract rate), but the shipowner would be liable for any loss or damage to the goods unless he or she can prove one of the exceptions available to a common carrier, and also that the damage would have occurred even if there had been no deviation[3].

The charterer also is bound by some implied undertakings, the main one being that he or she will not ship dangerous goods, at least without notice to the shipowner. Many cases have arisen over the question of whether particular goods were dangerous. Undeclared explosives are obviously dangerous, but so also are any goods which might render the ship liable to detention[4]. The master of the ship must take reasonable steps to identify any dangerous cargo, and would be treated as having had notice if he had a reasonable opportunity to observe the dangerous character of the goods and did nothing. However, in the absence of such notice the shipper of dangerous goods is liable for losses caused. There are also a substantial number of statutory provisions for the identification of dangerous goods.

Another undertaking by the charterer which is implied, although it will usually also be expressly dealt with in the charterparty, is that the vessel will be used only between 'safe' ports. An elastic definition of 'safety' and also of a 'port' is frequently asserted by shipowners when any loss occurs to the ship in the vicinity of one of the ports nominated by the charterer.

FREIGHT

Although common non-maritime usage applies the term 'freight' to goods being carried, the correct use of the term is to denote the reward payable to the carrier for the carriage and arrival of the goods in a merchantable

---

1   *Rio Tinto Co Ltd v Seed Shipping Co* (1926) 42 TLR 381; *Kish v Taylor* [1912] AC 604, HL; *Stag Line Ltd v Foscolo, Mango & Co Ltd* [1932] AC 328, HL.
2   *Hain SS Co v Tait and Lyle Ltd* [1936] 2 All ER 597, HL.
3   *James Morrison & Co Ltd v Shaw, Savill and Albion Co Ltd* [1916] 2 KB 783, CA. This was a bill of lading case, but the decision illustrates the point for charterparties also.
4   *Mitchell v Steel* [1916] 2 KB 610.

condition, fit for delivery to the consignee. Strictly it should not be used for the payment made for the charter of a ship, unless the payment is based on the quantity of goods carried in the ship.

Freight is payable, in the absence of any other stipulation by the parties, only on delivery of the goods. If the goods are lost on the voyage, eg if the ship sinks, or if they are thrown overboard in a general average sacrifice, or, indeed, if they are not delivered at the port of destination for any reason other than the fault of the shipper sending the goods, then no freight is payable. This is quite distinct from the question of whether the carrier may be liable in damages for the loss. The carrier may be entitled to rely on a clause exempting him or her from liability for the loss, but the carrier is not entitled to payment if the goods do not arrive[1].

Advance freight

It is, however, common for parties to contract that the freight is due and payable on completion of loading, and thus before the ship even sets out. This is known as advance freight, and the important difference from the common law rule is that the carrier is still entitled to the freight even although the goods are lost on the voyage through some events for which the carrier is not liable. Thus once true advance freight has been paid it cannot be recovered if the voyage is abandoned[2] but it may not always be clear whether the parties have agreed on advance freight or whether the shipper has merely made a loan to the carrier towards the expenses of the voyage.

Back freight

Back freight may be payable by the shipper if the consignee of the goods does not appear at the port of destination to take delivery. The cost of unloading and storing, or transport to another destination is recoverable from the shipper as back freight[3].

Dead freight

Dead freight is payable by the shipper under a charterparty in which he or she is bound to load a full and complete cargo and payment is by reference to the tonnage shipped. If less than a full cargo is loaded, the shipowner has a claim for damages in respect of the extra freight which he or she would have earned if a full cargo had been shipped, and this extra amount is dead freight.

---

1 *Dakin v Oxley* (1864) 10 LT 268.
2 *Civil Service Co-op Society v General Steam Navigation Co* [1903] 2 KB 756, CA. The possible difference in Scots law (*Watson & Co v Shankland* (1871) 10 M 142) is probably to be explained as a decision on the terms of the particular contract.
3 *The Argos (Cargo ex) Gaudet v Brown* (1873) LR 5 PC 134.

DEMURRAGE

Demurrage[1] is an extremely important topic, usually arising in connection with voyage charters. Speed of loading or unloading is always vital to the shipowner, for his or her income from freight earned depends upon the number of charters he or she can complete. The quicker the turnaround time, the more freight-earning voyages can be fitted into a given time. While the shipowner controls the speed of the actual voyage, the pace of loading and unloading is controlled by the rate at which cargo is loaded by the charterer and taken away by the consignee. The charter will invariably include specification of a reasonable time for loading or unloading (the 'lay-days' or 'laytime') and the amounts to be paid for extra time taken ('demurrage'). This amount is likely to be fixed as a percentage of an internationally recognised New Worldscale. There has been a great deal of litigation, because the sums involved can be very large indeed. The standard Gencon charter fixes demurrage in terms of days, for a fixed number of days, but laytime is allowed by reference to hours. Much litigation arises over the precise meaning of the terms used in the infinite variety of circumstances which arise. If delay extends beyond the contractual demurrage period, the charterer remains liable in damages for the delay, but the amount of the damages is no longer liquidated, and may be extremely large. This non-contractual demurrage is usually called 'damages for detention', and is fixed by a court to reflect what the shipowner has in fact lost by the detention of his ship in port. The stipulated demurrage rate would be a starting point in the calculation of damages for detention, but other evidence might show that the true loss was higher or lower than the contractual demurrage. If the delay becomes so excessive as to amount to a repudiation of the contract by the charterer, the shipowner would be free to order his or her ship to leave in search of another charter.

If laytime is specified in days, the prima facie rule is that 'days' mean calendar days commencing at midnight, and that fractions of a day count as whole days. Thus if a laytime of six days is allowed, and loading took six days four hours, there would be a whole day of demurrage to pay. There will usually be provision in the charter for local holidays and Sundays, but in the absence of such provision, three lay days would be taken to mean three consecutive calendar days, irrespective of Sundays and holidays[2]. If 'running days' are specified, this has the same meaning, but 'working days' would mean the days on which work is normally done in the port in question. The phrase 'weather working days' excludes from the count not only non-working days in the port but also days on which weather conditions prevent work[3].

In addition to the calculation of the number of days, it is often a matter of importance to know when they begin to run. The charter may give some clarification, and Gencon, eg, specifies that the laytime begins at 1 pm if notice of readiness to load or discharge is given by the master of

1 For a detailed discussion of the many problems, see *Schofield Laytime and Demurrage* (3rd edn, 1996).
2 *Nielsen v Wait* (1885) 16 QBD 67.
3 *Reardon Smith Line Ltd v Ministry of Agriculture, Fisheries and Food* [1963] 1 All ER 545, HL.

the ship before noon, and at 6 am the next working day if notice is given during office hours after noon. Therefore the crucial point is often when notice of readiness may properly be given so as to establish when laytime begins.

For valid notice of readiness to be given, the ship must be an 'arrived ship' and it must in fact be ready to load or unload. When a ship is chartered for a voyage to a port, as opposed to a particular berth within the port (ie a 'port' charterparty as opposed to a 'berth' charterparty) it is treated as an arrived ship when it enters the commercial area of the port, even although it cannot immediately get a berth. The classic case is *Leonis SS Co Ltd v Rank Ltd*[1], where a ship chartered to a busy port had to wait for five weeks in a river forming part of the commercial area of the port before a berth became available. It was none the less held to be an arrived ship on anchoring in the river, irrespective of whether the physical act of loading was possible there. It seems that if a ship is at a place within the port limits where waiting ships usually lie, she will be held to have arrived[2].

In addition to having 'arrived', the ship must also be ready to load or unload before the laytime can commence. She is treated as ready if an inability to load is due to events within the charterer's control, but not if they are the owner's responsibility. Thus if all ships from a given area are subject to quarantine delays, this is the owner's responsibility and the ship is not ready, even although she is physically in the correct port. Laytime would not commence until the expiry of the quarantine which would be treated as an unforeseeable event preventing loading or unloading[3]. However, the possibility of strike action would not normally be regarded as unforeseeable, and would rarely excuse the charterer from failing to load within the laytime.

GENERAL AVERAGE

If goods are being transported by sea, one of the liabilities which their owner may face is being required to make a general average contribution to certain losses during the voyage. This is a complex topic, with effects wider than the rights and liabilities of cargo owners, but should be mentioned as one of the oldest specialties of maritime trade[4].

'Average' in this context is not used in the arithmetical sense, but in the special meaning of a loss. Three main interests are at risk in any given voyage: (1) the ship itself; (2) the cargo; and (3) the freight which will be earned on delivery of the goods. (If true advance freight has been contracted for, it is not, of course, at risk during the voyage, having been earned on loading the goods.) The general rule is the normal one that losses which are the result of a danger affecting one interest only must lie where they fall. However, to this general rule there is the important

1 [1908] 1 KB 499, CA.
2 *E L Oldendorff & Co GmbH v Tradax SA* [1974] AC 479: *Federal Commerce and Navigation Co Ltd v Tradax Export SA* [1978] AC 1, HL.
3 *Whites v SS Winchester Co* (1886) 13 R 524.
4 See Lowndes and Rudolf *General Average and York-Antwerp Rules* (11th edn, 1990).

exception, recognised by all maritime nations, that in some situations a loss is no longer a particular average lying where it falls, but a general average falling to be met rateably by all the interests at risk during the voyage. This arises when one or more of the interests is intentionally sacrificed for the benefit of the remainder when there is a danger threatening the whole voyage. The doctrine has been known so long as there has been seafaring[1] and the current statutory basis in the UK is the Marine Insurance Act 1906. It may be questioned whether the whole topic might not be better dealt with by individual insurance provision, but general average is still important in practice.

The three essential elements of general average are: (a) a common danger to all the interests at risk; (b) a voluntary jettison or sacrifice of some portion of the joint adventure; and (c) a successful outcome of the sacrifice.

Common danger

The danger must be real, and not merely believed to be real[2]. It must also be one common to all the interests at risk. Thus where the captain of a ship stranded on the Irish coast at the end of the eighteenth century was forced by a mob to sell his cargo of wheat at a low price, there was no danger to the ship itself and thus there was no general average[3].

Voluntary sacrifice

The acts must be extraordinary, the typical original examples being throwing cargo overboard to lighten ship or cutting away a mast, and not something reasonably to be regarded as incidental to the type of voyage[4]. It must also be voluntary, and therefore would not include cutting away a mast already broken in a storm or an action compelled by superior forces[5]. Deliberate beaching of a ship in danger of sinking may lead to difficult issues of whether it was either a sacrifice or voluntary, but expenses incurred in going to a port of refuge for repairs will probably be accepted as general average even if the damage itself is not[6].

Success

As the basis for general average is that the property saved by a sacrifice contributes to make up the loss to those whose property was sacrificed, the result is that if nothing is saved there is no basis for general average

---

1 *Lex Rhodia de jactu Digest* XIV, 2, 1.
2 *Joseph Watson & Son Ltd v Firemen's Fund Insurance Co of San Francisco* [1922] 2 KB 355; *Vlassopoulos v British and Foreign Marine Insurance Co Ltd* [1929] 1 KB 187.
3 *Nesbitt v Lushington* (1792) 4 Term Rep 783.
4 *Wilson v Bank of Victoria* (1867) LR 2 QB 203.
5 *Shepherd v Kottgen* (1877) 2 CPD 585; *Athel Line Ltd v Liverpool and London War Risks Association Ltd* [1944] KB 87.
6 *Australian Coastal Shipping Commission v Green* [1971] 1 QB 456, CA.

contribution[1]. Saving lives does not count as saving property, and therefore passengers and crew have no liability to make a general average contribution for having their lives saved. However, it is wise to insure against the possibility of having to pay a general average contribution if any goods are being shipped, as eg when a car is taken on a cross-Channel ferry.

1 *The Seapool* [1934] P 53.

4 Insurance

INSURANCE CONTRACTS AND INSURANCE LAW

The purpose of insurance

Insurance is, in essence, a mechanism whereby risk can be transferred to an insurer. Some risks (eg the destruction of one's home by fire) carry such severe financial consequences that it is not possible for one person to make adequate provision for the possibility of the occurrence of the risk. Insurance offers a means for a large number of people to contribute to a fund which will meet the cost of specific forms of loss or damage. As only a fraction of all the contributors are likely to suffer loss in any one year, the cost can be borne more easily by a large number than by an individual. This spreading of risk across large numbers makes it possible for insurers to charge premiums which represent only a fraction of the sums which can be recovered by an insured who suffers a loss.

Definition of an insurance contract

There is no statutory definition of an insurance contract. Organisations engaged in carrying on insurance business are regulated by the Insurance Companies Act 1982, but there is no definition of insurance business or an insurance contract given in the Act. In *Scottish Amicable Heritable Securities Association Ltd v Northern Assurance Co*[1], Lord Justice-Clerk Moncreiff defined insurance as a contract in which 'the insurer undertakes, in consideration of the payment of an estimated equivalent beforehand, to make up to the assured any loss he may sustain by the occurrence of an uncertain contingency'. It is essential that the insured stands to lose by the occurrence of the insured event and that the timing of the insured event is uncertain. The insured event itself does not have to be uncertain: in the case of life assurance, eg, death is a certain event, but its timing is uncertain and therefore it is an insurable risk. Uncertainty is determined at the time when the contract is concluded[2]. Nor is it necessary that the insurer agree to pay a sum of money to the insured on the occurrence of an insured event. In *Department of Trade and Industry v St Christopher Motorists Association Ltd*[3], it was held that the provision by the insurer of chauffeur services to motorists convicted of drink-driving offences was insurance even though payment was in a form other than money. This approach was clarified in the later case of *Medical Defence Union Ltd v Department of*

---

1 (1883) 11 R 287 at 303.
2 *Department of Trade and Industry v St Christopher Motorists Association Ltd* [1974] 1 All ER 395.
3 [1974] 1 All ER 395.

Trade[1], which held that insurance was a contract for 'the payment of money or for money's worth' but that the payment of some other form of benefit could not be considered to be insurance.

Insurance contracts should be distinguished from manufacturers' guarantees and cautionary obligations. The former, in particular, can appear similar to insurance contracts, in that they provide for the manufacturer to bear the cost of an uncertain event in the future, eg the breakdown of an appliance. The law has approached manufacturers' guarantees from the perspective of the related contract for sale of goods rather than from the perspective of risk transfer[2]. Nevertheless, where a retailer offers an extended warranty to a customer, which covers the risk of breakdown, this may amount to a contract of insurance if the elements outlined in the paragraph above are present[3]. Cautionary obligations, by contrast, are in their nature different to insurance contracts in that they are accessory and not primary obligations[4]. An insurance contract can be enforced against the insurer immediately following an insured event, whereas a cautionary obligation can only be enforced following the default of the debtor in the primary obligation.

TYPES OF INSURANCE

Indemnity

The most fundamental distinction is between indemnity and non-indemnity insurance. Indemnity contracts are intended to compensate the insured to the extent of his financial loss resulting from the occurrence of an insured event. Common examples are motor and home contents insurance. Non-indemnity contracts provide for the insurer to pay a specified amount on the occurrence of the insured event. They are used where the financial loss resulting from the occurrence of an insured event is not readily ascertainable. The most common form of non-indemnity insurance is life assurance[5]. As the loss resulting from a person's death cannot be known in the same manner as, eg, the cost of replacing a car component, the sum to be paid by the insurer under a life assurance contract is specified when the contract is agreed.

1 [1980] Ch 82 at 93, per Megarry V-C. The issue in this case was whether the Medical Defence Union was an insurer. It could, at its discretion, undertake or defend legal proceedings on behalf of members and could provide an indemnity in relation to awards arising from such proceedings. It was held that the discretionary power of the MDU prevented it having a contract with each member.
2 Eg manufacturers' guarantees are governed by the Unfair Contract Terms Act 1977 whereas insurance contracts are not. The approach can be justified on the basis that the manufacturer's guarantee forms an integral part of the goods purchased by the customer.
3 In this case the extended warranty is additional to the protection given to the customer by the terms implied into the contract of sale by the Sale of Goods Act 1979.
4 *Scottish Amicable Heritable Securities Association Ltd v Northern Assurance Co* (1883) 11 R 287 at 303, per Lord Moncreiff.
5 The use of the terms assurance and insurance leads to some confusion. 'Assurance' is associated primarily with life assurance, as the insured event (death) is an assured event. However, it is also common practice in marine insurance to refer to the insured as the assured, despite the fact that the contract is referred to as insurance (see the definition of a marine insurance contract in s 1 of the Marine Insurance Act 1906).

First party and third party

A distinction can also be drawn between first party and third party insurance. First party cover is intended to protect against the risk of loss of or harm to the insured property. Common examples of such insurance are the cover against causing damage to one's own car or having the contents of one's home stolen. Third party cover protects against the liability arising from damage caused to a third party. Motor policies, eg, provide cover for this risk both in relation to personal injury and property damage. Where third party cover is provided, the policy wording makes clear that the insurer will only be liable in situations in which there is a legal liability to a third party. The result is that the normal principles of delictual liability will be applied to determine if the insurer is liable for a claim.

Voluntary and compulsory

In the case of most types of insurance, the decision to insure is made voluntarily by the insured. However, there are some instances in which insurance is required by law. Two examples of this are third-party motor vehicle insurance and employers' liability insurance. Section 143 of the Road Traffic Act 1988 requires a vehicle to be insured in respect of death or bodily injury caused to any person or damage to property caused by the use of the vehicle on a road in Great Britain. Employers are required to insure against the risk of bodily injury or disease sustained by employees in the course of their employment by s 1(1) of the Employers' Liability (Compulsory Insurance) Act 1969.

Life assurance

In its simplest form, life assurance provides protection against the financial consequences of early death. Such policies can take two forms. A whole life policy provides for a sum to be paid on the death of the assured, whenever that occurs. A term policy provides for a sum to be paid if the assured dies during a certain period (eg ten years) and no sum is payable if the assured survives to the end of that period. The more complex forms of life assurance are those which combine protection against early death with an investment. The most common example is an endowment assurance, where part of the premium is invested by the insurer to provide the assured with a capital sum at the end of the policy term. This type of policy is frequently used in conjunction with mortgages and fulfils two functions: first, if the assured dies before the mortgage is repaid, the sum assured under the policy will repay the mortgage; second, if the assured survives to the end of the mortgage term, he or she will have a capital sum to repay the mortgage.

SOURCES AND STRUCTURE OF INSURANCE LAW

Insurance has a long history as a means of sharing the risks faced by merchants in their trading activities. Early forms of insurance involved merchants themselves rather than professional insurers assuming the risks of ships sinking or cargoes being lost, but as trade expanded and risk assessment became more complex, it became common for insurance to be underwritten[1] by insurers. The law relating to insurance underwent its most rapid development in the latter part of the eighteenth century. The influence of Lord Mansfield, Lord Chief-Justice of the King's Bench, was particularly evident in this period. By the time of Lord Mansfield's retirement in 1788, the basic principles of the common law governing insurance contracts had been put in place. The development of the law in Scotland[2] lent heavily on the law in England, which benefited from the emergence of London as an international centre for insurance and shipping.

Insurance continued to be governed primarily[3] by the common law until the passing of the Marine Insurance Act 1906. The Act codified the law relating to marine insurance. It specifically preserved the common law governing marine insurance in so far as it was not altered by the Act[4]. Other types of insurance are not covered by the Act[5]. However, there has always been a tendency on the part of the courts to extend the general principles of marine insurance to other types of insurance. This resulted from marine being the major class of business in the early days of insurance. As other types of insurance, such as fire and motor, were introduced, it was natural to look to the principles which had already been established for marine insurance. In *Thomson v Weems*[6] Lord Blackburn said: 'I think that on the balance of authority the general principles of insurance law apply to all insurances, whether marine, fire or life'. It follows that, to the extent that it states general principles of insurance law, the Marine Insurance Act 1906 corresponds to the common law governing non-marine contracts.

Insurance contracts do not fall within the scope of the Unfair Contract Terms Act 1977[7]. They are instead subject to the self-regulatory control of the insurance industry. The Statement of General Insurance Practice and the Statement of Long-Term Insurance Practice are subscribed to by members of the Association of British Insurers, to which the vast majority of insurers belong. The statements do not have the force of law, but they are generally observed and, if they were not, it is likely that legislation would be introduced to give them legal effect. The statements apply only to insurance taken out in a private capacity[8] and, within this sphere, they have the effect that insurers agree not to enforce their full legal rights. In the sphere of commercial insurance, where the insured and insurer are judged to be contracting on an equal footing, insurers retain their full legal rights.

1 The term 'underwrite' originates from the practice of subscribing the names of the persons bearing the risk ('underwriters') on the insurance contract.
2 For more detail on historical developments, see 12 *Stair Memorial Encyclopedia* para 801; Forte 'Marine Insurance and Risk Distribution in Scotland before 1800' (1987) Law and History Review 393.
3 As outlined below, legislation was introduced to control the abuse of insurance for the purpose of gambling.
4 1906 Act, s 91(2).
5 1906 Act, s 2(2).
6 (1884) 9 App Cas 671 at 684.
7 Schedule 1, para 1(a) of the 1977 Act disapplies ss 2–4 for the purposes of English law and s 15(3)(a)(i) disapplies ss 16–18 for the purposes of Scots law.
8 See the introductory text of each statement.

REGULATION OF INSURANCE BUSINESS

The Insurance Companies Act 1982

The Insurance Companies Act 1982 controls the carrying on of insurance business in the UK. Since its introduction, it has been amended on several occasions to bring it into line with the European Community Directives which give effect to the principles of freedom of establishment and services contained in the Treaty of Rome. An authorisation, issued by the Department of Trade and Industry (the DTI), is required by any person engaging in insurance business in the UK[1]. Before granting an authorisation, the DTI must be satisfied that the organisation will be soundly and prudently managed and that the individuals managing the organisation are fit and proper persons[2]. Once authorised, the business activities of an insurer are monitored by the DTI and particular emphasis is placed on the requirement to maintain the margin of solvency required by s 32 of the Act. The purpose of the solvency margin is to ensure that insurers have sufficient funds to pay claims on the policies which they have written. If the solvency margin is not maintained, or the interests of policyholders are being threatened in some other way, the DTI can intervene in the running of the business[3].

The Financial Services Act 1986

The Financial Services Act 1986 controls the carrying on of investment business in the UK. Investments are defined in Sch 1 of the Act. A life assurance policy is an investment for the purposes of the Act[4], but those policies which pay only on death and have no investment element are not regarded as investments. Section 3 of the Act requires any person conducting investment business to be authorised, irrespective of whether the business is conducted as principal or agent. However, s 22 provides that an insurer authorised under the Insurance Companies Act 1982 is automatically authorised to conduct investment business[5]. Insurance policies account for a large part of the investments made by private individuals. The detailed rules governing the marketing of life policies are formulated and enforced by the Personal Investment Authority, which is recognised as a self-regulating organisation under the Financial Services Act.

The Insurance Brokers (Registration) Act 1977

As noted above, an agent (eg an accountant, estate agent or solicitor) who engages in investment business requires authorisation under the Financial

---

1 Insurance Companies Act 1982, s 2(1). It is also possible to engage in insurance business in the UK through a branch or by way of freedom of services on the basis of an authorisation granted by another member state of the European Economic Area (EEA).
2 1982 Act, ss 5A and 7(3).
3 1982 Act, s 37.
4 The Financial Services Act 1986, Sch 1, para 10.
5 1982 Act, s 16, limiting an insurer's business to activities carried on for the purposes or in connection with its insurance business, must still be observed.

Services Act 1986. No authorisation is required to conduct business as an agent arranging non-life insurance policies. However, an agent conducting any type of insurance business who wishes to be described as a 'broker' must be registered under the Insurance Brokers (Registration) Act 1977. It is an offence under s 22 of the 1977 Act to use the designation 'broker' without being registered. In order to become registered an individual must satisfy the Registration Council established by the Act as to his qualifications, character and suitability. It remains possible to carry on business as an insurance agent without being registered, eg by using the designation 'insurance adviser' or 'insurance consultant'. However, such an agent will still require authorisation if he or she conducts investment business. The agent will also be required to make clear to customers whether he or she is providing independent advice in relation to investments or simply acting as a representative for a particular insurer[1].

INSURABLE INTEREST

The rationale for insurable interest

The principle of insurable interest is that only those who have a financial interest in the occurrence of the insured event should be permitted to enter into and claim under an insurance policy. The origins of insurable interest as a a legal principle lie in the abuse of early forms of insurance as a form of gambling. This typically involved a person taking out a life insurance policy on a person in whose life they had no financial interest. Although gambling contracts were void under the common law in Scotland[2], they could be enforced under the common law in England[3]. Parliament intervened to deter this abuse of insurance contracts by passing various Acts requiring insurable interest. As detailed below, the scope of these Acts does not make it entirely clear that insurable interest is a statutory requirement for all types of insurance. However, as the requirement of insurable interest is also recognised by the common law, the problem of the scope of the statutory requirement is of limited relevance. Bell[4] refers to the common law principle in the following terms:

> 'It is essential to the contract of insurance that there shall be a subject in which the insured has an interest, a premium given or engaged for, and a risk run'.

Marine insurance

Legislation requiring insurable interest was first introduced in the field of marine insurance. The Marine Insurance Act 1745 made marine policies lacking interest, or with no further proof of interest than the policy itself,

1 SIB Core Conduct of Business, r 4 and PIA, r 4.2.
2 The decision in *Bruce v Ross* (1787) Mor 9523 marked a change in the law as gambling contracts had previously been enforceable.
3 *Jones v Randall* (1774) Cowp 17.
4 Bell *Principles* s 457.

void. This Act was repealed by the Marine Insurance Act 1906. Section 4 of the Marine Insurance Act 1906 makes policies lacking insurable interest void. It is not necessary that the insured has an insurable interest at the time of entering into the contract provided the insured has such an interest at the time of the loss[1].

Life assurance

The statutory requirement

The Life Assurance Act 1774[2] made insurable interest a statutory requirement for life assurance policies. Where there is no insurable interest the contract is void. The statute is silent on the issue of when insurable interest must exist. However, it was held in *Dalby v India and London Life Assurance Co*[3] that insurable interest is required only at the time of insuring and not at the time of death. Dalby was a director of a life assurance company which insured the life of the Duke of Cambridge. This policy was reinsured[4] by the defendant company. The original policy was cancelled but the plaintiff kept paying the reinsurance premiums until the Duke died. The defendants then denied liability under the policy on the basis that the plaintiff had no interest at the time of the Duke's death. It was held that the defendant company (the reinsurer) was liable under the policy as the 1774 Act required interest only when the contract was entered into and not at the time of death.

The scope of insurable interest in life assurance

The Life Assurance Act 1774 does not define the circumstances in which there is an insurable interest in a person's life. However, the common law recognises that a person has an unlimited insurable interest in his or her own life[5]. Insurable interest in the life of a spouse is recognised both by common law[6] and by statute. Section 1 of the Married Women's Policies of Assurance (Scotland) Act 1880 provides that a married woman can effect a policy on the life of her husband for her own benefit. Section 2 of the Act[7] provides that the proceeds of a policy effected by a married[8] man or woman expressly for the benefit of his or her spouse or children (or both) are deemed to be a trust[9] for their benefit. In the case of all other relationships, whether within or outside a family, insurable interest can only exist

---

1   1906 Act, s 6(1).
2   1774 Act, s 1.
3   (1854) 15 CB 365.
4   Reinsurance is where an insurer insures a risk with another insurer.
5   *Griffiths v Fleming* [1909] 1 KB 805 at 821.
6   *Wight v Brown* (1845) 11 D 459.
7   1880 Act, s 2 (as amended by the Married Women's Policies of Assurance (Scotland) (Amendment) Act 1980, s 1).
8   The provision also applies to unmarried persons named in the policy as beneficiaries who later become the spouse of the person effecting the policy.
9   The effect of the policy proceeds being deemed a trust is that they do not form part of the deceased's estate on death but are paid directly to the beneficiary.

where there is a financial interest in the life of the assured. The financial interest can arise from a contractual relationship, common examples being agency, partnership and employment. In *Turnbull & Co v Scottish Provident Institution*[1], eg, a firm of merchants insured the life of their agent in Iceland, through whom they carried on a lucrative business, and were held entitled to recover the proceeds after his death. Insurable interest can also arise from a financial interest based on an obligation of aliment. Under s 1 of the Family Law (Scotland) Act 1985 parents owe an obligation of aliment to their children but children do not owe an obligation to their parents. It follows that parents do not have an insurable interest in the lives of their children[2].

Indemnity insurance

The requirement of insurable interest

In the case of non-marine indemnity insurance, the requirement of insurable interest is recognised both by common law[3] and statute. Despite its title, the Life Assurance Act 1774 applies to insurance on any event with the exception of 'ships, goods and merchandises'. This exception was removed in a manner which was not entirely satisfactory. The Marine Insurance Act 1788 required the insertion of the name of an interested party 'for insurances, on ships and on goods, merchandises or effects' but did not explicitly make insurable interest a condition for the validity of the contract. However, the common law principle (in Scotland) requiring insurable interest can be viewed as resolving any doubt in the statutory provisions. The same approach can be taken in relation to the issue of whether the Life Assurance Act 1774 applies to heritable property. While this question remains unresolved in England[4], it has been assumed in Scotland that the requirement of insurable interest applies to heritable property. For example, in *Arif v Excess Insurance Group Ltd*[5], it was held that one partner in an hotel business could not claim under a fire policy as both the fire policy and the title to the building were in the name of the other partner.

The scope of insurable interest in non-marine indemnity insurance

Bell describes the scope of insurable interest in the following terms[6]: 'Interest is not limited to property but extends to every real and actual advantage and benefit arising out of or depending on the thing to which it

1 (1896) 34 SLR 146, OH.
2 There is a statutory exception in the case of industrial life assurance under s 2 of the Industrial Assurance and Friendly Societies Act 1948.
3 Bell *Principles* s 457. The common law rule is rooted in the basic principle that wagering contracts are void in Scotland.
4 The Court of Appeal held in *Mark Rowlands Ltd v Berni Inns Ltd* [1986] QB 211, CA, that the Life Assurance Act 1774 did not apply to fire insurance on buildings: but this has been disputed.
5 1986 SC 317, OH.
6 Bell *Principles* s 461, referring to the English case of *Lucena v Craufurd* (1806) 2 B & PNR 269 at 302.

refers. But one cannot insure a mere expectancy'. Consequently, insurable interest extends beyond the ownership of heritable or moveable property. It can exist in relation to property which one does not own, subject to the existence of a financial interest. In *Fehilly v General Accident Fire and Life Assurance Corpn Ltd*[1], the issue arose as to whether a tenant of a ballroom had an insurable interest in the building. A clause in the lease obliged the tenant to keep the building in good repair but gave the tenant the option of terminating the lease if major work was required. When the building was destroyed by fire the tenant claimed the full value of the building from the insurer. The insurer argued that the tenant was entitled only to recover to the extent of his loss, namely the market value of the lease. It was held that the tenant did not have an insurable interest in the full value of the building as the lease did not require the tenant to repair the fire damage. The tenant could only recover the market value of the lease.

Insurable interest can also exist in relation to potential legal liabilities in contract or delict. For example, if the tenant in *Fehilly* had been contractually bound by the lease to reinstate the property following fire damage, he would have had an insurable interest in the full value of the building. Another example is the potential delictual liability which is insured under the third party section of a motor vehicle insurance policy.

FORMATION OF INSURANCE CONTRACTS

The proposal form

The normal contractual principles requiring an offer and an acceptance apply to insurance contracts. In some cases the offer is made by the proposer for insurance on the insurer's standard proposal form[2]. This asks for information about the proposer and the risk which is to be insured. The insurer then has the option of accepting the offer, or of making a counter-offer to the proposer. A potential difficulty is that the proposer is unlikely to be aware of the precise contract terms at the time of completing the proposal form. It can therefore be argued that there is no consensus at the time when the insurer accepts the proposal. This outcome is avoided by the inclusion in proposal forms of a statement that the proposer is applying for insurance on the insurer's standard terms[3]. It follows that, even if the reality is that the insured is not familiar with the standard terms, an objective analysis of contract formation[4] will result in there being consensus when the insurer accepts the proposal.

---

1 1982 SC 163, OH.
2 Proposal forms are not normally used for marine insurance or large commercial risks where the relevant information cannot be easily fitted into a standard format.
3 Even without this statement, it is submitted that there would be consensus if there were agreeement on the following essential terms of the contract: subject matter, risk, premium, duration and sum insured.
4 Following the approach in *Muirhead and Turnbull v Dickson* (1905) 7 F 686.

Contracts concluded by telephone

The general principles of contract formation apply equally to contracts concluded orally. Many forms of personal insurance are now agreed by telephone, with the proposer making an oral offer and the insurer giving an oral acceptance. It is normal practice for the proposer to be asked to sign a proposal form which contains the information given over the telephone, but the contract is normally concluded orally, prior to the signing of such a form[1]. The issue of consensus is also relevant here as the insured will not normally be familiar with the insurer's standard terms at the time that the contract is agreed. However, there are two ways in which consensus can be recognised in this situation. The first is to hold that there has been agreement on the essential elements of the contract, namely subject matter, risk, premium, duration and sum insured. The second is to apply the analysis adopted in *General Accident Insurance Corpn v Cronk*[2], in the context of a written proposal form, to an oral offer. It was held in this case that a proposal form would be presumed to be an offer made by the insured for insurance on the insurer's standard terms.

The cover note

Cover notes are temporary contracts of insurance issued by insurers pending the issue of an insurance policy or certificate. Their use is most common in relation to those classes of insurance where there is a statutory obligation to insure, eg motor insurance. For such types of insurance it is important that the insured has proof of insurance right from the start of the period of cover. However, as technology has enabled insurers to speed up the process of issuing policies, cover notes are now much less common than they were in the past. Where they are issued, they normally incorporate, by reference, the insurer's standard policy terms. This avoids the problem which arose in *Re Coleman's Depositories Ltd and Life and Health Assurance Association*[3]. In that case a company applied for employers' liability insurance and was issued with a cover note. The policy, which was issued later, required immediate notification of claims. However, the insured delayed reporting an accident which occurred between the issue of the cover-note and the policy. The insurer tried to avoid liability for the claim on the basis of the delay in notification but the court held that this term could not be implied into the cover note.

Agency and insurance contracts

The normal rules of agency apply to insurance contracts. However, the application of these rules to the formation of insurance contracts is not

---

1 The purpose of the written proposal is to provide a record of the information provided by the insured. However, as there is no legal requirement for such a written record it could be replaced by recording the conversation, as occurs eg in Stock Exchange transactions.
2 (1901) 17 TLR 233.
3 [1907] 2 KB 798.

always straightforward. The main difficulty is identifying the agent's principal. This problem arises from the manner in which insurance contracts are agreed. Virtually all agents (whether they are 'brokers' under the Insurance Brokers Registration Act 1977, independent agents or agents tied to a particular insurer) who conclude insurance contracts are remunerated by the insurer. There is therefore a prima facie case for regarding them as agents of the insurer. However, an agent (particularly an independent broker) also advises the insured and can therefore be seen to be the agent of the insured. While it has been held that a Lloyd's broker[1] is always the agent of the insured[2], there is no simple rule for other types of broker. In each case the position of the broker must be examined, particularly as regards the authority given by the insurer to the agent. An example of an agent being held to be the agent of the insurer is *Stockton v Mason*[3]. In this case, the insured advised his broker that he had changed his car from a Ford Anglia to an MG Midget. The broker confirmed that he would arrange for the change of car to be covered. The insured took this to mean that the existing cover for any authorised driver would apply to the MG. The plaintiff was injured as a passenger in the MG as a result of the negligent driving of the insured's son. On the same day the insured received a letter from the insurers stating that only he himself was covered to drive the MG. The issue was therefore whether the insurers were bound by the broker's statement. It was held by the Court of Appeal that the insurers were bound as the broker had implied authority to confirm temporary cover and had clearly led the insured to believe that the existing cover had been extended.

Problems relating to the status of agents have arisen particularly in the context of the disclosure of information during contractual negotiations. The source of these problems is the rule that a principal is deemed to know what his or her agent knows[4]. This issue is considered below under the heading 'Disclosure to intermediaries'.

GOOD FAITH, THE DUTY OF DISCLOSURE AND MISREPRESENTATION

The principle of good faith

The general principles of contract law do not require the parties to a contract to act in good faith towards each other either during contractual negotiations or at the time of the performance of the contract. There is a duty to avoid making misrepresentations to the other party but no duty to volunteer information or co-operate with the other party.

Insurance contracts are one of a category[5] of contracts in which there is an obligation of good faith imposed on the contracting parties. Lord

---

1 Ie a broker entitled to do business at Lloyd's of London.
2 *Roberts v Plaisted* [1989] 2 Lloyd's Rep 341, CA.
3 [1978] 2 Lloyd's Rep 430.
4 *Woolcott v Excess Insurance Co Ltd* [1979] 1 Lloyd's Rep 231.
5 For fuller discussion of this point, see Gloag *The Law of Contract* (2nd edn, 1929) pp 496–507.

President Inglis stated the common law in the following terms in *Life Association of Scotland v Foster*[1]: '... but contracts of insurance are in this, among other particulars, exceptional, in that they require on both sides uberrima fides [utmost good faith]'. The same principle is to be found in s 17 of the Marine Insurance Act 1906, which provides that if utmost good faith is not observed by either party, the contract can be avoided by the other.

The obligation to act in good faith applies to the contract of insurance at all times: during the negotiations; during the period of insurance; and at the time of making a claim. Both the insurer and the insured must act in good faith. Although the reported cases have dealt mainly with breaches of good faith by the insured, it is clear from the decision of the Court of Appeal in *Banque Financière de la Cité SA v Westgate Insurance Co Ltd*[2] that the insurer can also be in breach of the principle.

The duty of disclosure

Rationale for disclosure

The duty of disclosure is the element of the obligation of good faith which is relevant to contractual negotiations between the insurer and the proposer. The rationale for the duty was expressed by Lord Mansfield in the early case of *Carter v Boehm*[3] in the following terms:

> 'The specific facts upon which the contingent chance is to be computed lie most commonly in the knowledge of the insured only: the underwriter trusts to his representation and proceeds upon a confidence that he does not keep back any circumstance in his knowledge to mislead the underwriter into a belief that the circumstance does not exist, and to induce him to estimate the risk as if it did not exist'.

Thus, the essential elements which underlie the duty of disclosure are the superior knowledge of the insured in relation to the risk and the reliance of the underwriter on the information given by the insured.

What must be disclosed?

The duty of disclosure requires the proposer to disclose every material circumstance which is known to him or her[4]. The insurer is required to disclose any facts known to him or her, but not to the proposer, which would reduce the risk[5]. A failure to observe the duty of disclosure allows the other party to avoid the contract.

The proposer clearly cannot be expected to disclose information he or she does not know[6], but the proposer is assumed to know information which is common knowledge in his or her business[7]. The proposer is also

---

1 (1873) 11 M 351 at 359.
2 [1990] 1 QB 665, CA, affd [1991] 2 AC 249, HL.
3 (1766) 3 Burr 1905.
4 1906 Act, s 18(1).
5 *Banque Financière de la Cité v Westgate Insurance* [1990] 1 QB 665, CA.
6 *Joel v Law Union and Crown Insurance Co* [1908] 2KB 863 at 884, per Fletcher-Moulton LJ: 'The duty is a duty to disclose and you cannot disclose what you do not know'.
7 1906 Act, s 18(1).

assumed to know information which he or she could discover by making inquiries. For example, in *Highlands Insurance Co v Continental Insurance*[1], Continental insured the premises of a company in Tel Aviv which they reinsured with Highlands. The information provided to Highlands by Continental indicated that the premises were sprinklered. Following a fire, it was discovered that they were not and Highlands therefore refused to pay a claim. It was held that Continental had failed in its duty of disclosure by providing false information which could have been verified by making inquiries.

Where the proposer is asked for an opinion by the insurer, it is sufficient that the opinion is given to the best of the proposer's knowledge and belief[2]. There must, however, be a reasonable basis for the proposer's knowledge and belief. In *McPhee v Royal Insurance Co Ltd*[3], the owner of a cabin cruiser gave the wrong dimensions of his boat in a proposal for marine insurance. He had obtained these dimensions by telephoning the previous owner, not by taking them himself. The proposal form declared that it formed the basis of the contract and that the answers in it were true to the best knowledge and belief of the insured. The boat was destroyed by fire and the insurers refused to pay on the basis of the inaccuracy of the dimensions. It was held: (1) that it was not sufficient to show that the answers to the questions were untrue in fact – it had to be shown that they were untrue to the insured's best knowledge and belief ; (2) that to provide answers to the best of a person's knowledge and belief requires a reasonable basis for the answers; and (3) that the insured did not exercise due care and as a result misled the insurer in a material manner.

Criminal convictions must be disclosed where the character of the insured is a factor which will influence the insurer's decision. However, criminal convictions which are 'spent' under the provisions of the Rehabilitation of Offenders Act 1974 need not be disclosed to insurers. Rehabilitation periods under the Act vary according to the severity of the sentence and sentences over thirty months cannot be spent.

Duration of the duty of disclosure

The duty of disclosure lasts until the contract is agreed between the insurer and the proposer. There is no obligation to disclose information during the period in which the insurance is in force[4]. However, if the contract is renewed, the duty of disclosure revives at each successive renewal since each renewal is treated as a new contract. In *Lambert v Co-operative Insurance Society Ltd*[5], an 'all risks' policy covering jewellery was taken out by the insured in 1963. She failed to disclose at that time that her husband had been convicted for handling stolen goods. The policy was renewed each year until 1972. Prior to the last renewal in 1971, the insured's husband was convicted for two offences of dishonesty, but no disclosure was

---

1 [1987] 1 Lloyd's Rep 109.
2 *Life Association of Scotland v Foster* (1873) 11 M 351.
3 1979 SC 304.
4 *Banque Financière de la Cité SA v Westgate Insurance Co Ltd* [1990] 1QB 665, CA, [1991] 2 AC 249, HL.
5 [1975] 2 Lloyd's Rep 485.

made to the insurer. When some jewellery was lost in 1972, the insurer denied liability on the basis of non-disclosure at the time the contract was agreed initially and at renewal in 1971. It was held that the duty of disclosure was the same at the outset and at renewal and that the insurer could avoid liability on the basis of either instance of non-disclosure.

Disclosure to intermediaries

Insurance contracts are often entered into through an intermediary such as an insurance broker. The normal rules of agency apply in this situation but there can be some difficulty in identifying for whom an agent is acting. Almost all agents are paid by the insurer in the form of a commission but, despite this, the courts have held that there are situations in which an agent can be taken to be acting on behalf of the insured and not the insurer. The issue (sometimes referred to as 'transferred agency') is of considerable importance in the context of the duty of disclosure because a principal is deemed to know information known to his or her agent: it follows that, where an agent acts on behalf of an insurer, the insurer is deemed to know information known by the agent. Closely related to this issue is the question of whether a proposer is always bound by a signature on a proposal form.

The cases of *Bawden v London, Edinburgh and Glasgow Assurance Co*[1] and *Newsholme Bros v Road Transport and General Insurance Co Ltd*[2] illustrate the difficulties which can arise in agency situations. In *Bawden*, an illiterate proposer with one eye applied for accident insurance. The agent filled out the proposal form on his behalf . At the end of the proposal there was a declaration stating that the proposer had no physical infirmity. The proposer signed the proposal form and claimed under the insurance when he lost his good eye. The insurers tried to avoid liability on the basis of non-disclosure but the court held that the agent had acted for the insurer and therefore the insurer was aware of the insured's physical condition. In *Newsholme*, the agent entered incorrect information in the proposal despite being told the truth by the proposer. The proposer signed the proposal form in the knowledge that the information inserted by the agent was untrue. It was held[3] that the agent had acted for the insured and that the insured was bound by his signature. The result was that the insurer was able to avoid the policy on the basis of misrepresentation.

The approach adopted in *Bawden* was followed in *Stone v Reliance Mutual*[4], but the *Newsholme* approach is supported by the cases of *Biggar v Rock Life Assurance Co*[5] and *McMillan v Accident Insurance Co Ltd*[6]. While it is not possible in this situation to state a single principle governing 'transferred agency', several principles can be distilled from the cases:

(1) A signature on a proposal form will normally bind the proposer whether the document has been read or not (*Newsholme*).

1 [1892] 2 QB 534.
2 [1929] 2 KB 356.
3 *Bawden* was distinguished in this case.
4 [1972] 1 Lloyd's Rep 469, CA.
5 [1902] 1 KB 516.
6 1907 SC 484.

(2) An insurer's agent who acts fraudulently is acting outside his or her authority. Information fabricated by an agent cannot therefore be imputed to the insurer (*Biggar and Newsholme*).
(3) Where the insurer's agent acts honestly but induces the proposer to sign a proposal form in the belief that it is complete and correct, the insurer cannot avoid liability on the basis of non-disclosure (*Bawden*).

Material information: non-life assurance

The duty of disclosure requires each party to the contract to disclose every material circumstance known to him or her[1]. Section 18(2) of the Marine Insurance Act 1906 provides that: 'Every circumstance is material which would influence the judgment of a prudent insurer in fixing the premium, or determining whether he will take the risk'.

While the dictum of Lord President Inglis in *Life Association of Scotland v Foster*[2] suggested that materiality was to be judged in all forms of insurance[3] by reference to what a reasonable man would consider material, the decision of the Inner House in *Hooper v Royal London General Insurance Co Ltd*[4] makes clear that in the case of indemnity contracts, materiality is to be judged from the perspective of the prudent insurer. In that case, the pursuer, who had insured the contents of his home with the defender, failed to disclose a conviction for vandalism, despite there being a specific question relating to convictions in the proposal form. Shortly after the cover entered into force, the contents of the pursuer's home were destroyed by fire. The insurer refused to pay a claim on the basis of non-disclosure. The pursuer sued for payment on the basis that a non-disclosure could only be material if it would be considered as such by a reasonable person in the position of the insured. The court rejected that argument, holding that the test of the reasonable insurer was applicable to all insurance contracts with the sole exception of life cover.

Two issues have dominated recent judicial interpretation of the statutory definition of material information. The first is the meaning of 'influence'. Here, the focus has been on whether influence refers to a decisive influence or whether it simply refers to information which a prudent underwriter would wish to have but which would not necessarily change his mind on the decision to insure or the terms of insurance. The second major issue has been whether, in order to avoid a contract, an insurer simply has to prove non-disclosure or misrepresentation or whether it is necessary also to show that the non-disclosure or misrepresentation induced the insurer to enter into the contract.

In *Container Transport International Inc and Reliance Group Inc v Oceanus Mutual Underwriting Association (Bermuda) Ltd*[5], the Court of Appeal held that a fact can be material even if its disclosure would not have changed

---

1   1906 Act, s 18(1).
2   (1873) 11 M 351 at 359.
3   It can be assumed that the statutory definition of materiality in s 18(2) of the Marine Insurance Act 1906 would be excluded from this statement.
4   1993 SLT 679.
5   [1984] 1 Lloyd's Rep 476.

the decision of the underwriter either as to the acceptance of the risk or the premium and the terms on which it would be accepted. In order to avoid the policy, an insurer simply had to show that there was non-disclosure of material information. This case formulated the law in a manner which clearly favoured insurers, in that they could avoid liability for non-disclosure of information which had no effect on their decision to insure. The matter subsequently came before the House of Lords in the case of *Pan Atlantic Insurance Co Ltd v Pine Top Insurance Co Ltd*[1] in the form of two separate, but related, issues:

(1) Could a fact be material even if it would not have had any effect on a prudent insurer's decision to accept the insurance or the terms on which it was accepted? (ie was *CTI v Oceanus* correctly decided on this point?)
(2) In order for an insurer to avoid liability under a policy was it enough simply to show that there had been non-disclosure of a material fact or was it also necessary for the insurer to prove that the non-disclosure had induced him to enter into the contract?

On the first point, the House of Lords (by a majority of 3:2) followed the decision in *CTI v Oceanus*. On the second point the House of Lords unanimously overruled *CTI v Oceanus*, holding that it was necessary for an insurer to show that he had been induced into making the contract by the non-disclosure.

Neither *CTI* nor *Pan Atlantic* have been considered judicially in Scotland[2]. The general law of misrepresentation in Scotland requires inducement[3] for the avoidance of a contract, but this does not help solve the issue of the role of inducement in non-disclosure. It might well be that a Scottish court would choose to disregard the fusion of non-disclosure and misrepresentation achieved by the House of Lords in *Pan Atlantic* and allow avoidance of the contract for any non-disclosure which would have a decisive influence on a prudent insurer's decision to insure or the terms of insurance.

Materiality - life assurance

In the case of life assurance, it was established in *Life Association of Scotland v Foster*[4] that the test of materiality in Scotland is that of the reasonable insured. In that case the insured replied in the negative to a question asking if she had a rupture. She later died from rupture and it was discovered that, at the time of making the proposal, she did have a small swelling on her groin. However, she did not appreciate that this was a symptom of rupture. Lord President Inglis, delivering the leading judgment, observed that the insured was obliged only to state such facts as a reasonable per-

1 [1995] 1 AC 501, HL.
2 The opportunity to consider *CTI v Oceanus* was not taken in *Gifto Fancy Goods Ltd v Ecclesiatical Insurance Office plc* [1991] GWD 2-117, OH and the case was not cited in argument or referred to in the judgments in *Hooper v Royal London General Insurance Co Ltd*.
3 *Menzies v Menzies* (1893) 20 R (HL) 108. Misrepresentation is considered in more detail below.
4 (1873) 11 M 351.

son would consider likely to influence the insurer's decision to enter into a contract[1].

In England, the courts chose, in the context of life assurance, to follow the test of the reasonable insurer in determining materiality[2]. This resulted in the test being the same for both life and indemnity contracts. However, as far as Scotland is concerned, the recent decision of the Inner House in the case of *Hooper v Royal London General Insurance Co Ltd*[3] confirmed that there remains a distinction between life and indemnity contracts. Lord Justice-Clerk Ross justified the application of the reasonable insured test to life assurance on the basis that questions asked in a life assurance proposal form are 'subjective and not capable of assessment on any objective basis', whereas questions asked in indemnity proposal forms could be objectively ascertained[4].

Misrepresentation

Misrepresentation is the giving of false information to the other contracting party. It is in essence an act of deception and therefore different from non-disclosure which involves the withholding of information[5]. Misrepresentation can occur innocently, negligently or fraudulently. In all three instances, the general principles of contract law allow the contract to be avoided where one party has been induced by a misrepresentation into entering into the contract[6]. The Marine Insurance Act 1906 treats misrepresentation in the same manner as non-disclosure. Section 20(1) provides that there is a right to avoid the contract in the case of a material misrepresentation but there is no express reference to a requirement of inducement. The decision of the House of Lords in *Pan Atlantic* makes clear that, in England, inducement is required if the contract is to be avoided. While that decision is not binding in Scotland, it is likely that it would be followed as inducement is an essential element of the general principle of misrepresentation in Scotland.

The ABI Statements of Insurance Practice

In the context of private insurance, the position in relation to materiality is further complicated by the Statements of Insurance Practice. The Statement of General Insurance Practice in effect adopts the approach taken in *Hooper* to life assurance. Paragraph 2(b)(i) provides:

> 'An insurer will not repudiate liability to indemnify a policyholder:
>
> > (i) on grounds of non-disclosure of a material fact which a policyholder could not reasonably be expected to have disclosed'.

1   (1873) 11 M 351 at 359.
2   *Mutual Life Insurance Co of New York v Ontario Metal Products Co Ltd* [1925] AC 344, PC.
3   1993 SLT 679.
4   For a critique of this case, see Forte 'The materiality test in insurance' 1994 LMCLQ 557.
5   Despite the clear difference in principle, the distinction may be more difficult to maintain in practice. Eg if a question in a motor insurance proposal relating to previous accidents involving the insured is left blank when the insured has been involved in several, is this a non-disclosure or a misrepresentation?
6   *Menzies v Menzies* (1893) 20 R (HL) 108.

The Statement of Long Term Insurance Practice adopts a slightly different test by referring to the (specific) policyholder rather than a hypothetical policyholder.

However, in both cases it is clear that the reasonable insurer test of materiality cannot be used to avoid the contract on the basis of non-disclosure.

THE INSURANCE POLICY

Warranties: definition

Warranties are fundamental terms of an insurance contract. Section 33(1) of the Marine Insurance Act 1906 makes clear the type of obligation which can be the subject of a warranty:

> A warranty, in the following sections relating to warranties, means a promissory warranty, that is to say, a warranty by which the assured undertakes that some particular thing shall or shall not be done, or that some condition shall be fulfilled, or whereby he affirms or negatives the existence of a particular state of facts'.

Following this definition, warranties can be divided into two categories: (1) warranties relating to future facts and (2) warranties relating to past or present facts.

Warranties relating to future facts

The most common form of warranty is that relating to future facts. It requires the insured to conform to a certain pattern of behaviour during the period of cover. Examples of such warranties are that the insured is obliged to set a burglar alarm when premises are unoccupied (to deter burglars) or to maintain a sprinkler system in good working order at all times (to prevent the spread of fire).

Warranties relating to past or present facts

Where a warranty relates to past or present facts the insured affirms or negatives the existence of a particular state of facts at the time that the insurance contract is agreed. Where such a warranty relates clearly to the past and present, it will not be taken to apply to the future. For example in *Kennedy v Smith and Ansvar Insurance Co Ltd*[1], a proposer for motor insurance completed a proposal form together with an 'Abstinence and Membership Declaration' in which he stated that he was and had always been an abstainer from alcohol. The euphoria of victory in a bowling match led him to consume his first ever alcoholic beverage. Later, when driving home, he swerved off the road and his two passengers were killed. The insurers denied liability under the policy on the basis that at the time of the accident, the abstinence declaration was false as the

1 1976 SLT 110.

insured was under the influence of alcohol. The court held that the warranty could not be taken to cover the future conduct of the insured (despite this being the intention of the insurer) and therefore the insurer was liable to pay the claim. If the warranty is based on the opinion of the insured, it can relate only to facts which are known to the insured. For example, in *Hutchison v National Loan Life Fund Assurance Co*[1], the insured warranted that she had no disease and enjoyed good health. It was held that this did not form a warranty against any latent disease which could only be discovered by post mortem examination.

Warranties: identification

No special form of words is needed to create a warranty. It will often be the case that the word 'warranty' will be used, but this is not necessary. What is required is a form of words which makes clear that the relevant term is fundamental to the contract and that it requires strict compliance. It is possible, though no longer common, for commercial insurance policies to contain warranties created through the use of a 'basis of contract clause'. The effect of such a clause is to turn all the information given in the proposal form into a warranty relating to past or present facts[2]. Once this has occurred, any inaccuracy in the information given by the insured allows the insurer to avoid the contract, even if the information was not material to the insurer's assessment of the risk[3].

The consequences of breach of warranty

The consequences of a breach of warranty are made clear by s 33(3) of the Marine Insurance Act 1906:

> 'A warranty, as above defined [in section 33(1)], is a condition which must be exactly complied with , whether it be material to the risk or not. If it be not so complied with, then, subject to any express provision in the policy, the insurer is discharged from liability as from the date of the breach of warranty, but without prejudice to any liability incurred by him before that date'.

The case of *Dawsons Ltd v Bonnin*[4] illustrates the obligation of strict compliance with warranties. A proposer for motor insurance entered in the proposal form that a lorry was garaged in central Glasgow whereas in fact it was garaged on the outskirts of the city. The proposal form declared that it was to be the basis of the contract. The lorry was subsequently destroyed by fire. The fourth condition of the contract provided that any material misstatement or concealment on the part of the insured would render the policy void. The insurers disputed liability and the issue went to the House of Lords. It was held (1) that the misstatement in relation to

1 (1845) 7 D 467.
2 An example of such a clause is: 'I hereby confirm that the information contained in the proposal form is complete and accurate and will form the basis of the contract'.
3 *Unipac (Scotland) Ltd v Aegon Insurance Co (UK) Ltd* 1996 SLT 1197.
4 1922 SC (HL) 156.

the garage address was not material within the meaning of condition 4 but (2) that the 'basis of contract' clause had the effect of turning the garage address into a fundamental term of the contract and that in this situation it did not matter if the address was material within the meaning of condition 4 or not. It followed that the insurer could refuse to pay the claim. *Dawsons Ltd v Bonnin* was recently applied in the case of *Unipac (Scotland) Ltd v Aegon Insurance Co (UK) Ltd*[1]. In this case, the insured answered two questions in a proposal form incorrectly: one related to the length of time for which the company had carried on business at the premises and the other to whether they were the sole occupiers. The proposal form contained a basis of contract clause which purported to make all the information in it the basis of the contract. The insured argued that the basis clause only made material facts the basis of the contract but the court held that this particular basis clause had the effect of turning all the information in the proposal form into a warranty. The court recognised that the effect of its decision was to allow the insurer to avoid the contract for non-disclosure or misrepresentation of information which was not material to the insurer's assessment of the risk, but took the view that this outcome was '... simply a consequence of what the parties have agreed to by contract and parties are free to agree what they like'[2].

There is no need for the insurer to show a causal connection between the breach of warranty and a loss in order to avoid the contract. For example, in *Jones and James v Provincial Insurance Co Ltd*[3] the policy contained a warranty which provided that the insured was required to maintain his vehicle in an efficient condition. The warranty was not observed by the insured and when the vehicle was stolen the insurer was able to avoid liability for the theft despite there being no causal connection between the breach of warranty and the loss. However, the ABI Statements of Practice alter the position of insurers on this issue in the case of private insurance. The Statement of General Insurance Practice[4] and the Statement of Long-Term Insurance Practice[5] provide that an insurer will not refuse to pay claims where a breach of warranty has no connection with a loss unless fraud is involved. This effectively reverses the conclusion which was reached in *Jones and James v Provincial Insurance Co Ltd*.

Breach of warranty does not release the insurer from liability in relation to losses which have occurred before the breach. The breach operates to release the insurer only from any future liability under the policy. No specific action is required on the part of the insurer in order to be released[6] and the option is open to the insurer to waive the breach and allow the policy to remain in force[7].

1 1996 SLT 1197.
2 1996 SLT 1197 at 1202, per Lord Ross.
3 [1929] 35 Ll L Rep 135.
4 Statement of General Insurance Practice, para 2(b) (iii).
5 Statement of Long-Term Insurance Practice, para 3(b).
6 *Bank of Nova Scotia v Hellenic Mutual War Risks Association (Bermuda) Ltd, The Good Luck* [1992] 1 AC 233, HL.
7 1906 Act, s 34(3).

Exceptions

Most insurance policies contain some form of exception to the cover. They can be either general exceptions which apply to the whole policy (eg a motor policy which excludes the use of a car for business purposes) or specific exceptions which apply to a particular insured peril (eg a commercial vehicle policy which covers theft of goods from the vehicle, but not while the vehicle is left unattended overnight). The effect of the operation of an exception is that the insurer is off risk during the time that the exception operates but comes back on risk when the exception ceases to operate. For example, in *Roberts v Anglo-Saxon Insurance Ltd*[1], the insurer of a van insured for business use only was held to be off risk when the van was used by the insured to drive to his golf club but was back on risk once the insured returned to his work.

Construction of insurance contracts

The normal rules for the construction of contracts apply to insurance[2]. Words and expressions used in the policy are given their ordinary, everyday meaning unless it is clear that a technical usage is intended[3]. Of particular importance is the *contra proferentem* principle which requires any ambiguity in a contract to be construed against the *proferens* (the person relying on the ambiguous term). This principle was applied in *Kennedy v Smith and Ansvar Insurance Co Ltd*[4], discussed above, to determine whether a warranty covered the future conduct of the insured.

Assignation

The rights of the insured or the insurer under a contract of insurance can, in principle, be assigned to a third party[5]. There are, however, limitations on the extent to which assignation can take place. First, obligations involving *delectus personae* cannot be assigned[6]: this principle rules out the assignation of fire and motor policies where the identity of the insured is a fundamental part of the risk. Second, it is possible that the policy itself will contain a prohibition on assignation.

Where assignation is possible[7], it will only be effective if it is intimated to the insurer. The Policies of Assurance Act 1867 requires written intima-

---

1 (1927) 27 Ll L Rep 313.
2 *Smith v Accident Insurance Co* (1870) LR Exch 302 at 307.
3 See eg *Scragg v UK Temperance and General Provident Institution* [1976] 2 Lloyd's Rep 227, where the term 'motor racing' was held to have a technical meaning which excluded hill climbing in which each vehicle set off separately and raced against the clock.
4 1976 SLT 110.
5 Bell *Principles* s 520, referring to life assurance, states '... and as it is assignable, it is useful as a fund of credit'.
6 *Cole v CH Handasyde & Co* 1910 SC 68 at 73, per Lord President Dunedin.
7 Assignation occurs most commonly in life assurance. Although it results in a change in the person to whom the sum assured is payable, the life assured, and therefore the risk, remains the same. An assignation immediately following the conclusion of a life contract can effectively circumvent the requirement for insurable interest, but the courts have not limited assignation on this basis.

tion of 'the date and purport' of the assignation to be given to the insurer at a principal place of business, but there is no prescribed form of intimation. The rights of the assignee are governed by the principle *assignatus utitur jure auctoris* (the assignee assumes the rights of the cedent). An example of this in the context of insurance is the case of *Scottish Widows Fund and Life Assurance Society v Buist*[1]. The insured failed to disclose his addiction to alcohol at the time the contract was agreed. The policy was later assigned to a third party. When the insured died at the age of 30, the insurer sought to avoid the assignee's claim for payment. It was held that as the assignee stood in the same position as the cedent (the insured), the insurer could avoid the policy.

Third party rights

An insurance contract imposes obligations only on the insured and the insurer and therefore, in principle, third parties are not able to enforce the contract for their own benefit. This principle holds good even when a third party has a valid claim against the insured which is covered by an insurance policy. However, there are two important exceptions to this principle. First, s 1 of the Third Parties (Rights against Insurers) Act 1930 allows third parties with a valid claim[2] against an insured to proceed directly against the insurer if the insured becomes bankrupt or (in the case of a company) is wound-up. The effect of this provision is to create a statutory assignation of the insured's rights in respect of the particular claim to the third party[3]. Second, in the case of motor insurance, s 151 of the Road Traffic Act 1988 requires insurers to pay directly to third parties any sums covered by a motor insurance policy. To benefit from s 151, a third party must first obtain judgment against the insured and must give notice of the proceedings against the insured to the insurer, so as to allow the insurer the opportunity to defend the case.

CLAIMS

Proximate cause

In order to claim under an indemnity policy[4], the insured must show that loss or damage has been proximately caused by an insured peril. If loss or damage results from a cause other than an insured peril, the insurer is not liable[5]. The proximate cause of loss is the dominant or effective cause of that loss. It does not have to be the only cause of the loss, nor need it be the

---

1 (1876) 3 R 1078.
2 The claim must be established in legal proceedings against the insured: *Bradley v Eagle Star Insurance Co Ltd* [1989] AC 957 at 960, HL, per Lord Brandon.
3 *Post Office v Norwich Union Fire Insurance Society Ltd* [1967] 2QB 363 at 376, CA, per Harman LJ.
4 In the case of life assurance, it is necessary to show only that the event insured against (eg death) has occurred.
5 1906 Act, s 55(1).

cause which operates closest in time to the loss. For example, in *Leyland Shipping Co Ltd v Norwich Union Fire Insurance Society*[1] there were two possible causes of loss. A marine policy covering a ship contained an exclusion relating to damage caused as a result of hostilities. The ship was torpedoed 25 miles from Le Havre by a German submarine during the 1914–18 war. She was towed into port at Le Havre but subsequently ordered to anchor outside the harbour as it was feared that she would sink and block the harbour. At low tide the ship became grounded, took in water and sank. The insurers refused to pay the shipowner's claim on the basis that the proximate cause of the loss was the torpedoing, which was excluded. It was held that the torpedoing, not the grounding, was the proximate cause of loss.

Where two losses occur concurrently and it is not possible to say which is the proximate cause, there can be no claim if one of the causes is excluded. This situation occurred in *Wayne Tank and Pump Co Ltd v Employers' Liability Assurance Corpn Ltd*[2]. Wayne Tank and Pump (WTP) were engineers who installed machinery in a plasticine factory. They had a public liability policy with ELA which provided cover, inter alia, for damage caused by WTP at customers' premises. An exception to the cover was damage caused by the nature of goods sold or supplied on behalf of the insured. The machinery was switched on by a WTP employee before installation was complete, it caught fire and destroyed the factory. WTP were held liable to the factory owners in a separate action where it was established that there were two concurrent causes of the fire: (1) dangerous plastic material used by WTP (excluded); and (2) the premature switching-on of the machinery (covered). It was held by the Court of Appeal that the insurer was not liable as the exception should be allowed to operate to limit the insurer's liability.

The problem which arose in Wayne Tank can be avoided by the use of suitable contract terms. For example, in *Jason v British Traders Insurance Co Ltd*[3] Jason was a market trader who was injured in a crash when a wheel came off his van. He claimed under an accident insurance policy from BTI. The policy provided cover for accidents which were, independently of other causes, the direct and immediate cause of injury. There was also an exclusion in respect of injuries caused by any physical defect or infirmity which existed prior to an accident. Following the accident, Jason suffered a coronary thrombosis and was disabled for about a year. The medical evidence showed that the stress of the accident had contributed to the condition but that Jason would have probably suffered this in any event within three years because of his existing medical condition. It was held that the insurers were not liable as the accident was not the independent cause of injury.

The indemnity principle

The objective of the principle of indemnity is to put the insured in the position he would be in had the loss not occurred. For example, in *Hercules*

1   [1918] AC 350, HL.
2   [1974] QB 57, CA.
3   [1969] 1 Lloyd's Rep 281.

Insurance Co v Hunter[1], the defender insured with the pursuers certain mill machinery and materials in Glasgow for a sum of £1,450. The property was destroyed by fire but the insurers refused to pay £1,450 on the basis that the goods destroyed were of lower value. It was established that the defender had deliberately overvalued the machinery and decided that in a contract of indemnity it is the actual value of the property destroyed which the insured is entitled to recover and not the particular sum insured contained in the policy. The actual value of the goods was the value for which they could be sold.

There is no need for the principle of indemnity to be stated in the policy. If the nature of the policy is such that it is intended to compensate the insured to the extent of his or her loss, measured at the time it occurs, then the principle of indemnity applies. However, it is possible for the policy to provide that the principle of indemnity will not apply or that its application will be modified. This can occur in several ways:

(1) *Agreed value policy.* Agreed value policies are used for items which may be difficult to value when a loss occurs, such as works of art or antiques. The policy specifies the sum which is to be paid in the event of a total loss of the subject matter insured. Where there is a partial loss there is a pro rata adjustment made[2].

(2) *Replacement value or reinstatement policies.* A replacement value policy gives the insured the cost of replacing the item which has been destroyed and a 'reinstatement' policy obliges the insurer to restore the property to its condition before the damage occurred. Some policies may give the insurer the option of either paying the value of the property destroyed or reinstating. Once agreement has been reached on the payment of money, the insurer no longer has the option to reinstate

(3) *Excess clause.* An excess clause requires the insured to bear a certain amount of the loss but beyond this amount the insurer will be liable for the balance of the loss. It is common to find an excess clause in motor and home insurance policies because insurers regard such a clause as encouraging the insured to avoid a loss on the basis that it will not be possible to claim the entire loss from the insurer.

(4) *Franchise clause.* A franchise clause requires the insured to bear losses below a certain percentage of the sum insured; where there is a loss above this percentage, it is borne in full by the insurer. For example a 5 per cent franchise on a policy covering goods valued at £1,000 would require the insured to bear any loss below £50, but any loss over £50 would be borne in full by the insurer.

(5) *Average clause.* An average clause is designed to deal with the problem of under-insurance. Where goods are insured for less than their true value, the insurer will not receive a premium which reflects the full value of the goods. For example, where goods worth £150,000 are insured for only £100,000, the insurer receives a premium based on £100,000 but is in reality exposed to the possibility of the loss of any

1 (1836) 14 S 1137.
2 Eg a policy states the value of goods to be £100, but the real value before loss is £60. The value after a loss is £30. The insured's claim against the insurer will be for £50 (⅚ of £100).

£100,000 out of the total £150,000 of goods. An average clause prevents the insured from taking out a partial insurance and then recovering the full value of the goods which have been lost. It does this by adjusting the claim in relation to the proportion of the value of the goods which is insured[1]. The effect of this is that the insured is his own insurer for the portion of the value of the goods which is not insured.

Section 81 of the Marine Insurance Act 1906 provides that the principle of average applies to marine policies. In the case of other classes of insurance, it is necessary for there to be a specific clause providing for the application of the principle of average. If there is not, the insurer will not be able to reduce a claim on the basis that there has been under-insurance[2].

Subrogation

The principle of subrogation follows logically from the principle of indemnity. It operates so as to prevent the insured from recovering more than a full indemnity under the policy. The possibility of the insured gaining more than a full indemnity arises in situations where the insured may be able to recover his loss from a third party as well as from the insurer. For example, where motorist **A** negligently crashes into motorist **B**, **A** will be liable in delict to **B**. Assume that they agree that **A** will pay the cost of repairing **B**'s car (say £2,000). **B** then claims another £2,000 from his insurer under his comprehensive motor policy. In this situation, **B** will have received £4,000 in respect of a loss of only £2,000. The principle of subrogation would operate in this case to allow the insurer to claim £2,000 back from **B**.

Subrogation is a common law principle and will therefore apply without being referred to in the policy. It applies only to indemnity insurance and only when the insurer has paid a claim under the policy. In *Page v Scottish Insurance Corporation*[3], the insurer tried to exercise subrogation against a person who had caused damage to the insured's car. It was held that this could only be possible after the insurer had paid the insured's claim. Subrogation transfers from the insured to the insurer every right of the insured in contract or delict. This principle was applied in *Castellain v Preston*[4] where the insured was the vendor of a house which was burnt down between the conclusion of the contract for sale and the transfer of title. The contract provided for the risk to pass to the purchaser on conclusion of the contract. The vendor recovered the insurance money from the insurers and the purchaser then paid the price (as he was obliged to do under the contract). It was held that as the insurers had fully indemnified the vendor for his loss, the purchase price had to be passed to the insurers as they became subrogated to his rights once they had paid the claim.

In most cases the insured's rights in contract and delict will be passed to the insurer automatically when a claim is paid. However, there are cir-

---

1   In the example cited, a loss of £30,000 would result in a claim for £20,000 ie ($^{100}/_{150}$ x £30,000).
2   *Sillem v Thornton* (1854) 3 E & B 868.
3   (1929) 33 Ll L Rep 134.
4   (1883) 11 QBD 380, CA.

cumstances in which this will not occur. One is where the policy contains a contractual exclusion of subrogation. This occurred in the case of *Mark Rowlands Ltd v Berni Inns Ltd*[1]. A lease provided that the landlord was obliged to insure the property and that the tenant was to pay an additional insurance rent. The property was damaged by fire, the insurer paid the landlord's claim under the policy and then tried to exercise a right of subrogation against the tenant. It was held that the effect of the lease was to prevent the landlord recovering damages from the tenant for any loss covered by insurance and as the landlord had no right of action against the tenant, the insurer could have no action.

A second situation where subrogation will not apply is where the loss has been caused by the insured or by a co-insured. In the case of the insured causing the loss, the insurer can have no right of action because the insured has no right of action against himself or herself and there is therefore nothing to transfer by way of subrogation. In the case of *Simpson & Co v Thomson*[2] a ship ran down and sank another belonging to the same owner, William Burrell. The underwriters of the sunken ship paid its value to Burrell and then made a claim against him on the basis that his other ship had caused the damage. It was held that this claim was not possible as Burrell could not have sued himself and the underwriters stood in his position once they had paid the claim. Of course, had the owner of the other ship been a third party such a claim would have been possible. In *Petrofina (UK) Ltd v Magnaload Ltd*[3], Magnaload were sub-contractors involved in the construction of an extension to an oil refinery. The insurance policy provided cover for the work in progress and the construction equipment. Following the collapse of a crane, the owner of the refinery claimed on the policy for damage caused to the contract works by the crane's collapse. The insurers then attempted to exercise subrogation rights against Magnaload, who were the sub-contractors responsible for the operation of the crane. It was held that as Magnaload were one of the parties insured by the policy, it was not possible for the insurers to exercise subrogation.

Contribution

Contribution relates to the rights of insurers among themselves. It applies in situations in which a loss is covered by more than one policy (eg where a bag stolen from a car is covered both by home contents insurance and by motor insurance). In this situation, an insurer who pays the insured's claim in full is entitled to recover a proportion of the claim from the other insurer (ie one-half if two, one-third from each if three).

In order to avoid paying a claim in full in cases of double insurance, insurers often use rateable proportion clauses which provide that they are only liable for their rateable proportion of the loss. However, as was held in *Legal and General Assurance Society Ltd v Drake Insurance Co Ltd*[4], where there is double insurance and each policy has a rateable proportion clause,

1 [1986] 1 QB 211.
2 (1877) 5 R (HL) 40.
3 [1984] QB 127.
4 [1992] 1 All ER 283, CA.

any payment made voluntarily by an insurer in excess of his rateable proportion cannot be recovered from the other insurer.

Fraudulent claims

A claim is fraudulent if it is based on substantial falsehood and is intended to secure a payment greater than the insured's entitlement. Some exaggeration in the value of a claim is part of the normal process of negotiation between insured and insurer, but a claim which is several times the real value of the loss is indicative of fraud. The effect of a fraudulent claim is that the insurer has the right to avoid all liability under the policy, not just liability for the claim to which the fraud relates. The reason for this is that a fraudulent claim is a breach of the duty of good faith. For example, in *The Litsion Pride*[1], the insured attempted to claim for the loss of a ship during the Iran-Iraq war. The ship had sailed into a war zone, for which the policy required a large additional premium. When the ship was sunk by a helicopter attack the insured concocted false documents to give the impression that the failure to notify the insurers of entry into the war zone was due to an innocent oversight. It was held that the insurer could avoid the policy *ab initio* or reject liability for the particular claim and allow the policy to continue in existence.

The Insurance and PIA Ombudsman Schemes

The Insurance Ombudsman Bureau (IOB), established in 1981, provides a means for policyholders to make complaints relating either to a claim under a policy or to the marketing and administration of a policy. Membership of the IOB is voluntary, but over 90 per cent of insurers belonging to the Association of British Insurers are members. The jurisdiction of the IOB extends only to insurance purchased in a private capacity and does not cover any form of commercial insurance. A complaint can be made to the IOB only if it has been rejected by the senior management of the insurer concerned. Binding awards can be made by the IOB up to a value of £100,000 but any award above that figure acts only as a recommendation to the company. The IOB is required to take account of good insurance practice as well as the relevant law.

The creation of the Personal Investment Authority in 1994 as the regulator for firms selling investments directly to the public has resulted in the work of the IOB being effectively confined to non-life insurance, with the PIA Ombudsman taking responsibility for life assurance. Membership of the PIA Ombudsman scheme is compulsory for PIA members. Awards made by the PIA Ombudsman cannot exceed £50,000 in the case of life assurance policies regulated by PIA[2]. In the case of life policies not regulated by PIA, companies may voluntarily accept the jurisdiction of the PIA Ombudsman in relation to complaints, in which case the limit for awards is £100,000 (in line with the IOB).

---

1 *Black King Shipping Corpn and Wayang v Massie, The Litsion Pride* [1985] 1 Lloyd's Rep 437.
2 As far as insurance is concerned, this means life policies with a savings element.

5 Commercial paper – negotiable instruments

NEGOTIABLE INSTRUMENTS AND PAYMENT OF DEBT

In paying a debt the debtor's money is transferred to the creditor. This transfer of funds may be effected by two methods. The first is payment in cash or its equivalent, and into the latter category fall negotiable instruments such as bills of exchange, cheques and promissory notes. The second is the cashless transfer of funds, using credit transfers and direct debits, whereby money is transferred directly from the debtor's bank to that of the creditor. Negotiable instruments are a convenient and versatile way of paying business debts, and the law relating to their use ensures that these benefits are maintained. That law was codified in the Bills of Exchange Act 1882, which applies to cheques and promissory notes as well as to bills, and this statute remains the principal source of the rules regulating the use of commercial paper. The law applicable to cheques has needed periodic revision and the Cheques Acts of 1957 and 1992 embody these changes.

BILLS OF EXCHANGE IN CONTEXT

This book contains chapters on the sale of goods and on the carriage of goods, transactions which are frequently linked. In a contract for the sale of goods between a Scottish business and an overseas buyer, the seller may be obliged to arrange to have the goods transported to and insured for the benefit of the buyer (eg a CIF contract). There is also the matter of how payment is to be effected. One option, termed 'open account' trading, is for the seller simply to invoice the buyer and to receive payment directly from the latter. Open account trading, however, has two major disadvantages. Firstly, the seller has no assurance that he or she will be paid promptly and, moreover, has lost control of the goods supplied. Secondly, the buyer does not necessarily wish to pay promptly and has no assurance that the goods are of satisfactory quality. Where payment is made by bill of exchange the tensions between buyer and seller in an export transaction can be substantially reduced. Utilising a service offered by many banks, exporter and importer may arrange for payment to be made under a collection arrangement. Here the seller presents a bill of exchange in his or her favour to his or her bank together with any documents (eg bills of lading, invoices, insurance certificates) called for by the buyer. These are forwarded to the buyer's bank and released to the buyer when he or she accepts the bill. A good example of this process at work is to be seen in *Credito Italiano v M Birnhak & Sons Ltd*[1]. Here the sellers drew

1 [1967] 1 Lloyd's Rep 314, CA.

a bill of exchange, dated 14 February, on the buyers which was payable on 20 May. The sellers then had the buyers 'accept' the bill (ie promise to pay on 20 May) and thereafter 'discounted' it with their own bank. Discounting simply means that the seller negotiates the bill to the bank in return for payment of slightly less than its face value: the difference in value giving the bank its margin of profit. As the holder of the bill of exchange, the bank was entitled to payment from the buyer on the date of maturity of the instrument (ie 20 May). What benefits accrued to the buyers and sellers in this situation? The buyers obtained the goods quickly, but enjoyed a period of almost three months' credit (during which they could use or resell them) before having to honour the bill by paying the bank. At the same time the sellers did not have to wait three months for payment. It is not difficult to appreciate the importance of bills of exchange in financing international trade.

NEGOTIABILITY – THE KEY CONCEPT

A negotiable instrument is a piece of paper representing a right to payment: though its effect is quite different from other instruments indicating the existence of this right. Suppose, eg, that Smith borrows £5,000 from Jones and grants her a personal bond acknowledging the debt. Suppose further that Jones owes £5,000 to Black. In order to settle her debt with Black, Jones could assign to Black her right to be paid by Smith. But assignation of a right to payment is a more cumbersome method of transfer than using a negotiable instrument, since it must be intimated to the debtor before the assignee acquires a preferential right to payment[1]. Furthermore, when Jones assigns to Black her right to receive payment from Smith, that is exactly what Black gets – Jones' right. If Jones' right to payment is defective or invalid, then, in accordance with the principle *assignatus utitur jure auctoris*[2], Black acquires no better right to payment than Jones had and Smith may successfully plead against Black any defence available to him against Jones[3]. In contrast to the assignation of a right to payment is its transfer by means of a negotiable instrument. If Jones draws a bill of exchange on Smith, in favour of Black, this confers on Black the right to be paid by Smith when he presents the instrument to Smith without need for prior intimation. 'When transferred', a negotiable instrument 'passes in its own *corpus* the thing it represents without intimation'[4]. Moreover, where the party to whom a negotiable instrument has been negotiated takes it in good faith, and unaware of any defect in the transferor's title, then the transferee acquires a better title to be paid than the transferor had:

1 Stair *Institutions* III, 1,6; Bell *Commentaries* II, 16; *Grigor Allan v Urquhart* (1887) 15 R 56.
2 'The assignee exercises the right of his or her cedent'.
3 *Scottish Widows' Fund and Life Assurance Society v Buist* (1876) 3 R 1078; *Buist v Scottish Equitable Life Assurance Society* (1878) 5 R (HL) 64.
4 *Connal & Co v Loder* (1868) 6 M 1095 at 1102, per Lord Neaves.

'The general rule of law is undoubted, that no-one can acquire a better title than he himself possesses: *Nemo dat quod non habet*. To this there are some exceptions, one of which arises out of the rule of the law merchant as to negotiable instruments. These being part of the currency, are subject to the same rule as money: and if such an instrument be transferred in good faith, for value, before it is overdue, it becomes available in the hands of the holder, notwithstanding fraud which would have rendered it unavailable in the hands of a previous holder'[1].

Finally, all signatories to a negotiable instrument are guarantors of payment to the holder thereof[2].

A negotiable instrument is effectively a document of title to money and can transfer the holder's title to be paid by being 'negotiated'. Where a negotiable instrument is drawn in favour of a named party or 'order' it is negotiated by indorsement plus delivery to another party. Where it is drawn in favour of the bearer of the instrument, then delivery alone transfers the right to payment. But not all instruments representing the holder's title to something are negotiable instruments. A bill of lading, eg, is a document of title to goods carried as cargo, and, depending on how it is expressed, it may be negotiated by either indorsement and delivery (an order bill of lading) or simply by delivery (a bearer bill of lading)[3]. However, a bill of lading is not a negotiable instrument since it cannot *per se* confer a better title on the holder than his predecessor had[4].

An instrument will be treated as negotiable when it is recognised as such either by statute, or by commercial or trade custom and usage. In addition to bills of exchange, cheques and promissory notes, the following are regarded as being negotiable instruments: bearer bonds and debentures; bearer scrip; treasury bills; dividend warrants. Postal and money orders are not negotiable instruments, nor is a building society withdrawal form[5]. A bank draft, however, may be treated as a bill of exchange or promissory note[6].

HOLDER IN DUE COURSE – THE KEY PARTY

The legislation confers rights and remedies on the holders of negotiable instruments. But some holders enjoy better rights than others and it is best to deal with this now.

Holder

A bill of exchange will either specify a person to whom payment is authorised or simply state that the sum drawn is payable to the bearer of the

1 *Whistler v Forster* (1863) 14 CBNS 248 at 257, per Willes J.
2 Bills of Exchange Act 1882, ss 54–56, 66, 88–89. This statute will be referred to hereinafter as the '1882 Act'.
3 A 'straight' bill of lading, where the consignee is named but the words 'or order' are omitted, is not negotiable unless it expressly stipulates that it may be transferred.
4 *Simmons v London Joint Stock Bank* [1891] 1 Ch 270, CA.
5 *Weir v National Westminster Bank plc* 1993 SC 515.
6 A bank draft is drawn by a bank on itself. The holder of such a draft may treat it as either a bill of exchange or a promissory note: 1882 Act, s 5(2); *Universal Import Export GmbH v Bank of Scotland* 1995 SLT 1318.

instrument. In either case the party entitled to claim payment is the payee, and, where the bill is in the possession of that party, he or she is a holder. Where the payee indorses and delivers an order bill to another person, the indorsee then becomes the holder. Where the instrument is payable to bearer, then the party to whom it is delivered becomes the holder[1]. Clearly possession of an instrument is central to the definition of what constitutes a holder.

The rights enjoyed by the holder of a bill of exchange (or of a cheque or promissory note) are, in certain important respects, of less consequence than those of the holder in due course. Nevertheless, they are quite extensive. The holder has the ability to negotiate the bill[2] and to convert a blank indorsement on an order bill into a special one[3]. Where a bill, which states that it is payable at a fixed period after its date, is undated, the holder may insert the correct date. The holder may also insert the date on which it was accepted if the acceptance of a bill states that it will be payable at a fixed period after the date of acceptance[4]. Only the holder, or his or her agent, may present a bill for acceptance or payment[5]. The holder enjoys the right to have a duplicate of a bill which he or she has lost (provided that the bill was not overdue at that time)[6]. Finally, the holder has the right to demand payment of the bill and to sue for it if need be[7]. However, any defect in the title of prior parties to the bill affects the holder's right to payment.

It does not follow that the holder of a bill is necessarily its true owner. Suppose, eg, that Right draws a bill on Proper, which is payable to bearer, and gives that bill to Good. If Crook steals the bill from Good then Crook becomes the holder because he is in possession of a bill payable to bearer. But although Crook is the holder, Good remains the true owner of the bill.

Holder for value

A holder for value is a holder who either gives valuable consideration for the bill or who takes a bill where consideration has been given by a prior party to it[8]. The doctrine of consideration is a feature of English law and forms no part of Scots law. It has been said with reference to bills of exchange that: 'According to the law of Scotland onerosity of a bill is to be assumed'[9].

Holder in due course

Status as a holder in due course is incremental, since no one can be a holder in due course unless already a holder and a holder for value[10].

1 1882 Act, s 2 ('holder').
2 1882 Act, s 31(1).
3 1882 Act, s 34(4).
4 1882 Act, s 12.
5 1882 Act, ss 41(1)(a), 45(3).
6 1882 Act, s 69.
7 1882 Act, s 38(1).
8 1882 Act, s 27(1),(2).
9 *Law v Humphrey* (1876) 3 R 1192 at 1193, per Lord President Inglis. There is a presumption that anyone whose signature appears on a bill has given value for it: 1882 Act, s 30(1).
10 1882 Act, s 29(1).

There is a presumption that the holder of a bill is also a holder in due course, but this is rebuttable on the ground that 'the acceptance, issue, or subsequent negotiation of the bill is affected with fraud, duress, or force and fear, or illegality'[1]. If challenged, the onus of proving that he or she took the bill as a holder in due course rests on the holder, who must satisfy the following criteria prescribed by s 29(1) of the 1882 Act.

The bill must be complete and regular

Where a bill or note lacks any of the essential requirements prescribed by the 1882 Act (eg the drawer's signature is absent, or no payee is identified) it is not complete. Where such as bill is negotiated, the transferee does not become a holder in due course. However, if the holder, within a reasonable time of receiving the bill[2], corrects any omissions[3], he or she then becomes a holder in due course. A bill or promissory note is irregular where something on it should arouse suspicion: eg an unauthenticated erasure, or where the payee's indorsement does not replicate the payee's name as shown on the face of the bill[4]. Although s 29(1) talks of the bill being complete and regular 'on the face of it', indorsements are usually on the back of the bill and, as the last example shows, these are treated as being regular. Clearly, the wording of the provision is not interpreted literally[5].

The bill must not be overdue

Suppose that a bill is payable on 12 May 1997. If it has not been paid by that date it is overdue. If an overdue bill is negotiated the transferee will be a holder and may also be a holder for value, but cannot be a holder in due course. Furthermore, no one who takes an overdue bill from such a holder can become a holder in due course[6]. There is a rebuttable presumption that an undated indorsement on an order bill indicates that the bill was negotiated before it became overdue. If an indorsement bears a date which is later than the date of maturity of the bill, the presumption does not arise[7].

If the bill has been dishonoured, the holder must be unaware of that fact

A bill may be dishonoured either by non-acceptance or by non-payment[8]. If the person to whom the bill is negotiated knows that the drawee has refused to accept the bill or has refused to pay it, he or she cannot be a holder in due course[9].

---

1 1882 Act, s 30(2).
2 1882 Act, s 20(2).
3 1882 Act, s 20(1).
4 *Arab Bank Ltd v Ross* [1952] 2 QB 216, CA.
5 *Yeoman Credit Ltd v Gregory* [1963] 1 All ER 245.
6 1882 Act, s 36(2).
7 1882 Act, s 36(4).
8 1882 Act, ss 43 and 47.
9 1882 Act, s 36(5).

The holder must have acted in good faith when taking the bill

The 1882 Act defines 'good faith' as acting honestly and does not infer dishonesty from negligent conduct[1]. There is also a rebuttable presumption that a holder always takes in good faith[2]. Suppose, however, that Red owes £25,000 to Brown and Brown knows that Red is bankrupt. So Brown persuades Red to draw an order bill of exchange for £25,000 on Blue payable to Red, who then negotiates the bill to Brown. This rather obvious ploy is an attempt by Brown to obtain payment in preference to Red's other creditors. Brown cannot be a holder in due course when he has so obviously acted in bad faith[3].

The holder must not have notice of any defect in the title of the person who negotiated the bill to him

This last requirement indicates that a holder in due course is a holder to whom a bill has been *negotiated*[4]. Consequently, although a holder, the payee can never be a holder in due course. The drawer of a bill or note does not negotiate this to the payee, the drawer 'issues'[5] (ie delivers) it to the payee[6]. Where the party negotiating the bill has obtained it, or its acceptance, by fraud, duress, force and fear, or by some other unlawful means (eg theft), or for some illegal consideration, then his or her title is defective. His or her title is also defective where he or she negotiates the bill in breach of faith or in circumstances amounting to fraud[7]. Suppose, eg, that Crook persuades Good to draw a bill or cheque in his favour by fraudulently misrepresenting to Good that payment is due to him. Crook's title to the instrument is defective. If Crook then negotiates the bill or cheque to Soft, Soft will be a holder in due course if he does not know how Crook came by the instrument. But if Soft does know, then he cannot be a holder in due course[8].

The creditor under a regulated consumer credit agreement and the owner under a regulated consumer hire agreement cannot accept payment in the form of a negotiable instrument, other than a cheque or bank notes. Nor can a negotiable instrument of any kind be taken as security for the discharge of a regulated agreement[9]. Furthermore, a cheque taken in payment cannot be negotiated to anyone other than a bank[10]. A holder who contravenes this rule creates a defect in his title[11]. Where a bill of exchange is taken when it should not have been proffered, the taker does not become a holder in due course and has no right to enforce payment

1 1882 Act, s 90. See also *Lipkin Gorman v Karpnale Ltd* [1992] 4 All ER 512, HL.
2 1882 Act, s 30(2).
3 *Banca Popolare di Novara v John Livanos & Sons Ltd* [1965] 2 Lloyd's Rep 149.
4 1882 Act, s 29(1)(b).
5 The first delivery of a bill or promissory note to a holder is termed the 'issue':1882 Act, s 2.
6 *RE Jones Ltd v Waring and Gillow Ltd* [1926] AC 670, HL.
7 1882 Act, s 29(2). The list in this subsection is not exhaustive.
8 *Whistler v Forster* (1863) 14 CBNS 248.
9 Consumer Credit Act 1974, s 123(1), (3). There is an exception to the statement in the text where the creditor or owner does not act in the course of his business (ie non-commercial agreements).
10 1974 Act, s 123(2).
11 1974 Act, s 125(2).

thereunder[1]. But anyone to whom such a bill is negotiated, and who takes it in good faith and for value, and without notice of any defect in the title of the transferor, will be a holder in due course[2]. Likewise, where a cheque has been negotiated to someone other than a bank, the holder of the cheque will be a holder in due course, provided that he or she is unaware of the defect in title of the transferor.

The holder in due course enjoys advantages denied to other parties to a bill. As a holder he or she obviously has the right to demand payment and to sue for this if need be[3]. But, unlike a mere holder, the holder in due course's right to payment is unaffected by a defect in the title of the drawer or of any prior holders of the bill[4]. Suppose, eg, that Good draws a bill of exchange on Hope which is payable to bearer and gives this to Nice. Nasty steals this and, although not the true owner of the bill, he is, nonetheless, its holder. Nasty negotiates this bill by delivering it to Honest. If Honest satisfies the statutory criteria he takes the bill as a holder in due course and becomes its true owner. And as owner, Honest holds the bill free from the defective title of Nasty to the instrument and will be able to enforce payment of the bill. The entitlement of a holder in due course to payment from a party liable on the bill is unaffected by any personal defence which that party may have against a prior party to the bill[4]. The fourth indorser of a bill may, eg, request payment from the third indorser. The third indorser must pay and may not, eg, argue that he or she gave value to the second indorser in the erronious belief that money was due to the second indorser.

NEGOTIATION – THE PROCESS

In order to derive the benefits of negotiability four steps need to be taken: (1) the bill must be drawn in compliance with the statutory definition of what constitutes an enforceable bill of exchange; (2) the bill must be transferred in the manner required by the 1882 Act; (3) negotiation is only effective if done in the way prescribed by the Act; and (4) the bill must be presented for payment and, sometimes, for acceptance. These requirements will now be examined.

Step 1: Drawing an enforceable bill of exchange

A bill of exchange must satisfy the requirements identifiable from the definition of a bill in s 3(1) of the 1882 Act. Forms of bills can be purchased from printers or stationers and, in the case of cheques, are supplied by banks to customers with current accounts. However, even a pre-printed cheques can be incorrectly completed (eg the drawer might forget to sign

1 1974 Act, s 125(1).
2 1974 Act, s 125(4).
3 1882 Act, s 38(1).
4 1882 Act, s 38(2).

it) and a bill of exchange written on a business's stationery or on a blank piece of paper may be incorrectly worded. An incorrectly worded bill of exchange will not be treated as a negotiable instrument and the parties will lose the benefits of negotiability[1]. An example of a bill of exchange is set out below and after that the statutory definition found in s 3(1). Each requirement in that definition has been numbered to correspond with the essential features of the specimen bill.

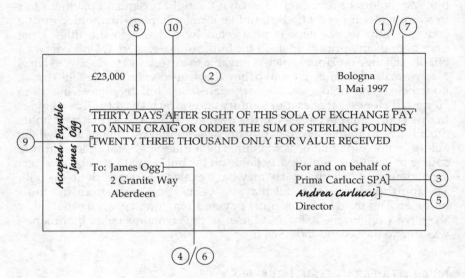

A bill of exchange is (1) an unconditional order (2) in writing, (3) addressed by one person (4) to another, (5) signed by the person giving it, (6) requiring the person to whom it is addressed (7) to pay (8) on demand or at a fixed or determinable future time (9) a sum certain in money (10) to or to the order of a specified person, or to bearer[2].

The parties to this bill are: (a) the drawer (Prima Carlucci SPA) who prepared the bill; (b) the drawee (James Ogg) who was ordered to pay it; and (c) the payee (Anne Craig) who is to receive payment. Since in the example the drawee has indicated his acceptance of the drawer's order to him to pay[3], he is referred to as the 'acceptor'. Sometimes, where payment is to be made by a bankers' documentary credit, the letter of credit may specify that a bill of exchange is to be drawn in a set[4]. Where only one bill of exchange is required this may be referred to (as in the example above) as a 'sola' bill.

---

1 1882 Act, s 3(2).
2 'A cheque is a bill of exchange drawn on a banker payable on demand': 1882 Act, s 73. 'A promissory note is an unconditional promise in writing made by one person to another signed by the maker, engaging to pay, on demand or at a fixed or determinable future time, a sum certain in money, to, or to the order of, a specified person or to bearer': s 83(1).
3 1882 Act, s 17(1).
4 For the rules applicable to bills drawn in a set, see 1882 Act, s 71. A set comprises two or three bills as specified.

'An unconditional order'

The instrument must order the drawee to pay. If it merely requests or suggests payment it is not a bill of exchange. But a bill which states 'Please Pay' is still an order to the drawee to make payment[1]. The order to the drawee must be unconditional. In *Bavins Junr and Sims v London and South Western Bank Ltd*[2], an instrument which directed the drawee to pay on condition that the receipt annexed to it was signed by the payee was held not to be a cheque. But in *Nathan v Ogdens Ltd*[3], an instrument which requested the payee to sign a receipt was held to be a bill of exchange. The difference in result may be explained in this way. The first instrument told the drawee to pay only when satisfied that the receipt had been signed. That is not an unconditional order to the drawee. In the second case the instruction to sign the receipt was addressed to the payee and not to the drawee. There was no linkage between these sets of orders, the payee was ordered to sign the receipt, the drawee was ordered to pay regardless of whether the receipt had been signed or not. 'Pay Smith £3,000 from the proceeds of the sale my etchings' or 'Pay Jones £1,790 out of my rents with you' are not unconditional orders. There is no certainty that there are funds to meet payment, so the order to pay is predicated on the condition that adequate funds exist[4].

'In writing'

Bills of exchange must be in writing and writing is taken to include print, typescript and 'other modes of reproducing words in visible form'[5]. Although electronic bills of exchange are known in other countries (eg France), they are not used in the UK. Their introduction would require the 1882 Act to be amended[6].

'Addressed by one person to another'

There must be a drawer and a drawee and the drawee, if unnamed, must be indicated with reasonable certainty[7]. This is necessary since the holder must know to whom the bill should be presented for acceptance or payment. Drawer and drawee may be the same person, as, eg, where a branch of the Bank of Caledonia issues a draft drawn on its head office. Strictly speaking this cannot be a bill of exchange since the instrument is not addressed by one party to another. However, where drawer and drawee are the same person, the holder has the option of treating the instrument

---

1 *Airdrie Provost v French* (1915) 31 Sh Ct Rep 189. A promissory note stating that its maker 'agrees' to pay is valid: *McTaggart v MacEachern's Judicial Factor* 1949 SC 503, OH.
2 [1900] 1 QB 270, CA.
3 [1905] 94 LT 126, CA.
4 1882 Act, s 3(3).
5 1882 Act, s 2; Interpretation Act 1978, s 5 and Sch 1.
6 This has been recommended: *Report of the Review Committee on Banking Services: Law and Practice* (the Jack Report) (Cm 622) (1989) recommendation 8(9).
7 1882 Act, s 6(1).

as either a bill of exchange or a promissory note[1]. A bill drawn on joint drawees is valid but not one drawn on alternative or successive drawees[2].

'Signed by the person giving it'

Until a bill is signed by the drawer it remains inchoate and unenforceable as a bill. That signature may, however, be added at some later time[3]. A signature must be subscribed[4] and may be handwritten in ink or pencil (rather risky). Notarial execution is competent where the drawer is blind or illiterate. A stamped signature is probably valid[5] but not a stamped company name[6]. Signature by initials is competent[7] but has two drawbacks: (a) the drawer has to prove that the signature is his or hers and that this was his or her usual mode of signing; and (b) summary diligence cannot be done on a bill or promissory note which requires to be proved before it can be accepted or paid[8]. It appears that signature by mark is sufficient where this is the drawer's normal mode of signature[9]. The use of a trade (or an assumed) name binds the signatory as though he or she had used his or her real name and the signature of a firm name is equivalent to the signature of all of the partners[10].

When company officers, such as directors, sign cheques they must be careful not to do so in a manner which makes them (and not the company) liable. An officer who signs as the acceptor of a bill drawn on his or her company is personally liable to pay the bill if the company is wrongly named[11]. An officer signing a bill of exchange or company cheque must do so in a manner which clearly indicates that this is done in a representative capacity, acting as the company's agent, otherwise there is personal liability on the bill[12]. Here are three different ways in which a bill drawn by a company might be signed:

A	B	C
Anne Smith, Director	Corgarff Gardens Ltd	For and on behalf of
Ian Wilkie, Secretary	*Anne Smith*, Director	Corgarff Gardens Ltd
Corgarff Gardens Ltd	*Ian Wilkie*, Secretary	*Anne Smith*, Director
		Ian Wilkie, Secretary

1 1882 Act, s 5(2); *Universal Import Export GmbH v Bank of Scotland* 1995 SLT 1318. The holder also has this option where the drawee is fictitious or lacks contractual capacity.
2 1882 Act, s 6(2). The drawer or indorsers of a bill may, however, name a 'referee in case of need' (ie someone to whom the holder can look to, should he or she so choose, if the bill is dishonoured by non-acceptance or non-payment): 1882 Act, s 15. This practice is virtually obsolete.
3 1882 Act, s 20.
4 Bell *Principles* s 323.
5 *Goodman v J Eban Ltd* [1954] 1 QB 550; *Lazarus Estates Ltd v Beasley* [1956] 1 QB 702, CA.
6 *Lazarus Estates Ltd v Beasley* above.
7 Bell *Principles* s 323.
8 See generally *Summers v Marianski* (1843) 6 D 286.
9 As might be the case where, eg, the drawer is illiterate. Bell *Principles* s 323; *Brown v Johnstoun* (1662) Mor 16802; *Cockburn v Gibson* 8 Dec 1815 FC. See also Cusine and Meston 'Execution of Deeds by a Mark' (1993) 38 JLSS 270.
10 1882 Act, s 23.
11 Companies Act 1985, s 349(4); *Scottish and Newcastle Breweries Ltd v Blair* 1967 SLT 72, OH. The company may, however, choose to pay the bill.
12 1882 Act, s 26(1).

Smith and Wilkie are personally liable where the bill is signed in manner **A**. Their designations, 'Director' and 'Secretary', simply describe their position as company agents but do not indicate that when they signed the bill they were acting as its agents[1]. Smith and Wilkie would not, however, be held personally liable for signing in manner **B**. Placing the company's name before their signatures indicates that the bill is the company's and not the officer's[2]. **C** is undoubtedly the safest way of signing an instrument. Use of the words 'per pro' or 'For and on behalf of' indicate clearly that the bill is that of the company and that the officers have signed when acting on its behalf[3]. Where the signature is 'per pro' (*per procurationem*), however, it operates as notice to any holder of the bill that the principal (drawer) is only liable where the agents (officers) were acting within the scope of their actual authority[4]. Where the signature is 'for and on behalf of' a company, the apparent authority of the officers to sign all bills may be assumed[5].

'To pay on demand or at a fixed or determinable future time'

Bills of exchange are either 'demand bills' or 'time bills' according to when they are payable[6]. A demand bill, as the name suggests, is one which is payable whenever the payee so demands. A time bill will only be paid at a specific time. Sections 10 and 11 of the 1882 Act define demand and time bills respectively by reference to the way in which the order to pay on the face of the bill is expressed. A bill of exchange will be treated as a demand bill when it orders the drawee to pay (a) on demand; or (b) at sight; or (c) on presentment of the bill; or (d) does not state when it is payable[7]. Furthermore, if a bill is accepted or indorsed when it is overdue, then, it is regarded as payable on demand[8]. A cheque, while it orders a bank to pay the payee, does not specify when this should be done. Consequently a cheque is a demand bill and is defined as 'a bill of exchange drawn on a banker payable on demand'[9].

Where an instrument which acknowledges a loan promises to repay it 'by' a specific date, that date is a deadline and the drawer has the option of repaying before the deadline is reached. Such an instrument may be treated as a receipt, but it is not a promissory note since it is not payable at a 'fixed or determinable future time'[10]. A bill which states that it is payable 30 days after the date on which it was drawn is a time bill. The specimen bill above is also a time bill because it is payable 30 days after it is

---

1 *Brebner v Henderson* 1925 SC 643; *Brown v Sutherland* (1875) 2 R 615; *McMeekin v Easton* (1889) 16 R 363.
2 *Chapman v Smethurst* [1909] 1 KB 927, CA (promissory note); *Bondina Ltd v Rollaway Shower Blinds Ltd* [1986] 1 All ER 564, CA (cheque).
3 Companies Act 1985, s 37; *Brebner v Henderson* 1925 SC 643.
4 1882 Act, s 25.
5 Chalmers and Guest *Bills of Exchange* (14th edn, 1991), pp 209–213.
6 Promissory notes may also be payable on demand or at a fixed or determinable future time: 1882 Act, s 83(1).
7 1882 Act, s 10(1).
8 1882 Act, s 10(2).
9 1882 Act, s 73.
10 1882 Act, s 83(1); *Claydon v Bradley* [1987] 1 All ER 522, CA.

presented to the drawee for acceptance (ie 30 days after the drawee has sight of the bill)[1]. In both instances the bill complies with the requirement that payment be ordered at a 'fixed or determinable future time'[2]. If a bill dated 1 May were payable 30 days after date, payment would be due on 31 May not on 30 May. In calculating the time for payment, the date from which time begins to run is excluded but the day on which payment is due is included[3]. A bill expressed to be payable '10 days after date', but which omits to state the date on which it was drawn, is not, however, invalid as a result of the omission[4]. But since it is impossible to ascertain the date on which payment should be made, the holder of such a bill may insert the date on which it was issued[5]. Were a bill to declare that it was payable *'after* sight' it would be invalid since there is no fixed or determinable time for payment. A dated instrument expressed to be payable 'at 90 days', the word 'sight' having been deleted, has been held not to be a valid bill[6]. However, where a bill payable so many days after sight has been accepted, but the acceptance is not dated, the holder may insert the date on which it was accepted[7].

Where an instrument is not payable at a fixed period after date or sight, it will still be a valid bill of exchange if it orders payment to be made 'after the occurrence of a specified event which is certain to happen, though the time of happening may be uncertain'[8]. So an instrument which declares that it is payable on White's death is valid, whereas one payable on his fiftieth birthday is not. White's death is an event which is certain to happen one day, even though its date cannot be predicted in advance. But White's fiftieth birthday is not an event which is certain to happen; he might not live that long. So the order to pay is contingent on White's survival to fifty and 'an instrument ... payable on a contingency is not a bill'[9]. Such a bill would not be revalidated should White actually reach his fiftieth birthday. With one exception, an invalid time bill does not automatically become a demand bill. That exception applies to a bill which is accepted or indorsed after it has become overdue. So if a bill payable 30 days after 1 May was presented and accepted on 4 June, it would be overdue, but it would then be payable on demand against the acceptor or anyone who indorsed it after 31 May[10].

'A sum certain in money'

An instrument which orders payment to be made other than in money (eg in goods)[11] cannot be either a bill of exchange or promissory note[12]. In

1 1882 Act, s 11.
2 1882 Act, s 3(1).
3 1882 Act, s 14(2).
4 1882 Act, s 3(4).
5 1882 Act, s 12.
6 *Korea Exchange Bank v Debenhams (Central Buying) Ltd* [1979] 1 Lloyd's Rep 548, CA.
7 1882 Act, s 12.
8 1882 Act, s 11(2).
9 1882 Act, s 11.
10 1882 Act, s 10(2). For the position of the acceptor and indorsers see ss 18(2) and 36.
11 *Dixon v Bovill* (1856) 3 Macq 1, HL (iron rails); *McDonald v Belcher* [1904] AC 429, CA (gold dust).
12 For the definition of a promissory note, see the 1882 Act, s 83(1) .

Dickie v Singh[1] the pursuer argued that the following was a promissory note:

> 'I Mr Chanan Singh do hereby agree to pay Dickie and Renton the sum of £950 to be paid at the rate of £50 per month. First payment due on the first day of every month commencing February 1st 1969. Also the present staff to be employed and paid by myself for the next two weeks'.

Since this instrument promised to do something additional to making payment it was not treated as a promissory note. The sum must be certain and specific. 'Pay £500 together with all other sums due' is not an order to pay 'a sum certain in money'. However, 'Pay £500 with interest at the rate of 12.5 per cent' is an order to pay a precise sum and an instrument containing this direction is valid[2]. If there is a discrepancy between the sum expressed in words and the sum expressed in figures, the former is taken to be the amount payable[3].

'To or to the order of a specified person, or to bearer'

Bills are also classified by the 1882 Act as 'bearer' and 'order' bills[4]. Whether a bill is a bearer or an order bill depends on how the payee is designated. In a bearer bill the payee is stated to be the bearer[5]. In an order bill the payee is either the person so named or the person referred to as his or her order. Such a bill must also not prohibit transfer[6].

Bearer bills	Order bills	Invalid bills
Pay Bearer	Pay Daniel Allan	Pay Cash
Pay John Smith or Bearer	Pay Daniel Allan or Order	Pay Cash or Order

A cheque made out to 'Cash' or to 'Cash or Order' is not an order bill since 'cash' is not a synonym for 'specified person'. Nor is it a bearer bill since it does not state that it is payable to bearer[7]. An instrument payable to 'Cash or Bearer' might be treated as payable to bearer[8].

Step 2: signing and delivering the instrument

To be liable on a bill or cheque one has to do two things: (1) sign it[9]; and (2) deliver it to the party intended[10]. 'Delivery' means either the actual or

---

1 1974 SLT 129.
2 1882 Act, s 9(1). A sum is also certain if payable in stated instalments, or stated instalments with the proviso that if an instalment is missed the whole sum is payable, or in accordance with either a stated rate of exchange or one which may be ascertained from the bill.
3 1882 Act, s 9(2).
4 1882 Act, s 8(2). This classification also applies to cheques and promissory notes.
5 1882 Act, s 8(3). A bill is also a bearer bill where the only or the last indorsement is a blank one.
6 1882 Act, s 8(4).
7 *Orbit Mining and Trading Co Ltd v Westminster Bank Ltd* [1963] 1 QB 794, CA.
8 *Chalmers and Guest* p 29.
9 1882 Act, s 23.
10 1882 Act, s 21(1). See *Martini & Co v Steel and Craig* (1878) 6 R 342. Delivery is also required in the case of a promissory note: 1882 Act, s 84.

the constructive transfer of possession[1]. So the drawer of a bill incurs no liability to the payee unless and until he or she signs as drawer and then 'issues' it to the payee (actual delivery) or to the payee's agent (constructive delivery). The drawee is not liable to the payee until he or she signs the bill as 'acceptor' and then redelivers it to the payee. An indorser, having signed as such, must then deliver the bill to the indorsee in order to become liable to the latter. There are, however, three exceptions to the rule that delivery is a prerequisite for liability. The first is where the drawee notifies acceptance to the payee or to anyone else entitled to payment[2]. The second is a rebuttable presumption that a bill which is not in the possession of any of its signatories has been validly and unconditionally delivered to a holder[3]. The third is that where the bill is in the hands of a holder in due course there is an irrebuttable presumption that all signatories agreed to its delivery[4]. Suppose, eg, that Mustard draws a bearer bill on White which Black steals from her office, before it is posted to Green, and then negotiates it to Blue. Although this bill has not been issued, its valid delivery to Blue is conclusively presumed if he does not know that the bill was stolen and takes it in good faith and for value. In an action by Blue against Mustard for payment of the bill, the latter cannot argue that the bill is unenforceable because it was never issued.

Step 3: negotiating the instrument

A bill of exchange is negotiated by transferring it in such a way as to make the transferee a holder of the bill[5]. In the case of bearer bills, the bearer is the holder and negotiation is effected simply by the bearer delivering the instrument to another[6]. The holder of a bearer bill who negotiates it in this way is termed a 'transferor by delivery'[7]. Because his or her signature is not needed to negotiate a bearer bill, a transferor by delivery is not liable on it[8]. However, as between a transferor by delivery and his or her immediate transferee, the former warrants that the 'bill is what it purports to be' (eg that a signature is not a forgery or that the bill has not been materially altered); that he or she has the right to transfer it (ie that his or her title is not defective); and also that he or she is 'unaware of any fact which renders it valueless' (eg that the drawer and drawee were insolvent)[9].

The holder of an order bill is the payee and any subsequent indorsee[10]. Consequently, order bills are negotiated by delivery plus the holder's indorsement to another[11]. It is, however, important to note that the first delivery or 'issue' of a bill by the drawer to the payee does not constitute

---

1 1882 Act, s 2.
2 See the proviso to s 21(1) of the 1882 Act.
3 1882 Act, s 21(3).
4 1882 Act, s 21(2).
5 1882 Act, s 31(1).
6 1882 Act, s 31(2). Section 2 of the Act defines a 'holder' as being, inter alia, the bearer.
7 1882 Act, s 58(1).
8 1882 Act, s 58(2).
9 1882 Act, s 58(3). The position is the same for promissory notes payable to bearer: s 89(1).
10 1882 Act, s 2.
11 1882 Act, s 31(3); *RE Jones Ltd v Waring and Gillow Ltd* [1926] AC 670, HL.

its negotiation by the former to the latter[1]. Since a bill is not negotiated to the payee, the payee cannot, therefore, be treated as a holder in due course. This is because negotiation to a party is a precondition for that party satisfying the statutory criteria for being a holder in due course[2]. The remainder of this section concentrates on three issues: (a) the consequences of not indorsing an order bill when delivering it to another; (b) the different types of indorsement and their effect; and (c) cheque crossings.

Non-indorsement

Where the holder of an order bill simply delivers it to another without indorsing it, this does not prevent the transferee from suing on the bill in his or her own name[3]. Nevertheless, such a transferee is seriously disadvantaged when it comes to enforcing payment. Because the bill has not been negotiated in the prescribed manner, the transferee is not a holder, being neither the payee nor an indorsee, and cannot be a holder in due course if not a holder in the first place[4]. Nor is the transferee regarded as a bearer, since the bill was not drawn payable to bearer in the first place[5]. Logically, therefore, the transferee acquires the bill subject to any defects in the right of the transferor to obtain payment: 'the holder of the bill must, if it be payable to order, obtain an indorsement, . . . Until he does so, he is merely in the position of an assignee . . . and has no better right than his assignor'[6]. The 1882 Act reflects this view exactly[7]. Because non-indorsement of an order bill has so serious an effect, the transferee of such a bill has the right to return it to the transferor and insist that it be indorsed[7]. However, only the first transferee enjoys this right. This is because s 31(4) refers to a 'holder' who transfers a bill without indorsing it. Since the first transferee is not a holder, unless and until the indorsement of the transferor is obtained, further transfer by the first transferee of an unindorsed bill cannot be transfer by a holder.

Types of indorsement

The general rule is that an indorsement must appear on the bill itself[8]. But where a promissory note was a constituent part of a document, an indorsement written on the back of that document, though not on the back of the part which was the note, was held valid[9]. If there is no space left for writing an indorsement, as may happen where an order bill has been negotiated frequently, a paper slip, termed an 'allonge', may be attached

1 *RE Jones v Waring and Gillow Ltd* above.
2 1882 Act, s 29(1)(b).
3 *Hood v Stewart* (1890) 17 R 749. The English courts, however, take the view that a transferee cannot sue in his or her own name on an unindorsed bill: *Chalmers and Guest* p 301.
4 1882 Act, s 29(1) defining a holder in due course.
5 1882 Act, s 8(3). While it is true that a blank indorsement on an order bill converts it into a bearer bill, this cannot help the transferee in the situation where there is no indorsement..
6 *Whistler v Forster* (1863) 14 CBNS 248 at 257, per Willes J.
7 1882 Act, s 31(4).
8 1882 Act, s 32(1). The same holds true for cheques and promissory notes.
9 *KHR Financings Ltd v Jackson* 1977 SLT (Sh Ct) 6.

to the bill and further indorsements written thereon. An indorsement written on a copy of a bill of exchange is valid if the bill was either issued or negotiated in a country which permits the use of copy bills[1].

Normally indorsements are found on the back of a bill, but there is nothing which forbids their appearance on its face. The 1882 Act envisages four types of indorsements and, depending on the type used, their effect may be: (1) to prevent negotiation; (2) to affect negotiability; and (3) to alter the nature of the bill. The various types of indorsement are depicted below. Each and its effects are then discussed.

A   B   C   D

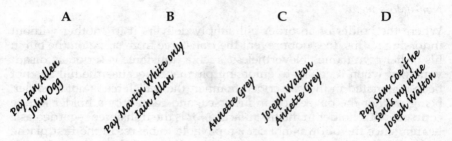

Type **A** is a special indorsement. A special indorsement is one where the indorser signs and also specifies the indorsee to whom the bill is payable. Had Ogg written, 'Pay Ian Allan or Order', and signed it, that too would be a special indorsement[2].

Type **B** is a restrictive indorsement. It instructs the drawee that payment should only be made to White[3]. Further negotiation is prohibited[4] and the bill ceases to be negotiable[5]. Consequently, should White indorse the bill to Black, Black would not hold a negotiable instrument and could not, therefore, obtain a title which was better than White's. A bill which has been restrictively indorsed loses its negotiable quality forever[6]. White could not override the restrictive indorsement by a special indorsement to Black. Had Allan written, 'Pay Martin White for the account of Peter Jones', that too would be a restrictive indorsement. Allan's indorsement makes it clear that White does not become owner of the bill, with the right to collect payment for himself, but that he is merely Allan's agent to collect and apply payment to Jones. A restrictive indorsement may, however, be worded in a way which permits transfer of the bill. For example, if Allan's indorsement read, 'Pay Martin White *or order* for the account of Peter Jones', it is clear from the words 'or order' that White can transfer the bill to Brown to collect payment in order to see that Jones is paid[7].

---

1 1882 Act, s 32(1). Allonges are rarely used on 'inland bills', ie bills drawn and payable within the British Islands or drawn within these on someone resident therein: 1882 Act, s 4(1).
2 1882 Act, s 34(2).
3 1882 Act, s 35(2).
4 1882 Act, s 35(1).
5 1882 Act, s 8(1): 'When a bill contains words prohibiting transfer, or indicating an intention that it should not be transferable, it is valid as between the parties thereto, but it is not negotiable'.
6 1882 Act, s 36(1)(a).
7 1882 Act, s 35(2).

However, a restrictive indorsement which permits transfer does not revive the negotiability of the bill. Consequently, Brown's right to collect payment is no better than White's[1].

Type **C** is a blank indorsement. The indorser, Annette Grey, has signed the back of the bill but no indorsee is identified[2]. A blank indorsement turns an order bill into a bearer bill[2] which can then be negotiated by delivery alone[3]. Blank indorsements are undesirable for security reasons. Suppose that Grey, having blank indorsed the bill delivers it to Walton. Crook, however, steals the bill and presents it to the drawee for payment. Since this bill is now payable to bearer, if the drawee pays Crook without knowledge of the theft, then he is not liable to pay Walton[4]. To protect the holder of a blank indorsed order bill, the 1882 Act permits the holder to convert the blank indorsement into a special indorsement by adding his or her name above the indorser's signature[5]. This is what Walton has done in the example above. It will be apparent from what has been said that a bill may begin life as an order bill, become a bearer bill, and then revert to being an order bill. But a bill which starts out as an bearer bill cannot be converted into an order bill by adding a special indorsement[6].

Type **D** is a conditional indorsement. If the drawer's order to the drawee is conditional the bill is unenforceable as a bill of exchange[7]. But a condition in an indorsement can be ignored by the payee[8].

Cheque crossings

The bank on which a crossed cheque is drawn (the paying bank) will not pay cash to the holder of that cheque. It will only pay the proceeds of the cheque to the holder's own bank (the collecting bank). So crossing a cheque decreases (though it does not eliminate) the risk of payment being made to a party who is not entitled to receive it. Crossings must appear on the face (not the reverse) of cheques[9]. Any crossing of the type permitted by the 1882 Act is deemed to be a material part of the cheque, which, if obliterated or altered, renders the cheque void against everyone except the person who made, or was responsible for making, the alteration[10].

The several types of crossing permitted by the 1882 Act are depicted below. Crossings which do not bear the name of the bank to which payment must be made (types **A-D**) are termed 'general' crossings[11]. Crossings which designate the bank to which payment must be made (types **E-F**) are termed 'special' crossings[12]. General crossings require the

1 1882 Act, s 35(3).
2 1882 Act, s 34(1).
3 1882 Act, s 31(2).
4 *Auchteroni & Co v Midland Bank Ltd* [1928] 2 KB 294.
5 1882 Act, s 34(4).
6 *Chalmers and Guest* p 312, citing *Miller Associates (Australia) Pty Ltd v Bennington Pty Ltd* [1975] 7 ALR 144.
7 1882 Act, s 3(1),(2).
8 1882 Act, s 33.
9 1882 Act, s 76(1),(2): 'Where a cheque bears across its face . . .'.
10 1882 Act, ss 78, 64(1). However, s 77 sanctions certain alterations made by holders and banks.
11 1882 Act, s 76(1).
12 1882 Act, s 76(2). Special crossing of cheques is rare today.

use of two parallel transverse lines. Special crossings do not require this, though lines are usually added[1]. The 'Account Payee' (type **G**) crossing was only given statutory effect in 1992, though it was regarded as a valid crossing long before that[2].

A   B   C   D   E   F   G

(crossing diagram with labels: A '& Co'; B '& Co / Not Negotiable'; C; D 'Not Negotiable'; E 'Bank of Caledonia'; F 'Bank of Caledonia / Not Negotiable'; G 'A/C Payee')

It is important to appreciate that a cheque which is crossed 'Not Negotiable' is still transferable. Since a negotiable instrument is capable of passing to a transferee (who is a holder in due course) a better title than that of the transferor, then to state that a cheque is 'not negotiable' is to deprive it of its status as a negotiable instrument and, consequently, to treat it as any other document representing a right to be paid: ie, the transferee's right to payment will be no better than that of the transferor[3]. The effect of the 'not negotiable' crossing has been described with clarity:

> 'The section [s 81] does not say that the person to whom the payee of the cheque gives a crossed cheque marked "not negotiable" shall not become the transferee of the cheque, but merely that he shall not take a better title than that which the person from whom he took it had. *The transferability of the cheque is not affected by the words "not negotiable" but only its negotiability*'[4].

The only effective way to prevent a cheque being transferred by the payee is to cross it 'Account Payee': 'Where a cheque is crossed and bears across its face the words "account payee" or "a/c payee", either with or without the word "only", the cheque shall not be transferable, but shall only be valid as between the parties thereto'[5]. The account payee crossing is found on most pre-printed cheques, and such cheques will only be collected for the payee named thereon and no one else. A bill of exchange crossed 'not negotiable' has been held not to be transferable[6].

Imagine that Gardner draws a cheque for £500, crossed 'A/C Payee', on his bank, the Bank of Caledonia, in favour of Butcher. The cheque is posted to Butcher, who banks with Scotia Bank plc. Butcher will present

---

1 1882 Act, s 76(1),(2).
2 *Akrokerri (Atlantic) Mines Ltd v Economic Bank* [1904] 2 KB 465.
3 1882 Act, s 81.
4 *Great Western Rly Co v London and County Banking Co Ltd* [1900] 2 QB 464 at 474–475, CA, per Vaughan Williams LJ (emphasis added). See also [1901] AC 414 at 418, HL, per Lord Halsbury LC; *Universal Guarantee Pty Ltd v National Bank of Australasia Ltd* [1965] 2 All ER 98, PC.
5 1882 Act, s 81A (added by Cheques Act 1992, s 1).
6 *Hibernian Bank Ltd v Gysin and Hanson* [1938] 2 KB 384. Sections 81 and 81A of the 1882 Act apply only to 'crossed cheques'. In the case of a bill, 'not negotiable' can be read as 'indicating an intention that [the bill] should not be transferable': s 8(1).

this cheque to the branch of Scotia Bank plc where he has his current account and the cheque will now enter the clearing process. That process has been neatly summarised thus: 'A cheque moves from collecting to paying bank and draws or sucks the funds in the opposite direction'[1]. Butcher's branch-bank is called the 'collecting bank' because it collects the proceeds of the cheque. Gardener's branch-bank is, for obvious reasons, termed the 'paying bank'. (This cheque clearing process may be achieved either by physical transfer of cheques or by the electronic transmission of information about these. If the former method is employed, then, Butcher's branch sends the cheque to the Scotia Bank's clearing office which, in turn, sends it to the Bank of Caledonia's clearing office from where it will be sent to the branch of that bank where Gardner has his current account. Gardener's branch will then pay the proceeds of the cheque to Butcher's branch. This process will take from three to five days to accomplish. Electronic presentation of Gardner's cheque, however, permits 'truncation' of the clearing process[2]. Butcher's bank will transmit information about Gardner's cheque, but not the cheque itself, to the latter's bank which will debit his account. This process clearly is faster than the physical transfer of paper.) Suppose, however, that Baker steals the cheque from Butcher and takes it to the branch of the Bank of Caledonia where Gardner keeps his account. Gardener's bank must not pay the proceeds of this cheque to Baker. If it does, then it will have to recredit Gardener's account with the £500[3]. Furthermore, since the cheque was in Butcher's possession when it was stolen[4], and since Butcher was its 'true owner', the Bank of Caledonia will also have to make good Butcher's loss[5].

Step 4: presenting an instrument for acceptance or payment

Once the payee or a subsequent holder has possession of a bill, cheque, or promissory note and wishes payment he must present (ie deliver) it to the drawee. The 1882 Act refers to two types of presentment – presentment for acceptance and presentment for payment. From this one might conclude that negotiable instruments must first be presented for acceptance and then be presented a second time for payment. This is not so. There is no general requirement that bills must be presented for acceptance[6]. Indeed, neither cheques nor promissory notes can be presented for acceptance. Since a cheque simply orders the drawer's bank to take money from the drawer's own account, acceptance is unnecessary Furthermore cheques are payable on demand[7], and bills payable on demand do not need to be presented for acceptance. Because a promissory note represents the

---

1 *Report of the Review Committee on Banking Services: Law and Practice* (the Jack Report) (Cm 622) (1989), App E323.
2 Rules concerning electronic presentation of cheques came into force on 28 November 1996: the Deregulation (Bills of Exchange) Order 1996, SI 1996/2993. These are further discussed later.
3 1882 Act, s 79(2); *Phillips v Italian Bank Ltd* 1934 SLT 78, OH.
4 Except where a creditor requests remittance by post, the debtor remains liable to make payment if the cheque is lost or stolen: *Robb v Gow Bros and Gemmell* (1905) 8 F 90; *Coats v Glasgow Corpn Gas Dept* (1912) 28 Sh Ct Rep 38.
5 1882 Act, s 79(2).
6 1882 Act, s 39(3).
7 1882 Act, s 73.

maker's promise to pay, logically, his or her promise does not require his or her further acceptance thereof[1]. Bills payable on sight or on presentment need not be presented for acceptance. Why then will a bill be presented for acceptance?

Presentment for acceptance

It has already been noted that discounting a bill is easier when it has been accepted. Moreover, a bill accepted prior to its date of maturity is much easier to negotiate. And where a bill is payable after sight, presentment (within a reasonable time) is necessary to calculate the date of maturity[2]. Another reason for presenting a bill for acceptance (the doing of summary diligence) will be discussed later.

What does acceptance of a bill do? The answer is straightforward. Acceptance converts the drawee into its acceptor who, as such, promises to obey the drawer's order to pay[3]. The holder of an accepted bill knows that payment is *almost* guaranteed when it is subsequently presented to the acceptor for payment. There are two reasons for this note of qualification.

The first, is because s 54(1) of the 1882 Act provides that the acceptor 'engages that he will pay [the bill] according to the tenor of his acceptance'[4]. This means that, although the drawee may choose to accept it without qualification (a general acceptance), he or she is nonetheless entitled to impose conditions to be satisfied before payment will be made (a qualified acceptance)[5]. For example, a contract for the sale of goods might specify that payment is to be made by bill of exchange drawn on the buyer for the purchase price of the goods. The buyer (as drawee) might accept the bill as follows: 'Accepted payable on condition that the goods conform to description as per bill of lading.' This is a qualified acceptance and payment will only be made if the condition is met[6]. However, the holder of a bill is entitled to a general acceptance and is, therefore, justified (1) in refusing to take a qualified acceptance and (2) in treating the bill as dishonoured by non-acceptance[7]. A holder is best advised not to take a qualified acceptance because, unless they have authorised the holder to do so, or agree to it thereafter, the drawer and any prior indorsers are no longer under any liability to ensure payment[8]. The drawer and any prior indorsers to whom the holder has notified the qualified acceptance will be deemed to have agreed to it unless they notify their dissent within a reasonable time of receiving notice[9]. The drawee may grant partial accep-

---

1   1882 Act, s 89(3).
2   1882 Act, s 39(1). See also ss 14(3) and 40(1).
3   1882 Act, ss 17(1), 54(1).
4   Although a promissory note is not presented for acceptance, the liability of its maker is similar to that of an acceptor and, consequently, he 'engages that he will pay it according to its tenor': 1882 Act, s 88.
5   1882 Act, s 19(1).
6   1882 Act, s 19(2)(a). The subsection gives further examples of qualified acceptances.
7   1882 Act, s 44(1).
8   1882 Act, s 44(2).
9   1882 Act, s 44(3).

tance of a bill[1]: eg, where the acceptance of a bill drawn for £1000 states – 'Accepted payable £500 only'. The holder may take this, since it gives him or her half of the amount drawn, and treat the bill as dishonoured as regards the sum outstanding. In this case, the drawer and prior indorsers remain liable on the bill provided the holder notifies them of the partial acceptance[2].

The second reason for qualification, rests on the fact that the drawee may dispute certain matters with the presenter of the bill. Where a person who holds a bearer or order bill as a holder in due course requests the acceptor to make payment, the acceptor cannot refuse that request by arguing that (a) the drawer does not exist; (b) the drawer's signature is not genuine but a forgery; and (c) the drawer lacks capacity or authority to draw the bill[3]. Furthermore, and because indorsement is necessary for the negotiation of order bills, the acceptor of such a bill cannot refuse payment on the grounds that either the drawer or the payee lacked capacity to indorse the bill[4]. However, since the 1882 Act says nothing about the genuineness of indorsements, the acceptor can refuse payment, even to a holder in due course, on the grounds that either the drawer's or the payee's indorsement is forged or that it is unauthorised[4].

What happens if the drawee refuses to accept a bill of exchange[5]? Because one cannot be liable as a drawer, indorser, or acceptor of a bill unless one signs it as such[6], the drawee who refuses to sign his acceptance of the bill incurs no liability on it. But, the drawer has (self-evidently) signed the bill, as have any indorsers, and they are, prima facie, liable to pay the holder[7]. An inland bill[8] which has been refused does not, subsequently, have to be presented for payment but confers on the holder the right to seek immediate payment from the drawer and any prior indorsers[9]. So presentment for acceptance speeds up a holder's right of recourse. But this right is contingent upon the holder notifying the dishonour to the drawer and indorsers[10]. Notification may be written, oral, or inferred from the fact that the bill has been returned to the drawer or an indorser[11]. It follows that a drawer or indorser to whom notice of dishonour has not been given, is no longer liable on the bill[12]. But non-acceptance does not mean that the bill cannot be negotiated thereafter, and, if it is, the

1 1882 Act, s 19(2)(b).
2 1882 Act, s 44(2).
3 1882 Act, s 54(2)(a). In the case of a promissory note, the maker cannot, in a question with the holder in due course, deny the existence of the payee and his capacity to indorse it: s 88.
4 1882 Act, s 54(2)(b),(c).
5 One option, preserved by s 65 of the 1882 Act, but obsolete in practice, is for someone who is not a party to the bill to accept it 'for honour supra protest'. See also ss 66–68.
6 1882 Act, s 23.
7 1882 Act, s 42.
8 An inland bill is one 'which is or on the face of it purports to be (a) both drawn and payable within the British Islands, or (b) drawn within the British Islands upon some person resident therein. Any other bill is a foreign bill': 1882 Act, s 4(1).
9 1882 Act, s 43(2).
10 1882 Act, s 48.
11 1882 Act, s 49(5),(6).
12 1882 Act, s 48.

drawer or indorser to whom notice is not given remains liable to a holder in due course[1]. Notice of dishonour looks like this:

MacStrang, Geddes & Co
Solicitors and Notaries Public
Garden House, 21/25 Pitt Road
ABERDEEN AB9 2ZX
Telephone: 01224-658967 Fax: 01224-650967

To Grampian Widgets Ltd   24 November 1996
Gateside Square West
Aberdeen AB12 7YJ

TAKE NOTICE that a bill for £5,000 (five thousand pounds sterling) drawn by you under date 6 September 1996 on Sparke & Plugg Electronics Ltd, 18 Beckett Street, Aberdeen, payable one month after date, has been DISHONOURED by non-acceptance and that you are held responsible therefor.

Lucy MacStrang

Agent for ABCA plc

Partners: L MacStrang MA LLB NP; J Geddes LLB NP; B Cox LLB Dip LP NP

It will be seen from the example that the notice was served on behalf of the holders, ABCA plc, by their solicitor. Notice of dishonour may either be given by the holder or by an agent for the holder and, if it is given by the latter, notice may be in the agent's own name or in the holder's name[2].

With a foreign bill[3], giving notice is not enough to preserve the holder's right of recourse. Such a bill must be noted and protested[4]. But if the bill is presented for acceptance and refused, it need not be subsequently presented for payment[5]: again this speeds up the holder's right of recourse. Noting and protest are not necessary to preserve the holder's right of recourse in the case of an inland bill, but they are necessary if the holder wishes to do summary diligence on an inland bill[6]. Noting and protest are intended to supply incontrovertible proof of dishonour and, again, by presenting a bill for acceptance the holder speeds up his remedies.

If the holder of a bill sues the drawer or a prior indorser for reimbursement on the bill, the action is one for payment of a debt. Normally one requires a court decree before payment of a debt may be enforced by way of diligence. Summary diligence, however, as the term suggests, does not first require a decree and gives the holder a speedy chance to be reim-

---

1 1882 Act, s 48 proviso (1); *Dunn v O'Keefe* (1816) 5 M & S 282.
2 1882 Act, s 49(1),(2).
3 1882 Act, s 4(1).
4 1882 Act, s 51(2). In the case of a foreign promissory note, protest is unnecessary: s 89(4).
5 1882 Act, s 51(2). The bill may, however, be protested for non-payment at the holder's option: s 51(3).
6 1882 Act, s 98.

bursed from the debtor's property or earnings. Summary diligence is competent against the drawer and any prior indorsers of a bill which has been presented for either acceptance or payment and refused. But summary diligence cannot be done on a bill which is not, on its face, complete and regular: eg an undated bill[1], a bill which is signed with initials or by mark[2], or one which has been torn up[3]. It is important to note that summary diligence cannot be done on a cheque dishonoured by non-payment[4].

Noting and protest are separate procedures and normally done by a solicitor who is a notary public[5]. They must be done on the face of the bill and at the place where it was dishonoured[6]. A protest for non-acceptance must be registered within six months from the date of the bill; a protest for non-payment must be registered within six months of the date on which payment became due[7]. Registration is in the books of the court enjoying jurisdiction over the party against whom summary diligence is to be done[8]. A bill which has been protested for non-acceptance looks like this:

£5,000

26/11/96
p.n.acc.
L. Macstrang N.P.

Gateside Square West
Aberdeen
6 September 1996

One month after date pay ABCA plc or Order the sum of £5,000 (five thousand pounds sterling).

To: Sparke & Plugg Electronics Ltd
18 Beckett Street
Aberdeen

For and on behalf of
Grampian Widgets Ltd
Alan Jones
Director

If protested for non-payment the abbreviation 'p.n.p.' would appear on the face of the bill.

Normally the drawee who accepts a bill will write 'Accepted' on it and add his signature: though his signature alone is enough to render him liable as acceptor[9]. If the drawee adds the name of his bank, this authorises

---

1 Bell *Principles* s 343.
2 *Munro v Munro* (1820) Hume 81 (initials); *Macintosh v Macdonald* (1828) 7 S 155 (mark).
3 *Thomson v Bell* (1850) 12 D 1184.
4 *Glickman v Linda* 1950 SC 18, OH.
5 1882 Act, s 94. Where a notary is unavailable at the place where the bill is dishonoured, a householder or 'substantial' resident may sign a certificate attesting the bill's dishonour.
6 1882 Act, s 51(6).
7 *McNeill & Son v Innes, Chambers & Co* 1917 SC 540.
8 Wilson *The Scottish Law of Debt* (2nd edn, 1991) para 19.6.
9 1882 Act, s 17(2)(a).

the bank to make payment when the bill is presented to it and to debit his account accordingly[1]. It is usual for the acceptance to be written on the bill's face, but there is no reason why this cannot be written on its back. A bill can be accepted even before the drawer signs it and even an inchoate bill (one which, though signed, lacks one or more of the other prerequisites for the creation of a valid bill under s 3(1)) may be accepted[2]. An overdue bill may be accepted, as may one previously dishonoured by non-acceptance or even non-payment[3]. The holder of a bill which has been negotiated, but which is simply stated to be payable 'after sight', should present it for acceptance within a reasonable time or negotiate it again[4]. Presenting such a bill for acceptance at the earliest opportunity reduces the risk of not being paid should the drawee become insolvent.

Presentment for payment

A bill, other than one payable on demand, which has been accepted should be presented on the date payment is due[5]. A demand bill does not need to be presented for acceptance, but must be presented for payment within a reasonable time[6]. If this is not done, the drawer and indorsers are discharged. Presentment must occur during the business day and at the 'proper' place[7]. The proper place will be that specified as the place of payment in the bill, failing which, at the drawee's or acceptor's address as shown in the bill, or, where this is not shown[8], at the drawee's or acceptor's place of business if known, and if not 'at his ordinary address if known'. If all else fails, presentment may be made to the drawee or acceptor wherever he can be found or at his last known place of business or residence[9]. Presentment is excused if, having tried one's best, the drawee or acceptor cannot be found[10]. In this last case, the bill is dishonoured when it becomes overdue and remains unpaid[11].

Otherwise, a bill is dishonoured by non-payment when the drawee or acceptor refuses to pay it or when payment cannot be obtained[12]. Where a bill has been presented for acceptance and refused, then, if notice of dishonour was given to the drawer and any prior indorsers, it is not necessary to notify them again that it has been dishonoured by non-payment[13].

---

1 *Banca Popolare di Novara v John Livanos & Sons Ltd* [1965] 2 Lloyd's Rep 149.
2 1882 Act, s 18(1). For inchoate instruments, see 1882 Act, s 20.
3 1882 Act, s 18(2).
4 1882 Act, s 40(1). Failure to do either discharges the drawer and prior indorsers: s 40(2). Guidance as to what constitutes a reasonable time is provided by s 40(3).
5 1882 Act, s 45(1).
6 1882 Act, s 45(2). This provision does not apply to cheques which are dealt with by s 74.
7 1882 Act, s 45(3).
8 Failure to specify where a bill is drawn or where it is payable does not invalidate the bill: 1882 Act, s 3(4).
9 1882 Act, s 45(4)(a)–(d).
10 1882 Act, s 46(2).
11 1882 Act, s 47(1)(b).
12 1882 Act, s 47(1)(a).
13 1882 Act, s 48(2). If, however, the bill was accepted after notice of dishonour by non-acceptance was given, but thereafter payment was refused, notice of non-payment will have to be given to preserve a right of recourse.

The rules as to notice of dishonour by non-acceptance also apply to dishonour by non-payment[1].

If a cheque is not presented for payment within a reasonable time (which current banking practice regards as being no more than six months from the date of issue) the drawer is not discharged unless he suffers loss in consequence of the delay[2]. Where a promissory note is payable at a particular place, then it must be presented for payment there in order to render its maker liable thereon; otherwise such presentment is unnecessary[3]. Presentment for payment of a promissory note is, however, necessary if an indorser is to be liable[4]. From the perspective of the collecting bank, presentment for payment of a cheque through the clearing process described earlier may take several days. The law has, however, recently been altered to expedite matters.

In the case of cheques, presentment for payment 'at the proper place' still means presentment at the branch of the bank on which the cheque is drawn. If, however, the paying bank specifies that presentment for payment may be made at an address other than the one printed on the cheque, then, the cheque may, as an alternative, be presented, by the collecting bank, at that other address[5]. This facilitates the truncation of cheques by permitting the central office of the paying bank to process cheques without having to send them to the branch where the drawer has his cheque account.

As an alternative to the physical presentment of a cheque by the collecting bank to the paying bank, the former may collect payment after transmitting, to the latter, electronic information concerning the 'essential features' of the cheque[6]. These essential features are: (1) the serial number of the cheque; (2) the code which identifies the banker on whom the cheque is drawn; (3) the account number of the drawer of the cheque; and (4) the amount as entered by the drawer[7]. Unlike physical presentment of a cheque, electronic presentation does not have to occur during business hours[8]. Even where electronic presentation has been made, the paying bank enjoys the right to request physical presentment of the cheque in question. This right, however, must be exercised 'before the close of business on the next business day' following electronic presentation of the cheque[9]. But such a request does not amount to dishonour of the cheque by non-payment[10]. The paying bank would be likely to exercise this right where fraud is suspected and where only actual sight of the cheque would confirm or allay suspicion[11].

1 1882 Act, s 49.
2 1882 Act, s 74(1).
3 1882 Act, s 87(1).
4 1882 Act, s 87(2).
5 1882 Act, s 74A, added by the Deregulation (Bills of Exchange) Order 1996, SI 1996/2993, r 3. The alternative address at which cheques may be presented must be published by notice in the London, Edinburgh and Belfast Gazettes. Such notice may be cancelled by publication of a subsequent notice to that effect in these Gazettes.
6 1882 Act, s 74B(1) (added by the Deregulation (Bills of Exchange) Order 1996, r 4).
7 1882 Act, s 74B(6).
8 1882 Act, s 74B(2).
9 1882 Act, s 74B(3).
10 1882 Act, s 74B(4).
11 It is thought that 'high value cheques' will still require to be physically presented to paying banks: *Electronic Presentation of Cheques: A Consultative Document from HM Treasury* (1996) para 43.

Presentment and assignation

We have seen that a drawee who refuses to accept or pay a bill or note drawn on him is not liable to the holder. There is, however, an important qualification to this. The 1882 Act provides that, in Scotland, presenting a bill for acceptance or, where acceptance is unnecessary, for payment has the effect of assigning the drawer's funds (which are held by the drawee) to the holder[1]. Presenting a cheque for payment has the same effect on the drawer's account with the paying bank[2]. The position has been summed up in the following terms: 'There is no doubt that a bill of exchange, of which acceptance is refused, . . . is equivalent to an intimated assignation, and though a cheque on a bank is not in all respects the same as a bill of exchange, yet in certain circumstances it must operate to the same effect'[3]. Where there is no credit balance in the drawer's account, then, clearly, there is nothing to be assigned to the holder[4]. However, where the drawee holds funds which are partially able to pay the amount in the bill or cheque these are assigned to the holder when the instrument is presented to the drawee. Suppose, eg, that Red owes Black £161. He draws a cheque for that amount and sends it to Black. However, Red only has £135 in his current account. When Black's bank (the collecting bank) presents this cheque to Red's bank (the paying bank) for payment, the right to have that £135 is assigned to Black on presentment of the cheque. If Red were subsequently to become bankrupt with £156 in his current account, the trustee in bankruptcy would only be entitled to £21 because the balance is now Black's property[5]. But if the drawee holds several accounts for the drawer which, when looked at overall, show that the latter is overdrawn, then the drawee does not hold funds available for the payment of a bill drawn on an account which is in credit. Imagine that Red has three accounts with his bank, two of which are overdrawn to the tune of £2,000 each, and one of which has a credit balance of £1,000. If Red draws a cheque on this last account for £900, what is left in that account does not cover his overall debt to the bank which stands at £3,900. Consequently, it cannot be said that the drawee holds sufficient available funds for the payment of the bill and, therefore, presentment of the cheque for £900 does not operate as an assignation[6]. As Lord President Dunedin said when considering the application of s 53(2) of the 1882 Act: 'It seems to me quite clear that the expression "where the drawee of a bill has in his hands funds available for the payment thereof", must mean funds as upon a true state of the accounts between the two parties concerned'[7].

---

1   1882 Act, s 53(2).
2   *British Linen Co Bank v Carruthers and Fergusson* (1883) 10 R 923; *James Kirkwood & Sons v Clydesdale Bank Ltd* 1908 SC 20. It may be noted that a bank is contractually bound to honour its customers' cheques provided their accounts contain sufficient funds to permit this: *King v British Linen Company* (1899) 1 F 928; *Royal Bank of Scotland v Skinner* 1931 SLT 382, OH; *Lipkin Gorman v Karpnale Ltd* [1992] 4 All ER 409, CA; *National Bank of Greece SA v Pinios Shipping Co No 1* [1990] AC 637.
3   *British Linen Co Bank v Carruthers and Fergusson* (1883) 10 R 923 at 926, per Lord President Inglis.
4   *Sutherland v Royal Bank of Scotland plc* 1997 SLT 329, OH.
5   *British Linen Co Bank v Carruthers and Fergusson* above.
6   *James Kirkwood & Sons v Clydesdale Bank Ltd* 1908 SC 20.
7   *James Kirkwood & Sons v Clydesdale Bank Ltd* 1908 SC 20 at 25.

Because presentment of a cheque may operate as a statutory assignation of the sum drawn, this causes problems where the drawer contacts his bank and countermands payment[1]. If presentment assigns funds in the drawer's account, the paying bank cannot thereafter recredit the drawer's account with the sum drawn. In these circumstances the bank will pay the money into a suspense account until the drawer and payee resolved their difficulties. This can be a protracted process, so s 75A of the 1882 Act[2] disapplies s 53(2) by the simple expedient of deeming the paying bank to have no funds available to pay the drawer's cheque if and when it receives the drawer's countermand of payment. But s 75A applies only to cheques and, consequently, s 53(2) is not disapplied in the case of bills. Furthermore, s 75A does not apply to cheques which are backed by a cheque guarantee card.

FRAUD AND FORGERY

Use of commercial paper carries with it the risk that instruments may fall into the wrong hands and that payment may be made to someone who is not entitled to it. This section looks at how bills are forged and at the effect of forgery. Since readers are most likely to encounter cheque forgeries in practice, attention is paid to the protection banks enjoy when dealing with forged cheques[3].

Bill and cheque frauds are often perpetrated in one of two ways, either by the fraudster inventing a payee or inventing a transaction. Both share a common feature, namely, the presence of a forged indorsement. Suppose, eg, that an accounts' clerk is employed to prepare bills and cheques for signature by his employer and prepares an instrument in favour of a payee whose name the clerk has made up. The clerk gets his employer to sign it and then forges the invented payee's indorsement in his favour. In the case of a cheque the clerk will then pay this into his own bank account, or he may, if the cheque permits this, negotiate it to another in return for payment. In the case of a bill he may either present this for payment or negotiate it to another in return for payment[4]. Alternatively, our dishonest accounts' clerk may prepare an instrument in favour of a payee with whom his employer does business. Here the employer signs because the employee has untruthfully represented that another transaction with the payee has occurred and that payment is now due. The clerk will then forge the payee's indorsement and present it to his bank for payment, in the case of a cheque, or to the drawee in the case of a bill. In both cases, these may also be negotiated to another in return for payment[5].

1 A bank's obligation to honour a customer's cheques is 'determined' (ie revoked) by the latter countermanding payment. The obligation is also determined on being notified of a customer's death: 1882 Act, s 75.
2 Added by the Law Reform (Miscellaneous Provisions) (Scotland) Act 1985, s 11(b).
3 The banks' obligations to drawers and payees are not affected where electronic presentment is made: 1882 Act, s 74B(5).
4 *Clutton v Attenborough & Son* [1897] AC 90, HL.
5 *Vinden v Hughes* [1905] 1 KB 795.

A forged (or unauthorised) signature on a bill or cheque is severe in its effect. The general rule is that no one whose signature has been forged (or is unauthorised), whether as drawer, acceptor, payee or indorser, is liable on the instrument[1]. Applying the general rule, therefore, a paying bank cannot debit the drawer's account where the drawer's signature has been forged or added without authorisation to a cheque. In *Kreditbank Cassel GmbH v Schenkers Ltd*[2], a branch manager employed by the defendants drew and indorsed bills of exchange on their behalf without authority to do so. He signed cheques in the defendants' name, had them accepted by a company in which he had an interest, indorsed them, and sent them to a German company which discounted them with the plaintiffs. When the bills were dishonoured the plaintiffs sued the defendants as drawers of the bills. It was decided that the bills in question were forgeries and that the defendants were not liable on them. A holder in due course has no right to payment from a person whose indorsement has been forged.

Section 24 is bad news for the holders of instruments which, normally, confer a title to payment free from defects on holders who have taken them in goods faith[3]. So, the 1882 Act provides for exceptions to the general rule. One exception, already noted, is the rule that the acceptor of a bill cannot refuse to pay a holder in due course on the ground that the drawer's signature, as such, is a forgery[4]. Another exception exists where the payee is either fictitious or non-existing.

Section 7(3) of the 1882 Act provides that 'where the payee is a fictitious or non-existing person the bill may be treated as payable to bearer'. Bearer bills, it will be recalled, are negotiated by delivery alone without the need for indorsement[5]. Therefore it follows that an indorsement on a bearer bill, whether genuine or forged, is disregarded and that s 24 does not come into play. So, provided that the payee is fictitious or non-existing, an order bill bearing a forged indorsement is treated as a bearer bill, and the drawee who honours it is entitled to debit the drawer's account with the sum drawn. Unfortunately, the 1882 Act does not define the terms 'fictitious' and 'non-existing' and judicial attempts to do so have not always been helpful.

Non-existing payee

Clearly the payee is non-existing when dead, in the case of a person; dissolved, in the case of a company; or not yet in being, such as an unborn child or unincorporated company[6]. However, even a living person may be treated as 'non-existing', a result which comes about in the following way:

1 1882 Act, s 24. See *Strathmore Group Ltd v Credit Lyonnais* 1994 SLT 1023, OH, where it was averred that a director's signature as acceptor of two bills of exchange drawn on a company was a forgery.
2 [1927] 1 KB 826, CA. See also *Weir v National Westminster Bank plc* 1993 SC 515.
3 The onus of proving that the signature alleged to be forged is, in fact, genuine, rests on the holder who seeks to enforce the instrument: *British Linen Co v Cowan* (1906) 8 F 704; *McIntyre v National Bank of Scotland Ltd* 1910 SC 150.
4 1882 Act, s 54(2)(a). The acceptor is not precluded from refusing payment where it is the drawer's indorsement which has been forged.
5 1882 Act, s 31(2).
6 *Chalmers and Guest* p 47.

An accounts' clerk is trusted to prepare cheques for his employer's signa-ture. He makes out a cheque payable to a 'George Brett' (a name which he has made up) for work which, he untruthfully says, Brett has done. His employer signs the cheque and the clerk forges the payee's indorsements in his favour and then negotiates it to a third party, who is unaware of what has been going on, in return for payment. When the clerk's employer discovers the fraud, she sues the third party for repayment of the proceeds of the cheque. This action will not succeed because the payee, 'George Brett' is non-existing. Why? The clerk invented a name in order to induce his employer to draw the cheque. But the drawer did not actually know when she signed the cheque whether the payee was a real (ie existing) or imaginary (ie non-existing) person. And where the drawer of a bill or cheque does not actually know whether the named payee really exists or not, then that payee will be treated as non-existing. In consequence, the cheque is treated as payable to bearer, the forged indorsement is ignored, the drawer is liable, and the third party keeps the proceeds of the cashed cheque. It does not matter that there really is someone out there called George Brett, what is important is that the drawer did not know of the existence of a person of that name to whom she thought payment was owed[1].

Fictitious payee

Where the drawer knows that the payee exists, then clearly that payee cannot be regarded as non-existing. However, a payee known to the drawer may still be fictitious and the bill treated as payable to bearer. Suppose, eg, that the accounts' clerk knows that his employer regularly accepts bills drawn on her by John Smith which are payable to Grampian Widgets. The clerk therefore makes out a bill drawn by John Smith on his employer and payable to Grampian Widgets and forges Smith's signature as drawer. His employer accepts the bill payable at a named bank and the clerk then forges Grampian Widgets' indorsement in his favour and indorses the bill to someone else in return for a cash payment. The payee really exists, but the true drawer of this bill is the dishonest clerk and not John Smith. However, neither the true, nor the ostensible, drawer of this bill intended the payee to be paid. In fact, it can be said that what the true drawer of the bill did was to create the fiction that payment was owed to the payee in order to manipulate affairs to his advantage. Because this instrument will be treated as a bearer bill, the bank may debit the ostensi-ble drawer's account[2].

One further scenario must be understood. Our accounts' clerk prepares a cheque in favour of a firm with which his employer regularly does busi-ness. However, the transaction in respect of which the cheque has been prepared did not really take place. His employer signs the instrument, the clerk forges the payee's indorsement, and then pays it into his bank account. The drawer of this cheque: (1) knows that the payee is real or

1 *Clutton v Attenborough & Son* [1897] AC 90, HL.
2 *Bank of England v Vagliano Brothers* [1891] AC 107, HL.

existing; and (2) intends that that payee should be paid. Consequently, this cheque cannot be treated as a bearer bill and the general rule regarding forged indorsements kicks back into place. The drawer of the cheque will not be liable to anyone taking it after the forged indorsement was placed on the bill[1]. But will the paying bank be entitled to debit the drawer's account if it pays out on the cheque? And will the collecting bank be liable to the drawer if the paying bank is not? The possibilities are now explored.

Protecting the paying bank

Where the drawer's signature is forged

Where the drawer's signature is forged the paying bank is not entitled to debit the drawer's account[2]. The usual explanation for this is that the bank has been negligent in not spotting that its customer's signature has been forged[3]. It is, of course, quite unrealistic to expect that the paying bank's employees should be able to memorise the signatures of all of their customers. Perhaps a more justifiable basis for the rule is that in the case of a cheque bearing the forged signature of the drawer, the bank's customer has not truly authorised its payment. But the drawer is barred from founding on the forgery of his or her signature if, eg, he or she knows that it has happened and delays notifying the bank[4]. It may be added that if the drawer, whose signature is genuine, draws cheques in a manner which facilitates fraud, the paying bank may debit his or her account[5]. If a stolen cheque card is used in conjunction with a stolen chequebook to purchase goods (the thief forging the signature of the owner of the chequebook and card), it may be that the bank is bound by the promise to pay contained in the cheque card and must honour the cheque, although unable to debit the drawer's account[6].

Where an indorsement is forged

The paying bank usually cannot tell if an indorsement is forged or not. It might, however, be able to tell if the circumstances are somewhat unusual in the case of a cheque which it is asked to pay out on. Consequently, s 60 of the 1882 Act provides that a bank which pays out on a cheque bearing a forged or unauthorised indorsement is entitled to debit the drawer's account, provided that it has acted in good faith[7] and in the ordinary course of business[8]. Suppose, eg, that a cheque for £250,000, made payable

1 *Vinden v Hughes* [1905] 1 KB 795; *North and South Wales Bank Ltd v Macbeth* [1908] AC 137, HL.
2 *Orr and Barber v Union Bank of Scotland* (1854) 1 Macq 513, HL.
3 *Clydesdale Bank v Royal Bank of Scotland* (1876) 3 R 586.
4 *Greenwood v Martins Bank Ltd* [1933] AC 51, HL.
5 *London Joint Stock Bank Ltd v Macmillan and Arthur* [1918] AC 777, HL.
6 *First Sport Ltd v Barclays Bank plc* [1993] 3 All ER 789, CA. Here the card stated that it could only be used by an 'authorised signatory' and the bank argued that the thief was not such a person. The court determined that where a payee acts in good faith and has no reasonable ground for suspecting that the actual signatory is anyone other than the authorised signatory, the disclaimer was inapplicable.
7 1882 Act, s 90 defines what is meant by good faith.
8 1882 Act, s 60 also applies to demand bills drawn on a bank.

to Trans-Global Widgets plc, is appropriated by a dishonest postman who forges the payee's indorsement in his favour and presents it for payment. If the bank pays him it does so in circumstances which ought to have made it suspicious: would a multinational corporation really negotiate a cheque for quarter of a million pounds to a postman? A bank which paid out in these circumstances would not be justified in debiting the drawer's account[1]. Section 80 of the Act applies to crossed cheques which bear a forged indorsement[2]. In this situation, the paying bank may debit the drawer's account provided that: (1) the cheque was paid to another bank; (2) the paying bank acted in good faith; and (3) the paying bank acted without negligence[3]. But although the bank may debit its customer's account, provided that the cheque has come into the hands of the payee, the drawer is deemed to have paid the payee and does not have to make payment again.

Where an indorsement is absent or irregular

Sections 60 and 80 of the 1882 Act overlap, but both are intended to protect the paying bank against forged indorsements. Section 1(1) of the Cheques Act 1957 protects the paying bank which pays out against an unindorsed or irregularly indorsed cheque provided that payment is made in good faith and in the ordinary course of business.

Prior to the passing of the Cheques Act 1957 a paying bank required a payee to indorse cheques in its favour before paying out on these. This was a time-consuming way of doing business, but it was necessary if the bank wished to obtain the protection offered by s 60 of the 1882 Act. If the indorsement was not that of the person entitled to payment but rather a forged indorsement, purporting to be that of the person so entitled, the bank was protected by s 60. Section 1(1) of the Cheques Act 1957 abolishes the need for indorsement of cheques. However, the banks[4] have taken the view that the payee's indorsement is still needed where a cheque is to be paid over the counter and in cash, and also where order cheques are to be credited to an account other than that of the original payee (in other words where the original payee has negotiated the cheque to another). Where such an indorsement can be described as irregular, a bank which pays out on the cheque may safely debit the drawer's account, provided, of course, that there is nothing to arouse its suspicion about the cheque.

It must be remembered that an irregular indorsement is not the same as an invalid one, and a regular indorsement may turn out to be invalid:

> 'Regularity is a different thing from validity. . . . On the one hand an indorsement which is quite invalid may be regular on the face of it. Thus the indorsement may be forged or unauthorised and, therefore, invalid under section 24 of the [1882] Act, but nevertheless there may be nothing about it to give rise to any suspicion. The bill is then quite regular on the face of it. Conversely, an indorsement which is quite irregular may nevertheless be

---

1   *Auchteroni & Co v Midland Bank Ltd* [1928] 2 KB 294.
2   This includes cheques crossed 'account payee' or 'a/c payee': 1882 Act, s 80 (amended by the Cheques Act 1992, s 2).
3   If the cheque is crossed generally payment may be to any bank, if crossed specially, payment must be made to the bank nominated by the crossing.
4   Committee of London Clearing Bankers, Circular dated 23 September 1957.

valid. Thus, by a misnomer, a payee may be described on the face of the bill by the wrong name, nevertheless, if it is quite plain that the drawer intended him as payee, then an indorsement on the back by the payee in his own true name is valid and sufficient to pass the property in the bill'[1].

An example of an irregular indorsement is found in *Arab Bank Ltd v Ross*[2]. In this case the designated payee in two promissory notes was 'Fathi and Faysal Nabulsy Company'. The notes were indorsed by the payee in favour of the Arab Bank which discounted them. The indorsements read: 'Fathi and Faysal Nabulsy' without the addition of the word 'Company'. The Court of Appeal determined that the indorsements were irregular since they did not specify the indorser's full name.

Protecting the collecting bank

Where the payee of a cheque presents it to his or her bank, the bank may collect the sum shown on the cheque and, having done so, then credit that sum to the payee's account. Alternatively, the payee's bank may credit his or her account with the sum and then collect that sum from the paying bank on its own behalf. In the former case the collecting bank has acted as the payee's agent in collecting the proceeds of the cheque. In the latter case, however, it cannot be assumed that the collecting bank was acting on its own behalf and as the legitimate owner of the cheque. The capacity in which the collecting bank operates when collecting payment of a cheque is always a question of fact[3]. If, eg, the payee's bank gives him or her cash for the cheque (ie buys the cheque from the payee), then, despite the fact that the amount represented by the cheque will be credited to the payee's account, the bank becomes a holder for value and may also be a holder in due course. But what is the bank's position if the payee has no title to the bill in the first place?

Under English law, a bank which collects payment for itself or for the payee is liable under the tort of conversion to the true owner of the cheque. However, s 4(1) of the Cheques Act 1957 protects an English collecting bank against liability to the true owner of the cheque where it has acted in good faith and without negligence. But conversion is an English concept and s 4(1) has no real application in Scotland. It is, however, possible to indicate with reasonable certainty what the position of the collecting bank is under Scots law. If the bank collects in a representative capacity only, as agent for its customer, it incurs no liability to the true owner of the cheque[4]. If the collecting bank gives value for an unindorsed cheque and otherwise satisfies the criteria for being a holder in due course, it also incurs no liability[5]. But the collecting bank will be liable to the true owner of the cheque where it has given value for, and taken in return, a cheque from someone who does not qualify as a holder. Suppose, eg, that Crook steals a cheque which is payable to Good. He then opens a

1 *Arab Bank Ltd v Ross* [1952] 2 QB 216 at 226, CA, per Lord Denning MR.
2 [1952] 2 QB 216.
3 *McLean v Clydesdale Bank Ltd* (1883) 11 R (HL) 1.
4 *Clydesdale Bank v Royal Bank of Scotland* (1876) 3 R 586.
5 1957 Act, s 2.

current account with the Bank of Caledonia, giving his name as Good. The true owner of the cheque is the real Good. Crook cannot be a holder of the cheque, being neither the payee nor an indorsee[1]. The Bank of Caledonia has not taken the cheque from a holder and, consequently, remains liable to reimburse the real Good with the proceeds of the collected cheque.

THE LIABILITY OF PARTIES TO A BILL OF EXCHANGE

'No person', states s 23 of the 1882 Act, 'is liable as drawer, indorser, or acceptor of a bill who has not signed it as such'. Having signed as such, a holder in due course 'may enforce payment against all parties liable on the bill'[2]. However, the right of recourse enjoyed by a party who has made payment only lies against *prior* parties liable on the bill. Reproduced immediately below are the front and back of an inland bill. This will be used to explain the liability of the parties whose signatures appear on it.

Accepted for and on behalf of
Tayside Flanges Ltd
Alistair Watson, Director

£25,000

Aberdeen
3 January 1997

At sixty days after date pay to Gordon Pirie or order the sum of sterling pounds twenty five thousand only for value received.

For and on behalf of
Grampian Widgets Ltd
Ian Wallace
Director

To Tayside Flanges Ltd
Grote House
Dundee

Alistair Watson

Frank Steele
Gordon Pirie

Gordon Hailes
Frank Steele

William Anderson
Gordon Hailes

Gregor MacSween
William Anderson

Raymond Coyle
Gregor MacSween

Peter Grant
Raymond Coyle

Drawer (Grampian Widgets Ltd)

The drawer promises that the bill will be accepted and paid according to its tenor when presented to the drawee. Should Tayside Flanges Ltd dishonour this bill, either by non-acceptance or non-payment, then

---

1 1882 Act, s 2 ('holder').
2 1882 Act, s 38(2).

Grampian Widgets Ltd, as drawers, will be obliged to compensate the holder or an indorser who has had to pay it. However, Grampian Widget Ltd's liability is conditional on notice of dishonour having been given to them[1]. Since this is an inland bill, it does not need to be noted and protested in order to hold the drawers liable on it[2]. Had it been a foreign bill, then it would have been necessary to protest it in order to have a right of recourse against the drawer and indorsers[3]. It is also possible for the drawer of this bill to exclude liability to a holder. This is done by adding after the signature the words 'sans recours' or its English equivalent 'without recourse to me'[4].

Acceptor (Tayside Flanges Ltd)

Since Tayside Flanges Ltd have accepted this bill without qualification (ie generally), they have now become the party primarily liable on it[5]. And having given their general acceptance to this bill, Gordon Pirie does not need to present it to them for payment in order fix Tayside Flanges Ltd with liability on it[6]. Effectively, therefore, Tayside Flanges Ltd guarantee payment of the bill to a holder in due course. For example, if Peter Grant asks them to pay him, Tayside Flanges Ltd could not refuse to do so on the ground that Grampian Widgets Ltd's signature was forged. As we have already seen, the acceptor of a bill cannot deny to a holder in due course 'the existence of the drawer, the genuineness of his signature, and his capacity and authority to draw the bill'[7]. Furthermore, because this bill is payable to the order of a third person (ie to Gordon Pirie or to his order), Tayside Flanges Ltd cannot deny to Peter Grant the existence of Pirie nor his capacity to indorse the bill to Frank Steele[8]. However, if it were the case that Gordon Pirie had not really indorsed the bill to Frank Steele, but rather that Steele had forged Pirie's indorsement to him, then, Tayside Flanges Ltd would be able to plead the forgery in justification of their refusal to pay Grant[8].

Aval (Alistair Watson)

Watson signed the acceptance on the face of the bill in his representative capacity as agent for Tayside Flanges Ltd. However, on the back of the bill, the first indorsement is that of the payee, Gordon Pirie, whose purpose in indorsing the bill was to transfer his right to payment to Frank Steele. So what does the presence of Watson's signature, on its own, represent?

1 1882 Act, s 55(1)(a).
2 1882 Act, s 51(1).
3 1882 Act, s 51(2).
4 1882 Act, s 16(1).
5 1882 Act, s 54(1).
6 1882 Act, s 52.
7 1882 Act, s 54(2)(a).
8 1882 Act, s 54(2)(c).

Watson is not the holder of the bill, and, since only a holder can indorse a bill[1], Watson cannot be taken to have signed the bill as an indorser. However, s 56 of the 1882 Act provides that: 'Where a person signs a bill otherwise than as drawer or acceptor, he thereby incurs the liabilities of an indorser to a holder in due course'. Watson's signature may be termed an 'aval' and its purpose is to guarantee payment of the bill to a holder in due course[2]. Of course, as we have already seen, Tayside Flanges Ltd, as acceptors of the bill, also guarantee that it will be paid to the holder in due course. But now the holder in due course enjoys two, independent, guarantees of payment. Watson's guarantee 'backs' that of Tayside Flanges Ltd. This double guarantee will make discounting this bill much easier. However, the aval only operates in favour of a holder in due course. It does not benefit Pirie since the payee is not a holder in due course.

Indorsers (Pirie, Steele, Hailes, Anderson, MacSween and Coyle)

These persons are the indorsers of the bill. Pirie, of course, was also the payee before he negotiated this bill. There is a rebuttable presumption that indorsements are made in the order in which they appear[3]. So we may presume, until the contrary is proved, that Pirie indorsed the bill first and that Raymond Coyle was the bill's last indorser. A bill will not, however, be regarded as incomplete or irregular should the sequence of indorsements prove not to be in strict chronological order[4], even where the indorsement which is out of sequence is a restrictive one[5]. But it is important to establish the order in which indorsements were made since an indorser's liability is to the holder or to any *subsequent* indorsers.

Like the drawer, the indorser of a bill promises that it will be accepted and paid according to its tenor. The indorser further promises (again like the drawer) that should the bill be dishonoured he will compensate the holder or a subsequent indorser who has had to pay it, provided notice of dishonour has been given to him[6]. But an indorser who is called upon to make payment on a bill which has been dishonoured, has, as has been noted, the right to be repaid by the drawer[7]. It is, however, open to an indorser to indorse the bill 'sans recours' and this has the effect of excluding his liability to the holder[8]. Where an indorser is called upon to pay by another party to the bill who satisfies the criteria for being a holder in due course, that indorser cannot dispute the 'genuineness and regularity in all respects of the drawer's signature and all previous indorsements'[9]. Finally, the indorser cannot deny, either to the person to whom he indorses the bill or to any subsequent indorsee that: (1) the bill 'was at the

1 1882 Act, s 31(3).
2 *G and H Montage GmbH v Irvani* [1990] 1 WLR 667, CA.
3 1882 Act, s 32(5).
4 *Lombard Banking Ltd v Central Garage and Engineering Co Ltd* [1963] 1 QB 220.
5 *Yeoman Credit Ltd v Gregory* [1963] 1 All ER 245.
6 1882 Act, s 55(2)(a).
7 1882 Act, s 55(1)(a).
8 1882 Act, s 16(1).
9 1882 Act, s 55(2)(b).

time of his indorsement a valid and subsisting bill' and (2) 'that he had then a good title thereto'[1].

With reference to the sample bill above, let us assume the following facts: (a) the bill was stolen from Gordon Hailes by a thief who forged Hailes' indorsement to William Anderson; (b) Tayside Flanges Ltd refused to pay Peter Grant when he presented the bill to them for payment on the ground (which is entirely justifiable) that Hailes' signature was a forgery; and (c) that Grant otherwise fulfils the requirements for being treated as a holder in due course. So we have a situation where the last holder of this bill stands to lose the money which he paid for it. Section 24 of the 1882 Act is very clear as to the consequences flowing from a forged indorsement on a bill of exchange. That signature is 'wholly inoperative' and, as a result, Grant has 'no right to retain the bill' or 'to enforce payment thereof against any party thereto'. So Hailes has the right to redelivery to him of the bill. But s 55(2)(b) protects Grant in this situation and, in effect, disapplies s 24. Three people have indorsed this bill since the forgery of Hailes' signature occurred, William Anderson, Gregor MacSween and Raymond Coyle. And as indorsers, these three are 'precluded from denying to a holder in due course [Peter Grant] the genuineness . . . of . . . *all* previous indorsements' – and that includes the forged indorsement. So Grant may require either Anderson, MacSween, or Coyle to pay him what he paid for the bill. If he obtains payment from Coyle, then Coyle has a right of recourse against either MacSween or Anderson. But when Anderson is required to pay out on the bill his only right of recovery (for what it is worth) is against the thief and forger.

Accommodation parties and accommodation bills

A bill will always be easier to discount where the financial standing of one of the parties liable on it is well-known and respected. Bearing this in mind, bills of exchange are sometimes used to raise money quickly on the basis of the financial probity of someone other than the drawer. For example, suppose that Poor needs to find £20,000 quickly but cannot do so on a favourable overdraft basis. Poor may reach an accommodation with Rich, whose financial standing is high in the business community, which will allow Poor to acquire the money he needs. This is how it can be done: Poor draws a bill of exchange for £20,000, payable to himself, on Rich. Rich does not actually owe Poor £20,000 but he accepts the bill, which is expressed to be payable five months after date. Poor then takes his accepted bill to the bank which is happy to give him £20,000 (minus its charge for discounting the bill) because the bank knows that the bill has been accepted by someone whose credit is good. Rich hopes that Poor will repay him the £20,000 within the five months so that Rich will then be in a position to pay the bank on the date of maturity of the bill. Someone 'who has signed a bill as drawer, acceptor or indorser, without receiving value therefor, and for the purpose of lending his name to some other person' is known as an accom-

1   1882 Act, s 55(2)(c).

modation party[1]. And where, as is the case here, the accommodation party is also the acceptor, the bill is known as an accommodation bill[2].

Poor will, of course, have negotiated this bill to the bank in order to have it discounted and the bank will, therefore, be a holder for value. It is quite probable that the bank will know that Rich was only an accommodation party and that Poor has, in the jargon used, been 'raising the wind' or 'flying a kite'. So what will happen if Poor does not manage to repay Rich before the bill's date of maturity? The answer is very simple: 'An accommodation party is liable on the bill to a holder for value; and it is immaterial whether, when such holder took the bill, he knew such party to be an accommodation party or not'[3]. Rich will have to honour the bill and pay the bank. Should Poor and Rich both be bankrupt on the date of maturity of the bill, the bank may rank on both estates for the full amount of the bill. However, in accordance with the rule that a debt cannot be ranked twice on the same estate, Rich cannot rank on Poor's estate for payment of any dividend[4].

DISCHARGE OF BILLS

A distinction must be observed between discharge of a bill, cheque, or promissory note and discharge of the parties to these. A bill may be discharged by its payment, where the acceptor becomes its holder, by renunciation, cancellation, alteration, or prescription.

Payment

Because the acceptor of a bill is the party who is primarily liable thereon, it follows, in logic, that payment by the acceptor must discharge the bill and the liability of all of the parties to that bill. In the case of cheques, which are not accepted, payment by the drawee discharges the cheque. A promissory note is discharged when paid by the maker. This is, in fact, what the 1882 Act says[5]. Where the acceptor or drawee of a bill of exchange (or someone acting on their behalf) pays it *at* or *after* its date of maturity, then, provided that the payment is made to the holder of the bill 'in good faith and without notice that [the holder's] title to the bill is defective' the bill is discharged. As a consequence of discharge, the bill, cheque or note ceases to be negotiable[6]. Yet despite the cessation of negotiability on payment, the legislation confers on the acceptor or drawee the right to demand possession of the bill from the holder[7]. It is advisable to exercise

1 1882 Act, s 28(1); *McLelland v Mackay* (1908) 24 Sh Ct Rep 157.
2 A bill can only be an accommodation bill where the accommodation party is the acceptor.
3 1882 Act, s 28(2).
4 Goudy *Bankruptcy* (4th edn, 1914), pp 574–576; Wilson *The Scottish Law of Debt* (2nd edn, 1991) para 23.9; *Anderson v Mackinnon* (1876) 3 R 608.
5 1882 Act, s 59(1). For promissory notes, see s 89(1). See also *Coats v Union Bank of Scotland Ltd* 1929 SC (HL) 114.
6 1882 Act, ss 36(1), 89(1).
7 1882 Act, s 52(4). This provision, which requires physical presentation and delivery of bills, is disapplied in cases where cheques have been electronically presented: 1882 Act, s 74C.

this right since it is arguable that if this is not done, and the instrument gets back into circulation, the party who paid the bill may be personally barred from founding on that payment in a question with a holder who took the instrument in good faith[1].

With equal logic, when payment is made by the drawer or an indorser, whose liability is secondary to that of the acceptor, the bill is not discharged[2]. This is necessary since a drawer who has had to pay out on a bill enjoys a right of recourse against the acceptor, and an indorser who pays has a right of recourse against the acceptor, the drawer and all prior indorsers[3].

In the case of an accommodation bill, payment by the acceptor does not discharge the bill. It would be unfair were this to be so since it would deprive the accommodation party of a right of recourse against the real obligant, namely, the accommodated party. Consequently, an accommodation bill is discharged when paid by the party who has been accommodated[4]. The accommodated party obviously has no right of recourse if he pays.

Acceptor becomes holder

Although possession of a bill by the party who is liable on it raises a presumption of payment[5], it does not necessarily signify that the bill has been discharged. However, where the acceptor of a bill becomes the holder at or after its date of maturity, then, provided that he becomes a holder in his own right and not as an agent for another, the bill is discharged[6]. This is logical and a statutory application of the principle that 'where the same person in the same capacity becomes both creditor and debtor in the same obligation, the debt is extinguished *confusione'*[7]. The situation envisioned is this: a bill for £3,000, payable on 2 April 1997, is drawn on Smith. It is presented for acceptance on 14 February 1997, duly accepted by Smith and, thereafter, is negotiated, ultimately, to Jones who owes Smith £3,000. Jones, therefore, negotiates the bill to Smith on (or after) 2 April 1997. On 2 April, which is the date of maturity of the bill, Smith, who is already the acceptor of this bill, becomes the holder also. Smith is now in the paradoxical position of both owing and being owed £3,000, and so the debt is extinguished and the bill discharged. The same is true where the maker of a promissory notes becomes its holder[8].

---

1 See *Chalmers and Guest* pp 483–484. It will be remembered that where a holder takes a dated bill after the date of maturity he or she cannot be a holder in due course since the bill is overdue: 1882 Act, s 29(1)(a). But it might not be obvious to the holder of a demand bill that it is overdue, and a promissory note payable on demand is not deemed overdue simply because it has been in circulation for longer than might be thought reasonable: s 86(3).
2 1882 Act, s 59(2). The same is true for promissory notes.
3 1882 Act, s 59(2).
4 1882 Act, s 59(3).
5 Erskine *Institute* III, 4, 5.
6 1882 Act, s 61.
7 *Wilson* para 14.3; Bell *Principles* s 580.
8 1882 Act, s 89(2).

Renunciation

A bill may be discharged by the holder's renunciation of his or her rights against the acceptor[1]; and such renunciation releases the acceptor and all other parties to it from liability thereon. In the case of a promissory note, renunciation by the holder discharges the note and releases the maker and other parties from liability[2]. However, once again, a holder in due course occupies a privileged position. Should the holder of a bill which has been renounced subsequently negotiate it to a holder in due course, the latter, provided he or she has not been notified of the renunciation, may oblige the acceptor to pay him or her[3]. To be effective, however, renunciation by the holder of his rights against the acceptor (or maker of a promissory note) must: (1) be made at or after the date of maturity of the instrument; (2) be absolute and unconditional; (3) be in writing or, alternatively, the bill (or note) may be delivered to the acceptor (or maker)[4]. A written account by his nurse, that the holder of a promissory note on which payment was due had said on his deathbed that he forgave the maker the debt and, furthermore, that he wished the note to be destroyed when found, was held not to discharge the note. His recorded statement, it was said, did not 'absolutely and unconditionally' renounce his right to payment by the maker of the note. It only represented an intention to renounce it[5].

Instead of renouncing his or her rights against the acceptor of a bill, the holder may choose to renounce these rights against any other party liable on the bill and this may even be done before the date of maturity[6]. While such renunciation will discharge the liability of the particular party so chosen, and also of parties to the bill who come after him or her, the liability of parties prior to the chosen party remains unaffected and, of course, the bill itself is not discharged[7]. Once again, a holder in due course is protected if he or she takes the bill without notice of the renunciation[8]. Renunciation of individual liability is best put in writing since there is some doubt as to whether only delivery of the bill to the acceptor, but not to the individual concerned, would be effective. In the case of a cheque, eg, there could be no delivery to an acceptor since, as has been seen, cheques are not accepted. Some support for the view that delivery to someone other than the acceptor would be competent may be derived from *Westminster Bank Ltd v Zang*[9], where the view was expressed that a bank did not possess a lien over a cheque which had been returned to the payee. In other words, the bank did not enjoy a right of action as a holder in due course because it had surrendered possession of the cheque.

---

1 1882 Act, s 62(1).
2 1882 Act, s 89.
3 1882 Act, s 62(2).
4 1882 Act, s 62(1).
5 *Re George, Francis v Bruce* (1890) 44 Ch D 627.
6 1882 Act, s 62(2).
7 *Chalmers and Guest* p 528.
8 1882 Act, s 62(2).
9 [1966] AC 182, HL.

Cancellation

A bill may be discharged by being cancelled by the holder or his or her agent, provided that (1) the cancellation is intentional and (2) it is quite clear from the bill itself that it has been cancelled[1]. Consequently, a 'cancellation' which is not written on the bill itself, but rather on a separate instrument, is insufficient to discharge the bill. The safest course is for the holder or his or her agent to write 'cancelled' across the face of the bill. If the holder or his or her agent intentionally cancels the signature of any party liable on a bill, then that party is discharged[2]. Logically, the cancellation of a party's liability should also result in the cancellation of the liability of any other parties to the bill who would have looked to that party had they been called on to make payment. And this is what the legislation also provides for[2]. Bearing in mind what has already been said about the liabilities of parties to a bill of exchange, let us suppose that Smith draws a bill on Jones which is payable to Black and that Black indorses it in favour of Brown, Brown in favour of White, and White in favour of Green. If Green cancels Black's signature this not only discharges Black but also Brown and White who normally, if called upon to pay by Green, would have enjoyed a right of recourse against Black. Cancellation of Smith's signature (as drawer) or that of Jones (as acceptor) discharges all of the indorsers. And because the drawer enjoys a right of recourse against the acceptor, where the former has had to pay because of the latter's failure to do so, cancellation of Jones' signature also discharges Smith. It would appear to be the case, therefore, that cancellation of the acceptor's signature is tantamount to cancellation of the bill itself. If a bill is cancelled unintentionally, or without the holder's authority, or as the result of a mistake, the cancellation is inoperative[3]. So where a bank agent who had offered to obtain payment for the holders of a bill which had been protested for non-payment, informed them of the conditions under which the acceptors were prepared to pay but then, without obtaining the holders' authorisation, collected payment and returned the bill to the acceptors for cancellation, it was held in an action against the bank that the bill had been cancelled without the holders' authority[4]. The onus of proof that cancellation was unintentional, mistaken, or unauthorised, rests on the party so alleging[5].

Alteration

The material alteration of a bill of exchange or acceptance thereof, when this is done without the agreement of all of the parties liable on it, avoids the instrument. Of course the party who makes the unauthorised alteration remains liable on the bill, as does any party who authorises that alteration or agrees to its making. A holder in due course enjoys the usual protection in such a situation but only if the alteration is not apparent[6]. An

1 1882 Act, s 63(1). Cheques and promissory notes may also be cancelled in this manner.
2 1882 Act, s 63(2).
3 1882 Act, s 63(3).
4 *Bank of Scotland v Dominion Bank* (1891) 18 R (HL) 21.
5 1882 Act, s 63(3).
6 1882 Act, s 64(1). The position is the same for cheques and promissory notes.

alteration must, however, be deliberate and not accidental for the bill to be discharged[1]. Furthermore, 'alteration' is not interpreted restrictively as referring only to the changing of existing information on a bill, as where the date, sum payable, or time and place of payment are changed, it also includes additions and deletions. If, eg, the holder of a bill which has been accepted generally adds, without the acceptor's consent, the place where it is to be paid, that addition constitutes a material alteration[2].

Not all alterations, however, result in a bill being avoided. We have already noted that the holder of an undated bill or acceptance may, in certain circumstances, insert a date[3] and that a holder may convert a blank indorsement into a special one[4]. Nor does the completion of an inchoate instrument[5] constitute an alteration. Although a crossing is a material part of a cheque, which, as a general rule, it is unlawful to obliterate, add to, or alter, some alterations are nonetheless permitted[6]. The holder of a cheque, eg, may: (1) cross it either generally or specially where it is uncrossed; (2) cross it specially where it is already crossed generally; and (3) add the words 'not negotiable' to a cheque crossed generally or specially. In addition, a banker to whom a cheque is crossed may cross it specially to another banker for collection. And a collecting banker to whom an uncrossed cheque, or one crossed generally, is sent, may cross it specially to himself or herself.

The material alteration of a cheque poses certain difficulties. In *London Joint Stock Bank Ltd v Macmillan and Arthur*[7] a clerk obtained his employers' signature to a cheque on which the sum expressed payable in figures was £2, but where the space for expressing the sum payable in words was left blank. The clerk converted the sum expressed in figures to £120 by inserting the numbers 1 and 0 before and after the 2 and completed the blank space by inserting the words 'one hundred and twenty pounds'. The drawers' bank was held to be entitled to debit their customers' account with £120. In this situation, even though the alteration is not apparent, a bank is not protected by s 64(1) because it is not a holder in due course. However, a bank's customers are under a duty to take reasonable care to guard against forgery when preparing cheques. If a customer fails in this duty and the bank, in good faith and without negligence, pays the cheque, then, it is entitled to debit its customer's account with the full amount it has paid. It may be noted, however, that the courts have proved unwilling to extend the customer's duties to the bank beyond the duty to prepare cheques in a manner which does not facilitate fraud, and a duty to notify the bank of forgeries as soon as these are discovered[8]. There is considerable authority for the view that a customer does not owe the bank a duty to organise its system for the preparation of cheques in such a way as to prevent the occurrence of forgeries[9].

1 *Hong Kong and Shanghai Banking Corpn v Lo Lee Shi* [1928] AC 181, PC.
2 1882 Act, s 64(2). The list of alterations deemed material by this subsection is not exhaustive.
3 1882 Act, s 12.
4 1882 Act, s 34(4).
5 1882 Act, s 20.
6 1882 Act, s 77.
7 [1918] AC 777, HL.
8 On this duty see *Greenwood v Martins Bank Ltd* [1933] AC 51, HL.
9 *Tai Hing Cotton Mill Ltd v Liu Chong Hing Bank Ltd* [1986] AC 80, PC. See also: *London Intercontinental Trust Ltd v Barclays Bank Ltd* [1980] 1 Lloyd's Rep 241; *Wealdon Woodlands (Kent) Ltd v National Westminster Bank Ltd* (1983) 133 NLJ 719.

Prescription

Bills of exchange, cheques and promissory notes are extinguished by operation of the short negative five-year prescription[1]. The prescriptive period commences from the date on which the obligation under the instrument becomes enforceable[2]. In the case of an instrument payable on demand, the period begins to run from midnight on the date shown on the instrument. If payment is due on a fixed date in the future, the prescriptive period starts to run on that date, and where the instrument is payable at a fixed period after sight it commences on the midnight after the period of notice has expired.

---

1 Prescription and Limitation (Scotland) Act 1973, s 6(1), Sch 1, para 1(e).
2 1973 Act, s 6(3).

6 Rights in security

Introduction

'A right in security' is 'any right which a creditor may hold for ensuring the payment or satisfaction of his debt, distinct from, and in addition to, his right of action and execution against the debtor under the latter's personal obligation'[1].

THE PROTECTION OF CREDITORS

The purpose of rights in security is to protect the position of secured creditors against the potential insolvency of their debtors. A secured creditor is one who holds some form of security right against the debtor. In principle all creditors are entitled to be paid. But what if the debtor becomes insolvent (ie his or her debts are greater than his or her ability to repay the sums owed)? In such a situation, an unsecured creditor may receive only partial repayment of his or her debt and may not even receive repayment at all. A secured creditor, however, enjoys the extra protection conferred by his or her security: ie the creditor's right to those assets of his or her debtor over which the creditor holds a security or his or her right to proceed against another person for the debt.

CLASSIFICATION OF RIGHTS IN SECURITY

The term 'rights of security' covers two quite distinct forms of security depending on the nature of the right constituted. There are real rights (*iura in re*), which confer rights against specified property of the debtor, often referred to as the 'subject' of the security right. These 'real rights' are 'good against the world': ie they allow the holder to defeat the claims of all other creditors and to claim the right to sell or to claim ownership over the property in question. Such real security rights are called rights in security, in the 'narrow' or strict sense of the term, and may be granted over heritable (ie land and buildings) or moveable (eg cars or ships) property. The term 'rights in security' can also be used in a broader sense to include any legal means by which the creditor increases the likelihood of being repaid. In this sense 'rights in security' can cover any additional personal rights (*iura in personam*), and confer rights on a creditor against persons. These personal rights are against a named person other than the actual debtor. A

---

1 Gloag and Irvine *Law of Rights in Security and Cautionary Obligations* (1897) pp 1–2. See also Erskine *Institute* III, 3, 61; Bell *Principles* s 245.

personal security right is called a 'cautionary obligation' the English law equivalent is 'guarantee' or 'surety'.

Rights in security (*iura in re*)

GENERAL PRINCIPLES

Rights in security over property operate by the debtor granting a real right of security in favour of the creditor over some or all of the property that the debtor owns. The security must be a real, rather than a mere personal, right in order to allow it to defeat the claims of the debtor's other creditors should the debtor become insolvent. For this reason sequestration is often spoken of as the 'acid test' of a security.

Property in Scots law is classified as heritable (immovable), moveable, corporeal and incorporeal. Each of these classes has its own distinctive type of security and, in addition, all classes of property owned by limited companies may be covered by a special type of security known as a floating charge. The position may be summarised as follows:

Type of property	Type of security
Heritable property	Standard security
Moveable property	Pledge, lien and hypothec
Incorporeal property	Assignation plus intimation
Property owned by companies	Floating charge

THE NECESSITY OF DELIVERY TO THE CREDITOR

The general rule governing property transfer in Scots law is expressed in the 'great maxim'[1] *traditionibus, non nudis pactis, transferuntur rerum dominia* (the ownership of things is transferred by delivery and not by bare agreement) and this principle therefore also applies to the creation of rights in security over property. Accordingly, subject to certain exceptions, a contract or deed on its own is insufficient to create a right in security, there must also be some form of delivery. The bare contract (*nudum pactum*) creates only a personal right, it is the delivery (*traditio*) which creates the real right. 'There is no principle more deeply rooted in the law than this, that in order to create a good security over subjects delivery must be given. If possession be retained no effectual security can be granted'[2].

---

1 *Orr's Tr v Tullis* (1870) 8 M 936 at 950, per Lord Neaves.
2 *Clark v West Calder Oil Co Liquidators* (1882) 9 R 1017 at 1033, per Lord Shand.

OBLIGATIONS OF THE SECURITY HOLDER

Although the primary purpose of a right in security is to protect the creditor in whose favour the security is granted, the security holder also has certain obligations to the debtor. Should the creditor have to enforce his or her security by compelling the sale of the security subjects, then the provisions of the security agreement and of the general law, common or statute, must be strictly observed.

The law imposes obligations on security holders who are in possession of the subjects of those securities, since, it must be remembered, they hold those subjects merely as security and not as owners. The main obligations are: (1) to restore to the owner, on redemption of the debt, the exact property given in security[1]; (2) to take reasonable care of property held and to have some regard for the debtor's interests[2]; and (3) not to use property held in security unless specifically authorised to do so. In *Waddell v Hutton*[3] the creditor held certain company shares in security when a rights issue, at advantageous terms to existing shareholders, was made. The creditor, who failed to inform the debtor of the offer, and did not take advantage of it personally, was found not to have exercised reasonable care in the matter. If the security subject is accidentally destroyed this does not extinguish the obligation of the debtor to repay his debt[4]. It has been held that the wearing of jewellery held on pledge by the wife and daughter of the pledgee does not constitute a fundamental breach of the contract of pledge[5].

CORPOREAL MOVEABLES

Pledge

Delivery

Pledge is the conventional common law security that applies to corporeal moveable property. By 'conventional' it is meant that the existence of the security is created by contract between the parties: in other words, with the express consent of the owner of the goods in question. The contract of pledge is 'limited to corporeal moveables which pass from hand to hand'[6]. The debtor who owns the goods pledged in security is known as the pledger and the creditor who holds the goods in security is known as the pledgee. The maxim *traditionibus, non nudis pactis, transferuntur rerum dominia* applies and, accordingly, the contract of pledge alone merely creates a personal right. To constitute a real right the contract of pledge must be accompanied by delivery of the goods into the possession of the

1 *Crerar v Bank of Scotland* 1921 SC 736; 1922 SC (HL) 137.
2 Bell *Principles* s 206.
3 1911 SC 575.
4 *Syred v Carruthers* (1858) EB & E 469.
5 *Wolifson v Harrison* 1977 SC 384.
6 *Hamilton v Western Bank of Scotland* (1856) 19 D 152 at 165, per Lord Deas.

creditor. If there is no delivery then no security right is created. As was remarked in *Pattison's Tr v Liston*: '[I]t is quite certain that an effectual security over moveables can only be effected by delivery of the subject of the security'[1]. And in *Moore v Gledden* it was opined that: 'Possession in moveables is like Sasine in heritage. It is the badge of a real right'[2].

The right of pledge is lost if the creditor surrenders possession of the security subjects: 'In the pledge of moveables, the creditor who quits possession of the subject loses the real right he had upon it'[3]. However, the pledged subjects do not necessarily always have to be in the physical possession of the pledgee. As already noted[4], a pledgee who allowed his wife and daughter to wear jewellery held in pledge was said not to have lost possession and hence not to have lost his security right. Where goods represented by a bill of lading are pledged, with a concurrent power to sell, the pledgee does not relinquish possession by delivering the bill to his agent in order to achieve their sale[5].

The delivery of the subjects must be real[6], and s 62(4) of the Sale of Goods Act 1979 prevents evasion of this general rule by means of a fictitious sale. But defining what counts as a fictitious sale can often be highly problematic[7]. There are three types of delivery: actual, symbolic or constructive.

ACTUAL DELIVERY

Actual delivery is simply the physical transfer of goods from the debtor to creditor. This can take the form of the transportation of the goods by the debtor to the creditor, or by the latter assuming control of the premises in which the goods are housed. In *West Lothian Oil Co Liquidator v Mair*[8], possession of the key to a yard surrounded by a fence was held to constitute delivery of the barrels stored within the yard. This case can be contrasted with *Pattison's Tr v Liston*[9] where a contract of pledge had been granted over some furniture and the keys to the house in which the furniture was situated were handed over to the creditor for the purposes of letting the property. Here it was held that there had been no delivery because the creditor held the keys merely as agent of the debtor for the purposes of letting the house and not in his capacity as secured creditor.

CONSTRUCTIVE DELIVERY

Constructive delivery is the term applied to delivery when the goods are in the custody of an independent third party and not with the creditor. It is only competent when four requirements are satisfied[10]:

1 (1893) 20 R 806 at 813, per Lord Trayner.
2 (1869) 7 M 1016 at 1022, per Lord Neaves.
3 Erskine *Institute* III, 1, 33. See also Bell *Principles* s 206: 'the security expires with loss of possession'; *Hunter & Co v Slack and Hyland* (1860) 22 D 1166.
4 *Wolifson v Harrison* 1977 SC 384.
5 *North-Western Bank Ltd v Poynter, Son and Macdonalds* (1894) 22 R (HL) 1; (1894) 21 R 513.
6 *Orr's Tr v Tullis* (1870) 8 M 936.
7 The problem is discussed later.
8 (1892) 20 R 64.
9 (1893) 20 R 806.
10 *HD Pochin & Co v Robinows and Marjoribanks* (1869) 7 M 622.

(1) The custodier must be an independent third party. In *Anderson v McCall & Co*[1], a firm of grain merchants granted as security a document transferring ownership of a quantity of the grain to the lender. The firm went bankrupt and the lender sought to rely on his security. However, the grain was held in a store controlled by an employee of the firm and, accordingly, it was held that as the goods were not in the custody of an independent third party then there was no constructive delivery.

(2) Intimation must be made to the third party that he holds the goods on behalf of the lender[2].

(3) Goods must be specifically ascertained and identified. In *Hayman & Son v McLintock*[3], a flour merchant sold, and received payment for, a number of sacks of flour. The sacks were located in a store with nothing on them to indicate to whom they were to be delivered. However, the seller had given the buyer delivery orders for the sacks sold and these were initimated to the storekeeper. A competition then arose on the seller's sequestration, between the buyer and the seller's trustee, and it was held that no property in the goods had passed, as a consequence of constructive delivery, since the orders did not identify the sacks which were to be delivered against them.

(4) The obligation or order to deliver the goods must be unqualified. In *Mackinnon v Max Nanson & Co*[4] a delivery order in favour of the creditor which purported to act as security for a loan nevertheless allowed the debtor to remove such of the goods as he required in the course of his business. It was held that as the obligation was qualified there was no valid right of security.

SYMBOLIC DELIVERY

Symbolic delivery is only competent in certain specific situations. The two main examples are goods on ships and goods held by mercantile agents. Goods on ships are covered by bills of lading. A bill of lading is the authority for unloading goods from a ship and transfer of the bill is recognised as symbolic of the transfer of the goods themselves. In *Hayman & Son v McLintock*[5] the holders of a bill of lading covering 750 sacks which formed part of a larger group of sacks, and held as security from the now insolvent owner, were held to have good title to the relevant sacks. Pledge by a mercantile agent of documents of title to goods operates as a pledge of the goods themselves[6]. Consequently, a mercantile agent can do what his principal cannot, namely, create a security over goods without the need for delivery of those goods.

In commerce delivery is usually constructive or symbolic because normally it is troublesome and expensive for commercial lenders to store

1 (1866) 4 M 765.
2 *Rhind's Tr v Robertson and Baxter* (1891) 18 R 623. See also *Inglis v Robertson and Baxter* (1898) 25 R (HL) 70.
3 1907 SC 936.
4 (1868) 6 M 974.
5 1907 SC 936.
6 Factors Act 1889, s 3.

goods. Moreover, the debtor can rarely afford to lose possession of the goods pledged since these are often part of his or her stock in trade without which the debtor may have little hope of making the money with which to pay off his or her debts.

Enforcement

Should the debtor fail to repay his debt then the pledge holder will eventually be entitled to sell the goods in question. Normally this requires a warrant from the court: '. . . the subject of the pledge cannot be sold without the order of a judge, which is obtained on a summary application to the sheriff'[1]. However, there is no need for the court's consent where a debtor has authorised sale at the time of loan, which is standard practice for commercial loans, or for loans involving pawn which are regulated under the Consumer Credit Act 1974.

Pawn and the Consumer Credit Act 1974, sections 114 to 122

Pawn is a type of pledge which is partially regulated by ss 114 to 122 of the Consumer Credit Act 1974 and defined as 'any article subject to a pledge'[2]. The provisions of the 1974 Act apply to consumer transactions for loans of amounts not exceeding £15,000[3]. A debtor is defined as a consumer if he or she is a 'person other than a body corporate'[4]. Accordingly the Act applies only where credit for goods up to £15,000 is given to individuals. Such transactions are classified by the Act as 'consumer credit agreements'[5]. The person pledging the item is known as the 'pawnor' and the person taking the security as the 'pawnee'. In return for the article the pawnee must provide a pawn receipt in the prescribed form[6] and failure to do so is an offence[7]. It is also an offence to take a pawn from a minor[8]. A pawn is redeemable at any time within six months after it was taken[9], or for a longer period as agreed by the parties[10]. A pawn is redeemed by the pawnor surrendering the pawn-receipt together with payment of the amount owing to the pawnee[11]. If the pawn has not been redeemed within the appropriate period then it may still be redeemed until the pawn is realised or becomes the property of the pawnee in accordance with the terms of the agreement[12]. Where the redemption period is six months and the credit does not exceed £25, the pawn becomes the property of the pawnee at the end of the redemption period[13]. A pawn can be realised

---

1 Bell *Principles* s 207.
2 Consumer Credit Act 1974, s 189(1).
3 1974 Act, s 8(2).
4 1974 Act, ss 8(1), (2) and 189(1).
5 1974 Act, s 8(2).
6 1974 Act, s 114(1).
7 1974 Act, s 115.
8 1974 Act, s 114(2).
9 1974 Act, s 116(1).
10 1974 Act, s 116(2).
11 1974 Act, s 117(1).
12 1974 Act, s 116(3).
13 1974 Act, s 120(1)(a).

only after the pawnee has given the pawnor notice of his intention to sell and notice of the asking price together with other details[1].

Lien

General

A lien is the right of a creditor to retain the property of his or her debtor that is presently in the possession of the creditor until such time as the debt has been repaid: lien is sometimes (though inaccurately)[2] referred to as a right of retention[3]. Lien is an implied common law security over corporeal moveables: ie the existence of the security is automatically implied by operation of the common law without any need for the consent of the owner of the goods in question. The advantages of this are obvious: the creditor gets a security right automatically and without need for any legal formalities, so lien is a useful self-help remedy. As with pledge, a right of lien is a real right and will defeat the claims of the other creditors of the debtor. A right of lien arises in two main circumstances: in contracts of sale (unpaid seller's lien) and in contracts for services (eg repairer's lien, carrier's lien, warehouser's lien).

The necessity of possession

A right of lien is implied only where the goods are in the possession of the holder with the consent of the owner[4], and the right may be waived by express agreement or by custom[5]. A right of lien exists only for as long as the goods are in the creditor's possession. As Bell states: 'A person possessed of property, and entitled to a lien, loses it the moment he quits his possession'[6]. Where an unpaid seller who had previously surrendered possession subsequently repossessed the goods without the consent of the buyer this was held not to revive the right of lien[7]. Where, however, the seller regains possession with the consent of the buyer then, subject to the intentions of the parties, it may be held that the right of lien revives[8].

Effect and enforcement of liens

Where a right of lien has been exercised, the owner of the goods is deprived of his or her right to use or possess these until the debt to the holder has been paid[9]. Should the owner fail to pay then the holder has the right to sell the goods after obtaining judicial authority or even without it in the case of a repairer's lien.

1 1974 Act, ss 120(1)(b) and 121.
2 Gloag and Henderson *The Law of Scotland* (10th edn 1995) (eds Wilson, Forte) para 19.19.
3 Bell *Principles* s 1410.
4 Bell *Commentaries* II, 89.
5 Bell *Commentaries* II, 91.
6 Bell *Commentaries* II, 89.
7 *London Scottish Transport Ltd v Tyres (Scotland) Ltd* 1957 SLT (Sh Ct) 48.
8 *Hostess Mobile Catering v Archibald Scott Ltd* 1981 SC 185, OH.
9 Bell *Commentaries* II, 91.

Special and general liens

Liens are traditionally categorised as special or general. Bell explains the difference between the two thus:

> 'The right of Retention, or Lien, is of two kinds; namely, Special and General. 1. SPECIAL RETENTION, or LIEN, is the right of withholding or retaining property or goods which are in any one's possession under a contract, till indemnified for the labour or money expended on them. This sort of retention is a favourite of the law. 2. GENERAL RETENTION, or LIEN, is a right to withhold or detain the property of another, in respect of any debt which happens to be due by the proprietor to the person who has the custody; or for a general balance of account, arising on a particular train of employment'[1].

Special liens

A special lien is widely implied, a 'favourite', as Bell put it, by the law and is the right of any workman who repairs an object to retain possession of that object until he has been paid. The two main types of special lien are the repairer's lien and the unpaid seller's lien.

REPAIRER'S LIEN

Any person who repairs an object has a lien over that object for the price of the repair, except, that is, where the goods repaired are the subjects of a hire-purchase contract which prohibits the creation of liens by the hirer[2].

UNPAID SELLER'S LIEN

By virtue of s 39 of the Sale of Goods Act 1979, an unpaid seller has a right of lien over the sale goods and he or she may exercise this right even where property in the goods has already passed to the buyer under the terms of the contract[3]. After giving due notice and reasonable time to pay, the unpaid seller may resell the goods and also claim damages for any loss incurred through the buyer's breach of contract[4]. As with lien generally the unpaid seller loses his or her security right the moment he or she surrenders possession: eg when the seller delivers the goods to a carrier or to the buyer or the buyer's agent[5].

General liens

General liens, in contrast, are restricted to those few situations specifically acknowledged by the law. Four liens are generally categorised as being general, namely, those of factors, bankers, solicitors and innkeepers.

1 Bell *Commentaries* II, 87.
2 *Lamonby v Arthur G Foulds Ltd* 1928 SC 89.
3 Sale of Goods Act 1979, s 39(1)(a).
4 1979 Act, s 48(3).
5 1979 Act, s 43(1)(a),(b).

BANKER'S LIEN

The banker's lien is a general lien implied by law and held by the bank as security against sums owed to the bank by the customer. The lien covers those negotiable instruments (ie bills of exchange, cheques and promissory notes) belonging to the customer which are in the possession of the bank[1]. Items deposited with a bank for safekeeping cannot be the subject of a lien[1] unless, that is, the bank has advanced money to its customer against retention of those items[2]. However, the banker's lien only confers a right to retain the customer's property, it confers no right to sell it[2].

FACTOR'S LIEN

A factor or mercantile agent (the terms are interchangeable) is someone who in the customary course of business acts as an agent and is employed to trade with his or her principal's property (which is in his or her possession) for a profit[3]. It includes dealers and for the purposes of lien has been held to include auctioneers and stockbrokers.

INNKEEPER'S LIEN

The innkeeper's lien is of great antiquity and gives the innkeeper the right to retain any goods or baggage brought into the hotel by the guest until the guest has paid his or her bill[4]. There is fairly little reported authority on the nature and scope of the innkeeper's lien. In the leading modern case, *Bermans and Nathans Ltd v Weibye*[5], it was held that the innkeeper's lien applies to all of the possessions brought into the hotel by guests, regardless of whether or not these are owned by the guest. But the lien does not extend to goods delivered to the inn by a third party and which belong to that third party. Also by statute the innkeeper's lien does not apply to any vehicle, any property left in a vehicle or to any live animal[6]. Should the guest still be unable or unwilling to pay his or her bill then, after six weeks have elapsed, the innkeeper has the right to sell the goods by auction under the terms of the Innkeeper's Act 1878. There is some authority for the proposition that the lien does not extend to any claim for loss or damages to the hotel's fabric caused by the guest. In *Ferguson v Peterkin*[7], an innkeeper claimed that guests had damaged a wardrobe door and refused to surrender possession of their luggage. It was held that the right of retention did not extend to damages claims and the guests were in turn awarded damages for the illegal detention of their property.

SOLICITOR'S LIEN

A solicitor has a general lien over all of his or her client's papers which are in the solicitor's possession (eg contracts, title deeds, wills, etc) to cover

1 *Brandao v Barnett* (1846) 12 Cl & Fin 787, HL.
2 *Robertson's Tr v Royal Bank of Scotland* (1890) 18 R 12.
3 Factors Act 1889, s 1(1).
4 Bell *Principles* s 1428.
5 1983 SC 67.
6 Hotel Proprietors Act 1956, s 2(2).
7 1953 SLT (Sh Ct) 91.

any unpaid bills, expenses or advances made in the ordinary course of his or her business as a solicitor[1]. The right consists only of the right to retain the documents, and does not extend to a right to dispose of them[2]. It does not cover any cash advances or money lent to a client except where such advance is directly concerned with his role as solicitor[3]. In *Christie v Ruxton*[4], a solicitor was acting for a client in the purchase of a property, but also provided a cash advance to the client. It was held that the solicitor had a lien over the title deeds for the expenses incurred but not for the cash advance. The lien does not extend to unpaid accounts incurred on a client's behalf but for which the solicitor is not personally liable to make payment[5]. A trustee in sequestration, or the liquidator of a company, may demand production of all relevant papers belonging to a client to allow him or her to ingather the insolvent party's estate. However, this does not affect the solicitor's legal rights as surrender of the documents is made by him or her under the implied reservation of the lien, and the solicitor will rank as a preferred creditor[6]. A solicitor who acts in the dual capacity of agent for the borrower and also for the lender cannot retain possession of title deeds granted in security for the loan until the borrower pays off debts due to that solicitor[7]. In *Yau v Ogilvie & Co*[8] a solicitor, whose fee had not yet been paid by a client, was held to have a lien over the client's papers even though the latter wished return of these in order to sue the solicitor for professional negligence.

Hypothec

General

A hypothec is a security over moveables that does not require possession to be effective. There are two types of hypothec, conventional and legal, and these are only available where the law, whether common law or statute, makes specific provision for their existence.

Conventional hypothecs

Conventional hypothecs are created by express agreement and are used to create securities over ships and aircraft. The commercial need for a non-possessory security over ships and planes is obvious. These are extremely costly items and can only make money if at sea or in the air. Consequently, to be effective, such securities must be non-possessory in nature. There are three such hypothecs presently recognised by Scots law: a mortgage over a ship, an aircraft mortgage, and bonds of bottomry and respondentia.

---

1 Bell *Principles* s 1438; *Paul v Meikle* (1868) 7 M 235.
2 *Ferguson and Stuart v Grant and Wemyss* (1856) 18 D 536.
3 *Wylie's Exrx v McJannet* (1901) 4 F 195.
4 (1862) 24 D 1182.
5 See also *Grand Empire Theatres Ltd Liquidator v Snodgras* 1932 SC (HL) 73.
6 Bankruptcy (Scotland) Act 1985, s 38(4) (sequestration); Insolvency Act 1986, s 144 (liquidation). See also *Adam and Winchester v White's Tr* (1884) 11 R 863.
7 *Paterson v Currie* (1846) 8 D 1005.
8 1985 SLT 91, OH.

SHIP MORTGAGES

The appropriate form of security for a ship is a ship mortgage. The instrument creating the security must be registered in the Register of Shipping to be effective[1]. Ship mortgages rank in the order in which these are listed in the Register[2] but after bonds of bottomry or maritime liens.

AIRCRAFT MORTGAGE

The appropriate form of security for an aircraft is an aircraft mortgage, which is in the same general form as a ship's mortgage[3].

BONDS OF BOTTOMRY AND BONDS OF RESPONDENTIA

Bonds of bottomry and bonds of respondentia are still competent but rarely met with in practice now: advances in modern communications have caused their demise.

A bond of bottomry creates a right in security over a ship and a bond of respondentia creates a right in security over a cargo. A ship's master has implied authority to grant a bond of bottomry if the ship, which is in a foreign port, is unable to continue on its voyage without an advance of money, and no money can be obtained on the personal credit of the vessel's owner[4]. It is only where communication with the owner is impracticable, an unlikely event given the global communication networks available today, that the master may grant a bond on his own authority. The bond is effective without any requirement for possession or registration. Since the purpose of such bonds is to enable the vessel to arrive at its destination, it follows that where several bonds have been granted, it is the last one which is preferred[5].

A bond of respondentia over a ship's cargo may also be granted by the master if an advance is necessary for the continuation of the voyage. Again, where possible, the master should try to contact the owner of the cargo but if this is not possible he may grant the bond on his own authority.

Legal hypothecs

Legal hypothecs are those implied by the common law, in certain specified circumstances, without need for the consent of the owner of the goods in question.

LANDLORD'S HYPOTHEC

A landlord's hypothec[6] is automatically held for specified arrears of rent. The maximum period of rent covered is one year and the hypothec is

---

1 Merchant Shipping Act 1995, s 16 and Sch 1.
2 1995 Act, Sch 1, para 8(1) – subject to the registrar being given a priority notice: para 8(2).
3 Civil Aviation Act 1982, s 86.
4 Bell *Principles* ss 452, 455.
5 Bell *Principles* s 456.
6 There is also the implied hypothec of a feudal superior for unpaid feuduty. Since feuduties have nearly all been redeemed this is seldom met with and is not discussed here.

enforced by a special procedure called 'sequestration for rent' which must be raised, within three months from the end of the period claimed for, in the sheriff court[1]. It extends over the moveable goods, including any stock-in-trade, belonging to the tenant which are situated within the leased subjects. It does not extend to moveables owned by someone other than the tenant. In *Bell v Andrews*[2] it was held that the landlord's hypothec did not apply to a piano owned by the tenant's daughter. However, in a commercial context, the courts have been prepared to widen the scope of the landlord's hypothec to include property not belonging to the tenant. In *Scottish and Newcastle Breweries Ltd v City of Edinburgh District Council*[3] the landlord's hypothec for the lease of a public house was held to extend to beer kegs belonging to a brewery because they were deemed to be part of the regular stock-in-trade of a public house. Likewise, in *Dundee Corporation v Marr*[4], the landlord of premises leased as a cafe was held to have a hypothec over a jukebox situated with the premises but rented by the tenant from a third party[5].

SOLICITOR'S HYPOTHEC

A solicitor has a hypothec for expenses incurred on behalf of a client whilst pursuing an action, and it extends over any sum (typically an award for damages) awarded by a court to his or her client. It is implemented by the solicitor moving for decree on his or her own behalf as agent-disburser. This claim is now preferable to that of any other creditor and, unusually, can be claimed even after the client has been sequestrated. It is a hypothec because the money is not in the possession of the solicitor but in the hands of the defender to the action raised by the solicitor's client. It may also be claimed against any property recovered in the course of the action[6].

Maritime hypothecs

Rather confusingly maritime hypothecs are generally referred to as maritime 'liens' and may be claimed by certain specified parties. The unpaid crew of a ship have a maritime lien for their wages and cannot contract out of their right[7]. Likewise the master has a lien for his wages and for any disbursements made[8]. Salvors have a lien for any sum expended in the course of the salvage of the vessel[9], as do repairers for ships repaired[10].

1 *Young v Welsh* (1833) 12 S 233.
2 (1885) 12 R 961.
3 1979 SLT (Notes) 11.
4 1971 SC 96.
5 Nevertheless, the position, even in the commercial context, is far from clear. See *Pulsometer Engineering Co Ltd v Grace* (1887) 14 R 316 (sample goods on display in commercial premises held not to be covered); *Edinburgh Albert Buildings Co Ltd v General Guarantee Corpn Ltd* 1917 SC 239 (no hypothec over rented piano on the ground that the subjects were leased fully furnished).
6 Solicitors (Scotland) Act 1980, s 62(1).
7 Merchant Shipping Act 1995, s 39(1).
8 1995 Act, s 41.
9 *Harmer v Bell, The Bold Buccleugh* (1851) 7 Moo PCC 267.
10 *Barr and Shearer v Cooper* (1875) 2 R (HL) 14; *Ross and Duncan v Baxter & Co* (1885) 13 R 185.

Contracts for moveables which are functionally equivalent to securities

Creditor-to-debtor sales and retention of title clauses

Because of the problems created by the need for delivery for the constitution of a valid right in security (other than in those cases where a hypothec is available or where the creditor is strong enough to demand a floating charge), lawyers have developed contract terms which, while they do not create an actual right in security, nevertheless function as such in practice. In the context of corporeal moveables the most important of these is the retention of title clause, often used where there is a creditor-to-debtor sale (eg where the goods are sold on credit) and generally referred to as a 'Romalpa clause' after the first case in which these were recognised[1]. There has never been any doubt that a seller can retain title over goods until he or she is paid for those goods, as this is explicitly provided for in ss 17 and 19 of the Sale of Goods Act 1979. Accordingly, clauses to this effect, sometimes known as 'simple' retention of title clauses, were always valid[2]. But the Scottish courts found so called 'all sums' retention of title clauses (which provide that title in the goods will not pass until all sums due by the buyer to the seller have been paid)[3] more problematic. The problem with all sums clauses was the argument that these, which in effect allow a form of security for the seller, fall foul of s 62(4) of the Sale of Goods Act 1979. This subsection specifically provides that the provisions of the Act that allow transfer of property without delivery[4], are not to apply to the creation of securities. The Inner House in the 1980s took the view that 'all sums' clauses were invalid because they violated s 62(4)[5]. But in *Armour v Thyssen Edelstahlwerke AG*[6], the House of Lords reversed this trend, holding that 'all sums' clauses', if properly phrased, are effective, being merely a straightforward application of the provisions of ss 17 and 19 of the 1979 Act, and that s 62(4) is irrelevant in this situation. Accordingly, a properly drafted retention of title clause will afford the unpaid seller protection against the insolvency of his buyer as regards the goods he has sold, provided that these are still identifiable.

Debtor-to-creditor sales and transfer of title clauses

Another method by which creditors may try to protect their interests is by having the debtor transfer ownership of some of his or her goods to the creditor: eg by a sale and lease-back agreement. Here the contrast between

---

1 *Aluminium Industrie Vaassen BV v Romalpa Aluminium Ltd* [1976] All ER 552, CA.
2 *Archivent Sales and Development Ltd v Strathclyde Regional Council* 1985 SLT 154, OH; *Zahnrad Fabrik Passau GmbH v Terex Ltd* 1985 SC 364, OH.
3 The difference between a simple retention of title clause and an all sums clause is analogous to the distinction between a special and a general lien.
4 Sale of Goods Act 1979, s 17(1) provides that property in the goods passes when intended to pass, without any requirement for delivery.
5 *Deutz Engines Ltd v Terex Ltd* 1984 SLT 273, OH; *Armour v Thyssen Edelstahlweke AG* 1986 SLT 452, OH.
6 1990 SLT 891, HL.

the law of sale and the law of security is highlighted. A contract for the sale of goods requires no delivery, property passing when intended to pass, and so a real right of ownership in the goods may be created without the buyer-creditor actually taking possession. But a contract for security, of course, requires delivery in order to create a real right. In transactions of this kind, rather than a retention of title by the seller-creditor, as we find in Romalpa clauses, there is a transfer of title by the seller-debtor. The problem with transfers of title by seller-debtors is that such transactions are likely to be considered 'sham sales' and contrary to s 62(4) of the Sale of Goods Act 1979. The difficulty lies in interpreting the rather opaque wording of this provision, and the cases on the topic are contradictory. The common interpretation[1] of the case law on s 62(4) is that the Scottish coursts, in cases such as *Robertson v Hall's Tr*[2], have derived two principles from it. Firstly, that they must consider the 'true intentions' of the parties in order to decide whether or not the contract is one of sale or security. Consequently, if it is found, having regard to all the circumstances, that the parties intended to create a security right and not a sale, so that the transaction is really a security in the form of a sale, then it must satisfy the requirements of a security, and delivery will be essential if the security is to be a properly constituted real right. Under this approach, where the buyer-creditor allows the debtor-seller to retain possession of the goods, (as, eg, in a sale and lease-back arrangement), there is a danger that the creditor will be deemed to have no real right should the debtor become insolvent. However, it can be argued that the cases which support this view are based on a misunderstanding of s 62(4). A contrary view[3], there-fore, is that the correct approach is that taken by the Inner House in *Gavin's Tr v Fraser*[4]. In *Gavin's Tr* the court stressed that the intention men-tioned in s 62(4) is contractual intention. This view argues that what s 62(4) requires is the discovery of the true intention of the parties simply by reference to the contractual intentions embodied in the relevant con-tract. Should those intentions disclose a contract of sale then it is the law of sale that will apply, regardless of whether one of the background motives of the buyer was to obtain security for his loan.

INCORPOREAL MOVEABLE PROPERTY

Assignation

Incorporeal moveable property includes any sort of obligation owed by one party to another excluding those in relation to heritable property. This includes debts, insurance policies, company shares, and intellectual prop-erty rights such as copyright and patents. Once again the civilian principle *traditionibus, non nudis pactis, transferuntur rerum dominia* applies, and,

---

1 Most clearly set out in Carey Miller *Corporeal Moveables in Scots Law* (1991) ch 11.
2 (1896)·24 R 120. See also *Jones & Co's Tr v Allan* (1901) 4 F 374; *Rennet v Mathieson* (1903) 5 F 591.
3 Argued by Styles 'Debtor-to-Creditor Sales and the Sale of Goods Act 1979' (1995) JR 365.
4 1920 SC 674.

therefore, there is a two-stage process to create a right in security over incoporeal moveables. There is a contract which creates the personal right (in the form of an assignation), followed by the equivalent of delivery (in the form of an intimation to the debtor that the obligation has been assigned): 'Intimation of an assignation to the debtor is the equivalent of delivery of a corporeal moveable and is necessary to complete the title of the assignee'[1]. The party who assigns the property is known as the 'assignor' or 'cedent', and the party to whom it is assigned is known as the 'assignee' or 'cessionary'. The assignee gets all the rights previously held by the assignor, which means, on the application of the maxim *assignatus utitur jure auctoris*, that the assignee will receive no better title than that held by the assignor. Thus in *Scottish Widows' Fund and Life Assurance Society v Buist*[2], where an insurance policy was void on account of false statements made by the insured, it was held that this defect operated equally against any claim by the assignee.

Mere possession of a document of title to an obligation confers no interest in that obligation. For example, in *Wylie's Exrx v McJannet*[3], a solicitor, in order to cover advances that he had made to a client, persuaded him to take out a life assurance policy. The solicitor retained the policy and paid all the premiums for the client. The client died, but as there had been neither assignation nor imitation of the policy to him, it was held that the solicitor had no right to the proceeds thereof[4]. It should be noted that some obligations cannot be assigned if this is prohibited by a term in the contract constituting them. Insurance policies, eg, sometimes prohibit assignation.

If there is assignation but no imitation then, as only a personal obligation[5] (a *ius in personam*) has been created, that right will be of no avail in an insolvency situation. However, the personal obligation will still bind the parties so that the cedent is still obliged to the appropriate creditor: 'Though . . . intimation be a necessary solemnity to assignations, yet the assignation alone will be sufficient against the cedent'[6]. That intimation is essential was highlighted in the case of *Strachan v McDougle*[7] where the assignee failed to intimate the assignation of a life assurance policy to the insurance company until after the death of the insured. In these circumstances it was held that the prior arrestment of the proceeds of the policy by another party had priority over the claims of the assignee. The requirement of intimation is unknown in England where mere possession of a document of title confers an equitable mortgage upon the holder. It is worth keeping this in mind since it possible that questions may arise as to the relevant jurisdiction in a particular instance.

1 *Gallemos Ltd (In Receivership) v Barratt Falkirk Ltd* 1990 SLT 98 at 101, per Lord Dunpark.
2 (1876) 3 R 1078; *Buist v Scottish Equitable Life Assurance Soc* (1878) 5 R (HL) 64.
3 (1901) 4 F 195.
4 See also *Strachan v M'Dougle* (1835) 13 S 954 and *Bank of Scotland v Hutchison Main & Co Ltd Liquidators* 1914 SC (HL) 1.
5 Stair *Institution* III, 1, 6–10; *Campbell's Trs v Whyte* (1884) 11 R 1078; *Allan v Urquhart* (1887) 15 R 56.
6 Stair *Institution* III, 1, 15.
7 (1835) 13 S 954.

Formalities

Assignation

For certain categories of obligation an assignation must be in writing (eg those pertaining to interests in land)[1]. However, while there is no general obligation to use writing, in practice assignations are always made in writing since this is clearly the safest course. The Transmission of Moveable Property (Scotland) Act 1862 provides forms, or styles, for assignations but these need not be followed: 'If anything is settled in the law of Scotland, it is that no words directly importing conveyance are necessary to constitute an assignation, but that any words giving authority or directions, which if fairly carried out will operate a transference, are sufficient to make an assignation'[2]. For a deed to be valid as an assignation, however, two things are essential. First, the intention to transfer an obligation must be clear. Second, that intention must be a present and not a future one: 'Any words which express a present intention to transfer are sufficient as an assignation'[3]. Thus in *Gallemos Ltd (In Receivership) v Barratt Falkirk Ltd*[4] a deed containing the far from clear expression 'reserve the right to the contra' was held not to constitute an assignation. A mere agreement or intention to assign at a future time does not constitute an assignation and confers no right at all upon the purported assignee[5].

Intimation

Intimation may be express or implied from the surrounding circumstances. Express intimation is usually done in writing and in accordance with the methods set out in s 2 of the Transmission of Moveable Property (Scotland) Act 1862. These are: (1) delivery of a certified copy of the assignation done by a notary public; or (2) postal delivery of a certified copy sent by either the assignee or his or her agent followed by written acknowledgment of receipt of the copy of the assignation from the debtor. Intimation may be implied, eg, where an assignee raises an action against the debtor founding on the assignation[6]. In such circumstances the debtor can hardly be unaware that an assignation has occurred. Naturally intimation is unnecessary where the assignee is himself or herself the debtor[7].

---

1   Examples include the Registration of Leases (Scotland) Act 1857, s 3(1) and Sch A, and the Conveyancing and Feudal Reform (Scotland) Act 1970, s 14, Forms A, B.
2   *Carter v McIntosh* (1862) 24 D 925 at 933, per Lord Justice-Clerk Inglis.
3   *McCutcheon v McWilliam* (1876) 3 R 565 at 571, per Lord Justice-Clerk Moncreiff. See also *Gallemos Ltd (In Receivership) v Barratt Falkirk Ltd* 1990 SLT 98.
4   1990 SLT 98.
5   *Bank of Scotland v Hutchison, Main & Co Ltd Liquidators* 1914 SC (HL) 1.
6   *Whyte v Neish* (1622) Mor 854.
7   *Browne's Tr v Anderson* (1901) 4 F 305.

PROPERTY OWNED BY COMPANIES – THE FLOATING CHARGE

General

The floating charge is the conventional statutory security that applies to all categories of property, moveable and heritable, owned by a limited company. The floating charge is a unique form of security and the law governing it is subject to many peculiarities. It has its origins in the English law of equity[1], was imported into Scots law only in 1961, and still bears many of the marks of its origins in the law of the Courts of Chancery. Accordingly it fits only with difficulty into the general scheme of Scots property law. As a creature of statute, born out of the English law of equity, there is no requirement for the application of the civilian principle that delivery or its equivalent is necessary for the constitution of a real right, and possession by the holder of the security is not required. But although the floating charge may disturb the conceptual neatness of Scots law, there is no doubting its importance in modern commercial life.

Creation and operation

The legislative provisions governing floating charges in Scotland are largely contained in ss 410 to 424 and ss 462 to 466 of the Companies Act 1985, and in ss 50 to 71 of the Insolvency Act 1986. Neither statute gives a full definition of the nature of a floating charge and its character has to be deduced from the interaction of the respective provisions of the two Acts and the general law. Only an incorporated company may grant a floating charge and accordingly it is not competent for private individuals or partnerships to grant this form of security[2].

The creation of a floating charge is a two-stage process: ie execution of a deed, followed by its registration. To create a valid security right the deed must be registered within 21 days of the date of its execution[3]. Provided that this is done within the statutory period, the charge takes retrospective effect from the date of its execution. If, however, the deed is not registered within 21 days, then it is of no effect and no valid security has been created[3]. Registration is with the Registrar of Companies in Scotland and a certificate of registration issued by the Registrar is conclusive evidence as to the date of registration. Once the charge has been created it exists in a rather strange manner. The floating charge confers a conditional right of security on the holder over a company's property at any time prior to its attachment. This means that any property which is disposed of prior to attachment automatically ceases to be covered by the floating charge, while any property that is acquired by the company automatically becomes subject to the charge. In other words, the charge 'floats' over company property.

1 The floating charge was first recognised by the Court of Appeal in Chancery in *Re Panama* (1870) 5 Ch App 318.
2 Companies Act 1985, s 462(1).
3 1985 Act, s 410(2).

Enforcement of a floating charge: 'attachment'

The vast majority of loans secured by a floating charge will be repaid in accordance with the terms of the constituting deed. And on full repayment the floating charge is automatically discharged. The process of enforcing a floating charge is known as 'attachment' or 'crystallisation'. A floating charge crystallises either on the winding up of a company[1] or on the appointment of a receiver by the floating charge holder[2]. A floating charge holder is entitled to appoint a receiver either on the occurrence of any event specified in the deed creating the charge, or, on the occurrence of any event specified in s 52(1) of the Insolvency Act 1986 which, in the latter case, basically amounts to defaulting on the loan. When a floating charge crystallises it then has effect as if it were a fixed security[3]. The point was well put by Lord President Emslie in *Forth & Clyde Construction Co Ltd v Trinity Timber & Plywood Co Ltd*: 'The intention [of the Act] appears to me to be that the holder of the floating charge shall, on the appointment of a receiver, enjoy all the protection in relation to any item of attached property that the holder of a fixed security over that item thereof would enjoy under the general law'[4]. In other words the floating charge becomes a fixed charge and a real right on attachment[5].

The potential range of subjects caught by the attachment of a floating charge has been reduced by the recent and controversial case of *Sharp v Thomson*[6]. In this case the House of Lords held that where a disposition (conveying heritable property) was delivered to the buyers, the price had been paid and entry taken, the buyers acquired a 'beneficial interest' in the property. The buyers did not, on delivery of the disposition, acquire a real right to the property, that still depended on their registration of title. But, a floating charge which only crystallised *after* delivery of the disposition to the buyers was held not to attach to the property disponed. It is important to remember that the House of Lords arrived at this decision, not at the expense of 'the ordinary law on the transference of moveables or immoveables'[7], but by construing the term 'property' in s 462(1) of the Companies Act 1985 as having a different meaning from that employed in 'the ordinary law'. The message of *Sharp v Thomson* has been described thus: 'The effect of the decision is that, once a disposition of land is delivered and the price paid, the purchaser ceases to be at risk from the holder of a floating charge'[8].

---

1   1985 Act, s 463(1).
2   Insolvency Act 1986, s 53(7). See also *Sharp v Thomson* 1997 SCLR 328, HL.
3   1986 Act, s 53(7).
4   1984 SC 1 at 10, per Lord President Emslie.
5   *National Commercial Bank of Scotland Ltd v Telford Grier Mackay & Co Ltd Liquidators* 1969 SC 181.
6   1997 SCLR 328, HL, overturning, in some but not all aspects, the decision of the First Division.
7   1997 SCLR 328 at 344E, per Lord Clyde.
8   Reid 'Jam Today: *Sharp* in the House of Lords' 1997 SLT (News) 79 at 80.

Ranking

A very important matter in the actual operation of floating charges is the question of ranking, ie the relative priority of the floating charge in relation to any other securities or other competing legal rights over the property of the debtor company. Ranking is a complex issue that is governed by two statutory provisions, s 60 of the Insolvency Act 1986 and s 464 of the Companies Act 1985, and also, in many cases, by a ranking agreement contained in the floating charge itself.

Section 60 of the Insolvency Act 1986

By virtue of s 60 of the 1986 Act there are five categories of creditor entitled to payment before the holder of the charge. These are, in order of priority:

(1) the holder of a fixed security which is over property subject to the floating charge and which ranks prior or equal to the floating charge;
(2) anyone who has effectually executed diligence on any property subject to the floating charge;
(3) creditors in respect of all costs incurred by or on behalf of the receiver;
(4) the receiver in respect of his liabilities, charges and expenses; and
(5) preferential creditors entitled to payment, such as the Inland Revenue, in respect of taxes still owing, and employees for unpaid wages[1].

Section 464 of the Companies Act 1985

Section 464(1) of the 1985 Act provides that the deed creating the floating charge may contain a ranking agreement, regulating its relative priority with subsequent securities, and/or a prohibition on the creation of further securities. Regardless of any ranking agreement, however, a fixed security 'arising by operation of law' has priority over the floating charge[2]. This is generally thought to cover those securities that arise by implication of the general law (as opposed to those explicitly agreed to by the debtor) such as liens and the landlord's hypothec. This approach was confirmed in *Grampian Regional Council v Drill Stem (Inspection Services) Ltd (in receivership)*[3], where the sheriff held that a landlord's hypothec for rent arrears had priority over the claim of the floating charge holder. Where there is no ranking agreement, the order of priority is:

(1) fixed securities which have been constituted as real rights before the floating charge has attached rank in priority over floating charges;
(2) floating charges rank with each other according to the time of registration; and
(3) charges for registration which arrive in the same post rank equally[4].

---

1 Insolvency Act 1986, ss 60(1)(e), 59, 386 and Sch 6.
2 Companies Act 1985, s 464(2).
3 1994 SCLR 36.
4 1985 Act, s 464(3), (4).

CORPOREAL HERITABLE PROPERTY – THE STANDARD SECURITY

General

The standard security is the statutory security that applies to corporeal heritable property. Created by the Conveyancing and Feudal Reform (Scotland) Act 1970, and broadly following the model of the English 'mortgage', the standard security is quite commonly, though also erroneously, referred to by laymen by its English name. Since 1970[1] the standard security has been the only kind of security which may be created over heritage. As usual, the civilian principle, *traditionibus, non nudis pactis, transferuntur rerum dominia*, applies to the creation of securities over corporeal heritable property, and, once again, therefore, we have the familiar two-stage process of a contract, which creates a personal right, and registration, which creates a real right.

The deed creating the standard security must be in one of the two prescribed forms, A and B, laid down in Sch 2 of the 1970 Act[2], and Sch 3 sets out 'standard conditions' which are automatically imported into the standard security[3]. These standard conditions impose obligations on the debtor with regard to the maintenance, repair, and insurance of the subjects in respect of which the security is granted. The parties are, however, free to vary or exclude these conditions as they wish, except for those relating to the sale, foreclosure and redemption of the subjects[4]. Any purported variation in contravention of s 11(3) of the 1970 Act is void and unenforceable[5]. For example, standard condition 6 prohibits the granting of a lease by the debtor without permission of the creditor. Should the debtor contravene condition 6 without the creditor's permission, then, not only is the debtor in breach of his or her obligation, but the lease can be reduced by the creditor. Where, however, the creditor knows that a lease is already extant, or that one is to be granted, then the lease cannot subsequently be reduced since that would be acting in bad faith[6].

Execution of the deed, however, as already noted, creates only a personal right and there is no real right until the deed is registered[7] in the Register of Sasines or the Land Register as appropriate. Registration of the deed, therefore, operates as the legal equivalent, for heritable property, of delivery for moveable property.

---

1 Previously there were three forms of security used for heritable subjects: the bond and disposition in security; the cash credit bond and disposition in security; and the ex facie absolute disposition qualified by backletter. These ceased to be competent on the coming into force of the 1970 Act with effect from 29 November 1970. For a brief account of their nature, see Crerar *The Law of Banking in Scotland* (1997) pp 332–334.
2 1970 Act, s 9(2) and Sch 2. Form A is a combined personal obligation to repay the debt and a grant of security. Form B is only a grant of security used where the personal obligation to repay is constituted in a separate deed.
3 1970 Act, s 11(2).
4 1970 Act, s 11(3). The non-variable standard terms are standard condition 11, which governs redemption, and standard conditions 8, 9 and 10, which govern sale and foreclosure.
5 1970 Act, s 11(4)(b).
6 *Trade Development Bank v Warriner and Mason (Scotland) Ltd* 1980 SC 74.
7 1970 Act, s 11(1).

Ranking

More than one standard security can be granted over the same property, and where this occurs the respective ranking of the securities is by date of registration unless this is varied by the parties in a ranking agreement[1]. If a second security is granted, then the first creditor's security will be restricted to the sums already advanced, or obliged to be advanced under the contract (together with interest on these advances and expenses and outlays reasonably incurred), provided that the first creditor has received notice of the second security[2]. In competition with a floating charge, as we have seen, provided that the standard security has been 'constituted as a real right' before crystallisation of the floating charge, it will prevail[3]. However, s 464(1) of the Companies Act 1985 provides that the floating charge may contain a prohibition or restriction on creating a fixed security or other floating charge[4].

Default

Naturally, the debtor is obliged to fulfil his or her obligations under the standard security. But the debtor will be deemed to be in default in three situations: (1) where a calling-up notice has been served but not complied with[5]; (2) where there has been a failure to comply with any other requirement arising out of the security; and (3) where the proprietor (not the debtor) of the security subjects becomes insolvent[6].

The remedies open to a creditor on the debtor's default are contained in Sch 3, standard condition 10, unless otherwise contracted for. These include the power to sell the security subjects[7], the power to enter into possession of the security subjects[8], the power to effect repairs to those subjects[9], and the power to apply to the court for an order of foreclosure[10]. These powers are in addition to any other remedies that may be available to the debtor arising from the contract of loan[11]. However, the remedies contained in standard condition 10 must be used only for the purpose of the creditor recovering his or her loan and the creditor must not otherwise unduly harm the interests of the debtor. In *Armstrong, Petitioner*[12] it was said:

1 1970 Act, s 13.
2 1970 Act, s 13(1).
3 Companies Act 1985, s 464(3), (4)(b).
4 *AIB Finance Ltd v Bank of Scotland* 1993 SC 588.
5 A calling-up notice requests payment of the debt. It is discussed in more detail later.
6 1970 Act, Sch 3, standard condition 9(1). See also standard condition 9(2) defining the situations in which the debtor will be deemed to be insolvent.
7 1970 Act, Sch 3, standard condition 10(2).
8 1970 Act, Sch 3, standard condition 10(3). Once possession is obtained the security holder has the right to let the subjects (standard condition 10(4)) and any leases granted by the debtor over the subjects are transferred to the creditor (standard condition 10(5)).
9 1970 Act, Sch 3, standard condition 10(6).
10 1970 Act, Sch 3, standard condition 10(7).
11 1970 Act, s 20(1).
12 1988 SLT 255 at 258A, per Lord Jauncey.

'A creditor's primary interest will normally be the recovery of the debt due to him and I do not consider that he has unlimited discretion as to which one or more of the powers he exercises. If the value of the heritage is likely to exceed the sum of the debt, his interest is to have the heritage sold and to account for the surplus of the debt to the debtor. . . . A heritable creditor cannot use his powers for the primary purpose of advancing his own interests at the expense of the debtor when he has the alternative of proceeding in a more equitable manner'.

Where the security subjects are sold the creditor is obliged by s 25 of the 1970 Act to advertise the sale and to take all reasonable steps to ensure that the price is the best that can be 'reasonably obtained'[1]. What constitutes a reasonable price falls to be determined at the time when the subjects are sold and not by reference to any possible (but unquantifiable) hope of an increase in the value at some future point. In *Dick v Clydesdale Bank plc*[2] the debtor objected to some land near a town having been sold for agricultural purposes, rather than for commercial purposes which would have commanded a higher price. The court held that although a debtor had the right to object to a sale on the grounds that a reasonable price was not obtained, in this particular case, selling the land for agricultural purposes was perfectly reasonable since no planning permission for non-agricultural use had been granted. Any surplus left over after payment of the secured debt falls to the debtor or to his or her representative such as a trustee in bankruptcy[3]. A debtor cannot prevent the creditor exercising his or her right to sell the subjects, once the debtor is in default, merely because their value is less than the amount of the outstanding debt or because the debtor has offered to resume payment of the debt[4].

Enforcement

Calling-up notice

Where payment of the debt is in arrears, or the creditor, subject to the terms of the loan agreement, requires discharge of the debt, and failing such discharge to exercise his or her statutory remedies (above), then the security may be enforced by a calling-up notice[5]. This notice must be in the style prescribed by Form A of Sch 6. A calling-up notice must give the debtor at least two months[6] to pay, failing which, the creditor can enforce his or her remedy to exercise such of the rights under standard condition 10 in Sch 3 as he or she deems appropriate, in order to gain possession and sell the property[7]. If the debtor is still in physical possession he or she must remove himself or herself.

---

1 The burden of proving that a creditor is in breach of the statutory duty rests on the debtor: *Associated Displays Ltd v Turnbeam Ltd* 1988 SCLR 220, Sh Ct.
2 1991 SC 365.
3 1970 Act, s 27.
4 *Halifax Building Society v Gupta* 1994 SC 13.
5 1970 Act, s 19 and Sch 3, standard condition 8.
6 The period of notice may be varied by the terms of the security agreement.
7 1970 Act, s 20. Other remedies exist but sale of the subjects is the most common.

Notice of default and warrant from court

Where there is a breach of the agreement other than a failure to comply with a calling-up notice, then there are two remedies open to the holder of a standard security. First, provided that the fault complained of is remediable, such as failure to maintain property or to take out insurance, the creditor may serve a notice of default on the debtor. The debtor then has at least one month in which to comply with the notice and rectify the fault complained of[1]. Second, the creditor may apply to the sheriff court for a warrant to exercise any of the remedies that he or she would be entitled to exercise as if there had been a failure to comply with a calling-up notice. This procedure is available even where the default complained of is irremediable[1].

Cautionary obligations (*ius in personam*)

GENERAL

We have already seen how a creditor may obtain protection against default by a debtor by means of a real right in security over some thing (*ius in re*) belonging to the debtor. Another type of security is one that takes the form of a right against a third party (*ius in personam*) in the event of the debtor's default. Most frequently this is achieved by finding someone willing to give his or her personal guarantee that, in the event of the debtor defaulting, he or she will honour the debt. Such a guarantee is known in Scots law as a cautionary obligation.

Caution involves three separate parties: the principal debtor (or obligant), whose liabilities are guaranteed; the creditor, to whom the principal debtor owes the money or obligation, and the cautioner who guarantees the liabilities of the principal debtor. The purpose of caution is, as already outlined, in effect to insure the creditor against the possible default of the principal debtor by creating an obligation, on the part of the cautioner, to honour that debt on the default of the principal debtor. Since a cautionary obligation creates a personal right only, its value is limited to cases where the cautioner is solvent and has sufficient assets to honour the debt. Caution is also an 'accessory' obligation because the cautioner's liability is in addition to the primary liability of the principal debtor. It follows, therefore, that the cautioner's liability can never be greater than that of the principal debtor. 'The obligation of a cautioner', it has been said, 'is not an independent obligation, but is essentially conditional in its nature, being properly exigible only on the failure of the principal debtor to pay at the maturity of his obligation'[2].

Cautionary obligations are mostly governed by the common law and there is no statutory definition of the term. The classic definition, there-

1 1970 Act, s 21(1).
2 *City of Glasgow District Council v Excess Insurance Co Ltd* 1986 SLT 585 at 588G, per Lord Justice-Clerk Ross.

fore, is that given by Bell: 'Cautionry is an accessory obligation, or engagement, as surety for another, that the principal obligant shall pay the debt or perform the act for which he has engaged, otherwise the cautioner shall pay the debt or fulfil the obligation'[1]. It has been said that the law of caution in Scotland is governed by the same general principles as the English law on the corresponding concept of 'surety'[2]. As caution is an accessory obligation, its existence requires the existence of a principal debt. If the debt has been repaid then, obviously, there can be no cautionary obligation. Likewise, where the principal debtor's obligations are void for want of capacity or illegality there can be no cautionary obligation[3]. Where, however, the principal obligation is void through want of capacity[4] and the cautioner is aware of that fact, it has been held, on grounds of personal bar, that the cautioner is still bound[5]. It is difficult to see how this principle could be extended to contracts void for illegality or contrary to public policy.

CATEGORISATION

Cautionary obligations are distinguished into proper and improper caution. In proper caution the cautioner is explicitly liable as cautioner for the debts of the principal debtor to the creditor[6]. And where there is more than one cautioner, each is impliedly liable only for his or her pro rata share of the debt to the creditor. In improper caution the cautioner is jointly and severally liable with the principal debtor as a co-obligant to the creditor. In effect this means that vis-à-vis the creditor, the cautioner and principal debtor are both considered to be principal debtors; but between themselves the cautioner still stands in the relation of cautioner to the principal debtor and is entitled to claim relief from the principal debtor for payment of the debt.

CONSTITUTION

There are three ways of constituting a cautionary obligation.

Express agreement where the cautioner is liable to a named creditor

The simplest way in which a cautionary obligation can be created is where the cautioner grants a guarantee to a particular, identified creditor for the liabilities of the principal debtor. In such circumstances it is a matter of construction of the terms of the offer as to whether an express acceptance

---

1 Bell *Principles* s 245.
2 *Aitkens's Trs v Bank of Scotland* 1944 SC 270 at 279, per Lord Justice-Clerk Cooper.
3 *Garrard v James* [1925] Ch 616.
4 Capacity to grant caution is governed by the usual rules of contract and by the Age of Legal Capacity (Scotland) Act 1991.
5 *Stevenson v Adair* (1872) 10 M 919.
6 *Wallace v Gibson* (1895) 22 R (HL) 56.

by the creditor is needed to establish the cautioner's liability or whether liability is automatically implied on the provision of credit to the principal debtor[1].

Contracts where the creditor is not a party to a contract of caution

Caution can also arise where the cautioner gives a general undertaking to the principal debtor that he or she will guarantee the latter's debts to unspecified third parties. In such situations where the guarantee is for the debts of the debtor then the creditor must show reliance upon that guarantee in order to establish that the cautioner is obliged to him or her[2].

Caution by implication of law

In certain circumstances a cautionary obligation may arise by implication of law. The two main examples are said to be the liability of a partner for the debts of the firm[3], and the liabilities of the parties to a bill of exchange[4].

FORMALITIES

The Requirements of Writing (Scotland) Act 1995, s 1(2)(a)(ii)[5], provides that 'a gratuitous unilateral obligation *except* an obligation undertaken in the course of business' must be made in writing and signed by the granter in accordance with s 2 of the Act. Because of this provision a cautionary obligation must be in writing unless it is undertaken in the course of business or is not a unilateral gratuitous obligation. But where the cautionary obligation is not gratuitous, or is to be regarded as part of a bilateral transaction, or has been undertaken in the course of a business, then there is no requirement that the agreement be in writing. On the application of normal principles of contract, because in many cases caution is a unilateral obligation, there will be no need for any express acceptance by the creditor. Where the cautionary obligation is undertaken by more than one cautioner, all the cautioners must agree or none shall be bound. In *Scottish Provincial Assurance Co v Pringle*[6], the creditor agreed to provide a loan that was to be guaranteed by four cautioners. Three of the named cautioners signed, but the debtor merely forged the signature of the fourth cautioner. It was held that none of the purported cautioners was bound.

---

1 *Wallace v Gibson* (1895) 22 R (HL) 56.
2 *Fortune v Young* 1918 SC 1.
3 Partnership Act 1890, s 9. Cautionary liability here is predicated on the joint and several liability of partners for the firm's debts. For detailed discussion of joint and several liability, see ch 9 'Partnership' below.
4 Bills of Exchange Act 1882, s 55 (discussed in more detail in ch 5 'Commercial Paper' above.
5 The previous provision was contained in the Mercantile Law Amendment (Scotland) Act 1856, s 6 which was repealed by s 14(2) and Sch 5 of the 1995 Act.
6 (1858) 20 D 465.

ENFORCEMENT

At common law, in proper caution, the cautioner had the right to the 'benefit of discussion': ie the creditor had to 'do diligence' against the principal debtor before he or she could proceed against the cautioner. As an implied legal right this was abolished by s 8 of the Mercantile Law Amendment (Scotland) Act 1856, which provided that the benefit of discussion exists only where it is expressly contracted for, which in practice is seldom. This means that a creditor can proceed directly against a cautioner for payment of the debt on the default of principal debtor: ie the creditor can demand payment from the cautioner once the principle debtor has defaulted. If the cautioner fails to pay, the creditor then enjoys all the usual remedies of an unpaid creditor, including the right to do diligence if necessary. However, bonds of caution often contain a 'consent to summary diligence' clause which allows the creditor to do diligence against the cautioner without the need to have the court's consent.

EXTENT OF THE CAUTIONER'S LIABILITY

Because caution is an accessory obligation it follows that the liability of the cautioner can be no greater than that of the principal debtor[1]. Liability for the debt includes any interest due, unless this is explicitly excluded by the terms of the bond, and any other expenses reasonably incurred by the creditor in trying to enforce his or her rights[2]. Furthermore, because of the onerous nature of a contract of caution, the cautioner's obligations are construed narrowly[3] and will not exceed those of the principal debtor unless explicitly stated.

CAUTIONER'S RIGHTS

The cautioner's rights can vary according to a number of factors and, consequently, are not to be viewed as a package enjoyed by him or her in every instance. The individual rights, however, are as follows.

Benefit of discussion

The benefit of discussion applies only to proper caution. In proper caution each cautioner also has the right to the 'benefit of division': ie each cautioner is only liable to the creditor for his or her pro rata share of the debt.

1 *Jackson v McIver* (1875) 2 R 282.
2 *Struthers v Dykes* (1847) 9 D 1437.
3 *Aitken's Trs v Bank of Scotland* 1944 SC 270.

Right of relief against the principal debtor

On payment of debt by the cautioner, he or she has a right of relief against the principal debtor[1]. In many cases this right is unlikly to be worth much for two reasons. Firstly, if the principal debtor had been able to pay the debt, then the creditor would not have demanded payment from the cautioner. Secondly, the cautioner has no right of relief where the principal debtor is sequestrated or liquidated. The right of relief is subject to prescription after five years from the date of the payment of the debt[2]. It is possible, by contract, for the cautioner to waive his or her right of relief either unconditionally or on certain specified conditions[3].

Right of relief against co-cautioners

Where there is more than one cautioner then, amongst themselves, each is liable on a pro rata basis and, accordingly, where any cautioner pays more than his or her share he or she is entitled to pro rata relief from the co-cautioners[4].

Right to assignation of debt and securities

On payment of the debt by the cautioner, he or she has the right to the assignation of the debt[5], any securities held for that debt by the creditor[6], and any diligence done on the debt[7]. This right applies only after full payment of the principal debt has been made[8]. A cautioner also enjoys a right to share in the benefit of securities which a co-cautioner has obtained from the principal debtor[9], but not from someone else[10].

MISREPRESENTATION

Caution is not a contract *uberrimae fidei* (of the utmost good faith) and accordingly there is no general duty of disclosure owed by the principal debtor to the cautioner. Whether or not the cautioner is allowed to resile from the contract on the ground that he or she was misled depends on the circumstances that led the cautioner to make the contract.

---

1 'Cautioners, on making payment of the debt, or any portion of the debt, have a right to relief and indemnification against the principal debtor, to the full extent to which they have been made answerable for him. This right of relief on the part of the cautioner against the principal debtor, on whose account he has made payment, arises *de jure* without any formal assignation by the creditor': *Gloag and Irvine* pp 796–797, approved in *Smithy's Place Ltd v Blackadder and McMonagle* 1991 SLT 790 at 795C–E, OH.
2 *Smithy's Place Ltd v Blackadder & McMonagle* 1991 SLT 790.
3 *Williamson v Foulds* 1927 SN 164, OH.
4 *Marshall & Co v Pennycook* 1908 SC 276.
5 *Ewart v Latta* (1865) 3 M (HL) 36; *Thow's Tr v Young* 1910 SC 588.
6 *Scott v Young* 1909 1 SLT 47, OH.
7 See also Bell *Principles* s 255.
8 *Ewart v Latta* (1865) 3 M (HL) 36.
9 Bell *Commentaries* I, 367.
10 *Scott v Young* 1909 1 SLT 47, OH.

Misrepresentation by the principal debtor

A misrepresentation by the principal debtor does not free the cautioner[1]. However, where the debtor is in a position to exert undue influence on the cautioner, due to the nature of their relationship, it may be possible that the cautionary obligation would be struck down on that ground[2].

Failure by the creditor to disclose information

The creditor's failure to disclose information that he or she possesses about the principal debtor should not free the cautioner. There is long-standing authority to this effect: 'It is well settled that it is not the duty of a bank to give any information to a proposed cautioner as to the state of accounts with the principal debtor'[3]. But now, following *Smith v Bank of Scotland*[4], it would appear that where the creditor has constructive notice of the potential undue influence of the principal debtor over the cautioner, then the creditor's failure to warn the cautioner of the potential risks may result in the cautionary obligation being set aside.

Actual misrepresentation by the creditor

Positive misrepresentation by a creditor will allow the cautioner to resile, provided, of course, that the cautioner relied on the misrepresentation (even if it was innocent)[5]. However, under s 6 of the Mercantile Law Amendment (Scotland) Act 1856, as interpreted by the courts, it was formerly held that only written misrepresentations could be relied upon, which allowed creditors to make verbal representations with impunity. This provision was repealed by the Requirements of Writing (Scotland) Act 1995 and, accordingly, a cautioner can rely on a verbal misrepresentation to release him from his obligation.

TERMINATION OF CAUTIONARY OBLIGATIONS

As an accessory obligation, the most common way in which the obligation of the cautioner is terminated is when the debtor's obligation, for whatever reason, is extinguished. There are several specific ways in which the contract of caution may be terminated.

Payment of principal debt by the obligant

Payment of the principal debt by the obligant will extinguish the cautionary obligation unless the caution is continuing in nature. If the creditor

1 *Young v Clydesdale Bank Ltd* (1889) 17 R 231.
2 *Smith v Bank of Scotland* 1997 GWD 21-1004, HL. For discussion of this troublesome decision, see Gretton 'Sexually Transmitted Debt' 1997 SLT (News) 195.
3 *Young v Clydesdale Bank* (1889) 17 R 231 at 240, per Lord Adam. See also *Royal Bank of Scotland v Greenshields* 1914 SC 259. Both cases were followed in the Outer and Inner House in *Mumford v Bank of Scotland; Smith v Bank of Scotland* 1994 SLT 1288, OH; 1996 SLT 392.
4 1997 GWD 21-1004, HL.
5 *Royal Bank of Scotland v Ranken* (1844) 6 D 1418.

discharges the principal debtor without the cautioner's consent or without qualifying the discharge, so as not to affect the cautioner's right of relief, then the cautioner is discharged[1]. The discharge of the principal debtor by virtue of his or her bankruptcy does not extinguish the obligation of the cautioner[2]. If a new debt is substituted for the existing one, that is novation. Novation of the original debt incurred by the principal debtor discharges the cautioner[3]. But assignation of that debt (which merely substitutes a new creditor for the original one) does not discharge the cautioner[4]. A cautionary obligation guaranteeing payment of a fixed amount on a continuous account (eg a current account with a bank) may be extinguished where, the obligation having ended, the principal debtor continues to make payments into the account. Each payment made thereafter by the principal debtor will gradually reduce the debt and, coequally, the sum covered by the cautionary obligation. Eventually, sufficient payments may be made to extinguish the sum guaranteed by the cautioner[5].

Prejudicial conduct by creditor

As caution is an onerous contract the creditor must do nothing which prejudices the position of the cautioner[6]. Examples of such prejudicial conduct are granting more time to the principal debtor to pay[7] and altering the contract without the cautioner's consent[8].

Where the sum guaranteed is limited to a specified amount then it has been held that the cautioner is not prejudiced merely by the fact that the creditor advances the debtor sums in excess of that limit. Two cases illustrate this point. In *Bank of Scotland v MacLeod*[9], where the cautioner guaranteed the debts of the principal debtor to the sum of £15,000, it was held that the cautioner was not prejudiced merely because the bank loaned the debtor a total of £27,400. Likewise, in *Huewind Ltd v Clydesdale Bank plc*[10], the cautioner's liability was in the form of a 'top slice' guarantee, limited to a total of £1 million, for the debts of the principal debtor over £800,000. The creditor eventually advanced a total of a little over £2.3 million to the principal debtor. The cautioner objected that allowing a debt well above £1.8 million had increased the risk to them and asked to be released from the cautionary obligation. It was held, however, that there had been no prejudice to the cautioner and the cautionary obligation was upheld.

1 Bell *Principles* s 260; *Wallace v Donald* (1825) 3 S 433 (NE 304).
2 Bankruptcy (Scotland) Act 1985, s 60.
3 *Hay and Kyd v Powrie* (1886) 13 R 777.
4 *Bradford Old Bank Ltd v Sutcliffe* [1918] 2 KB 833, CA.
5 This is the result of the application in this context of the 'rule in *Clayton's Case*', ie *Devayne's v Noble* (1816) 1 Mer 529. See also *Hay & Co v Torbet* 1908 SC 781.
6 *Lord Advocate v Maritime Fruit Carriers Co Ltd* 1983 SLT 357, OH.
7 *C and A Johnstone v Duthie* (1892) 19 R 624.
8 Bell *Principles* s 259; *NG Napier Ltd v Crosbie* 1964 SC 129.
9 1986 SC 165.
10 1995 SLT 392, OH.

Discharge of co-cautioners without consent of others

Where there is more than one cautioner, then the discharge of any cautioner by the creditor, without the consent of the others, results in the automatic discharge of all the others[1].

Prescription

Cautionary obligations prescribe after five years[2]. The prescriptive period begins to run from the date of the default by the principal debtor. In *City of Glasgow District Council v Excess Insurance Co Ltd*[3], an insurance company were cautioners for a building contractor engaged to carry out work for Glasgow District Council. The contractor defaulted under the contract on 8 July 1976 but the council did not raise an action against the insurance company until 7 June 1983, and, accordingly, the court held that the obligation had been extinguished by prescription. In the case of bank guarantees, which normally bear to be payable on demand, it would appear that the prescriptive period commences from the time that a demand is made[4].

The right of relief of a cautioner against the principal debtor is also governed by the quinquennial prescriptive period but in this situation the prescriptive period runs from date of the payment of the debt by the cautioner not the date of the demand by creditors[5].

Death

A cautioner's death has no effect on the existence of the obligation, as a person's obligations as well as their assets transmit to their representatives. Indeed, if the guarantee is continuing in nature it may continue until it is expressly revoked[6]. However, although the creditor is under no obligation to inform a deceased cautioner's representatives of the existence of the cautionary obligation, failure to do so, coupled with the continuation of advances to the principal debtor, may allow the representatives to escape liability on grounds of equity[7]. The death of a co-cautioner does not of itself terminate the cautionary obligation of the other cautioners[8].

The death of the principal obligant frees the cautioner from any future liability but liability remains for any debts of the principal obligant existing at the time of his or her death. In *Woodfield Finance Trust (Glasgow) Ltd v Morgan*[9] the cautioners had guaranteed the rental payments on a television used by a relative. The cautioners were found to be liable for arrears of rental at the time of their relative's death, but not for that portion of the rental period remaining after the hirer's death. The death of creditor does not affect the cautioner's liability for existing debts at the time of death.

1 Mercantile Law Amendment (Scotland) Act 1856, s 9. See also *Royal Bank of Scotland plc v Welsh* 1985 SLT 439.
2 Prescription and Limitation (Scotland) Act 1973, s 6, Sch 1, para 1(g).
3 1986 SLT 585, OH.
4 *Royal Bank of Scotland Ltd v Brown* 1982 SC 89.
5 *Smithy's Place Ltd v Blackadder & McMonagle* 1991 SCLR 512, OH.
6 *British Linen Co v Monteith* (1858) 20 D 557.
7 *Caledonian Banking Co v Kennedy's Tr* (1870) 8 M 862.
8 *Beckett v Addyman* (1882) 9 QBD 783, CA.
9 1958 SLT (Sh Ct) 14.

7 Bankruptcy

INTRODUCTION

The concept of bankruptcy

The term 'bankruptcy' is not a technical term: it does not have a precise technical meaning. Bankruptcy may be used to mean insolvency or the formal judicial procedure of sequestration or informal arrangements with creditors which may follow on from such insolvency.

Company and non-company debtors

Although companies may, of course, become insolvent, the term bankruptcy is usually confined to non-company debtors. Companies are not subject to sequestration: the appropriate procedures applicable to insolvent companies are mostly contained in the Insolvency Act 1986 and are beyond the scope of this book[1].

The legislation

Much of the modern law of bankruptcy is contained in the Bankruptcy (Scotland) Act 1985 as amended (hereinafter referred to as 'the 1985 Act'), supplemented by the Bankruptcy (Scotland) Regulations 1985[2] as amended. The Scottish law of bankruptcy is quite distinct from the corresponding law in the rest of the UK.

The Act implemented with some modifications the relevant recommendations of the Scottish Law Commission's *Report on Bankruptcy and Related Aspects of Insolvency and Liquidation*[3] and represented a major restatement of the law of bankruptcy. It has been subject to various consequential amendments which will not be separately considered. It has also been extensively amended by the Bankruptcy (Scotland) Act 1993, as a result of the unexpected results of some of the new provisions it introduced. In particular, the 1985 Act introduced public funding of sequestrations where there were insufficient assets to pay a dividend. In such cases, the fees and outlays of the trustee administering the sequestration were made payable from public funds to the extent that there were insufficient assets in the estate to meet them. Combined with new provisions making access to the sequestration process by the debtor himself easier, this resulted in a

---

1 For company insolvency in Scots law, see St Clair and Drummond Young *The Law of Corporate Insolvency in Scotland* (2nd edn, 1992); D Bennett *Palmer's Company Insolvency in Scotland* (1993).
2 SI 1985/1925.
3 (Scot Law Com no. 68) (1982).

massive increase in the number of sequestrations, many of which were cases attracting public funding. The government regarded the consequent increase in public expenditure as unacceptable. The 1993 Act was therefore passed with a view, inter alia, to making access to the sequestration process by the debtor more difficult and reducing the costs to the public purse by altering the arrangements for dealing with cases where there were few or no assets. These amendments have resulted in some further major changes to the law.

INSOLVENCY

Introduction

Just as the term bankruptcy has no precise technical meaning, so the term insolvency is not a technical term and has several different meanings. The consequences of a debtor's insolvency for himself or herself and others will often depend on which type of insolvency is involved.

Absolute insolvency

Absolute insolvency occurs where the debtor's total liabilities exceed his or her total assets. It is sometimes referred to as 'balance sheet' insolvency although that term is really misleading. The debtor may still be paying his or her bills as they fall due, and may remain absolutely insolvent without any action being taken against him or her. If, however, a debtor who is absolutely insolvent disposes of assets other than for full consideration, unfairly favours some creditors over others, or generally carries out transactions which may be regarded as a fraud on his or her creditors, these transactions may be challenged at a later date[1]. This is because the common law regards a debtor who is absolutely insolvent as a trustee for his or her creditors[2], although the term should not be interpreted literally[3].

Practical insolvency

Practical insolvency occurs where a debtor cannot pay his or her bills as they fall due. The debtor may not be absolutely insolvent: ie his or her total assets may exceed his or her total liabilities, but he or she has no ready cash to pay debts. Practical insolvency, particularly in a business context, is usually caused by cash flow problems. The debtor becomes unable to pay his or her own bills because his or her own creditors are late in paying, perhaps for the same reasons, creating a chain of delayed payments. Practical insolvency of itself may entitle a creditor to exercise various remedies against the debtor: eg, the Sale of Goods Act 1979 specifically provides for an unpaid seller to exercise various remedies

---

1 See below.
2 Bell *Commentaries* II, 170; *Caldwell v Hamilton* 1919 SC (HL) 100.
3 *Nordic Travel Ltd v Scotprint Ltd* 1980 SC 1 at 9, per Lord President Emslie.

where the debtor is insolvent, and the definition of insolvency adopted by the 1979 Act is essentially one of practical insolvency. Where there is no such specific provision, unpaid creditors may resort to remedies available under the general law. They may try informal action first: writing to the debtor, threatening to cut off further supplies, perhaps a solicitor's letter. If these do not produce payment, they may resort to court action. If a creditor obtains a decree for payment against the debtor but remains unpaid, the creditor is entitled to carry out diligence against the debtor's assets. In certain cases, the creditor may be entitled to do diligence without first obtaining a court decree, eg, if the document constituting the debt is registered for execution[1]. Diligence may or may not result in the creditor being paid. If the debt remains unpaid, the debtor may in turn be rendered apparently insolvent.

Apparent insolvency

The concept of apparent insolvency was introduced by the 1985 Act[2]. A debtor[3] can be made apparently insolvent in a number of ways which are detailed in s 7 of the 1985 Act. These are as follows.

(1) Where the debtor is sequestrated in Scotland or made bankrupt in England or Wales or Northern Ireland[4]. Sequestration is the judicial procedure whereby the debtor's assets are taken away from him or her and distributed amongst his or her unpaid creditors. Bankruptcy is the equivalent procedure in England, Wales and Northern Ireland.
(2) Where the debtor has given *written* notice to his or her creditors that he or she has ceased to pay his or her debts in the normal course of business[5].
(3) Where the debtor has granted a trust deed for creditors[6]. A trust deed for creditors is a device whereby a debtor transfers all or part of his or her assets to a trustee, who distributes them amongst the debtor's creditors according to their rights without the involvement of the court[7].
(4) Where a charge for payment has been served on the debtor and the debtor has not paid within the time allowed in the charge[8].
(5) Where a poinding or other seizure of the debtor's moveable property has taken place to enforce a summary warrant for the recovery of rates or taxes and the debtor does not pay within fourteen days of the poinding or other seizure[9]. What is covered by the phrase 'other

---

1 A detailed discussion of diligence is, however, beyond the scope of this book. The principal Scottish texts on diligence generally are Graham Stewart *The Law of Diligence* (1898) and Maher and Cusine *The Law and Practice of Diligence* (1990). On inhibitions and adjudications, see Gretton *The Law of Inhibition and Adjudication* (2nd edn, 1996).
2 It replaced the concept of 'notour bankruptcy' to which references may still sometimes be seen.
3 For the definition of debtor, see 'Applying for sequestration' below.
4 1985 Act, s 7(1)(a).
5 1985 Act, s 7(1)(b).
6 1985 Act, s 7(1)(c)(i).
7 See below.
8 1985 Act, s 7(1)(c)(ii).
9 1985 Act, s 7(1)(c)(iii).

seizure of the debtor's moveable property' is not clear, but it has been held that it does not include a wages arrestment[1].

(6) Where a decree of adjudication in security or for payment of any of the debtor's estate is granted[2].

(7) Where the debtor's effects are sold as a result of a sequestration for rent[3].

(8) Where a receiving order is made against the debtor in England or Wales[4].

(9) Where a creditor has served a statutory demand for payment of debt on the debtor and the debtor has failed, within three weeks of its service, *either* to pay the debt or debts due or find security for their payment *or* to intimate to the creditor by recorded delivery post that he denies the existence of the debt or that he or she denies that it is due at that time[5]. A statutory demand for payment of debt may be served only where the creditor is owed a liquid debt or debts of at least a prescribed amount[6] and evidence of the debt or debts must be attached to the demand[7]. It must be served personally on the debtor by an officer of court. The three-week time limit is strictly observed[8].

In situations (3) to (8) inclusive, s 7 provides that the debtor will not in fact be held to be apparently insolvent if it is shown that at the time he or she was willing and able to pay his or her debts as they fell due. It would be up to the debtor to establish this. Such a situation is, however, likely to be rare.

A debtor's apparent insolvency may have practical effects. It is not uncommon for contracts or leases, eg, to provide for termination (or the option of termination) of the agreement or other stipulated effects in the event of, inter alia, apparent insolvency. It also has two main effects as a matter of law. First, it will affect certain types of diligence done by creditors within certain time limits. Secondly, it may render the debtor liable to have his or her estates sequestrated[9]. A debtor's estates may be sequestrated in some cases without his or her being apparently insolvent: this is why s 7 provides that sequestration is one of the events which can make a debtor apparently insolvent. In other cases, however, sequestration may be sought *only* if the debtor is apparently insolvent.

An insolvent debtor may be able to restore himself or herself to solvency, or continue in a state of insolvency, without suffering any serious consequences. If the insolvency is serious, however, or continues for any substantial period of time, it is more likely that the debtor will be forced

---

1 *Mackay, Petr* 1996 SCLR 1091, Sh Ct. The Scottish Office is currently consulting on whether the law regarding this and a number of other matters concerning the constitution of apparent insolvency should be changed: see *Apparent Insolvency, A Consultation Paper on Amending the Bankruptcy (Scotland) Act 1985* (July 1997).
2 1985 Act, s 7(1)(c)(iv).
3 1985 Act, s 7(1)(c)(v).
4 1985 Act, s 7(1)(c)(vi).
5 1985 Act, s 7(1)(d).
6 As at the date at which the law is stated in this work, the amount is £750.
7 *Lord Advocate v Thomson* 1994 SCLR 96.
8 *Guthrie Newspaper Group v Morrison* 1992 GWD 22-1244.
9 It is not technically correct to speak of the sequestration of a debtor, only of sequestration of his or her estates, although the former usage is common.

to take action himself or herself to try to deal with his or her insolvency, or will have action forced upon him or her by impatient creditors. The debtor may apply for or have forced upon him or her sequestration of his or her estates, or he or she may be able to avoid sequestration by adopting a number of extra-judicial alternatives. Sequestration is considered first.

SEQUESTRATION

Definition

Sequestration was described briefly above as the judicial procedure whereby the debtor's assets are taken away from him and distributed amongst his unpaid creditors. It has been defined more fully as

> 'a judicial process for attaching and rendering litigious the whole estate, heritable and moveable, real and personal, of the bankrupt, wherever situated, in order that it may be vested in a trustee elected by the creditors, to be recovered, managed, sold and divided by him, according to certain rules of distribution'[1].

That definition remains an accurate description of the process of sequestration currently embodied in the Bankruptcy (Scotland) Act 1985 as amended.

Outline of procedure

Applications for sequestration are made by petition to the appropriate court. When sequestration is awarded, an interim trustee is appointed by the court. The interim trustee may be a private insolvency practitioner, usually an accountant or solicitor who has the relevant qualifications, or the Accountant in Bankruptcy, a public official who has various functions in relation to sequestrations. As the name suggests, the interim trustee takes care of matters in the interim until a permanent trustee can be put in place. The permanent trustee then gathers in the debtor's assets, sells them and distributes them to the creditors, all according to the rules laid down in the Act. Commissioners may in some cases be appointed to advise and assist the trustee in carrying out these functions. In certain cases, principally those where there are few or no assets, the normal procedures are modified in order to save time and money. There are two types of modified procedure, Sch 2 procedure and summary administration. Once the administration of the debtor's estate has been completed, the sequestration is brought to an end. The debtor receives a discharge in respect of most of his or her pre-sequestration debts; the trustee also receives a discharge in respect of his or her conduct of the sequestration.

---

1 Bell *Commentaries* II, 283.

Applying for sequestration

Whose estate may be sequestrated?

The estate of any of the following is subject to sequestration:

(1) a living individual;
(2) a deceased individual, his or her executor or a person entitled to be appointed as his or her executor;
(3) a trust;
(4) a partnership or limited partnership within the meaning of the Limited Partnerships Act 1907 including, in either case, a dissolved partnership;
(5) a body corporate or unincorporated body.

This is the combined effect of ss 5, 6 and 73(1) of the 1985 Act. Section 5 of the Act makes provision for the sequestration of the estate of living or deceased debtors. Section 6 makes provision for sequestration of other estates. Section 5(1) of the Act provides that the estate of 'a debtor' may be sequestrated in accordance with the Act. 'Debtor' is in turn defined in s 73(1) of the Act as including, without prejudice to the generality of the expression: an entity whose estate may be sequestrated by virtue of s 6 of the Act; a deceased debtor; his or her executor or a person entitled to be appointed the executor of a deceased debtor. The entities whose estate may be sequestrated by virtue of s 6 are: trusts; partnerships, including dissolved partnerships; bodies corporate or unincorporated bodies; and limited partnerships, including dissolved partnerships, within the meaning of the Limited Partnerships Act 1907.

Sequestration of the estates of any of the partners may be sought at the same time as sequestration of the estates of a partnership, and the petition for sequestration of the estates of any of the partners may be combined with that for sequestration of the partnership[1]. However, there is no joint award of sequestration: the sequestrations remain distinct and the various estates must be administered separately[2]. It is not otherwise competent to combine petitions for sequestration, eg, to petition for the sequestration of the estates of a husband and wife, unless they are actually in partnership[3].

Section 6(2) of the Act specifically states that it is incompetent to sequestrate the estate of a registered company[4] or any entity in respect of which an enactment provides, expressly or by implication, that sequestration is incompetent[5], although such companies and entities may be made apparently insolvent[6].

1   1985 Act, s 6(5).
2   *Royal Bank of Scotland plc v J & J Messenger* 1991 SLT 492, OH.
3   *Campbell v Dunbar* 1989 SLT (Sh Ct) 29.
4   Ie companies registered under the Companies Act 1985 or the former Companies Acts within the meaning of that Act: 1985 Act, s 6(2).
5   It is probably also incompetent, therefore, to sequestrate the estate of an unregistered company, since provision is made for the winding up of such companies in the Insolvency Act 1986.
6   1985 Act, s 7(4).

Who may apply?

Section 5 of the 1985 Act, as amended by the 1993 Act, prescribes who may petition for sequestration of the estates of a living or deceased debtor; s 6 prescribes who may do so in the case of a trust, partnership[1], body corporate or unincorporated body. The effect of these sections is as follows:

(1) in all cases, the debtor[2] may petition for sequestration with the concurrence of a qualified creditor or creditors;
(2) in all cases, a qualified creditor or creditors may petition for sequestration if the debtor is apparently insolvent[3];
(3) a living individual may also petition for sequestration of his or her own estates without the concurrence of a qualified creditor or creditors providing that the total amount of his or her debts (including interest) at the date of presentation of the petition is not less than £1,500, an award of sequestration has not been made against the debtor in the period of five years prior to the presentation of the petition[4] and *either* the debtor is apparently insolvent[5] *or* he or she has granted a trust deed which has failed to become protected[6];
(4) in the case of a living individual, the trustee acting under a trust deed may petition for sequestration if one or more of the following conditions is satisfied:
   (a) the debtor has failed to comply with an obligation imposed on him or her by the trust deed with which he or she could reasonably have complied;
   (b) the debtor has failed to comply with any instruction or requirement reasonably imposed by the trustee; or
   (c) the trustee avers that it is in the best interests of the creditors that an award of sequestration be made[7].

A qualified creditor is one who is owed by the debtor, as at the date of presentation of the petition, a debt or debts[8] amounting to not less than £1,500[9]. In calculating the sums due by the debtor, the creditor is allowed to include interest which has legally accrued on the debt for this

---

1 Including a limited partnership or, in either case, a dissolved partnership. For ease of reference, the word partnership is used here to include limited or, in either case, dissolved partnerships unless otherwise stated or the context otherwise requires.
2 In the case of a trust 'the debtor' means the majority of the trustees (1985 Act, s 6(3)(a)), and in the case of a body corporate or an unincorporated body, it means a person authorised to act on behalf of the body.
3 See 'Apparent insolvency' above.
4 The five-year period is calculated back from the day preceding the day of presentation of the petition.
5 See 'Apparent insolvency' above. For this purpose, however, the debtor is not regarded as being apparently insolvent by reason only of having granted a trust deed or given notice to his or her creditors that he or she has ceased to pay his or her debts in the ordinary course of business under s 7(1)(b): 1985 Act, s 5(2B). This restriction is currently the subject of consultation by the Scottish Office with a view to possible amendment: see *Apparent Insolvency, A Consultation Paper on Amending the Bankruptcy (Scotland) Act 1985* (July 1997).
6 1985 Act, s 5(2), (2B). For the concept of protected trust deeds, see 'Trust deeds' below.
7 1985 Act, s 5(2), (2C).
8 'Debts' includes liquid or illiquid debts, but not future or contingent debts.
9 This is the figure as at the date at which the law is stated in this work: it may be altered from time to time by statutory instrument.

purpose[1]. Qualified creditors means creditors who have debts amounting to that sum between them[2].

Section 8 of the 1985 Act sets out certain time limits for presentation of a petition. For example, a creditor's petition for sequestration must be presented within four months of the constitution of the debtor's apparent insolvency[3].

Which court?

Jurisdiction is dealt with in s 9 of the 1985 Act. Sequestration is competent in both the sheriff court and the Court of Session, but the majority of petitions are presented in the sheriff court. Any award of sequestration made in the Court of Session will be remitted to the appropriate sheriff court thereafter[4]. In the case of a living or deceased debtor, jurisdiction is established if the debtor had an established place of business[5] or was habitually resident[6] within Scotland (in the case of a Court of Session petition) or the sheriffdom (in the case of a sheriff court petition) at any time in the year immediately preceding the presentation of the petition or date of death[7]. In addition, the Court of Session has jurisdiction in respect of sequestration of the estates of a partner of a firm if there is a current sequestration in relation to that firm, even if these grounds of jurisdiction are not established in relation to him[8]. In the case of the entities which may be sequestrated under s 6 of the Act, jurisdiction is established if the entity had an established place of business within Scotland or the sheriffdom (as appropriate) at any time in the year immediately preceding the presentation of the petition[9] or was constituted or formed under Scots law and at any time carried on business[10] within Scotland or the sheriffdom as appropriate.

The award of sequestration

Debtor petitions

In the case of a petition by the debtor, if the court is satisfied that matters are in order procedurally, it must award sequestration 'forthwith' unless cause is shown why sequestration cannot be competently awarded[11].

1 *Arthur v HM Advocate* 1993 SCCR 130.
2 1985 Act, ss 73(1) and 5(4).
3 1985 Act, s 8(1)(b).
4 1985 Act, s 15(1).
5 'Established place of business' is not defined, but means something more than temporary or transitory.
6 The concept of habitual residence is not defined, but again it implies something more than temporary, and probably even something more than ordinary, residence: see McBryde's annotations to s 9 of the 1985 Act in Scottish Current Law Statutes.
7 Note that it is *at any time* within that year: this is to cater for the situation where the debtor has ceased carrying on business or has ceased to be habitually resident prior to presentation of the petition.
8 1985 Act, s 9(3).
9 The comments made in relation to individuals apply *mutatis mutandis*.
10 Carrying on business is different from having an established, or indeed any, place of business. This test may therefore be satisfied where the other would not.
11 1985 Act, s 12(1). For a discussion of when sequestration cannot competently be awarded, see 'Reasons for refusing sequestration' below.

Non-debtor petitions

Where the petition is not presented by the debtor, the court grants a warrant to cite the debtor to appear before the court on a given date in order to allow him or her the opportunity to put forward any reason why sequestration should not be awarded[1]. The warrant must be served on the debtor not more than fourteen and not less than six days before the date fixed by the court[1]. For that reason, although service by post is competent, most often the petition will be served by sheriff officers (messengers-at-arms in the case of a Court of Session petition) in order to ensure that these time limits are complied with. At the hearing, if the court is satisfied that matters are in order procedurally, it must award sequestration 'forthwith' unless s 12(3A) applies[2]. Section 12(3A) states that sequestration shall not be awarded if *either* cause is shown why sequestration is incompetent *or* the debtor forthwith pays or satisfies, or produces written evidence of payment or satisfaction of, or gives or shows that there is sufficient security for the payment of, both the debt which gave rise to his or her apparent insolvency and any other debts due to the petitioning or concurring creditor[3].

Non-discretionary and summary nature of sequestration

The 1985 Act does not allow the court any discretion in deciding whether to award sequestration. If matters are in order procedurally, the court must award sequestration, unless the matters specified above[4] apply[5].

Furthermore, the court must award sequestration 'forthwith'. This means immediately. Sequestration is a summary remedy[6]. The court should not normally sist or continue the petition unless one of the matters specifically provided for is raised at the hearing[7] *and* the matter is not capable of being determined at the hearing but requires further inquiry[8]. In some cases, a sist or continuation has been granted for other reasons[9], including to allow the debtor further time to pay, but it is thought that a sist or continuation for time to pay, to allow a cheque to clear or for any other reason except in the most exceptional circumstances, is incompetent[10].

---

1 1985 Act, s 12(2).
2 1985 Act, s 12(3).
3 For further discussion of s 12(3A), see 'Reasons for refusing sequestration' below.
4 See further 'Reasons for refusing sequestration' below
5 See eg *Sales Lease Ltd v Minty* 1993 SCLR 130.
6 *Scottish Milk Marketing Board v A and J Wood* 1936 SLT 470. See also *Royal Bank of Scotland plc v Aitken* 1985 SLT (Sh Ct) 13; *Campbell v Sheriff* 1991 SLT (Sh Ct) 37; *Sales Lease Ltd v Minty* above.
7 *Royal Bank of Scotland plc v Forbes* 1987 SC 99; *Sales Lease Ltd v Minty* above.
8 *Royal Bank of Scotland plc v Forbes* above; *Racal Vodac Ltd v Hislop* 1992 SLT (Sh Ct) 21; *Sales Lease Ltd v Minty* above.
9 See eg *Chris Hart Business Sales Ltd v Campbell* 1993 SCLR 383, Sh Ct (pursuers interdicted from proceeding with sequestration).
10 Although the contrary argument has been advanced: see Stewart '"Forthwith" and Avoiding Sequestration' 1995 SLT (News) 19 and reply by McKenzie '"Forthwith" and Avoiding Sequestration: Some Observations' 1995 SLT (News) 151.

Reasons for refusing sequestration

The first reason for which the court may refuse sequestration is that matters are not in order procedurally. In the case of a debtor petition, the court must be satisfied that:

(1) the petition has been presented in accordance with the provisions of the 1985 Act;
(2) the petition is presented with the concurrence of a qualified creditor *or* the debtor, if a living individual, satisfies the conditions for petitioning without the concurrence of a qualified creditor; and
(3) in the case of a petition for sequestration of the estate of a living or deceased debtor, the requirements of s 5(6) and s 5(6A) have been complied with[1]. These are, respectively, that the petitioner has sent a copy of the petition to the Accountant in Bankruptcy on the day the petition is presented[2], and that the debtor has lodged with the petition a statement of assets and liabilities and sent a copy to the Accountant in Bankruptcy.

In the case of a non-debtor petition, the court must be satisfied that:

(a) proper citation has been made of the debtor;
(b) the petition has been presented in accordance with the provisions of the Act;
(c) the provisions of s 5(6) of the Act (see above) have been complied with; and
(d) in the case of a petition by a creditor, the debtor is apparently insolvent[3] *or* in the case of a petition by the trustee under a trust deed, that the averments of the trustee in relation to the debtor's failure or failures under s 5(2C) are true[4].

In addition, it should be noted that the Act requires a petitioning or concurring creditor to produce an oath in prescribed form, which must have attached to it evidence of the creditor's debt or debts.[5]

If the court is not satisfied in relation to any of these matters, it may refuse to award sequestration. It will not necessarily do so, however. For example, if the court is not satisfied that the debtor has been properly cited, it may order re-service rather than refusing the petition outright.

The second reason for which sequestration may be refused is that cause is shown why sequestration cannot competently be awarded[6]. The Act

---

1 1985 Act, s 12(1).
2 As to how this requirement may be satisfied, see *Scottish & Newcastle Breweries plc v Harvey-Rutherford* 1994 SCLR 131.
3 Where the debtor is averred to be rendered apparently insolvent as a result of s 7(1)(d) of the 1985 Act (unsatisfied statutory demand for payment of debt), the requirement of *Lord Advocate v Thomson* 1994 SCLR 96, that evidence of the debt or debts should have been attached to the statutory demand before it will be held to be competent to constitute apparent insolvency should be noted.
4 1985 Act, s 12(3).
5 1985 Act, s 11(1), (5). It should be noted that the requirement to produce evidence of the debt or debts along with the oath is a separate requirement from the requirement to attach such evidence to a statutory demand for payment of debt if that is relevant: *Lord Advocate v Thomson* above.
6 1985 Act, s 12(1) (debtor petitions) and s 12(3A) (non-debtor petitions).

does not give any guidance as to what is meant by this phrase, but examples may be found in case law. For instance, in *Unity Trust Bank plc v Ahmed*[1], the creditor averred that the debtor was apparently insolvent as a result of the expiry of a charge for payment served on him without payment having been made. The creditor had also served a statutory demand on the debtor, however, and the period allowed for payment under the statutory demand had not expired at the time the petition was presented. The court held that the creditor had presented the debtor with 'directly contrary ultimata' and refused the petition as incompetent[2].

The third reason for which sequestration may be refused, which applies only to non-debtor petitions, is that the debtor *forthwith* pays or satisfies specified debts, produces written evidence of payment or satisfaction of these debts or gives or shows that there is sufficient security for the payment of these debts. The debts in question are those which gave rise to his apparent insolvency *and* any other debts due to the petitioning or concurring creditor[3].

It is not uncommon for the debtor to appear at the hearing and offer to make payment. As discussed above, however, sequestration is a summary remedy and the court will (or should) not continue the petition to allow the debtor further time to make payment. It is thought that in order to escape sequestration on this ground, the debtor would require to make payment in advance of the hearing date so that the creditor is in possession of cleared funds by the hearing date, or make payment on the hearing date in cash or by banker's draft. If the debtor tendered a cheque, the creditor would have no guarantee that the cheque would be honoured, and it is thought that the creditor would not be obliged to accept payment in this form, nor would the debtor be entitled to dismissal of the petition on tendering such a cheque. If payment is made, the court may dismiss the petition but award expenses against the debtor.

If the debtor alleges that he or she has paid or otherwise satisfied the debt, again the qualification that evidence of this must be produced 'forthwith' implies that the debtor must produce any such evidence at the hearing. The court should not continue the petition to allow it to be produced at a later stage.

If the debtor wishes to escape sequestration by offering to give sufficient security for payment of the debt or demonstrate that this already exists, the requirement that this must also be done 'forthwith' (ie at the hearing) may cause him or her considerable difficulties. For example, it may be difficult for the debtor to produce a security at the hearing, or there may be dispute about the validity or sufficiency of the security. It has been held that notwithstanding this, the court should be able to be satisfied at the hearing if it is to refuse sequestration, but in certain circumstances further procedure may be necessary to enable these matters to be established[4].

1 1993 SCLR 53, Sh Ct.
2 See also *Racal Vodac Ltd v Hislop* 1992 SLT (Sh Ct) 2 (dispute over the identity of the debtor).
3 1985 Act, s 12(3A)(b).
4 See *Royal Bank of Scotland plc v Forbes* 1987 SC 99. See also *National Westminster Bank plc v W J Elrick & Co* 1991 SLT 709, OH. For a full discussion of the difficulties with this provision, see McKenzie 'Avoiding Sequestration by Provision of Sufficient Security' 1993 SLT (News) 269.

Finally, the court may refuse to award sequestration if there are concurrent proceedings for sequestration or an analogous remedy pending before another court or there has already been an award of sequestration or an analogous remedy[1].

A decision to refuse sequestration is subject to appeal[2].

Date of sequestration

The date of sequestration is important because many effects and time limits are linked to it. In the case of a debtor petition, the date of sequestration is the date of the *award* of sequestration[3]. In any other case, the date of sequestration is the date on which the *original* warrant to cite the debtor is granted[4].

Registration of court order

Section 14 of the 1985 Act requires the clerk of the court to send a certified copy of the relevant order to the Keeper of the Register of Inhibitions and Adjudications and a copy of the order to the Accountant in Bankruptcy 'forthwith' after the date of sequestration. This means a copy of the order making the award in the case of a debtor petition, and a copy of the warrant to cite in non-debtor cases[5]. The order is registered in the Register of Inhibitions and Adjudications and has the effect of an inhibition against the debtor[6], ie, it prevents him or her from dealing with his or her heritable property. This effect lasts for three years, unless there is earlier recorded a certified copy of an order refusing the sequestration[7], recalling the sequestration[8], or granting discharge on composition[9]. The initial period can be extended for further periods of three years by the recording of a memorandum to that effect by the trustee[10].

Recall of sequestration

General

Although refusal to award sequestration is subject to appeal, a decision to award sequestration is not. An award of sequestration may, however, be recalled by the Court of Session in certain circumstances. The general rules for recall of sequestration are contained in ss 16 and 17 of the 1985 Act, and there are special rules where recall is sought by a non-entitled spouse of the debtor seeking to protect his or her occupancy rights in the

1 1985 Act, s 10.
2 1985 Act, s 15(3).
3 1985 Act, s 12(4)(a).
4 1985 Act, s 12(4)(b).
5 1985 Act, s 14(5).
6 1985 Act, s 14(2).
7 As provided for under 1985 Act, s 15(5)(a).
8 As provided for under 1985 Act, s 17(8)(a).
9 As provided for under 1985 Act, Sch 4, para 11. Discharge on composition is discussed further below.
10 1985 Act, s 14(4).

matrimonial home. Where recall is competent, it should be sought rather than any other remedy[1].

Grounds for recall

Recall may be applied for by the debtor, any creditor, the interim or permanent trustee, the Accountant in Bankruptcy or any other person having an interest[2]. The court may recall the sequestration if it is satisfied in all the circumstances, including those arising after the date of sequestration, that it is appropriate to do so[3]. It has a very wide discretion[4]. Section 17(1) of the 1985 Act provides three specific grounds on which the court may recall the sequestration, without prejudice to the general power to do so. These are as follows.

(1) The debtor has paid his or her debts in full or provided sufficient security for their payment[5]. The funds must have come from an outside source, or from assets which do not vest in the trustee, since the debtor is not in a position to deal with assets which have vested in the trustee.
(2) The majority in value of the creditors reside in a country other than Scotland and it is more appropriate to have the sequestration there[6].
(3) One or more other awards of sequestration or analogous awards have been made[7]. The grounds of jurisdiction are designed to avoid this, and s 10 allows the court to sist or refuse a sequestration if the existence of another award or pending proceedings is known to the court before an award of sequestration is made. Nonetheless, it is possible for more than one award of sequestration to made be made and accordingly recall of an award in such a case is specifically provided for. The court has discretion to recall any other award which has been made in preference to the one in respect of which the petition has been presented[8]. This may be appropriate, eg, if the administration in the other case is less advanced.

Time limits

Where the petition is based on any of the specific grounds set out in s 17(1) of the 1985 Act, the petition may be presented at any time. If the administration of the estate has reached an advanced stage, this will be a factor in whether the court will exercise its discretion to recall. In any other case, the petition must be presented within ten weeks of the award of sequestration[9].

1 *Spence v Davie* 1993 SLT 217, OH.
2 1985 Act, s 16(1).
3 1985 Act, s 17(1).
4 See eg *Button v Royal Bank of Scotland* 1987 GWD 27-1019 (recall refused as debtor's proposed scheme too uncertain); *Royal Bank of Scotland plc v Gillies* 1987 SLT 54; *Wright v Tennent Caledonian Breweries Ltd* 1991 SCLR 633; *Archer Car Sales (Airdrie) Ltd v Gregory's Tr* 1993 SLT 223, OH.
5 1985 Act, s 17(1)(a), and see *Martin v Martin's Tr* 1994 SLT 261, OH.
6 1985 Act, s 17(1)(b).
7 1985 Act, s 17(1)(c).
8 1985 Act, s 17(2).
9 1985 Act, s 16(4).

Effect

The effect of recalling the sequestration is to put the debtor and anyone else affected by it back in the same position, so far as possible, as they would have been in had the sequestration not been granted[1]. The court has power to make any necessary orders to achieve this[2]. It will also make provision for payment of the interim and, if appropriate, permanent trustee[3], and may make various orders in relation to expenses[4].

Refusal of recall

The court may refuse to recall an award of sequestration. It may also make an order that the sequestration continue subject to such conditions as it thinks fit[5].

Recall by non-entitled spouse

Where the debtor's estate includes a property which is a matrimonial home in which the debtor's spouse has occupancy rights under the Matrimonial Homes (Family Protection) (Scotland) Act 1981, the non-entitled spouse who has such occupancy rights may apply to the court for recall of the debtor's sequestration on the ground that the purpose of the sequestration was wholly or mainly to defeat the spouse's occupancy rights[6]. The court may make any other appropriate order to protect the occupancy rights instead of recalling the sequestration[7].

The interim trustee

Appointment of interim trustee

An interim trustee will be appointed in every sequestration: normally at the time sequestration is awarded[8]. The petitioner may have nominated someone to act as interim trustee in the petition[9]. In order to be eligible for appointment, such a person must be resident within the jurisdiction of the Court of Session, be qualified to act as an insolvency practitioner[10] and have given an undertaking to act as interim and, if necessary, permanent trustee[11]. If no such person is nominated or the court declines to appoint the person nominated, the Accountant in Bankruptcy will be appointed as interim trustee[12]. In practice, a private insolvency practitioner will usually

1 1985 Act, s 17(4).
2 1985 Act, s 17(3).
3 1985 Act, s 17(3)(a)
4 1985 Act, s 17(3)(b) and s 17(7).
5 1985 Act, s 17(6).
6 1985 Act, s 41(1).
7 1985 Act, s 41(1)(b).
8 See 'Award of sequestration' above.
9 1985 Act, s 2(1).
10 In accordance with ss 388 and 389 of the Insolvency Act 1986: see 1985 Act, s 73(1).
11 These requirements are set out in s 2(3) of the 1985 Act and must be averred in the petition.
12 1985 Act, s 2(2).

agree to act only if it appears there are at least enough assets to pay his fees, since public funding is no longer available.

In a non-debtor petition, an interim trustee may be appointed before the award of sequestration is made[1]. Unless the debtor consents, the petitioner must show a good reason for such an appointment. For example, if the debtor has a business which requires to be competently run in the interim, or there is a danger that he or she will dispose of assets, an immediate appointment may be justified.

Replacement of interim trustee

The interim trustee may require to be replaced for any one of a variety of reasons.

Where the interim trustee dies in office, the court will appoint a new interim trustee[2]. Where a private insolvency practitioner is interim trustee and no longer wishes to act in the sequestration, he or she must apply to the court for permission to resign[3]. The court will permit this where *either* the trustee is unable to act (eg because he or she no longer qualifies as an insolvency practitioner or because he or she is seriously ill) *or* the court is satisfied that he or she has behaved in such a way that he or she should no longer be interim trustee[4]. In such a case, the court will appoint a new interim trustee[5].

The interim trustee may also be removed by the court on application of the debtor, a creditor or the Accountant in Bankruptcy on the same grounds[6] *or* following on a report to the court by the Accountant in Bankruptcy that he or she has failed to perform any of his or her duties without reasonable excuse[7]. In either case, the court will appoint a new interim trustee[8].

Functions of interim trustee

In essence, the interim trustee is a caretaker who is appointed to preserve the position until the appointment of the permanent trustee who will administer and finally distribute the debtor's estate to the creditors. This is reflected in s 2 of the 1985 Act which sets out the general functions of the interim trustee and prescribes two of the interim trustee's functions as being to safeguard the debtor's estate[9] and to administer the sequestration process[10] pending the appointment of a permanent trustee.

1 1985 Act, s 2(5).
2 1985 Act, s 13(5). (Section 13 substituted by the Bankruptcy (Scotland) Act 1993, Sch 1, para 2.)
3 1985 Act, s 13(3).
4 1985 Act, s 13(3) referring to paras (a) and (b) respectively of s 13(2).
5 1985 Act, s 13(4).
6 1985 Act, s 13(2).
7 1985 Act, s 1A(2). The court may, however, simply censure the interim trustee or make some other appropriate order.
8 1985 Act, s 13(2) and s 13(1) respectively.
9 1985 Act, s 2(4)(a).
10 1985 Act, s 2(4)(d).

The interim trustee must also ascertain what the debtor's assets and liabilities are[1] and the reasons for the debtor's insolvency[2]. The trustee will be able to obtain information to enable him to fulfil these functions by using the powers conferred on him by the Act. The debtor is also obliged to provide him with a statement of assets and liabilities, a document in prescribed form containing details of the debtor's assets, liabilities, income and expenditure and such other information as may be prescribed[3], which will assist him with this task. In the case of a debtor petition, this document will already have been lodged with the court, and the debtor simply requires to send a copy of it to the interim trustee[4]. In other cases, the debtor must prepare one and send it to the trustee[5].

The interim trustee's final function is to provide information to the Accountant in Bankruptcy, even after he or she has ceased to act in the sequestration[6].

Powers of interim trustee

Notwithstanding the nature of the interim trustee's position as essentially that of a caretaker, he or she does in fact have extensive powers. These are mainly set out in s 18, which deals with interim preservation of the estate. The interim trustee can give the debtor directions about the running of his or her estate[7]. The debtor can appeal against these if he or she thinks that they are unreasonable, but must comply with them in the meantime[8]. This power will often be utilised where there is a business, and the interim trustee wants to be sure that it is run so as to preserve it so far as possible for the creditors. Alternatively, he or she has the power to carry on the debtor's business himself[9] or, rather more drastically, to close it down[10]. The interim trustee is given the latter two powers, along with a number of others specifically to enable him to carry out the functions discussed above. The other powers which the interim trustee is given under s 18 include:

(1) The right to recover from the debtor money, valuables or documents relating to his or her business or financial affairs[11] and to place them in safe custody[12].
(2) The right to sell or otherwise dispose of perishable goods[13]. Normally, disposal of the estate would be a matter for the permanent trustee, but in the case of perishable goods, it may be necessary to act immediately so that the value of the goods, if not the goods themselves, is retained for the estate.

1   1985 Act, s 2(4)(c).
2   1985 Act, s 2(4)(b).
3   1985 Act, s 73(1) as amended.
4   1985 Act, s 19(1).
5   1985 Act, s 19(2).
6   1985 Act, s 2(4)(e).
7   1985 Act, s 18(1).
8   1985 Act, s 18(4).
9   1985 Act, s 18(2)(h).
10   1985 Act, s 18(2)(g).
11   1985 Act, s 18(2)(a).
12   1985 Act, s 18(2)(b).
13   1985 Act, s 18(2)(c).

(3) The power to inventory the debtor's property[1].
(4) The right to make the debtor carry through any transaction which he or she has already entered[2], eg a contract for sale of the debtor's house.
(5) The right to take out or maintain insurance policies for the debtor's business or property[3] – essential in case it should be stolen or otherwise damaged or destroyed.
(6) The right to borrow money if this is necessary to safeguard the debtor's estate[4], eg to complete the purchase of an asset so as to preserve it as part of the estate.

The interim trustee can exercise all of these powers automatically. There are some other things which he may obtain only by applying to the court. These are:

(a) A warrant to enter and search the debtor's house or business premises[5]. Court involvement is necessary because of the invasion of the debtor's privacy.
(b) Any other order for the purpose of safeguarding the debtor's estate[6]. This is a catch-all provision. An example of the type of order which can be made under this subsection can be seen in the case of *Scottish & Newcastle plc, Petitioner*[7], where the court authorised the interim trustee to sell licensed premises (a power which, as discussed above, he would not otherwise have) in the special circumstances of that case.

The interim trustee also has the power to request the debtor, the debtor's spouse and any other person the trustee thinks can give him or her information about the debtor's financial affairs to appear before him or her and give such information[8]. The trustee can also if necessary ask for an order for any of these persons to appear before the sheriff to be examined in private to gain the information[8].

Duties of interim trustee

Where the debtor has not petitioned for his or her own sequestration, the interim trustee has a duty to notify the debtor of the interim trustee's appointment[9]. The interim trustee must also advertise his or her appointment in all cases[10].

The interim trustee must also take the necessary steps to safeguard the debtor's estate. Although not directly expressed as a duty in the 1985 Act, it is the interim trustee's basic function.

Once the interim trustee receives the debtor's statements of assets and liabilities, he or she must prepare a 'statement of affairs' which sets out what he or she knows about the debtor's financial position. The interim

1 1985 Act, s 18(2)(d).
2 1985 Act, s 18(2)(e).
3 1985 Act, s 18(2)(f).
4 1985 Act, s 18(2)(h).
5 1985 Act, s 18(3)(b).
6 1985 Act, s 18(2)(c).
7 1992 SCLR 540.
8 1985 Act, s 20(4).
9 1985 Act, s 2(7).
10 1985 Act, s 15(6).

trustee must give a view on whether he or she thinks any of the debtor's unsecured creditors will receive any money from the sequestration[1]. If the interim trustee is a private insolvency practitioner, he or she must send a copy of the debtor's statement of assets and liabilities and his or her own statement of affairs to the Accountant in Bankruptcy along with his or her comments about what he or she believes caused the insolvency and the debtor's role in bringing it about[2].

Where the interim trustee is a private insolvency practitioner, he or she must also call a meeting of all the creditors[3]. This is known as the statutory meeting[4]. He or she must notify all known creditors and the Accountant in Bankruptcy of the details of the meeting and invite creditors to submit claims in the sequestration[5].

Where the interim trustee is the Accountant in Bankruptcy, the statutory meeting is not compulsory. The Accountant must tell creditors whether he or she intends to call the meeting or not[6]. If the Accountant does not, any creditor can request the calling of the meeting[7], and the Accountant must call it if creditors representing at least one-quarter of the value of the debts request it[8]. If the meeting is called, the procedure is substantially the same as in the case where the interim trustee is a private insolvency practitioner[9].

The statutory meeting

If held, the statutory meeting is an opportunity for the creditors to get together, to exchange information and, if appropriate, to choose the permanent trustee who will administer the debtor's estate.

It is chaired initially by the interim trustee, whose first task is to decide whether to accept claims already submitted by creditors[10]. Only creditors whose claims have been accepted and who are not otherwise disqualified[11] can vote in any election to choose the permanent trustee. The interim trustee makes available the debtor's statement of assets and liabilities and his or her own statement of affairs[12] (which most creditors will already have received with the notice of the meeting), answers questions[13], gives his or her opinion on the likelihood of the unsecured creditors receiving any payment[14] and, if necessary as a result of further information disclosed at the meeting, prepares (or indicates he or she will prepare) a revised statement of affairs[15]. He or she must thereafter send any such

1   1985 Act, s 20(1).
2   1985 Act, s 20(2).
3   1985 Act, s 21(1).
4   1985 Act, s 20A.
5   1985 Act, s 21(2).
6   1985 Act, s 21A(2).
7   1985 Act, s 21A(4).
8   1985 Act, s 21A(5).
9   1985 Act, s 21A(6), (7) and (8).
10   1985 Act, s 23(1)(a).
11   1985 Act, s 24(3).
12   1985 Act, s 23(3)(a).
13   1985 Act, s 23(3)(b).
14   1985 Act, s 23(3)(c).
15   1985 Act, s 23(3)(d).

revised statement to the creditors[1]. The meeting then moves on to the election of the permanent trustee[2].

Discharge of interim trustee

Once the permanent trustee is in place, the interim trustee may wish to obtain a discharge. Where the interim trustee has himself or herself become the permanent trustee, he or she will not usually bother to do so since his or her ultimate discharge as permanent trustee will cover his or her actings as interim trustee also.

The procedure where the interim trustee is a private insolvency practitioner is set out in s 27 of the 1985 Act; where the interim trustee is the Accountant in Bankruptcy, the procedure is set out in s 26A. Assuming the discharge is granted, the interim trustee cannot thereafter be sued by either the debtor or any of the creditors for any of his or her acts or omissions in carrying out his or her functions as interim trustee, except for fraud[3].

The permanent trustee

Selection of permanent trustee

There must be a permanent trustee in every sequestration[4], but there may only be one permanent trustee at a time: a joint appointment is not permissible[5]. The permanent trustee may be either elected at the statutory meeting, if held, or appointed by the sheriff. It has been said that the difference between election and appointment is crucial to the understanding of the whole 1985 Act[6].

The Accountant in Bankruptcy is not eligible to be elected as permanent trustee[7], although he or she may become permanent trustee by other means[8]. If a permanent trustee is elected at the statutory meeting, the interim trustee makes a report to that effect to the sheriff who confirms the permanent trustee in office[9]. At the same time the interim trustee may apply for a certificate of summary administration[10].

Where a permanent trustee is not elected, a different procedure will be followed. This may happen where:

(1) the Accountant in Bankruptcy is interim trustee and there has been no statutory meeting;
(2) no creditors who are eligible to vote attend the statutory meeting;

---

1 1985 Act, s 23(5).
2 1985 Act, s 24(1).
3 1985 Act, s 27(5) (private insolvency practitioner), s 26A(7) (Accountant in Bankruptcy).
4 1985 Act, s 3(1).
5 *Inland Revenue Comrs v MacDonald* 1988 SLT (Sh Ct) 7.
6 McBryde *Bankruptcy* (2nd edn, 1995) pp 88–89.
7 1985 Act, s 24(2).
8 See below.
9 1985 Act, s 25(2). Objections are dealt with in s 25(1)(b), (3), (4) and (5).
10 1985 Act, s 25(2A).

(3) no permanent trustee is elected at the statutory meeting for some other reason.

In the first case, the Accountant in Bankruptcy as interim trustee will report the circumstances of the sequestration to the sheriff[1] and the Accountant or his or her nominee will be appointed permanent trustee[2]. The Accountant in Bankruptcy may apply for a certificate of summary administration[3]. Where this is not applied for or not granted, the sequestration will proceed as a Sch 2 case[4].

In the other two cases, the interim trustee will report the outcome of the statutory meeting to the sheriff[5] and, where the interim trustee is a private insolvency practitioner, he or she will also notify the Accountant in Bankruptcy[6]. In either case, where the interim trustee is a private insolvency practitioner, he or she will be appointed as permanent trustee[6] and may apply for a certificate of summary administration[7]. Where this is not applied for or not granted, the sequestration will proceed as a Sch 2 case[8]. Where the interim trustee is the Accountant in Bankruptcy, the Accountant or his or her nominee will be appointed as permanent trustee[9] and he or she may also apply for a certificate of summary administration[10]. Again, where this is not applied for or not granted the sequestration will proceed as a Sch 2 case.[11]

In any case where the Accountant in Bankruptcy is interim trustee and applies for and is granted a certificate of summary administration, the Accountant or his or her nominee will be appointed as permanent trustee[12].

Replacement of permanent trustee

Where the permanent trustee dies in office, the commissioners or, if there are no commissioners, the Accountant in Bankruptcy, are required to call a meeting of the creditors for the election of a new permanent trustee[13].

Where the permanent trustee wishes to resign, he or she must apply to the court for permission to do so. The grounds for resignation are the same as those applicable to resignation of an interim trustee[14], and where either applies, the application will be granted. The application may be granted unconditionally, in which case the commissioners or, if there are no commissioners, the Accountant in Bankruptcy, are required to call a

---

1 1985 Act, s 21B(1).
2 1985 Act, ss 21B(2) and 25A.
3 1985 Act, s 21B(2)(b).
4 1985 Act, s 25A(3).
5 1985 Act, s 24(3A) (where the interim trustee is the Accountant in Bankruptcy) and s 23(4) (where the interim trustee is a private insolvency practitioner).
6 1985 Act, s 23(4).
7 1985 Act, s 23(4A).
8 1985 Act, s 24(5).
9 1985 Act, s 24(3A) applying s 25A.
10 1985 Act, s 23(3B).
11 1985 Act, s 25A(3).
12 1985 Act, ss 23A(4) and 25A.
13 1985 Act, s 28(3).
14 1985 Act, s 28(1).

meeting of the creditors for the election of a new permanent trustee[1]. Alternatively, the application may be granted subject to election of a new permanent trustee[2], in which case, the resigning permanent trustee must call the appropriate meeting of creditors[3]. If no new permanent trustee is elected at any such meeting, the Accountant in Bankruptcy or his or her nominee is appointed by the court and the sequestration thereafter proceeds as a Sch 2 case[4].

The permanent trustee may be removed in several ways on different grounds. He or she may be removed by the creditors at a meeting of creditors called for that purpose if they also elect a new permanent trustee[5], without any reason being given. He or she may be removed following on a report to the court by the Accountant in Bankruptcy that he or she has failed to perform any of his or her duties without reasonable excuse[6]. He or she may be removed from office by the court on the application of a commissioner, the debtor, a creditor or the Accountant in Bankruptcy on substantially the same grounds as he or she may apply for his or her own resignation[7]. Finally, the permanent trustee may be removed by the court on the application of the commissioners, the Accountant in Bankruptcy or a person representing at least a quarter in value of the creditors on cause shown other than those grounds[8]. In the three latter cases, the commissioners or, if there are no commissioners, the Accountant in Bankruptcy, are required to call a meeting of the creditors for the election of a new permanent trustee[9]. Again, if no new permanent trustee is elected at any such meeting, the Accountant in Bankruptcy or his or her nominee is appointed by the court and the sequestration thereafter proceeds as a Sch 2 case[10].

Functions of permanent trustee

The essential function of the permanent trustee is to gather in the debtor's estate (so far as the interim trustee has not already done so), to realise it and to distribute it to the creditors according to their respective rights, returning any surplus to the debtor in the unlikely event that there is such a surplus. This is reflected in s 3 of the 1985 Act, which sets out the permanent trustee's functions, and which gives as his or her first two functions the recovery, management and realisation of the debtor's estate[11] and distribution of the estate among the debtor's creditors according to their respective entitlements[12].

1 1985 Act, s 28(2)(a).
2 1985 Act, s 28(1A).
3 1985 Act, s 28(2)(b).
4 1985 Act, s 28(5) applying s 25A.
5 1985 Act, s 29(1)(a).
6 1985 Act, s 1A(2). Alternatively, the court may simply censure the permanent trustee or make some other appropriate order.
7 1985 Act, s 28(6), (9).
8 1985 Act, s 29(1)(b).
9 1985 Act, s 29(5) and (6).
10 1985 Act, s 29(8) applying, inter alia, s 28(5) above.
11 1985 Act, s 3(1)(a).
12 1985 Act, s 3(1)(b).

The permanent trustee must also ascertain the debtor's assets and liabilities[1] and the reasons for the debtor's insolvency[2], both tasks which the permanent trustee has in common with, and which were already begun by, the interim trustee. These are part of the permanent trustee's functions as well because the interim trustee may have been unable to complete these tasks in the short time available to him or her, and further information may emerge in the course of the permanent trustee's administration.

The permanent trustee must also keep a record of the progress of the sequestration by means of a sederunt book[3], into which important documents are inserted, and keep regular accounts[4], which can be inspected by the debtor, the creditors and the commissioners, if any[5]. A private insolvency practitioner must also provide information to the Accountant in Bankruptcy, even if he or she has ceased to act as permanent trustee[6].

Commissioners

The permanent trustee may be supervised and advised by commissioners[7]. Commissioners are creditors or their mandatories elected by other creditors in accordance with the procedure laid down in s 30 of the 1985 Act. There may be up to five commissioners[8], although it is not necessary to have any at all. If commissioners are elected, the permanent trustee must consult them about recovery, management and realisation of the debtor's estate[9]. The permanent trustee is obliged to have regard to their advice[10] although this does not necessarily mean that he or she must follow it. The consent of the commissioners is required for certain matters[11].

Commissioners cannot be elected in cases being dealt with under the abbreviated procedures in Sch 2[12]. Accordingly, commissioners will not be competent in almost all summary administration cases either, since Sch 2 applies to all summary administration cases with one exception[13].

Vesting of the estate

Act and Warrant

Following confirmation of the permanent trustee's appointment or his or her appointment by the court, the sheriff clerk issues to him or her an act and warrant. The act and warrant vests, as at the date of sequestration, the whole estate of the debtor in the permanent trustee for the benefit of the creditors[14].

1 1985 Act, s 3(1)(d).
2 1985 Act, s 3(1)(c).
3 1985 Act, s 3(1)(e).
4 1985 Act, s 3(1)(f).
5 See 'Commissioners' below.
6 1985 Act, s 3(1)(g), (5).
7 1985 Act, s 4.
8 1985 Act, s 30(1).
9 1985 Act, s 39(1).
10 1985 Act, s 3(2).
11 1985 Act, ss 39(2) and 65(1).
12 1985 Act, s 4.
13 See 1985 Act, Sch 2A, para 5.
14 1985 Act, s 31(1). See also 'Definition of estate' below.

Effect of vesting

In general terms, the effect of vesting is to divest the debtor of ownership of the assets which the 1985 Act provides will vest in the permanent trustee, and to transfer ownership of those assets to the permanent trustee. Section 31 achieves this effect by providing that:

(1) in relation to heritable property, the act and warrant has the effect of a decree in an action of adjudication in implement of sale as well as in such an action for payment and in security of debt[1]; and
(2) in relation to moveable property, where such property would normally require delivery or possession or intimation of its assignation to transfer title, the act and warrant vests the property in the permanent trustee as if delivery, possession or intimation had taken place at the date of sequestration[2].

Nature of trustee's right to property

The trustee generally acquires a real right to moveable property of the debtor, but in some cases further steps will be necessary to complete his title to property if a real right to the property is desired: eg, registration of shares in a company. This has generally been regarded as necessary on the basis that if he does not do so, there is a danger that a prior transferee of the debtor may obtain a good title preferable to that of the trustee by completing his own right to the property in question before the trustee does so[3]. This position may, however, have changed as a result of the decision of the House of Lords in *Sharp v Thomson*[4].

The trustee does not acquire a real right to heritage. In order to obtain a real right to heritage, the trustee requires to take the necessary steps to complete his or her title: usually recording a title to the heritage in his or her own name, as trustee, in the Register of Sasines or registering such a title in the Land Register[5]. The trustee will not always go to the trouble of doing so since he or she may deal with the property without completing title in this way. It has generally been accepted, however, that if the trustee does not do so, or if he or she delays in doing so, there is the risk that someone else to whom the debtor has granted a title prior to the sequestration will be able to record his or her title first and so obtain a real right to the property which will be preferred to the trustee's right. This is the so-called race to the register. Once again, however, this position may have changed as a result of the decision in *Sharp v Thomson*[6].

Tantum et tale

The trustee does not, in general, acquire any better right to the estate which has vested in him or her under the 1985 Act than the debtor had

---

1 1985 Act, s 31(1)(b).
2 1985 Act, s 31(4).
3 *Morrison v Harrison* (1876) 3R 406, which concerned shares in a company.
4 1997 SCLR 328, HL.
5 Where the debtor himself or herself had only an uncompleted right to the heritage, the trustee may complete title in the trustee's own or the debtor's name: 1985 Act, s 31(3).
6 1997 SCLR 328, HL.

and the trustee's title is therefore generally subject to any limitations which affected the debtor's title[1]. Thus if, eg, the debtor's title is reducible, then the trustee's title is also reducible: an example would be an insurance policy which was voidable because of the debtor's non-disclosure. The trustee is said to take the property *tantum et tale*.

This principle is part of the common law[2] and is not explicitly mentioned in the Act, except to the extent that the Act specifically states in s 33(3) that the vesting of property in the trustee under the Act is without prejudice to the rights of secured creditors which are preferable to the right of the trustee[3]. In other words, the property vests in the trustee subject to any such security. The secured creditor remains free to enforce his security without regard to the sequestration, subject only to certain restrictions placed on heritable creditors and a trustee's right to require the creditor to surrender any security on payment of its value[4].

Definition of estate

Section 31(1) of the 1985 Act vests 'the whole estate of the debtor' in the permanent trustee. This in turn is defined by s 31(8) as the debtor's whole estate as at the date of sequestration, wherever situated, including any income or estate vesting in the debtor on that date, and any rights which the debtor was entitled to exercise in relation to his property[5].

Certain types of property deserve special mention, as they may give rise to difficulties, namely foreign property, damages, pensions and property to which the debtor has title but in which he or she has no beneficial interest.

FOREIGN PROPERTY

Although s 31(8) states that the debtor's property 'wherever situated' vests in the trustee, whether the trustee will actually be able to enforce his or her right to property outwith Scotland, and recover and/or realise it for the benefit of the creditors, will depend on whether his or her right is recognised by the legal system of the country where the property is situated[6].

DAMAGES

In general, damages which have been paid to the debtor and form part of his or her estate will vest in the trustee under s 31(8). Damages which are paid to the debtor during the sequestration will also vest in the trustee except those which are in the nature of income. These rules apply equally

---

1   Although it is not clear whether the trustee's right to the debtor's home is affected by occupancy rights of a non-entitled spouse under the Matrimonial Homes Act 1991: see McBryde *Bankruptcy* (2nd edn, 1995) pp 204–207 and further sources there cited.
2   The leading case is *Heritable Reversionary Co Ltd v Millar* (1892) 19 R (HL) 43.
3   See also 1985 Act, s 51(6) and 'Ranking' below.
4   1985 Act, Sch 1, para 5(2) and see 'Amount of claim' below.
5   1985 Act, s 31(8).
6   The position within the UK is regulated by s 426 of the Insolvency Act 1986. For a full discussion, see Anton *Private International Law* (2nd edn, 1990) ch 29.

to damages in the form of solatium for personal injury. However, the right to *raise* an action for solatium is personal to the debtor, and does not vest in the trustee[1]. The trustee cannot raise an action for solatium, although he or she can raise an action for patrimonial loss[2]. The trustee may, however, sist himself in any action which has been raised by the debtor and thereby obtain payment of any damages ultimately awarded, including solatium. Where the trustee chooses not to sist himself or herself in any such action, he or she will have no right to the damages if these are paid after the debtor's discharge[3]. The trustee could, however, apply for deferral of the debtor's discharge in order to secure them[4].

PENSIONS

Whether or not a debtor's right to a pension vests in the trustee depends on the type of pension. In general terms, where the debtor has a personal pension, the policy will vest in the trustee because it comes within the definition of estate in s 31(8) unless, perhaps, there is a valid forfeiture clause. Because of the principle that the trustee takes the property *tantum et tale*, he or she will not be able to obtain payment of any sums due under the pension until they become payable in terms of the pension policy (usually on retirement). The trustee will, however, be entitled to all sums due under the policy[5], even if they are paid after the debtor's discharge. Where the debtor is a member of an occupational pension scheme, in general the pension will not vest in the trustee, although the debtor may be required to make a contribution to the estate out of pension income[6]. There are also now provisions for recovering excessive contributions to pensions on the statute book, although these are not in force at the time of writing[7]. A full discussion of the complexities of pensions is beyond the scope of this work[8].

PROPERTY: DEBTOR HAS TITLE TO BUT NO BENEFICIAL INTEREST IN

A situation may arise where a debtor has transferred property to another prior to his sequestration, but the transferee has not completed his or her title: eg where the debtor has transferred shares to another but the transfer has not been registered, or the debtor has transferred heritage to another but the title has not been recorded or registered as appropriate. It has traditionally been accepted that in such a situation, since the debtor still retains the title to the property at the date of sequestration, it vests in

1 See *Muir's Tr v Braidwood* 1958 SC 169; *Watson v Thomson* 1991 SC 447.
2 *Muir's Tr v Braidwood* above.
3 *Coutt's Tr v Coutts* 1996 SCLR 1026, Sh Ct.
4 The issue of the treatment of damages for personal injury in sequestration was considered by the Scottish Law Commission in 1988, but following consultation, they recommended no change in the present law: *Consultation Paper on the Law of Bankruptcy: Solatium for Personal Injury/Future Wage Loss* (February 1994).
5 1985 Act, s 32(1).
6 1985 Act, s 32(4) and see 'Acquierenda' below.
7 See 'Challengeable transactions' below.
8 For a more detailed discussion of some of the relevant issues, see Talman 'Sequestration and Pension Rights' 1994 SLT (News) 105 and, especially, Gordon 'The Effect of Bankruptcy on Personal Pensions' (1997) 42 JLSS 329.

the trustee and there is then a 'race' between the original transferee and the trustee to complete title, whoever does so first obtaining the right to the property. However, as a result of the decision of the House of Lords in *Sharp v Thomson*[1], there may be some doubt as to whether that remains the case.

The case was actually concerned with receivership. A company had sold a flat to purchasers. After the price had been paid and the title deed delivered to the purchasers, but before the deed had been recorded by them, a receiver was appointed to the company. The question was whether the flat, to which the company still had title, was part of the company's 'property and undertaking' and so caught by the receivership. The House of Lords held that although title remained with the company, it had no beneficial interest in the flat, which had been sold, and therefore it could not be regarded as part of the company's 'property and undertaking' so as to be caught by the receivership.

The implications of the decision are a matter of considerable debate[2]. If the scope of the decision cannot be regarded as confined to receivership, it is arguable that in a similar situation involving a sequestration, property which the debtor had conveyed away would not vest in the trustee even although the debtor still had title to it, on the basis that since the debtor had no longer any beneficial interest in it, it could not be regarded as part of his or her estate. It is suggested that such an extension of the case beyond receivership would be unfortunate. Further case law or legislation will, however, be required to clarify the position.

Property excluded from vesting

Certain property is specifically excluded from vesting in the trustee. Section 33 of the 1985 Act excludes from vesting property which is exempt from poinding for the purposes of protecting the debtor and his or her family[3]. It also excludes property which the debtor holds in trust for another[4].

Acquirenda

Section 31 of the 1985 Act deals with the vesting of the estate as at the date of sequestration. But what of income or property acquired by the debtor after that date? This is covered by s 32. Income which derives from the estate vested in the permanent trustee vests in the permanent trustee, but any other income received by the debtor, eg from employment, vests in the debtor himself or herself or herself[5]. The trustee may, however, apply to the court for an order requiring the debtor to pay over to the trustee any

1 1997 SCLR 328, HL.
2 See eg KGC Reid *Jam Today: Sharp* in the House of Lords' 1997 SLT (News) 79; R Rennie 'Sharp v Thomson: The Final Act' (1997) 42 JLSS 130; JG Birrell '*Sharp v Thomson*: The Impact on Banking and Insolvency Law' 1997 SLT (News) 151; DJ Cusine 'Sharp v Thomson: The House of Lords Strikes Back' (1997) 26 Property Law 5; Guild '*Sharp v Thomson* – A Practitioner's View' (1997) 42 JLSS 274.
3 1985 Act, s 33(1)(a). The property so exempted is defined in s 16 of the Debtors (Scotland) Act 1987.
4 1985 Act, s 33(1)(b). See *Council of the Law Society of Scotland v McKinnie* 1991 SCLR 850.
5 1985 Act, s 32(1).

income which is in excess of the sum the court considers suitable for the debtor's own aliment and any 'relevant obligations' which he or she may have[1]. 'Relevant obligations' are aliment[2], periodical allowance and child support under the Child Support Act 1991[3]. However, in determining a suitable amount to allow for any relevant obligation, the court is not bound by any prior decree or agreement fixing the amount of aliment or periodical allowance. Therefore, if the debtor is obliged to pay his ex-wife periodical allowance of £500 per month under a divorce decree, the court fixing the amount allowable as a relevant obligation for this purpose will not be bound to allow all of the £500 as a relevant obligation. The Act does not contain any guidelines as to how the court is to decide on what is a suitable amount for the debtor's aliment and his relevant obligations. In the case of *Brown's Tr v Brown*[4], it was made clear that there is no 'formula' for calculating the sum which is to be paid over to the trustee. That case did, however, set out a number of principles to be applied by the court in deciding the amount. These included balancing the interests of the creditors and the debtor, considering the total amount of debts and how much the creditors are likely to receive in the sequestration and the principle that the debtor should not have much free income after the payment to the trustee. The debtor, the permanent trustee or any other interested person may apply to the court to have any order varied or recalled if circumstances change[5].

Creditors of the debtor cannot use diligence to attach post-sequestration income in order to satisfy pre-sequestration debts[6]. They can, however, attach it in relation to debts which arose after the sequestration and which are not therefore included in the sequestration. But, it would appear that if the debtor is entitled to benefits, the Secretary of State for Social Security may make deductions from these benefits in relation to pre-sequestration debts in the form of loans to the debtor from the Social Fund, on the grounds, inter alia, that the deductions are not diligence[7].

Property which is acquired by the debtor after the date of sequestration but before his or her discharge, and which would have vested in the trustee if it had belonged to the debtor on the date of sequestration, vests in the trustee[8]. Thus if the debtor receives, eg, an inheritance or gift, this will vest in the trustee and not the debtor. The debtor is not free to deal with the property in any way[9]. He or she must notify the permanent trustee of any assets he or she acquires[10].

---

1 1985 Act, s 32(2).
2 As defined in the Family Law (Scotland) Act 1985: Bankruptcy (Scotland) Act 1985, s 32(3)(a).
3 1985 Act, s 32(3).
4 1995 SLT (Sh Ct) 2.
5 1985 Act, s 32(5). For instance, the debtor may lose the job which gave rise to the income, or he or she may obtain a better paid job allowing the amount payable to the trustee to be increased. The debtor is under an obligation to notify the permanent trustee of any change in his or her financial circumstances, failure to do so being an offence: 1985 Act, s 32(7).
6 1985 Act, s 32(5).
7 *Mulvey v Secretary of State for Social Security* 1997 SCLR 348.
8 1985 Act, s 32(6).
9 See eg *Alliance and Leicester Building Society v Murray's Tr* 1994 SCLR 19.
10 1985 Act, s 32(7). Failure to do so is an offence.

Post-sequestration dealings with estate

The corollary of the fact that the debtor's property vests in the permanent trustee is that the debtor is not allowed to deal with such property after the date of sequestration. Any dealing by the debtor with any of the property which vests in the permanent trustee under s 31 is invalid so far as the permanent trustee is concerned[1]. There are, however, a number of exceptions to this rule in order to protect the position of innocent third parties who were unaware of the sequestration and that the debtor consequently had no right to deal with the property[2]. These are as follows.

(1) Where the permanent trustee has abandoned the property to the debtor[3]. The permanent trustee may do this if he or she decides for some reason that it is not worthwhile to claim the property: eg he or she may consider it is not worth the expense of recovering it. The permanent trustee may abandon it expressly or impliedly.
(2) Where the permanent trustee has expressly or impliedly authorised the dealing[4].
(3) Where the trustee has otherwise acted in such a way as to be personally barred from challenging the debtor's action[5].
(4) Where the third party was obliged to the debtor and carried out his or her obligation[6], eg by paying the debtor a debt which was due to him or her.
(5) Where the debtor has sold goods and the purchaser has paid the debtor for them or is willing to pay the trustee[7].
(6) Where the transaction is a banking transaction in the ordinary course of business[8], eg honouring a cheque or allowing a withdrawal from an account.

In all cases, the party dealing with the debtor must have been unaware of the sequestration and must have had no reason to believe the debtor's estate had been sequestrated[9]. Otherwise, the transaction will not be protected.

Recovery of estate

Once the permanent trustee has been issued with an act and warrant, he or she will start to gather in the debtor's property. As discussed above, the trustee must, however, consult with the commissioners, if there are any, or failing them the Accountant in Bankruptcy, about recovery as well as management and realisation of the estate[10], and must comply with any

1 1985 Act, s 32(8).
2 1985 Act, s 32(9).
3 1985 Act, s 32(9)(a)(i).
4 1985 Act, s 32(9)(a)(ii).
5 1985 Act, s 32(9)(a)(iii).
6 1985 Act, s 32(9)(b)(i).
7 1985 Act, s 32(9)(b)(ii).
8 1985 Act, s 32(9)(b)(iii).
9 Note that it is the knowledge of the *party to the transaction* which is relevant, not that of any agent actually carrying out the transaction on the party's behalf: *Minha's Tr v Bank of Scotland* 1990 SLT 23, OH.
10 1985 Act, s 39(1).

directions given to him or her by the creditors[1], the court[2] or the Accountant in Bankruptcy[3] in this respect.

Section 38 of the 1985 Act empowers the permanent trustee to take possession of all the estate which has vested in him or her *and* any document in the debtor's possession or control which relates to the debtor's financial affairs[4].

Section 38 also empowers the trustee to have access to and to copy any such documents in the hands of third parties[5]. A third party who refuses to co-operate can be ordered to do so by the court[6]. The permanent trustee can also require delivery of the debtor's title deeds (eg, the deeds of his or her house) or any other documents of the debtor even where the holder of the deeds or documents claims a lien over them (eg, a solicitor claiming a lien over title deeds pending payment of his or her account)[7]. The holder of the deeds or documents will, however, still be entitled to the benefit of any lien to which he or she would otherwise have been entitled if he or she had not had to hand them over to the permanent trustee[8].

Recovery of information

The permanent trustee may need to obtain further information about the debtor's estate and financial affairs. The trustee will wish to be certain that all the estate to which he or she is entitled or may be entitled has been identified and that he or she knows all that needs to be known to administer the estate properly and to obtain the maximum return for the creditors. The permanent trustee is given extensive powers to recover information from the debtor and various other persons, some of which, as discussed above, apply equally to the interim trustee.

Appearance before trustee

Under s 44(1) of the 1985 Act, the permanent trustee may request the debtor[9], the debtor's spouse or any other person whom the trustee believes has relevant information to appear before him or her and give information on the debtor's assets, the debtor's dealings with them, or the debtor's conduct in relation to his or her business or financial affairs. There is no sanction for failing to comply with such a request or for failing to give information, but the subsection allows the trustee, if he or she is not satisfied, to apply to the sheriff for a private examination of any of these persons under s 44(2).

---

1 1985 Act, s 39(1)(a).
2 On application of the commissioners: 1985 Act, s 39(1)(b).
3 If there are no commissioners: 1985 Act, s 39(1)(c).
4 1985 Act, s 38(1).
5 1985 Act, s 38(2).
6 1985 Act, s 38(3).
7 1985 Act, s 38(4).
8 1985 Act, s 38(4), and see *Findlay (Liquidator of Scottish Workmen's Assurance Co Ltd) v Waddell* 1910 SC 670.
9 Where the debtor is an entity rather than an individual, the reference is taken to be to a person representing the entity: 1985 Act, s 44(4) (eg a partner or trustee).

Private examination

The sheriff has a discretion whether or not to order a private examination. If he or she does so, the person to be examined is cited to attend before the sheriff in private[1] and failure to appear without reasonable excuse is an offence[2]. The examination is conducted on oath[3], and therefore a charge of perjury may result if it is subsequently discovered that the examinee has failed to tell the truth. The trustee or his or her legal representative may question the examinee about the debtor's assets, the debtor's dealings with them, or the debtor's conduct in relation to his or her business or financial affairs. If the examinee is someone other than the debtor, the debtor may also ask questions[4]. The examinee is not excused from answering questions because the answers may be incriminating, but the answer to a question is not admissible in evidence in subsequent criminal proceedings (except those for perjury)[5]. Nor is confidentiality an excuse for failing to answer a question, unless the other person in the confidential relationship is not called for examination[5]. The examinee may be ordered to produce any relevant documents in his or her custody or control and to deliver such documents or copies thereof to the permanent trustee[6].

Public examination

Under s 45 of the 1985 Act, the trustee may apply to the sheriff for a public examination of the debtor or any of the other persons mentioned above[7]. Where the Accountant in Bankruptcy, the commissioners or at least one-quarter in value of the creditors request the Accountant to do so, he or she must apply for such an examination[8]. In the case of a public examination, the sheriff has no discretion and must grant the order[9]. There is an elaborate procedure for publicising the examination[10]. Failure on the part of the person ordered to attend the examination to do so without reasonable excuse is an offence[11]. A public examination is held in open court. Otherwise, the provisions relating to the conduct of private examinations discussed above apply equally to a public examination, with the additional feature that creditors may also attend and ask questions at a public examination[12].

1 On a date not less than eight and not more than sixteen days after the date of the order: 1985 Act, s 44(2).
2 1985 Act, s 44(3).
3 1985 Act, s 47(1).
4 1985 Act, s 47(2).
5 1985 Act, s 47(3).
6 1985 Act, s 46(4).
7 Such a request may only be made not less than eight weeks before the end of the first accounting period unless cause is shown, when it may be permitted at any other time: 1985 Act, s 45(1).
8 1985 Act, s 45(1)(b).
9 1985 Act, s 45(2).
10 1985 Act, s 45(3). The permanent trustee is required to publish a notice in the Edinburgh Gazette and to send a notice to all known creditors and advise them of their right to participate in the examination, although he or she does not appear to be obliged to inform the debtor. Where the examination is of someone other than the debtor, the trustee must also inform the debtor and advise the debtor of his or her right to participate in the examination.
11 1985 Act, s 45(4).
12 1985 Act, s 47.

The court may grant a warrant to arrest a debtor or any other person ordered to attend a private or public examination and have them taken to the place of examination if it considers that such a step is necessary to secure their attendance[1]. There is also, however, provision to have evidence taken on commission if attendance is impossible for a good reason[2].

Challengeable transactions

General introduction

It was indicated above that where a debtor was absolutely insolvent, any disposal of his or her assets other than for full consideration, any favouring of one creditor over another or any transaction generally regarded as a fraud on his or her creditors might subsequently be the subject of challenge, as a result of the principle that the debtor, once insolvent, is a trustee for his or her creditors. This means *all* of the debtor's creditors, not just some that he or she happens to favour: it is another basic principle of insolvency law that creditors should be treated equally (*pari passu*), although in fact this principle is imperfectly applied[3]. The law therefore allows transactions which flout these basic principles to be challenged, with a view to returning any assets disposed of in violation of them to the debtor's estate where they will be available to all creditors equally.

The 1985 Act makes specific provision for the challenge of certain types of transaction. In addition, certain transactions may be challenged at common law independently of any statutory right of challenge. Traditionally, the transactions challengeable at common law have been divided into two categories which coincide with two of the types of transaction for which statutory provision is made: gratuitous alienations and unfair preferences[4]. McBryde, in the leading modern textbook on bankruptcy, argues that this division may not accurately reflect the principles involved. He argues persuasively that a proper analysis of the cases shows rather a general principle of striking at any transaction which is a fraud on the creditors, and the cases cannot necessarily be categorised in this way. Since he himself points out[5], however, that his treatment in most cases will not give an appreciably different result in practice, the more traditional analysis of the common law is adopted in this text.

---

1 1985 Act, s 46(1). In the case of a debtor residing in Scotland, the warrant is granted by the sheriff; in the case of a debtor residing in another part of the UK, the warrant may be granted either by the sheriff or the Court of Session, and may be enforced throughout the UK. The warrant is granted on the application of the permanent trustee.
2 1985 Act, s 46(2).
3 See 'Ranking' below.
4 Goudy *Bankruptcy* (4th edn, 1914). Goudy's treatment has been followed by most other writers in the field. The current statutory provisions on gratuitous alienations and unfair preferences supersede those contained in the Bankruptcy Act 1621 and the Bankruptcy Act 1696, which dealt with gratuitous alienations and fraudulent (as they were then known) preferences respectively.
5 *Bankruptcy* (2nd edn, 1995) p 289.

Gratuitous alienations

The statutory provisions governing challenge of gratuitous alienations are contained in s 34 of the 1985 Act.

The section applies only where the estate of the debtor has been sequestrated, the debtor has granted a trust deed which has become protected, the estate of a deceased debtor has been sequestrated within twelve months of his or her death or a judicial factor has been appointed to the estate of a deceased debtor[1].

It allows the permanent trustee, the trustee under the trust deed, the judicial factor and creditors whose debts were incurred before the sequestration, trust deed or death[2] to challenge transactions where 'any of the debtor's property has been transferred or any claim of the debtor has been discharged or renounced'[3]. This is very wide. Therefore, if the debtor transfers his house to his wife[4], or gives her money[5], or discharges his right to claim to legal rights in a deceased relative's estate, or renounces his rights under a contract[6], all of these transactions are alienations to which the section would apply.

Only alienations which took place within certain time limits are challengeable under s 34. The alienation must have taken place within the five years preceding the sequestration, trust deed or death if it was made to an 'associate' of the debtor; if made to anyone other than an associate, it must have taken place within the two years preceding the sequestration, trust deed or death. This can be illustrated diagrammatically:

```
                    5 years (associate)
I---------------------------------------------------------- I
                                                             I   date of sequestration,
                        2 years (non-associate) I   granting of trust deed
                        I------------------------------ I   or death
```

'Associate' is defined in s 74 and encompasses a variety of relatives and business relationships. In the case of an individual debtor, someone is an associate of the debtor if they are:

(1) a spouse, ex-spouse or reputed spouse of the debtor[7];
(2) a relative, defined as brother, sister, uncle, aunt, nephew, niece or any other lineal ascendant or descendant (eg parent, child, grandparent, grandchild), including relationships of the half-blood and illegitimate, step and adopted children, of the debtor[8];
(3) a spouse, ex-spouse or reputed spouse of a relative of the debtor[9];
(4) a relative of the debtor's spouse, ex-spouse or reputed spouse[9];
(5) the spouse, ex-spouse or reputed spouse of a relative of the debtor's spouse, ex-spouse or reputed spouse[9];

1 1985 Act, s 34(2).
2 1985 Act, s 34(1).
3 1985 Act, s 34(2)(a).
4 See eg *Matheson's Tr v Matheson* 1992 SLT 685.
5 See eg *Cay's Tr v Cay* 1997 SCLR 556, OH.
6 See eg *Ahmed's Tr v Ahmed (No 2)* 1993 SLT 651, OH.
7 1985 Act, s 74(2),(4).
8 1985 Act, s 74(4).
9 1985 Act, s 74(2),(4).

(6) a (business) partner of the debtor[1];

(7) a spouse, ex-spouse, reputed spouse or relative of the debtor's (business) partner[1];

(8) an employee or employer of the debtor[2].

Firms and members of the firm are also associates of each other for this purpose[3].

The challenge may be resisted if the defender is successful in establishing any of the defences listed in s 34(4). These are as follows.

(a) The debtor was absolutely solvent immediately or at any other time after making the alienation[4]. Assume eg that the debtor transferred his house to his wife on 1 February, and the date of sequestration was 1 June. If on 2 February his assets exceeded his liabilities, the defence would be established, even if this were no longer true by 28 February. Similarly, it would be established if his assets were less than his liabilities on 2 February, but exceeded them on 28 February or on any other date between 2 and 28 February.

(b) The alienation was made for adequate consideration[5]. Consideration in this context generally means money or money's worth, although it may take a variety of forms[6]. In *McFadyen's Tr v McFadyen*[7], the court said that in the absence of a definition in the 1985 Act, consideration must be given its ordinary meaning 'as something which is given or surrendered in return for something else'[8] and that it must be 'something of material or patrimonial value which could be vindicated in a legal process'[9]. The consideration must be intended to be consideration for whatever has been given at the time it was exchanged – it cannot later be plead as amounting to consideration if it did not have that character at the time[10]. In order to be adequate, the consideration need not necessarily represent the best value that could have been obtained (eg on a sale)[11], but it has been held that the term 'adequate' does imply an objective assessment, and the consideration should be 'not less than would reasonably be expected in the circumstances, assuming that persons . . . were acting in good faith and at arm's length from each other'[12].

---

1 1985 Act, s 74(3).
2 1985 Act, s 74(5).
3 1985 Act, s 73(3).
4 1985 Act, s 34(4)(a).
5 1985 Act, s 34(4)(b).
6 Eg in *John E Rae (Electrical Services) Linlithgow Ltd v Lord Advocate* 1994 SLT 788, OH, the issue of an exemption certificate by the Inland Revenue was held to be capable of amounting to adequate consideration; in *Cay's Tr v Cay* 1997 SCLR 556, OH, the assumption of responsibility for another's debts was similarly held to be capable in principle of amounting to adequate consideration.
7 1994 SLT 1245.
8 1994 SLT 1245 at 1248I.
9 1994 SLT 1245 at 1248J-K. See also *Cay's Tr v Cay* above, where it was held that an undertaking to fulfil an obligation of aliment did not fall within this definition.
10 *McFadyen's Tr v McFadyen* above. See also *Matheson's Tr v Matheson* 1992 SLT 685.
11 *Short's Tr v Chung* 1991 SLT 472 at 475A-B. See also *Lafferty Construction Ltd (in liquidation) v McCombe* 1994 SLT 858, OH, and *McLuckie Brothers Ltd v Newhouse Contracts Ltd* 1993 SLT 641, OH.
12 *Lafferty Construction Ltd v McCombe* 1994 SLT 858 at 861D-E.

(c) The alienation was a permitted gift[1]. This means that it was either a birthday, Christmas or other conventional gift[2] (eg a mother's day gift) or a charitable gift to a non-associate of the debtor[3]. In either case, the gift must have been reasonable in all the circumstances. It would probably not be reasonable for the average debtor to make a birthday present of his house to his wife. If, however, the debtor was at the time of the gift a millionaire, a gift to his wife of a holiday cottage in France might be perfectly reasonable.

If none of the above defences is successfully established, s 34(4) requires the court to grant decree of reduction, restoration of the property or such other redress as appropriate. Reduction would normally be appropriate, eg, where the alienation involved the transfer of heritable property. An order for restoration of the property would normally be appropriate, eg, where the alienation was of moveable property transferred by delivery, there being no deed to reduce. If property has been transferred by the original transferee to a third party, the challenger may not be able to recover the property itself, since a third party who has acquired the property in good faith and for value is protected from any challenge under the section[4]. In such a situation, 'other redress' would be appropriate, eg payment of the value of the property by the original transferee.

In *Short's Tr v Chung*[5], the court stated that reduction was the principal remedy if applicable. If reduction was not applicable, restoration of the property would be ordered. Only if neither of these was applicable would the court grant 'other redress'. Since the challenger will normally be seeking the return of any alienated property to the debtor's estate, this approach will not normally cause any difficulty. However, assume that the debtor had transferred his house to his wife. The result of the decision is that the challenger would be able to reduce the deed implementing the transfer, but apparently could not ask the court to allow the wife to keep the house and pay him its value. This can have harsh results, particularly if the transferee has in fact given consideration for the alienation, but this has been found to be inadequate. The case of *Short's Tr v Keeper of the Registers of Scotland*[6] has also highlighted a difficulty with reduction of a disposition of heritable property under the section. Where the property is registered in the Register of Sasines, reduction essentially has the effect of restoring the property to the debtor's estate. But *Short's Tr v Keeper of the Registers of Scotland* shows that it may not have this effect if the property is registered in the Land Register. In such a case, the challenger may well have preferred 'other redress', but this would not appear to be possible in the light of the earlier decision.

The types of transaction which will be challengeable at common law are similar to those which are challengeable under the 1985 Act[7]. However, there are a number of important differences between the common law and

---

1 1985 Act, s 34(4)(c).
2 1985 Act, s 34(4)(c)(i).
3 1985 Act, s 34(4)(c)(ii).
4 1985 Act, s 34(4).
5 1991 SLT 472.
6 1996 SC (HL) 1.
7 Goudy *Bankruptcy* (4th edn, 1914) p 23.

the statutory provisions: some of these make it harder to succeed in a challenge at common law, others may allow a challenge to be brought at common law in circumstances where a statutory challenge would not be possible. The principal differences are as follows.

(i)   Under s 34, the challenger only needs to show that there has been an alienation, and it is up to the defender to show that one of the defences applies if he or she wishes to resist the challenge. At common law, it is up to the challenger to establish both that the alienation was gratuitous (ie for nothing or for inadequate consideration) *and* that the debtor was absolutely insolvent at the time of the alienation and remained so up to the date of challenge. This makes the challenger's task more difficult.
(ii) Under s 34, the alienation must have taken place within specific time limits. At common law, there are no time limits. This means that a challenge at common law would be possible where a statutory challenge was impossible because the alienation took place outwith the time limits in s 34.
(iii) There is no need to wait for sequestration or any of the other events described above to occur before a challenge can be brought. It may be made at any time after the alienation has taken place. Of course, prior to sequestration or any of the other defined events, the only person in a position to challenge would be a creditor. A creditor may be reluctant to incur the expense of bringing proceedings since the asset is not transferred to the creditor but restored to the debtor's estate, where it is subject to the diligence of all creditors. In certain circumstances, however, it might be worthwhile.

The challenger must show that the transaction was to the prejudice of lawful creditors, but it is not necessary to show that the debtor intended to defraud the creditors by his or her actions. The conjunction of insolvency and the gratuitous nature of the transaction is sufficient to infer the necessary fraud.

A statutory title to challenge gratuitous alienations at common law is conferred on the permanent trustee, a trustee acting under a protected trust deed and a judicial factor by the Act[1].

Unfair preferences

The statutory provisions governing unfair preferences are contained in s 36 of the 1985 Act. They have been made as similar as possible to those on gratuitous alienations.

As with the statutory provisions governing gratuitous alienations, s 36 comes into play only where the estate of the debtor has been sequestrated, the debtor has granted a trust deed which has become protected, the estate of a deceased debtor has been sequestrated within twelve months of his or her death or a judicial factor has been appointed to the estate of a deceased debtor[2]. It allows the permanent trustee, the trustee under the trust deed, the judicial factor and creditors whose debts were incurred before the

1   1985 Act, s 34(8).
2   1985 Act, s 36(1).

sequestration, trust deed or death[1] to challenge certain transactions the debtor may have carried out with a view to recovering what has been lost from the debtor's estate as a result of such transactions for distribution among all the creditors.

The transactions affected by s 36 are those which have 'the effect of creating a preference in favour of a creditor to the prejudice of the general body of creditors'[2]. In other words, transactions which favour one creditor at the expense of the others. Such transactions are struck at because they violate the principle that creditors should be treated equally on insolvency. An example would be the granting of a security for an unsecured debt[3]. The creditor to whom such a security is granted is thereafter in a more favourable position – instead of simply having to take a share of the debtor's assets along with other unsecured creditors, he or she now has a priority claim on the assets over which the security is granted. The other (unsecured) creditors are prejudiced because the pool of assets on which they have a claim has been reduced to the extent of the new security. It is important to note that both elements (the favouring of one creditor and disadvantage to the general body of creditors) are necessary. If one is present without the other, the transaction will not be challengeable.

Only transactions which become completely effectual within the period of six months prior to the date of sequestration, granting of the trust deed or debtor's death are challengeable under this section. The time at which any particular transaction becomes 'completely effectual' depends on the type of transaction and the particular circumstances of the case[4]. There has been some debate over whether a transaction is caught by the section if it was made completely effectual within the six months, but the original agreement to carry it out was outwith that time limit. It has been argued that such a transaction is not caught because it is not 'voluntary', ie, it could not be legally compelled. The previous statutory provisions required the transaction to be voluntary. It is suggested that the better view is that it is caught, because s 36 makes no mention of any such requirement, although it is accepted this view represents a change from the previous law[5]. The time limit is obviously very short.

Some types of transaction are specifically stated not to be challengeable[6]. These are as follows.

(1) Transactions in the ordinary course of trade or business[7]. Whether or not a transaction falls into this category depends on the circumstances in each case. Reference may need to be made to the specific practices in particular trades.

1 1985 Act, s 36(4).
2 1985 Act, s 36(1).
3 See *McCowan v Wright* (1853) 15 D 494.
4 Eg, a transaction involving heritage will become completely effectual on the recording of the title deed. See also *Masson's Tr v W & J Bruce (Builders) Ltd* (6 March 1997, unreported), Peterhead Sh Ct discussed in 1997 Bus LB 27–4 (mandates); *Craiglaw Developments Ltd v Wilson* 1997 GWD 21–1050 (deposit receipts).
5 See McKenzie 'Gratuitous Alienations and Unfair Preferences on Insolvency' (1993) 38 JLSS 141 and letter in response thereto by DP Sellar (1993) 38 JLSS 215. See also McBryde *Bankruptcy* (2nd edn, 1995) p 317.
6 1985 Act, s 36(2).
7 1985 Act, s 36(2)(a).

(2) Payments in cash for debts actually due[1]. This exception is linked to the previous one in respect that a cash payment will usually be a payment in the course of trade, but it need not be. Cash includes coins and banknotes and probably also cheques, banker's drafts and bills[2].

(3) Transactions involving reciprocal obligations[3]. Transactions falling under this exception are commonly referred to as '*nova debita*'. They are unobjectionable because the debtor's estate is not diminished. It follows, therefore, that the obligations undertaken must be of a strictly equivalent value in order to fall within this exception[4].

(4) The granting of a mandate authorising payment of arrested funds to the arresting creditor[5]. This exception removes the doubt under the previous law as to whether such a transaction was an unfair preference or not.

It should be noted, however, that transactions falling within the terms of head (2) or (3) above will not be excepted if they were collusive with the purpose of prejudicing the general body of creditors[6]. The creditor's knowledge of the debtor's insolvency is necessary, but not sufficient, for collusion[7].

As with s 34, if there is a successful challenge, the court must grant decree of reduction, restoration of the property or such other redress as appropriate[8]. Again, a third party who has acquired the property in good faith *and* for value is protected from any challenge under the section[8].

Although *Short's Tr v Chung*[9] was a case dealing with gratuitous alienations under s 34 of the Act, it is thought that the principles laid down in that case would apply equally to unfair preferences under s 36. Since the wording of the two sections on this point is identical, it would be strange if it did not. The problems arising from that decision have been discussed.

The same types of transaction will be challengeable at common law as under statute with this important qualification: at common law, the transaction must be voluntary. This means that it could not have been legally compelled[10]. This is different from the current statutory provisions. As with gratuitous alienations, there are a number of other important differences between the common law and the statutory provisions, some of which make it harder to succeed in a challenge at common law, others allowing the possibility of a challenge at common law where a statutory challenge would not be possible. The principal differences are as follows.

(a) Under s 36, the preference must have taken place within a very short time limit. At common law, there is no time limit. A challenge at common law would therefore be possible where a statutory challenge was impossible because the preference took place outwith the time limit in s 36.

1 1985 Act, s 36(2)(b).
2 The authoritative exposition of this and the preceding exception is to be found in *Whatmough's Tr v British Linen Bank* 1932 SC 525; on appeal, 1934 SC (HL) 51.
3 1985 Act, s 36(2)(c).
4 *Nicoll v Steelpress (Supplies) Ltd* 1992 SCLR 332.
5 1985 Act, s 36(2)(d).
6 1985 Act, s 36(2)(b) and (c) respectively.
7 *Nordic Travel Ltd v Scotprint Ltd* 1980 SC 1.
8 1985 Act, s 36(5).
9 1991 SLT 472.
10 *Nordic Travel Ltd v Scotprint Ltd* above.

(b) There is no need to wait for sequestration or any of the other events described above to occur before a challenge can be brought. It may be made at any time after the preference has taken place. Of course, prior to sequestration or any of the other defined events, the only person in a position to challenge would be a creditor. A creditor may be reluctant to incur the expense of bringing proceedings for the same reasons as discussed in connection with gratuitous alienations.

(c) The categories of exempt transactions may not correspond directly with those enumerated in s 36. McBryde[1] argues that the types of transaction excepted under statute and, with the exception of mandates, commonly listed as the exceptions at common law also, can only be regarded as examples and not definitive categories. If that is so, a transaction exempted under s 36 might be challengeable at common law.

The challenger must show that the debtor was aware of his or her insolvency in order to establish that the transaction was fraudulent, but it is not necessary to prove that the debtor intended to defraud the creditors by his or her actions. The conjunction of insolvency and the preferential nature of the transaction is sufficient to infer the necessary fraud.

A statutory title to challenge fraudulent preferences at common law is conferred on the permanent trustee, a trustee acting under a protected trust deed and a judicial factor by the Act[2].

Payments into occupational pension schemes

The Pensions Act 1995 inserts important new provisions into the 1985 Act concerning recovery of excessive pension contributions. Section 95(2) of the 1995 Act adds three new sections to the 1985 Act, ie ss 36A, 36B and 36C. At the time of writing, these provisions are in force only for the purposes of the making of regulations, but will be discussed in anticipation of their coming into force in due course.

These sections provide that where the debtor has made contributions to an occupational pension scheme[3] within the five years preceding the sequestration, or such contributions have been made on his behalf, the permanent trustee can apply to the court for an order[4]. The court will determine if 'excessive contributions' have been made, and if so may make any order it thinks fit for restoring the position to what it would have been if such excessive contributions had not been made[5]. 'Excessive contributions' are those which have unfairly prejudiced the debtor's creditors[5]. In determining whether the contributions did unfairly prejudice the debtor's creditors, the court has to consider particularly whether any of the contributions were made for the purpose of putting assets beyond the reach of creditors; whether the total contributions made during the five-year period were excessive in view of the debtor's circumstances at the time they were made and whether the level of benefits under this and any other occupational pension scheme is excessive in all the circumstances[6].

1 *Bankruptcy* (2nd edn, 1995) p 317.
2 1985 Act, s 36(6).
3 As defined by s 1 of the Pension Schemes Act 1993.
4 1985 Act, s 36A(1).
5 1985 Act, s 36A(2).
6 1985 Act, s 36A(3).

The court's discretion as to the type of order it can make is unfettered, but it is specifically provided that it can make orders requiring a payment by the trustees of the pension scheme to the permanent trustee or reducing the benefits available under the scheme or otherwise adjusting it[1]. The court is not affected by the fact that the benefits are unassignable[2]. Orders can be varied, rescinded or reviewed on the application of interested persons[3].

Orders on divorce

Section 35 of the 1985 Act makes special provision for the situation where the debtor has been divorced and was ordered to make payment of a capital sum and/or to transfer property to his or her ex-spouse in the divorce action.

A trustee in sequestration, a trustee under a protected trust deed for creditors or a judicial factor on the estate of a deceased debtor can apply to the court to have any such order recalled. The section applies only where the relevant order was made within the five years prior to the debtor's sequestration or the granting of a trust deed by the debtor for creditors which subsequently became protected[4] or the sequestration of, or appointment of a judicial factor to, the estate of a deceased debtor. In addition, the debtor must have been absolutely insolvent when the order was made or have been made absolutely insolvent by the order[5]. It is up to the trustee or judicial factor to prove this.

If these conditions are satisfied, the court has discretion to recall the order and order the ex-spouse to repay all or part of the money paid to him or her under the order or to return all or part of the property transferred to him or her under the order. If property transferred under the order has been sold, the court can order the ex-spouse to hand over all or part of the proceeds of sale[6]. In making its order, the court is directed to have regard to all the circumstances, including the financial and other circumstances of the ex-spouse[6].

The section clearly and intentionally puts the interests of creditors before the interests of the debtor's ex-spouse. Particularly since a payment or transfer may be affected many years after it is made[7], this might in some cases cause hardship to a spouse who has to repay sums received or re-transfer property. The section does not, however, appear to be much used[8].

1 1985 Act, s 36B(1).
2 1985 Act, s 36C(1).
3 1985 Act, s 36B(7).
4 Discussed further below.
5 1985 Act, s 35(1)
6 1985 Act, s 35(2).
7 The time period involved could be well in excess of the five-year period within which such orders are challengeable, since a challenge may not be brought until after the administration of the estate has been going for some time.
8 For a good discussion of financial provision on divorce and sequestration, see McBryde 'Financial Provision on Divorce and Sequestration' 1996 SLT (News) 389.

Extortionate credit transactions

Normally, if a person makes a bad bargain which is not in other respects challengeable (for instance, because of misrepresentation or coercion), then they are simply stuck with it. Debtors in financial difficulties may, however, be so desperate for money that they will enter into transactions, particularly credit transactions, on very disadvantageous terms. This is ultimately to the detriment not only of the debtor, but of other creditors. To prevent unfairness to other creditors, s 61 of the Act allows the permanent trustee to challenge credit transactions entered into by the debtor within the three-year period prior to his sequestration if such transactions are or were extortionate[1]. 'Extortionate' means the agreement required 'grossly exorbitant' payments or otherwise 'grossly contravened the ordinary principles of fair dealing'[2]. These concepts are not further defined. If the court is satisfied that the transaction was extortionate, it has very wide powers to re-open the transaction. It may order all or part of the agreement to be set aside, vary the terms of the agreement, require repayment of money paid under the agreement to the permanent trustee, order any property taken as security to be surrendered to the permanent trustee and/or order an accounting[3]. Any sums or property returned to the permanent trustee under this section vest in the trustee[4] and are then distributed by him or her to the creditors as part of the estate.

Effect of sequestration on diligence

Creditors who have done diligence against a debtor will be in a more favourable position than other creditors who have not done so because diligence gives the creditor who has carried it out a preferential right to the assets affected by the diligence. As a general rule, diligences affecting any particular asset rank in date order, so that the creditor who is quickest in carrying out diligence will usually gain the greatest advantage. Therefore, if **A** arrests the debtor's bank account, all other things being equal, **A** will have first call on any funds in the account caught by the arrestment; if **B** subsequently arrests the same bank account, **B** will have next claim on any balance left after payment of the sums due to **A**; and so on.

However, the very purpose of insolvency law is to ensure that once a debtor has become insolvent, any remaining assets are distributed fairly amongst all of his or her creditors. In order to achieve this, the law makes provision for diligence carried out within certain time periods to be regulated so that creditors who have carried out such diligence do not in fact gain any preference over other creditors who have either carried out diligence more belatedly or not carried out any diligence at all.

The law regulates diligence occurring within certain periods around both apparent insolvency and sequestration itself.

1 1985 Act, s 61(1),(2).
2 1985 Act, s 61(3).
3 1985 Act, s 61(4).
4 1985 Act, s 61(5).

On apparent insolvency

The rule here is that arrestments and poindings which take place within the period sixty days prior to and four months after apparent insolvency are equalised, ie they are treated as if they had all taken place on the same date[1]. This can be illustrated diagramatically:

arrestments and poindings equalised

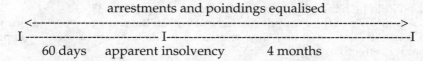

Further, if there is a judicial process relating to the arrestments or poind-ings (eg an action of multiple poinding), any creditor producing liquid grounds of debt or a decree for payment within the period is also entitled to share equally in the assets affected by the diligence[2]. In this way, no creditor gains any advantage over the others.

There may be multiple constitutions of apparent insolvency, in which case the periods surrounding each apparent insolvency may overlap. This causes special problems which are outwith the scope of this book[3].

It should be noted that these provisions do not apply to inhibitions: inhibitions are *not* affected by apparent insolvency.

On sequestration

The position on sequestration is regulated by s 37 of the 1985 Act. Inhibitions, arrestments and poindings which take place within the period sixty days prior to the sequestration and at any time thereafter are cut down, that is they are equalised with the sequestration and do not secure any preference for the creditor in competition with the sequestration[4]. Again, this can be illustrated diagramatically:

inhibitions, arrestments and poindings cut down

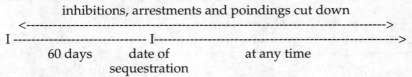

Any estate affected by such an arrestment or poinding, or the proceeds of sale thereof, must be handed over to the trustee[5]. It would seem that this includes money which has been paid to the arresting creditor as a result of an arrestment which has been cut down even although the result of the payment is that the arrestment no longer subsists. In *Johnston v Cluny*

---

1 1985 Act, s 75(1)(b), Sch 7, para 24(1). This is subject to the proviso that any such arrest-ment which is executed on the dependence of an action is followed up without undue delay: Sch 7, para 24(2).
2 1985 Act, Sch 7, para 24(3).
3 For a good review of the problems involved, see McBryde *Bankruptcy* (2nd edn, 1995) p 330. See also Gretton 'Multiple Notour Bankruptcy' (1983) 28 JLSS 18 and *Equalisation of Diligences* (Scot Law Com Discussion Paper no. 79) (1988).
4 1985 Act, s 37(2) (inhibitions) and s 37(4) (arrestments and poindings).
5 1985 Act, s 37(4). The same requirement does not apply in the case of an inhibition, because inhibitions do not attach to specific assets.

Estates Trs[1], the court held in such a situation that the arresting creditor was entitled to keep the money paid to him, but s 37(4) applies to an arrestment 'whether subsisting or not' at the date of sequestration, which appears to alter the result of that case[2]. A creditor carrying out an arrestment or poinding within the sixty-day period prior to sequestration is, however, entitled to payment of certain expenses out of the estate which has had to be handed over to the trustee as a result of s 37(4)[3].

A poinding of the ground[4] carried out within the sixty-day period prior to sequestration or at any time thereafter is likewise 'cut down', except that it is effective to secure certain interest[5].

Where sequestration preceded by apparent insolvency

Where sequestration is preceded by the debtor's apparent insolvency, the two sets of rules discussed above may overlap. This will happen if sequestration occurs within four months of apparent insolvency[6]. In such a case, all arrestments and poindings within the period sixty days prior to apparent insolvency up to the date of sequestration and at any time after sequestration will be cut down. This is because s 37(1) provides that the sequestration itself is to be regarded as having the effect of the appropriate diligence on the debtor's property[7], although it is not actually a diligence of itself[8]. Applying the rule on apparent insolvency discussed above, any arrestments or poindings carried out within the period sixty days prior to and four months after apparent insolvency are equalised. This includes the sequestration itself. Therefore any arrestments and poindings are equalised with the sequestration, and do not have any preference to it, even although they are outwith the sixty days prior to the sequestration itself. They are effectively cut down[9]. Again this can be illustrated diagramatically:

---

1 1957 SC 184.
2 There is, however, debate as to the exact effect of s 37(4) and the extent to which the effect of *Johnston v Cluny Estates Trs* has been altered. The debate is beyond the scope of this text, but see St Clair and Drummond Young *The Law of Corporate Insolvency in Scotland* (2nd edn, 1992).
3 1985 Act, s 37(5). Again, this provision does not apply to inhibitions because they do not attach to specific property.
4 Poinding of the ground is a particular diligence available to the creditor in any real security entitling him or her to attach and sell corporeal moveables on the ground belonging to the debtor.
5 1985 Act, s 37(6).
6 This will in fact be quite common, since apparent insolvency is a pre-requisite of applying for sequestration in a number of cases, most notably in the case of a creditor petition, and a creditor petition must be presented within four months of apparent insolvency.
7 Ie a decree of adjudication of the debtor's heritable property and an arrestment in execution and decree of furthcoming, an arrestment in execution and warrant of sale and a completed poinding in relation to the debtor's moveable property.
8 See *Sinclair v Edinburgh Parish Council* 1909 SC 1353; *G and A Barnie v Stevenson* 1993 SCLR 318, Sh Ct.
9 See *Stewart v Jarvie* 1938 SC 309.

                    arrestments and poindings cut down
<--->

I------------------------I--I
  60 days   apparent   4 months
               insolvency
                              I------------------------I----------------------------------->
                                  60 days   date of   at any time
                                               sequestration

It is the overlap of the date of sequestration and the period surrounding apparent insolvency which is important. If the date of sequestration occurs after the end of the four-month period following apparent insolvency, then the diligences affected by the apparent insolvency will be equalised with each other, but will not be cut down by the sequestration. Once again, the position will be complicated if there are multiple constitutions of apparent insolvency.

Diligence unaffected by sequestration

Diligence carried out outwith the periods provided for in s 37 will not be affected by the sequestration. If the asset affected by the diligence is still part of the debtor's estate, ie it has not been transferred to the creditor as a result of the diligence[1], it will have vested in the permanent trustee and will require to be handed over to him[2]. However, the diligence creates a security over the asset[3] so that the trustee takes the asset subject to such security[4]. The creditor will therefore have a preferential claim to be paid from the assets affected by the valid diligence[5]. In the case of an inhibition, because it does not attach to specific assets, the valid preference is given effect to by ranking the inhibition as if post-inhibition creditors did not exist. This is a complex subject beyond the scope of this book[6].

Management and realisation of estate

Management and realisation of estate generally

The permanent trustee is given extensive powers to manage the debtor's estate pending its realisation and distribution to the creditors. As previously discussed, the trustee must, however, consult with the commissioners, if there are any, or failing them the Accountant in Bankruptcy, about management and realisation of the estate[7], and he or she must comply with any directions given to him or her by the creditors[8], the court[9] or the

---

1 Eg, as a result of an action of furthcoming following on an arrestment.
2 *Berry v Taylor* 1992 SCLR 910, OH.
3 It comes within the definition of security contained in s 73(1).
4 1985 Act, s 33(3).
5 *Gordon v Millar* 1842 4 D 352
6 See McBryde *Bankruptcy* (2nd edn, 1995) pp 340–342; Graham Stewart *The Law of Diligence* (1898); Gretton *The Law of Inhibition and Adjudication* (2nd edn, 1996).
7 1985 Act, s 39(1).
8 1985 Act, s 39(1)(a).
9 On application of the commissioners: 1985 Act, s 39(1)(b).

Accountant in Bankruptcy[1]. The exception to this is that the trustee does not have to comply with any directions given to him or her by the creditors or the Accountant in Bankruptcy if he has to sell perishable goods and he or she believes the directions will adversely affect the sale price[2].

Powers of permanent trustee

Section 39(2) empowers the trustee to do the following things if they would benefit the estate.

(1) The trustee may carry on the business of the debtor. The trustee may wish to do this, eg, to preserve goodwill and enable the business to be sold as a going concern. Sale as a going concern will usually realise more than simply selling the individual assets.
(2) The trustee may raise, defend or continue any court actions concerning the estate. This allows the trustee, inter alia, to recover assets.
(3) The trustee may create a security over any part of the estate. The trustee may need to do this if he or she needs, eg, to borrow money. This might be necessary, eg, to allow the trustee to complete contracts where failure to do so would result in either a loss or a lesser gain to the estate than would be obtained by completing them (even taking into account the cost of the borrowing).
(4) The trustee may make payments or incur other liabilities in order to obtain property under a right or option which is part of the estate. For example, if the debtor had an option to purchase shares, the trustee might wish to exercise that option and pay for the shares if he or she can then sell them at a profit for the benefit of the creditors.

Where there are commissioners, the trustee needs their consent, or the consent of the creditors or the court, to exercise these powers.

Contracts

The permanent trustee may adopt any of the debtor's pre-sequestration contracts if he or she considers the adoption would be beneficial to the estate, unless such adoption is precluded by the express or implied terms of the contract itself[3]. The trustee must decide whether to adopt the contract within a reasonable time, otherwise he or she will be held to have abandoned it[4]. Any other party to the contract may force the issue by writing to the trustee requesting a decision. In such a case, the trustee must decide to adopt or refuse to adopt the contract within twenty-eight days of receipt of the request, or such longer period as the court may allow[5]. If the trustee does not respond in writing to the request within the appropriate period, he is deemed to have refused to adopt the contract[6]. If the trustee

1 If there are no commissioners: 1985 Act, s 39(1)(c).
2 1985 Act, s 39(6).
3 1985 Act, s 42(1).
4 *Crown Estate Comrs v Liquidators of Highland Engineering Ltd* 1975 SLT 58, OH (although the case involved a liquidator, the same principles apply).
5 1985 Act, s 42(2).
6 1985 Act, s 42(3).

refuses to adopt a contract, the other party may have a claim for damages for breach of contract in the sequestration[1].

In addition, the trustee may enter into new contracts if such contracts would be beneficial to the administration of the estate[2]. This may be necessary if, eg, the trustee is running the debtor's business prior to selling it.

There are special provisions regarding contracts for the supply of gas, electricity, water and telecommunications services. Where the supply is for the purposes of carrying on the debtor's business, the suppliers of these utilities may make it a condition of continued supply that the trustee personally guarantees payment in respect to future supplies, but may not make it a condition of continued supply that pre-sequestration debts are paid[3].

The trustee is personally liable on both pre-sequestration contracts adopted by him[4] and new contracts entered into by him[5] unless such liability is specifically excluded. He or she is, however, entitled to a right of relief against the estate.

Sale of estate

The trustee may sell the debtor's heritable or moveable property by public sale or private bargain[6], although there are special rules where heritable property is subject to a security. It is specifically provided that the trustee's failure to comply with the various procedural requirements in respect to realisation, such as the need to consult with the commissioners or the Accountant in Bankruptcy or to follow their directions, will not affect the validity of the purchaser's title[7].

Heritable property subject to a security

Where heritable property is subject to a valid prior security (or securities), s 39(4) of the 1985 Act sets out special rules regarding the sale of the property. In essence, the trustee or the heritable creditor must intimate his or her intention to sell the property to the other, and once he or she has done so, the other is precluded from taking steps to sell the property[8]. If, however, a trustee or a heritable creditor, having intimated his or her intention to sell, then delays unduly in doing so, the other may obtain the authority of the court to go ahead and sell the property[9]. Where the trustee is selling the property, he or she requires the concurrence of any heritable creditor or creditors *unless* he or she obtains a sufficiently high price to discharge all the securities[10].

---

1 *Crown Estate Comrs v Liquidators of Highland Engineering Ltd* above.
2 1985 Act, s 42(4).
3 1985 Act, s 70. This section also applies to trustees under trust deeds, which are discussed below.
4 *Dundas v Morison* (1857) 20 D 225 (rent arrears due under a lease adopted by the trustee).
5 *Mackessack & Son v Molleson* (1886) 13 R 445 (charterparty).
6 1985 Act, s 39(3).
7 1985 Act, s 39(7).
8 1985 Act, s 39(4)(b).
9 1985 Act, s 39(4)(c).
10 1985 Act, s 39(4)(a).

The family home

In order to prevent hardship to the debtor's family, who might otherwise be liable to be evicted from their home where that home or the debtor's interest in it has vested in the trustee as part of the debtor's estate, s 40 of the 1985 Act provides some limitation on the trustee's powers to dispose of the debtor's right or interest in his or her 'family home'. Family home is defined as a home which was occupied *immediately before the date of sequestration* by either:

(1) the debtor and spouse; or
(2) the debtor and a child of the family[1]; or
(3) the debtor's spouse or former spouse[2].

If the property does not fall within that definition, eg the debtor lives there alone, or with a friend or cohabitee, there are no restrictions on the disposal of the debtor's interest in the property. The debtor and his or her family and any other occupants, unless they have proprietorial rights of their own in the property, for instance as co-owners, may be evicted by the trustee in order to allow the trustee to dispose of the debtor's interest. If the property does fall within the definition of family home, however, the trustee requires to obtain either the relevant consent or the authority of the court before selling or disposing of the debtor's interest in the home. Relevant consent is defined in s 40(4). Where the home is occupied by a spouse or former spouse of the debtor, it is the consent of the spouse or former spouse which is required, irrespective of whether the debtor is also living in the home. Where there is no spouse or former spouse occupying the home, but the home is occupied by the debtor and a child of the family, it is the debtor's consent which is required.

If the trustee is unsuccessful in obtaining the relevant consent, he or she must apply to the court for authority to sell or dispose of the family home. The court may refuse the application, postpone it for up to twelve months to allow the family time to find alternative accommodation or grant it subject to any conditions which it thinks fit[3]. The court has a very wide discretion as to the nature of any conditions which it may attach to the grant of the application[4]. In reaching its decision, the court must have regard to all the circumstances of the case, including the needs and financial resources of the debtor's spouse or former spouse and any child of the family, the interests of the creditors and the length of time the home has been occupied by the debtor's spouse, former spouse or child of the family before and after the sequestration[4]. These factors also apply where the trustee is seeking a division and sale of the family home (where the debtor is not the sole owner and the other owner or owners will not consent to the sale of the property) or an order for vacant possession[5]. The way in which

---

1   'Child of the family' includes any child or grandchild of the debtor or his or her spouse or former spouse, and any person who has been brought up or accepted by either the debtor or his or her spouse or former spouse as if he or she were a child of the debtor or his or her spouse or former spouse, whatever their age: 1985 Act, s 40(4).
2   1985 Act, s 40(4).
3   1985 Act, s 40(2).
4   *McMahon's Tr v McMahon* 1997 SCLR 439.
5   1985 Act, s 40(3).

the court balances these factors can be seen in the case law. For example, in *Salmon's Tr v Salmon*[1], the debtor's only real asset was the family home, but the debtor's wife, who had only slender resources of her own, and the couple's sixteen-year old son, who was still at school and so had no independent resources either, continued to reside there. The home had been the family home for sixteen years, including the sixteen months since the sequestration. The court granted the order for sale of the home, but delayed enforcement of the decree for four months. In contrast, in the case of *Gourlay's Tr v Gourlay*[2], the court refused the trustee's application in exceptional circumstances[3]. Each case will, however, turn on its own facts.

It should be noted that s 40 only applies where the family home is being disposed of the trustee. Where a heritable creditor is selling the property, the section does not apply even if the property falls within the definition of family home[4].

Abbreviated procedures

Abbreviated procedures generally

In certain cases, the normal procedures in the sequestration are modified to allow the sequestration to be completed more speedily and with less expense. There are two types of abbreviated procedure, Sch 2 procedure and summary administration. In most summary administration cases, the modified procedures in Sch 2 will also apply.

Schedule 2 procedure

Cases to which the modified procedures in Sch 2 apply are often referred to as small assets cases, although not all cases falling within the schedule are such cases. The modified procedure in Sch 2 applies in the following circumstances:

(1) where the Accountant in Bankruptcy is the interim trustee but does not call a statutory meeting and is therefore appointed permanent trustee[5];
(2) where the Accountant in Bankruptcy applies for and is granted a certificate of summary administration[6];
(3) where no creditor entitled to vote attends the statutory meeting or no permanent trustee is elected at the meeting for some other reason and the permanent trustee is therefore appointed by the court[7];

---

1 1989 SLT (Sh Ct) 49.
2 1995 SLT (Sh Ct) 7.
3 See also *Hunt's Tr v Hunt* 1995 SCLR 973, Sh Ct, where the trustee's application was also refused in slightly more dubious circumstances.
4 Indeed, this may be one reason why a trustee would be happy for the heritable creditor to undertake to sell the property rather than do so himself or herself.
5 1985 Act, s 21B(2) and s 25A.
6 1985 Act, s 23A(4) and s 25A.
7 1985 Act, s 24(3A) and s 25A where the interim trustee is the Accountant in Bankruptcy; s 24(4) and (5) where the interim trustee is a private insolvency practitioner.

(4) no permanent trustee is elected to replace one who has resigned, died[1] or been removed[2];
(5) all summary administration cases *except* those where the permanent trustee has been elected[3].

The main differences from the normal applicable procedures are that:

(a) a modified act and warrant is issued[4];
(b) there are simplified procedures for replacing the permanent trustee[5];
(c) there are no commissioners and, where a case has started off normally and become a Sch 2 case later, existing commissioners cease to hold office[6];
(d) where the permanent trustee is the Accountant in Bankruptcy, he or she need not consult with anyone regarding recovery, management and realisation of the estate and he or she does not need consent for any of the actions normally requiring it[7];
(e) a private insolvency practitioner permanent trustee requires the consent of the Accountant in Bankruptcy to apply for a public or private examination[8];
(f) there are modified procedures regarding accounts where the permanent trustee is the Accountant in Bankruptcy[9].

Summary administration (Schedule 2A procedure)

Summary administration was introduced by the Bankruptcy (Scotland) Act 1993 to deal with 'small assets' cases, and applies where the assets and liabilities of the debtor fall within specified limits. A certificate of summary administration may be applied for by the interim trustee whether he or she is the Accountant in Bankruptcy or a private insolvency practitioner. It may be applied for in the following circumstances:

(1) where the petition is a debtor petition, the Accountant in Bankruptcy may apply for a certificate of summary administration within seven days of the award of sequestration[10], but this will be granted only where he is interim trustee[11];
(2) where the Accountant in Bankruptcy is the interim trustee and does not call a statutory meeting, he or she may apply[12];

1 1985 Act, s 28(5) and s 25A.
2 1985 Act, s 29(8) and s 25A.
3 1985 Act, Sch 2A, para 5.
4 1985 Act, Sch 2, para 2(2).
5 Sch 2, paras 3, 4.
6 1985 Act, Sch 2, para 6.
7 1985 Act, Sch 2, para 7. A private insolvency practitioner permanent trustee requires only the consent of the Accountant in Bankruptcy rather than the normal consents.
8 1985 Act, Sch 2, para 8.
9 1985 Act, Sch 2, para 9.
10 1985 Act, s 12(1A).
11 See 1985 Act, s 23A(9).
12 1985 Act, s 21B(2).

(3) where no creditor entitled to vote attends the statutory meeting or no
   permanent trustee is elected for some other reason[1];
(4) where the permanent trustee is elected[2].

The court must grant the application where the debtor's liabilities
(excluding secured liabilities) are less than £20,000 and the debtor's assets
(excluding heritage and any other property which would not vest in the
permanent trustee) are less than £2,000[3].

The debtor, a creditor, the permanent trustee or the Accountant in
Bankruptcy may apply to the court for the withdrawal of the certificate of
summary administration at any time[4].

The main differences from the normal procedure in summary administration cases are:

(a) the permanent trustee is required to carry out his or her functions only
   to the extent that he or she thinks it would be of financial benefit and
   in the interests of the creditors to do so[5] in other words, the trustee
   need not waste time and resources carrying out extensive investiga-
   tions he or she thinks would be fruitless or produce nothing of worth
   to the creditors;
(b) the permanent trustee is required to obtain a report from the debtor of
   his current position every six months[6];
(c) a private insolvency practitioner permanent trustee is subject to directions from the Accountant in Bankruptcy[7].

As discussed above, in all summary administration cases except those
where the permanent trustee has been elected, the modifications to normal procedure contained in Sch 2 also apply[8].

Creditors' claims

General

In order to obtain their share of the debtor's assets, creditors must actually
make a claim in the sequestration process. They should be aware of the
sequestration process: if they are known to the interim trustee as a result
of information obtained by the trustee from the debtor or the debtor's
records, they will have received information from him or her about the
sequestration inviting them, inter alia, to submit claims. Alternatively,
they may have seen the sequestration advertised or heard about it from
other sources.

---

1 1985 Act, s 24(4A) (private insolvency practitioner interim trustee); s 24(3B) (Accountant
   in Bankruptcy interim trustee).
2 1985 Act, s 25(2A).
3 1985 Act, s 23A(1), (2). These limits are subject to alteration by regulation: s 72A.
4 1985 Act, s 23A(5). The procedure is specified in s 23A(6) to (8).
5 1985 Act, Sch 2A, para 1.
6 1985 Act, Sch 2A, para 2.
7 1985 Act, Sch 2A, para 3.
8 1985 Act, Sch 2A, para 5.

Submission of claims

Creditors must submit their claims on a prescribed form[1] which requires details of the debt (or debts) due and any security for the debt. They must attach evidence of the debt (eg invoices or a court decree). Claims may be submitted to the interim trustee or at a later stage to the permanent trustee. If a claim has been submitted to the interim trustee and wholly or partly accepted by him or her, the creditor does not need to submit it again to the permanent trustee[2]. However, the permanent trustee is not bound by the interim trustee's decision on the claim[2].

A creditor may submit a different claim at a later stage[3], eg where a mistake was made in calculating the original claim.

In appropriate circumstances, claims may be made in foreign currency[4]. Such claims are converted into sterling at the rate of exchange applying at close of business on the date of sequestration[5]. Foreign creditors may be allowed to submit claims informally[6].

Adjudication

The process whereby the permanent trustee accepts or rejects creditors' claims is known as adjudication[7]. The permanent trustee has the power to ask a creditor or any other person who may have it to produce further evidence regarding the claim so that the trustee can decide on the validity or amount of the claim[8]. If the person asked refuses or delays in producing the evidence, the trustee can ask for them to be privately examined before the sheriff[9]. The procedure is the same as for a private examination under s 44[10].

The creditor or the debtor can appeal to the sheriff if they are dissatisfied with the trustee's decision on a claim[11].

Amount of claim

The amount which a creditor may claim is determined according to the rules laid down in Sch 1 of the Act[12]. Basically, the creditor may claim the amount of principal and interest due at the date of sequestration[13]. Interest must be legally due, eg under a contract or in terms of a court decree.

---

1 1985 Act, ss 22(2), 48(3).
2 1985 Act, s 48(2).
3 1985 Act, s 48(4).
4 1985 Act, s 22(6).
5 1985 Act, ss 23(1)(a), 49(3).
6 1985 Act, ss 22(3), 48(3).
7 See 1985 Act, s 49. For a discussion of the mechanics of adjudication and some of the problems which can arise, see Aird 'The Liquidator, the Permanent Trustee and the Adjudication of Complicated Claims' (1997) 42 JLSS 229.
8 1985 Act, s 48(5)(a), (b).
9 1985 Act, s 48(5).
10 1985 Act, s 48(6).
11 1985 Act, s 49(6).
12 1985 Act, s 22(9).
13 1985 Act, Sch 1, para 1(1).

There are special rules relating to certain types of claim which may be mentioned briefly.

(1) Claims for aliment and periodical allowance will be allowed only if the payments are being made under a court decree or formal written agreement and the spouses or ex-spouses are living apart[1].
(2) Debts depending on a contingency are valued and only that value may be claimed[2].
(3) Where there has been a judicial composition under the 1985 Act[3], and the sequestration is revived, a creditor must deduct anything paid under the composition from his or her original claim[4].
(4) Where the sequestrated estate is that of a partner in a firm, and the claim is for a partnership debt, the creditor must deduct the value of any claim against the partnership itself[5].
(5) A secured creditor must deduct the value of his or her security (as estimated by him or her) from the amount of his or her claim, unless he or she surrenders it for the benefit of the debtor's estate[6]. If a secured creditor has already realised his or her security, eg by selling the property secured, he or she may claim for the balance of his or her debt after deduction of the net proceeds of the security[7].

Ranking

It is a basic principle of insolvency law is that creditors should be treated equally. However, this principle is imperfectly applied. There are different categories of creditors and some of these are given priority over others. Section 51 of the 1985 Act lays down an order of priority for distribution of the funds in the debtor's estate. Section 51(6) specifically states, however, that this is without prejudice to (1) the rights of secured creditors which are preferable to those of the trustee[8] and (2) any preference to be accorded to the holder of a lien over title deeds which had to be delivered to the trustee in terms of the Act[9].

Secured creditors have already been mentioned. Creditors who have a valid security constituted prior to the sequestration and which is not challengeable by the trustee (eg as an unfair preference) will have a right to the property which is preferable to that of the trustee. They are effectively insulated from the effects of sequestration, at least in so far as the value of the security is sufficient to cover their claims against the debtor. The debtor's property vests in the trustee subject to existing third party rights, and as discussed above, this includes validly constituted securities. The secured creditor will therefore have first claim on the property before it

1 1985 Act, Sch 1, para 2.
2 1985 Act, Sch 1, para 3.
3 See 'Discharge by composition' below.
4 1985 Act, Sch 1, para 4.
5 1985 Act, Sch 1, para 6.
6 1985 Act, Sch 1, para 5(1).
7 1985 Act, Sch 1, para 5(3).
8 It will be recalled that the debtor's property vests in the trustee subject to the rights of secured creditors which are preferable to that of the trustee – 1985 Act, s 33(3) and see 'Vesting' above.
9 See 'Recovery of estate' above.

can be applied in payment of the debts listed in s 51. Subject to the provisions regarding securities over heritable property discussed above, the security holder is essentially free to enforce his or her security and retain the proceeds or sufficient of them to pay his or her debts. As discussed above, if the security has already been realised, the creditor will simply retain the net proceeds up to the value of his or her debt, and if the proceeds of the security were insufficient to pay the creditor fully, claim in the sequestration for any remaining balance of his or her debt. Such a claim, unless it falls into one of the other categories set out in s 51, would be an ordinary debt as defined in that section. The trustee may require a secured creditor to discharge, convey or assign his or her security to the trustee, but only on payment of the value of the security[1], so that his or her priority is preserved. Where particular property is affected by more than one security, the normal rules of ranking of securities will apply[2].

Secured creditors include those who have carried out diligence which has *not* been struck down by the sequestration. Such creditors are also therefore effectively insulated from the sequestration process and, as discussed above, are entitled to keep the proceeds of their diligence or, if the property affected by the diligence has vested in the trustee, to be paid from the proceeds of the property attached by the diligence in priority to other creditors or, where the diligence in question is an inhibition, to be given priority by treating the inhibiting creditor as if debts incurred after the inhibition did not exist, and adjusting the sums otherwise due to creditors under s 51 accordingly.

The position of the holder of a lien has already been discussed[3].

Subject to the rights of secured creditors which are preferable to those of the trustee and any preference to be accorded to the holder of a lien over title deeds which had to be delivered to the trustee in terms of the Act, s 51 sets out the following order of priority of payment.

(1) The interim trustee's outlays and remuneration.
(2) The permanent trustee's outlays and remuneration.
(3) In the case of a deceased debtor, reasonable deathbed and funeral expenses and reasonable expenses of administering the estate. Any expenses which are not reasonable will not have priority, but will rank as an ordinary debt.
(4) Reasonable expenses of a petitioning or concurring creditor.
(5) Preferred debts. These are defined in Part I of Sch 3 of the Act. Formerly, extensive categories of debts due to taxing and rating authorities were treated as preferential debts, but these preferences have been considerably reduced. Currently, preferred debts of this type are: first, certain sums due to the Inland Revenue, including PAYE contributions which were or ought to have been deducted from the wages or salaries of employees during the twelve months prior to the date of sequestration or, in the case of a deceased debtor, the date of death[4]; secondly, certain sums due to Customs and Excise, including

---

1 1985 Act, Sch 1, para 5(2) sets out when the trustee can insist on this.
2 These rules are discussed in ch 6 above.
3 See 'Recovery of estate' above.
4 1985 Act, Sch 3, paras 1 and 7.

VAT in the six months prior to the date of sequestration or, in the case of a deceased debtor, the date of death[1]; thirdly, certain sums in respect of social security contributions, including certain National Insurance contributions which the debtor should have made[2]; and fourthly, certain sums owed by the debtor in relation to occupational or other pension schemes[3].

Certain sums due to employees are also treated as preferred debts[4], including arrears of wages for a period of up to four months prior to the date of sequestration or, in the case of a deceased debtor, the date of death (subject to a prescribed limit[5]) and accrued holiday pay[6]. Where the debtor has borrowed money in order to pay wages, with the result that the employees were paid and therefore have no, or a reduced, preferential claim, the lender who advanced the money will have a preferential claim for so much of the money advanced as was used to pay wages which would otherwise have been the subject of a preferential claim by the employees, subject to the same limits as the employees themselves (ie four months arrears up to the current prescribed limit)[7]. In order for the lender to obtain this preference in place of the employees, however, the money must have been specifically advanced for that purpose. In practice, it will usually be the bank who has lent the money, and they will open a separate wages account in order to have proof the monies were advanced for that purpose.

It should be noted that interest on preferred debts incurred prior to the date of sequestration is *not* treated preferentially[8]. It is treated as an ordinary debt. This is different from the normal position where the amount of the claim includes interest accrued prior to the date of sequestration.

(6) Ordinary debts. These are the bulk of the debts in the normal sequestration, defined as debts which are not secured and not mentioned in any of the other categories set out in s 51.

(7) Interest on preferred and ordinary debts between the date of sequestration and date of payment. This is paid at either the rate which would normally have applied (eg under the contract) or the rate prescribed by statutory instrument, whichever is higher[9].

(8) Postponed debts. These are defined by s 51(3).

Any surplus remaining after all these debts have been paid will be returned to the debtor[10]. Such a situation would, however, be very uncommon.

---

1 1985 Act, Sch 3, paras 2 and 7.
2 1985 Act, Sch 3, paras 3 and 7.
3 1985 Act, Sch 3, para 4.
4 1985 Act, Sch 3, paras 5 and 7.
5 1985 Act, Sch 3, para 5(1). As at the date at which the law is stated in this work, the limit is £800: SI 1985/1925, reg 14 (amended by SI 1986/1914).
6 1985 Act, Sch 3, para 5(2).
7 1985 Act, Sch 3, para 3.
8 1985 Act, s 51(1)(e).
9 1985 Act, s 51(1)(g), (7).
10 1985 Act, s 51(5).

Abatement

With the exception of the first two categories listed above where there is only one creditor, namely the interim trustee and permanent trustee respectively, in most cases there will be multiple creditors in each of the remaining categories. The trustee pays the debts in each category in turn, working down the list. However, since in the normal case there will be insufficient funds to pay all creditors in full, a stage will be reached where there is not enough money left to pay all of the creditors in a particular category.

Section 51(4) provides that all the debts in any particular category rank equally, and that if there is insufficient funds to pay all the creditors in any particular category in full, their debts will abate in equal proportions. In other words, the trustee will not pay some of the creditors in the category and not others, or give some creditors a higher percentage of their debt than others. Each will receive the same proportion of their debt as the others. This can be illustrated as follows:

Sum remaining for distribution   £200

Creditors in category	amount of debt
Fred	£100
Joe	£300
Total debts in category	£400

Obviously, there are insufficient funds to pay both creditors in full. The rule that the debts abate in equal proportions is therefore applied. This results in Fred receiving £50 and Joe receiving £150 of the £200 available. This is calculated by working out the appropriate percentage to be paid to each creditor and then applying it to their individual debts.

$$\% \text{ payable to each creditor} = \frac{\text{sum available for distribution}}{\text{total debts in category}} \times 100$$

$$= \frac{200 \times 100}{400}$$

$$= 50\%$$

Apply this to the individual debts:

Fred	£100 x 50%	£50
Joe	£300 x 50%	£150
		£200

Joe therefore receives more than Fred, but equality of treatment is maintained because each has received the same percentage of their debt.

Where each creditor is not paid in full, but receives only a proportion of his debt, he is said to receive a dividend. In our example, Fred and Joe received a dividend of 50 pence in the pound, ie 50 pence for each £1 that they were due.

Accounting periods

The sequestration is divided into accounting periods of six months, or such other period as may be agreed by the permanent trustee and the commissioners (or the Accountant in Bankruptcy if there are no commissioners)[1]. The permanent trustee makes up accounts of his administration in respect of each of these periods[2] and, where appropriate, will make interim payments of dividend to creditors in respect of each accounting period[3]. Final accounts will be made up at the end of the sequestration, when all estate has been gathered in and realised and all distributions have been made.

Defects in procedure

It is obvious that the procedure involved in all aspects of sequestration is complex. On occasion, matters will be overlooked, time limits will not be complied with and generally mistakes will be made. These need not, however, be fatal. Section 63 allows the sheriff to make various orders which can effectively cure most problems, including failure to comply with time limits.

The debtor

Effects of sequestration generally

The consequences of insolvency generally are not so harsh as they were historically, where non-payment of debts might result, eg, in imprisonment or exile. Nonetheless, the consequences of sequestration for the debtor (and indirectly his or her family) are still extremely serious. Most of these have already been discussed. The debtor loses almost all of his or her assets, and this will probably include his or her home. Any assets that the debtor may acquire after the sequestration and prior to his or her discharge also go to the trustee to be applied in payment of his or her debts. If the debtor is earning, he or she may be required to contribute part of the earnings to the trustee. The debtor is restricted in his or her dealings. The debtor has various obligations laid on him or her by the Act and may be subject to private or public examination. In addition, the debtor is disqualified from holding certain public offices (such as being a Member of Parliament), and may be disqualified from carrying on his or her trade or profession (eg as a solicitor). The debtor may not obtain credit without disclosing that he or she is an undischarged bankrupt, and even after discharge, may have difficulty in obtaining credit.

Duty to co-operate with permanent trustee and other duties

Various specific duties are laid on the debtor by the 1985 Act, a number of which have already been considered in context, such as the duty to comply with the interim trustee's instructions regarding the management of the debtor's estate under s 18 and the duty to provide a statement of assets

1 1985 Act, s 52(2). Where the Accountant in Bankruptcy is the permanent trustee, he or she may simply determine alternative accounting periods: 1985 Act, s 52(2)(b)(ii).
2 1985 Act, s 52(1).
3 1985 Act, s 52(3).

and liabilities to the interim trustee under s 19. In addition to these specific duties, there is also a general duty to co-operate with the permanent trustee. Section 64(1) requires the debtor to take 'every practicable step' which is necessary to enable the permanent trustee to carry out his or her functions under the Act. This would include signing documents, which is specifically mentioned in s 64(1), and other things such as completing tax returns, instructing agents, instructing the transfer of property (eg property abroad which the trustee might not otherwise be able to recover) and so on.

Offences

Bankruptcy no longer renders the debtor liable to imprisonment of itself. However, the 1985 Act creates a number of criminal offences for failure to comply with its provisions. For example, it is an offence punishable by fine or imprisonment for the debtor to fail without reasonable excuse to follow a direction of the interim trustee relating to the management of the debtor's estate[1] or to fail without reasonable excuse to provide the interim trustee with the statement of assets and liabilities required by s 19[2]. Other examples have been mentioned elsewhere[3]. Section 67 also lists a number of general offences such as making false statements in relation to his assets or business or financial affairs[4] or destroying, damaging, concealing or removing from Scotland any assets or relevant documents[5]. Some offences may be committed by persons other than the debtor. For example, the offence of destroying, damaging, concealing or removing from Scotland any assets or relevant documents may also be committed by anyone acting in the debtor's interests, whether with or without the debtor's authority[5]. There are also common law offences such as 'away-putting of assets'.

The permanent trustee has a duty to report suspected offences to the Accountant in Bankruptcy[6], who may in turn refer the matter to the Lord Advocate for prosecution. Commission of offences is taken seriously. In *Shevlin v Carmichael*[7], the debtor was sentenced to three months imprisonment for concealing assets.

Discharge

Automatic discharge

Unless the debtor's discharge is deferred, he or she will be automatically discharged three years after the date of sequestration[8], irrespective of whether administration of the estate is still continuing or not. The debtor

1 1985 Act, s 18(5)(a)(i).
2 1985 Act, s 19(3), (4).
3 See eg 'Recovering information' (private and public examinations).
4 1985 Act, s 67(1).
5 1985 Act, s 67(2).
6 1985 Act, s 3(3).
7 1991 GWD 36-2173.
8 1985 Act, s 54(1).

may apply to the Accountant in Bankruptcy for a certificate of discharge as evidence of discharge[1], but the discharge is effective whether or not the debtor obtains the certificate. Section 55 of the 1985 Act describes the effect of the discharge. The debtor is discharged within the UK[2] of all debts and obligations for which he or she was liable at the date of sequestration, with very few exceptions. The exceptions are:

(1) liability to pay fines or other penalties payable to the Crown[3];
(2) liability to forfeit money deposited in court under s 1(3) of the Bail (Scotland) Act 1980[4];
(3) liability for fraud or breach of trust[5];
(4) liability for aliment or periodical allowance which could not be claimed in the sequestration[6];
(5) the obligation to co-operate with the permanent trustee under s 64[7]. This exception is necessary because the debtor may be discharged before the administration of the estate is complete.

Any property which the debtor acquires which would have vested in the permanent trustee during the sequestration will vest in the debtor after his or her discharge. The debtor may deal with it as he or she wishes and it cannot be attached by creditors for pre-sequestration debts[8]. The debtor will no longer be disqualified from holding public office.

Deferment of discharge

Section 54 of the 1985 Act makes provision for the debtor's automatic discharge to be deferred. An application to have the discharge deferred may be made by the permanent trustee or any creditor, and should be made within two years and nine months of the date of sequestration[9]. The applicant is ordered to serve a copy of the application on the debtor and, if the applicant is a creditor, on the permanent trustee[10]. The debtor is ordered to lodge in court a declaration that he or she has made a full surrender of his or her estate and has delivered to the trustee every document under his or her control relating to his or her estate and business and financial affairs[11]. If the debtor does not lodge the declaration, the discharge is automatically deferred for up to two years. If he or she does, a hearing is fixed and the permanent trustee (or the Accountant in Bankruptcy if the permanent trustee has been discharged) lodges in court a report on the debtor's assets and liabilities, financial and business affairs, the sequestration

1 1985 Act, s 54(2).
2 The effect of the discharge in foreign law is a matter for the foreign law applying its rules of domestic and private international law.
3 1985 Act, s 55(2)(a).
4 1985 Act, s 55(2)(b).
5 1985 Act, s 55(2)(c).
6 1985 Act, s 55(2)(d).
7 1985 Act, s 55(2)(e).
8 Other than those which, as detailed above, are not affected by the discharge.
9 1985 Act, s 54(3).
10 1985 Act, s 54(4). Service need only be made on the permanent trustee if he or she is not discharged.
11 1985 Act, s 54(4).

generally and the debtor's conduct in relation to his or her affairs and the sequestration. At the hearing, the debtor, the applicant or any creditor can make representations[1]. Following the hearing, the application may be refused or the discharge deferred for a period of up to two years[2].

In the normal case, the hearing will take place prior to the date for the debtor's automatic discharge, and so a decision on deferral will be taken before the debtor is automatically discharged. In some cases, however, it may not be possible to hold the hearing prior to the date when the debtor is automatically discharged. In *Clydesdale Bank plc v Davidson*[3], it was held that so long as the application was made timeously, it did not matter that it was not disposed of before the three-year period expired. The automatic discharge is effectively suspended pending the outcome of the application. Where the application is not presented timeously, eg because the trustee has overlooked the time limit, he or she will need to ask the court to extend the time limit to allow him to lodge the application late. In *Whittaker's Tr v Whittaker*[4], it was held that in such cases, there was a two stage process – dealing with the trustee's request to be allowed to lodge the application late, and then dealing with the application itself. It was held further that in the situation where the first was dealt with before the three years expired but not the second, and also where both could not be dealt with before the three years expired, the discharge was automatically suspended in the same way as had happened in *Clydesdale Bank plc v Davidson*. Earlier cases had taken the more cautious approach of interim deferment of the discharge if either or both of the applications could not be dealt with prior to the expiry of the three years[5].

The Act does not give any guidance as to the grounds for deferring a discharge. Some good reason will, however, be required. This was emphasised in *Crittal Warmlife Ltd v Flaherty*[6], where deferment for four years to allow the trustee to claim the debtor's pension was refused. In *Watson v Henderson*[7], however, deferment was granted to allow the trustee to sist himself in an action for reparation by the debtor. It has been held that the debtor's conduct alone can justify deferral of the discharge[8], although it is suggested that the better view is that although conduct is undoubtedly relevant, it is only one factor and ought not to be used as the sole ground for deferring a discharge.

If discharge is deferred, the debtor may apply at any time thereafter for

---

1 1985 Act, s 54(6). Curiously, this would seem to exclude the permanent trustee if he or she is not the applicant. It is also unclear how 'any creditor' other than a creditor applicant would be in a position to make representations, since there is no provision for notification of creditors or advertisement, so that they would appear to be able to find out only by chance.
2 1985 Act, s 54(6).
3 1993 SCLR 428.
4 1993 SCLR 718, Sh Ct.
5 *Pattison v Halliday* 1991 SLT 645, OH.
6 1988 GWD 22-930. See also *Whittaker's Tr v Whittaker* 1993 SCLR 718, Sh Ct.
7 1988 SCLR 439.
8 *Nicol's Tr v Nicol* 1996 GWD 10-531. See also Jones 'Deferral of Debtor's Discharge' (1995) 40 JLSS 388.

a discharge[1]. Further applications for deferment may be made by the permanent trustee or a creditor[2].

Discharge by composition

The debtor may also obtain his or her discharge if he or she makes an acceptable offer of composition. A composition is an agreement between the debtor and his or her creditors whereby the creditors agree to discharge the debtor on part payment of their debts. Such compositions are competent at common law and may be used as an alternative to the sequestration process[3]. They may also be used, however, to bring the sequestration process to an end[4]. In the latter case, such compositions are known as judicial compositions and the procedure for concluding a judicial composition is set out in Sch 4 of the 1985 Act.

The debtor may make an offer of composition at any time after the issue of the act and warrant to the permanent trustee[5]. The offer is put to the commissioners or, if there are no commissioners, the Accountant in Bankruptcy[6], for a decision on whether the offer should be put to the creditors[7]. The composition must propose payment of at least 25 pence in the pound[7]. If it is submitted to the creditors, and if a majority in number and at least two-thirds in value of them accept it[8], the offer goes to the sheriff for approval[9]. The sheriff fixes a hearing[10]. If the composition is approved by the sheriff, there is further sundry procedure and thereafter the debtor and the permanent trustee will be discharged[11] and the sequestration brought to an end[12]. The debtor is re-invested in his assets[13] and can use them to generate the income needed to make the payments agreed in the composition.

If the debtor defaults or for some other reason the composition cannot continue, the composition may be recalled, and the sequestration will be revived[14].

The attraction of this procedure for the debtor is that if his or her offer of composition is accepted, discharge may be obtained more quickly than is provided for under s 54.

1   1985 Act, s 54(8). A suitably modified version of the procedure for the original application for deferment is followed.
2   1985 Act, s 54(9). The same procedure applies as in the original application for deferment.
3   See 'Extra-judicial alternatives to sequestration' below.
4   1985 Act, s 56.
5   1985 Act, Sch 4, para 1.
6   1985 Act, Sch 4, para 2.
7   1985 Act, Sch 4, para 3.
8   1985 Act, Sch 4, para 5.
9   1985 Act, Sch 4, para 6.
10 1985 Act, Sch 4, para 7.
11 1985 Act, Sch 4, para 11.
12 1985 Act, Sch 4, para 13.
13 1985 Act, Sch 4, para 16(a).
14 1985 Act, Sch 4, para 17.

End of sequestration

Generally

The debtor's discharge by composition under s 56 and Sch 4 will bring the sequestration to an end unless it is subsequently revived. However, the debtor's automatic discharge under s 54 will not have that effect *per se*, although of course the administration of the estate may have been completed by or prior to that time. If it has not, however, the administration of the estate will continue even after the debtor's discharge, until everything has been completed. Thereafter, the permanent trustee will apply for his or her own discharge and in practical terms bring the sequestration to an end.

Discharge of permanent trustee

Where the permanent trustee is a private insolvency practitioner, the procedure for obtaining his or her discharge is set out in s 57 of the 1985 Act. The application for discharge is made to the Accountant in Bankruptcy[1]. The debtor and the creditors are allowed an opportunity to make representations to the Accountant[2], who then decides whether or not to grant it on the basis of the documents submitted by the permanent trustee and any representations which are made to him[3]. The Accountant's decision is subject to appeal to the sheriff[4].

Where the permanent trustee is the Accountant in Bankruptcy, the procedure is set out in s 58A. The Accountant notifies the debtor and the creditors that he or she has put in motion the procedure for his or her discharge[5], and they may appeal to the court against such discharge[6]. If no appeal is made or is dismissed, the Accountant is duly discharged[7].

In either case, the permanent trustee cannot thereafter be sued by either the debtor or any of the creditors for any of his or her acts or omissions in carrying out his or her functions as permanent trustee[8]. The discharge also covers the trustee's actings as interim trustee if he or she has not already obtained a discharge as interim trustee[9]. The discharge does not, however, relieve the trustee of liability for fraud[10].

EXTRA-JUDICIAL ALTERNATIVES TO SEQUESTRATION

Informal arrangements with creditors

A debtor may enter into informal arrangements with creditors in order to avoid sequestration. Examples of such arrangements might include a

1 1985 Act, s 57(1)(c).
2 1985 Act, s 57(2).
3 1985 Act, s 57(3).
4 1985 Act, s 57(4). That appeal is final: s 57(4A).
5 1985 Act, s 58A(4).
6 1985 Act, s 58A(5).
7 1985 Act, s 58A(7).
8 1985 Act, s 57(5) (private insolvency practitioner), s 58A(7) (Accountant in Bankruptcy).
9 1985 Act, s 57(5) (private insolvency practitioner), s 58A(9) (Accountant in Bankruptcy).
10 1985 Act, s 57(5) (private insolvency practitioner), s 58A(7) (Accountant in Bankruptcy).

scheme of instalment payments, or a simple moratorium where creditors agree to postpone further action for an agreed period of time. The success of such informal arrangements depends on a number of factors, including the number of creditors; how early the debtor approaches them; the manner in which the debtor approaches them; precisely what the debtor can offer them; how patient or otherwise they are prepared to be; how bad a state the debtor's affairs are in; the reason for the debtor's difficulties and whether there is any real prospect of improvement in the situation.

Composition contracts

Composition contracts have already been discussed briefly above. They are a more formal arrangement between the debtor and his creditors. Usually, the debtor will retain his or her assets in order to generate the income necessary to pay the creditors as agreed in the contract. The creditors will agree to accept a lesser sum than the full amount due in settlement of their debts. This will usually be paid by instalments. All creditors participating in the agreement must, however, be treated rateably.

The difficulty with composition contracts is that in order to have any real chance of success, it is almost always necessary to get all creditors to agree to be bound by them, although it is perfectly competent at common law to have a composition with only some creditors. Any creditor who is not included in the contract or does not agree to be bound by it may carry on with action against the debtor. In most cases, such action would probably prevent him from being able to fulfil his part of the contract, eg, through being deprived of assets, or the use of them. The kinds of factors which will affect whether it is possible to get creditors to agree to a composition contract will be the same as those discussed in the preceding section.

If the debtor fails to fulfil his part of the agreement, eg by failing to pay agreed instalments in full or on time, creditors may pursue the debtor for payment of the full amount of the original debt less any sums paid under the composition contract, and may claim such sum in any subsequent sequestration.

Trust deeds for creditors

Trust deeds generally

A debtor who wishes to avoid the formal sequestration process may choose to grant a trust deed for creditors instead. A trust deed is a document whereby a debtor conveys all or as many as he or she chooses of his or her assets to a named trustee to be administered for the benefit of his or her creditors and settlement of his or her debts. The deed normally conveys to the trustee the same assets as would vest in a trustee in sequestration. The trustee will usually administer the assets in much the same way as a trustee in sequestration, but he or she can only act in accordance with the powers granted to him or her in the trust deed. A carefully drawn deed will give the trustee all the necessary powers.

Although trust deeds are creatures of the common law, the 1985 Act does contain a number of provisions which apply to all trust deeds. These are contained in Sch 5. Thus, the debtor, trustee or any creditor can insist on the trustee's accounts being audited and his or her remuneration fixed by the Accountant in Bankruptcy whether the trust deed makes alternative provision for these matters or not[1]; the trustee is given rights and obligations regarding the recording of certain notices in the Register of Inhibitions and Adjudications[2]; the lodging of a claim by a creditor stops the running of prescription in the same way as it does in sequestration[3] and, unless the trust deed otherwise provides, the amount of a creditor's claim is to be valued in the same way as in sequestration[4].

As with composition contracts, the difficulty with trust deeds is that if all creditors do not agree to the debtor's affairs being administered in this way, by *acceding* to the trust deed, creditors who do not accede can carry on with independent action, including sequestration. In order to prevent this where the majority of creditors do agree (or at least do not object) to the trust deed procedure, the 1985 Act provides that a trust deed may become protected in certain circumstances.

Protected trust deeds

The concept of a protected trust deed was introduced by the 1985 Act. It provided for the trust deed to become protected if a defined majority of the creditors acceded to it and certain other conditions were satisfied. Few trust deeds became protected, however, and so the conditions for a trust deed becoming protected were amended by the 1993 Act. It is now the case that if the deed itself satisfies certain conditions, and if the trustee follows certain procedures and a defined percentage of the creditors *do not object* within a specified time limit, the trust deed will become protected.

The conditions which must be satisfied for a trust deed to become a protected trust deed are set out in Sch 5. The trustee under the deed must be someone who would be able to act as trustee in the debtor's sequestration[5]. The trustee must publish a notice in prescribed form[6] and then within a week send a copy of the deed, the notice and other prescribed information to all known creditors[7]. If a majority in number, or at least a third in value, of the creditors notify the trustee in writing of their objection to the trust deed within five weeks[8], it will not become protected. If not, it will become protected, provided that immediately on the expiry of the five weeks the trustee sends a copy of the trust deed to the Accountant in Bankruptcy with a certificate endorsed on it stating that he or she has not received the required objections[9]. Creditors who do not object are effectively deemed to have acceded to the deed.

The effect of the trust deed becoming protected is, in simple terms, to

1 1985 Act, Sch 5, para 1.
2 1985 Act, Sch 5, para 2.
3 1985 Act, Sch 5, para 3.
4 1985 Act, Sch 5, para 4.
5 1985 Act, Sch 5, para 5(1)(a).
6 1985 Act, Sch 5, para 5(1)(b).
7 1985 Act, Sch 5, para 5(1)(c).
8 1985 Act, Sch 5, para 5(1)(d).
9 1985 Act, Sch 5, para 5(1)(e).

prevent any creditor, even one who objected to it, from carrying on with independent action. In terms of para 6(a)(i) of Sch 5 any creditor who objected to the deed has no higher right to recover his or her debt than one acceding to it. Similarly, any creditor who did not receive the relevant notice from the trustee has no higher right to recover his or her debt than one acceding to it[1]. However, an objecting creditor or one who did not receive the relevant notice is given the right to apply for sequestration within six weeks of the original notice published by the trustee[2]. The court may award sequestration if it considers it is in the best interests of creditors to do so[3]. Such a creditor may also apply for sequestration at any other time if he or she alleges that the distribution is or is likely to be unfairly prejudicial[4]. In such a case the court will only award sequestration if it is satisfied that this is true[5].

The debtor is also prevented from applying for sequestration during the currency of the trust deed[6].

1 1985 Act, Sch 5, para 6(a)(ii).
2 1985 Act, Sch 5, para 7(1)(a).
3 1985 Act, Sch 5, para 7(2).
4 1985 Act, Sch 5, para 7(1)(b).
5 1985 Act, Sch 5, para 7(3).
6 1985 Act, Sch 5, para 6(b).

8 Agency

INTRODUCTION

Nature and purpose of agency

Agency is the relationship which exists when someone, instead of acting personally, engages or permits someone else to act on his or her behalf in a legal relationship with a third party. Agency may be distinguished from mandate by the fact that mandate is gratuitous, where one person is empowered to act on behalf of another without reward, but agency is onerous, in that the agent receives some reward[1].

Academic writers have spent considerable effort in trying to summarise the concept of agency and to describe the features which distinguish agency from other legal relationships, such as that between an employer and an independent contractor[2]. Fridman, eg, notes that:

> 'It seems virtually impossible to define agency except in terms of its consequences. A person is an agent only in so far as his acts can result in some alteration of the legal situation of the one for whom he acts or purports to act'[3].

He goes on to argue that agency may exist, at least for certain purposes, even where no consent and no contract can be found as between principal and agent[4]. Such cases are limited however, and it is equally arguable either that the legal relationship is not truly one of agency[5], or that there is at least implied consent, as, eg, in the case where a receiver appointed by the holder of a floating charge is deemed by statute to be the agent of the company for certain purposes[6], even though the receiver may incur personal liability in certain circumstances[7]. It can be argued that the company, in granting the floating charge and agreeing to its terms, gives consent to the appointment of a receiver under the terms of the floating charge and, therefore, to the legal consequences of such an appointment[8].

---

1 Bell *Commentaries* I, 506.
2 See eg Fridman *The Law of Agency* (7th edn, 1996) ch 1; Bowstead and Reynolds *The Law of Agency* (16th edn, 1996) ch 1. See also *Trojan Plant Hire Co Ltd v Durafencing (Northern) Ltd* 1974 SLT (Sh Ct) 3.
3 *Fridman* p 11. See too *Bowstead and Reynolds* pp 17–20.
4 *Fridman* pp 15–16.
5 *Branwhite v Worcester Works Finance Ltd* [1969] 1 AC 552, HL. But see Consumer Credit Act 1974, s 56(2) which creates a deemed agency in certain circumstances. As to the scope of s 56(2), see *UDT v Whitfield* [1987] CCLR 60; *Forthright Finance Ltd v Ingate* (14 May 1997, unreported), CA; cf *Powell v Lloyds Bowmaker Ltd* 1996 SLT (Sh Ct) 117.
6 Insolvency Act 1986, ss 57(1), 57(1A).
7 1986 Act, s 57(2).
8 For a contrary view, see *Fridman* p 19.

The most common effect of the contract of agency is to create a direct contractual relationship between the principal and a third party, in consequence of the agent's activities. In this sense there are two contracts which have to be noted – that between the agent and the principal, and that between the principal and the third party. The first contract gives rise to questions concerning the rights and duties of the agent and principal as between themselves: eg, when will the agent be entitled to remuneration for acting on the principal's behalf and to what extent is the principal entitled to expect that the agent will act solely for the principal's benefit in any transaction? The second contract, between the principal and the third party, gives rise to questions such as whether the agent's acts will bind the principal in all circumstances and whether the principal will be liable to the third party for everything done by the agent. Some commercial arrangements, such as distribution agreements between manufacturers and dealers, or franchise agreements, are distinguishable from agency in that they do not result in contracts being made on behalf of the manufacturer or franchisor. In such cases the distributor/dealer or franchisee will act as principal in selling the manufacturer's goods to third parties and will be liable on contracts as such. This question tends to arise particularly in the case of motor vehicle dealerships, where the dealer may be styled as a 'sole agent', but the legal position may be that the dealer is acting on his or her own account in selling vehicles to the public.

The creation of a direct contractual relationship between the principal and the third party is not, however, the only possible consequence of the agency relationship. It may result in the creation of delictual obligations where, eg, the principal becomes liable for wrongs done by the agent in the course of a transaction.

Different types of agent

Agents may act in many different circumstances and the extent of their ability to affect the principal's relationships with third parties may vary considerably, depending on what types of agent they are. What is usual in a particular trade or profession will be a relevant consideration, and this factor will be explored further when discussing the extent of an agent's authority. For example, the position of a solicitor or law agent will differ from that of an auctioneer, an estate agent or a stockbroker. The law recognises a distinction between 'general' agents and 'special' agents. A general agent is one who has authority to act for the principal in all matters, or in all matters falling within the scope of the agent's particular business or profession. A special agent is one whose authority to act is limited to a particular act or to representing the principal in a particular transaction not in the ordinary course of his business or profession. An example of this distinction is seen in *Morrison v Statter*[1], where the duties of the head shepherd on Statter's farm included overseeing other farm workers, but did not include buying and selling sheep unless he had special instructions to do so. On one occasion the shepherd bought sheep from Morrison without instructions from Statter. In an action by Morrison for the loss he

1 (1855) 12 R 1152.

incurred when Statter refused to pay, it was held that as the shepherd had no special authority and as there had been no course of dealing from which it could be inferred that he had authority, Statter was not liable for the shepherd's actions. General agents are recognised as being vested with implied authority in various matters, but in the case of special agents, the third party should always check on the precise terms of the agent's authority. Certain 'mercantile agents' have in the customary course of their business authority to buy and sell goods and their powers to dispose of goods are expressly recognised by statute[1]. 'Commercial agents' are now recognised as a separate category of agents whose rights and duties are defined by legislation[2]. A commercial agent for this purpose is a self-employed intermediary who has continuing authority to negotiate (or negotiate and conclude) the sale or purchase of goods on behalf of a principal, but the definition excludes persons acting in their capacity as officers of a company, partners and insolvency practitioners[3], as well as agents whose activities are unpaid, agents operating on commodity exchanges and certain Crown Agents[4].

CONSTITUTION OF AGENCY

Capacity

Both the principal and the agent must be legally capable of acting in their respective roles. The normal rules of contract as to nonage apply[5]. A principal cannot confer on an agent any authority which the principal himself or herself could not exercise. For example, a company which has not yet been incorporated has no capacity to act as a legal person and cannot therefore act as a principal[6]. A partnership is recognised in Scots law as having a separate personality[7] and obligations undertaken by partners and other agents of the firm may bind the firm as principal[8]. An unicorporated association such as a club has no legal personality and cannot act as principal, with the result that committee members or others transacting for the benefit of the club may be personally liable[9]. The relationship of agency cannot be created after the death of the 'principal'[10].

---

1 Factors Act 1889; Factors (Scotland) Act 1890.
2 Commercial Agents (Council Directive) Regulations 1993, SI 1993/3053.
3 Ibid, reg 2(1).
4 Ibid, reg 2(2).
5 These rules are to be found in the Age of Legal Capacity (Scotland) Act 1991.
6 *Tinnevelley Sugar Refining Co Ltd v Mirrlees, Watson and Yaryan Co Ltd* (1894) 21 R 1009; Companies Act 1985, s 36C.
7 Partnership Act 1890, s 4(2).
8 1890 Act, ss 5, 6.
9 *Thomson and Gillespie v Victoria Eighty Club* (1905) 43 SLR 628; *Cromarty Leasing Ltd v Turnbull* 1988 SLT (Sh Ct) 62.
10 *Lord Advocate v Chung* 1995 SLT 65.

Express appointment

No special form is normally required for the constitution of agency. In the case of a commercial agency, the commercial agent and principal are each entitled to receive from the other, on request, a signed written document setting out the terms of the agency contract including any terms subsequently agreed[1]. Sometimes an agency will be created expressly by formal written agreement, eg where a power of attorney is granted by a principal to enable another person to act in his or her absence. If so, the writing will be the measure of the rights of the parties and will be fairly strictly construed[2]. The agency may, however, be created expressly by oral agreement and, in the absence of writing, the agency may be proved by any competent evidence[3].

Implied appointment

As indicated above, the agency relationship may arise where the agent has been expressly appointed to act, either orally or in writing. The agency relationship may also arise by implication. In some circumstances an agency is implied by the actings of the parties. For example, in *Neville v C and A Modes*[4] it was held that employing a person as a shop manager impliedly conferred authority on that person to protect the employer's property from shoplifters, as such authority would normally be conferred on an employee in that position[5]. In *Barnetson v Peterson Bros*[6], where a shipbroker had rendered various necessary services to a ship on charter, it was held that the master of a ship was impliedly the agent of the owners, and that the owners were directly liable to the shipbroker. In some cases an agency, or at least the extent of the agency, is implied by the terms of a particular statute. For example, by operation of law every partner in a firm becomes an agent of the firm and the other partners for the purpose of the business of the partnership[7]. The extent of the agency, however, is implied by the type of business in which the partnership is involved.

Ratification

Normally the relationship of principal and agent is established prior to the agent's actings on behalf of the principal. Sometimes, however, the relationship is created by the principal subsequently ratifying the acts of the agent. In such cases, the ratification is retrospective and takes effect from the time of the agent's acts[8]. Ratification may be express, or implied from the conduct of the principal[9]. Effectively, therefore, it is as if the principal

1 Commercial Agents (Council Directive) Regulations 1993, reg 13.
2 *Park v Mood* (1919) 1 SLT 170, OH.
3 *Pickin v Hawkes* (1878) 5 R 676; *Ross v Cowie's Exrx* (1888) 16 R 224.
4 1945 SC 175.
5 See too *Mackenzie v Cluny Hill Hydropathic Co Ltd* 1908 SC 200.
6 (1902) 5 F 86.
7 Partnership Act 1890, s 5.
8 *Alexander Ward & Co Ltd v Samyang Navigation Co Ltd* 1975 SC (HL) 26.
9 *Ballantine v Stevenson* (1881) 8 R 959.

had expressly or impliedly appointed the agent to act before the actings in question took place. The possibility of ratification may arise where the agent had no authority at all in the first place, or where the agent had some authority but exceeded that authority. Certain conditions have to be fulfilled before ratification is effective.

Existence of the principal

The first condition for effective ratification concerns the existence of the principal. Ratification will be possible only if the principal was in existence at the time of the agent's purported actings on his or her behalf. For example, until a company has been incorporated it has no legal capacity and cannot act as a principal[1]. Any contract which purports to be made by or on behalf of a company before it has been formed will, subject to any agreement to the contrary, be binding on the person who purports to act for the company or as agent for it and that person will be personally liable on it[2]. It is not legally possible for a company to adopt or ratify a pre-incorporation contract and the only way of achieving this effect is for the parties to agree to substitute a new contract to be made with the company itself once it has been incorporated. Alternatively, it might be argued that the object of the contract was to confer a benefit on a third party (the company) and that therefore the company has a *jus quaesitum tertio*, enabling it to sue upon the contract[3].

Known or identifiable principal

The second condition for effective ratification is that the agent must have made it clear to the third party that he or she was acting on behalf of a known or identifiable principal. In other words the agent should have made it clear that he or she was not acting in his or her own name but as an agent. If the agent contracted in his or her own name with an undeclared intention to act on behalf of someone else, when in addition the agent had no prior authority to act for that other person, then the undisclosed principal cannot ratify the contract at a later stage. This is illustrated by the case of *Keighley Maxsted & Co v Durant*[4], where Roberts, a corn merchant, had been authorised by Keighley Maxsted to buy wheat at a certain price. He failed to buy it at the authorised price and later, without authorisation, contracted with another merchant to buy wheat at a higher price. He did not say at the time of this contract that he was acting as an agent. The next day Keighley Maxsted agreed to take the wheat. In the end, however, neither Roberts nor Keighley Maxsted took delivery of the wheat and they were sued for the price. On the question of whether Keighley Maxsted had ratified the contract, it was held that a contract made by someone who means to contract on behalf of another but has no

---

1   *Kelner v Baxter* (1866) LR 2 CP 174; *Tinnevelly Sugar Refining Co Ltd v Mirrlees Watson and Yaryan Co Ltd* (1894) 21 R 1009.
2   Companies Act 1985, s 36C. See also *Phonogram Ltd v Lane* [1982] QB 938, CA.
3   See *Cumming v Quartzag Ltd* 1980 SC 276. See also MacQueen 'Promoters' Contracts, Agency and the Jus Quaesitum Tertio' 1982 SLT (News) 257.
4   [1901] AC 240, HL.

authority to do so, cannot be ratified by that other party unless the person making the contract has said, at the time of its making, that he is acting for a principal. If the circumstances indicate that the transaction is being undertaken on behalf of a partnership, or that the parties are undertaking a joint adventure (ie a partnership for one particular purpose), it may be possible to argue that an agency relationship exists, despite the fact that no disclosure of the principal has been made to the third party[1].

Capability of principal to authorise transaction

The third condition for effective ratification is that the principal must have been capable, at the time of the agent's actings, of authorising the acts in question. This is illustrated by *Boston Deep Sea Fishing and Ice Co Ltd v Farnham*[2], where a question arose as to the tax liability of a firm of Fleetwood trawler owners who had managed a French trawler during the war at a time when the trawler's French owners were alien enemies. It was held that the French owners were legally incompetent to run the trawler at the time in question and therefore could not ratify the Fleetwood agents' actions.

Timely ratification

Where the validity of an action depends on its being done within a certain time, it has been held that it will not be valid as an act of the principal unless it is ratified by the principal within the time limit. An example of this is seen in *Goodall v Bilsland*[3], which concerned an application for renewal of a public house licence. A solicitor was given authority to lodge objections at the licensing court. There was a time limit for appeals to be made to the Licensing Appeal Court. The solicitor, without consulting his principal, lodged an appeal to the Licensing Appeal Court but it was held that his actings could not be made valid by ratification after the period allowed for appeal had expired. It has been held in England that, notwithstanding the expiry of a limitation period, it was competent for the liquidators of a company to ratify the commencement, without authority, of an action by solicitors on behalf of the company[4]. In that case however, it appears that not all the causes of action pleaded were statute-barred[5]. In a case where the defenders' solicitors marked an appeal without authority and then did not proceed with the appeal, as a result of which decree passed against the defenders, it was argued by the defenders that the proceedings were null because of the agent's lack of authority and that this entitled the defenders to succeed in an action of reduction[6]. It was held, however, that an action of reduction was inappropriate in these circumstances, and it was noted by the court that the authorities cited did not in any case support a general proposition that a solicitor requires a specific

---

1 For further discussion of this point, see 1 *Stair Memorial Encyclopaedia* para 625, where the case of *Lockhart v Moodie & Co* (1877) 4 R 859 is considered.
2 [1957] 3 All ER 204.
3 1909 SC 1152.
4 *Presentaciones Musicales SA v Secunda* [1994] 2 All ER 737, CA.
5 [1994] 2 All ER 737 at 746, per Dillon LJ.
6 *Riverford Finance v Kelly* 1991 SLT 300, OH.

mandate before he can mark an appeal to the Court of Session from the sheriff court[1].

Necessity

In England certain cases have been treated as creating a special category of agency, to which the term 'agency of necessity' is applied. These are cases where one person is regarded by law as justified in taking action for the benefit of another in an emergency[2], even although there may have been no prior contractual relationship between the parties. The cases traditionally recognised by English law as falling into this category relate mainly to the powers of a ship's master to contract in relation to the ship and its cargo[3]; the powers of a carrier by land to care for the goods if there is no one to receive them at their destination[4]; and in the case of bills of exchange, the acceptance of a bill for the honour of the drawer[5]. In the first two cases, the application of the agency of necessity doctrine depends on the impracticability of communication with the principal[6] and on there being some sort of real emergency. Inconvenience alone will not enable someone to act as an agent of necessity. For example, in a case where furniture had been stored on behalf of another party for several years and it was eventually felt that it was taking up too much space, considerable effort was made, to no avail, to contact the owner to have it removed. The furniture was eventually auctioned but it was held that there was no emergency compelling its sale and that therefore the sellers were not acting as agents of necessity[7]. It has been argued that much of the notion of agency of necessity, as understood in English law, could and should be treated more flexibly nowadays within the general law relating to implied and apparent authority[8]. The issue has also been raised by another commentator as to whether English law ought to extend the scope of agency of necessity by embracing a wider principle of reimbursement akin to the Roman law doctrine of *negotiorum gestio*[9], although Fridman, who raises the issue, concludes that it is better to deal with certain types of cases separately under the law of restitution rather than invoke the full consequences of the agency relationship[10].

In Scots law, the somewhat broader principle of *negotiorum gestio* has been the basis of decisions in cases which in England might have been tested against the criteria applicable to agency of necessity. *Negotiorum gestio* is described as:

1   1991 SLT 300 at 301, per Lord Morton of Shuna.
2   See *Bowstead and Reynolds* pp 145 ff.
3   Eg *Tronson v Dent* (1853) 8 Moo P C 419.
4   Eg *Great Northern Rly Co v Swaffield* (1874) L R 9 Exch 132; *China Pacific SA v Food Corpn of India, The Winson* [1982] AC 939, HL.
5   Bills of Exchange Act 1882, ss 65–68; *Hawtayne v Bourne* (1841) 7 M & W 595.
6   *Springer v Great Western Railway Co* [1921] 1 KB 257, CA. See too *Industrie Chimiche Italia Centrale and Cerealfin SA v Alexander G Tsavliris & Sons Maritime Co, The Choko Star* [1990] 1 Lloyd's Rep 516, CA.
7   *Sachs v Miklos* [1948] 2 KB 23, CA.
8   *Bowstead and Reynolds* p 152.
9   *Fridman* pp 143–144.
10 *Fridman* p 144.

'the management of the affairs of one who is absent or incapacitated from attending to his own affairs, spontaneously undertaken without his knowledge, and on the presumption that he would, if aware of the circumstances, have given a mandate for such interference. An obligation is thence raised ... to the effect of indemnifying the *negotiorum gestor*'[1].

In *Fernie v Robertson*[2], a question arose as to who was liable to pay for repairs done to the house of an elderly woman who later died. The house had passed to her son as heir-at-law, but the repairs had been instructed by her daughter who had cared for her during her senility and had instructed tradesmen to carry out the essential repairs in question. It was held that the heir-at-law was liable to pay for the repairs and that the daughter had been acting as *negotiorum gestrix* on behalf of her mother, since there was no doubt that the mother would have had to have the repairs done if she had been able to attend to her own affairs. The same principle would apply where a tenement flat has been left empty by its owner and a burst pipe causes flooding in the property below. A plumber called in by a neighbour, acting as *negotiorum gestor*, would have a right of action against the absent owner for the cost of repairing the pipe. Another example of the effect of the operation of this principle is seen in the case of *AS Kolbin & Sons v United Shipping Co Ltd*[3], where it was held that the *gestor* is liable for any loss caused by his failure to exercise the care and diligence which a prudent man would have shown in relation to his own property.

Holding out

Sometimes an agent, who has had authority at one time but whose authority has been withdrawn, may continue to bind the principal in transactions with third parties. In other words the law recognises that the consequences of the agency relationship may continue, despite the fact that the agent's actual authority to act has been withdrawn. This recognition of an 'apparent' rather than an 'actual' agency is based on the principle of personal bar, so that where the principal holds the agent out as having authority, or fails to inform third parties that the agent no longer has authority, the principal is then barred from denying that the agent has authority to act on his or her behalf and will be bound by the agent's acts as if the agent had been authorised. This notion of the principal 'holding out' someone as agent is bound up with the question of the agent's 'ostensible' or 'apparent' authority and is explored further under that heading below.

Operation of law

In some cases a person becomes an agent by operation of law. For example, s 5 of the Partnership Act 1890 states that 'Every partner is an agent of the firm and his other partners for the purpose of the business of the partnership...'. A person appointed as a receiver is deemed to be the agent of

1 Bell *Principles* s 540.
2 (1871) 9 M 437.
3 1931 SC (HL) 128.

the company for certain purposes[1], and a person appointed as the administrator of a company under an administration order is deemed, in exercising his or her powers, to act as the company's agent[2].

RELATIONSHIP BETWEEN AGENT AND PRINCIPAL

The agent's authority

Generally speaking, the principal is not bound in a contract with a third party if the agent acts without the authority of the principal although, as noted above, the principal may ratify the agent's unauthorised act and so become a party to the contract. It is important to note, however, that the law recognises various types of authority which the agent may possess and that if the agent is acting within the scope of any of these authorities, the principal may be bound. Each of these types of authority is looked at in turn.

Express authority

The agent may bind the principal if the agent is acting with authority which has been expressly conferred on him or her by the principal. This is the most straightforward type of authority.

Implied authority

The agent may bind the principal if the agent is acting with the implied authority which an agent has to do anything which is necessary to carry out his or her commission. An example of this is seen in *Park v Mood*[3], where agents were given power to lease property and it was held that there was implied in this a power to remove the tenants. Similarly it is implied that an agent has authority to do anything which is usual in his or her trade or profession. For example, where an architect employed on a particular job had the plans measured by a surveyor and the surveyor claimed his fees directly from the principal, it was held that in the circumstances the architect was the general agent of the employer for all purposes necessary for carrying out the agreed work[4]. Where a principal wishes to restrict the powers of the agent, such restriction would only be effective if it was notified to the third party[5].

---

1 Insolvency Act 1986, ss 57(1), 57(1A), but note the qualification in repect of personal liability in s 57(2).
2 1986 Act, s 14(5).
3 *Park v Mood* (1919) 1 SLT 170, OH.
4 *Black v Cornelius* (1879) 6 R 581; cf *Knox and Robb v Scottish Garden Suburb Co Ltd* 1913 SC 872; *WT Partnership v Nithsdale District Council* 1996 GWD 15-866. See too *Watteau v Fenwick* [1893] 1 QB 346; *Barry, Ostlere and Shepherd Ltd v Edinburgh Cork Importing Co* 1909 SC 1113.
5 Eg see Partnership Act 1890, ss 5, 8.

Apparent authority

Express and implied authority are sometimes described as 'actual' authority, in that they are forms of authority which the agent actually has. The agent, however, may also bind the principal if the agent is acting not with actual authority but with apparent or, as it is sometimes called, ostensible authority. This is authority which the agent appears to have, but does not actually have. In this case authority appears to exist because of some representation by the principal that the agent is authorised to act on the principal's behalf. In other words, the agent is being held out by the principal as having authority and the principal is then personally barred from denying this[1]. There are two instances where it usually arises. The first is where authority was conferred at one stage on the agent but has been withdrawn. Unless the principal notifies the third party of this change, the principal may be held liable for contracts made under the agent's apparent authority. The second case is where the agent has exceeded the express authority he or she has been given, but because of previous dealings between the agent and the third party, where the agent had wider authority, the third party is led to think that the agent has the same degree of authority which he or she had in those previous dealings. An example is seen in the case where a travelling salesman had called on a particular firm for many years. He was authorised to collect payment by crossed cheque made payable to the company. Several times, however, he was paid with a cheque made out to him personally and money was embezzled. In an action for payment of money due to the principal, it was held that the payments to the agent had been valid since the customer had no reason to believe that the agent was not entitled to receive payments in that way, particularly since the principal's attention had been drawn to the practice previously but it was allowed to continue[2]. In a similar case, where the agent embezzled money but the principal had no knowledge of the agent's practice of receiving payment by way of a blank cheque, and could not be said to have represented to the third party that the agent had authority to receive payment in this way, it was held that the principal was entitled to sue the third party for payment[3]. It is the possibility of the principal being held liable on a contract made within the agent's apparent authority which makes it necessary for notice to be given when a partner leaves a firm, so that the firm is no longer liable for the actings of an apparent partner[4].

Duties of the agent

The rights and duties of the agent may be dealt with expressly in the contract between the principal and the agent. In the case of commercial

---

1 *Thomas Hayman & Sons v American Cotton Oil Co* (1907) 45 SLR 207; cf *British Bata Shoe Co Ltd v Double M Shah Ltd* 1980 SC 311; *Armagas Ltd v Mundogas SA* [1986] AC 717, CA; *Capital Land Holdings Ltd v Secretary of State for the Environment (No 2)* 1995 GWD 32-1652, OH.
2 *International Sponge Importers Ltd v Andrew Watt & Sons* 1911 SC (HL) 57.
3 *British Bata Shoe Co Ltd v Double M Shah Ltd* 1980 SC 311.
4 Partnership Act 1890, s 36.

agents[1], the relevant regulations require that the agent 'must look after the interests of his principal and act dutifully and in good faith'[2]. Under the general law, the agent has several basic legal responsibilities. These are: to carry out instructions; to exercise reasonable skill and care; not to delegate work; to account for transactions he or she undertakes on the principal's behalf; and to act in good faith.

To carry out instructions

The agent has a duty to carry out what he or she has been instructed to do and if the agent fails to do so will be liable for any loss which the principal incurs. For example, where a merchant instructed a carter to deliver goods for shipment on a particular vessel, and the goods were put on the wrong vessel, the carter was held liable for the value of the goods when the ship was lost[3]. A commercial agent must make proper efforts to negotiate and, where appropriate, conclude the transactions he or she is instructed to take care of, must communicate to his or her principal all the necessary information available to him or her and must comply with reasonable instructions given by the principal[4].

To exercise reasonable skill and care

The agent must exercise due skill and care. Failure to do so will render the agent liable for any resulting damage[5]. The standard of skill and care expected has been stated as that 'of a prudent man in managing his own affairs'[6]. Where the agent is a professional person, he or she must show the degree of skill and knowledge and exercise the care of a reasonably competent and careful member of the profession in question[7]. Even where the agent acts gratuitously, he or she may be liable for failure to exercise reasonable skill and care[8]. The agent, however, is not bound to do something which an agent in his or her position would not normally be expected to do. For example, where normal practice varied as to the time when agents would advise shipments, and an agent sent notice by the first post during business hours after a shipment, it was held that the agent was not bound to advise the principal sooner, even although the delay meant that the principal had not taken out insurance to cover the shipment before it had been lost[9].

1　As defined in the Commercial Agents (Council Directive) Regulations 1993, SI 1993/3053, reg 2.
2　Ibid, reg 3(1).
3　*Gilmour v Clark* (1853) 15 D 478. See too *Alexander Graham & Co v United Turkey Red Co Ltd* 1922 SC 533; *Balsamo v Medici* [1984] 2 All ER 304.
4　Commercial Agents (Council Directive) Regulations 1993, reg 3.
5　*Stiven v Watson* (1874) 1 R 412.
6　Bell *Commentaries* I, 516.
7　*Cooke v Falconer's Representatives* (1850) 13 D 157.
8　*Copland v Brogan* 1916 SC 277.
9　*Hastie v Campbell* (1857) 19 D 557.

Non-delegation

There is a general presumption that an agent has a duty to act in person and not to delegate his or her work. This general presumption rests on the maxim *delegatus non potest delegare*, meaning that a person to whom authority has been delegated must do himself or herself what he or she has been commissioned to do. It is recognised, however, that there are many exceptions and that in many cases the agent will be either expressly or impliedly authorised to delegate. For example, in some circumstances it will be implied that an architect has authority to delegate certain work to a surveyor[1]. Where delegation is permissible, rights and duties then exist between the principal and the sub-agent. This is seen in the case of *De Bussche v Alt*[2], where a sub-agent employed to sell a ship had difficulty in finding a buyer and bought it himself for the minimum price. It was soon resold at a profit and it was held that the sub-agent was liable to account for the profit to the principal. Where a sub-agent fails in his or her duties, the main agent may be liable[3].

To account

The agent has a duty to account to the principal for transactions the agent undertakes on the principal's behalf. If there is some deficiency which the agent cannot explain, he or she will be liable to make this good, even if dishonesty cannot be proved. This is illustrated by the case of *Tyler v Logan*[4], where the manager of a shoe shop was held liable to make up a deficiency which came to light at a stocktaking, even although there was no evidence of dishonesty .

To act in good faith

An agent is generally under an overriding duty to act solely for the benefit of the principal in all matters connected with the commission, but it is clear that this does not always preclude an agent from acting for other principals too. The wording of any contract between the agent and the principal may be relevant to the question of conflicting interests. For example, in *Lothian v Jenolite Ltd*[5] the defenders appointed Lothian as sole distributors in Scotland but then terminated the contract because Lothian had agreed to sell the goods of one of their competitors as well. The Second Division considered the question of whether there was implied in the agency contract a condition that the agent would not enter into a contract which would cause a potential conflict of interests, but decided that this kind of term could not be implied. Such a term had to be expressly stated[6]. So although the mere fact of acting for one principal does not exclude an agent acting for others, there is a danger that the agent will act

1 *Black v Cornelius* (1879) 6 R 581; cf *Knox and Robb v Scottish Garden Suburb Co Ltd* 1913 SC 872.
2 (1878) 8 Ch D 286, CA.
3 *Mackersy v Ramsay, Bonar & Co* (1843) 2 Bell App 30.
4 (1904) 7 F 123.
5 1969 SC 111.
6 See eg *Alexander Graham & Co v United Turkey Red Co Ltd* 1922 SC 533.

improperly, eg by using confidential information from one source to gain advantage for another principal. This is what happened in *Liverpool Victoria Friendly Society v Houston*[1], where a former insurance agent supplied a confidential list of members to a rival society and it was stated by the court that 'the law implies a contract that the information shall not then or afterwards be ... disclosed to a third party'. The agent therefore was not entitled to make use of this information and was also held liable in damages for the loss of business which his former employer had suffered as a result[2].

If the agent's personal interests conflict with his or her duties to the principal, the agent should disclose the circumstances to the principal so that the principal may consent to the agent's acts. Otherwise the agent may be held liable to account for any secret profit made out of his or her position[3]. 'Secret profit' refers to any financial advantage which an agent receives, over and above what he or she is entitled to receive from the principal[4]. In addition to any civil remedies available to the principal, an agent who corruptly accepts or agrees to accept any reward for doing anything in relation to the principal's affairs may be liable to criminal penalties under the Prevention of Corruption Acts 1906 and 1916. The rather broadly-worded legislative requirements that a commercial agent 'must look after the interests of his principal and act dutifully and in good faith'[5] do not appear to conflict with the requirements under the general law.

Rights of the agent against the principal

The agent has certain rights which he may enforce against the principal, namely a right to remuneration; a right to relief; and a lien over the principal's property in his possession.

Remuneration

The agent has a right to remuneration. The amount of the agent's remuneration or commission may be expressly provided for in the contract of agency but if not it will be fixed according to what is customary in the particular trade or profession. Failing this, it will be fixed on a *quantum meruit* basis (ie as much as he or she has earned)[6]. In the case of commercial agents, the relevant regulations provide that, in the absence of agreement, the agent will be entitled to the customary remuneration in the place where the activities are carried on and, failing that, to reasonable remuneration taking into account all aspects of the transaction[7]. The duty of the

---

1 (1900) 3 F 42.
2 (1900) 3 F 42 at 47, per Lord Pearson.
3 *Boardman v Phipps* [1967] 2 AC 46, HL; *Regal (Hastings) Ltd v Gulliver* [1967] 2 AC 134, HL; *Industrial Development Consultants Ltd v Cooley* [1972] 2 All ER 162; *Logicrose Ltd v Southend United Football Club Ltd* [1988] 1 WLR 1256.
4 *Industries and General Mortgage Co v Lewis* [1949] 2 All ER 573; *Trans Barwil Agencies (UK) Ltd v John S Braid & Co Ltd* 1988 SC 222.
5 Commercial Agents (Council Directive) Regulations 1993, reg 3(1).
6 *Kennedy v Glass* (1890) 17 R 1085.
7 Commercial Agents (Council Directive) Regulations 1993, reg 6(1).

principal to pay remuneration arises only when the agent has earned it, but the problem which may arise is how to determine when the agent has earned it. In the case of commercial agents, detailed rules about entitlement to commission on transactions concluded both during the agency contract and after its termination, including rules about apportionment between new and previous agents, are contained in the 1993 Regulations[1]. In other cases, much depends on the wording (if any) of the agency contract. The case of *Dudley Bros & Co v Barnet*[2] provides a good illustration, where estate agents had contracted to find a purchaser for a lease and stated their commission 'in the event of business resulting through our efforts'. They found a suitable purchaser but the principal said he had accepted an offer from someone else. It was held that the estate agents, on finding a person willing to contract on the terms required, were entitled to their commission. In *Luxor (Eastbourne) Ltd v Cooper*[3] however, where the agent was denied commission because a sale did not take place although a willing purchaser had been introduced, it was held that a term could not be implied in the agreement to the effect that the principal would not dispose of the property himself nor act in such a way as to prevent the agent from earning his commission[4]. In contrast, in *Alpha Trading Ltd v Dunnshaw-Patten Ltd*[5], it was held that a term could be implied which entitled the agents to recover the amount of their commission. In that case, the agents had introduced a buyer to the principal, who was selling certain goods, and a contract for the sale of the goods was made. The seller, however, failed to perform the contract and the agents argued successfully that they were entitled to damages for breach of an implied term that the principal would not break the contract with the third party and thus deprive the agents of their commission. In *Chris Hart (Business Sales) Ltd v Currie*[6], it was held that, on a correct interpretation of the contract between principal and agent, estate agents were entitled to commission where missives had been completed for the sale of a public house but then fell in terms of a suspensive condition when the purchaser failed to obtain the transfer of the licence. In *Stuart Wyse Ogilvie Estates Ltd v Bryant*[7] it was held that estate agents were entitled to their fee in terms of an agency agreement. In that case the seller had intimated that he wished to withdraw the property from sale, arguably triggering termination of the agency agreement, but he then accepted an offer from a purchaser who had been introduced during the period of the agency. It was held that since the agreement was not terminated until the requisite period of notice had expired, it was still operative when missives were concluded and in any case the purchaser had been introduced during the period when the estate agent had sole selling rights.

1 Ibid, regs 7–12. See *Kontogeorgas v Kartonpak AE* [1997] 1 CMLR 1093.
2 1937 SC 632.
3 [1941] AC 108, HL.
4 See too *Marcan Shipping (London) Ltd v Polish Steamship Co* [1989] 2 Lloyd's Rep 138, CA.
5 [1981] QB 290.
6 1992 SLT 544.
7 1995 GWD 27-1429.

Relief

The agent has a right to be relieved of all liabilities and reimbursed for losses and expenses incurred in carrying out the undertaking. For example, a principal was held liable to relieve stockbrokers when he instructed them to sell shares which he did not have and the stockbrokers were held liable to pay damages to the purchaser[1]. The duty of the principal to reimburse the agent may be expressly stated in the contract of agency, but usually it will be implied and therefore the extent of the principal's liability depends on the kind of business the agent is employed to do. An agent is entitled to be indemnified for the costs of defending an action as long the agent is acting within the scope of his or her authority[2]. Where a firm of solicitors granted a letter of obligation, relying on inaccurate information supplied by the principal, and then incurred expense in instructing building works and settling an action raised against them, it was held that they were entitled to recover their expenses[3]. In another case it was held that a company director, who had incurred expenses in defending himself on criminal charges relating to fraudulent misappropriation of the company's funds and the fraudulent issue of a prospectus, was not entitled to be indemnified on the ground that his alleged actions were not actions which it was his duty to do and the expenses were not incurred in the discharge of his duties as the company's agent but were incurred as a personal misfortune[4].

Lien

The agent has a lien over the principal's property in his possession, such as money, goods or documents of debt, and by this lien can secure payment of his or her remuneration. Apart from the general lien which is recognised by the custom of certain trades and professions, eg the banker's lien[5] and the solicitor's lien[6], factors or mercantile agents have a general lien over the principal's property which has come into their possession in the course of their employment[7]. This general lien extends to stockbrokers[8] and auctioneers[9]. It covers all claims which the agent may have against the principal arising out of the agency, including commission or other remuneration, reimbursement of expenses and other relief. Accountants do not have a general lien for the whole of their professional account, but have a special lien over papers in their possession for the particular work done in connection with those papers[10].

---

1 *Stevenson & Sons v Duncan* (1842) 5 D 167. See too *Robinson and Fleming v Middleton* (1859) 21 D 1089.
2 *Re Famatina Development Corpn Ltd* [1914] 2 Ch 271.
3 *Marshall Wilson Dean & Turnbull v Feymac Properties Ltd* 1996 GWD 22-1247.
4 *Tomlinson v Scottish Amalgamated Silks Liquidator* 1935 SC (HL) 1.
5 Bell *Principles* s 1451.
6 *Paul v Meikle* (1868) 7 M 235; *Drummond v Muirhead and Guthrie Smith* (1900) 2 F 585.
7 Bell *Principles* s 1445; *Sibbald v Gibson and Clark* (1852) 15 D 217. See too *Powdrill v Murrayhead Ltd* 1996 GWD 34-2011, OH.
8 *Glendinning v John D Hope & Co* 1911 SC (HL) 73.
9 *Miller v Hutcheson and Dixon* (1881) 8 R 489.
10 *Findlay (Liquidator of Scottish Workmen's Assurance Co Ltd) v Waddell* 1910 SC 670.

RELATIONSHIP OF THIRD PARTIES TO AGENT AND PRINCIPAL

Contractual liability

The purpose of agency is to enable the agent to effect legal relations between the principal and third parties. In dealings with third parties, however, the agent may act in one of several different ways and the question as to whether liability for the agent's acting will fall on the agent, or on the principal, or on both, will depend generally on the manner in which the agent contracts. Broadly, there are two ways in which the agent may operate. First, the agent may contract expressly as agent on behalf of a disclosed principal, either on behalf of a named principal or on behalf of a principal who is unnamed but whose existence has been disclosed. Second, the agent may contract without disclosing the existence of the principal at all, so that it appears to the third party that the agent is contracting as principal himself or herself. Each of these cases, and its consequences, will now be considered.

Agent acts expressly as agent for a named or identifiable principal

Where an agent, who has authority to do so, contracts on behalf of a named principal, the general rule is that the agent is not a party to the contract, cannot sue on it and is not liable to be sued on it[1]. The same applies where the principal has not been named specifically but is nevertheless identifiable. For example, in the case of *Armour v TL Duff & Co*[2], steamship owners and brokers ordered goods to be supplied to a named ship. The supplier sent the account to Duff & Co, believing they were the owners of the ship, but they refused to pay and it was held that they had been acting effectively as agent for a disclosed principal since the third party could have ascertained the name of the ship's owners from the Register of Shipping. It is recognised, however, that in certain circumstances the agent may be personally liable even where he or she is acting for a named principal. Whether the agent is liable or not will depend on the wording of the contract or the intention of the parties. The custom of a particular trade or profession may be that an agent incurs personal liability even when contracting as an agent. For example, solicitors have been held personally liable on certain undertakings given in the course of transactions on behalf of clients[3], and, unless a disclaimer is made, will be liable for fees and outlays when employing another solicitor on a client's business[4]. Where an agent is contracting for a foreign principal, the facts and the custom in a particular trade may indicate that the agent may be personally liable, but the fact that the principal is foreign does not in itself raise any presumption to that effect[5].

1 *Stone & Rolfe Ltd v Kimber Coal Co Ltd* 1926 SC (HL) 45; *McIvor v Roy* 1970 SLT (Sh Ct) 58.
2 1912 SC 120.
3 *British Paints Ltd v Smith* (1960) SLT (Sh Ct) 45; *Johnston v Little* 1960 SLT 129, OH; *Muirhead v Gribben* 1983 SLT (Sh Ct) 102. Cf *Digby Brown & Co v Lyall* 1995 SCLR 572.
4 Solicitors (Scotland) Act 1980, s 30.
5 *Millar v Mitchell* (1860) 22 D 833; *Teheran-Europe Co v ST Belton (Tractors) Ltd* [1968] 2 QB 545, CA.

An agent may be personally liable if he or she contracts on behalf of an unincorporated body which cannot be sued as an entity[1], although in some such cases, where it is possible to identify clear responsibilities amongst those responsible for management, it may be possible to argue that those (eg a management committee) who have endorsed the agent's acts, should be liable as principal[2]. Where an agent purports to act on behalf of a company which has not yet been formed, the agent will incur personal liability subject to any agreement to the contrary[3]. Where, in dealings with the Inland Revenue, the son of a deceased person purported to act as the 'personal representative' of the deceased, although he was not a trustee or executor, no agency was created and he was held to be personally liable on the undertakings given to the Inland Revenue[4].

Agent acts expressly as agent for an unnamed principal whose existence is disclosed

Where an agent, who has authority, contracts expressly as agent but does not identify the principal for whom he or she acts, the position is, on the whole, the same as if the principal had been named. The issue is likely to revolve around the question of whether the third party entered the contract looking to the credit of the unnamed principal or to the credit of the agent and, as in the case of a named principal, the custom of a particular trade may be relevant. The question of liability becomes more critical, however, if in the end of the day the agent refuses to disclose the identity of the principal and thus denies the third party a remedy against the principal. In such a case, the agent may be held liable[5], but it may be necessary to assess all the facts and circumstances to ascertain whether the third party ought to have known or could readily have discovered the identity of the principal, or had relied on the credit of the agent, as in one case where a firm of builders had carried out work on the instructions of architects against a background of prior dealings in which the architects had acted as agents for a client who had since died[6].

It should be noted that where an agent contracts expressly as agent for a disclosed principal, the agent warrants that he or she has the necessary authority and may be liable to the third party for any loss incurred through breach of the agent's implied warranty[7].

Agent acts as apparent principal

Where an agent with authority contracts ostensibly as principal, the position generally is that both the agent and the 'hidden' principal are liable on the contract and are entitled to sue upon it. This case, where an agent

---

1 *Cromarty Leasing Ltd v Turnbull* 1988 SLT (Sh Ct) 62.
2 *Thomson and Gillespie v Victoria Eighty Club* (1905) 43 SLR 628.
3 Companies Act 1985, s 36C.
4 *Lord Advocate v Chung* 1995 SLT 65.
5 *Gibb v Cunningham & Robertson* 1925 SLT 608. See too *Brydon v Muir* (1869) 7 M 536.
6 *P & M Sinclair v Bamber Gray Partnership* 1987 SLT 674. See too *Boyter v Thomson* 1995 SCLR 1009, HL.
7 *Anderson v Croall & Sons Ltd* (1903) 6 F 153.

has authority but does not tell the third party that he or she is acting as agent, can be distinguished from the case where an agent acts ostensibly as principal and does not have any authority to act as agent, although he or she may intend to contract for the benefit of someone else. In the latter case, an example of which is seen in *Keighley Maxsted & Co v Durant*[1], the supposed principal cannot sue or be sued on the contract. In the former case, the agent renders himself or herself personally liable because the third party naturally thinks that the agent is the principal and has no one else to look to for performance of the contract. In this type of case, however, it is established that the principal may disclose himself or herself and sue on the contract and, once the principal's identity has been established, he or she may be sued on the contract. An example is seen in *Bennett v Inveresk Paper Co*[2] where a contract was made by Bennett, acting through a London agent, for the supply of paper to him in Australia. The paper was found to be damaged upon arrival and it was held that Bennett had title to sue on the contract even although the supplier had not known of him at the time the contract was made.

In this type of case, where the third party seeks eg to have the contract performed or to raise an action against the other contracting party, and the identity of the principal has been revealed, the third party must elect whether to sue the agent or the principal. In other words, the liability of the agent and the principal is alternative liability rather than joint and several liability[3]. Once the third party has elected whether to sue the agent or the principal, that election is final[4]. A question which sometimes arises however is how to decide when an election has been made. Raising an action against one party is not conclusive evidence of election[5], although where an action was raised against an agent and the principal became known during the course of a proof, it was held that by continuing the action to decree, the third party had elected to treat the agent as the debtor and that the agent was therefore entitled to counterclaim for damages against the third party[6]. In certain circumstances a party's conduct may amount to election, as in the case where a horse bought at auction had been warranted to be a good worker but was found to be unsound. The owner's name was disclosed and the buyer returned the horse to him and brought an action against both the auctioneer and the original owner. It was held that returning the horse to the original owner constituted an election to treat him as the party responsible and that this precluded an action against the auctioneer[7].

Delictual liability

Broadly speaking the general principles relating to vicarious liability, whereby an employer may be held liable for the wrongful or negligent

---

1 [1901] AC 240.
2 (1891) 18 R 975. See too *Siu v Eastern Insurance Co Ltd* [1994] 2 AC 199, PC.
3 *David Logan & Son Ltd v Schuldt* (1903) 10 SLT 598, OH; *British Bata Shoe Co Ltd v Double M Shah Ltd* 1980 SC 311.
4 Bell *Commentaries* I, 537.
5 *Meier & Co v Küchenmeister* (1881) 8 R 642.
6 *A F Craig & Co v Blackater* 1923 SC 472. See too *James Laidlaw & Sons Ltd v Griffin* 1968 SLT 278.
7 *Ferrier v Dods* (1865) 3 M 561.

acts of his or her employee committed within the scope of his or her employment[1], apply to the relationship of principal and agent. In the case of agency, the test of whether the principal is vicariously liable will be whether the agent was acting within the scope of his or her authority[2]. One example is the provision made in s 10 of the Partnership Act 1890, which imposes vicarious liability on the firm for loss or injury caused by any wrongful act or omission of any partner acting in the ordinary course of the business of the firm, or with the authority of his or her co-partners. This section also illustrates another important aspect of vicarious liability, namely, that the original wrongdoer remains liable, and the third party has a choice as to whether to sue the principal (in this case the firm) or the agent (in this case the partner). Where a question arises as to possible vicarious liability, it will be important to consider whether the relationship is truly that of agency, with the agent acting within the scope of his or her authority, or is perhaps that of employer and independent contractor acting outwith the control of the employer, since in the latter case the principle of vicarious liability will not necessarily apply[3]. It is interesting to note, however, that the Crown is vicariously liable for the delicts of its servants or agents, including independent contractors[4].

TERMINATION OF AGENCY

The agency relationship may be terminated either by an act of the parties or by operation of law.

By act of the parties

If there is an express provision in the agency contract for termination, it will terminate according to that provision[5]. The agency may be brought to an end by subsequent mutual agreement of the parties. Alternatively there may be a unilateral act by one of the parties ending the agency. It is possible, but unusual, for the agency to be irrevocable by the principal without the agent's consent[6], but in any case where the principal does revoke the agent's authority, the principal should be careful to ensure that he or she will not be bound by any further transactions entered into by the agent, on the basis that principal continues to hold out the agent as having authority. Notice of withdrawal of the agent's authority should be given to those with whom the agent has had dealings and, depending on the cir-

1 Bell *Principles* s 547.
2 *Laing v Provincial Homes Investment Co Ltd* 1909 SC 812 at 827–829; *Percy v Glasgow Corpn* 1922 SC (HL) 144 at 151, per Viscount Haldane. See too *Armagas Ltd v Mundogas SA* [1986] 1 AC 717, CA.
3 For further discussion, see *Fridman* ch 13; *Bowstead and Reynolds* ch 8, paras 8-174 to 8-194; Gloag and Henderson *The Law of Scotland* (10th edn, 1995) (eds Wilson, Forte et al) pp 539–548.
4 Crown Proceedings Act 1947, ss 2, 38(2).
5 *Brenan v Campbell's Trs* (1898) 25 R 423; *Stuart Wyse Ogilvie Estates Ltd v Bryant* 1995 GWD 27-1429.
6 *Premier Briquette Co Ltd v Gray* 1922 SC 329.

cumstances, it may be advisable to give notice more generally[1]. Where, however, the third party dealing with the agent should have been put on inquiry, the principal may not be liable[2]. Where the principal revokes the agent's authority, or where the agent renounces his or her agency, there may be (depending on interpretation of the contract) breach of an express or implied term of the agency contract and consequent liability for damages[3].

By operation of law

The contract of agency may be terminated by operation of law. The death of either the principal or the agent will operate to terminate the contract[4]. Insanity may also operate to terminate the contract, on the ground that in general an insane person cannot validly contract, but it is arguable that the temporary insanity of the principal will not result in termination of the agency[5]. The bankruptcy or liquidation of the principal operates to terminate the agency[6]. As regards the insolvency of the agent, the question may depend on whether it is an express or implied term of the contract of agency that the agent will continue to be solvent. As in the general law of contract, where it becomes impossible or illegal to perform the contract, the contract will be terminated by operation of law[7].

Termination of commercial agency contracts

Some special rules apply in relation to the termination of commercial agency contracts. A commercial agency contract concluded for a fixed period, which continues to be performed by both parties after that period has expired, is deemed to be converted into an agency contract for an indefinite period[8]. Where the contract is for an indefinite period, either party may terminate it but must give at least the minimum period of notice. This period depends on how long the contract has been in force and ranges from one month for the first year of the contract to three months for the third year commenced and subsequent years[9]. Only in exceptional circumstances or where one party has failed to carry out his or her obligations under the contract, may the contract be terminated with immediate effect[10]. A commercial agent is entitled to either indemnity or

---

1 See eg Partnership Act 1890 ss 36(1), (2).
2 *North of Scotland Banking Co v Behn Möller & Co* (1881) 8 R 423.
3 *Galbraith and Moorhead v Arethusa Shipping Co Ltd* (1896) 23 R 1011; *North American & Continental Sales Inc v Bepi (Electronics) Ltd* 1982 SLT 47; cf *Patmore & Co v B Cannon & Co Ltd* (1892) 19 R 1004; *SS State of California Co Ltd v Moore* (1895) 22 R 562.
4 *Life Association of Scotland v Douglas* (1886) 13 R 910.
5 *Wink v Mortimer* (1849) 11 D 995. See too Law Reform (Miscellaneous Provisions) (Scotland) Act 1990, s 71, relating to formal appointments of agents by factory and commission or power of attorney.
6 *McKenzie v Campbell* (1894) 21 R 904; *SS State of California Co Ltd v Moore* (1895) 22 R 562.
7 *Boston Deep Sea Fishing and Ice Co Ltd v Farnham* [1957] 3 All ER 204.
8 Commercial Agents (Council Directive) Regulations 1993, reg 14.
9 Ibid, regs 15, 22.
10 Ibid, reg 16.

compensation on termination of the contract (eg where the principal continues to derive substantial benefit from customers as a result of the agent's efforts[1]) or where the agent is unable to amortise costs and expenses incurred on the advice of his or her principal[2]. The agent must notify his or her principal within one year of termination that he or she intends to pursue his or her entitlement[3], and in certain circumstances payment will be excluded, eg where the principal was justified in terminating the contract immediately[4], or the commercial agent, with the agreement of the principal, assigns his or her rights and duties under the contract to another person[5].

1 Ibid, reg 17(3).
2 Ibid, reg 17(7).
3 Ibid, reg 17(9).
4 Ibid, reg 18(a).
5 Ibid, reg 18(c).

9 Partnership

INTRODUCTION

Sources of partnership law

The law which applies to partnerships is derived from several sources, primarily the Partnership Act 1890, a codifying statute which assimilated much, but not all, of the Scots and English law. Prior to that the law had been developed by the courts in each jurisdiction, giving rise to some differences in the case law. In many instances these differences were attributable to differences in other relevant branches of the law in the two jurisdictions[1]. The 1890 Act provides in s 46 that existing rules of equity and common law are to continue in force except where they are inconsistent with the provisions of the Act. In addition to the rules in the 1890 Act and the case law on partnerships arising from the Act and prior to it, a number of other relevant rules are found in statutes such as the Companies Act 1985, the Business Names Act 1985 and the Limited Partnerships Act 1907. Many rules of the law of property, the law of contract and the law of delict are also particularly relevant to partnerships.

Meaning of 'partnership'

The partnership is a form of business organisation, used as a trading medium by many different types of businesses, ranging from small family businesses, run by perhaps only two or three persons, to international firms of accountants with hundreds of partners. The statutory definition of partnership is 'the relation which subsists between persons carrying on a business in common with a view of profit', but excluding the relation between the members of a registered company or other incorporated body[2]. The expression 'business' includes every trade, occupation or profession[3]. There must be an intention to make a commercial gain from the business[4]. Even where parties carrying on a business have made no express agreement to do so in partnership, it is possible that a partnership may be inferred from the circumstances and that as a result the legal rules relating to partnerships will apply to govern their relationship with persons dealing with them and also their relationship amongst themselves.

---

1 For a discussion of the historical influences on Scots partnership law, see Clark *The Law of Partnership and Joint Stock Companies according to the Law of Scotland* (1886).
2 Partnership Act 1890, s 1: hereinafter referred to as the 1890 Act.
3 1890 Act, s 45.
4 *Religious Tract and Book Society v Inland Revenue* (1896) 23 R 390; cf *Inland Revenue Comrs v Falkirk Temperance Cafe Trust* 1927 SC 261.

Choice of partnership as a business medium

In some cases a partnership is the obvious choice of medium for carrying on a particular business. The rules of certain professions, notably dentistry and medicine, point to the suitability of using the partnership form[1]. For example, statutory rules prohibit corporate bodies from carrying on the business of dentistry except in very limited circumstances[2]. Some professions, including the legal profession, which previously required business to be carried on in partnership (except in the case of sole practitioners), now permit the use of a registered company subject to certain safeguards for those dealing with the company[3]. A new form of limited liability partnership for professions has been proposed, with the object of enabling businesses in regulated professions to adopt a form of organisation which is now available in a number of other jurisdictions[4]. In many cases, however, and particularly in the case of trading firms, the choice of business medium may be made from a number of options such as the sole trader, partnership, limited partnership, private limited or unlimited company or public limited company registered under the Companies Act 1985. Whilst taxation considerations will often play a major part in deciding on the most suitable business medium, there are other factors which are relevant. For example, the extent and cost of complying with the relevant legal regime may influence choice.

Relatively little formality is involved in setting up a partnership, even where a formal agreement is to be drawn up. For small businesses particularly, the Companies Acts impose a considerable burden of administration, despite attempts in recent years to 'deregulate' in respect of smaller companies: eg by relaxing some of the requirements in relation to audited accounts. Privacy in financial matters is generally easier to achieve in a partnership, as there is no requirement of public disclosure of the partnership accounts. There may also be more flexibility in managing a partnership, where the partners may simply agree amongst themselves on changes to their original agreement, although unanimity amongst the partners will be required for certain major changes such as the introduction of a new partner. In a registered company, formal alterations to a company's memorandum and articles of association will require a certain majority. The creation of a variety of different membership rights may be easier to achieve in a company, where different classes of share can be created to reflect different interests, and it may be easier to transfer shares to outsiders, although there may be provisions in the company's memorandum and articles restricting such transfers. The likely future borrowing requirements of the business may be an important consideration. Where a lender requires security for repayment of a loan, companies, unlike partnerships, may grant a floating charge over any of the company's property[5]. In a limited company, the liability of the members is limited to the

---

1 For discussion, see Banks *Encyclopaedia of Professional Partnerships*.
2 Dentists Act 1984, ss 42–44.
3 See eg Solicitors (Scotland) Act 1980, s 34(1A); Solicitors (Scotland) (Incorporated Practices) Practice Rules 1987.
4 *Limited Liability Partnership : A New Form of Business Association for Professions* (Department of Trade and Industry, 1997).
5 Companies Act 1985, s 462.

amount they agree to subscribe for shares (or, in the case of a company limited by guarantee, the amount they guarantee to contribute in a winding up of the company). The liability of partners, on the other hand, is an unlimited joint and several liability for the debts and obligations of the firm. Although limitation of liability is often heralded as the most obvious reason for forming a company rather than a partnership, this advantage is reduced in many cases by the fact that banks and other lenders will often require personal guarantees from directors of companies, in addition to other forms of security. For some businesses, start-up finance may be more readily available if the business is carried on in a particular form: eg a co-operative formed under the Industrial and Provident Societies Acts 1965–1978. Where two or more existing organisations or other persons decide to embark on a new joint project, they may choose either to form a new registered company for the purpose, or to embark on the joint venture as a partnership governed by the Partnership Act 1890 or, if the purpose of the project is to co-operate in carrying on certain types of business activity across national frontiers, to form a European Economic Interest Grouping, a body corporate in which each member will have unlimited joint and several liability for the debts and liabilities of the grouping[1]. Other European initiatives have resulted in proposals for a European Company (Societas Europaea) and other forms of European business association such as a European Co-operative Society and a European Mutual Society[2]. In many cases however, after all the factors have been considered, it is the relative privacy in financial matters which persuades business persons to opt for a partnership, despite the consequent exposure to personal liability.

Different types of partnership

Most partnerships take the form of general trading partnerships, sometimes referred to simply as 'general partnerships'. A partnership which is formed for only one particular transaction or is limited in its purpose or duration is a 'joint adventure' or 'joint venture'[3]. A joint adventure, such as a fishing trip undertaken for profit, is simply a species of partnership and in most essential respects is not distinguishable from general partnership[4]. An agreement to develop a particular piece of land, with provision for sharing of profits between the parties, is a typical example of a joint venture[5]. A distinctive form of partnership is provided for under the Limited Partnerships Act 1907, which provides a legal mechanism for persons to invest capital in a firm without risk of further liability. A limited partnership must be registered as such[6] and there must be at least one general partner who has unlimited liability for the debts of the business and who will take part in the management of the firm, and at least one limited

1 See European Economic Interest Grouping Regulations 1989, SI 1989/638.
2 For discussion of these, see *Palmer's Company Law* paras 16.418–16.429.
3 For discussion, see *Miller on Partnership* (2nd edn 1994, by G Brough) ch 15.
4 See *Mair v Wood* 1948 SC 83 at 86, per Lord Cooper.
5 *White v McIntyre* (1841) 3 D 334.
6 Limited Partnerships Act 1907, s 5.

partner whose liability is limited to the amount contributed on entering the firm but who is not entitled to take part in the management of the firm[1]. A limited partner who participates in management loses the benefit of limited liability[2]. Similar restrictions as apply to general partnerships regarding the maximum number of members apply to limited partnerships too[3].

Different types of partner

It is not necessary that the partners should be natural persons and it is quite competent to form a partnership between an individual and a company or between two or more companies. By creating a partnership where all the partners are limited companies, a form of limited liability can be achieved, but such a partnership is subject to rules requiring preparation and disclosure of accounts[4]. Sometimes a distinction is made between a 'salaried partner' and a 'profit-sharing' partner. Since a partner is ultimately liable jointly and severally for the firm's debts, there appears to be a degree of inequity in calling someone a partner and exposing him or her to unlimited liability but at the same time simply paying that person a salary in the same way as any other employee. The term 'salaried partner' has, therefore, given rise to some debate about the precise status of such a person. Can a person be a true partner if he or she does not share in the profits of the firm? The question of partners' rights to share in profits, in the absence of other agreement, is discussed below, but it may be useful at this stage to note that in practice, on accepting an offer to become a partner on a fixed salary, the person's name will usually appear as a partner on the firm's notepaper and it will be announced that he or she has become a partner in the firm. Often such a person will be indemnified by the other partners against any liability for losses, by virtue of the partnership agreement. In *Stekel v Ellice*[5] Megarry J observed that:

> '*Quoad* the outside world it often will matter little whether a man is a full partner or a salaried partner; for a salaried partner is held out as being a partner, and the partners will be liable for his acts accordingly. But within the partnership it may be important to know whether a salaried partner is truly to be classified as a mere employee, or as a partner. ... It seems to me impossible to say that as a matter of law a salaried partner is or is not necessarily a partner in the true sense. He may or may not be a partner, depending on the facts. What must be done, I think, is to look at the substance of the relationship between the parties; and there is ample authority for saying that the question whether or not there is a partnership depends on what the true relationship is, and not on any mere label attached to that relationship'.

1 1907 Act, s 4.
2 1907 Act, s 6(1).
3 Companies Act 1985, s 716; Limited Partnerships (Unrestricted Size) (No 1) Regulations 1971, SI 1971/782; Limited Partnerships (Unrestricted Size) (No 2) Regulations 1990, SI 1990/1580; Limited Partnerships (Unrestricted Size) (No 3) Regulations 1992, SI 1992/1027.
4 Partnerships and Unlimited Companies (Accounts) Regulations 1993, SI 1993/1820.
5 [1973] 1 All ER 465 at 472, 473, per Megarry J.

It has been suggested that in general, rather than treating salaried partners as merely being 'held out' as partners, it is preferable to view them as full partners in the firm whose rights, as between the partners, have been varied in a number of ways[1] and this appears to be the better view, certainly where there is clear evidence that it has been announced to the outside world that someone is to become a partner.

CONSTITUTION OF PARTNERSHIP

Partnership contract

As noted above, the statutory definition of partnership is 'the relation which exists between persons carrying on a business with a view of profit'[2]. The Partnership Act 1890 does not state how this relation arises, but it is clearly based on a consensual contract, either express or implied[3]. The best evidence of the agreement is provided where the partnership agreement is in writing, but the existence of a partnership may also be established by any other competent evidence. For example, where parties had shared an office and office staff, had kept ledgers to cover their joint interests and had sent out accounts jointly, it was established that a partnership existed[4]. All the circumstances must be considered in deciding whether a partnership exists. It was argued recently by a London-based surveyor working with a firm of surveyors, which had offices in Scotland and London, that he was a partner only in the 'London partnership', which was separate and distinct from the Scottish partnership. His name was not on the notepaper used in Scotland and he did not share in the profits of the Scottish business. Taking into consideration a number of factors relating to the organisation of the business, it was decided by the Inner House (reversing the decision of the Outer House on this point) that the London firm was a separate entity, and that the London-based surveyor was a partner only in the London firm and was therefore not liable along with the partners in the Scottish firm for a negligent valuation by a partner in the Scottish firm[5]. A common economic interest will not always be regarded as sufficient to indicate a partnership or a joint venture, since some degree of common interest is involved in any contractual commercial enterprise. For example, where parties had entered into what was effectively a commercial rent-sharing scheme relating to a single asset, it was held that no partnership or joint venture existed. There was no sharing of profit and loss, no *delectus personae*, and no trace of mutual agency, all factors which might be indicative of partnership. In terms of the detailed agreement, payments representing a return on the capital invest-

---

1 *Miller on Partnership* p 152. For further discussion, see Styles 'The Salaried Partner' (1994) 39 JLSS 254.
2 1890 Act, s 1(1).
3 See Stair *Institutions* I, 16, 1; Bell *Commentaries* II, 510, 511.
4 *Morrison v Service* (1879) 6 R 1158.
5 *Mortgage Express Ltd v Dunsmore Reid & Smith* 1996 GWD 40-2295, IH; 1996 GWD 10-590, OH.

ment were to be made and there was nothing which inferred the existence of a partnership in order to make the scheme capable of operating effectively[1]. The whole circumstances of the case must be looked at and even where parties expressly declare that they are not to be held partners, a partnership may still be constituted[2]. Where there is no express agreement, agreement may be implied by the conduct of the parties, having regard to the statutory rules provided for determining the existence of partnership[3].

Statutory rules

The Partnership Act 1890 provides rules for determining whether a partnership does or does not exist[4]. These are a re-enactment of rules originally contained in 'Bovill's Act', which was passed in 1865 to regulate the liabilities of persons sharing profits. The first rule is that owning property jointly or in common does not of itself create a partnership, even where profits from its use are shared[5]. The second rule is that the sharing of gross returns does not of itself create a partnership[6]. The third rule relates to the sharing of profits, as opposed to gross returns. Until the case of *Cox v Hickman* was decided in 1860[7], there had been an irrebuttable presumption at common law that participation in the profits of a business was sufficient to establish the relation of partnership. In *Badeley v Consolidated Bank*[8] it was decided that the fact that two persons are sharing in the profits of a business will, in the absence of explanation, lead to the conclusion that a partnership exists; but if participation in profits is merely one of a set of relevant facts, all the circumstances must be considered in arriving at the real intention of the parties. The statutory rule embodies this approach by providing that the receipt by a person of a share of the profits does not of itself create a partnership, although it is prima facie evidence of partnership[9]. The Act gives five examples of instances where the question of profit-sharing may arise:

(1) where someone receives payment of a debt out of the profits of a business[10];
(2) where a servant or agent is remunerated by way of a share in the profits[11];
(3) where the widow or child of a deceased partner receives part of the profits as an annuity[12];

---

1 *Dollar Land (Cumbernauld) Ltd v CIN Properties Ltd* 1996 SLT 186, OH.
2 *McCosh v Brown & Co's Tr* (1890) 1 F (HL) 86; *Stewart v Buchanan* (1903) 6 F 15.
3 1890 Act, s 2.
4 1890 Act, s 2. For a full discussion of these rules, see *Miller on Partnership* ch 3.
5 1890 Act, s 2(1). See also *Moore v Dempster* (1879) 6 R 930; *Davis v Davis* [1894] 1 Ch 393.
6 1890 Act s 2(2); *Clark v GR and W Jamieson* 1909 SC 132; *Cox v Coulson* [1916] 2 KB 177.
7 (1860) 8 HL Cas 268.
8 (1888) 38 Ch D 238, CA.
9 1890 Act, s 2(3).
10 1890 Act, s 2(3)(a).
11 1890 Act, s 2(3)(b).
12 1890 Act, s 2(3)(c).

(4) where someone receives a loan in connection with a business and the contract provides that the lender is to receive a share of the profits or a rate of interest varying with the profits[1]; or
(5) where someone sells the goodwill of a business and receives a portion of the profits as payment[2].

In all these cases, the whole circumstances will be relevant in deciding whether or not a partnership exists.

Content of partnership agreement

The partnership agreement regulates the relations of the partners amongst themselves. Many of the disputes which arise in relation to partnerships, particularly where a partner dies or retires, are due to lack of foresight in drafting the partnership agreement. In the absence of contrary agreement, certain provisions of the 1890 Act will apply[3]. For example, the Act provides that if nothing to the contrary has been agreed between the partners, all partners are entitled to share equally in the capital and profits of the business and must contribute equally towards the losses[4]. If a question arises which is not covered by the agreement or by the terms of the 1890 Act, it will be determined according to general principles[5].

A specific statement in the partnership agreement of what constitutes partnership property[6], and the partners' entitlement to share in the firm's assets, may help to resolve any dispute at a later stage. Some thought should also be given to the question of how an outgoing partner's share is to be ascertained[7] and whether, eg, it is to be payable in a lump sum or in instalments. Goodwill is sometimes ignored or written off, but if it is treated as an asset of the firm some arrangement for its valuation and purchase should be specified: eg by way of a preferential share of the profits or an annuity. The possible taxation implications when a partner leaves the partnership should also be considered so that provision can be made if necessary for appropriate indemnities to be given.

Restrictive covenants are commonly found in partnership agreements but must be carefully drafted if they are to be enforceable[8]. Apart from general matters of administration, such as the preparation of accounts, provision is sometimes also made for a power of expulsion, notice of retiral, and assignation of a partner's share. The agreement will often also contain provision for reference of any disputes to arbitration[9].

---

1 1890 Act, s 2(3)(d).
2 1890 Act, s 2(3)(e).
3 1890 Act, ss 19–31.
4 1890 Act, s 24, para (1).
5 See *Smith v Jeyes* (1841) 4 Beav 503 at 505, per Lord Langdale.
6 See 'Partnership property' below.
7 See 'Ascertainment of retiring or deceased partner's share' below.
8 *Scottish Farmers' Dairy Co (Glasgow) Ltd v McGhee* 1933 SC 148; *Anthony v Rennie* 1981 SLT (Notes) 11; *Deacons v Bridge* [1984] AC 705; *Dallas McMillan and Sinclair v Simpson* 1989 SLT 454, OH; *Cameron v Mathieson* 1994 GWD 29-1740.
9 For further discussion of the contents of a partnership agreement, see Banks *Lindley & Banks on Partnership* (17th edn, 1995) ch 10.

Number of partners

By definition partnership requires the association of two or more persons. A general restriction on the size of partnerships is contained in the Companies Act 1985, which prohibits the formation of partnerships of more than twenty persons, except for solicitors, accountants and members of a recognised stock exchange (in which cases the partners must be professionally qualified as specified in the Act), and certain partnerships carrying on re-insurance business[1]. In addition, the Secretary of State has power to provide for further exemptions from the general restriction and has exercised this power in relation to a number of types of professional partnership where a specified proportion of partners must be professionally qualified, namely: surveyors, auctioneers, valuers, estate agents, land agents and estate managers, actuaries, consulting engineers, building designers, loss adjusters, insurance brokers, town planners; certain multinational lawyers' partnerships; certain partnerships involving Stock Exchange member firms; and partnerships of patent agents and registered trade mark agents. These exemptions are set out in an extensive series of regulations[2].

Capacity

The general law governing capacity to contract applies to contracts of partnership. For example, an insane person has no power to contract and is therefore incapable of becoming a partner. A person between sixteen and eighteen years of age has full capacity to contract on his or her own behalf, and the general right to have a transaction set aside before the person reaches the age of twenty-one, on the ground that it was greatly prejudicial, does not apply to any transaction entered in the course of the young person's trade, business or profession[3]. Where war breaks out and a partner becomes an alien enemy, the partnership is dissolved[4].

Discrimination

Statutory rules exist to guard against sexual or racial discrimination[5]. These rules apply to any arrangements for determining whether someone should be offered a partnership, to the terms of the offer of partnership, to refusing or deliberately offering someone a partnership, and in relation to the rights of existing partners.

---

1 Companies Act 1985, s 716.
2 Eg, in relation to surveyors, auctioneers, valuers, estate agents, land agents and estate managers), see the Partnerships (Unrestricted Size) (No 1) Regulations 1968, SI 1968/1222 (amended by SI 1994/644); and in relation to actuaries see, the Partnerships (Unrestricted Size) (No 11) Regulations 1996, SI 1996/262.
3 Age of Legal Capacity (Scotland) Act 1991, s 3(2)(f).
4 *Hugh Stevenson & Sons v AG für Cartonnagen-Industrie* [1918] AC 239, HL.
5 See Sex Discrimination Act 1975, ss 1–4, 11; Race Relations Act 1976, s 10.

Illegality

A partnership entered for the purpose of committing a crime or deriving profit from an illegal activity will be illegal[1]. Where a partnership does not comply with the statutory limits on membership it is also illegal and each member will have unlimited liability for the debts of the association[2]. A partnership which contravenes the rules of a particular profession as regards membership may be illegal or a penalty may be imposed, depending on the terms of the relevant statute. Where a partner in a solicitor's firm accidentally failed to renew his practising certificate, it was held that this rendered the firm illegal and caused its dissolution[3].

Duration

It is often provided in the partnership agreement that the partnership is to be of a certain duration: eg three years. This avoids the partnership being defined as a 'partnership at will', which may be dissolved at any time by a partner giving notice to the other partners[4]. An agreement to continue the partnership for a particular length of time may be inferred, but the duration of a lease of the partnership premises will not be deemed a conclusive indication of an agreement that the partnership is to continue for that length of time[5]. Where a partnership is for an agreed term and continues after the term without further agreement, it becomes a partnership at will and the rights and duties of the partners remain the same as before, but only so far as is consistent with the incidents of a partnership at will[6]. This means that any provision in the previous agreement fixing the duration of the partnership is not effective and the partnership may be dissolved by notice at any time.

Firm name

The partnership business may be carried on under the name or names of an individual (a 'social' name, such as 'Adams and Smith') or under a descriptive name (such as 'The Muffin Shop'). Where the name does not consist of the surnames (or, in the case of companies which are partners, the corporate names) of all partners, or those names with certain permitted additions, the controls imposed by the Business Names Act 1985 will apply. The Act prohibits the use of certain business names and requires approval to be given by the Secretary of State for others. It also requires disclosure of certain information such as the name of each partner, in business documents, at the business premises and on request by anyone dealing with the firm in the course of business and provides civil and criminal penalties for failure to do so.

---

1 *Michael Jeffrey & Co v Bamford* [1921] 2 KB 351; *Lindsay v Inland Revenue* 1933 SC 33.
2 *Shaw v Benson* (1883) 11 QBD 563, CA; *Greenberg v Cooperstein* [1926] 1 Ch 657.
3 *Hudgell Yeates & Co v Watson* [1978] QB 451.
4 1890 Act, s 26.
5 *McNiven v Peffers* (1868) 7 M 181; *Miller v Walker* (1875) 3 R 242.
6 1890 Act, s 27.

Personality of the firm

In both Scotland and England persons who have entered into partnership with one another are called collectively a 'firm'[1]. In Scotland, unlike England, legal recognition has always been given to the partnership as a persona separate from those composing it[2]. This concept is embodied in s 4(2) of the Partnership Act 1890 which states that:

> 'In Scotland a firm is a legal person distinct from the partners of whom it is composed, but an individual partner may be charged on a decree or diligence directed against the firm, and on payment of the debts is entitled to relief pro rata from the firm and its other members'.

The persona of the firm, however, is not identical to the full separate legal personality of a corporation. Although it enables contracts to be entered in the firm name, and although the liability of the firm must be established in an action against the firm, at the end of the day the partners are jointly and severally liable for the debts of the business[3]. In practice, however, the firm is seen by outsiders and by the partners themselves as a distinct entity with a distinctive business name, a separate bank account and separate partnership accounts showing the partners as debtors or creditors of the firm. Events such as the retirement or death of a partner, or the introduction of a new partner, are of considerable legal significance, but in practice the business will often appear to the outsider to continue smoothly as before. Even in England, where s 4(2) does not apply and the firm remains legally merely the aggregate of the individual partners, the firm – with its business name and separate accounts – tends to be thought of in practice as a separate entity.

RELATIONSHIP BETWEEN PARTNERS AND OUTSIDERS

Agency of partners

The common law rule that a partner is entitled to bind the firm by acts done on its behalf for carrying on in the usual way the business done by the firm was given statutory effect in s 5 of the Partnership Act 1890 as follows:

> 'Every partner is an agent of the firm and his other partners for the purpose of the business of the partnership; and the acts of every partner who does any act for carrying on in the usual way business of the kind carried on by the firm of which he is a member bind the firm and his partners, unless the partner so acting has in fact no authority to act for the firm in the particular matter, and the person with whom he is dealing either knows that he has no authority, or does not know or believe him to be a partner'.

The liability of the firm depends, therefore, on whether the partner has authority, but that authority may be actual or apparent.

---

1 1890 Act, s 4(1).
2 Bell *Principles* s 35.
3 1890 Act, s 9.

Partner acting with actual authority

A partner may be granted express authority under the terms of the partnership agreement to act in a certain way, but this is not something which will be within the knowledge of a third party and so s 5 of the 1890 Act defines the extent of the partner's authority by reference to the purposes of the firm. The partner's authority, therefore, depends on the nature of the business, although certain acts have come to be recognised as characteristic of some businesses. It has been held, eg, that a partner in a trading firm has implied authority to borrow money necessary for the firm's business and to bind the firm for its repayment[1]. Where, however, a partner in a building firm borrowed money from a moneylender at an interest rate of 40 per cent and used the proceeds for his own purposes, it was held that the firm was not bound and that the moneylender must bear the loss, as his suspicions should have been aroused when it appeared that a firm of good repute required to borrow money at this rate[2].

Partner acting with apparent authority

Even where a partner's actual authority is lacking, or is restricted in some way, the firm will be bound nevertheless by acts done for carrying on in the usual way business of the kind carried on by the firm, unless the third party knows that the partner lacks authority or does not know or believe him to be a partner. The partners may have placed some limitation on the authority of one of the partners, but notice of the restriction must have been given to third parties if the firm is to avoid liability[3]. The extent of a partner's apparent authority will be defined by reference to what appears to the third party to be usual in the particular type of business. For example, where a partner in a firm whose business was car repairs and lock-up garages sold a car, the firm was held bound even although the sale of cars was excluded in terms of the partnership agreement[4].

Acts outwith the course of business

Where a partner pledges the firm's credit for a purpose apparently not connected with the firm's ordinary course of business, the firm is not bound unless it has specially authorised the transaction[5]. The partner will incur personal liability, as in the case of *Fortune v Young*[6], where a partner signed a letter guaranteeing the financial standing of an individual and it was held that the partner, not the firm, was liable. Similarly, the firm will not be bound where a partner grants an undertaking in his or her own private interest, even where the partner grants that undertaking in the firm name[7].

1 *Bryan v Butters Bros & Co* (1892) 19 R 490.
2 *Paterson Bros v Gladstone* (1891) 18 R 403.
3 1890 Act, s 8.
4 *Mercantile Credit Co Ltd v Garrod* [1962] 3 All ER 1103.
5 1890 Act, s 7.
6 1918 SC 1.
7 *Walker v Smith* (1906) 8 F 619.

Acts done and documents executed on behalf of the firm

The firm is bound by an act or instrument relating to the firm's business, done or executed in the firm name (or in any other manner showing an intention to bind the firm) by any authorised person[1]. This means that it is not only partners who have authority to bind the firm and the other partners. Any other agent acting with authority may bind the firm and its partners.

Admissions and representations

An admission or representation made by any partner concerning the partnership affairs, and made in the ordinary course of its business, is evidence against the firm[2].

Notice to partner

Notice given to any partner who habitually acts in the partnership business, of any matter relating to partnership affairs, operates as notice to the firm, except where a fraud on the firm is committed by or with the consent of that partner[3]. The phrase 'any matter relating to partnership affairs' will not, however, be interpreted so as to embrace matters which relate solely to the partner-client relationship, where the partner may have a duty not to communicate information[4].

Joint and several liability of partners

The firm is primarily liable, to an unlimited extent, on its obligations. This principle applies irrespective of the amount of capital employed in the business. Every partner is liable jointly and severally for all the debts and obligations of the firm incurred while he or she is a partner[5]. This liability of the partners is regarded as an accessory liability, so that the partners are effectively cautioners for the firm, and in order to impose liability on the partners the debt must first be constituted against the firm. An individual partner may then be charged on a decree or diligence directed against the firm and on payment of the debts is entitled to relief pro rata from the firm and the other partners[6]. The fact that any one partner may be liable for the whole amount of the partnership debts, albeit with the right to reclaim whatever has been paid from the other partners proportionately, serves as a warning that one's fellow partners should be chosen with caution.

1 1890 Act, s 6. See too the Requirements of Writing (Scotland) Act 1995, s 7(7), Sch 2, para 2.
2 1890 Act, s 15.
3 1890 Act, s 16.
4 *Campbell v McCreath* 1975 SLT (Notes) 5, OH.
5 1890 Act, s 9.
6 1890 Act, s 4(2).

Liability of incoming partner

Section 17(1) of the Partnership Act 1890 provides that a person who is admitted as a partner into an existing firm does not thereby become liable to the creditors of the firm for anything done before he or she became a partner. The fact of becoming a partner therefore will not in itself make the incoming partner liable for anything done before he or she became a partner, but the whole facts and circumstances must be looked at. For example, where a partner is assumed and in effect there is simply a continuance of the old firm with the addition of a new partner, it may well be that the new partner will be taken to have assumed personal liability. This is because where the whole assets of a firm are transferred to a new firm consisting of the partners of the original firm with one or more additional partners, an equitable presumption arises at common law that the new firm assumes the liabilities of the old firm[1]. If, however, an incoming partner has contributed substantial capital to the firm, he or she may not be liable for prior debts of the business, on the basis that there is intended to be a clean break as regards the financial arrangements and a new start is to be made with a different capital structure[2]. Liability for prior debts might also be settled by agreement between the partners and the creditors of the firm or, in the case of debts incurred after the new partner joins the firm, by evidence that creditors are dealing with the former trader rather than the new firm[3]. Where a continuing running account is operated with a creditor, the rule in *Clayton's Case*[4] (whereby the earliest credit item is applied to wipe out the earliest debt item) may apply and have the effect of imposing liability on an incoming partner for prior debts of the firm.

Liability of retiring partner for prior debts or obligations

Section 17(2) of the Partnership Act 1890 provides that a partner who retires from the firm does not thereby cease to be liable for partnership debts or obligations incurred before his or her retirement. It is further provided that a retiring partner may be discharged from any existing liabilities by an agreement to that effect between himself or herself and the other members of the firm as newly constituted and the creditors; and this agreement may be either express or inferred as a fact from the course of dealing between the creditors and the firm as newly constituted[5]. It is not enough that there is an agreement between the retiring partner and the remaining partners[6], even where the retiring partner has lodged with them sufficient money to pay the debts[7]. The question of the applicability

1 *Heddle's Exrx v Marwick and Hourston's Tr* (1888) 15 R 698; *Miller v MacLeod and Parker* 1973 SC 172. See also *Clark v Clark* 1989 GWD 7-300.
2 *Thomson and Balfour v Boag & Son* 1936 SC 2. See also *Henry Nelmes & Co v James Montgomery & Co* (1833) 10 R 974.
3 *Re Warwick, ex parte Whitmore* (1838) 3 Deac 365; *British Homes Assurance Corpn Ltd v Paterson* [1902] 2 Ch 404.
4 *Devaynes v Noble, Clayton's Case* (1816) 1 Mer 572. See also Wilson *The Scottish Law of Debt* (2nd edn, 1991) para 12.5.
5 1890 Act, s 17(3).
6 *Campbell v Cruickshank* (1845) 7 D 548; *Muir v Dickson* (1860) 22 D 1070.
7 *Milliken v Love and Crawford* (1803) Hume 754.

of s 17(2) in an action of damages against a firm alleging professional negligence was considered in *Welsh v Knarston*[1], where the firm had been dissolved, and a proof was allowed in the Inner House to ascertain the precise circumstances of retiral.

Liability of retiring partner for later debts and obligations

Where a retiring partner has not given adequate notice of retirement, that partner may be liable, as an apparent member of the firm, for debts and obligations incurred after retirement. It is provided in s 36(1) of the 1890 Act that where a person deals with a firm after a change in its constitution, he or she is entitled to treat all apparent members of the old firm as still being members of the firm until he or she has notice of the change. The Act does not specify what form the notice is to take in the case of former or existing customers. In practice a circular may be sent to them to ensure that they are made aware of the change, although changes in the particulars appearing on business letters and other documents probably also give notice to existing customers. In the case of persons who had no dealings with the firm before the change, the Act provides that an advertisement in the appropriate Gazette is sufficient notice[2]. A retired partner who has not been known to the person dealing with the firm to be a partner is not liable for firm debts contracted after his or her retirement[3]. However, a retiring partner who represents himself or herself or 'knowingly suffers' himself or herself to be represented as a partner is liable as a partner to anyone who has given credit to the firm on the faith of any such representation[4]. In *Tower Cabinet Co Ltd v Ingram*[5] it was held that a retiring partner did not 'knowingly suffer' himself to be represented as a partner where, after his retirement, an order for goods was placed on notepaper from which his name had not been deleted and which he had failed to destroy before he left the firm. It was also held in that case that the retiring partner was protected from liability as an apparent partner as he had not been known to the third party as a partner before the dissolution of the firm.

Liability of deceased and bankrupt partners' estates

The estate of a deceased partner is severally liable for unsatisfied debts and obligations incurred while he or she was a partner, subject in England and Ireland to the prior payment of the deceased partner's separate debts[6]. The estate of a partner who dies or becomes bankrupt is not liable for partnership debts contracted after the date of death or bankruptcy respectively[7].

1 1972 SLT 96.
2 1890 Act, s 36(2).
3 1890 Act, s 36(3).
4 1890 Act, s 14(1).
5 [1949] 2 KB 397.
6 1890 Act, s 9.
7 1890 Act, s 36(3).

Effect of changes in the firm on obligations

In general, where a continuing guarantee or cautionary obligation has been given either to a firm or to a third person in respect of the firm's transactions, any change in the constitution of the partnership will revoke the liability of the cautioner in respect of future transactions[1]. If, however, it can be shown that continuing liability was intended or assented to[2], the cautioner may remain liable. Any contract which involves an element of *delectus personae* may be terminated on a change in the constitution of the firm, according to the general rules applicable to such contracts[3]. Contracts of employment are not revoked merely by a change in the constitution of the firm, or the conversion of a partnership into a limited company[4].

Liability incurred by 'holding out'

Where a person is not a partner in a firm but represents himself or herself as a partner, or 'knowingly suffers' himself or herself to be represented as a partner, that person may be personally barred by his or her conduct from denying that he or she is liable as a partner, in any question with a third party who has given credit to the firm on the faith of the representation. This type of liability, based on 'holding out', is established under s 14 of the 1890 Act and the liability arises whether the representation has or has not been made or communicated with the actual knowledge of the apparent partner suffering it to be made. The circumstances covered in s 14 may include cases where the apparent partner either by spoken or written words or by conduct has represented himself or herself or suffered himself or herself to be represented as a partner[5].

Liability of the firm for wrongs

The liability of the firm for wrongs is governed by the terms of s 10 of the 1890 Act:

> 'Where, by any wrongful act or omission of any partner acting in the ordinary course of the business of the firm, or with the authority of his co-partners, loss or injury is caused to any person not being a partner in the firm, or any penalty is incurred, the firm is liable therefor to the same extent as the partner so acting or omitting to act'.

This section imposes vicarious liability on the firm. In other words, the injured party may sue either the partner who has done the wrong or the firm. In many cases the injured party will prefer to sue the firm as it may be wealthier than the individual partner or it may have insurance cover. If liability is to be established against the firm, however, it has to be proved

---

1 1890 Act, s 18.
2 *Aytoun v Dundee Banking Co* (1844) 6 D 1409; *Miller v Thorburn* (1861) 23 D 359.
3 *Garden, Haig-Scott and Wallace v Prudential Approved Society for Women* 1927 SLT 393, OH.
4 Employment Rights Act 1996 s 218; Transfer of Undertakings (Protection of Employment) Regulations 1981, SI 1981/1794.
5 1890 Act, s 14(1).

that the partner was acting in the ordinary course of the business of the firm, or that he or she was acting with the authority of his or her co-partners. What is within the ordinary course of the business of a firm will depend on the type of firm involved. In *Kirkintilloch Equitable Co-operative Society v Livingstone*[1] one of the partners in an accountancy firm held an appointment as auditor of an industrial and provident society. The audit fee was paid into the firm and the auditor was assisted in the audit by employees of the firm. It was held that a relevant case had been stated against the auditor's former co-partners, the firm having been dissolved. The extent of the firm's liability to a third party who relies on information supplied by the firm will depend on the circumstances. This is illustrated by the increasing number of cases relating to auditors' liability[2]. The firm is not liable for the wrongful act or omission of a partner which causes loss or injury to one of his or her co-partners[3]. The partner who commits the wrongful act remains responsible[4]. Special provision is made in s 11 of the 1890 Act for liability in respect of the misapplication of money or property received for or in the custody of the firm and in s 13 for liability in respect of the improper employment of trust property for partnership purposes[5]. The firm itself may be liable for a statutory offence where the terms of a particular statute allow this. For example, it was held in one case that a firm could be liable for an offence under the Trade Descriptions Act 1968, being a 'body corporate' within the meaning of that Act[6].

Liability of partners under sections 10 and 11 of the 1890 Act

Where liability has been established against the firm for wrongs under s 10 or 11 of the 1890 Act, every partner then becomes liable jointly with his or her co-partners and also severally, for everything for which the firm, while he or she is a partner, becomes liable under these sections[7]. This is the same sort of accessory liability as arises under s 9 of the Act in relation to debts and obligations of the firm, and depends on the liability of the firm having been established first. Where a firm of surveyors was held liable for a negligent valuation by one of its partners working from an office in Scotland, it was held, as has already been noted, that all of the partners in the Scottish firm were liable, but that the surveyor who was based in London was not liable as he was a partner only in the London firm[8].

Liability of incoming, retiring and deceased partners for wrongs

It is arguable that an incoming partner may be jointly and severally liable for the consequences of the negligence of his co-partners in a transaction

1　1972 SC 111.
2　Eg *Caparo Industries plc v Dickman* [1990] 2 AC 605. Cf *Twomax v Dickson McFarlane and Robinson* 1982 SC 113, OH; 1984 SLT 424, IH; *James McNaughton Paper Group Ltd v Hicks Anderson & Co* [1991] 2 QB 113; *ADT Ltd v BDO Binder Hamlyn* [1996] BCC 808.
3　1890 Act, s 10; *Mair v Wood* 1948 SC 83.
4　*Parker v Walker* 1961 SLT 252, OH.
5　For discussion of these provisions, see 16 *Stair Memorial Encyclopaedia* paras 1045, 1048.
6　*Douglas v Phoenix Motors* 1970 SLT (Sh Ct) 57. Cf *Bennett v Richardson* [1980] RTR 358, CA.
7　1890 Act, s 12.
8　*Mortgage Express Ltd v Dunsmore Reid & Smith* 1996 GWD 40-2295.

begun before but completed after his introduction as a partner[1]. Where a partner has retired, or the firm has been dissolved, that partner's liability for the negligent acts of his or her former co-partners while he or she was a partner does not cease on retirement or dissolution[2]. Likewise, the estate of a deceased partner may be liable for wrongful acts done while the deceased was a partner[3].

MANAGING THE FIRM: THE RELATIONSHIP OF PARTNERS WITHIN THE FIRM

Contractual aspects

The rights and obligations of the partners amongst themselves are governed essentially by the partnership contract. The express terms of this contract may be found in a written contract of co-partnery or, in the absence of agreement, may be implied by the provisions of the Partnership Act 1890. Whether the terms of the agreement are defined by a partnership contract or by the terms of the Act, they may be varied by consent of all the partners and this consent may be express or inferred from a course of dealing based on the agreed alteration[4].

Good faith

Partnership is a relationship of good faith and the partners are in the position of fiduciaries towards the firm and each other both when negotiating for a partnership[5] and during the subsistence of the partnership[6]. Certain duties arising from this relationship of good faith are considered below.

Duty to account

One aspect of the requirement of good faith is that 'partners are bound to render true accounts and full information of all things affecting the partnership to any partner or his legal representatives'[7]. Non-disclosure of information, depending on the circumstances, may give rise to a claim for damages[8]; otherwise an action may be raised for accounting and payment of any balance due[9]. A partner will be entitled to an accounting even where he or she has been in breach of the partnership agreement in not devoting enough time to the business[10].

1 *Tully v Ingram* (1891) 19 R 65.
2 *Kirkintilloch Equitable Co-operative Society v Livingstone* 1972 SC 111; *Welsh v Knarston* 1973 SLT 66.
3 *Sawyer v Goodwin* (1867) 36 LJCh 578; *Blyth v Fladgate* [1891] 1 Ch 337 at 366.
4 1890 Act, s 19.
5 *Adam v Newbigging* (1888) 13 App Cas 308, HL; *Manners v Whitehead* (1898) 1 F 171.
6 See 1890 Act, ss 28–30; *Brenner v Rose* [1973] 2 All ER 535.
7 1890 Act, s 28.
8 *Ferguson v Mackay* 1985 SLT 94, OH.
9 *Smith v Barclay* 1962 SC 1.
10 *Park v Park* 1970 SLT (Notes) 59, OH.

Duty not to make a private profit

'Every partner must account to the firm for any benefit derived by him without the consent of the other partners from any transaction concerning the partnership, or from any use by him of the partnership property, name or business connection'[1]. Another example of the requirement of good faith, this statutory duty is a reflection of the general principle of the law of agency that an agent must account for any secret profits. The phrase 'any transaction concerning the partnership' embraces only transactions forming part of the business of the firm and appears to exclude such matters as the method by which a partner raises his or her capital[2]. Where information obtained in the course of the firm's business is used by a partner to make a secret profit in a transaction which is not within the firm's business, he or she is not liable to account for this profit[3]. Where a partner, before the expiry of the lease of the partnership premises, obtained a new lease in his own name and carried on the same business as an individual, it was decided that he was liable to account to his former partner for a share of his profit[4]. The provision that every partner is accountable for private profits applies also to transactions undertaken after a partnership has been dissolved by the death of a partner, by any surviving partner or by the representatives of the deceased partner[5].

Duty not to compete with the firm

A further aspect of the requirement of good faith is expressed in s 30 of the 1890 Act which provides that: 'If a partner, without the consent of the other partners, carries on any business of the same nature as and competing with that of the firm, he must account for and pay over to the firm all profits made by him in that business'. Where three brothers had arranged a partnership carrying on business as rivet, bolt and nut manufacturers, and the following year one of them purchased a separate rivet, bolt and nut manufacturing business, it was held that he was bound to account to the firm for the profits from that business[6].

Management of partnership affairs

In the absence of express or implied agreement between the partners, their rights and duties will be determined by the rules provided in s 24 of the 1890 Act. For example, subject to any agreement to the contrary, every partner may take part in the management of the partnership business[7] and where any difference arises as to ordinary matters connected with the partnership business, the question may be decided by a majority of the

1 1890 Act, s 29(1).
2 *Lonsdale Hematite Iron Co v Barclay* (1874) 1 R 417; *Cassels v Stewart* (1881) 8 R (HL) 1.
3 *Aas v Benham* [1891] 2 Ch 244.
4 *McNiven v Peffers* (1868) 7 M 181.
5 1890 Act, s 29(2); *Laird v Laird* (1855) 17 D 984.
6 *Pillans Bros v Pillans* (1908) 16 SLT 611, OH.
7 1890 Act, s 24, para (5).

partners, but no change may be made in the nature of the partnership business without the consent of all the existing partners[1]. It is also provided that no person may be introduced as a partner without the consent of all the existing partners[2]: an example of the application of *delectus personae* to partnership. Again, however, this is subject to any agreement between the partners and it may be provided in the partnership agreement, eg, that a partner has the right to nominate his or her successor or that the representative of a deceased partner has the right to be admitted to the partnership in his or her place. Such provisions are in effect a prospective consent to the assumption of a new partner.

Right to indemnity

Every partner has a right to be indemnified by the firm in respect of payments made and personal liabilities incurred by him or her 'in the ordinary and proper conduct of the business of the firm'[3]. This right may be limited by agreement, eg by setting a limit on the expense which a partner may incur and for which he or she may claim indemnity. There is a further duty to indemnify every partner in respect of payments made and personal liabilities incurred 'in or about anything necessarily done for the preservation of the business or property of the firm'[4], which suggests that this indemnity rests on the principles applicable to *negotiorum gestio*, where action needs to be taken urgently to safeguard the firm's business or property.

Remuneration and profit-sharing

Subject to any express or implied agreement between the partners, no partner is entitled to remuneration for acting in the partnership business[5]. Sometimes a contrary agreement will be made, as in the case of 'salaried partners', or where, eg, it is desired that certain active partners should receive a salary before the profits are divided amongst all the partners. As regards sharing in the profits, in practice there will often be an agreement amongst the partners for an unequal division of profits, but the statutory rule is that, in the absence of agreement, all partners are entitled to share equally in the capital and profits of the firm and must contribute equally towards the losses sustained by the firm[6]. Where the partnership agreement makes clear and specific provision for profit-sharing, any alteration to that agreement will have to be evidenced[7].

Interest on advances and on capital

Subject to any contrary agreement, a partner who makes any payment or advance to the firm over and above the amount of capital he or she has

1 1890 Act, s 24, para (8).
2 1890 Act, s 24, para (7).
3 1890 Act, s 24, para (2)(a).
4 1890 Act, s 24, para (2)(b).
5 1890 Act, s 24, para (6).
6 1890 Act, s 24, para (1).
7 *Heaney v Downie* 1997 GWD 9-393.

agreed to subscribe is entitled to interest at a rate of 5 per cent per annum from the date of the payment or advance[1]. A partner is not entitled however, before the ascertainment of profits, to interest on the capital subscribed by him or her, unless there is an agreement to the contrary[2].

Access to partnership books

Subject to any agreement between themselves, the partners have a right of access to the partnership books, which are to be kept at the principal place of business[3]. This right of access was recognised at common law, and a partner was entitled to inspect and copy the books himself or herself or through an agent (usually an accountant)[4]. The right to inspect the books does not entitle the partner or the agent to use the information obtained for an extraneous or injurious purpose[5]. Apart from this, however, a difficult situation may arise where a partner is in dispute with the firm, or has died, and objection is taken by the other partners to the inspection of the firm's books by the partner's legal adviser or executor (who may be a solicitor in a competing firm). It is to safeguard against problems such as these that partners may wish to make provision in the partnership agreement for inspection of the books in such circumstances by an independent accountant.

Breach of partners' obligations

Interdict has been granted in several cases where it has been shown that some of the partners were intending to do something injurious to the interests of the others, or something contrary to the express or implied provisions of the partnership agreement[6]. The courts will look closely at what was agreed amongst the partners[7]. It appears that although the courts are willing to consider awarding damages for breach of fiduciary duty (eg where full disclosure of information has not been made to a partner in the negotiation of the terms of the partnership[8], or where a partnership has been dissolved suddenly and files removed clandestinely by some of the partners who have decided to set up a competing firm[9]), damages will not be granted readily[10]. The partners complaining may decide that the best remedy is to expel a partner[11] or seek a dissolution of the

1 1890 Act, s 24, para (3).
2 1890 Act, s 24, para (4).
3 1890 Act, s 24, para (9).
4 *Fife Bank v Halliday* (1831) 9 S 693; *Cameron v McMurray* (1855) 17 D 1142.
5 *Trego v Hunt* [1896] AC 7, HL; *Bevan v Webb* [1901] 2 Ch 59, CA.
6 *Taylor & Sons v Taylor* (1823) 2 S 157 (NE 143); *Learmonth v Leadbetter* (1841) 3 D 1192; *Brown v Adam* (1848) 10 D 744; *Hunter v Wylie* 1992 SLT 1091, OH. See also *Roxburgh v Seven Seas Engineering Ltd* 1980 SLT (Notes) 49, OH; *Patience v Milne* 1991 GWD 3-172, Sh Ct.
7 *Duff v Corsar* (1902) 10 SLT 27, OH.
8 *Ferguson v Mackay* 1985 SLT 94, OH. See too *Dean v MacDowell* (1878) 8 Ch D 345, CA.
9 *Finlayson v Turnbull* 1996 GWD 17-1014, OH.
10 *Leslie v Lumsden* (1856) 18 D 1046; *MacCredie's Trustees v Lamond* (1886) 24 SLR 114.
11 See 'Expulsion of a partner' below.

firm[1]. Another possible remedy is to seek the appointment of a judicial factor[2]. An action for an accounting would be appropriate where a partner is in breach of the duty to account for private profits[3] or profits made from a business carried on in competition with the firm[4].

Expulsion of a partner

No majority of the partners can expel any partner unless a power to do so has been conferred by express agreement between the partners[5]. In exercising any power of expulsion which has been conferred, the partners must act in good faith and an expulsion may be declared void if it is proved that the expelling partners have abused their power. For example, the expelled partner in *Blisset v Daniel*[6] proved that one of his co-partners had organised the expulsion following a disagreement and also that the expulsion had been kept a secret from him until after he had been induced to sign accounts which would bind him after expulsion. In that case the court declared the expulsion void and restored the expelled partner to his rights as a partner in the firm[7]. Apart from expulsion, dissolution is the only alternative method of forcing a partner to leave the firm, although it would not be unlawful to persuade a partner to leave the firm unless bad faith or undue influence could be proved[8].

Partnership property

The question whether particular property is partnership property may arise in a number of different circumstances. For example, partnership assets may have to be identified and valued on a final dissolution of the firm, or on the death of a partner in order that the deceased partner's estate may be valued. Uncertainty sometimes arises where property is held in the name of a partner but is used in the business of the firm. The partnership agreement may define which assets are to be treated as partnership property but in the absence of agreement the provisions of the 1890 Act will have to be considered. The Act provides that all property and interests in property originally brought into the partnership or acquired, whether by purchase or otherwise, on account of the firm or for the purposes and in the course of the partnership business, are partnership property, and must be held and applied by the partners exclusively for the purposes of the partnership and in accordance with the partnership agreement[9]. Unless a contrary intention appears, property bought with money belonging to the firm is deemed to have been bought on

1 See 'Dissolution by the court' below.
2 *McKenzie v Lodge* 1988 GWD 24-1044.
3 1890 Act, s 29.
4 *Stewart v North* (1893) 20 R 260; *Pillans Brothers v Pillans* (1908) 16 SLT 611, OH.
5 1890 Act, s 25.
6 (1853) 10 Hare 493.
7 See too *Wood v Woad* (1874) LR 9 Exch 190; *Green v Howell* [1910] 1 Ch 495, CA.
8 *Tennent v Tennent's Trs* (1870) 8 M 10.
9 1890 Act, s 20(1).

account of the firm[1]. The whole circumstances will be taken into account in deciding whether particular property has been acquired on account of the firm[2]. Sometimes it will be clear that property is partnership property, eg where heritable property is conveyed to some or all of the partners as trustees for the firm[3]. Apart from land held by feudal tenure, which cannot be held in the firm name but must be held by partners in trust for the firm, property (including leases) may be held in the firm name or by partners in trust for the firm. Where partners are co-owners of heritable property, however, that property is not necessarily partnership property and it is provided in the 1890 Act that where partners derive profits from heritable estate of which they are co-owners, but which is not partnership property, they are to be regarded as co-owners of any property which they purchase out of these profits to be used in like manner, in the absence of any agreement to the contrary[4]. A partner's interest in the partnership property is a right to a *pro indiviso* share of the firm's assets[5]. The partner's interest is treated as moveable estate in succession[6]. The nature of a partner's interest in the partnership property is important where partnership property is to be insured as it is the partnership, rather than the individual partners, which has an insurable interest in partnership property[7]. The nature of the partner's interest in the partnership property is also important to the question of diligence, in that the interest of the partner may be arrested in the hands of the firm by his separate creditors while the firm is a going concern[8]. It is clear that specific property cannot be arrested, but only the interest of the partner in any surplus assets once realised[9]. A partner's share in the partnership may be assigned. Since the interest of the partner is an incorporeal moveable right, it must be transferred by assignation followed by intimation to the firm[10]. The presumption that no person may be introduced as a partner without the consent of all existing partners[11] extends to the transfer of a partner's share to a third party, so that a partner cannot, without the agreement of his partners, assign his or her share so as to make the assignee a partner in the firm; and in the absence of consent, the assignee has no right to interfere in the management, to require any accounts, or to inspect the partnership books[12]. The assignee is entitled only to receive the assigning partner's share of the profits and must accept the account of profits agreed by the partners[12]. On a dissolution, the assignee is entitled to the assigning partner's share of the assets and is entitled to an account as from the date of the dissolution[13].

1 1890 Act, s 21.
2 *McNiven v Peffers* (1868) 7 M 181; *Davie v Buchanan* (1880) 8 R 319.
3 *Morison v Miller* (1818) Hume 720. See too 1890 Act s 20(2); and Styles 'Why Can't Partnerships Own Heritage?' (1989) 34 JLSS 414.
4 1890 Act, s 20(3).
5 See Gretton 'Who Owns Partnership Property?' 1987 JR 163.
6 1890 Act, s 22 (repealed in respect of England by Trusts of Land and Appointment of Trustees Act 1996, ss 25(2), 27 and Sch 4).
7 *Arif v Excess Insurance Group Ltd* 1986 SC 317, OH.
8 Bell *Commentaries* II, 536. As to arrestment after dissolution of money due to the firm, see *Finlayson v Turnbull* 1993 GWD 7-506, OH.
9 *Parnell v Walter* (1889) 16 R 917.
10 See, however, *Hill v Lindsay* (1846) 8 D 472.
11 1890 Act, s 24, para (7).
12 1890 Act, s 31(1).
13 1890 Act, s 31(2).

DISSOLUTION

Meaning of dissolution

Confusion is sometimes caused by the different ways in which the term 'dissolution' is used. It is used to describe the case where the firm is dissolved and wound up completely, in which case the rules provided in s 44 of the 1890 Act concerning the order for distribution of assets on a final settlement of accounts are particularly relevant. The term 'dissolution' is also used to describe the legal position where a firm as presently constituted ceases to exist: eg where a partner leaves the firm but an arrangement is made to satisfy the rights of the retiring partner and the remaining partners carry on the business in what appears to be the same way as before, under the same firm name. In this case, although everything appears to the outside world to be as before, except that a partner has retired, the old firm has really come to an end and its assets have been transferred to a new firm, albeit one carried on under the same business name. In this case, one of the most relevant statutory provisions is s 36 of the 1890 Act, concerning the rights of persons dealing with the firm against apparent members of the firm. This provision has already been discussed.

Reasons for dissolution

There are many reasons why a partnership might be dissolved. The partnership agreement may specify that certain events will give rise to dissolution, or the partners may mutually agree to a dissolution. The contract of partnership may be rescinded where a partner has been induced by fraud or misrepresentation to enter into it and in such a case the rules in s 41 of the 1890 Act apply to safeguard the rights of the party entitled to rescind. Where a partnership was originally entered for a fixed term, it is dissolved at the expiry of that term; and where it was for a single adventure or undertaking, it is dissolved on the termination of the adventure[1]. Where illegality arises after the constitution of a partnership, either because it becomes unlawful for the particular partners to carry on the business or where the nature of the business itself becomes unlawful, the partnership is automatically dissolved regardless of any agreement between the partners to the contrary[2]. Unless there is a contrary agreement between the partners, the partnership will also be dissolved on the death or bankruptcy of any partner and it may be dissolved by the court. These grounds are considered separately below.

Any provision in the partnership agreement specifying the length of notice required for dissolution must be adhered to and where a partner is in material breach of the partnership agreement, as in a case where partners withdrew capital from the firm without the consent of the other profit-sharing partners, contrary to the agreement, he or she may not

1 1890 Act, s 32, para (b).
2 1890 Act, s 34.

validly invoke a right to dissolve the firm[1]. An arbitration clause in the partnership agreement may be sufficiently wide to allow a dispute, as to whether a partnership should be dissolved, to be submitted to arbitration[2].

Notice of dissolution

In a partnership at will, where no fixed term for the duration of the partnership has been agreed upon, any partner may determine the partnership at any time by giving notice to the other partners[3], and where the partnership at will was originally constituted by deed, a notice in writing signed by the partner giving it will be sufficient notice[4]. Although it has been held that intention to dissolve may be implied from actings of the parties[5], the best practice in all cases is to give notice in writing. The Act provides that where notice is given, the partnership will be dissolved as from the date mentioned in the notice or, if no date is mentioned, as from the date of communication of the notice[6].

Dissolution by death or on sequestration

Subject to any agreement between the partners, a partnership will be dissolved on the death or bankruptcy of any partner[7]. 'Bankruptcy' means sequestration under the Bankruptcy (Scotland) Acts[8]. The partnership will not be dissolved where the partnership agreement stipulates, eg, that a bankrupt partner is to cease to be a partner and makes some provision for the ascertainment and payment of his share by the firm as a going concern.

Dissolution by the court

Section 35 of the 1890 Act provides a number of grounds on which a partnership may be dissolved by the court on the application of a partner. In the case of mental incapacity of a partner, the application may be made by another specified person[9]. The court may also decree a dissolution where a partner in any other way becomes permanently incapable of performing his part of the partnership contract[10], or where a partner has been guilty of conduct prejudicial to the business[11]. Breach of the partnership agreement

---

1 *Hunter v Wylie* 1993 SLT 1091, OH.
2 *Hackston v Hackston* 1956 SLT (Notes) 38, OH. Cf *Semple v Macnair and Crawford* (1907) 15 SLT 448, OH.
3 1890 Act, s 26(1).
4 1890 Act, s 26(2).
5 *Jassal's Exrx v Jassal's Trs* 1988 SLT 757, OH.
6 1890 Act, s 32.
7 1890 Act, s 33(1).
8 1890 Act, s 47(1).
9 1890 Act, s 35, para (a).
10 1890 Act, s 35, para (b): but see *Eadie v MacBean's Curator Bonis* (1885) 12 R 660; *MacCredie's Trs v Lamond* (1886) 24 SLR 114.
11 1890 Act, s 35, para (c).

or other conduct, in matters relating to the partnership business, which destroys mutual confidence may also give rise to a dissolution by the court[1]. For example, where a partner obtained money by signing the firm name on a cheque and absconding with the proceeds, it was held that mutual trust had been destroyed and an order for dissolution was competent[2]. Where the business can only be carried on at a loss, a dissolution by the court may be decreed[3]. The final ground on which the court may decree a dissolution is when circumstances have arisen which in the opinion of the court render it just and equitable that the partnership be dissolved[4]. The procedure for seeking a dissolution by the court will be either a petition or an ordinary action, depending on whether the parties are at variance over matters requiring further investigation or inquiry by means of a proof[5]. The appointment of a judicial factor on the partnership estate might be sought if there are no partners competent to wind up the partnership[6], or if notice of dissolution has been given but a partner fears for the partnership property under the management of another partner in the meantime[7].

Consequences of dissolution

Where a change in the firm's constitution has taken place, eg by the retirement of a partner, the interest of creditors is protected by the provision in s 36 of the 1890 Act that apparent partners of the firm will remain liable until notice of the change has been given. This provision is discussed above in relation to the liability of retiring partners for debts and obligations of the firm. On the dissolution of the firm or the retirement of any partner, any partner is entitled to publicly notify this[8], thus enabling partners to protect themselves by ensuring that proper notice is given of dissolution or retirement. It is important that proper notice is given from the point of view not only of the retiring partner but also of the firm and any partners who succeed to the firm's business. The partners have a continuing authority to wind up the firm's affairs and the extent of this authority will now be considered.

Continuing authority of partners to wind up firm's affairs

At the date of dissolution a number of obligations undertaken by the firm will usually exist. It is provided in s 38 of the 1890 Act that:

> 'After the dissolution of a partnership the authority of each partner to bind the firm, and the other rights and obligations of the partners, continue notwithstanding the dissolution so far as may be necessary to wind up the

1   1890 Act, s 35, para (d).
2   *Thomson* (1893) 1 SLT 59.
3   1890 Act, s 35, para (e).
4   1890 Act, s 35, para (f). See too *Cleghorn* (1901) 8 SLT 409, OH; *Baird v Lees* 1924 SC 83.
5   *Wallace v Whitelaw* (1900) 2 F 675; *Macnab v Macnab* 1912 SC 421; *Anderson v Blair* 1935 SLT 377, OH.
6   *Thomson* (1893) 1 SLT 59. See too *Eadie v McBean's Curator Bonis* (1885) 12 R 660.
7   *McCulloch v McCulloch* 1953 SC 189; *McKenzie v Lodge* 1988 GWD 24-1044.
8   1890 Act, s 37.

affairs of the partnership, and to complete transactions begun but unfinished at the time of the dissolution, but not otherwise.

Provided that the firm is in no case bound by the acts of a partner who has become bankrupt; but this proviso does not affect the liability of any person who after the bankruptcy represented himself or knowingly suffered himself to be represented as a partner of the bankrupt'.

The effect of this provision has been considered in a number of cases. In *Inland Revenue Commissioners v Graham's Trustees*, Lord Reid observed that:

> 'The surviving partners have the right and duty to complete all unfinished operations necessary to fulfil contracts of the firm which were still in force when the firm was dissolved ... In my opinion section 38 does not make the surviving partners parties to the firm's contracts and so keep those contracts alive. That would involve a radical change in Scots law. But I see no difficulty in holding that this section does require unfinished operations to be completed under the conditions which would have applied if the contract had still existed'[1].

In *Dickson v National Bank of Scotland Ltd*[2], the House of Lords held that a partner's continuing authority under s 38 extended to indorsing the firm's name on a deposit receipt and uplifting trust money payable to the firm, eight years after the firm's dissolution. In a case where a partnership was converted into a limited company, it was held that an action for payment of damages on a transaction begun but not completed at the date of dissolution of the partnership was competently raised in the name of the firm and the partners[3]. Partners of a dissolved firm having continuing authority under s 38 may be liable for professional negligence in respect of transactions begun but not completed at the date of dissolution, one example being the case of solicitors who failed to raise an action which then became time-barred[4]. Where a lease has been entered into in the firm name, it will depend on the terms of the lease as to whether it may be continued. For example, the lease may provide that it is to lapse on dissolution of the partnership, or it may permit assignation, in which case it may be assigned before dissolution. Alternatively, there may have been a clear intention when the lease was entered that it was to be a contract with the 'house', rather than with the firm as constituted at that point in time, and in that case it would be arguable that a change in the constitution of the firm on death or retirement of a partner would not operate to terminate the lease[5].

Partners' rights in the application of property

On dissolution, every partner is entitled to have the property of the partnership properly applied as between creditors, the firm and the partners, and for that purpose any partner or his representative is entitled to apply

1 1971 SC (HL) 1 at 121.
2 1917 SC (HL) 50.
3 *Brown v Canon Co Ltd* (1898) 6 SLT 90, OH. See also *Grierson, Oldham & Co Ltd v Forbes, Maxwell & Co Ltd* (1895) 22 R 812.
4 *Welsh v Knarston* 1973 SLT 66.
5 *Walker v McKnights* (1886) 13 R 599; *Inland Revenue Comrs v Graham's Trs* 1971 SC (HL) 1; *Jardine-Paterson v Fraser* 1974 SLT 93, OH; *Lujo Properties Ltd v Green* 1996 GWD 8-463, OH.

to the court to wind up the affairs of the firm[1]. The conduct of the winding up is, however, primarily a matter for the surviving, solvent partners[2]. Where the conduct of a partner administering the winding up gives rise to the concern that the rights of his or her co-partners may be defeated, or where there is a serious difference between the partners, a judicial factor may be appointed[3]. A judicial factor will not generally be personally liable for the firm's debts incurred during the factory[4]. Where one partner has paid a premium, as opposed to a contribution of capital, on entering a partnership for a fixed term, and the partnership is dissolved before the expiry of that term, the court may in appropriate circumstances order repayment of the premium or part of it[5]. Payment of a sum in this way, purely as the price of being admitted as a partner, no longer appears to be a common practice. Where a partnership contract is rescinded on the ground of fraud or misrepresentation, the party entitled to rescind is given certain protections in relation to any capital contributed by him or her[6] and any payments he or she has made to creditors in respect of partnership liabilities[7]. The party entitled to rescind is also entitled to be indemnified against all the debts and liabilities of the firm by the person responsible for the fraud or misrepresentation[8]. In certain circumstances an outgoing partner will be entitled to receive either interest at a rate of 5 per cent on the amount of his or her share of the partnership assets, or, at his or her option, a share of profits made after dissolution and attributable to the use of his or her share in the partnership assets[9]. This might happen eg where profits have been made from use of a deceased partner's share during a substantial delay in winding up[10]. Another example is seen in *Hugh Stevenson & Sons v AG für Cartonnagen-Industrie*[11] where one partner became an alien enemy on the outbreak of war and the business was carried on by the other partners. In such a case the enemy partner's share of the assets and share of any profits attributed to the use of his or her share must be set aside for him or her and will be payable on termination of the war. Difficult questions can arise as to what proportion of profits are attributable to the use of the outgoing partner's share and this is a question for the court to determine, taking into account such factors as the nature of the business and the skill and diligence of the remaining partners[12]. When a partner dies or retires, and the business is carried on by the surviving or continuing partners, the amount due from the surviving or continuing partners in respect of the deceased or outgoing partner's share is, subject to any agreement between the partners, a debt accruing at the date of dissolution or death[13]. Where one partner has

---

1 1890 Act, s 39.
2 *Thomson* (1893) 1 SLT 59.
3 *Allan v Gronmeyer* (1891) 18 R 784; *Carabine v Carabine* 1949 SC 521.
4 *Scottish Brewers Ltd v J Douglas Pearson & Co* 1995 SCLR 799, Sh Ct.
5 1890 Act, s 40.
6 1890 Act, s 41, para (a).
7 1890 Act, s 41, para (b).
8 1890 Act, s 41, para (c).
9 1890 Act, s 42.
10 *Barclay's Bank Trust Co Ltd v Bluff* [1982] Ch 172.
11 [1918] AC 239.
12 *Simpson v Chapman* (1853) 4 De G M & G 154; *Manley v Sartori* [1927] 1 Ch 157; *Popat v Shonchhatra* [1997] 3 All ER 800, CA.
13 1890 Act, s 43.

retained all the assets on a dissolution and sequestration of the firm's estates, it is competent in exceptional circumstances to charge compound interest against him or her in respect of the partnership assets in his or her hands[1].

Ascertainment of retiring or deceased partner's share

The question of ascertaining what is due to an outgoing partner or to the representatives of a deceased partner, as their share, is one of the most common problems which arise in practice in relation to partnerships. The problem can be avoided in many cases by considering, at the outset, what provision should be made in the partnership agreement for such an eventuality; but if the agreement is not clearly and carefully worded, the wording itself can give rise to a costly dispute over its interpretation. For example, the agreement may provide that the outgoing partner's share of capital is that standing at his or her credit in the balance sheet of the preceding year, but may not specify the basis on which 'capital' is entered in the accounts. In such a case, the partnership agreement and the intentions of the partners in relation to the accounts will have to be considerd carefully, as it is clear from the case law that the accounts may be intended to be conclusive for one purpose but not for another. An example is seen in the case of *Clark v Watson*[2], where the partnership agreement between two dentists provided that, on the death of either of them, all the partnership property was to become the property of the remaining partner, and the representatives of the deceased partner were to be paid a sum for goodwill, a share of the profits up to the date of death, and the capital standing at the credit of the deceased partner 'in the Accounts of the Partnership'. There was no reference in the agreement to a particular balance sheet or to accounts being prepared at the date of dissolution. Previous annual accounts had shown the heritable property at its original cost plus the cost of renovations and improvements. It was held that in the absence of a reference in the agreement to a specific balance sheet, the deceased partner's share of capital must be ascertained by drawing up a balance sheet as at the date of his death and that all the assets of the partnership must be entered at their fair value at that date. This decision follows several others where the courts have taken the view that, in the absence of agreement to the contrary, an outgoing partner will be entitled to have assets entered in the final accounts at a real or market valuation[3]. A different outcome is seen in the case of *Thom's Exrx v Russel and Aitken*[4]. In that case it was held that on a true construction of the partnership agreement a particular meaning was to be given to 'capital' as distinct from assets, and that the deceased partner's share, which was to include 'the share standing at his credit in the capital of the firm', was restricted to a share in the book value of the capital and did not fall to be calculated by reference to the fair value of the heritage at the date of death. In addition the court found that the

---

1 *Roxburgh Dinardo & Partners' Judicial Factor v Dinardo* 1992 SC 188.
2 1982 SLT 450, OH.
3 *Cruickshank v Sutherland* (1922) 92 LJ Ch 136, HL; *Shaw v Shaw* 1968 SLT (Notes) 94, OH; *Noble v Noble* 1965 SLT 415, affd 1983 SLT 339 (Appendix).
4 1983 SLT 335, OH.

partners, in the continuance of the partnership, had demonstrated clearly by their actings in relation to other deceased and incoming partners that there was no intention that any basis other than book values should be used to determine an outgoing partner's share.

Final settlement of accounts

The rules to be applied in a final settlement of accounts between the partners are set out in s 44 of the 1890 Act but, as with many other provisions of the Act, they apply subject to any agreement. It is provided that:

> 'Losses, including losses and deficiencies of capital, shall be paid first out of profits, next out of capital, and lastly, if necessary, by the partners individually in the proportion in which they were entitled to share profits'[1].

So in a case where the partners have contributed capital in unequal shares but have shared equally each year in profits and losses, and there is a deficiency in capital on final settlement, each partner is liable, in the absence of agreement, to contribute an equal share of the deficiency[2]. If, however, one partner is insolvent and unable to contribute to such a loss, the other partners are not liable to make up his or her share of the loss before the available capital is distributed rateably[3].

Bankruptcy of partnerships

As a consequence of its separate legal personality, the estate of the firm may be sequestrated under the provisions of the Bankruptcy (Scotland) Act 1985. The petition for sequestration may be at the instance of the partnership with the concurrence of a qualified creditor or creditors[4], or at the instance of a qualified creditor or creditors if the firm is apparently insolvent[5]. A qualified creditor is one who, at the date of presentation of the petition, is a creditor in respect of liquid or illiquid debts (other than contingent or future debts), whether secured or unsecured, which amount to not less than £1,500[6]. Both the sheriff court and the Court of Session have jurisdiction in sequestration proceedings[7].

Apart from sequestration under the terms of the Bankruptcy (Scotland) Act 1985, other insolvency procedures are available in relation to partnerships under various statutes enabling them, in certain cases where the partnership has had a place of business in England and Wales, to be wound up as unregistered companies[8], to make voluntary arrangements or to be the subject of an administration order[9].

1 1890 Act, s 44, para (a)
2 *Wood v Scoles* (1866) 1 Ch App 369; *Binney v Mutrie* (1886) 12 App Cas 160, PC.
3 *Garner v Murray* [1904] 1 Ch 57.
4 Bankruptcy (Scotland) Act 1985, s 6(4)(a).
5 1985 Act, s 6(4)(b). See also s 8(1)(b).
6 1985 Act, s 5(4) (amended by the Bankruptcy (Scotland) Act 1993, s 3(3)).
7 1985 Act, s 9(2), (4). See too ss 16,17. Sequestration is dealt with more fully in ch 7 on bankruptcy above.
8 Insurance Companies Act 1982, ss 53, 54; Financial Services Act 1986, s 72; Insolvency Act 1986, s 221(1); Banking Act 1987, s 92(1), (2); Insolvent Partnerships Order 1994, SI 1994/2421 (amended by SI 1996/1308).
9 Insolvent Partnerships Order 1994 (amended by SI 1996/1308).

10 Intellectual property

General

This chapter focuses on three of the four main pillars of intellectual property law: copyright, patents and trade marks. The fourth pillar – dealing with the protection of the industrial design of mass-produced goods – is also commercially important but has been omitted here for reasons of space[1].

Copyright

INTRODUCTION

Economic importance of copyright

The renamed Ministry of Culture has recently emphasised the need to promote a 'creative economy' in Britain involving the arts and entertainment industries[2]. Figures collated in the early 1990s suggest that businesses which are primarily dependent on copyright protection account for at least 3.6 per cent of the gross domestic product (GDP) and generate £17,000 million annually. Over 800,000 people are employed in publishing, broadcasting, the record industry, film-making, the performing arts, software houses and retailing. If the economic contribution of industries with substantial dependence on copyright is also taken into account, the GDP figure increases to 5.4 per cent and the number employed rises to 1.3 million[3]. Another way of gauging the importance of copyright material as a valuable national resource is to estimate the probable impact of copyright piracy in the UK. The Intellectual Property Institute currently estimates that commercial copyright infringement costs businesses £1,000 million in annual turnover and threatens up to 100,000 jobs.

Stimulus to cultural activity

The economic value of copyright protection should not obscure the fact that the existence of meaningful copyright laws is also a matter of considerable cultural and social importance. In theory, copyright law should

---

1 For a thorough examination of designs law, see Fellner *Industrial Design Law* (1995).
2 See *The Art Newspaper* (June 1997) p 4.
3 See Price *The Economic Importance of Copyright* (1993) pp 1–2.

stimulate a virtuous cycle of creative activity which produces economic benefits for authors and producers while at the same time ensuring that society as a whole gains from the introduction of new works. This largely unchallenged view is best summed up by the World Intellectual Property Organisation:

> 'The higher the level [of copyright protection], the greater the encourage-
> ment of authors to create; the greater the number of a country's intellectual
> creations, the higher its renown; the greater the number of productions in
> literature and the arts, the more numerous their auxiliaries in the book,
> record and entertainment industries; and indeed, in the final analysis,
> encouragement of intellectual creation is one of the basic prerequisites of all
> social, economic and cultural development'[1].

Public interest

While the existence of copyright protection can undoubtedly be beneficial to both the author and the public at large, it would considerably overstate the position to claim that 'copyright is an instance in which the public good fully coincides with the claims of individuals'[2]. Any survey of the current law of copyright soon reveals that copyright producers have invariably been successful in pursuing their case for greater protection not only at Westminster but also increasingly with the European Commission in Brussels. As a result, the interests of authors and producers have tended to predominate over the legitimate interests of copyright users. This has led one English High Court judge who specialises in intellectual property law to suggest that the trend in UK copyright law is towards providing 'an over-abundance of protection to the monopoly right owner'[3]. Over against this trend, competition law can – and does – intervene in the public interest to control the exercise of copyright in exceptional cases[4]. It may be, however, that the balance of copyright law has now tilted so far in the direction of producers that a fundamental reappraisal of copyright is required[5].

Nature of copyright protection

The essence of copyright is that the copyright owner has, subject to certain 'fair dealing' exceptions, the right to prevent copying of any substantial part of his material. The owner's position has recently been strengthened by the introduction of a longer period of protection so that the owner now benefits from copyright throughout his or her lifetime and for 70 years after his or her death. This might be compared with the mere 20 years' protection which a patented invention enjoys in the UK. Unlike patents, copyright offers an automatic form of protection; there is no copyright

1 Preface to WIPO Guide to the Berne Convention, quoted by Dixon and Hansen 'The Berne Convention Enters the Digital Age' [1996] EIPR 604 at 607.
2 James Madison, quoted by Davies *Copyright and the Public Interest* (1994) p 3.
3 Laddie 'Copyright: Over-strength, Over-regulated, Over-rated?' [1996] EIPR 253 at 256.
4 See especially *RTE and Independent Television Productions v EC Commission* [1995] 4 CMLR 718.
5 As eg Laddie suggests: [1996] EIPR 253 at 260.

equivalent of the patent register. It is commonly thought that copyright symbols or notices must be put on the author's work but there has never been any requirement to do so in the UK. Copyright notices are commonly used in practice as a simple – though largely ineffective – way of discouraging potential infringers. Such notices are, in fact, only essential where the author wants to ensure copyright protection abroad in the 80 or so countries which have ratified the Universal Copyright Convention[1]. As far as protection under domestic law is concerned, copyright is available to authors in the UK as soon as a qualifying category of work is recorded on any semi-permanent medium (paper, canvas, film, audio or video tape and so on).

The most important principle in copyright law is not explicitly stated anywhere in the Copyright, Designs and Patents Act 1988[2] but has been repeatedly emphasised by the courts. Copyright does not protect general ideas or information as such; it only protects the expression of ideas or information in the form in which these have been recorded by the author. As Erle J put it in a House of Lords case in 1855, 'copyright is a claim not to ideas, but to the order of words [or ideas], and that this order has a marked identity and a permanent endurance'[3]. Perhaps the best modern example of this principle in operation can be found in *Komesaroff v Mickle*[4]. The plaintiff claimed artistic copyright in his design of a glass box containing various shades of coloured sand which could be moved around to create different pictures. The court held that the sand pictures were only temporary and lacked the degree of permanance necessary to be protected by copyright.

TYPES OF COPYRIGHT

Copyright material under the 1988 Act falls into two categories: primary or author's copyright; and secondary or entrepreneurial copyright.

Primary copyright

The 1988 Act recognises the existence of copyright in four primary forms: (1) literary; (2) dramatic; (3) musical; and (4) artistic works. In each case, the author, artist or musician must have produced an 'original' work to receive protection.

Originality

The term 'original' in s 1(1) of the 1988 Act does not mean that the author should have produced something which is new or unprecedented. The originality standard in copyright law is a minimal one: it simply requires

---

1 Universal Copyright Convention, art 3.
2 Hereinafter referred to in footnotes as 'CDPA 1988'.
3 *Jeffreys v Boosey* (1855) 10 ER 681 at 703.
4 [1988] RPC 204, Vict SC.

the author to have produced the material by dint of his or her own, independent efforts. In *London University Press Ltd v University Tutorial Press Ltd*[1], the court had to consider whether degree exam papers were 'original' literary works. There was evidence that sufficient independent effort had been put into revising previous exam questions so as to give copyright to the latest set of degree papers. Thus Peterson J[2] concluded that 'the papers originate from the author and are not copied by him from another book or papers'.

The courts have emphasised that there are no hard-and-fast rules to determine the amount of skill and labour required to establish originality. It will always be a question of degree, depending on the facts of each particular case. What emerges from the case reports is a relaxed, *de minimis* approach: business letters consisting of less than 100 words[3], lists of practising solicitors[4] and football coupons[5] have each been recognised as 'original' copyright material because there was evidence that the author had devoted sufficient effort and skill in producing the relevant work. On the other hand, the Privy Council was not convinced that originality was present in *Interlego AG v Tyco Industries Inc*[6]. Artistic copyright was claimed in the design drawings for Lego bricks. The drawings simply repeated an earlier set of drawings with only a few minor alterations in the marginal text and accompanying figures. The court refused to recognise artistic copyright on the basis that insufficient skill and labour had gone into producing the second set of drawings.

Provided the author's effort goes beyond a minimal level of personal effort, copyright will be recognised even if someone else has independently come up with the same result. If **A**'s sketch or poem is the same as **B**'s, each is entitled to a separate copyright in their respective masterpiece so long as the result was achieved by independent effort.

Literary works

Literary copyright is the oldest form of copyright material recognised by the law. The current scope of protection is found in s 3(1) of the 1988 Act. Literary copyright protects any work 'which is written, spoken or sung' provided that the work is 'original' (and not copied) and has been recorded in some way (s 3(2)). The definition of literary work includes 'a table or compilation' and computer software. The quality or style of the work is unimportant so long as the author has displayed evidence of more than minimal, independent creative effort[7].

Not every collection or use of words qualifies for copyright protection. Names, titles and advertising slogans are regarded as having insufficient

1 [1916] 2 Ch 601
2 [1916] 2 Ch 601 at 609.
3 *Tett Bros Ltd v Drake & Gorham Ltd* [1928-35] MCC 492.
4 *Waterlow Directories Ltd v Reed Information Services Ltd* [1992] FSR 409.
5 *Ladbroke (Football) Ltd v William Hill (Football) Ltd* [1964] 1 All ER 465.
6 [1989] AC 217, PC.
7 See eg *London University Press Ltd v University Tutorial Press* [1916] 2 Ch 601 at 608, per Peterson J.

substance to be protected[1]. For instance, protection has been refused in the case of the invented company name 'Exxon'[2]; the weekly magazine title 'Church and State'[3]; and song title 'The Man Who Broke the Bank at Monte Carlo'[4]. The Privy Council allowed Twentieth Century Fox to use the latter song title as the title for one of their films on the basis that copyright was being claimed in 'a few obvious words'[5]. Those who devise or trade under distinctive names or titles may succeed in applying for trade mark registration under the Trade Marks Act 1994. It is understood, for instance, that Paul Gascoigne has registered 'Gazza' as a trademark in respect of certain categories of goods. The common law action of passing off also provides a remedy where goodwill or a customer base has been built up under a particular trade name[6].

Dramatic works

Original dramatic material receives copyright protection if it has been recorded in some way[7]. The 1988 Act uses the term 'dramatic work' to cover any set of recorded instructions on how a work is to be played or choreographed[8]. If a championship iceskater performs a new routine which follows a recorded sequence, the routine will be protected as a dramatic work. It follows from this that spontaneous or improvised dramatic performances cannot be the subject of copyright protection. In *Seltzer v Sunbrook*[9], the US District Court for the District of California refused to recognise dramatic copyright in the performance of a roller skating competition because the conduct and ultimate success of the various teams was not 'foreordained by [the] author's controlling plan'.

It is an interesting – and commercially important – question whether the format of television shows is protected by dramatic copyright. The Privy Council's view in *Green v Broadcasting Corporation of New Zealand* was that the format of such shows is probably too insubstantial to attract copyright[10]. Hughie Green had devised the television talent show 'Opportunity Knocks' and claimed dramatic copyright in his inimitable catchphrases and the use of a clapometer to gauge audience reaction. The Privy Council dismissed his appeal from the New Zealand courts on the ground that these elements in the show lacked sufficient prominence to possess dramatic character or substance.

---

1 It was suggested in *Shetland Times Ltd v Wills* 1997 SLT 669 at 671, OH, that newspaper headlines could qualify as a literary work but this will rarely be the case since most headlines are too short or are not the product of sufficient independent skill and labour. But see *Lamb v Evans* [1893] 1 Ch 218, CA (elaborate headings given in four languages held to be an original literary work).
2 *Exxon Corpn v Exxon Insurance Consultants International Ltd* [1982] Ch 119, CA.
3 *Primrose Press Agency Co v Knowles* (1885) 2 TLR 404.
4 *Francis Day and Hunter Ltd v Twentieth Century Fox Corpn Ltd* [1940] AC 112, PC.
5 [1940] AC 112 at 123, per Lord Wright.
6 Artistic copyright can, however, be used to protect the design of a masthead used to display a title: *Sun v Daily Mirror* (1988) Times, 27 June (injunction granted to prevent *Daily Mirror* adopting a masthead substantially similar to that used by *The Sun*).
7 CDPA 1988, s 3(2).
8 CDPA 1988, s 3(1).
9 [1936-45] MacG Cop Cas 337 at 342.
10 [1989] 2 All ER 1056, PC.

Musical works

Music attracts copyright when it is recorded and its composition represents the product of independent effort. The originality required may only involve the arrangement of a few notes or chords. The four chords used in Channel 4's signature tune have been held to constitute an original musical work[1]. The definition of musical work in s 3(1) covers only the composer's melody or harmony. For instance, if Andrew Lloyd Webber writes a new musical, the score will be protected as a musical work but the lyrics will attract literary copyright. Dramatic copyright would protect Lloyd Webber's written instructions to the performers on how to play the characters.

Artistic works

Artists and photographers enjoy copyright protection where they have recorded the product of their own labour and skill. The 1988 Act indicates that artistic quality or aesthetic merit is irrelevent to copyright status except, it would seem, in the case of works of 'artistic craftsmanship'.

GRAPHIC WORKS

Paintings, drawings and other graphic works such as maps and plans enjoy artistic copyright under s 4(1)(a) 'irrespective of artistic quality'. The same applies to photographs and works of sculpture. The definition of photograph refers to the 'recording of light or other radiation on any medium on which an image is produced'[2]. This is clearly wide enough to cover videograms and holograms. The courts have held that works of sculpture need to possess artistic character or represent an artistic statement before they qualify for copyright. The New Zealand Court of Appeal, for instance, has held that a frisbee disc is not a work of sculpture because it is an essentially functional object[3].

On the other hand, it is clear that artistic merit or excellence it is not essential for a piece of sculpture to be protected by copyright. For example, many of the art critics may have dismissed Damien Hirst's dead sheep or Carl Andre's famous piece in the Tate Gallery 'as anything but art' but copyright law would regard either arrangement as a work of sculpture because the artist intended the work to be a thought-provoking visual statement.

WORKS OF ARCHITECTURE

The 1988 Act also gives architects artistic copyright in works of architecture. It is generally assumed – though not explicitly stated in the Act – that this form of copyright arises irrespective of the artistic quality of the work. The term 'works of architecture' is defined in s 4(1)(b) to cover buildings

1 *Lawson v Dundas* (1985) Times, 13 June.
2 CDPA 1988, s 4(2).
3 *Wham-O Manufacturing Co v Lincoln Industries Ltd* [1985] RPC 127, CA.

328 Intellectual property

and models for proposed buildings[1]. It follows from this definition that models of existing buildings (such as a scale model of the Houses of Parliament) are not protected by this form of copyright. Design drawings and plans are, of course, protected as graphic works under s 4(2).

WORKS OF ARTISTIC CRAFTSMANSHIP

The final category of artistic copyright offers protection to what are called 'works of artistic craftsmanship'. The phrase first appeared in the Copyright Act 1911 but has never been defined by Parliament. Various obiter comments in the case reports indicate the belief that the term would cover such things as hand-made furniture, stained glass windows and certain pieces of jewellery. After more than half a century, the House of Lords was required to tackle the issue of interpretation directly in *George Hensher Ltd v Restawile Upholstery (Lancs) Ltd*[2]. The case concerned the alleged artistic copyright in the prototype of a 'boat shaped' three piece suite which was said to have been copied by the defendants. Reliance was placed on the prototype because there were no design drawings. The House of Lords unanimously held that the prototype, consisting of a tubular metal frame with pieces of cloth attached, was clearly a functional and temporary work which lacked artistic character.

The apparently implicit requirement in s 4 of the 1988 Act to show artistic quality in the case of works of artistic crafstmanship begs the question of how the courts are to determine whether the relevant work possesses sufficient artistic quality to be protected by copyright. While the prototype in *Hensher* was unhesitatingly refused artistic copyright on the facts of the case, none of the judges could agree on the proper test to determine the presence of artistic craftsmanship. Lord Reid[3] proposed a 'popular opinion' test of whether 'any substantial section of the public genuinely admires and values a thing for its appearance' even although 'many others may think it meaningless or common or vulgar'. At the other extreme, Lord Kilbrandon[4] felt that the craftsman's 'conscious intention' when he set out to create the work was not merely 'important' (as Lord Reid was prepared to concede) but paramount. If the work fell short of the author's original aspirations, the views of other craftsmen should determine whether the author was producing a work of artistic craftsmanship.

Lord Morris proposed a middle way between popular opinion and the artist's intention. He felt that the issue should be determined by the consensus view among various experts in the relevant area of artistic crafstmanship[5]. The difficulty with Lord Morris' approach is that it is essentially circular: the court cannot determine who the relevant experts are without first of all knowing what a work of artistic craftsmanship is under the Act.

---

1 The term 'building' is defined in s 4(2) of the 1988 Act as including any fixed structure so that designs of bridges and piers are protected by artistic copyright.
2 [1976] AC 64, HL.
3 [1976] AC 64 at 78, HL.
4 [1976] AC 64 at 97, HL.
5 [1976] AC 64 at 82, HL.

Secondary copyright

Introduction

The 1988 Act affords protection to various secondary or derivative copyrights which usually arise where an entrepreneur – such as a record or film company – brings together various primary copyrights in a single work (eg a new CD or film). Secondary copyrights are available in the case of: (1) films; (2) sound recordings; (3) broadcasts; (4) cable programmes; and (5) published editions. In each case, the producer of the relevant secondary work receives a distinct copyright over and above the primary copyrights which are represented in that work. For example, a new film invariably generates or brings together at least five primary and secondary copyrights. The primary copyrights include the script (literary work), background or incidental music (musical work) and costumes or scenery (artistic works). The film as a collected sequence of sounds and pictures is entitled to its own secondary copyright. In addition, the film's soundtrack (made up of dialogue, music and other sounds) is given separate copyright as a sound recording under the 1988 Act.

The need for originality is still a feature in the case of secondary copyrights, although the requirements differ slightly depending on the type of derivative work involved.

Sound recordings

Secondary copyright in sound recordings was first recognised under the Copyright Act 1911. By virtue of s 5(1) of the 1988 Act, any recording of sounds 'from which the sounds may be reproduced' is protected. The Act goes on to emphasise that the choice of recording medium is irrelevant to the copyright status of the recording itself. It is also apparent that the nature or quality of the recording plays no part under s 5(1). The originality requirement in the case of sound recordings simply means that the recording should not be a copy of a previous sound recording.[1] Thus, for instance, if **A** and **B** simultaneously make separate tape recordings of the one o'clock gun salute at Edinburgh Castle, each obtains copyright under s 5 in his or her own, independently-made recording. This copyright would be infringed if a copy was made of either of the original recordings without permission. The person who copies one of the original recordings will not obtain any sound recording copyright of his or her own. This is the case even if the copier makes his or her copy with the copyright owner's permission[1].

Films

The term 'film' is widely defined in s 5(1) to mean 'a recording on any medium from which a moving image may by any means be produced'. The definition is therefore broad enough to take in feature films and commercial videos, as well as home videos captured on camcorder or cine film. Originality is satisfied so long as the film is not an authorised or unauthorised copy of a previous film[1].

1 CDPA 1988, s 5(2).

Broadcasts

Broadcasts which transmit ' visual images, sounds or other information' are protected under s 6 of the 1988 Act. This clearly covers television and radio broadcasts, regardless of whether they transmit live or pre-recorded programmes. Reference to transmission of 'visual images' also brings tele-text services within the ambit of this form of secondary copyright. There is an important proviso to the definition which states broadcasts should only involve transmission by 'wireless telegraphy'. Satellite broadcasts are therefore within the scope of s 6. However, where the broadcasts are carried to the viewer 'by a material substance' (such as fibre optic cables), broadcast copyright is not available although the transmission may qualify for cable programme copyright under s 7(1).

The definition in s 6 also refers to the broadcast being one which is capable of being lawfully received by the public. This is mainly relevant to subscription television companies whose broadcasts will attract copyright where the programmes can only be viewed with the aid of decoding equipment issued by them[1].

In terms of originality, a broadcast will not attract copyright if it infringes copyright in another broadcast or cable programme[2].

Cable programmes

Secondary copyright is conferred on cable programmes under s 7(1) of the 1988 Act. Any broadcast which is transmitted by wireless telegraphy is excluded from cable programme copyright. The originality requirement under s 7(6) means that cable programmes are denied protection if they involve the reception and immediate re-transmission of a broadcast. Copyright is also removed from cable programmes which infringe copyright in other cable programmes or broadcasts.

In *Shetland Times Ltd v Wills*[3], the court had to consider whether the pursuers' web site on the Internet was a cable programme service. The definition of 'cable programme service' in s 7(1) refers to a service which consists 'wholly or mainly in *sending* visual images, sounds or other information' by means of a telecommunication system. Lord Hamilton held that the definition prima facie covered the pursuers' web site since the web site sent information to the user when the site was accessed. The court rejected the argument that the web site was an interactive cable programme service under s 7(2)(a) and therefore not entitled to copyright. In Lord Hamilton's view, the fact that the web site welcomed suggestions or comments from users was not 'an essential element in the service, the primary function of which [was] to distribute news'[4]. Interim interdict was therefore granted to prevent the defenders from taking headlines and text appearing in the pursuers' web site and reproducing them in their own web site.

1 CDPA 1988, s 6(2).
2 CDPA 1988, s 6(6).
3 *Shetland Times Ltd v Wills* 1997 SLT 669, OH.
4 1997 SLT 669 at 671.

Published editions

Publishers can rely on copyright to protect the typographical arrangement of published editions of literary, dramatic or musical works[1]. The protection extends to the arrangement of text or other non-artistic material on the printed page. Commercially, this form of copyright can be particularly important where there is a steady demand for reprinted editions of out-of-copyright material. For instance, copyright in Jane Austen's works expired last century but, because television has revived interest in her work, there is still a considerable market for re-published editions of her novels which are set out in an attractive format. To receive copyright, publishers must satisfy the originality requirement in s 8(2). This means that the publisher's typographical arrangement should not copy the arrangement of previous editions.

AUTHORSHIP AND OWNERSHIP OF COPYRIGHT

General rule

Copyright in literary, dramatic, musical and artistic works first belongs to the author or artist who recorded the work in tangible form[2]. As we have seen, the test of authorship is whether the would-be author or artist put a substantial amount of his or her own skill and effort into producing or executing the final work. In the case of sound recordings, the first owner of the sound recording copyright is the producer of the recording[3]. To comply with Community law, the 1988 Act has recently been amended so that copyright ownership in films now vests in the producer and principal director as joint authors[4]. The 'producer' of a sound recording or film is taken to be 'the person by whom the arrangements necessary for the making of the sound recording or film [were] undertaken'[5].

Joint authorship

The possibility of joint authorship in any type of copyright work is recognised under s 20(1) of the 1988 Act. Joint authorship arises where two or more authors have collaborated in the execution of a work and the contribution of each author in the final work is not distinct from that of the other or others. Merely contributing good ideas or helpful revisions does not usually make the 'constructive critic' a joint author; authorship only belongs to the person who actually executes the work[6].

---

1 CDPA 1988, ss 1(1)(c) and 8.
2 CDPA 1988, s 11(1).
3 CDPA 1988, s 9(2)(aa).
4 CDPA 1988, s 9(2)(ab), implementing EC Council Directive 92/100 (OJ L346, 27.11.92, p 61) on rental and lending rights so as to give principal directors copyright ownership for the first time in the UK.
5 CDPA 1988, s 178.
6 See eg *Wiseman v Weidenfeld and Nicolson* [1985] FSR 525.

Commissioned work

If the copyright work was commissioned by a client, the copyright still belongs to the author unless the parties agree otherwise[1]. For instance, the photographer who is hired to take the official photographs at a wedding owns the artistic copyright in the photographs. The client can avoid this result by getting a written assignation or transfer of copyright from the commissioned author[2]. The assignation can take place either before or after the work has been created[3].

Employee authors

There is one major exception to the rule that copyright belongs to the author and this relates to employee authors. Where the work is produced by an employee acting 'in the course of employment', the employer auto-matically becomes the copyright owner[4]. The rationale is that the employee has simply produced what his employer has paid him to do[5]. Employer and employee remain free under s 11(2) to agree a different result; for instance, some employees may be able to negotiate joint author-ship in certain cases. The employee retains copyright if he or she can show that the work was produced outside the express or implied terms of his or her contract of employment. In *Byrne v Statist Co*[6], copyright in a transla-tion produced for the employer was held to belong to the employee because it was produced in the employee's own time and he had negoti-ated a separate fee for the work. Similarly, in *Stevenson Jordan and Harrison Ltd v McDonald and Evans*[7], an accountant published his lecture notes after his employer had paid his travelling expenses and given him secretarial assistance in writing the lectures. The court held that the copyright belonged to the accountant. It was not part of an accountant's duties to give lectures; he was employed to advise clients.

Transfer of copyright

Copyright can only be transferred to a new owner if the previous owner has assigned his or her copyright interest in writing[8]. As an item of incor-

1 CDPA 1988, s 11(1).
2 Even if assignation does not take place, the client enjoys a statutory right of privacy in respect of private and domestic photographs: CDPA 1988, s 85. This would eg prevent the photographs being exhibited in the photographer's shop window or published without the consent of the person who commissioned the photographs: see Lord Beaverbrook's remarks during the passage of the Copyright Bill in 495 HL Official Report (5th series) col 608 (29 March 1988).
3 See CDPA 1988, ss 90 and 91.
4 CPDA 1988, s 11(2).
5 See eg Lord Beaverbrook's remarks that 'if an author wants the security of employment and relies on the employer to provide materials, the guidance, and is paid for doing it, then it is only right that the employer owns any resulting copyright': 493 HL Official Report (5th series) col 1092 (23 February 1988).
6 [1914] 1 KB 622.
7 [1952] RPC 10, CA.
8 CDPA 1988, s 90. Assignation can take place in advance of the copyright work being cre-ated: s 91.

poreal moveable property, copyright can be the subject of a bequest under a will or, if there is no valid will, it will pass to a new owner under the rules of intestate succession[1].

PERIOD OF COPYRIGHT

Differing terms across the European Union

The period of copyright protection has recently been extended following the UK's implementation of the Copyright Term Directive 93/98[2]. The purpose of the Directive was to prevent varying terms of protection across the European Union operating as an artificial barrier to the free movement of goods within the Single Market. The problem was highlighted in *EMI Electrola GmbH v Patricia Im-und Export*[3], where copyright in various sound recordings had expired under Danish law but was still in force in Germany. Copies were made in Germany and delivered to Denmark before being re-exported to Germany. The European Court of Justice held that the copyright owner in Germany was entitled to prevent these imports under German copyright law even though this amounted to a barrier to the free movement of goods which had been lawfully placed on the market in another member state.

EC Directive 93/98

The EC Commission responded to the problem of differing periods of protection by proposing a Directive which levelled up national copyright laws to the longest term available in any member state. Most member states, including the UK, has previously followed the 'life plus 50 years' rule agreed as a minimum term under art 7 of the Berne Copyright Convention. German law, however, had extended this term in 1965 to the author's life plus 70 years and this was the period chosen for EC Council Directive 93/98.

Primary copyright works

In implementing EC Council Directive 93/98, the Duration of Copyright Regulations 1995[4] have extended the term of protection for literary, dramatic, musical and artistic works to the author's lifetime plus 70 years after his or her death[5]. This means, for instance, that the copyright in a novel written by a young author in 1997 could potentially last for nearly a century and a half.

1 CDPA 1988, s 90
2 EC Council Directive 93/98 (OJ L290, 24.11.93, p 9).
3 (Case 341/87) [1989] ECR 79, ECJ.
4 Duration of Copyright and Rights in Performances Regulations 1995, SI 1995/3297. For a comprehensive examination of the implications of the 1995 Regulations, see Adams and Edenborough ' The Duration of Copyright in the UK' [1996] EIPR 590.
5 The 70 years of posthumous copyright begin to run from the end of the calendar year in which the author or artist died: CDPA 1988, s 12(2).

Secondary works

In the case of films, the 1995 Regulations extend the period of copyright to 70 years after the death of the last to die of (1) the principal director, (2) the author of the screenplay, (3) the author of the dialogue or (4) the composer of the music specifically composed for and used in the film[1]. This extended period for film copyright also applies to film sound tracks[2]. Sound recordings enjoy 50 years' protection from the time the recording is made where the recording is not released or played in public[3]. If the recording enters the public domain during the 50-year period, it will enjoy a fresh period of 50 years' protection running from the date of release[4]. Copyright in television and radio broadcasts lasts for 50 years from the date when the broadcast was made. The same period also applies to programmes included in a cable programme service[5].

Performers

Performers are entitled to protect their performance for 50 years from the date of performance. If they decide to release a recording of the performance within that period, the performers are entitled to a fresh period of protection for 50 years running from the date of release[6].

Revived copyright

The 1995 Regulations also deal with the difficult issue of revived copyrights in works where the copyright had expired before 31 December 1995. If the relevant work was still in copyright anywhere in the European Economic Area on 1 July 1995, the expired copyright is deemed to have been revived in the UK at one minute past midnight on 1 January 1996. For example, if an author died in 1940, his or her copyright would previously have expired on 31 December 1990. However, under the 1995 Regulations, literary copyright will automatically have been revived on 1 January 1996 and will now expire on 31 December 2010. The revived copyright belongs to the person who owned it immediately before it expired; if the owner is no longer alive or, in the case of a company or partnership, has ceased to exist, the copyright vests in the original author or the author's personal representatives[7].

---

1 CDPA 1988, s 13B(2).
2 CDPA 1988, s 5B(2). If the film sound track had been treated purely as a sound recording and not as part of the film, the period of protection would have been shorter (50 years from the date of making or release). The protection applies to film sound tracks which existed before 1 January 1996: Duration of Copyright Regulations 1995, reg 26.
3 No account is taken of unauthorised releases or playing in public: CDPA 1988, s 13A(3).
4 CDPA 1988, s 13A(2).
5 CDPA 1988, s 14(2). It is not possible to extend the 50-year period by repeating the broadcast or cable programme.
6 CDPA 1988, s 191(2). No account is taken of the release or public playing of unauthorised recordings.
7 Duration of Copyright Regulations 1995, reg 19.

Those who have previously exploited material in which copyright has now revived are protected under the 1995 Regulations. Any infringement of revived copyrights is excused if it took place before 1 January 1996. A similar exemption is given to anyone who made arrangements before 1 January 1995 to exploit or market material which is now back in copyright[1]. Where someone proposes to exploit a revived copyright for the first time after January 1996, they must first apply to the copyright owner for a statutory licence by giving reasonable notice of the intention to exploit and indicating when exploitation is to be begin. The owner is obliged to grant a licence but he can insist on payment of a reasonable royalty. If the parties cannot agree on royalties, the Copyright Tribunal will fix an appropriate figure[2].

Publication right

Where copyright has expired in a previously unpublished work, anyone choosing to publish it for the first time is now entitled to a publication right 'equivalent to copyright' for a period of 25 years from the date of publication[3]. This new publication right applies to previously unpublished literary, dramatic, musical and artistic works, as well as to films. The publisher has to satisfy two important conditions: he or she must be a national of a state in the European Economic Area and first publication must take place within the EEA. The publication right allows the publisher to prevent any communication of the published work to the public, including making it available on an electronic retrieval system.

COPYRIGHT INFRINGEMENT

Historically, the concept of copyright infringement involved the making of unauthorised copies of the author's work. Over the years, Parliament has broadened the scope of copyright protection to cover other forms of unauthorised and economically detrimental use. At the same time, various 'fair dealing' exceptions or defences have been included in the legislation to allow users to make use of copyright material in certain circumstances without the threat of infringement proceedings.

Infringing use of copyright material can result in primary or secondary infringement. The various types of primary infringement impose strict liability for breach of copyright so that the infringer cannot plead ignorance as a defence. In contrast, liability for secondary infringement depends on proof that the infringer knew or had reason to believe that he or she was committing a breach of copyright.

1 1995 Regulations, reg 23.
2 1995 Regulations, reg 24.
3 See Copyright and Related Rights Regulations 1996, SI 1996/2967, regs 16 and 17.

Primary infringement

Overview

The copyright owner's exclusive rights are found in s 16 of the 1988 Act and breach of any of these rights without the owner's licence is a form of primary infringement. In summary, the owner's exclusive rights relate to (1) copying, (2) issuing or lending copies to the public, (3) public performance, (4) broadcasting and (5) adaptation of his or her work. These rights are breached if they are exercised by an unauthorised party anywhere in the UK. As we have noted, the recurring feature of the various categories of primary infringement is the fact that the infringer incurs strict liability for breach of copyright. It is therefore not open to the defender to plead innocence as a defence to an action for infringement. The court will, however, refuse a claim for damages if the defender did not know or have reason to suspect that he or she was exploiting copyright material[1]. Liability for primary infringement falls on individuals and legal entities such as limited companies and partnerships in Scotland. Company directors or employees can be held jointly liable along with the company if they actively participate in the act of infringement[2]. Indeed anyone who 'authorises' another person to carry out an act of primary infringement is himself or herself treated under s 16(2) as a primary infringer[3].

Causal connection

Liability for primary infringment occurs where the defender has taken, directly or indirectly, all or a 'substantial part' of the pursuer's work in producing his or her own work[4]. The essence of breach of copyright is the existence of a causal connection between the original work and the infringing version. The causal connection is not broken by the fact that the defender may never have seen the original work and has relied on secondhand copies[5]. Applying the same logic, the courts are unlikely to dismiss an infringement claim where the defender has probably had access to the original work but maintains he or she cannot recall reading or hearing it (usually called 'subconscious copying')[6]. Another principle which is important to the idea of infringement is the fact that copyright law does not prevent the taking of general ideas or concepts. It is different matter, however, when it comes to the taking of detailed ideas such as the complex narrative sequence in a novel or play.

---

1 CDPA 1988, s 97(1).
2 *C Evans & Sons Ltd v Spritebrand Ltd* [1985] FSR 267, CA.
3 See further 18 *Stair Memorial Encyclopaedia* paras 1067–1069.
4 CDPA 1988, s 16(3).
5 See *House of Spring Gardens v Point Blank* [1985] FSR 327, discussed by Phillips and Firth in *Introduction to Intellectual Property Law* (3rd edn, 1995), p 177, in which the Irish Supreme Court found that there had been infringement where the defendant had never seen the original pattern but was given detailed instructions by someone who had seen it on how to produce a substantially similar version.
6 See further Laddie, Prescott and Vitoria *The Modern Law of Copyright* (2nd edn, 1994) pp 82–84.

Substantial part

Any form of infringement must involve the taking of the whole or 'any substantial part' of the original work. This phrase is not defined in the 1988 Act despite attempts to insert a definition when the Bill was being debated by the House of Lords in 1988. The government spokesman rejected the idea of a definition partly to maintain flexibility and partly because the courts were already following a well-established approach to the issue of substantiality. Looking at the case reports, it soon becomes apparent that the term 'substantial' leads the courts mainly to focus on the volume and importance of the material taken as it first appeared in its original context. In the leading case of *Ravenscroft v Herbert*[1], Brightman J emphasised that while the court will certainly look at the volume of material taken, 'quality is more important than quantity'. In many instances, however, volume and quality or significance are inextricably linked questions of fact and degree[2]. For instance, in a case concerned with musical copyright, the Court of Appeal[3] held that 'it is quite right to consider whether or not the amount of the musical march that is taken so slender that it would be impossible to recognise it'. More recently, the same court considered that a single frame taken from a film made for television was 'part of the film of which it forms an integer' because one could readily identify the source from which it was taken[4].

The upshot is that are no hard-and-fast rules about what is 'substantial' and each case will always turn on its own facts. The taking of four lines of a poem or song has been held to be infringement in one case but not in another[5]. In *Moorhouse v University of New South Wales*, the High Court of Australia held that a single short story of 12 pages amounted to a substantial part of a collection of 20 short stories[6]. The Court of Appeal found 28 bars, lasting 50 seconds, from the tune 'Colonel Bogey' amounted to 'a substantial, a vital and an essential part' of the original four-minute tune[7]. At the opposite end of the spectrum, the author of a book on the trials of Oscar Wilde unsuccessfully claimed that his copyright had been breached when a film company took large extracts from his book without permission. The book contained lengthy verbatim extracts from the transcripts of the court proceedings which the author had copied from an earlier work by someone else. Assessing the significance or importance of these extracts, the court found that the large sections taken by the film company did not constitute a substantial part of the author's book[8]. An infringement action was also dismissed in *Rees v Melville* where the basic idea for a play involved a sudden marriage of convenience to a beggar girl in order to stop the family fortune being inherited by someone else. The court

1 [1980] RPC 193 at 203.
2 See Bently 'Sampling and Copyright' [1989] JBL 405 at 406–407.
3 *Hawkes & Sons Ltd v Paramount Film Service Ltd* [1934] 1 Ch 593 at 604, CA, per Lord Hanworth MR.
4 See *Spelling Goldberg Productions v BPC Publishing Ltd* [1981] RPC 283 at 297, CA, per Buckley LJ.
5 Cf *Kipling v Genatosan* [1923-1928] MacG Cop Cas 203 (Kipling's poem 'If'); and *Chappell & Co Ltd v D C Thompson & Co Ltd* [1928–1935] MacG Cop Cas 467 (song 'Her Name is Mary').
6 *Moorhouse v University of New South Wales* [1976] RPC 151, Aust HC.
7 *Hawkes & Sons (London) Ltd v Paramount Film Service* [1934] Ch 593, CA.
8 *Warwick Film Productions Ltd v Eisinger* [1969] 1 Ch 508.

found that the author of the second play undoubtedly drew his inspiration from the idea behind the first play but had then gone on to develop his own, rather different narrative in considerable detail[1].

Competing works

While 'substantial part' infringement largely depends on the quantity and quality of the material taken, Brightman J's dictum in *Ravenscroft v Herbert* indicates that competition can also be a relevant factor. This allows the courts to consider whether both works were aimed at the same audience or, as one American judge has put it, 'the degree in which the [defender's] use may prejudice the sale, or diminish the profits of the original work'[2]. In one nineteenth-century case[3], the defendants regularly published four entries a week from the plaintiffs' lists which normally contained 400 entries. The court found that the parties were in direct competition and held that the small amount of copying was an infringement of the plaintiffs' copyright. It was similarly relevant to a finding of infringement in *Ravenscroft* that both publications were aimed at the same general readership even though the plaintiff's book was historical in nature and the defendant's was essentially a thriller[4]. In contrast, in the *Cambridge University Press* case, described by the judge as 'very near the line', CUP's claim narrowly failed because a student text containing a selection of 13 Hazlitt essays was not thought likely to prejudice the market for the full published set of 127 essays[5].

Before considering the various forms of primary infringement in some detail, it is worth re-emphasising that copyright is breached in each case even if the defender was acting in good faith. Unless the defender possessed an appropriate licence from the copyright owner, the defender can only avoid strict liability by showing that copyright did not exist or that his or her use of the material was covered by one of the permitted acts sanctioned under the legislation.

Copying

Copying of literary, dramatic, musical or artistic works is a widely defined form of infringement which takes place whenever that work is 'reproduced in any material form'. The concept of copying includes 'storing the work in any medium by electronic means'[6]. Temporary or incidental copying also infringes the owner's copyright[7]. This means that loading a computer program onto the temporary working memory (or RAM) of a computer in order to run the program amounts to copying the program even though the copy is lost when the computer is switched off[8]. Across

1 [1911–1916] MacG Cop Cas 168.
2 *Folson v Marsh* 2 Story 100 at 116 per Story J.
3 *Trade Auxiliary Co v Middlesborough & District Tradesmen's Protection Association* (1888) 40 Ch D 425.
4 *Ravenscroft v Herbert* [1980] RPC 193.
5 *Cambridge University Press v University Tutorial Press* [1923–1928] MacG Cop Cas 349.
6 CDPA 1988, s 17(2).
7 CDPA 1988, s 17(6).
8 For further discussion, see Bainbridge *Introduction to Computer Law* (3rd edn, 1996) chs 3 and 4.

the whole spectrum of copyright material, the making of identical copies of the copyright owner's work clearly amounts to a breach of copyright.

ESTABLISHING A PRIMA FACIE CASE

The pursuer does not need to prove actual, physical copying by the defender to succeed in an infringement action. The courts will draw a strong inference of copying where the works are identical or possess a striking degree of similarity, particularly if the pursuer can show that his or her own work was already in the public domain before the defender's work appeared. Proof of similarity, coupled with proof of access to the original work, is invariably sufficient to set up a presumption of copying so as to shift the onus to the defender to rebut the case against him or her[1]. To overcome a prima facie case of copying, the court in *Corelli v Gray*[2] identified three possible lines of defence: (1) both pursuer and defender have heavily borrowed or relied on the same common source; (2) the defender's work was independently created; or (3) the pursuer has in fact copied the defender. The case omits to mention a fourth possible defence: that the nature of the subject matter dictates that the two versions are bound to be highly similar or identical. This would be the case, for instance, in the case of street maps or tables of information[3]. However, copying can still be proved in such cases if the defender has copied the pursuer's deliberate mistakes[4].

INDIRECT COPYING

As the leading authors[5] on the subject point out, copyright also offers protection against altered copying, where the copier has adapted or disguised his or her source. The 1988 Act refers to indirect copying as a form of infringement and, as with cases of direct copying, allegations of indirect or altered copying involve consideration of whether the alleged copier has taken or 'lifted' a substantial part of the original work[6]. The upshot is that a clever or sophisticated copier cannot escape liability merely by changing the phrasing, dialogue or setting used in the original version. Thus the party who selects the most appealing items from an earlier compilation and presents them in a different form or style is liable to found guilty of infringement. In a successful infringement action against a defendant who had picked out the most interesting bits from 300 pages of compiled information and reproduced them on a single page, the court found that an important part of the original selection had been reproduced[7].

---

1 See eg *Francis Day and Hunter Ltd v Bron* [1963] 1 Ch 587, CA.
2 (1913) 29 TLR 570.
3 See eg *Lamb v Evans* [1893] 1 Ch 218 at 224, CA, per Lindley LJ.
4 See *Laddie, Prescott and Vitoria* p 84.
5 See *Laddie, Prescott and Vitoria* pp 86–87.
6 See CDPA 1988, s 16(3)(b).
7 *Graves v Pocket Publications Ltd* [1936-1945] MacG Cop Cas 236.

TRANSLATIONS

Perhaps the best example of altered copying is the translation of a work into another language; the words used are different but the underlying detail remains and so the translator will have breached copyright if he or she has translated a significant portion of the original material[1].

DIMENSION-SHIFT COPYING

The 1988 Act identifies dimension-shift copying as another form of altered copying which amounts to infringement. Copyright in a two-dimensional artistic work is breached when a three-dimensional version is produced and vice versa[2]. In the *Popeye* case, artistic copyright in the well-known, spinach-eating cartoon character was held to have been breached when the defendants produced Popeye dolls and mechanical toys without a licence from the copyright owner[3].

SUBCONSCIOUS COPYING

One problem which the courts have occasionally had to tackle is so-called 'subconscious copying' where the defender argues that he or she cannot consciously have reproduced the copyright work because he or she cannot recall having read or heard it on a previous occasion. The few authorities on the issue indicate that subconscious copying is probably not a defence to an allegation of copying[4]. In such cases, the copyright owner's action will succeed if there is proof – or at least a strong inference – that the defender was familiar with the work which is alleged to have been copied[5].

PARODIES

While American copyright law is prepared to uphold satire or parody as a defence, the UK courts refuse to hold that even genuine literary or artistic parodies do not infringe copyright in the original version[6]. Cases of parody or satire will therefore turn on whether the defender has reproduced a 'substantial part' of the original work. As always, this is a question of fact and degree and it may involve a commercial assessment of whether both versions are competing for the same audience or market[7]. In an Australian case[8], the copyright in the script for a television advert featured

---

1 See CDPA 1988, s 21.
2 CDPA 1988, s 17(3).
3 *King Features Syndicate Inc v O & M Kleeman Ltd* [1941] 2 All ER 403, HL.
4 See *Francis, Day and Hunter Ltd v Bron* [1963] Ch 587 at 614, CA, per Willmer LJ holding that subconscious copying 'may' amount to an infringement, whereas Upjohn LJ thought that the issue 'remains entirely open' (617). Diplock LJ supported the former approach on the basis that the copier's knowledge of infringement is not a necessary ingredient in a claim for breach of copyright.
5 See *Ricordi & Co Ltd v Clayton & Waller Ltd* [1928-1935] MacG Cop Cas 154 at 162, per Luxmoore J.
6 See eg Gredley and Maniatis 'Parody: A Fatal Attraction?' [1997] EIPR 339 at 341-342.
7 See *Schweppes Ltd v Wellingtons Ltd* [1984] FSR 210, in which Falconer J held that the drinks label 'Schlurppes' infringed the artistic copyright in Schweppes' label for tonic water.
8 *AGL Sydney Ltd v Shortland County Council* (1989) 17 IPR 99, discussed in *Laddie, Prescott and Vitoria* p 102.

a young couple moving into an new home and extolling the virtues of gas to an unenlightened builder. In response, the defendants produced a very similar advert where the builder was persuaded by the couple to install electricity. The court dismissed the defence of parody and held that the electricity advert reproduced a substantial part of the original version.

Distribution

The copyright owner is entitled to control the distribution or release of the original work and each and every copy to the public[1]. The right applies to all forms of copyright material[2] and is sometimes known as the distribution or issuing right because it allows the owner to put copies into circulation for the first time anywhere in the world[3]. The upshot is that s 18(2) allows the owner to hold the defender strictly liable for copyright infringement whenever the owner first issues the original work or a copy to the public. The distribution right is limited to the initial issue to the public. Subsequent distributions cannot be attacked as primary infringement under s 18 but they can be prevented as a form of secondary infringement under s 22 or 23 (see below).

Rental or lending

The copyright owner can prevent the rental or lending of copies of his or her work to the public under s 18A of the 1988 Act. Until recently, the rental right was confined to sound recordings, films and computer programs. However, with a few exceptions[4], the right now extends to all forms of copyright material. The term 'rental' means 'making a copy of the work available for use, on terms that [the copy] will or may be returned, for direct or indirect economic or commercial advantage'. The owner's lending right relates to the right to control making copies available for use 'otherwise than for direct or indirect economic or commercial through an establishment which is accessible to the public'. Public libraries clearly fall within the scope of the lending right but school or university libraries do not[5]. Certain forms of lending are deemed not to infringe the lending right: public libraries can lend books to each other without the need for a licence, and books covered by the public lending right scheme[6] can be issued to readers with impunity[7]. In the case of both rental and lending rights, copyright is not infringed if copies of the work are made available for public exhibition only or for 'on-the-spot reference use'[8]. There is also

---

1 CDPA 1988, s 18(1).
2 Eg it allows broadcasters to control the release of CDs and videos of radio and television programmes.
3 CDPA 1988, s 18(2) (substituted by Copyright and Related Rights Regulations 1996, SI 1996/2967, reg 9).
4 Ie buildings or models for proposed buildings; works of applied art; broadcasts; and cable programmes.
5 Lending by educational establishments is expressly declared not to be an infringement of the lending right: CDPA 1988, s 36A.
6 For a good description of the public lending right scheme, see *Phillips and Firth* ch 15.
7 See CDPA 1988, ss 18A(4) and 40A.
8 CDPA 1988, s 18A(3).

an exemption in respect of copies made available to be shown or performed in public.

FILMS

Section 93A of the 1988 Act contains a special provision dealing with the ownership of the rental right in films. An author who concludes a film production agreement with the film's producer is presumed to have transferred any rental right in the film to the producer. The author remains free to negotiate retention of the rental right. In addition, the author retains the right if the film uses screenplay, dialogue or music which he or she specifically wrote for that particular film. If the author is deemed to have transferred his or her rental right, he or she is still entitled under s 93B to 'equitable remuneration' from the film's producer (or his or her successors in title) in respect of the film's rental. If the parties cannot reach agreement, the Copyright Tribunal can be asked to fix the amount payable to the author and how it should be paid.

Public performance

The copyright owner enjoys the sole right to perform his work in public or to licence others to do so[1]. Any mode of visual or acoustic presentation is potentially a form of infringement. In the case of sound recordings, films broadcasts and cable programmes, the owner's right covers the playing or showing of the work in public. The key phrase 'in public' is not defined in the 1988 Act but a series of cases, brought by the Performing Right Society on behalf of copyright owners, has clarified when a performance will fall into this category. The most important factor is not the place of performance or the size of the audience but, rather, the economic relationship between the audience and the copyright owner. The courts will therefore ask whether the performance satisfies part of the public demand for the work so as to reduce the owner's potential income. Thus it has been held to be a performance 'in public' to perform a copyright play before members of a village branch of the Women's Institute[2]; to play records to 600 employees working on the factory floor even though visitors were denied access[3]; and to play live music in the lounge of a football supporters' club where only members and invited guests were in attendance and the main purpose of the evening seems to have been to watch a football match on television[4].

Liability for breach of s 19 of the 1988 Act falls on the organiser of the performance or the playing in public. Performers or disc jockeys are specifically exempt under s 19(4) from primary liability.

Broadcasting and cabling

The unauthorised inclusion of a copyright work in television or radio broadcast or cable programme is another form of primary infringement[5].

1 CDPA 1988, s 19.
2 *Jennings v Stephens* [1936] Ch 469, CA.
3 *Ernest Turner Electrical Instruments Ltd v Performing Right Society Ltd* [1943] 1 Ch 167, CA.
4 *Performing Right Society Ltd v Rangers FC Supporters' Club, Greenock* 1974 SC 49.
5 CDPA 1988, s 20.

In the *Shetland Times* case,[1] the court held that the pursuers' web site was a protected cable programme under s 7(1) of the 1988 Act. By publishing material taken from the pursuers' web site on their own web site, the defenders had prima facie breached copyright and interim interdict was granted.

Adaptation

Section 21 of the 1988 Act provides that 'adaptation' of an original copyright work constitutes infringement. The term 'adaptation' includes translations of literary and dramatic works and dramatisation of non-dramatic works. It also includes turning a story into picture form and producing a new arrangement of a piece of music.

In the case of computer programs, the original program is adapted if it is converted into a different computer language or code; for instance, the defender would be liable under s 21(4) if he or she was able to reverse-engineer or decompile the program's object code so as to arrive at its source code[2]. In the latter case, the decompiler has a defence if he or she can show that it was necessary to disassemble the program in order to obtain the information required to achieve the inter-operability or compatability of the decompiled program with another of the defender's programs[3].

Secondary infringement

Secondary infringement largely concerns commercial dealings with copyright material and those who give assistance to primary copyright infringers. The main types of secondary infringement caught under ss 22 to 26 of the 1988 Act include: (1) importing pirate copies; (2) possessing, selling or hiring pirate copies; (3) making or possessing equipment which is designed to make pirate copies; and (4) providing premises or equipment for an infringing public performance. In contrast with the strict liability which attaches to primary copyright infringement, each type of secondary infringement depends on proof that the infringer knew or at least had 'reason to believe' that he or she was commerically exploiting copyright material.

Knowledge required

The test for secondary infringement is an objective one: would a reasonable person, in possession of the same facts as the defender, have formed the reasonable belief that a breach of copyright was being committed[4]? It has been argued[5] that the defender might be able to avoid liability if he or she can show that, despite the facts in his or her possession, he or she actually believed that he or she was not infringing copyright. It is submitted

1 *Shetland Times Ltd v Wills* 1997 SLT 669 at 671, OH.
2 See further Bainbridge *Introduction to Computer Law* (3rd edn, 1996) pp 36–38.
3 CDPA 1988, s 50B.
4 See the Court of Appeal's decision in *LA Gear Inc v Hi-Tech Sports Inc* [1992] FSR 121, CA, applied in *ZYX Music GmbH v King* [1997] 2 All ER 129, CA.
5 See *Laddie, Prescott and Vitoria* p 526.

that this line of argument is unlikely to succeed if a reasonable person would objectively have evaluated the same facts in a different way. Clearly the easiest way to fix secondary infringers with the requisite knowledge is to send them a warning letter[1].

Public performance

In the case of unauthorised public performance of copyright material, the person who gave permission for a 'place of public entertainment' to be used for the performance becomes a secondary infringer[2]. The premises covered by s 25 includes premises which are mainly occupied for other purposes but which are still made available for hire 'from time to time' for the purposes of public entertainment[3]. Caretakers or managers accepting bookings of church halls and community centres are therefore potentially liable as secondary infringers. Such individuals can escape liability if they can show that they believed on reasonable grounds that the performance would not infringe copyright. The defence is cast in such a way that the onus of ascertaining the copyright position rests with the person giving permission for the premises to be used by the performers. As the government spokesman on the Bill confirmed in the House of Lords, the person giving permission must 'take positive steps to check that those using his premises have whatever licences are necessary rather than just sit[ting] back assuming everything is in order'[4].

Public showings

In the case of unauthorised public showings of films or sound recordings, liability for secondary infringement falls on the person who supplied the necessary equipment[5], the occupier of the premises who gave permission for the equipment to be brought onto the premises[6] and the person who supplied the copy of the film or sound recording which was shown in public[7].

DEFENCES

Generally

Copyright has never been viewed as a complete or absolute monopoly so that certain non-commercial dealings (eg research or news reporting) are not regarded as infringing acts. The 1988 Act includes certain 'permitted acts' which, as s 28(1) confirms, 'may be done in relation to copyright

---

1 See eg *ZYX Music GmbH v King* [1995] 3 All ER 1 at 18, per Lightman J.
2 CDPA 1988, s 25(1).
3 CDPA 1988, s 25(2).
4 See Lord Beaverbrook, 493 HL Official Report (5th series) col 1141 (23 February 1988).
5 CDPA 1988, s 26(2).
6 CDPA 1988, s 26(3).
7 CDPA 1988, s 26(4).

works notwithstanding the subsistence of copyright'. Unlike the US Copyright Act, which has a single, broad defence of 'fair use', the UK legislation permits over 30 detailed defences which each have their own particular qualifying conditions; for reasons of space, only the main permitted acts can be outlined here.

Two propositions do, however, apply to all the defences available under the 1988 Act. The defences only come into play where a substantial part of the original work has been taken by the defender. Moreover, each defence is to be construed independently, so that failure to establish one does not preclude success under another[1].

Research or private study

Section 29(1) of the 1988 Act permits 'fair dealing' with a literary, dramatic, musical or artistic work for 'research or private study' purposes. The defence does not therefore cover infringing use of sound recordings, films, broadcasts and cable programmes. Despite attempts by publishers to exclude commercial research from the defence, s 29(1) nevertheless applies to both private and commercial research so 'that the flow of information that business needs is not unduly restricted'[2]. The term 'private study' is not defined but in *Sillitoe v McGraw-Hill Book Co (UK) Ltd* it was held to mean that a commercial publisher could not rely on the defence when it published a set of study notes for students which contained long extracts from the author's published work[3]. It appears, therefore, that the defence is limited to the efforts of individual researchers or students acting on their own behalf. Librarians are, however, permitted under s 29(3) to make a single copy on behalf of a researcher[4]. There is no statutory guidance on when a researcher's dealing with a work is 'fair' but case law indicates that the courts will consider the volume and importance of the material which has been used[5]. The defence is available even if the original source is not acknowledged in any way.

Criticism or review

This 'fair dealing' defence allows copyright material to be used for the purposes of criticism or review[6]. In the *Clockwork Orange* case, the Court of Appeal reiterated that the defence existed to prevent copyright owners deciding who could or could not review their work, when they could review it and which clips they could use[7]. The author and source of the

---

1 CDPA 1988, s 28(4).
2 See Lord Beaverbrook, 493 HL Official Report (5th series) col 1153 (23 February 1988).
3 [1983] FSR 545.
4 For the full extent of the requirement on librarians only to make a single copy, see CDPA 1988, ss 38–40. Other specific exceptions apply to librarians and archivists making a single replacement copy in order to preserve an item which might otherwise be lost (s 42) or providing a single copy of an unpublished work to a researcher (s 43).
5 See Lord Denning in *Hubbard v Vosper* [1972] 2 QB 84, CA.
6 CDPA 1988, s 30(1).
7 *Time Warner Entertainment Co Ltd v Channel 4 Television Corpn plc* [1994] EMLR 1, CA.

quoted material needs to be 'sufficiently acknowledged' for the reviewer to benefit from s 30(1)[1]. The judge in the *Sillitoe* case[2] held that the requirement to acknowledge also meant that the reviewer had to indicate that the author or anyone else has any 'copyright position or claims' in respect of the original work. It is suggested that this conclusion is not justified by the definition of 'sufficient acknowledgement'[3] or indeed on practical grounds[4].

The availability of the defence clearly depends on the presence of commentary or analysis alongside the work which has been quoted. The reviewer's criticism can be directed towards the author's style as well as his or her underlying thought or philosophy. What is fair dealing in any given case is always a question of fact and degree so that, as Lord Denning remarked in *Hubbard v Vosper*, the final conclusion 'must be a matter of impression'[5]. The court will take into account the number and the extent of the quotations or extracts. It would also consider the use made of the extracts and, in particular, whether the reviewer was motivated by a desire to offer genuine criticism or merely to gain an advantage over a competitor. The proportions involved would also weigh heavily with the court; long extracts and short comments may be regarded as unfair but the reverse ratio may be permissible.

Reporting current events

This exception allows copyright material, other than photographs[6], to be used in reporting current events[7]. If the material is included in a newspaper or magazine, the defence is only available if the author's name and the title of the work are acknowledged[8]. On grounds of practicality, acknowledgment on air is not required in the case of television or radio broadcasts or cable programmes[9]. The defence has been successfully used against the BBC during the 1990 World Cup when a satellite television company were held entitled to use short excerpts from the BBC's live broadcasts to report the outcome of matches. Scott J held that the World Cup matches were clearly current events at the time and, moreover, that the clips used were no more than was necessary to report the relevant match[10].

---

1 CDPA 1988, s 178.
2 See *Sillitoe v McGraw-Hill Book Co (UK) Ltd* [1983] FSR 545 at 565 per Judge Davies.
3 Which merely refers to 'an acknowledgement identifying the work in question by its title or other description, and identifying the author': CDPA 1988, s 178.
4 See Phillips '"Sufficient Acknowledgement" of Literary Works' (1984) 100 LQR 179.
5 [1972] 2 QB 84, CA.
6 Hence freelance photographers can exploit their work by offering exclusive rights to the media outlet which is willing to pay the highest fee: see Prime *The Law of Copyright* (1992) pp 122–123.
7 CDPA 1988, s 30(2).
8 CDPA 1988, ss 30(2) and 178.
9 CDPA 1988, s 30(3). In any event, incidental inclusion of copyright material in such media is not treated as breach of copyright: s 31(1).
10 *British Broadcasting Corpn v British Satellite Broadcasting Ltd* [1991] 3 All ER 833.

Public interest

In addition to the above fair dealing defences, the courts are free under s 171(3) of the 1988 Act to recognise that the 'public interest' may override any attempt by the copyright owner to prevent or restrict publication of copyright material. The intention is 'to leave in the hands of the courts the task of dealing with those exceptional cases where it is necessary to balance public criteria with the rights of copyright owners'[1]. The courts will only uphold the public interest defence in very restricted circumstances. In *Beloff v Pressdram Ltd*, for instance, Ungoed Thomas J[2] held that the public interest could only be used to justify uncovering 'misdeeds of a serious nature and importance to the country [which] are clearly recognisable as such'. Examples covered by the public interest defence included breach of national security, fraudulent activity or other conduct 'destructive of the country or its people' and 'matters medically dangerous to the public'.

The same cautious approach to the defence is evident more recently in *Lion Laboratories Ltd v Evans*[3], where Griffiths LJ emphasised that 'there is a world of difference between what is in the public interest and what is of interest to the public'. In this case, the Court of Appeal allowed the Daily Express to publish a leaked company memo because it was in the public interest to reveal that a breathalyser giving inaccurate readings was being used by the police to secure convictions for drunken driving. The court stressed that the decision was not intended to be a 'mole's charter' for employees or public servants with a strong sense of moral outrage to leak material which could then be published with impunity in the media.

Pursuer's own work breaches copyright

It is sometimes argued as a defence that the pursuer should be barred on grounds of public policy from enforcing copyright in material which itself infringes a third party's copyright[4]. In such cases, the fact that the pursuer has infringed copyright does not prevent the pursuer enjoying copyright in his or her own work. In a recent case, for instance, the plaintiff was held entitled to his or her own copyright in the 'disco' version of a song which was notably different from the copyright owner's original version of the song[5]. Moreover, the House of Lords has held that an infringer cannot automatically rely on the fact that the pursuer's work breaches copyright as a defence[6]. At least in cases of technical and innocent infringement 'involving no moral obloquy against a third party', the pursuer can enforce his copyright against the defender 'subject to his obligations to

1 See Lord Beaverbrook 491 HL Official Report (5th series) col 77 (8 December 1987).
2 [1973] 1 All ER 241 at 260.
3 [1985] QB 526 at 553, CA.
4 See the argument of counsel (ultimately rejected by Robert Goff J) in *Redwood Music Ltd v Chappell & Co Ltd* [1982] RPC 109 at 120. The current basis for such arguments is found in CDPA 1988, s 171(3), which allows the courts to prevent or restrict enforcement of copyright on grounds of public interest.
5 *ZYX Music GmbH v King* [1995] 3 All ER 1.
6 *British Leyland Motor Corpn v Armstrong Patents Co Ltd* [1982] FSR 481 at 502.

account to the original author for his due share of any recovery'[1]. It remains an open question whether a pursuer who has deliberately infringed a third party's copyright would be allowed to enforce his or her copyright against an infringer.

REMEDIES FOR INFRINGEMENT

Primary and secondary infringers and those who authorise their actions can only be sued in Scotland in the Outer House of the Court of Session; the sheriff court has no jurisdiction over copyright actions. Title to sue for infringement rests with the copyright owner[2] and the owner's exclusive licensee[3] who enjoy concurrent rights and remedies[4]. The rule about concurrent remedies does not apply to interim interdict so that either party can apply for an interdict to prevent threatened or continuing copyright infringement[5].

Interim interdict

Interim interdict will be granted if there is an arguable case of infringement and the balance of convenience lies in the petitioner's favour. The respective financial positions of the parties is clearly a relevant factor in assessing the balance of convenience; it becomes particularly important where one party is likely to be put out of business as a result of the grant or refusal of an interdict. In a recent case[6] the balance of convenience favoured the grant of interim interdict where the defenders' activities had just begun and had not caused loss to date but there was 'a clear prospect of loss of potential advertising revenue in the foreseeable future'. The fact that an interdict is sought (even unsuccessfully) may lead the parties to agree a licence on terms which are mutually beneficial.

Damages

In cases where infringement is ultimately proved or admitted, damages can be awarded to compensate the pursuer for loss of sales or royalties. To assess the measure of loss where the copyright owner and his or her exclusive licensee have concurrent rights of action, the court is obliged to consider the terms of the licence between the parties and any pecuniary remedy already awarded or available to either of them in respect of the infringement[7]. The quantum of award may be calculated on the basis of a

---

1 See *ZYX Music GmbH v King* [1995] 3 All ER 1 at 10, per Lightman J.
2 CDPA 1988, s 96(1).
3 CDPA 1988, s 101(1). Exclusive licensees enjoy the right to exploit copyright in the manner authorised under the licence to the exclusion of the copyright owner.
4 CDPA 1988, s 101(2).
5 CDPA 1988, s 102(3).
6 See *Shetland Times Ltd* v *Wills* 1997 SLT 669 at 672, OH.
7 CDPA 1988, s 102(4)(a).

fair licensing fee where the pursuer does not exploit the copyright directly but licences others to do so[1]. In cases where the pursuer directly exploits the copyright as part of his or her business, damages will reflect the loss of profits sustained as a result of sales going to the infringer[2]. If the court accepts the infringer's defence of innocence, damages cannot be awarded at all[3]. The innocence defence only covers the defender's lack of knowledge of the existence of copyright; it does not extend, for instance, to cases where an innocent mistake is made about which party can properly give copyright permission[4]. Refusal of damages on grounds of innocence is confined to cases involving primary infringers; secondary infringers are not liable unless requisite knowledge is proved.

Additional damages

In addition to ordinary compensatory damages, the court has the discretion under s 97(2) of the 1988 Act to award additional damages where the justice of the pursuer's case requires such an award. The use of the word 'additional' had been interpreted at first instance to mean that the court can award damages under s 97(2) in addition to other forms of relief available under the 1988 Act. These decisions meant that an award of additional damages could still be made where the pursuer has applied for an accounting of the defender's profits[5]. This view of the legislation has now been expressly overruled by the Inner House in *Redrow Homes Ltd v Bett Brothers plc*[6]. Lord McCluskey held that additional damages was not 'a free-standing right sui generis which is capable of being added on to any other remedy, including damages'[7]. The ordinary meaning of the statutory provisions meant that 'additional damages' under s 97(2) entailed the award of damages 'which are added to or somehow inflate other damages'[8]. It is therefore not possible to claim additional damages in an infringement action where an account of profits is sought.

While some courts have taken the view that additional damages are designed to punish or deter gross breaches of copyright, judges in more recent cases appear to be inclining to the view that the purpose is to provide extra compensation[9]. The 1988 Act singles out the flagrancy of the defender's infringement as one of the important factors to be considered but this should not be seen as a pre-condition for an award of additional damages[10]. The term 'flagrant' is not defined in s 97(2) but has been held

1 *Stovin-Bradford v Volpoint Properties Ltd* [1971] 3 All ER 570, CA.
2 *Birn Bros Ltd v Keene & Co Ltd* [1918] 2 Ch 281.
3 CDPA 1988, s 97(1).
4 See *Byrne v Statist Co* [1914] 1 KB 622.
5 *Cala Homes (South) Ltd v Alfred McAlpine Homes (East) (No 2)* 1995 FSR 36 and *Redrow Homes Ltd v Bett Bros plc* 1996 SLT 1254.
6 1997 SCLR 469.
7 1997 SCLR 469 at 479.
8 1997 SCLR 469 at 481.
9 See *Cala Homes (South) Ltd v Alfred McAlpine Homes (East) (No 2)* 1995 FSR 36 at 42, per Laddie J; and *Redrow Homes Ltd v Bett Bros plc* 1997 SCLR 469 at 481, per Lord McCluskey.
10 See *ZYX Music GmbH v King* [1995] 3 All ER 1 at 19, per Lightman J.

to refer to 'deliberate and calculated copyright infringements'[1]. Additional damages are not therefore appropriate in the case of infringement activities committed during the period when the infringer was unaware that copyright subsisted in the relevant work[2].

Section 97(2) also directs the court to have regard to 'any benefit accruing' to the infringer by reason of the infringement[3]. In *Ravenscoft v Herbert*, this was held to mean that the infringer must be shown to have reaped a pecuniary advantage greater than the damages he would otherwise have to pay[4]. Additional damages were awarded in *ZYX Music GmbH v King* against a record distributor who knew he was handling pirate copies but proceeded 'without any pangs of conscience' to exploit these copies 'for all it was worth'. Lightman J held that ordinary compensatory damages did not adequately reflect the distributor's profit which had largely arisen because he was able to get a copy of what proved to be a No 1 hit single into the UK record charts before the original version was released[5].

Awards of additional damages are not restricted to cases where commercial interests or reputation have suffered as a result of the infringer's conduct. Thus additional damages have been awarded for the acute distress caused by a national newspaper publishing family photographs featuring someone who had recently been murdered by the IRA[6].

Accounting of profits

Few pursuers invoke s 96(2) of the 1988 Act to seek an accounting and payment of the defender's profits[7]. As an alternative remedy to damages, the purpose of an accounting is to get the infringer 'to give up his ill-gotten gains to the party whose rights he has infringed'[8]. Although theoretically attractive[9], an accounting of profits is rarely sought in practice 'because [it] very seldom result[s] in anything satisfactory to anybody'[10]. It will often be difficult to calculate the total profits derived from an infringement, particularly where the infringement only partly contributed to the infringer's final work. In any event, the courts will only award an accounting of net profits after deduction of production costs[11]. Various obiter dicta have suggested that an appropriate figure representing the infringer's own skill and labour should be set against gross profits where the infringer acted honestly[12]. Without referring to these dicta, Millet J

1 *Ravenscroft v Herbert* [1980] RPC 193 at 208 per Brightman J.
2 See *Redrow Homes Ltd v Bett Bros plc* 1997 SCLR 469 at 478.
3 CDPA 1988, s 97(2)(b).
4 [1980] RPC 193 at 208.
5 [1995] 3 All ER 1 at 19.
6 *Williams v Settle* [1960] 2 All ER 806, CA.
7 See Bently 'Accounting for Profits Gained by Infringement of Copyright' [1991] EIPR 5.
8 See *Colbeam Palmer Ltd v Stock Affiliates Property Ltd* (1968)122 CLR 25 at 32, per Windeyer J, quoted in Bently 'Account of Profits for Infringement of Copyright' [1990] EIPR 106.
9 Eg innocence is not a defence: CDPA 1988, s 97(1).
10 *Siddell v Vickers* (1892) 9 RPC 152 at 163, per Lindley LJ.
11 See *Potton Ltd v Yorkclose* [1990] FSR 11, in which the infringer's profits from the sale of houses built in infringement of the plaintiff's designs were subject to a deduction in respect of necessary construction costs.
12 See eg *Redwood Music Ltd v Chappell & Co Ltd* [1982] RPC 109 at 132.

held in *Potton Ltd v Yorkclose Ltd* that the infringer was entitled to deduct just allowances for his time and effort[1].

In cases where the copyright owner and an exclusive licensee have concurrent rights of action for infringement of copyright, the court is not permitted to direct an accounting of profits in favour of one of the parties where the other party has already been awarded damages or an accounting of the defender's profits[2]. Where an accounting of profits is directed, the court is obliged to order a just apportioning of the profits between the copyright owner and the exclusive licensee, subject to any agreement between them[3].

Infringing copies

The copyright owner can ask the court to exercise its discretion under s 99 to order the delivery up of infringing copies which are in the possession, custody or control of another in the course of that other party's business[4]. The court can also entertain an application for delivery up in respect of equipment which is specifically designed or adapted to make infringing copies of a particular copyright work where the possessor knew or had reason to believe that the equipment had been or was to be used to make infringing copies[5]. In either case, the copyright owner must apply for the order within six years from the date when the infringing copy or equipment was made[6]. Where infringing copies or equipment are delivered up, the court has the separate power to order that these items should be forfeited to the copyright owner or destroyed[7].

Seizure

In addition to his or her right to apply for a delivery order, the copyright owner enjoys the statutory 'self help' remedy of seizure which, in restricted circumstances, allows the owner to remove and detain infringing copies without going to court[8]. The remedy applies only to infringing copies which are immediately available for sale or hire in the course of a business[9]. The right of seizure is restricted to premises to which the public have access where the trader is not using these premises as his or her regular place of business. To prevent a possible breach of the peace, seizure

---

1　[1990] FSR 1.
2　CDPA 1988, s 102(4)(b). This rule applies even if the copyright owner and the exclusive licensee are not joined as parties to the same infringement action.
3　CDPA 1988, s 102(4)(c).
4　CDPA 1988, s 99(1)(a). The possessor would be guilty of secondary infringement under s 23(a) if he or she knew or had reason to believe that the copies in his or her possession were infringing copies.
5　CDPA 1988, s 99(1)(b). The possessor in such cases would also be guilty of secondary infringement under s 24.
6　CDPA 1988, s 113.
7　CDPA 1988, s 114.
8　See CDPA 1988, s 100.
9　Eg it could be used where pirate copies are on sale at a street market or car boot sale if the remaining conditions in s 100 are met.

can only take place if the owner or the owner's agent gives the local police advance notice of the time and place of the proposed seizure. The seizure must not involve the use of force and, if infringing copies are seized, a formal notice must be left at the premises.

CRIMINAL OFFENCES

Criminal liability under the 1988 Act depends on proof that the accused knew or had reason to believe that he or she was handling infringing material or breaching copyright. The copyright offences mirror some of the types of activity which give rise to civil liability for secondary infringement. Offences fall into three distinct categories: (1) making or dealing with infringing copies[1]; (2) making or possessing equipment specifically designed or adapted for making infringing copies of a particular copyright work[2]; and (3) causing a copyright work to be performed or played in public[3].

Where a company is proved to have committed a copyright offence, the directors, managers and other similar officers of the company will also be found guilty of the same offence if it is proved that it was committed with their consent or connivance[4].

Penalties

If the accused is convicted on summary complaint of making infringing copies for sale or hire, importing infringing copies for non-domestic use or distributing copies as part of a business or not, he or she faces up to six months in prison and/or a level 5 fine. In serious cases, such offences can be tried on indictment, where the maximum penalty is two years' imprisonment and/or an unlimited fine[5]. For all other copyright offences[6], the accused can only be prosecuted on summary complaint and, if convicted, faces six months' imprisonment and/or a level 5 fine[7].

The court can order the accused to deliver up infringing copies to the copyright owner if it is satisfied that these copies were in the accused's custody, possession or control at the time he or she was arrested or charged[8]. An order can be made whether or not the accused is convicted of the copyright offence. The court also has the power to order the permanent forfeiture or destruction of infringing copies which have been delivered up in compliance with an earlier order requiring delivery[9].

1　Which includes importation and distribution: CDPA 1988, s 107(1).
2　CDPA 1988, s 107(2).
3　CDPA 1988, s 107(3).
4　CDPA 1988, s 110(1).
5　CDPA 1988, s 107(4).
6　Eg sale or hire of infringing copies in the course of a business, or causing a copyright work to be shown or performed in public.
7　CDPA 1988, s 107(5).
8　CDPA 1988, s 108.
9　CDPA 1988, s 114.

MORAL RIGHTS

The UK's need to comply with the Berne Copyright Convention 1886[1] has resulted in the reluctant inclusion of moral or non-economic rights in the 1988 Act[2]. The introduction of explicit moral rights represented a significant departure from the traditional British view that copyright was solely an economic right given to authors allowing them to exploit their work for commercial gain[3]. In contrast, Continental European copyright systems have readily embraced the concept of moral rights because they view the author's work as an expression of his personality. As a consequence, Continental jurisdictions have happily legislated to ensure that the author is entitled to control how his or her work is represented to the public where the copyright belongs to someone other than the original author. This high view of human creativity is best exemplified in French and German copyright law where it has been remarked that moral rights have been 'placed in high position, equal at least to the economic rights; the moral rights essential, the economic in a sense only consequential'[4].

Implementation of the Berne Convention

The UK's approach to the moral rights contained in the 1988 Act retains a strongly pragmatic flavour. The notion that commercial interests should not be hampered by overly-strong moral rights is reflected in the various exceptions specifically created to protect the position of employers, publishers and software houses. Moreover, the new rights are significantly undermined by the recognition that they can be lost by formal or informal waiver[5].

Four specific moral rights are recognised in the 1988 Act: (1) the right to be named (paternity right); (2) the right to prevent derogatory treatment (integrity right); (3) the right to prevent false attribution of authorship; and (4) the right to privacy in respect of photographs and films commissioned for private and domestic purposes. Strictly speaking, only the paternity and integrity rights are derived from the Berne Convention.

Paternity right

Authors[6] and film directors have the right to be identified as such in a 'clear and reasonably prominent' manner on each copy of their work[7]. The

---

1 Ie the Convention for the Protection of Literary and Artistic Works (Berne, 9 September 1886; 77 BFSP 22; C 5167) (the Berne Convention), art 6*bis*.
2 See remarks of Mr John Butcher, Under Secretary of State for Industry and Consumer Affairs: 'We defer to the Berne Convention to the extent that we need to sign it to get appropriate protection for our works and our intellectual and industrial property rights in other countries' (138 HC Official Report (6th series) col 181 (25 July 1988)).
3 For an account of the mixture of common law and statutory protection previously thought sufficient to comply with the Berne Convention, see *Phillips and Firth* pp 244–247.
4 See Cornish 'Authors in Law' (1995) 58 MLR 1 at 9.
5 See CDPA 1988, s 87.
6 Ie of literary, dramatic, musical or artistic works.
7 CDPA 1988, s 77.

same right also applies whenever the work is broadcast, shown or performed in public. Authors can also require their identity as the original author to be acknowledged on adaptations of their work. Architects have the right to be identified on a building[1] which has been constructed to their design[2].

NEED TO ASSERT PATERNITY

Somewhat controversially, the paternity right is not automatic; it must be asserted before it can be enforced[3]. This requirement was justified by the government on the basis that 'users of copyright material [must] know where they stand'[4]. The wording of the provision is ambiguous[5] but it is probably the case that an assertion made in the proper manner has retroactive effect[6]. The assertion requirement can be met by including a statement of assertion in a written assignation of the author's copyright to a new owner[7]. If assertion is effected through an instrument of assignation, the paternity right will bind the new owner and anyone claiming through him or her, irrespective of whether they have received actual notice[8].

Paternity can alternatively be asserted by a separate instrument in writing signed by the author or director[9]. This method would be appropriate in cases where the author has retained copyright but has agreed to licence exploitation of his or her work. Again, the statute is rather unhelpful because it does not make it entirely clear what is meant by an 'instrument in writing signed by the author or director'. The government spokesman indicated at the time that 'the presence of a name on a book is not indication of a claim'[10]. Assertions effected by the separate instrument only bind those who receive actual notice of the assertion[11]. To guard against the paternity right being ignored by third party infringers, authors would be well advised to stipulate in their instrument of assertion that each copy of the work should carry a notice of assertion[12].

---

1 The right is restricted to the first building of that design if several buildings are constructed: CDPA 1988, s 77(5).
2 Identification of an architect on a building must by appropriate means be visible to persons entering or approaching the building: CDPA 1988, s 77(7)(b).
3 The 1988 Act's insistence on the need for assertion probably breaches art 5(2) of the Berne Convention which flatly precludes any formalities in connection with the enjoyment or exercise of rights conferred on authors under the Convention.
4 See Lord Beaverbrook, 491 HL Official Report (5th series) col 352 (10 December 1987).
5 See CDPA 1988, s 78(1).
6 See Merkin *Copyright, Designs and Patents: The New Law* (1989) p 239, referring to the use of 'unless' rather than 'until' in s 78(1) and the remedies provision in s 78(5) which directs the court to take into account any delay in asserting paternity when considering damages for infringement.
7 CDPA 1988, s 78(2)(a).
8 CDPA 1988, s 78(4)(a). See also Lord Beaverbrook: assertion in an instrument of assignation 'binds the assignee or his successors absolutely. If the successors lose it, that is their problem' (491 HL Official Report (5th series) col 365 (10 December 1987)).
9 CDPA 1988, s 78(2)(b).
10 See Lord Beaverbrook 493 HL Official Report (5th series) col 1302 (25 February 1988).
11 CDPA 1988, s 78(4)(b).
12 Eg 'John Smith has asserted his right to be identified as the author of this work in accordance with ss 77 and 78 of the Copyright, Designs and Patents Act 1988'.

MANNER OF IDENTIFICATION

The author or director can stipulate in his or her assertion of paternity how he or she wishes to be identified; this can include the use of a pseudonym or initials or some other special form of identification[1]. If the author makes no express provision over the form of his or her identification, the parties bound by the author's notice are entitled to use any reasonable form of identification. While the 1988 Act entitles the author to clear and reasonably prominent identification on each occasion[2], the author's moral right does not allow him or her to dictate its size or precise location; an author cannot, for instance, insist that his or her name is placed on the spine of a book.

EXCEPTIONS

As noted above, the paternity right is qualified by numerous exceptions. Publishers successfully lobbied to ensure that employee authors did not enjoy the right over work produced in the course of employment[3]. The government accepted the argument that a single contributor to a multi-authored publication could hold up publication by threatening litigation if that contributor felt that his or her contribution had not been properly accredited. For broadly the same reason, self-employed authors are also denied the right of paternity in respect of the distinct contributions which they have made to collective works such as encyclopaedias and dictionaries[4]. Computer programmers are barred from asserting paternity, presumably on the basis that it would be inconvenient to have to trace and then acknowledge everyone who might have contributed to the production or updating of each program[5].

In addition to the author exceptions, the 1988 Act also removes the need to identify authors in news broadcasts which report current events. Quotations used in exam questions also do not need to be accredited; nor do statements made in Parliament or by judges in court proceedings[6].

CONSENT AND WAIVER

Where the paternity right has been asserted, the right is deemed to be personal to the author so that he or she cannot assign it to a third party during the author's lifetime. The same bar applies to those to whom the rights pass on the author's death[7]. However, the author's paternity right can be overridden under the statutory provisions dealing with consent and waiver which the government included to prevent copyright users being placed 'in an impossible position, with a sword of Damocles hanging over their heads'[8]. The author may consent to his or her work being used in a

1 CDPA 1988, s 77(8).
2 CDPA 1988, s 77(7).
3 CDPA 1988, s 79(3).
4 CDPA 1988, s 79(6).
5 CDPA 1988, s 79(2)(a).
6 CDPA 1988, s 79(4).
7 CDPA 1988, s 94.
8 See Lord Beaverbrook's remarks in 491 HL Official Report (5th series) col 397 (10 December 1987).

particular way without his or her authorship being acknowledged[1]. Verbal consent appears to be sufficient to bind both the author and his or her successors[2].

In addition to consent, the author can lose protection by surrendering or waiving paternity in advance. Waiver was defined during Parliamentary debate as 'giving up the right completely or to a limited extent without any particular act necessarily being in view'[3]. The parties may opt to put the waiver in writing but this is not required under the 1988 Act[4]. The terms of a express waiver can be as narrow or as wide as the parties choose: it can relate to works in general or only to specific works; it can be conditional or unconditional; and it can be revocable. If the author signs an expressly irrevocable waiver, he or she binds his successors who will then be barred from taking action in relation to the work concerned[5].

INFORMAL WAIVER

The 1988 Act also envisages the possibility of an informal waiver barring future enforcement by the author[6] and his and her successors[7]. The informal waiver provision is undoubtedly the most controversial provision in the whole moral rights scheme and it has attracted considerable criticism since it was first proposed[8]. The upshot of this provision is that the author's inadvertent conduct before or after an assertion of paternity may be sufficient to bar him or her from subsequently enforcing his or her moral right to be identified as the author of a particular work.

DURATION OF PATERNITY RIGHT

The paternity right lasts for the same period as copyright – the author's life plus 70 years[9].

TRANSMISSION

Because the paternity right is personal, it cannot be assigned to a new owner[10]. It can, however, transmit on death by virtue of a valid will or under the law of intestacy[11].

---

1 CDPA 1988, s 87(1).
2 CDPA 1988, s 95(4).
3 See Lord Beaverbrook, 493 HL Official Report (5th series) col 1338 (25 February 1988).
4 CDPA 1988, s 87(2).
5 CDPA 1988, s 87(3).
6 CDPA 1988, s 87(4).
7 CDPA 1988, s 95(4).
8 See eg Carty and Hodkinson 'Copyright, Designs and Patents Act 1988' (1989) 52 MLR 369 at 372–373.
9 CDPA 1988, s 86(1).
10 CDPA 1988, s 94.
11 CDPA 1988, s 95. Successors are, of course, bound by any consents or waivers granted during the rightholder's lifetime: s 95(4).

REMEDIES

Breach of the paternity right entitles the author to obtain interim interdict to prevent copies being released without his or her authorship being identified. Damages can also be claimed for a breach of statutory duty[1]. The court is required to take into account any delay in asserting paternity when considering remedies[2].

Integrity right

The 1988 Act allows authors and directors to take action against 'derogatory treatment' of their copyright work. The right of action exists only if the affected work has been released to the public[3]. The term 'treatment' refers to 'any addition to, deletion from or alteration to or adaptation of the work'[4]. The right to object to treatment can arise in respect of any part of the author's work[5]. Thus the removal of a key line of dialogue in play may amount to infringement of the author's integrity right[6].

NEED FOR MODIFICATION

The wording of the statutory definition of 'treatment' suggests that the integrity right is confined to modifying action in relation to the body of the work itself. It would appear, therefore, that unless the courts interpret the definition creatively, the act of destroying an author's work would not be actionable because there is nothing left to put before the public[7]. The need for modification also appears to exclude the integrity right from cases where the author wishes to object to the setting or context in which his or her work is placed[8]. The fact that the author's work has been relocated to a less favourable position would similarly appear to be outside the author's moral right[9].

In addition to these apparent exclusions, the 1988 Act expressly removes the right of integrity from translations of literary or dramatic

---

1 CDPA 1988, s 103(1).
2 CDPA 1988, s 78(5).
3 See CDPA 1988, s 80(3)-(6).
4 CDPA 1988, s 80(2)(a).
5 CDPA 1988, s 89(2).
6 See *Frisby v British Broadcasting Corpn* [1967] Ch 932. Broadcasters do, however, have the right to delete any material which offends against good taste or decency provided they carry a disclaimer disassociating the author or director from the alterations: CDPA 1988, s 81(6).
7 See *Phillips and Firth* p 250; and compare art 6*bis* of the Berne Convention which accords the integrity right in respect of 'any distortion, mutilation or other modification of, *or other derogatory action in relation to*' the work (emphasis added).
8 See eg the former Beatles' reported complaint that Michael Jackson, having acquired the copyright in many of their lyrics, was 'cheapening' their songs by allowing some of them to be used in television commercials: *The Independent,* 6 November 1995, p 6.
9 Cf Glasgow District Council's controversial removal of the specially-commissioned 'Strathclyde' murals from the foyer of the city's new concert hall in September 1991. The murals were initially re-erected in a rehearsal room at the Tramway Theatre but were later taken down and put into storage. The artist Ian McCulloch decided not to litigate over the removal after receiving legal advice that the definition of 'treatment' offered him little prospect of success.

copyright works[1]. Thus unlike the position in France, it is not possible in the UK for an author 'to object to a translation which murders his work or distorts its meaning'[2] although the translator could take action against modifications carried out to his translation[3]. The 1988 Act also declares that the integrity right is not available where the re-arrangement of a musical work involves no more than a change of key or register[4].

DEROGATORY TREATMENT

To succeed under the integrity right, the author must show that the treatment of his or her work is 'derogatory' in the sense that the modification 'amounts to a distortion or mutilation of the work or is otherwise prejudicial to the honour or reputation of the author or director'[5]. The test of prejudice to the author's honour or reputation appears to be objective, depending on whether the author's view was a reasonable one. In a recent unsuccessful action[6], the well-known cartoonist Bill Tidy complained that his honour or reputation had suffered because copies of his original cartoons had been reproduced in smaller dimensions. Rattee J. held that the artist's personal view had to be tested against evidence as to how the reduction in size of his work affected his reputation in the public mind. The author's own opinion about the treatment of his work is therefore important evidence but it does not determine whether that treatment was derogatory.

EXCEPTIONS

As with the paternity right, the right to object to derogatory treatment is qualified by a good number of exceptions. The right does not apply to material submitted by the author for publication in newspapers or magazines. Similarly, material submitted for publication in collective works of authorship such as dictionaries and encyclopaedias is not protected by the integrity right[7]. To preserve flexibility in the process of compiling and editing news reports, the right is removed in the case of any copyright work produced for the purpose of reporting current events[8]. Derogatory treatment of computer programs is also not actionable.

Employee authors or directors do not enjoy a right of integrity in relation to copyright material produced in the course of employment. However, the right to object to modifications will apply where the employee is identified as author or director. In such cases, liability for infringement will be avoided if the modified work carries a disclaimer

1 CDPA 1988, s 80(2)(a)(i).
2 See *Laddie, Prescott and Vitoria* p 1015.
3 See eg the Provincial Appeal Court of Barcelona's decision, reported in [1995] EIPR D-229, to uphold the award of damages in favour of a professor of translation who found that his translation into English had been modified so as to include numerous errors in syntax and spelling.
4 CDPA 1988, s 80(2)(a)(ii).
5 CDPA 1988, s 80(2)(b).
6 *Tidy v Trustees of the Natural History Museum* [1996] EIPR D-81.
7 CDPA 1988, s 81(4).
8 CDPA 1988, s 81(3).

when it is released to the public indicating in a 'clear and reasonably prominent manner' that the work has been subjected to treatment to which the employee has not consented[1].

Broadcasters are not subject to the integrity right where this would conflict with other statutory requirements placed upon them[2]. Thus the BBC can edit programmes to remove material which offends against good taste or decency or is likely to encourage crime or be offensive to public feeling. Commercial broadcasting companies are entitled to alter or remove material to avoid committing an offence. In both cases, liability to the author is avoided if a sufficient disclaimer disassociating the author or director from the altered version is broadcast along with the programme[3].

CONSENT AND WAIVER

Like the paternity right, the right to object to derogatory treatment can be lost or surrendered by consent or waiver which binds the author's heirs or successors[4].

DURATION OF INTEGRITY RIGHT

The integrity right lasts for the same period as copyright in the relevant work[5].

TRANSMISSION

The integrity right cannot be assigned during the author's lifetime but it will transmit on death to the author's heirs or successors[6].

REMEDIES

The usual remedies of interdict and damages for breach of statutory duty apply[7]. If the court thinks that interdict is an adequate remedy in the circumstances, it will grant interdict barring the prohibited act unless a disclaimer is published or broadcast dissociating the author or director from the treatment of his work. The court will approve the terms of the disclaimer and the manner in which it will be issued[8]. If a building is the subject of derogatory treatment, the architect has the right to have his or her name removed from the building[9].

False attribution

The right to prevent false attribution of authorship is the statutory counterpart to the moral right to be identified. The right is not provided for

1 CDPA 1988, ss 82 and 178.
2 CDPA 1988, s 81(6).
3 CDPA 1988, s 81(6) proviso.
4 CDPA 1988, ss 87, 95(1), (4).
5 CDPA 1988, s 86(1).
6 CDPA 1988, ss 94 and 95.
7 CDPA 1988, s 103(1).
8 CDPA 1988, s 103(2).
9 CDPA 1988, s 80(5).

under the Berne Convention but it previously existed under the Copyright Act 1956 where it was accorded in respect of literary, dramatic, musical and artistic works. False attribution of authorship in the case of such works remains actionable under the 1988 Act where the defender makes an express or implied statement of authorship. In *Noah v Shuba*[1], the court held that the publisher of a magazine was liable for false attribution where it printed a long quotation attributed to the plaintiff which contained two additional sentences written by someone else. Similarly in *Moore v News of the World*[2], a singer obtained damages from a Sunday newspaper when it published an article allegedly written by her which had largely been composed by a journalist. The 1988 Act extends the previous legislation by allowing film directors to object to a film being falsely attributed to them as director[3].

NEED FOR ATTRIBUTION TO REACH PUBLIC DOMAIN

The right to object to false attribution is confined to cases where the statement of authorship reaches the public domain. Thus infringement takes place where copies of the work carrying a false statement of authorship are issued to the public[4] or an artistic work is publicly exhibited with a false attribution[5]. If the work is publicly performed or broadcast, liability will depend on proof that the performer or broadcaster knew or had reason to believe that the attribution was false[6]. Authors can rely on the right to take action where they are falsely stated to have adapted a literary, dramatic or musical work. Similarly artists can object to false representations that a copy of an artistic work is one which they have made[7]. The statutory right also allows authors and directors to object to false attributions appearing in publicity material[8].

DURATION

The right to object to false attribution endures for 20 years after the alleged author's or director's death[9] so that infringements remain actionable by the deceased's personal representatives[10] who are entitled to recover damages on behalf of the estate[11].

CONSENT AND WAIVER

The right to take action in respect of false attribution can be lost if consent is given or the right is formally or informally waived[12].

1 [1991] FSR 14.
2 [1972] 1 QB 441, CA.
3 CDPA 1988, s 84(1).
4 CDPA 1988, s 84(2)(a).
5 CDPA 1988, s 84(2)(b).
6 CDPA 1988, s 84(3).
7 CDPA 1988, s 84(8).
8 CDPA 1988, s 84(4).
9 CDPA 1988, s 86(2).
10 CDPA 1988, s 95(5).
11 CDPA 1988, s 95(6).
12 CDPA 1988, s 87.

TRANSMISSION

Like the other moral rights, the right to object to false attribution is deemed to be a personal right which cannot be assigned[1].

REMEDIES

Where an action is well-founded, the pursuer can seek an interdict as well as an award of damages for breach of statutory duty[2]. In the few reported cases on false attribution, the amount of damages recovered has not exceeded £250[3]. The 1988 Act[4] leaves open the possibility of claiming damages for defamation or passing off in the same action for breach of statutory duty[5].

Right to privacy

The 1988 Act introduced a moral right to privacy in respect of photographs and films which were commissioned for private and domestic purposes[6]. Privately-commissioned videos are included on account of the fact that they satisfy the definition of a 'film'[7]. The right was created in recognition of the fact that the person who commissions the taking of a photograph or the making of a film does not own the copyright in the resultant work unless it is assigned to him[8]. The term 'commission' is not defined but it is probably wide enough to cover commissioned works which are undertaken for no payment[9]. Thus the privacy right would appear to be available, for instance, to someone who asks another person attending a private party to take a photograph. Provided the work resulting from the commission attracts copyright, the photographer owns the copyright but the person who commissioned the work[10] can prevent the issue of copies to the public or the public exhibition or broadcasting of the work[11]. Certain forms of publicity are deemed not to be an infringement of privacy and these mainly include the incidental inclusion of the work in a broadcast or film[12].

---

1 CDPA 1988, s 94. Publishers and record companies cannot therefore raise an action; only the author can do so.
2 CDPA 1988, s 103(1).
3 See eg *Noah v Shuba* [1991] FSR 14.
4 CDPA 1988, s 171(4).
5 Eg in *Noah v Shuba* [1991] FSR 14, the plaintiff received damages of £7,500 for defamation on the basis that the quotation falsely attributed to him offered readers grossly incompetent and dangerous advice on hygienic skin piercing.
6 The work must have been created on or after 1 August 1989.
7 See CDPA 1988, s 5(1).
8 Copyright in photographs and films vests in the maker of the work or, in the case of an employee, in his employer: CDPA 1988, ss 9 and 11 (as amended).
9 For a contrary view, see *Laddie, Prescott and Vitoria* pp 1027–1028.
10 But not any other person whose image is recorded in the photograph or film.
11 CDPA 1988, s 85(1). Publicity in relation to any substantial part of the commissioned work is actionable: CDPA 1988, s 89(1).
12 CDPA 1988, s 85(2).

DURATION

The privacy right lasts for the same period as the copyright in the photographs or film[1].

CONSENT AND WAIVER

As with the other moral rights, the right of privacy cannot be assigned[2] although it can be lost by consent or waiver[3]. In the case of jointly commissioned works, each commissioner enjoys an individual right of privacy so that the consent or waiver of one commissioner does not deprive the others of the moral right of privacy[4].

TRANSMISSION

The right of privacy transmits on death to the deceased's heirs and representatives[5].

REMEDIES

Where privacy in photographs has been infringed, the pursuer is entitled to the usual remedies of interdict and damages[6].

INTERNATIONAL PROTECTION OF COPYRIGHT

Copyright is a strictly territorial property right which only offers protection within national boundaries. Thus the 1988 Act grants qualifying authors[7] exclusive rights to exploit copyright material within the UK[8]. To ensure that British nationals gain copyright protection abroad, the UK is a party to international treaties which require member states to give foreign nationals the same degree of copyright protection as their own nationals enjoy under domestic law. The principle of reciprocal treatment is the basis for both the Universal Copyright Convention of 1952[9] and the Berne Convention[10], the latter having attracted over 100 signatories. The Berne Convention is the more important of the treaties because it lays down a

---

1 CDPA 1988, s 86(1).
2 CDPA 1988, s 94.
3 CDPA 1988, s 87.
4 Thus eg wedding photographs would usually be considered to be jointly commissioned works which could only be published if both husband and wife have waived the moral right of privacy: *Mail Newspapers plc v Express Newspapers plc* [1987] FSR 90.
5 CDPA 1988, s 95
6 CDPA 1988, s 103(1),
7 Ie those who have (1) a personal connection with the UK by virtue of nationality or residence at the time their work was first published; or (2) lack such a personal connection but have had their work first published in the UK. See further Cornish *Intellectual Property* (3rd edn, 1996) paras 10-34–10-40.
8 See CDPA 1988, s 16(1).
9 Ie the Universal Copyright Convention (Geneva, 6 September 1952; TS 66 (1957); Cmnd 289), art 2.
10 Berne Convention, art 5.

higher degree of mimimum protection which member states undertake to provide before their own nationals gain reciprocal protection in other Berne states. If a member state chooses to introduce domestic copyright laws which offer greater protection than the minimum standards prescribed under the Berne Convention, nationals from all other Berne states, including the UK, are entitled to that higher level of protection.

COMPUTER PROGRAMS

Scope of copyright protection

Because of the difficulties in patenting computer programs[1], copyright has proved to be an attractive means of protecting the investment expended by software houses and freelance programmers. The 1988 Act includes computer programs within the definition of 'literary work' so that they enjoy copyright protection throughout the programmer's lifetime plus 70 years after his or her death[2]. Fresh copyrights can arise where a program is modified or adapted if the changes are not insignificant[3]. Literary copyright also offers separate protection to the programmer's preparatory design material; for instance, the programmer's flowcharts and notes would be independently protected for the same period as the final program itself[4].

Infringement

Copyright in a program is infringed by direct or indirect copying[5]. In the case of direct, line-by-line copying, it is enough that the defender has made a transient or incidental copy[6] which has involved storing the program (or a substantial part thereof) 'in any medium by electronic means'[7]. An inference of copying is raised if there are sufficient similarities between the respective works and an opportunity of access has been proved. It is particularly telling in a case of alleged copying that there are resemblances 'in inessentials, the small, redundant, even mistaken elements of the copyright work'[8]. Thus the appearance of common spelling

---

1 Purely 'mental acts' cannot be patented and hence the Patents Act 1977, s 1(2) excludes programs 'as such' from patenting on the ground that they represent an electronic method of performing a mental act. Some programs can however be patented if the applicant can demonstrate that 'there is some technical effect which is more than just a software implementation of "mental steps"': Bainbridge, *Introduction to Computer Law* (3rd edn, 1996) p 5.
2 CDPA 1988, s 3(1)(b) and new s 12. Since most programs are written by several authors, the term of protection is the longest life plus 70 years.
3 *IBCOS Computers Ltd v Barclays Mercantile Highland Finance Ltd* [1994] FSR 275 at 289, per Jacob J.
4 CDPA 1988, s 3(1)(c).
5 CDPA 1988, ss 16(3) and 17(1).
6 CDPA 1988, s 17(6). Loading and running a program so that it is stored on a computer's random access memory would therefore amount to copying even though the copy is wiped from the memory as soon as the computer is switched off.
7 CDPA 1988, ss 16(3) and 17(2).
8 *Billhöfer Maschinenfabrik GmbH v TH Dixon & Co Ltd* [1990] FSR 105 at 123, per Hoffman J.

mistakes and the use of identical redundant code in both programs are material evidence of direct copying.

Where there is prima facie evidence of copying, the onus shifts to the defender to rebut the presumption against him or her. The defender can argue that the material was already in the public domain or that both parties derived the similar parts from a third party. The defender can also show that the similarity 'arises out of functional necessity – that anyone doing this particular job would be likely to come up with similar bits'[1]. If the court is satisfied that copying has taken place, it will then consider whether the copier has taken a 'substantial part' of the original program. In many cases, the issue will not be in doubt but in each instance the court will rely heavily on expert evidence before reaching a conclusion.

Adaptation as infringement

In addition to direct copying, the 1988 Act declares the unauthorised adaptation of a computer program to be an act of infringement. The concept of adaptation or indirect copying includes making an arrangement or altered version of a program. Translations of an original program into a different computer language or code are also deemed to be adaptations.[2] Indirect or non-literal copying of a program involves an attempt to copy the structure, functions and visual appearance of an original program where the infringer has possibly used a different underlying code. In other words, infringement takes place where the defender has tried to re-create the 'look and feel' of the program without necessarily engaging in line-by-line copying. While copyright will not stop the taking of general ideas or principles, it will prevent the copying of a detailed idea where this represents an 'overborrowing of the skill, labour and judgment which went into the copyright work'[3]. If there is prima facie evidence of non-literal copying, the court still has to consider whether a substantial part of the structure and design features of the original program has been taken.

User rights

Users of computer programs enjoy several defences under the 1988 Act. In the first place, lawful users of a program are permitted to make 'necessary' back-up copies[4]. The concept of lawful user includes not only the original licensed purchaser but also his or her successors in title or any other reasonably anticipated user[5]. Secondly, lawful users are allowed to copy or adapt a computer program in order to correct errors or for any other purpose 'necessary for lawful use'. This right is subject to any contractual provision to the contrary. Thus, for instance, a program can be

---

1 See *IBCOS Computers Ltd v Barclays Mercantile Highland Finance Ltd* [1994] FSR 275 at 296–297, per Jacob J.
2 CDPA 1988, ss 16(1)(e) and 21.
3 See *IBCOS Computers Ltd v Barclays Mercantile Highland Finance Ltd* [1994] FSR 275 at 302, per Jacob J.
4 CDPA 1988, s 50A.
5 Eg employees or freelance consultants engaged by the user.

decompiled to correct errors if the licence agreement does not prohibit error correction[1].

The 1988 Act also allows lawful users to decompile or disassemble a program in order to retrieve the information necessary to develop a new program which will interact with the decompiled program or other existing programs used by the user[2]. The user may, for instance, have purchased a spreadsheet program which he or she wants to operate in conjunction with the user's existing word processing program. The decompilation defence allows the user to disassemble the spreadsheet program in order to create a new compatible program which will allow the speadsheet program to interoperate with the word processing program. Decompilation is restricted to cases where the necessary information is not 'readily available' to the user. It remains an open question whether information is 'ready available' if the published details of the relevant information contain errors or the information, though accurate, is only available in return for a fee[3]. Any contractual provision purporting to prevent decompilation is void unless the term was part of an agreement entered into before 1 January 1993[4].

Patents

INTRODUCTION TO THE PATENT SYSTEM

The UK's patent system is frequently justified on the basis that it offers an important incentive to innovators and inventors to deploy their inventive talents to the full. However, the few empirical studies on the subject suggest that freelance inventors are motivated less by the prospects of gaining a patent to make money than they are by the challenge of problem-solving and the desire to produce something which is genuinely useful to society. Given that nearly 90 per cent of all patents are produced by employee inventors whose employers invariably own the patent, the patent system really operates as a form of incentive to businesses and venture capitalists who are considering whether to invest in research and development. The prospect of gaining an absolute monopoly for 20 years affords investors the reasonable possibility (but not, of course, the guarantee) of not only recouping their initial development costs but also of reaping significant returns in terms of sales income or royalty payments.

Nature of patent monopoly

The 'prize' on offer to the potential patent owner (or patentee) is a high one because the Patents Act 1977[5] will give him or her a full or absolute

1 CDPA 1988, ss 50A(2) and 50C.
2 CDPA 1988, ss 50B(1).
3 See Cornish *Intellectual Property* (3rd edn, 1996) p 453.
4 CDPA 1988, ss 50B(4) and 296A.
5 Referred to hereinafter in footnotes as 'PA 1977'.

monopoly over his or her invention. Not only does the owner enjoy the right to stop others copying the substance of his or her patent, he or she can also prevent other inventors making the same invention independently. In return for these monopoly rights, the patentee is required to disclose the substance of his or her invention to the world at large. This means that anyone can consult the detailed patent specification at the Patent Office. The Patent Office acts, therefore, as an accessible store of up-to-date technical information which is available to competitors who might be able to use the information to improve on the original patent and then seek a patent of their own. In theory at least, the patent system benefits not only inventors and their competitors, but also customers and consumers, whose power of choice is enhanced by the ability to select from a wider range of products available on the market.

Patent system

The UK patent system is administered by the Patent Office in Newport, Gwent. Headed by the Comptroller of Patents, the Office decides on the validity of patent applications filed under the Patents Act 1977. Parts of the Act give domestic legal effect to the European Patent Convention[1] (EPC) which established certain common criteria for patenting inventions. The EPC also established the European Patent Office (EPO) in Munich so that inventors in the UK are able to patent their invention in several EPC states by filing a single patent application. The working of the EPO will be considered separately below but, for present purposes, the importance of the EPO for the UK patent system lies in the fact that its decisions on interpretation of the EPC are increasingly cited by counsel before the UK courts in cases where interpretation of the corresponding provisions of the 1977 Act is in dispute.

The House of Lords had recently emphasised that while the EPO's decisions are not strictly binding on the UK courts, they have 'great persuasive authority' because they are decisions of expert courts (the EPO's Appeal Boards) and it would be 'highly undesirable' for the provisions of the EPC to be construed differently in the EPO from the way they are interpreted in national courts[2]. In theory, there should be what one judge has termed 'a two-way flow', with the EPO taking into account relevant UK decisions on the 1977 Act as much as the UK courts have 'due regard' for appropriate EPO Board of Appeal decisions[3]. The reality, however, is that a lack of House of Lords authority on interpretation of the 1977 Act and the frequency with which cases are appealed in the EPO means that the UK

---

1 Ie the Convention on the Grant of European Patents (Munich, 5 October 1973; TS 16 (1982); Cmnd 8510).
2 See *Merrell Dow Pharmaceuticals Inc v H N Norton & Co* [1996] RPC 76 at 82, per Lord Hoffman.
3 See *Gale's Application* [1991] RPC 305 at 323, CA, per Nicholls LJ, basing his view on the fact that the PA 1977 was intended by Parliament as a harmonising measure which would ensure close correspondence between domestic patent law and the EPC. Cf especially PA 1977, s 130(7).

courts have made little (if any) noticeable impact on the development of European patent law[1].

Application process

The task of scrutinising individual UK patent applications falls to the patent examiners in the Patent Office. The examiners are full-time members of staff who invariably have science or engineering backgrounds. Much of the patent examiner's training concentrates on the detailed consideration which he or she will have to give to a patent application before deciding whether the invention satisfies the stringent conditions for patentability imposed under the 1977 Act. The whole pre-grant examination process usually takes a minimum of three years from the time the original application is filed but a final decision can (and often does) take longer. Applicants do, however, have the assurance under the Act that the Patent Office has to complete its examination process within 54 months[2]. Unsuccessful applicants can appeal against the Patent Office's decision to the Outer House of the Court of Session[3] or the Patents Court[4] in England[5]. If the case is heard in the Outer House, it will come before the Patents Judge[6] who may be assisted by an expert assessor[7]. An appeal against the Patent Judge's decision on a point of law lies to the Inner House[8].

PATENTABLE INVENTIONS

Inventors can attempt to patent either new products or new processes. Applicants must meet all of the stringent patentability conditions imposed under s 1(1) of the 1977 Act. In short, this means that applicants must convince the Patent Office that their invention is (1) 'new'; (2) involves an 'inventive step'; (3) has industrial application; and (4) is not one of the categories of invention excluded from patentability on grounds of public policy[9].

1 See Floyd 'Novelty under the Patents Act 1977' [1996] EIPR 480 at 480–481 citing only six House of Lords cases interpreting the PA 1977 since it was enacted. Judgment in a seventh appeal has since been given in *Biogen Inc v Medeva plc* [1997] RPC 1.
2 PA 1977, s 20.
3 PA 1977, s 97(4).
4 The Patents Court is part of the Chancery Division of the High Court: PA 1977, s 96(1).
5 PA 1977, s 97(1).
6 As at the date of publication, the Patents Judge is Lord Johnston.
7 PA 1977, s 98(2). Cf the House of Lords' recent acknowledgment in *Biogen Inc v Medeva plc* [1997] RPC 1 of the 'invaluable assistance' provided both before and during the hearing by expert advisers on molecular biology.
8 PA 1977, s 97(5).
9 Logically, the scheme in PA 1977, s 1(1) suggests that the first question which should be asked is whether the substance of the proposed patent amounts to 'an invention' before considering whether the four conditions for patentability have been met. However, this prior question will 'almost invariably be academic' if the patentability criteria are met: *Biogen Inc v Medeva plc* [1997] RPC 1 at 41–42, per Lord Hoffman. But see Mustill LJ's emphasis on the possible need to revisit the (undefined) requirement of invention in future cases as technology develops: [1997] RPC 1 at 31–32.

Novelty

When the applicant files his or her patent application he or she is given a 'priority date', which is normally the date when the application was received by the Patent Office. The priority date is important because it determines the cut-off point used by the patent examiner when considering whether the substance of the proposed patent is, in fact, 'new' or already known. Novelty is judged in terms of the state of human knowledge (the 'state of the art') as it stood at the priority date. Section 2(2) of the 1977 Act indicates that information forms part of the state of the art (and so destroys the novelty of an invention) if it has 'at any time been made available to the public (whether in the UK or elsewhere) by written or oral description, by use, or in any other way'.

Written disclosure

Prior publication will destroy novelty even if the substance of the invention is published in an obscure technical journal which only enjoys a limited circulation in the UK. In the *Windsurfing* case[1], for instance, part of the design of a windsurfing sail and board was published in an American sailing magazine which had a small UK readership. The court held that the novelty claimed for the part of the design which featured in the magazine article had been destroyed by prior publication. There is long-standing authority to the effect that anticipatory disclosure can take place where several people have received the relevant publication but have not actually read it[2]. The EPO's Board of Appeal[3] has gone further than this and held that a single copy of a journal received by a library one day before the invention's filing date was nevertheless made available to the public on the date of receipt 'whether or not any member of the public actually knew it was available'.

Some forms of written disclosure are discounted under the 1977 Act. Thus the Patent Office is obliged to ignore published material which only reached the public domain because it has been unlawfully obtained[4] or disclosed in breach of confidence in the six months prior to the filing date[5].

Other forms of disclosure

Oral statements made before the priority date – for instance, giving a scientific paper at a conference – will be relevant to the question of novelty unless it could be shown that the hearers were under an obligation of confidentiality at the time[6]. Prior public use constitutes another form of

1   *Windsurfing International Inc v Tabur Marine (Great Britain) Ltd* [1985] RPC 59, CA.
2   *Pickard and Currey v Prescott* (1892) 9 RPC 195 (four copies of journal received by UK subscribers but none proved to have read article describing the invention).
3   *IBM/Ion etching (T534/88)* [1991] EPOR 18.
4   Eg where the information was stolen or obtained by surreptitious means.
5   PA 1977, s 2(4).
6   See the EPO's decision in *Hooper Trading* [1993] EPOR 6, where a lecture to an invited audience of skilled technicians was held to be an anticipatory disclosure as the audience were not under a duty of confidentiality.

anticipatory disclosure which destroys novelty. In *Merrell Dow*[1], the House of Lords emphasised that the prior use of a product only makes the invention part of the state of the art if the use communicates the necessary information on how the invention works or can be made. Thus in *Quantel Ltd v Spaceward Microsystems Ltd*[2], the circuitry of a computer had not been 'made available to the public' where the computer was demonstrated at an exhibition because 'no-one was allowed near the actual machine and no engineering description was given at all'. On the other hand, the fact that the essence of the invention was clearly visible in a place where the public had a legitimate right of access was fatal in the *Windsurfing* case[3]. The design for a flexible boom on a windsurfer was used on a quiet stretch of public beach on the Sussex coast. The Court of Appeal held that novelty was destroyed because visitors to the beach could see that the straight boom became a flexible arc when the windsurfer was being used.

Lack of novelty

Before leaving the question of novelty, it should be noted that the issue is is not only important at the stage before a patent is granted. Should the inventor receive a patent grant, a competitor can apply to the Comptroller of Patents or the court under s 72 of the 1977 Act to have the patent revoked on the ground that it was invalidly granted. This was, in fact, what happened in the *Windsurfing* case, where the patentee sued for infringement and was met by a successful counterclaim for revocation on grounds of lack of novelty. It therefore pays in some cases for the defender who is sued for infringement to engage the services of a patent agent. By undertaking a comprehensive literature search, the patent agent may find material which was in the public domain before the filing date which can then be used to mount a counter-attack on the validity of the pursuer's patent.

Inventive step

Assuming the applicant can demonstrate novelty, he or she then has to show that his or her invention 'involves an inventive step'[4]. This require-ment reflects the patent system's basic philosophy of only offering an absolute monopoly to genuinely inventive advances or breakthroughs. Inventions which merely represent an obvious or unimaginative exten-sion of the current state of technology are not deemed patentable for the simple reason that, in Buckley LJ's words, 'what is obvious cannot be inventive, and what is inventive cannot be obvious'[5]. The need to show an

---

1 See *Merrell Dow Pharmaceuticals Inc v H N Norton & Co* [1996] RPC 76 at 86, per Lord Hoffman
2 [1990] RPC 83 at 127, per Falconer J.
3 See *Windsurfing International Inc v Tabur Marine (Great Britain) Ltd* [1985] RPC 59. No case law exists on situations where the access to prior use of the invention was obtained unlaw-fully or without due authorisation.
4 PA 1977, s 1(1)(b).
5 *Beecham Group Ltd's (Amoxycillin) Application* [1980] RPC 261 at 290, CA, per Buckley LJ.

unobvious, inventive step is undoubtedly the most daunting hurdle facing the would-be patentee[1]. Even if the patent application is eventually successful, doubts about the presence of inventive step 'remains the largest single cause of uncertainty about the validity of patents and hence a frequent inflator of the scale and length of patent disputes'[2].

Hypothetical skilled practitioner test

What, then, amounts to a truly inventive step? According to s 3 of the 1977 Act, an invention involves an inventive step 'if is not obvious to a person skilled in the art'. The patent examiner is expected to judge the presence of inventive step from the standpoint of the hypothetical skilled technician in the relevant field. Case law indicates that this fictitious individual is not the leading expert[3] or an inventive genius[4] but someone of ordinary or average competence and skill who possesses the appropriate degree of common general knowledge necessary to enable him or her to be good at his or her job[5]. The hypothetical skilled technician is also deemed to be sufficiently interested in the problem which the invention claims to solve to apply his or her general knowledge to the problem in hand. Despite his or her presumed level of skill and interest, the hypothetical technician is assumed not to have any inventive imagination of his or her own[6].

Although the notional qualities mentioned above are expressed in terms of an individual practitioner, the courts have recognised that some inventions only come about when researchers with differing skills and expertise are brought together as a multi-disciplinary team to work on a particular project. In these cases, inventive step will be judged from the standpoint of what the Court of Appeal has described as a 'composite entity' – 'a team whose combined skills would normally be employed in that art'[7].

The courts are also prepared to recognise that the benchmark for inventive step is increased where researchers are working at the 'cutting edge' of new technology such as biotechnology or pharmaceuticals. As the Court of Appeal has put it in *Genentech*[8], the hypothetical practitioner or team working in a 'difficult art' should be deemed to possess the 'appropriate degree' of ability where the expectation in that area of technology is such that the technical skill involved 'consists in a substantial degree of an ability to solve problems'.

---

1 See eg Reid *A Practical Guide to Patent Law* (2nd edn, 1993) pp 34–35.
2 See Cornish *Intellectual Property* (3rd edn, 1996), para 5-30.
3 See eg *General Tire and Rubber Co v Firestone Tyre and Rubber Co Ltd* [1972] RPC 457 (opinion discounted of main witness because he was clearly one of the leading experts in the field with nearly 50 patents in his own right).
4 See *Gillette Safety Razor Co v Anglo-American Trading Co Ltd* (1913) 30 RPC 465 at 481, HL.
5 Guidelines for Examination in the EPO, Pt C, ch IV, s 9.6.
6 See eg *Windsurfing International v Tabur Marine* [1985] RPC 59 at 73–74, per Oliver LJ.
7 *General Tire and Rubber Co v Firestone Tyre and Rubber Co Ltd* [1972] RPC 457 at 482, 485.
8 *Genentech Inc's Patent* [1989] RPC 147 at 279.

Asssessing inventive step

Having identified the appropriate degree of common general knowledge and the relevant prior art as it stood at the priority date, the patent examiner then has to assess whether the applicant's inventive claims are, in fact, truly 'obvious' steps which the unimaginative, ordinary practitioner would have adopted to solve the particular problem which the invention claims to address. In effect, the examiner has to ask himself this question: assuming the ordinary practitioner *could* have taken the steps claimed by the applicant, was it likely that he *would* have done so[1]?

If the applicant's solution is one 'you go straight to'[2] or one the hypothetical practitioner would 'directly be led as a matter of course to try' in the expectation that it might produce a useful result[3], the patent application fails because the invention embodies an 'obvious', rather than an 'inventive', answer to the problem[4]. As Musthill LJ put it in *Genentech*, where the hypothetical practitioner could have come up with the inventor's solution 'with no more' than 'pertinacity, sound technique or trial and error' – and did not also need 'a spark of imagination' to do so – the inventive step requirement has not been fulfilled[5].

As with novelty, the presence of inventive step in a patent which has already been granted can be challenged by an action for revocation brought under s 72[6].

Industrial application

Like every other patent system, the UK patent system does not allow inventors who discover abstract information or develop a theoretical analysis of a particular problem to file an application with the Patent Office in an attempt to obtain a monopoly simply over that discovery or or theory on its own. The 1977 Act insists that inventions or discoveries should not simply exist as an elegant set of equations or formulae; they must be shown to be 'capable of industrial application'[7]. As s 4(1) confirms, an invention is capable of industrial application if it 'can be made or used in any kind of industry, including agriculture'. In short, then, patents are only awarded under the 1977 Act to inventions or discoveries which have a definite, practical use in industry.

---

1 See Paterson *The European Patent System* (1992 and supps) para 10-30; and *Japan Styrene/Foam articles* [1994] OJ EPO 154.
2 *American Cyanamid v Berk Pharmaceuticals* [1976] RPC 231 at 257.
3 *Olin Mathieson Chemical Corpn v Biorex Laboratories Ltd* [1970] RPC 157 at 187.
4 But note the difficulty of assessing inventive step in the field of biotechnology where the inventor has applied known technology to solve a known problem: see especially *Biogen Inc v Medeva plc* [1997] RPC 1 at 44–45, per Lord Hoffman. For criticism of the House of Lords in *Biogen*, see Spence 'Patents and Biotechnology' (1997) 113 LQR 368.
5 *Genentech Inc's Patent* [1989] RPC 147 at 276.
6 See eg the defendant's successful counterclaim in *Biogen Inc v Medeva plc* [1997] RPC 1 based on the contention that the invention was obvious at the priority date.
7 PA 1977, ss 1(1)(c) and 4(1).

Discoveries

The need to show industrial application emerges all the more explicitly in s 1(2) of the 1977 Act when it states that 'discoveries, scientific theories and mathematical methods' are unpatentable by themselves (however important they might be). Again, this bar is justified on the basis that such forms of invention consist of essentially abstract information which has yet to be applied constructively to solve a particular problem[1]. A 'discovery' or 'scientific theory' becomes patentable only if it discloses a concrete application or use for that information 'which results in a new product, or a new result, or a new process or a new combination for producing an old product or an old result'[2]. The inventor who has made an important discovery is accordingly free to obtain separate patents for individual products or processes which make use of the discovery, provided he or she shows that each product or process is individually capable of industrial application. What the inventor cannot do, however, is lay claim to a blanket patent monopoly over all products or processes inventions which may result from his or her discovery without also detailing the particular practical applications to which that discovery is claimed to give rise[3].

Non-patentable inventions

Some inventions which have a definite industrial application are nevertheless deemed to be unpatentable under the 1977 Act on grounds of public policy. Computer software, eg, cannot be patented as such because copyright is thought to be the more appropriate from of protection[4]. New methods of medical treatment or surgery on humans and animals are not patentable because such methods are considered to be too important to the continuance of human and animal life to be 'subjected to possible restraint or restriction by reason of any patent monopoly'[5]. The 'treatment' exception in s 4(2) refers to therapeutic methods and is generally assumed to bar the patenting of preventative as well as curative methods of treating illness or disease[6]. The upshot is that new pregnancy testing kits or contraceptive devices can be patented[7] but new methods of vaccination cannot[8]. New drugs, vaccines and items of medical equipment are, however, patentable because they are considered to be a means rather than a 'method' of treatment or therapy[9]. Thus, for instance, a drug company which discovers a cure for the AIDS virus or (perhaps less probably)

1 Eg the laws of gravity or the general theory of relativity could never be patented unless the particular theory led to a concrete invention, in which case the patent monopoly would be confined to the specific application of that theory.
2 See *Reynolds v Herbert Smith & Co Ltd* (1913) 20 RPC 123 at 126, per Buckley J.
3 See *Genentech Inc's Patent* [1989] RPC 147, discussed in detail in Vitoria et al (eds), *Encyclopaedia of UK and European Patent Law* para 5-233.
4 PA 1977, s 1(2)(c), recently analysed by Laddie J in *Fujitsu's Application* [1996] RPC 511. The Court of Appeal has since upheld this decision: see (1997) Times, 14 March.
5 See *Schering's Application* [1985] RPC 545 at 565 per Falconer J.
6 See *Encyclopaedia of UK and European Patent Law*, para 5-232, citing the unreported case *Unilever* (CIPA vol 12 no 6, p 262).
7 See *Schering AG's Application* [1971] RPC 337.
8 See *Unilever Ltd (Davis's) Application* [1983] RPC 219.
9 PA 1977, s 4(3).

the common cold should be able to patent its new drug under the 1977 Act.

Two other types of non-patentable invention deserve particular mention because of the growth in research in the UK into the genetic engineering of plants and animals[1]. These exceptions are found in s 1(3) and relate to inventions contrary to public morality and the patenting of certain categories of life form.

Immoral inventions

The bar in s 1(3)(a) of the 1977 Act on patenting inventions contrary to public morality is derived from the *orde public* provision in art 53(a) of the European Patent Convention (EPC). This states that inventions are not patentable if their exploitation would be 'generally expected' to encourage 'offensive, immoral or anti-social behaviour'. Objectors in the *Onco-mouse* case[2] opposed Harvard Medical School's application under art 53(a), arguing that it was immoral to allow a patent over a creature which had been genetically-engineered to produce its own cancer cells. They also argued that it was immoral to introduce the risk of uncontrolled dissemination of unwanted cancer genes. Harvard contended that the benefits offered by the 'Onco-mouse' were very considerable because it had been bred specifically for research into human anti-cancer treatment. The EPO resolved the morality arguments by balancing the risks (eg of suffering to animals) against the possible benefits of advancing human anti-cancer treatment and held that the benefits outweighed the objections.

In a later case[3] dealing with genetically engineered plant cells, the EPO's Board of Appeal held that morality in art 53(a) must be addressed by reference to the 'concerns or moral norms that are deeply rooted in European culture' but no guidance was given on how these norms might be established or used. The EPO was clear, however, that survey or opinion poll evidence taken in EPC states would not be conclusive because opinions on moral issues could readily change in the light of recent events. On the other hand, the Board of Appeal was prepared to hold that 'serious prejudice' to the environment was a relevant factor but again no guidance was offered on how this argument could be satisfactorily established. Finally, the EPO regarded the benefit/detriment test used in *Onco-mouse* as 'useful' but went on to indicate that it was only one possible way of deciding whether exploitation of a patent was contrary to morality. Again, the EPO failed to take the opportunity to elaborate on what alternative means might be used to assess patentability under art 53(a).

Biological inventions

The second exclusion from patentability is derived from art 53(b) of the EPC and relates to certain new 'life forms'. Section 1(3)(b) prohibits the

---

1 In an attempt to ensure that European biotech companies compete on an equal footing with US and Japanese companies, the European Parliament voted in July 1997 in favour of a proposed Biotechnology Directive which now goes back to the Council under the co-decision procedure: European Parliament News, July 1997, p 1.
2 *Harvard/Onco-mouse* [1991] EPOR 525.
3 *Plant Genetic Systems/ Glutamine synthetase inhibitors* [1995] EPOR 357.

patenting of new animal or plant varieties or 'any essentially biological process for the production of animals or plants'[1]. Basically, this means that higher life forms are not patentable in the UK or in any other EPC country. For example, those who selectively breed or cross-breed plants are essentially initiating a process of biological or sexual replication so that the results of such breeding programmes will not be patentable[2]. On the other hand, chemicals to control or eliminate pests could well be patentable if the view is taken that the chemicals do not involve an 'essentially biological process for the production of plants or animals'[3].

Not all life forms are outside the scope of patent protection. Following art 53(b), the 1977 Act explicitly permits[4] the patenting of *micro*biological inventions that exist in the form of micro-organisms or cells which are only visible with the aid of microscope. Thus new bacteria or cells lines can be patented even if they are subsequently applied to plants or animals. The *Onco-mouse* case[5] is clearly an example of the latter, where the EPO dismissed objections under art 53(b) and upheld an application to patent an animal 'whose germ cells and somatic cells contain an activated oncogene sequence introduced into said animal at a stage no later than the 8-cell stage'. The EPO held that an invention described in these terms in the patent application was a microbiological invention and not a variety of animal.

OBTAINING A PATENT

The inventor[6] must file an application with the Patent Office in the form of a 'specification' which describes the invention. The specification is usually accompanied by explanatory diagrams or drawings. As part of the application, the inventor is required to set out the inventive claims which are being made in respect of the product or process described in the specification[7]. Patent agents are usually involved in the drafting both the specification and inventive claims because, as one leading patent lawyer has put it, this is 'at once the most important and the most difficult aspect of applying for a patent'[8]. If errors are made in drafting, the validity of any subsequent patent can be challenged in revocation proceedings brought under s 72 of the 1977 Act. Because of the 'first to file' nature of the UK patent

1 PA 1977, s 1(3)(b).
2 See the EPO's decision in *Lubrizol* [1990] EPOR 173 holding that art 53(b) of the EPC did not apply where 'the totality and sequence of specified operations neither occur in nature nor correspond to the classical breeders' processes'. New plant varieties or groupings are protectable under the Plant Varieties and Seeds Act 1964 but similar legislation does not exist for new animal strains as such.
3 See Guidelines for Examination in the EPO, Pt C, ch IV, s 4.1, 4.3.
4 PA 1977, s 1(3)(b).
5 *Harvard/Onco-mouse* [1990] EPOR 501.
6 Or, more commonly, the inventor's employer: PA 1977, s 39(1) confirms that an invention belongs to the employer if it was made by an employee in the course of normal or specifically assigned duties. The employee is, however, entitled under PA 1977, s 13 to be identified as the inventor on any patent which is subsequently granted for the invention.
7 PA 1977, s 14(2).
8 See Reid *A Practical Guide to Patent Law* (2nd edn, 1993) p 66.

system, an inventor who has yet to work out the full implications of his or her invention can still secure the all-important 'filing date' by lodging a description of the invention and paying the filing fee[1]. The applicant then has 12 months to file the detailed specification and inventive claims.

Preliminary examination and search

Once a patent application is filed, it is subjected to a rigorous process of examination and search by a patent examiner. The examiner's first task is to carry out a preliminary examination to check that the applicant has complied with the various formalities laid down for a patent application. At this stage, the examiner will also carry out a preliminary search to identify existing UK patents and the more important items of technical literature which the examiner thinks will be needed to determine whether the invention is new and involves an inventive step[2]. The outcome of the examiner's preliminary examination and search allows the applicant to assess the viability of proceeding with his application. Should he or she decide to withdraw, the applicant's invention remains confidential – and will not therefore become part of the prior art – so long as it is the withdrawn before the application has been published by the Patent Office[3].

Substantive examination

If the application is not withdrawn or refused, the Patent Office will automatically publish it once more than 18 months have elapsed since the filing date[4]. The next stage in the process involves substantive examination of the application, which the applicant must specifically request[5]. The process of substantive examination allows the patent examiner to examine in detail whether the invention meets inter alia the novelty and inventive step requirements. If the examiner raises objections, possibly in the light of observations made by third parties after the patent application was published[6], the applicant has the opportunity to present arguments or amend his or her application[7]. In the rare event that the examiner and the applicant cannot agree, a formal hearing can take place before a senior examiner, with a right of appeal to the Patents Court or the Court of Session. To prevent protracted proceedings within the Patent Office, the whole examination process must be completed within 54 months of the filing date[8].

1 PA 1977, s 15(1).
2 PA 1977, s 17(4). The literature search does not need to be a complete trawl through the sources; the examiner is only required to carry out such investigation 'as in his opinion is reasonably practicable and necessary' to identify the relevant documents.
3 PA 1977, s 16(1).
4 PA 1977, s 16(1).
5 PA 1977, s 18(1).
6 Competitors have no right to present a case as such before the Patent Office; they are limited to making written observations which the examiner is obliged to consider: PA 1977, s 21.
7 PA 1977, s 18(3).
8 PA 1977, s 20.

Patent grant

If the patent application is successful, the patent grant is published. The patent will last for 20 years[1] from the filing date so long as the patentee pays the annual renewal fees[2]. The fees become payable in the fifth year and the patent will lapse if payment is not made within 6 months of falling due. If the patent lapses, the patentee has 12 months from the date of expiry to apply to the Patent Office for restoration[3]. Anyone who acts in good faith in the period between expiry and restoration has the right to continue exploiting the patented invention after restoration even though such exploitation would otherwise constitute infringement of the restored patent[4].

EXPLOITING A PATENT

Patents are incorporeal moveable property under Scots law.[5] They can be assigned or licensed or form the subject of a security in favour of a lender[6].

Assignation

An assignation must be in writing but there is no longer any requirement for the writing to be probative or holograph[7]. The assignee receives a real right over the patent when he or she receives the instrument of assignation and the assignation is registered in the Register of Patents.

Licences

Where the patent owner decides to retain ownership and licence others to exploit the patent, he or she has the option of granting: (1) an exclusive licence[8] which would give the licensee the right to exclude all others, including the patent owner[9]; (2) a sole licence which would allow both the owner and the sole licensee to exploit the patent; or (3) a series of licences, usually for a limited period and covering a specified territory, so that several licensees are permitted to exploit the patent at the same time. Patent

---

1 A maximum period of 25 years applies in the case of patented drugs which have been granted a supplementary protection certificate by the Patent Office under the Patents (Supplementary Protection Certificates for Medicinal Products) Regulations 1992, SI 1992/3091. Certificates are granted where there have been delays in the drugs receiving safety clearance from the medical authorities.
2 PA 1977, s 25(1), (3).
3 PA 1977, s 28.
4 PA 1977, s 28A.
5 PA 1977, s 31(2).
6 PA 1977, s 31. This provision extends 'to Scotland' which probably means that it applies where the patentee is domiciled in Scotland.
7 See Requirements of Writing (Scotland) Act 1995, s 14(1) and Sch 4.
8 As defined in PA 1977, s 130(1).
9 Perhaps the best-known example is Ron Hickman's patent over the 'Workmate' bench (*Hickman v Andrews* [1983] RPC 147, CA) which he exclusively licensed to Black & Decker.

licences do not require to be registered although the 1977 Act provides incentives to encourage registration[1]. Thus while exclusive licensees have the statutory right to sue infringers[2], failure to register an exclusive licence within six months of execution will deprive the licensee of the right to claim damages against an infringer[3]. Because the Patent Register is open to public inspection, what is registered is invariably a bare licence agreement, ensuring that commercially-sensitive details remain confidential to the licensor and licensee.

Licence of right

If the patent owner has trouble finding suitable licensees, he or she can ask the Comptroller of Patents to put an entry on the Patent Register indicating that the patent will be made available as of right to anyone who wishes to exploit it[4]. The Register will be amended so as to make the patent subject to a 'licence of right' so long as the owner has not already granted an exclusive licence . The parties are free to negotiate mutually acceptable terms but, if they cannot agree, the licensee is entitled to exploit the patent on terms fixed by the Comptroller.

Compulsory licence

To ensure that patents are not being under-exploited by the owner, the 1977 Act allows competitors to apply to the Comptroller for a compulsory licence or mandatory endorsation of a licence of right to exploit the patent[5]. Compulsory licence applications are rare and can only be made if three years have elapsed since the patent was granted. The competitor has to show that the patented invention is not being worked 'to the fullest extent that is reasonably practicable'. If a compulsory licence is granted, the Comptroller will determine its terms.

Crown licence

Occasionally Crown licences are obtained over patented inventions. The 1977 Act allows government departments to apply for a licence to permit the Crown to exploit a patent in the public interest[6]. The provisions apply to patents over drugs and medicines and inventions which can be used for defence purposes. In return for a Crown licence, the relevant government department must pay compensation equivalent to the amount which a willing licensee would have paid to a willing licensor.

1 Including the fact that entries on the Patent Register are deemed to be sufficient evidence of rights in a patent: PA 1977, s 32(9).
2 PA 1977, s 67.
3 PA 1977, s 68. An exception is made if registration was 'not practicable' within six months of execution and the licence was registered as soon as practicable thereafter.
4 PA 1977, s 46.
5 PA 1977, s 48.
6 See PA 1977, ss 55–59.

Security over a patent

Where a patent is used as a security, the security holder will receive either an ex facie absolute assignation along with a separate 'backletter' setting out the terms of the security or, more usually, an assignation expressly in security of his or her interest as lender[1]. The security holder only obtains a real right over the patent if the assignation is then registered in the Register of Patents[2].

Compensation for employee inventors

Where the patent owner successfully exploits a patented invention, the employees who were involved in developing that invention may be entitled to statutory compensation, in the form of a fair share of the benefit which the employer has derived, if they can show that the patent is of 'outstanding benefit' to the employer[3]. To date, it would appear that no employee has successfully applied to the Comptroller for compensation[4].

PATENT INFRINGEMENT

Patents are infringed by making or using a patented product without authorisation, or using a patented process in the knowledge that its use would be an infringement[5]. Whether infringement has taken place or not will depend on the construction placed on the patent specification. If the defender has taken those elements in the specification which together amount to the essential substance or 'pith and marrow' of the owner's invention, the defender will be liable for infringement[6].

DEFENCES

As a defence, it can be argued that the infringement was performed privately and for non-commercial purposes or that the infringing act was done for experimental purposes[7]. An alleged infringer has the right to continue doing what would otherwise constitute infringement if he or she was already making or using the patented invention in good faith before the invention's priority date[8]. The case reports[9] indicate that it is fairly common for defenders to attack the validity of the owner's patent by

1 See Sellar 'Rights in Security over "Scottish Patents"' (1996) 1 SLPQ 137 at 139–140.
2 PA 1977, s 33.
3 See PA 1977, ss 40–43.
4 On the difficulties facing employee inventors, see further Wotherspoon 'Employee Inventions Revisited' (1993) 22 ILJ 119.
5 PA 1977, s 60.
6 See further Wotherspoon 'Suing for Patent Infringement' (1995) 40 JLSS 26 at 26–27.
7 PA 1977, s 60(5).
8 PA 1977, s 64. 'Effective and serious preparations' carried out before the priority date are also not actionable if done in good faith.
9 See eg *Windsurfing International Inc v Tabur Marine (Great Britain) Ltd* [1985] RPC 59, CA.

counterclaiming for revocation of the patent on the basis that it lacked novelty or inventive step at the priority date[1]. The very fact that revocation is raised as an issue often leads to an early settlement of the dispute, with a licence on favourable terms being granted to the defender.

REMEDIES

The remedies available to a patent owner include interdict and damages. As an alternative to an award of damages, the patent owner can seek an account of the defender's profits. Neither pecuniary remedy is available if the infringer can show that he or she acted without knowing or having 'reasonable grounds' for supposing the existence of the patent[2]. The fact that the owner's product carried the word 'patent' or 'patented' is not sufficient to destroy the defender's innocence[2]; use of the patent number is strong but not conclusive evidence of the issue[3]. The safest course for the owner is to fix the infringer with the requisite knowledge by sending the infringer a letter notifying him or her of the existence of the patent[4].

If damages are awarded, the sum awarded is usually based on the notional royalty which a willing licensee would pay to a willing licensor. Where the patent owner has already granted licences, damages will be based on the going rate of royalty paid by licensees multiplied by the number of infringements[5].

INTERNATIONAL PROTECTION

Patents are strictly territorial property rights which only apply within the country which has granted the patent. In theory, an inventor in the UK is therefore faced with prospect of having to obtain separate patent protection in each of the 100 or more countries in the world which have their own patent system. The problem of territoriality has been mitigated, however, by the adoption of several international patent conventions which the UK has chosen to ratify.

The Paris Convention for the Protection of Industrial Property

The Paris Convention[6] is the oldest patent convention (the original version was signed in 1883) and it now boasts over 90 member countries. Article 2 of the Convention ensures 'national' treatment of UK inventors when they apply for patent protection in other Convention countries. The 'national

1 PA 1977, s 72.
2 PA 1977, s 62(1).
3 See Wotherspoon (1995) 40 JLSS 26 at 29.
4 PA 1977, s 70(5).
5 See *Meters Ltd v Metropolitan Gas Meters Ltd* (1911) 28 RPC 157 at 164–165. The alternative possibility of claiming damages based on loss of profits has recently been upheld by the Court of Appeal in *Gerber Garment Technology Inc v Lectra Systems Ltd* (1997) Times, 17 January. See also Moss and Rogers 'Damages for Loss of Profits in Intellectual Property Litigation' [1997] EIPR 425.
6 Ie the Convention for the Protection of Industrial Property (Paris, 20 March 1883; 74 BFSP 44; C 4043).

treatment' rule means that UK applicants are entitled to the same level of patent protection in the state receiving their patent application as domestic nationals would be entitled to receive in the same state. Because prior publication or use anywhere in the world invariably destroys the novelty of an invention, the Paris Convention also ensures that the filing of a patent application in one member state secures a right of priority for 12 months in all other Convention states[1].

The Patent Co-operation Treaty

One of the major drawbacks of the Paris Convention is that it does not remove the need to make separate national patent applications. In response to this difficulty, the Patent Co-operation Treaty (PCT)[2] was signed in 1970 in order 'to simplify and render more economical the obtaining of protection for inventions where protection is sought in several countries'. Over 80 countries have since adopted the PCT, including Australia, China, Japan, the UK and the USA[3]. The PCT allows a single so-called 'international patent application' to be filed with a 'receiving' patent office, which includes the UK Patent Office. By filing an international application, the applicant is deemed to have filed the application in that country and in all the other PCT countries designated in the application.

After filing, an international search for prior art is conducted by one of the international searching authorities (which again includes the UK Patent Office)[4]. This has the advantage of avoiding costly individual literature searches which would normally be required if separate patent applications had been filed in each of the designated countries. Following the search, the inventor's application and the search report are forwarded to national patent offices for substantive examination according to the domestic patent law of the relevant country. The CPC system means, therefore, that a single 'international application' can be turned into a bundle of national patents.

The European Patent Convention

Three years after the PCT was signed, the European Patent Convention (EPC) entered into force as a regional patent treaty within the PCT. The object of the EPC is to allow inventors to obtain a 'European Patent' by filing a single application with the European Patent Office (EPO) set up under the Convention. If the 'European Patent' application is successful, the applicant will receive a 'bundle' of national patents in as many of the 18 EPC countries[5] as he or she chooses to designate in his or her applica-

---

1 Paris Convention, art 4.
2 Ie the Patent Co-operation Treaty (Washington, 19 June 1970; TS 78 (1978); Cmnd 7340).
3 See Adams 'Success of the PCT' [1996] 5 EIPR D-160, reporting that several new states had joined the PCT and that 38,906 international applications were made in 1995.
4 Other international search authorities include the European Patent Office, and the national patent offices in Australia, Japan, Russia and the USA.
5 Ie the 15 EC member states plus Liechtenstein, Monaco and Switzerland.

tion. The EPC contains detailed provisions on the determination of important substantive issues such as novelty and inventive step and these have been incorporated into UK domestic patent law via the 1977 Act[1]. Since the EPO came into operation in 1978, UK inventors have increasingly opted to take out patents in several EPC states instead of applying for a purely UK patent.

The Community Patent Convention

As a further step towards completing the EC internal market[2] and eliminating unnecessary patenting costs[3], the Community Patent Convention (CPC)[4] was signed in 1975. When it is eventually ratified the CPC will enable inventors to obtain a single Community patent – instead of a bundle of national patents under the EPC – which can be granted, transferred and revoked across the whole of the European Union[5]. Discussions continue on the detailed implementation of the CPC and it will probably be some time before the option of obtaining a single Community patent is available to inventors.

Passing off

INTRODUCTION

The delict of passing off prevents a competitor imitating another trader's name or marketing device – such as a logo or the packaging of goods – so as to confuse the public and lead them to believe that the competitor's goods or services are those of the other trader[6]. An action of passing off is also appropriate where a trader misrepresents the quality, as opposed to the origin, of his or her goods or services. Many of the marketing devices which are protected by passing off can potentially be registered as trade

---

1 See especially PA 1977, s 130(7).
2 Most of the barriers to the free movement of goods which national patents might present have, however, already been removed by the European Court of Justice: see *Cornish* para 3.29.
3 Which is far from certain if Convention countries continue to insist (as a majority currently do) that a Community patent is translated in full into their own national languages: Vitoria et al (eds) *Encyclopaedia of UK & European Patent Law* para 1-207.
4 Ie the Convention for the European Patent for the Common Market (the 'Community Patent Convention') (Luxembourg, 15 December 1975; EC 18 (1976); Cmnd 6553; OJ L17, 26.1.76, p 1).
5 CPC, art 2(2).
6 The reverse scenario, where the defender claims that what are in fact the pursuer's products or services are the defender's, is actionable as inverse passing off: see eg *John Henderson & Son Ltd v Alexander Munro & Co* (1905) 7 F 636 at 639, per Lord President Dunedin, holding that the complainers would be injured by misleading 'attribution of the [engineering] experience of Henderson & Son to Munro & Co'. The leading English authority on inverse passing off is the Court of Appeal's decision in *Bristol Conservatories v Conservatories Custom Built* [1989] RPC 455, CA.

marks under the Trade Marks Act 1994. The fact that a device has been registered does not prevent the owner from suing for passing off as well as, or instead of, a breach of the 1994 Act[1]. In practice, owners of a registered trade mark will usually sue infringers under both the 1994 Act and the law of passing off in case the registered mark is held not to have been infringed[2].

Essence of passing off

In the leading Scottish case on passing off[3], Lord-Justice Clerk Wheatley held that there was 'ample authority for the proposition that the law of Scotland does not differ from the law of England in this field'. A valid claim in either jurisdiction depends on the relevant conduct taking place in a commercial or business context[4]. The basic purpose of passing off is to protect a trader's goodwill[5]. In particular, the object of the delict is to enable a trader to prevent his or her goodwill being appropriated by a competitor's representations which are liable to mislead the public[6]. The classic case of passing off involves the defender falsely suggesting that his or her goods or services originate from the pursuer or have some connection with the pursuer's business. In recent years, the courts have also recognised another form of passing off. This occurs when the defender markets his or her product using the same product name as the pursuer is already using to suggest to the public that his product possesses the same distinctive qualities as the pursuer's product does.

In summary, it can be said that the essence of passing off is not that the pursuer's goodwill has been appropriated[7] – which is to be expected in a competitive market – but rather that a competitor has misrepresented his or her own goods or services so as to damage the pursuer's goodwill and thereby cause him or her to lose custom or reputation[8].

Scope of protection

Passing off is likely to diminish in importance to traders generally as a result of the registration and infringement provisions of the Trade Marks Act 1994. The legislation makes it possible to register a wider range of

1 See Trade Marks Act 1994, s 2(2).
2 See eg *J & G Grant v Wm Cadenhead Ltd* 1995 GWD 34-1764, OH.
3 *Lang Bros Ltd v Goldwell Ltd* 1982 SLT 309 at 312. No authorities were actually cited in support of this broad proposition!
4 See eg Clive 'The Action for Passing Off' (1963) JR 117 at 123 where he states that 'passing off must take place in the course of a trade, business or profession'. For discussion of how far the courts have been prepared to extend the concept of business activity, see Wadlow *The Law of Passing Off* (2nd edn, 1995) paras 2.12–2.24.
5 However, the English courts do so on the basis that goodwill is a right of property, a proposition which the Scottish courts would resist: see Clive (1963) JR 117 at 125-127.
6 See 18 *Stair Memorial Encyclopaedia* para 1364.
7 Otherwise all competition resulting in appropriation of goodwill would potentially be actionable: see eg Lord Scarman's cautionary remarks in *Cadbury-Schweppes Ltd v Pub Squash Co Ltd* [1981] RPC 429 at 490–491.
8 See Clive (1963) J R 117 at 127, 130 citing Lord Hill Watson in *John Haig & Co Ltd v Forth Blending Co Ltd* 1954 SC 35 at 37.

marketing devices as trade marks than it was possible to do under the Trade Marks Act 1938. To take but one example, traders who marketed their product in a distinctively shaped bottle or container could not have registered the shape under the 1938 Act[1] and would have depended on passing off for protection[2]. Distinctive shapes which are capable of distinguishing the goods of one trader from those of others are now prima facie registrable as trade marks[3]. The 1994 Act also expands the concept of trade mark infringement to cover the use of a registered mark on similar goods or services[4]. Moreover, statutory trade mark law now allows owners of well-known foreign marks to sue for infringement even though they have no goodwill in the UK[5].

The cumulative effect of the changes introduced by the 1994 Act means that passing off actions in future will be concentrated on those areas where there are gaps in statutory trade mark protection[6]. These gaps include the need to protect the names of unique products such as 'Scotch whisky' and 'Champagne' and, more controversially, the themes used in advertising products or services[7]. Although distinctive shapes are now prima facie registrable as trade marks, certain shapes for containers or packaging will not to be registrable because they fall within one of the absolute grounds for refusal of registration[8]. For example, a shape which gives 'substantial value' to the goods cannot be registered as a trade mark and so passing off will continue to be a relevant form of protection against imitation. While the common law may protect shapes for containers or packaging, the courts have generally refused to extend protection to the shape of the product itself[9].

Another area where passing off may be used is in relation to the overall appearance or get up of brand goods. Typically brand goods are marketed using a combination of features including 'the shape and colour of the container, the shape, position and colour of the label, the typeface of the product name and information and even the colour of the product'[10]. In highly competitive markets for retail sales, rival producers are often tempted to market their own-brand of look-alike products which emulate the overall appearance of the leading brand. Sainsbury's Classic Cola is probably the best-known recent example of this phenomenon where the

---

1 See the refusal of the House of Lords to allow registration of the Coca-Cola bottle in *Coca-Cola Trade Mark Applications* [1986] RPC 421.
2 See *John Haig & Co Ltd v Forth Blending Co Ltd* 1954 SC 35 (interdict granted to prevent passing off of dimple-shaped whisky bottle); and *Reckitt and Colman Products Ltd v Borden Inc* [1990] 1 All ER 873, HL (injunction upheld to prevent misleading use of yellow, lemon-shaped container to market lemon juice).
3 See Trade Marks Act 1994, s 1(1).
4 1994 Act, s 10(2)
5 1994 Act, s 56.
6 See Annand and Norman *Blackstone's Guide to the Trade Marks Act 1994* (1994) ch 2.
7 Compare the differing judicial attitudes to copying the 'look and feel' of an advertising campaign in *Cadbury-Schweppes Pty Ltd v Pub Squash Co Pty Ltd* [1981] 1 All ER 213, PC (injunction refused) and *Elida Gibbs Ltd v Colgate-Palmolive Ltd* [1983] RPC FSR 95 (interlocutory injunction granted).
8 See the absolute grounds for refusal of shape registrations in the Trade Marks Act 1994, s 3(2).
9 See further 18 *Stair Memorial Encyclopaedia* para 1380.
10 See Carty 'Dilution and Passing Off' (1996) 112 LQR 632 at 661.

product was marketed with labels carrying the same colours and similar italic script to that found on Coca-Cola. Sales of Coca-Cola dropped by 20 per cent before Sainsbury's agreed to re-design their labels[1]. Since combinations of features used as get up do not qualify as a registrable 'sign' under the 1994 Act, passing off provides a potential means of preventing competitors diverting custom by adopting the 'look and feel' of the pursuer's brand[2].

Elements in passing off

While there are various judicial definitions of the elements required to establish passing off, the law will be examined below in terms of the 'classic trinity' of (1) goodwill, (2) misrepresentation and (3) damage. These criteria are increasingly favoured by pleaders[3] and judges[4] in preference to the more elaborate – and not identical[5] – criteria adopted by Lord Diplock and Lord Fraser in the *Advocaat* case[6].

GOODWILL

Definition of goodwill

Commercial goodwill has been broadly defined as 'the attractive force which brings in custom' and the 'benefit and advantage of the good name, reputation and connection of a business'[7]. A trader must establish that he or she possesses sufficient goodwill before he or she will be allowed to argue that customers have been misled by a competitor's misrepresentations. The pursuer's case depends on establishing that he or she has used 'visible symbols' – or badges of identity – on his or her goods or services to build up a store of customer goodwill. Relevant badges of identity include the use of brand names, logos, packaging and other forms of get up which 'become so associated in the minds of the public with [the] trader's goods as to be distinctive of the goods of [that] trader and no other'[8]. The classic type of trading goodwill is 'source goodwill'. It is created when customers are attracted by various elements in a trader's busi-

1 Carty (1996) 112 LQR 632 at 664.
2 See *Annand and Norman* pp 27, 62.
3 See eg *Treadwells Drifters Inc v RCL Ltd* 1996 SLT 1048, OH.
4 Starting in the House of Lords with Lord Oliver and Lord Jauncey in the *Jif lemon* case: *Reckitt and Colman Products Ltd v Borden Inc* [1990] 1 All ER 873 at 880 and 890, HL; and followed in the Court of Appeal by Nourse LJ in *Consorzio del Prosciutto di Parma v Marks and Spencer plc* [1991] RPC 351 at 368, CA.
5 See eg *Consorzio del Prosciutto di Parma v Marks and Spencer plc* [1991] RPC 351 at 368, CA, per Nourse LJ.
6 *Erven Warnink BV v J Townend & Sons (Hull) Ltd* [1979] 2 All ER 927 at 932-933 and 943–944, HL.
7 *Inland Revenue Comrs v Muller & Co's Margarine* [1901] AC 217 at 224, per Lord Macnaghten, quoted with approval by the Second Division in *Lang Bros Ltd v Goldwell Ltd* 1980 SC 237.
8 *John Haig & Co Ltd v Forth Blending Co Ltd* 1954 SC 35 at 37-38, per Lord Hill Watson.

ness which, taken together, have the 'power of attraction sufficient to bring customers home to the source' from which these elements emanate[1].

Product goodwill

Apart from source goodwill, the so-called 'drinks cases' – involving champagne[2], sherry[3], Scotch whisky[4] and advocaat[5] – indicate that goodwill can also cover products themselves if they have become distinctive badges of identity in their own right. The products must be marketed under a specific name (eg Scotch whisky) and they need to possess particular characteristics or follow a particular recipe which leads the public to buy them. All traders who produce goods with the same distinctive characteristics will share product goodwill and are entitled to prevent the name being used on products which do not possess these characteristics. The wine producers from the Champagne district of France have been particularly vigorous in defending product goodwill before the UK courts[6].

Pre-trading goodwill

The Australian courts have been prepared to hold that goodwill can be created by sufficient pre-launch advertising before a product or service is actually available to the public[7]. Attempts to argue this point do not appear to have reached the Scottish courts but recent English decisions indicate the possibility that heavy pre-launch advertising may be sufficient to generate trading goodwill[8].

Local goodwill

Goodwill is protectable regardless of whether it exists in a small locality or has been created nationally or internationally. The fact that a business is located in just one or two places does not necessarily prevent it acquiring national goodwill[9]. For instance, Harrods, the well-known department

1 *Inland Revenue Comrs v Muller & Co's Margarine Ltd* [1901] AC 217 at 224, per Lord Macnaghten.
2 See eg *J Bollinger v Costa Brava Wine Co Ltd* [1960] Ch 262.
3 *Vine Products Ltd v Mackenzie & Co Ltd* [1967] RPC 193.
4 See eg *John Walker & Sons Ltd v Douglas McGibbon & Co Ltd* 1972 SLT 128.
5 *Erven Warnink BV v J Townend & Sons (Hull) Ltd* [1979] 2 All ER 927, HL.
6 See Sir Thomas Bingham MR's remarks in the *Elderflower Champagne* case about goodwill in the name 'champagne' being 'tenaciously and vigorously protected' by the champagne houses: *Taittinger v Allbev Ltd* [1994] 4 All ER 75 at 93, CA. The Court of Appeal granted an injunction in the case preventing the defendants from marketing a drink called 'Elderflower Champagne' when the product was non-alcoholic and did not come from the Champagne district.
7 *Turner v General Motors Ltd* (1929) 42 CLR 352 (High Court of Australia), discussed in Wadlow *The Law of Passing Off* (2nd edn, 1995) para 2.25
8 See *British Broadcasting Corpn v Talbot* [1981] FSR 228 and *My Kinda Bones Ltd v Dr Pepper's Stove Co Ltd* [1984] FSR 289.
9 See eg the Court of Appeal's decision in *Chelsea Man Menswear Ltd v Chelsea Girl* [1987] RPC 189, CA where the plaintiffs were granted an injunction covering the whole of England when they had shops in London's Oxford Street, Leicester and Coventry.

store, has long enjoyed goodwill throughout the UK even though the business has only ever operated from a single store in London[1]. If, however, the pursuer's goodwill is purely local or regional, the court will grant an interdict which is restricted to the appropriate geographical area.

Foreign goodwill

There is long-standing House of Lords authority for the proposition that traders in the UK can protect foreign goodwill by relying on passing off to prevent goods being exported which are likely to damage that goodwill[2]. Activity abroad can also be restrained if the defender's actions amount to a wrong in the country concerned[3]. As far as the position of foreign traders suing in the Scottish courts is concerned, they probably need to have actually traded or have customers in Scotland – and not just possess an 'overspill' reputation – before they would have created protectable goodwill. However the issue has not been directly considered by the Scottish courts[4] and may now be largely academic in view of the new statutory right to prevent use of a 'well-known' foreign mark in the UK[5].

The statutory right was introduced by the Trade Marks Act 1994 and gives effect to the UK's obligation under the Paris Convention to protect well-known marks[6]. The Act protects foreign marks (whether registered abroad or not) even if the owner does not carry on business or have any goodwill in the UK[7]. The mark must be well-known in the UK for the owner to exercise the right; a substantial reputation abroad is not sufficient. The phrase 'well-known' is not defined in the Act but it is thought to mean that the mark must possesses a substantial degree of recognition in the UK[8]. The owner of the mark is entitled to interdict[9] if he or she can show that the defender is using a similar or identical mark on similar or identical goods or services. The pursuer must also show that the defender's use of the mark is likely to cause confusion. The right to obtain interdict is lost if the owner knowingly acquiesces in the mark being used in the UK for a continuous period of five years[10]. The owner is also barred from preventing continued use of a mark where use commenced in good faith before the Act came into force on 31 October 1994[11].

1 See *Harrods Ltd v Harrodian School Ltd* [1996] RPC 697 at 701, per Millett LJ.
2 *Johnston & Co v Orr Ewing & Co* (1882) 7 App Cas 219, HL. The Court of Session has recently emphasised that the exporter is liable regardless of whether his or her conduct would be actionable under the law of the country where the goods are being sent: *Wm Grant & Sons Ltd v Glen Catrine Bonded Warehouse Ltd* 1995 SLT 936 at 944, OH.
3 *James Burrough Distillers plc v Speymalt Whisky Distributors Ltd* 1989 SLT 561, OH.
4 See 18 *Stair Memorial Encyclopaedia* para 1367. The position in England appears to be that the presence of a distributor or agent handling orders on the foreign trader's behalf is probably sufficient but a significant reputation without customers is not enough: *Wadlow* paras 2.32–2.41.
5 Trade Marks Act 1994, s 56.
6 Paris Convention for the Protection of Industrial Property, art 6*bis*.
7 See Trade Marks Act 1994, s 56.
8 See Cornish *Intellectual Property* (3rd edn, 1996) para 16-17.
9 1994 Act, s 56(2). Damages are not available, probably because the Act only requires proof of likely confusion rather than likely damage.
10 1994 Act, s 48.
11 1994 Act, s 56(3).

MISREPRESENTATION

Misrepresentation has been described as 'the key which unlocks the door' in an action of passing off[1]. The defender must be shown to have made representations about his or her goods or services which are 'both untrue and also prejudicial to [the pursuer's] pecuniary interests'[2]. The defender's statements may involve a suggestion that he or she has some trading link with the pursuer (source or connection misrepresentation). Alternatively, the defender may have marketed his or her goods under a certain name to indicate that the goods possess particular qualities (product misrepresentation).

The *Advocaat* case[3] is a good example of the need to prove either source or product misrepresentation. The plaintiffs, along with other Dutch producers, manufactured an alcoholic drink known as 'advocaat' which was made from a mixture of spirit and eggs. The product possessed substantial goodwill in the UK. The defendants began selling a cheaper alcoholic drink called 'Old English Advocaat' which was made from dried eggs and Cyprus sherry. From the facts, it was clear that the source of the defendants' product was not being misrepresented. However, the defendants' use of the name 'advocaat' suggested that the product was 'endowed with recognisable and distinctive qualities' when in reality the public was getting egg-flip rather than advocaat[4]. The House of Lords therefore upheld the plaintiffs' action and granted an injunction to prevent the defendants continuing to engage in product misrepresentation.

Likelihood of confusion

Misrepresentation is established by showing 'that there is a likelihood of the public [in general] or the particular section of the public being misled' about the source or the qualities of the defender's goods or services[5]. The likely impact of the defender's statements is judged from the standpoint of reasonable members of the public 'who [are] representative of consumers of the goods or services in question'[6]. The reasonable person is assumed to be a person of average intelligence who does not act like 'a moron in a hurry' when purchasing[7]. Thus, for instance, in a Scottish appeal to the House of Lords[8], the court held that the 'average citizen of Kilmarnock' was unlikely to be confused between the Dunlop Tyre Co from England and a family business in Kilmarnock which sold and

---

1 18 *Stair Memorial Encyclopaedia* para 1364. English law also places misrepresentation at the heart of passing off: see *Wadlow* para 4.01.
2 *Charles P Kinnell & Co Ltd v Ballantine & Sons* 1910 SC 246 at 254, per Lord Skerrington. See also Clive (1963) JR 117 at 130.
3 *Erven Warnink BV v J Townend & Sons (Hull) Ltd* [1979] 2 All ER 927.
4 [1979] 2 All ER 927 at 987, per Lord Diplock.
5 *John Haig & Co Ltd v Forth Blending Co Ltd* 1954 SC 35 at 37, per Lord Hill Watson.
6 *Wadlow* para 6.23.
7 *Morning Star Co-operative Society Ltd v Express Newspapers Ltd* [1979] FSR 113 at 117, per Foster J, who held that only such a person buying newspapers would confuse The Morning Star with The (Daily) Star.
8 *Dunlop Pneumatic Tyre Co Ltd v Dunlop Motor Co Ltd* 1907 SC (HL) 15.

repaired cars under the name Dunlop Motor Co. More recently, the Court of Appeal held that misrepresentation was not made out if only a 'very small, unobservant section of society' would be confused[1].

The representative consumer is deemed to have only imperfect recollection of detail so that 'he has in his mind's eye a general idea of the appearance of the article, and he looks at the article not closely, but sufficiently to take in its general appearance'[2]. In the *Jif Lemon* case, Lord Oliver emphasised that the court needs to consider the way or setting in which the consumer encounters the goods before ruling on the question of likely confusion. The case concerned sales of lemon juice in yellow, lemon-shaped containers where purchasers largely bought the product in supermarkets. Account therefore had to be taken of the fact that, since supermarkets normally only provided one or at most two brands of lemon juice to choose from, the consumer was 'reliant on his own perception or recollection, unassisted by the opportunity of side-by-side comparison' of the competing products[3].

Proof of likely confusion

It is not necessary for the pursuer to prove instances of actual confusion though such evidence will obviously greatly assist his or her action for passing off[4]. Survey evidence is often led to show confusion but, as the House of Lords indicated in the *Jif Lemon* case, its admissibility will depend on the conditions in which the surveys were conducted, the format of the questions posed and the manner in which the questions were asked[5]. The pursuer does not need to prove fraud or intent to deceive to obtain an interdict[6]. The more problematic question is whether proof of fraud is necessary to obtain damages. The older authorities[7] appear to suggest that damages can only be obtained if fraudulent intention is present. One writer[8] has argued persuasively that more recent developments in the law of delict (starting with *Hedley Byrne*[9]) suggest that damages could be recovered if negligent misrepresentations caused financial loss. However, in the absence of direct case law on the point, the question of liability for negligent passing off remains an open one.

1 *Newsweek Inc v British Broadcasting Corpn* [1979] RPC 441 at 447, per Lord Denning MR, holding that 'ordinary, sensible members of the public' would not be confused by the BBC adopting the same title for a weekly current affairs programme as that used by the publishers of an American magazine.
2 *Pasquali Cigarette Co Ltd v Diaconicolas & Capsopolus* [1905] TS 472 per Solomon J, a South African case quoted in *Wadlow* para 6.23.
3 *Reckitt and Colman Products Ltd v Borden Inc* [1990] 1 All ER 873 at 881, HL, per Lord Oliver.
4 See eg *Great North of Scotland Rly Co v Mann* (1892) 19 R 1035 (interdict granted on evidence that several people had been taken to the wrong hotel).
5 See *Reckitt and Colman Products Ltd v Borden Inc* [1990] 1 All ER 873 at 881, HL, per Lord Oliver.
6 See *Great North of Scotland Rly Co v Mann* (1892) 19 R 1035 at 1041, per Lord McLaren.
7 *Great North of Scotland Rly Co v Mann* above.
8 See Clive (1963) JR 117 at 124–125.
9 *Hedley Byrne & Co Ltd v Heller & Partners Ltd* [1964] AC 465, HL.

DAMAGE

The final element in a passing off claim is the need to show that the defender's misrepresentations are likely to cause substantial damage to goodwill[1]. Damage normally has to be proved as a separate issue because injury to goodwill does not necessarily follow from customer confusion. In the *Stringfellows* case, eg, the defendants used a disco theme in their adverts to market a new product, 'Stringfellows' oven chips. The plaintiff owned 'Stringfellows', a famous night club in London, and was able to show that some members of the public might be misled into thinking that there was a connection between the chips and the night club. However, the plaintiff failed to establish actual damage to goodwill since membership and attendance at the club remained unaffected. The Court of Appeal also found that there was no real likelihood of damage and therefore reversed the trial judge's finding for the plaintiff[2]. However in cases of fraudulent conduct or where the parties are in direct competition, damage is normally inferred[3].

Damage to goodwill can take a variety of forms. Apart from loss of sales and diversion of trade to the defender, the pursuer's goodwill can suffer from an injurious association. Thus, eg, the court granted an interlocutory injunction to prevent use of the name 'Rolls Royce' on cars converted by the defendants because if 'inferior work was put out as being the work of Rolls Royce, [the likely damage] is quite incalculable and of very great financial harm to Rolls Royce'. A large part of Rolls Royce's goodwill was said to depend on their reputation for immaculate finish and engineering[4]. In an earlier case, the Court of Appeal granted an injunction to prevent the defendants trading as 'Annabel's Escort Agency' where the plaintiffs ran a high class night club known as 'Annabel's'. There was no evidence that the night club was likely to lose members or income but the court was concerned that the plaintiffs should not be 'tarred to some extent with the brush which the general public are inclined to think is appropriate to escort agencies'[5].

Relevant damage is not confined to the impact of the defender's misrepresentations on customers. It may be relevant to consider the effect on trading or commercial relationships with, for instance, suppliers[6], retailers[7] and agents or intermediaries[8].

REMEDIES

Interdict is the primary remedy for passing off and most petitioners are content to rest with interim interdict. An interim interdict is obtained by

1 See eg *Reckitt and Colman Products Ltd v Borden Inc* [1990] 1 All ER 873 at 880, 890, HL.
2 *Stringfellow v McCain Foods* (GB) Ltd [1984] RPC 501, CA.
3 *Wadlow* paras 3.10–3.11.
4 *Rolls Royce Motors Ltd v Zanelli* [1979] RPC 143 at 155, per Browne-Wilkinson J.
5 *Annabel's (Berkeley Square) Ltd v G Schock* [1972] RPC 838 at 845, per Russell LJ.
6 *Chelsea Man Menswear Ltd v Chelsea Girl Ltd* [1987] RPC 189, CA.
7 *Highland Distilleries Co plc v Speymalt Whisky Distributors Ltd* 1985 SC 1, OH.
8 *Provident Financial plc v Halifax Building Society* [1994] FSR 81.

establishing a prima facie case of passing off and persuading the court that the balance of convenience lies with the petitioner rather than the respondent[1]. If the case goes to a full hearing, the court may grant permanent interdict along with either damages or an accounting of the defender's profits. The petitioner must choose between damages and an accounting of profits; he or she is not entitled to claim both remedies[2]. Claims for damages may still be restricted to cases of fraudulent misrepresentation but, in any event, the sum to be awarded will be difficult to quantify. An accounting of profits is similarly problematic for a petitioner in terms of assessing the profits which must be disgorged[3].

Registered trade marks

INTRODUCTION

The conventional wisdom among marketing executives is that products are what businesses make, but brands are what people buy. The need to develop a clear and attractive product identity in the market is seen as crucial to commercial success. In the highly competitive market for air passengers, for instance, British Airways announced in June 1997 that it was to spend £60 million over five years in re-branding its corporate image[4]. The most obvious way to achieve product differentiation is to develop a distinctive trade name or logo which can be used in advertising and on the product itself. It is no surprise, then, to learn that in America the average citizen is reckoned to see over 1,500 trade marks a day[5]. The pulling power of successful brand names and logos is such that trade marks are increasingly entered as a separate item on company balance sheets. The accountancy profession may not agree on how trade marks should be valued but there is little doubt that the more successful brand names and logos can be among the most valuable commercial assets which a business possesses. The commercial importance of successful trade marks is illustrated by the results of an American survey of major brand names published in 1993. The survey concluded that MARLBORO was worth $40 billion, COCA-COLA worth $33 billion and INTEL worth $17.8 billion. The leading British brand, GUINNESS, was valued at $2.74 billion[6].

Registration versus passing off

The function of trade marks as a way of differentiating one brand of goods or services from another forms the basis for the Trade Marks Act 1994[7] and

---

1 See further 18 *Stair Memorial Encyclopaedia* paras 1398–1399.
2 *Treadwell's Drifters Inc v RCL Ltd* 1996 SLT 1048 at 1061, OH.
3 See 18 *Stair Memorial Encyclopaedia* para 1400.
4 (1997) Times, 11 June, p 5.
5 See Hughes *Freshfields Intellectual Property Yearbook 1997* (1996) p 94.
6 Survey conducted by *Financial World* and discussed in *Annand and Norman* p 10
7 See Trade Marks Act 1994, s 1(1). The legislation is referred to hereinafter as 'TMA 1994'.

the harmonising Trade Marks Directive[1] which the Act seeks to implement. If the trade mark owner decides (eg on grounds of cost) not to register his or her mark under the 1994 Act, he or she will have to rely on the common law of passing off to prevent a similar mark being used by his or her competitors. However, the common law suffers from several disadvantages. The pursuer would have to prove that he or she was entitled to use the mark. The mark must also have been used and be shown to have generated goodwill through use. The owner also has to show that goodwill is likely to be damaged by the defender's mark.

In contrast, registration under the 1994 Act gives the owner several acknowledged advantages over passing off. Registration of a mark is prima facie proof of the owner's entitlement to the mark. The owner can apply for registration before a mark has ever been used on goods or services so long as there is bona fide intention to use the mark after it has been registered. If the mark is registered, the owner can sue infringers without having to prove the existence of goodwill or that goodwill is likely to be damaged. The existence of a register of trade marks also means that competitors can consult the register before adopting a new mark which may conflict with the owner's mark.

On the negative side, the 1994 Act requires the owner to go through a registration procedure and satisfy the Registrar of Trade Marks that the proposed mark satisfies the requirements of the legislation[2]. For many small to medium sized businesses, the costs of applying for a trade mark will be a significant expense since the professional fees charged by trade mark agents will need to be paid in addition to registration fees. Costs are inevitably increased if the application is opposed by a competitor[3]. A successful applicant will have to pay renewal fees to the Trade Mark Office if the registered mark is to remain on the register[4]. The owner of a registered mark faces revocation of the registration if the mark has not been put to genuine use in the UK in the five years following registration[5].

Importance of the Trade Marks 1994 Act

Before examining the main features of the substantive law on registration and protection of registered trade marks, it is worth noting the commercial importance of the 1994 Act. The legislation repeals the Trade Marks Act 1938 and, at the same time, implements the Trade Marks Directive. In practical terms, this means that businesses can now register certain marks which it would have been difficult or impossible to register under the 1938 Act. Thus it is now possible to register the shape of goods and the packaging which accompanies goods. Sounds, scents and other sensory marks are also now capable of registration as trade marks. Implementing the Directive through the 1994 Act has also broadened the scope of trade mark infringement. Thus, for instance, competitors are now potentially liable if

1 See EC Council Directive 89/104 (OJ L40, 11.2.89, p 1), art 2.
2 See TMA 1994, ss 1, 3, 5 and 7.
3 See TMA 1994, s 38(2).
4 See TMA 1994, ss 42 and 43.
5 See TMA 1994, s 46.

they use a similar mark on dissimilar goods or services from those for which the owner's mark is registered. The 1994 Act also allows trade mark owners greater freedom to assign or license registered marks.

WHAT CAN BE REGISTERED?

The 1994 Act allows trade marks to be registered for goods or services[1]. Before it can be registered, a proposed mark must satisfy three requirements: it must be (1) a 'sign' within the meaning of the Act; (2) the sign must be capable of being represented graphically as an entry on the Trade Mark Register; and (3) the sign must be capable of distinguishing the applicant's goods or services from those of other businesses. If the proposed mark satisfies these requirements, it can then be registered unless it falls foul of one the statutory grounds of refusal. Various absolute grounds of refusal are found in s 3 and these relate to the characteristics of the proposed mark. In addition, ss 5 to 7 specify various relative grounds of refusal, which include similarity between the proposed mark and marks which are already on the register.

Registrable signs

It soon becomes apparent from reading s 1(1) how the scope for trade mark registration has been increased by the 1994 Act. The types of sign which can be registered may consist of words (including personal names), designs, letters, numerals or the shape of the goods or their packaging. The fact that the shape of the goods or their packaging can now be a registered as trade marks reverses previous decisions. In the *Coca-Cola* case[2], for instance, the House of Lords upheld the Registrar's refusal of trade mark registration for the distinctively-shaped cola bottle on the basis that 'a bottle is a container not a mark'. Since the 1994 Act came into force, the Coca-Cola Company has successfully re-applied for registration of the bottle as a trade mark[3].

Sensory marks

The 1994 Act does not actually mention colours, sounds, scents or tastes as registrable signs. However, the definition of 'trade mark' in s 1(1) is taken from art 2 of the Trade Marks Directive which was intended by the European Commission not to exclude any type of sign automatically from registration. The intention behind s 1(1) is therefore to permit the registration of distinctive signs of any kind. Thus, for instance, there is nothing to stop an applicant registering a distinctive colour or combination of colours so long as the colour mark is perceived by the public as distin-

---

1 Eg banks, hotels, car hire companies and dry cleaning firms can seek to register service marks which distinguish their services from those provided by competitors.
2 *Coca-Cola Trade Mark Applications* [1986] RPC 421, HL.
3 See *Annual Report of the Patent Office 1995–96* p 34.

guishing the applicant's goods or services[1]. Distinctive sounds or jingles can also be registered if they are capable of graphic representation[2]. The same applies to distinctive scents or smells such as the scented yarn which possessed 'a high-impact, fresh floral fragrance reminiscent of plumeria blossoms' which was recently registered in America[3]. There is no reason in principle why distinctive tastes or textures could not also be registered as trade marks under the 1994 Act.

Graphic representation

The need under s 1(1) for a proposed mark to be 'represented graphically' is derived from art 2 of the Trade Marks Directive. It ensures that the mark can be published in the Trade Marks Journal[4] so that objectors have an opportunity either to oppose registration or to make written observations on registrability to the Trade Marks Registry. If accepted for registration, the mark also has to be physically entered on the Register of Trade Marks[5] so that it can be consulted by others who may be considering making an application to register a mark. The graphic representation requirement can be met by expressing scents in terms of their chemical composition and musical sounds in the form of musical notation[6].

Distinctiveness

If the applicant's proposed mark lacks the capacity to distinguish his or her goods or services from those provided by competitors, the application will fail[7]. Cornish[8] suggests that this requirement will particularly come into play where attempts are made to register sensory trade marks which represent the primary characteristics of the products themselves. Thus, for instance, the fragrance of a new perfume or air freshner will probably be refused registration because the traditional function of trade mark law is to offer protection to marks added or applied to products rather than to the primary products themselves. On the other hand, the smell incorporated in shampoos or household cleaning fluids may be registrable as a mark since the smell is a secondary characteristic which functions as a means of distinguishing one such product from another.

---

1 See Lord Diplock's remarks in *Smith, Kline and French Laboratories Ltd v Sterling-Winthrop Group Ltd* [1976] RPC 511 at 533, HL, where he insisted that colour combinations are shown 'to serve the business purpose of a trade mark [and] do precisely what a trade mark is supposed to do: [indicate] to potential buyers that the goods were made by SKF and not by any other manufacturer'.
2 Previously marks had to be visual to be capable of registration: Trade Marks Act 1938, s 68(2).
3 *In re Celia Clark* (1990) 17 USPQ 2d 1238 (US Trademark Trial and Appeal Board).
4 TMA 1994, s 38(1).
5 TMA 1994, s 40(1).
6 See further Lyons 'Sounds, Smells and Signs' [1994] EIPR 540.
7 TMA 1994, s 1(1).
8 Cornish *Intellectual Property* (3rd edn, 1996) para 17-20.

Absolute grounds of objection

For public policy reasons, marks which satisfy the distinctiveness requirement may be refused registration under one of the absolute grounds for
refusal set out in s 3 of the 1994 Act.

Failure to satisfy section 1(1) of the 1994 Act

The first absolute ground of refusal is simply that the proposed mark fails
even to satisfy the requirements of s 1 of the 1994 Act. Hence the sensory
mark which has not been properly represented graphically will be refused
registration.

Devoid of distinctive character

The second ground of refusal bars registration of a sign or mark which is
devoid of any distinctive character. Common surnames[1] will probably
come into this category. Simple devices, such as the red stripe in toothpaste, will also probably be regarded as devoid of distinctive character[2].
Signs which prima facie lack distinctiveness can, however, be registered if
the applicant can show that the sign had acquired a distinctive character
through its use before registration was sought[3]. Thus the fact that the public is familiar with the proposed name or mark because it has already been
used by the applicant on his or her goods or services may be sufficient to
overcome what would otherwise be a bar to registration.

Descriptive signs

The next ground of refusal in s 3(1) of the 1994 Act prohibits registration
of purely descriptive signs. Geographical names are a good example of
signs which would potentially fall into this category. The policy behind
this bar on registration is that geograhical names should remain in the
public domain and be available to other traders who have a legitimate
interest in using the same name. The Act does, however, allow an exception to made if there is evidence that the applicant has already been using
the geographical name for trade mark purposes[4]. In other words, evidence
of distinctiveness acquired through actual use of the name may be sufficient to overcome the objection that the mark is purely descriptive. Thus,
eg, the whisky producers who produced whisky from their distillery in
Glen Livet have been held entitled to register THE GLENLIVET as a trade
mark for both single malt whisky and mineral water. Registration of the
geographical name for mineral water was allowed on the basis that the
public would assume that the product not only came from Glen Livet but

---

1 Consultation of telephone directories is an important means of determining the distinctiveness of surnames.
2 See *Unilever's (Striped Toothpaste No 2) Trade Mark* [1987] RPC 13.
3 See TMA 1994, s 3(1) proviso.
4 TMA 1994, s 3(1) proviso.

was also produced by the distillers who had already produced whisky under the same name[1].

Other examples of purely descriptive marks include laudatory names (eg PERFECTION for soap[2]) and names which refer to the character or quality of the goods (eg PRO FIT for golf clubs[3]).

Generic names

A further absolute ground for refusing registration under s 3 of the 1994 Act bars attempts to register signs which were initially distinctive but have since become customary in the trade or become generic names to the public[4]. Examples of generic names would include ASPIRIN, HOOVER, LINOLEUM and SHREDDED WHEAT. Other signs which would probably be considered to be customary would be pictures of grazing cattle on the side of dairy products or sheaves of wheat on the wrappers used to package loaves of bread.

Certain shapes

Distinctive shapes, which are now registrable under s 1 of the 1994 Act, are subject to specific grounds of absolute refusal set out in s 3(2). These grounds are found in art 3(1)(e) of the Trade Marks Directive and are derived from Benelux trade marks law. The first specific bar to registering a shape mark is triggered where the shape results from the nature of the goods themselves. This obviously covers shapes where the applicant has no realistic alternative but to produce his product (eg a football) in that particular shape.

The second barrier to shape registration applies in cases where the shape of the goods is 'necessary to obtain a technical result'. This category appears to overlap with the first but is presumably intended to go further than simply barring registration of shapes which have been adopted for purely functional reasons. It is probably meant to catch shapes whose main (but not sole) purpose is a technical one such as the shape which has been designed to make it easier for the consumer to use or store goods. Thus, for instance, the shape of a toothpaste tube or the shape of the plastic container designed to carry heavy liquids would probably be denied registration under the 1994 Act[5]. Where, however, the shape possesses a mainly non-functional purpose, it can be registered, as happened in 1995 with the COCA-COLA bottle.

The final category of excluded shape in s 3(2) concerns cases where the shape 'gives substantial value to the goods'. Thus registration is barred

---

1 See *Glenlivet Trade Mark* [1993] RPC 461 at 469 per Robin Jacob QC, justifying registration on the basis that 'only someone wanting to trade on the reputation of the whisky is now likely to go [to Glenlivet]. Whilst it is possible to do that honestly, it could only be done with considerable care. I think a fetter on such a trader is not harmful to the public interest. If he merely wants to sell mineral water there are plenty of other places to go'.
2 See *J Crosfield & Son's Application* [1910] 1 Ch 130.
3 See *True Temper Corpn's Application* [1978] EIPR, November, p 20 (Ireland's Trade Mark Controller).
4 TMA 1994, s 3(1)(d).
5 See *Annand and Norman* p 86.

where a particular shape is distinctive but the shape itself is a substantial element in its appeal to the consumer. The 'substantial value' exception is derived from Benelux law where the Dutch Supreme Court has reached opposite conclusions in cases dealing with the shape of cracker biscuits[1]. In the first case, trade mark registration was allowed in respect of the spiral shape of a cracker which was found to have increased the product's market value but not its 'intrinsic' value. However, the Dutch Supreme Court later refused registration for a round shape of biscuit. Minor differences in taste between competing biscuit products meant that the round shape added substantial market value to the product. In later appeals on the same point of law, the Benelux Court of Justice first held[2] that substantial increase in commercial value is the determining factor in assessing 'substantial value' but in a later case[3] considered that only a substantial increase in intrinsic value would bar registration of a shape[4].

The distinctive shape element in some products or their packaging plays such an important part in marketing that an authoritative decision on the interpretation of the 'substantial value' exception is keenly awaited in several sectors of the economy[5].

Contrary to public policy

In the general public interest, s 3 of the 1994 Act also places an absolute bar on registering marks which are 'contrary to accepted principles of morality'. The bar also applies to marks which would deceive the public as to nature, quality or geographical origin of the goods[6]. As far as the latter category is concerned, SAFEMIX was refused as a proposed mark for thermostatically controlled valves under the 1938 Act because it was considered to imply that the valves were safe in every circumstance when they were not[7]. Applications made in bad faith will also be refused under the Act[8]. While the Act allows registration to be obtained before a mark is ever used, the application will be refused if the applicant lacks the bona fide intention to use the mark. Thus, for instance, if the mark is simply being registered to prevent competitors using a similar mark, it can be refused by the Registrar[9].

1 See *Wokkels* [1985] BIE 23 (spiral shape allowed) and *Bacony Snack* [1989] NJ 835 (round shape refused), discussed in *Annand and Norman* pp 86–87.
2 *Burberrys I* (1991) 22 IIC 567, following the market value approach in *Bacony Snack* [1989] NJ 835.
3 *Burberrys II* [1992] NJ 596, approving the intrinsic approach to 'substantial value' in *Wokkels* [1985] BIE 23.
4 As Cornish wryly remarks, 'so much for precedent in the Benelux system': *Intellectual Property* (3rd edn, 1996) para 17-46.
5 See eg The Times Magazine, 17 May 1997, p 34, where the importance of bottle design in the highly competitive market for new perfumes is reported to be such that 'without a distinctive bottle it would be very hard to win'.
6 TMA 1994, s 3(3).
7 See *Safemix Trade Mark* [1978] RPC 397.
8 TMA 1994, s 3(6).
9 Should the applicant's bad faith only become apparent after registration, competitors or the Registrar can apply to have the mark removed: TMA 1994, s 47.

Relative grounds for refusal

Assuming the applicant's proposed mark does not fall foul under one of the absolute grounds for refusal, the Registrar may exercise his discretion under ss 5 to 8 and refuse registration if he considers that the mark conflicts with an 'an earlier trade mark' or 'earlier rights'.

Earlier trade marks

Earlier trade marks will probably have been discovered by the Registrar after he has carried out a mandatory search in the register of existing marks[1]. The Registrar's search for potentially conflicting marks which are already on the register has long been recognised as a thorough process with the result that only about 2 per cent of published applications are later opposed by competitors[2]. For present purposes, earlier trade marks means prior UK and Community trade marks[3]; the latter mark is obtained from the Community Trade Mark Office in Alicante[4]. The concept of earlier marks includes earlier trade mark applications which are eventually successful.

An earlier mark will conflict with a proposed mark if the marks are similar or identical and the goods or services which carry the marks are also similar or identical[5]. If an identical mark is used on identical goods or services, the Registrar will automatically refuse the application without any further inquiry[6]. Where the conflict turns on the supposed similarity of the two marks, s 5(2) of the 1994 Act requires the Registrar to consider whether there exists 'a likelihood of confusion on the part of the public, which includes the likelihood of association with the earlier trade mark'. This test for similarity is taken from the Trade Marks Directive, which in turn is commonly assumed to have derived its concept of similarity from Benelux law[7]. Thus the Dutch Supreme Court[8] has held that a likelihood of confusion arises where the later mark conjures up an image in the public mind which leads them to associate the later mark with the earlier mark[9].

This broad approach to likelihood of confusion is not entirely unknown in the UK. Thus the courts have refused to apply a stringent visual test when comparing marks since 'marks are remembered rather by general impressions or by some significant detail than by photographic recollection of the whole'[10]. In the case of words or names, the courts will also con-

1 As he is required to do by TMA 1994, s 37(2), but only to such extent as he considers necessary.
2 See DTI White Paper *Reform of Trade Marks Law* (Cmnd 1203) (1990) para 4.11.
3 For the full meaning of 'earlier trade mark', see TMA 1994, s 6.
4 And is made possible by the Community Trade Mark Regulation (see below), which allows businesses to apply for registration of a single Community-wide trade mark.
5 See TMA 1994, s 5(1) and (2).
6 TMA 1994, s 5(1).
7 But see Laddie J's trenchant reservations on the provenance of the wording in *Wagamama Ltd v City Centre Restaurants plc* [1995] FSR 713 at 726–728.
8 See *Monopoly v Anti-Monopoly* (24 June 1977), Dutch Supreme Court, cited by *Annand and Norman* p 99.
9 See also the expert testimony given (but ultimately rejected) in *Wagamama Ltd v City Centre Restaurants plc* [1995] FSR 713 at 724.
10 See *de Cordova v Vick Chemical Co* (1951) 68 RPC 103 at 106.

sider 'the variety of ways in which members of the target market will pro-
nounce the mark'[1]. Apart from the visual or phonetic impact of the two
marks, the possible effect of imperfect recollection on the part of the target
consumer is important because the consumer may not have the opportunity to compare the two marks side by side[1]. In short, the Registrar has to
assess the overall 'idea of the mark' where similarity is an issue[2].

Earlier rights

The concept of conflicting 'earlier rights' as a ground of objection covers
unregistered marks which are identical or similar to the mark which the
applicant is proposing to use. The owner of an unregistered mark is only
likely to succeed in his or her objection if he or she can satisfy the requirements for bringing a passing off action. Prior copyrights[3], design rights or
registered designs also fall into the category of potentially conflicting earlier rights[4] unless the owner of the earlier right consents to the trade mark
application[5]. Thus, for instance, in the *Oscar* case[6], the US Academy of
Motion Pictures would arguably have been successful in opposing
OSCAR as a proposed trade mark for radio and television equipment if
the Academy had been able to establish the subsistence of copyright in the
UK.

OBTAINING A TRADE MARK

The procedure for obtaining a registration of a UK trade mark under the
1994 Act is briefly as follows. Before filing an application, the owner can
carry out a preliminary search in the computerised Trade Marks Register
to check if there are any prior rights which might prevent the mark being
registered. After making a preliminary search, the applicant who proceeds to file an application must state which categories of goods or services are to be protected by the proposed mark. The register is (somewhat
arbitrarily) divided[7] into thirty-four classes of goods[8] and eight classes of
services[9]. However, unlike the 1938 Act, which required separate applica-

1 See *Wagamama Ltd v City Centre Restaurants plc* [1995] RPC 713 at 732, per Jacob J.
2 See further *Kerly The Law of Trade Marks and Trade Names* (12th edn, 1986) paras 17-08–
   17-09.
3 See eg *KARO STEP Trade Mark* [1977] RPC 255 at 274, per Whitford J, where the court
   emphasised that the owner of a registered mark must be able to claim 'that he has an
   absolute right to use it'. Any such claim would be bad 'if in fact on copyright grounds
   some third person is going to be in a position to stop the applicant using the mark at all'.
4 See TMA 1994, s 5(4).
5 TMA 1994, s 5(5). The Registrar no longer has the discretionary power which existed
   under TMA 1938 to override the owner's consent if this was in the public interest.
6 *OSCAR Trade Mark* [1979] RPC 173.
7 In accordance with the Nice International Arrangement: TMA 1994, s 34 and Trade Marks
   Rules 1994, SI 1994/2583, Sch 4. A Committee of Experts has proposed that some of the
   services currently covered by class 42 should be assigned to three new classes: see [1995]
   EIPR D-268.
8 Eg furniture (class 20); clothing (class 25); games (class 28).
9 Eg insurance and financial affairs (class 36); provision of food and drink, temporary
   accommodation (class 42).

tions to be made in respect of each proposed class, the 1994 Act permits a single application to cover multiple classes[1], though supplementary fees must be paid for each class[2]. Should the applicant succeed in registering a mark in a particular class simply to prevent it being used by competitors, the mark can be revoked if it is found not to have been put to genuine use in the five years following registration[3].

Objections

On receipt of the application, the Registrar will conduct a search of earlier marks to identify possible conflicts with the proposed mark. The mark is then examined in the light of the absolute and relative grounds of refusal. If the Registrar has objections, he must give the applicant the opportunity either to make representations or to amend the statement of goods or services specified in the original application[4]. Once the Registrar is satisfied that the owner has met the requirements of the 1994 Act, he must accept the application and publish it in the Trade Marks Journal[5]. Objectors have a strict period of three months from the date of publication in which to file a statement of opposition to the proposed mark[6].

Registration

If no opposition is filed or notified objections are overcome, the mark will be registered. The period of registration is backdated to the date when the application was filed[7]. The effect of this is to allow the owner to claim damages from the date of registration for infringements committed between the filing date and the date of registration[8]. The mark is initially registered for ten years running from the filing date. Registration can be renewed indefinitely for further periods of ten years[9] unless the mark is revoked (eg, for non-use).

INFRINGEMENT OF TRADE MARKS

An action for infringement of a UK trademark is confined to the Court of Session[10] and can only be brought in respect of infringements occurring in the UK. The right to take action commences at the date when the mark is entered on the Register of Trade Marks but the owner is entitled to seek

---

1 See TMA 1994, s 32(4).
2 Trade Marks Rules 1994, r 5.
3 TMA 1994, s 46.
4 TMA 1994, s 37(3).
5 TMA 1994, ss 37(5) and 38(1).
6 TMA 1994, s 38(2), and Trade Marks Rules 1994, r 13.
7 TMA 1994, s 40(3).
8 TMA 1994, s 9(3). The registered owner also benefits from the fact that registration is prima facie evidence of the validity of the registered mark, thus placing the burden of proof on the alleged infringer to challenge the mark's validity: TMA 1994, s 72.
9 TMA 1994, s 42.
10 Or the High Court in England, Wales and Northern Ireland: TMA 1994, s 75.

damages for infringements which have taken place in the period between the filing date and the eventual date of registration[1]. The pursuer is normally the trade mark owner but exclusive licensees[2] can sue if the licence from the owner permits the licensee to sue infringers[3]. In response to an infringement action, the defender may seek to challenge the validity of the owner's mark by counterclaiming for revocation of the registration or having the mark declared invalid[4].

As noted earlier, implementation of the Trade Marks Directive has resulted in a broader definition of trade mark infringement. One aspect of this is the fact that infringement under the 1938 Act involved a 'printed or other visual representation'of the owner's mark. This still remains by far the most likely form of infringing use under the 1994 Act but, in view of the possibility of registering sensory marks under the 1994 Act, the concept of infringement now includes non-graphic use or representation of the owner's mark (eg playing a jingle)[5].

Several forms of infringement are recognised under the 1994 Act. The various grounds of action described below apply both to 'old' marks registered under the 1938 Act and to 'new' marks registered under the 1994 Act[6].

Identical sign for identical goods or services

The clearest case of infringement involves use of an identical sign on the same goods or services as those specified in the owner's certificate of registration. The pursuer has no need to establish confusion in such cases[7]. In a recent case on use of an identical sign, the respondent attempted to publish a book about the pop group *Wet Wet Wet* under the title *A Sweet Little Mystery – Wet Wet Wet – The Inside Story*. The petitioner owned the trade mark *Wet Wet Wet* which was registered for books. Lord McCluskey rejected the argument that the respondent's intended use was not an infringement merely because the book was to carry a different typeface from that featured in the certificate of registration. It was enough that the respondent was using 'the highly unusual combination of the word 'wet' repeated for a total of three uses without any punctuation'[8]. However Lord McCluskey upheld the defence available to the respondent under s 11(2)(b) of the 1994 Act because he had honestly used the registered name to indicate the subject matter of the book.

1 TMA 1994, s 9(3).
2 Ie those who exercise the right to use the mark to the exclusion of all others, including the trade mark owner: TMA 1994, s 29(1).
3 TMA 1994, s 31(1).
4 See eg the successful challenge to validity sustained by Jacob J in *British Sugar plc v James Robertson & Sons Ltd* [1996] RPC 281.
5 TMA 1994, s 103(2).
6 See TMA 1994, Sch 3, paras 2(1) and 4(1), which apply the 1994 Act's infringement provisions to infringements of 'old' marks committed after 31 October 1994.
7 TMA 1994, s 10(1).
8 *Bravado Merchandising Services Ltd v Mainstream Publishing (Edinburgh) Ltd* 1996 SLT 597 at 603, OH.

Identical or similar signs for identical or similar goods or services

The second form of infringement under the 1994 Act is found in s 10(2). This provision envisages two forms of infringement: (1) using an identical sign for similar goods or services; and (2) using a similar sign for identical/similar goods or services. As such, s 10(2) represents an extension of the previous law which only recognised infringement where the defender had used a similar mark used on *identical* – not similar – goods or services to those covered by the owner's registration. The key concept of similarity is not, however, defined in either the 1994 Act or the Trade Marks Directive. In a few cases, the concept will be relatively straightforward to apply. Thus, for instance, where the defendant used a single descriptive word ('European') from the owner's trade mark to form part of his own title for a new publication, similarity was held not to exist because the word was in common, everyday use[1]. Words which are common to a particular trade (such as COLA or SELTZER) will not infringe if this is the only point of similarity between the defender's sign and the owner's mark[2].

Similarity

In more difficult cases of alleged similarity, Jacob J has recently stated that the court should, as a matter of principle, be cautious in finding against the infringer, particularly where the owner's mark is registered for only a narrow class of goods or services. Any attempt in such cases by the trade mark owner to expand the scope of his or her protection into a wide range of supposedly similar goods should be doomed to failure on the basis that 'if a man wants wide protection he can always ask for it [when applying for registration] and will get it only if his claim is justified'[3]. Jacob J lists several factors which the court may need to consider when determining the issue of similarity. These factors include: the respective uses of the respective goods or services; the respective users of the respective goods or services; the physical nature of the goods or acts of service; the respective trade channels through which the goods or services reach the market; where the goods are likely to be found in supermarkets or self-service stores and, in particular, whether they are likely to be found on the same or different shelves; and the extent to which the respective goods or services are competitive which may take into account, for instance, whether market research companies put the goods or services in the same or different sectors.

Applying these factors in *British Sugar*, Jacob J held that similarity did not exist between a toffee-flavoured spread labelled 'Robertson's Toffee Treat', which was sold by supermarkets alongside jams and preserves, and the plaintiff's 'Silver Spoon Treat', a dessert sauce or syrup designed for pouring onto ice cream. It was significant that the two products were

---

1 See *European Ltd v Economist Newspapers Ltd* [1996] FSR 431.
2 See *Coca-Cola Canada v Pepsi Cola Canada* (1942) 59 RPC 127 and *Re Demuth's Application* (1948) 65 RPC 342.
3 *British Sugar plc v James Robertson & Sons Ltd* [1996] RPC 281 at 296–297.

stocked by supermarkets in different places and were regarded by market researchers as falling within different market sectors.

Likelihood of confusion

Having established similarity, the pursuer bringing an action under s 10(2) of the 1994 Act then has to prove that, because of the similarity, 'there exists a likelihood of confusion on the part of the public, which includes likelihood of association with the trade mark'[1]. According to Jacob J[2], this limb in s 10(2) requires the court to assume that the owner is using his or her mark 'in a normal and fair manner in relation to the goods [or services] for which it is registered'. Making this assumption, the court then proceeds to make a 'mark for mark' comparison. In other words, the process of comparison discounts any 'external added matter or circumstances' beyond the defender's mark itself so as to remove the possibility of arguing that these external factors distinguish the defender's goods or services from those of the registered owner[3].

Inevitably, the judge's assessment of likelihood of confusion is going to be 'more a matter of feel than science' which goes beyond merely seeing the two marks placed side by side[4]. In particular, the way in which the target market is likely to recollect the marks (visually or phonetically) is a key issue[5]. This has to be balanced against the need to recognise that consumers do not possess a photographic memory. As the Privy Council has noted: 'marks are remembered rather by general impressions or by some significant detail than by photographic recollection of the whole'[6]. Imperfect recollection therefore plays an important part in the assessment of likely confusion, particularly where the owner's mark is an invented or artificial word which is regarded as meaningless by a large section of the target market.

The fact that the owner's mark is entirely meaningless makes imperfect recollection more likely. As a consequence, some members of the public will either think the two marks are the same or at least believe that they are associated with each other. Thus the word RAJAMAMA, used for an inexpensive restaurant providing Indian style food in London, has been held to infringe the name WAGAMAMA which had been registered for an inexpensive Japanese-style restaurant in London[7]. Similarly, the owners of the registered mark RUS, obtained for bricks and tiles, were able to show that the public was likely to be confused by the use of SANRUS for brick facings. There was a danger that the public would think that SAN-RUS products were being marketed by the registered owners[8].

1   Cf *British Sugar plc v James Roberston & Sons Ltd* [1996] RPC 281 at 294, per Jacob J on the danger of eliding the questions of similarity and confusion where the registered mark is a 'strong' one.
2   *Origins Natural Resources Inc v Origin Clothing Ltd* [1995] FSR 280 at 284.
3   See *Saville Perfumery Ltd v June Perfect Ltd and FW Woolworth Ltd* (1941) 58 RPC 147 at 161.
4   See *Wagamama Ltd v City Centre Restaurants plc* [1995] FSR 713 at 732, per Laddie J.
5   The Benelux Court of Justice is prepared to go further and consider 'conceptual resemblance' if the degree of resemblance evokes associations between the trade mark and the infringer's sign: *Union v Union Soleure* [1984] BIE 137, cited in *Annand and Norman* p 155.
6   *de Cordova v Vick Chemical Co* (1951) 68 RPC 103 at 106, PC.
7   *Wagamama Ltd v City Centre Restaurants plc* [1995] FSR 713.
8   *Ravenhead Brick v Ruabon Brick* (1937) 54 RPC 341.

Identical or similar signs for dissimilar goods or services

Section 10(3) of the 1994 Act represents the most obvious shift in the traditional concept of trade mark infringement. By enacting an optional provision in the Trade Marks Directive[1], UK law now recognises that the
distinctiveness of a well-established registered mark (eg KODAK,
NESCAFE, MARLBORO) can be diluted by someone using a similar or
identical mark on entirely different goods or services (eg KODAK furniture). The 1994 Act offers protection against dilution if the registered mark
has acquired a 'reputation' in the UK and the defender's use 'takes unfair
advantage of, or is detrimental to, the distinctive character or the repute of
the trade mark'.

Without due cause

The pursuer will only succeed in a claim for dilution if he or she can show
that his or her sign has been used 'without due cause'. The phrase is taken
from Article 13A of the Benelux Trade Marks Law 1971 and appears to
have been strictly construed by the Benelux Court of Justice to mean that
the action fails if the defender's use of the mark was necessary (eg to indicate the intended purpose of spare parts or components). As Annand and
Norman point out[2], the difficulty with this interpretation is that such uses
are already included as specific defences under s 11(2) of the 1994 Act.
Case law, especially from the European Court of Justice, is therefore
awaited to shed light on what is meant by lack of due cause.

Dilution

The defender's liability under s 10(3) of the 1994 Act depends on establishing that his or her use of the sign takes unfair advantage of, or is detrimental to, the distinctive character or repute of the registered mark. It is
enough, therefore, for the owner to show unfair advantage without also
having to prove detriment. However, it is also clear that, unlike s 10(2),
likelihood of confusion between the mark and the sign is not a formal
requirement under s 10(3). The latter point raises another difficulty with s
10(3): it seems to allow a right of action where dissimilar goods or services
carry a mark which has a reputation even though there is little or no likelihood that the consumer would be confused by the defender's use of the
mark or even associate the goods or services with the registered owner.

However, in two recent unreported cases, it would appear that the
courts have construed s 10(3) to mean that there must be a risk – and probably a likelihood – of confusion before infringement is made out[3]. It is suggested that this approach must be correct because to hold otherwise
would bring about the absurd result that trade marks with a reputation

---

1 EC Council Directive 89/104, art 5(2).
2 *Blackstone's Guide to the Trade Marks Act 1994* p 157.
3 See Black ' Baywatch: Sour Grapes or Justice?'[1997] EIPR 39, discussing *BASF v CEP (UK)
   plc* [1996] IPD 19(4) and *Baywatch Production Co v Home Video Channel Ltd* [1997] 4 CL 685.

would enjoy far stronger protection under s 10(3) against completely different goods and services than they would under s 10(2) against similar goods and services.

DEFENCES

If the defender's use is caught by s 10 of the 1994 Act, he or she may be able to rely on one of the statutory defences to a claim for trade mark infringement. Under s 11(2)(a), a registered mark is not infringed by a defender who has simply used his or her own name and address. The Trade Marks Act 1938[1] required good faith on the user's part but the 1994 Act refers instead to use which is 'in accordance with honest practices in industrial or commercial matters'[2]. The courts previously interpreted good faith as a subjective test of the user's intention or motives[3]. However, it would appear that the test of honesty under the 1994 Act is to be judged objectively[4].

In terms of s 11(2)(b), a trader is allowed to use the owner's registered mark to describe the characteristics of the product (eg quality, geographical origin). Again, the defence is qualified by the need to show that the use is in accordance with honest practices. Thus use of the registered mark WET WET WET in the title of a book about the pop group of the same name was not an infringement of the trade mark[5]. Honest use of a trade mark to indicate the intended purpose of a product or service (especially accessories or spare parts) is also a defence[6]. Thus, eg, retailers can advertise replacement parts or accessories without infringing a registered mark provided their statements are not misleading (eg by suggesting that the parts are made by the manufacturers of the main product).

Section 11(3) protects a trader who continuously used an unregistered mark 'in a particular locality' before the registered mark was used or registered. In other words, the trader can claim a prior right to use the particular mark but only in the locality where he or she has previously been using it. The terms 'continuous' and 'particular locality' are not defined in the 1994 Act. The trader would make out the defence if he or she satisfied the court that the unregistered mark would be protected by the common law of passing off[7].

---

1 TMA 1938, s 8(a).
2 TMA 1994, s 11(2) proviso.
3 *Baume & Co Ltd v AH Moore Ltd* [1958] Ch 907, CA.
4 *Barclays Bank plc v RBS Advanta* [1996] RPC 307.
5 *Bravado Merchandising Services Ltd v Mainstream Publishing (Edinburgh) Ltd* 1996 SLT 597, OH. See also *J & G Grant v Wm Cadenhead Ltd* 1995 GWD 34-1764, OH (use of 'Glenfarclas-Glenlivet' on whisky, despite objections from the owner of 'Glenfarclas' trade mark, held 'plainly' to be an indication of geographical origin where there was no evidence of dishonesty).
6 TMA 1994, s 11(2)(c).
7 See TMA 1994, s 11(3) proviso.

REMEDIES FOR INFRINGEMENT

Apart from interim or permanent interdict, the usual pecuniary remedies are available in cases of trade mark infringement[1]. Damages can be claimed to compensate the pursuer for loss of sales income. Injury to reputation or goodwill could form another head of claim if the infringer's goods or services are of inferior quality. Innocent infringement is not a defence to a claim for damages[2]. As an alternative to damages, the pursuer can elect to seek an accounting and payment of the defender's profits. This remedy is not available in cases where the defender had no knowledge of the pursuer's mark. Where the defender can be shown to have had the requisite knowledge, the accounting is limited to the profits made during that period of knowledge[3].

Infringing goods

The trade mark owner can ask the Court of Session or the sheriff court[4] for an order under s 16 of the 1994 Act requiring delivery up of infringing goods (eg in the hands of wholesalers). Following compliance with a delivery order, the same courts can be asked under s 19 to order destruction or forfeiture of the goods. Before making a decision, the court must notify anyone else having an interest in the goods so as to allow them an opportunity to be heard. If the court refuses the application, the person who had possession of the goods before they were delivered up under s 16 is entitled to their return.

Groundless threats

The victim of groundless threats of infringement proceedings can raise an action under s 21 of the 1994 Act against the trade mark owner[5]. The fact that the trade mark owner warns someone that a mark is registered in his or her name does not constitute a 'threat' for these purposes[6]. The remedy is aimed at cases where litigation is threatened but the owner's threats are unjustified because the victim's conduct does not amount to infringement or the trade mark is invalid[7]. The onus is on the trade mark owner to show that the victim's conduct constituted infringement.

The remedy is not open to parties who have applied the owner's mark to goods or their packaging. Nor can the recipients of threats use s 21 if they have imported the goods into the UK or supplied the services under

---

1 See TMA 1994, s 14(2).
2 See *Gillette UK Ltd v Edenwest Ltd* [1994] RPC 279.
3 *Spalding & Bros v AW Gamage Ltd* (1915) 32 RPC 273 at 283, HL.
4 This limited role for the sheriff court in trade mark cases is granted under TMA 1994, s 20.
5 No such remedy was available under the TMA 1938 although it was included in other intellectual property statutes: see Patents Act 1977, s 70 and Registered Designs Act 1949, s 26.
6 TMA 1994, s 21(4).
7 TMA 1994, s 21(2) and (3).

the offending mark. The parties who are most likely to bring an action against the trade mark owner are wholesalers and retailers who have not been responsible for applying the offending mark to goods or their packaging. If successful, the victim is entitled to an interdict to prevent the threats continuing and damages in respect of any loss he has sustained as a result of the threats[1].

EXPLOITATION OF TRADE MARKS

Assignation

The owner of a registered trade mark acquires incorporeal moveable property which can be assigned or licensed[2]. Trade mark applications can also be assigned[3]. Assignation can take place with or without the goodwill of a business[4]. Partial assignation was possible under the Trade Marks Act 1938 which meant that the owner could opt to assign the mark in relation to only some of the goods or services covered by his or her certificate of registration. The 1994 Act retains this option and permits two other forms of partial assignation: the owner can restrict the assignee's manner of use or the locality in which the mark is to be used[5]. These new options do not appear to be available if the owner seeks to apply either or both of the restrictions to only some of goods or services covered by the registered mark[6]. Registered trade marks and trade mark applications[7] can also be the subject of an assignation in security in favour of a lender[8].

To obtain a real right in the trade mark, the assignation must be in writing and signed by the assignor or on his or her behalf[9]. The assignee then has to have the assignation entered on the Register of Trade Marks. The 1994 Act gives the assignee a clear incentive to register the assignation as soon as possible after execution since failure to register within six months of the deed being signed bars a claim for damages for infringements committed in the period between execution of the assignation and its eventual registration[10].

Licences

Trade marks may be the subject of a general licence or a limited licence. Like a partial assignation, a limited licence places restrictions on the goods or services which may carry the mark; alternatively, the particular use or

1 TMA 1994, s 21(2).
2 TMA 1994, s 22.
3 TMA 1994, s 27.
4 TMA 1994, s 24(1).
5 TMA 1994, s 24(2).
6 Cf the real danger that partial assignations of any kind may lead to deception of the public with regard to the origin of goods or services: see *Annand and Norman* p 133 on the possibility of revocation on grounds of misleading use under TMA 1994, s 46(1)(d).
7 TMA 1994, s 27(1).
8 TMA 1994, s 24(5).
9 TMA 1994, s 24(3).
10 TMA 1994, s 25(4).

locality can be restricted[1]. Sub-licences are possible if the licence agreement permits this[2]. Licences and sub-licences are only effective if they are put in writing and signed by or on behalf of the licensor[3]. Either the licensor or the licensee must then apply for registration of the licence under s 25 of the 1994 Act.

The 1994 Act removes the need which existed under the 1938 Act to satisfy the Registrar that the licensor was entitled under the licence agreement to exercise a close degree of control over the licensee's subsequent use of the mark[4]. In particular, the Registrar would previously look for an appropriate quality control clause in the licence agreement which ensured that the licensee only applied the licensed mark to goods or services of a certain quality. The DTI's White Paper[5] confirms the reasons for removing the Registrar's scrutinising role in respect of registration of licences. While the licensing of trade marks was considered to be a bold step when it was introduced in 1938, the public is now largely accustomed to trade marks being licensed or franchised by businesses so that the likelihood of deception or confusion is significantly reduced. The DTI was also attracted to the simple notion that it was in the trade mark owner's own commercial interests to ensure that he or she continued to exercise effective control over the way in which licensees and franchisees used an important business asset.

INTERNATIONAL PROTECTION

A trade mark registered under the 1994 Act is a strictly territorial right which confers exclusive rights solely within the UK[6]. Other countries follow the same territorial approach to the granting of trade marks with the result that exporters need to make a whole series of national applications before they obtain protection abroad. As a consequence, businesses in the UK are faced with language barriers, procedural delays and multiplying costs if they seek to protect commercially important trade marks in foreign markets. In future, however, businesses seeking protection abroad will be able to take advantage of two important developments which took place in 1996: (1) the introduction of the Community trade mark system; and (2) the coming into force of the Madrid Protocol Concerning the International Registration of Marks.

Community trade mark

Serious discussions on establishing a single Community trade mark began in 1976 but did not reach fruition until the Community Trade Mark

1 TMA 1994, s 28(1).
2 TMA 1994, s 28(4).
3 TMA 1994, s 28(2).
4 TMA 1938, s 28(4). However, initial scutiny of the application to register was the Registrar's only possibility of exercising control over the licensed use of the mark; there was no power to terminate the registration if the licensor failed to ensure that a quality control clause was being observed: see Kerly *The Law of Trade Marks and Trade Names* (12th edn, 1986) para 13-31.
5 *Reform of Trade Marks Law* (Cmnd 1203) (1990) paras 4.34–4.37.
6 TMA 1994, s 9(1).

Regulation was adopted in December 1993[1]. The Regulation[2] has automatic legal effect in the UK[3] and allows applicants to apply for and obtain a single trade mark for goods or services which has equal effect throughout the entire European Community[4]. A Community trade mark is basically governed by the same substantive principles which appear in the Trade Marks Directive.

Applications

Applications for a Community trade mark can either be filed through a national trade mark office (such as the UK Trade Mark Office) or made directly to the Community Trade Mark Office (CTMO) in Alicante, Spain. If the application is made to a national office, it must ensure that the application is forwarded to the CMTO within two weeks[5]. The application is then subjected to substantive examination to check if any of the absolute grounds of refusal apply[6]. The CMTO also carries out a search of prior Community marks to ascertain any potentially conflicting earlier rights which might trigger one of the relative grounds of refusal[7]. At the same time, searches will be carried out by national trade mark offices which have agreed to carry out a search for prior national marks[8].

Opposition

After the search reports have been produced, they are sent to the applicant and the application is then published in the Community Trade Marks Bulletin[9]. The owners of prior Community registrations or applications will also be notified so that they can decide whether to oppose the application[10]. The CTM Regulation does not, however, provide for notification to the owners of prior national rights (eg prior copyright). Owners of prior rights therefore need to check the Community Trade Marks Bulletin regularly if they intend to oppose a Community trade mark application within the prescribed time limit.

Written grounds of opposition must be sent to the CMTO within three months of the application being published in the Bulletin[11]. While the CMTO is empowered to invite the parties to reach a friendly settlement[12], it will reject the application if one of the relative grounds of refusal is satisfied. The CMTO's decision can be appealed provided that a notice of appeal is filed within two months of the date of the decision[13]. Appeals are

---

1 For full discussion of the Community trade mark system, see *Annand and Norman* ch 14.
2 EC Council Regulation 40/94 (OJ L11, 14.1.94, p 1).
3 See also the Community Trade Mark Regulations 1996, SI 1996/1908.
4 CTM Regulation, art 1(2).
5 CTM Regulation, art 25.
6 CTM Regulation, art 38. Absolute grounds of refusal are listed in art 7.
7 For the relative grounds of refusal, see CTM Regulation, art 8.
8 CTM Regulation, art 39.
9 CTM Regulation, arts 39(5) and 40(1).
10 CTM Regulation, art 39(6).
11 CTM Regulation, art 42.
12 CTM Regulation, art 43(4).
13 CTM Regulation, art 59.

decided by a Board of Appeal consisting of three members who are independent of the CMTO[1]. Thereafter a decision is subject to judicial review by the EC's Court of First Instance[2].

Registration

If the CTM application is successful, the mark is registered for a period of ten years and may be renewed for further ten-year periods[3].

Assessment of CTM

The prospect of obtaining a Community trade mark which is valid throughout the EC has attracted a good deal of commercial interest. With over 30,000 applications in its first six months of operation in 1996, the CMTO had to recruit more staff to deal with the backlog which rapidly developed in processing applications[4]. There are, however, substantive drawbacks to the new system. The proposed mark must overcome the various absolute and relative grounds of refusal which may exist at both Community and national level. In other words, the proposed CTM must be acceptable under the domestic law in all member states. If registration is achieved, the CTM is still vulnerable to attack (eg by the owner of prior national rights) which can result in the CTM being lost altogether.

Another disadvantage of the system is that the CTM Regulation leaves the issue of infringement to be decided on by national courts. The infringer's domicile or place of establishment will usually determine the forum for proceedings but the rules do allow for a degree of 'forum shopping'[5]. Owners will therefore need to consider procedural and linguistic difficulties, as well as potential costs, when deciding which forum to choose[6].

The Madrid Protocol

The Madrid Agreement

For various reasons[7], the UK chose to stand outside the arrangements for an International Register of Marks when it was set up under the Madrid Agreement of 1891[8]. The Madrid Agreement allows an applicant who has already registered his or her mark in one of the contracting countries to have the mark put on the International Register maintained by the World

1 CTM Regulation, arts 130 and 131.
2 CTM Regulation, art 63.
3 CTM Regulation, art 46.
4 See [1996] EIPR D-338.
5 See CTM Regulation, arts 93 and 94.
6 See further Michaels *A Practical Guide to Trade Mark Law* (2nd edn, 1996) paras 3.91–3.92.
7 For full discussion of the Madrid Agreement and Protocol systems, see *Annand and Norman* ch 15
8 Subsequently revised on various occasions, the most recent taking place at Stockholm in 1967.

Intellectual Property Organisation (WIPO) in Geneva[1]. A mark placed on the International Register is automatically protected in each other contracting country designated by the applicant[2] unless that country refuses protection under its national law within 12 months[3].

The Protocol to Madrid Agreement

As the DTI White Paper noted, only 29 states were parties to the Madrid Agreement and several of these had minimal trade mark activity[4]. The difficulties which many countries had with the Agreement were ironed out at a diplomatic conference convened by WIPO in 1989. As a result, 28 countries including the UK signed a Protocol to the Agreement which sets up an alternative system for international registration of trade marks. The UK has since ratified the Protocol to the Madrid Agreement and the new registration arrangements came into force on 1 April 1996. It is now possible for someone who has registered or applied for a mark in the UK to apply via the UK Trade Marks Registry or the Community Trade Mark Office for international registration based on the UK mark[5].

Application procedure

The application to WIPO will designate which Madrid Protocol countries should receive the application[6]. After formal examination in Geneva, the application is then sent to the appropriate national offices to be dealt with in the same way as 'home' applications in the relevant country. National trade mark offices have a standard period of 12 months in which to object to an application. The 12-month period can be extended to 18 months (or longer) where the application is opposed by a third party and the contracting state notified WIPO when it signed the Protocol that extensions would be permitted beyond that period[7]. The application is considered separately under the domestic trade mark law of each designated state so that objections in one country do not affect registration in another.

Registration

If the application is successful, the applicant can look forward to receiving a bundle of national registrations. Registration lasts for a period of ten years and is renewed by WIPO for further ten year periods for all the designated states[8]. Should, however, the 'home' application or registration in the UK fail during the first five years, applications or registrations in all the other states fall with it[9]. This process of 'central attack' is not completely fatal as the applicant can opt to convert his or her international

1 Madrid Agreement, art 1
2 Madrid Agreement, art 4.
3 Madrid Agreement, art 5.
4 *Reform of Trade Marks Law* para 5.07.
5 Madrid Protocol, art 2.
6 Madrid Protocol, art 3*bis*.
7 Madrid Protocol, art 5.
8 Madrid Protocol, arts 6 and 7.
9 Madrid Protocol, art 6(3).

application into a series of national applications which will still enjoy the original filing date secured by the 'home' application[1]. The possibility of maintaining a number of national registrations after the 'home' registration has been lost is one of the clear attractions of the Protocol when compared with the 1891 Agreement. The question of infringement under the Protocol system of registration is dealt with under the domestic trade mark law in each contracting state.

Assessment of the Madrid Protocol

The UK ratified the Madrid Protocol in the expectation that participation in the new arrangements could save trade mark owners up to £15 million per annum on the costs of obtaining overseas registrations[2]. Clearly the major benefit of the 'one-stop shop' procedure under the Protocol is that the applicant acquires a number of national registrations through a single application without the disadvantage under the Community trade mark system of losing the entire application because of objections raised in only one contracting state. Moreover, once the initial five-year period has elapsed since the date of international registration, revocation of the mark within the UK does not affect the validity of the mark in other states which have registered it. Again, this stands in contrast to CTM registrations, which can be challenged at any time. On the other hand, the CTM system is open to anyone who is domiciled[3] in a Paris Convention country whereas the Madrid Protocol is a closed system which is only available to nationals of those states which have either ratified the Protocol or the Madrid Agreement.

Bridging the two systems

In an attempt to bridge the two systems, the European Commission has recently proposed that the EC should accede to the Madrid Protocol[4]. If the Council accepts the Commission's proposal, holders of a CTM will be able to secure international registration under the Protocol by filing an application with WIPO. Conversely, those who have secured international registration under the Protocol will be able to apply for CTM registration in order to obtain trade mark protection throughout the entire Community.

The Trade Mark Law Treaty

The Trade Mark Law Treaty was drafted under the auspices of WIPO and was adopted in October 1994[5]. It was initially signed by 35 countries,

---

1 Madrid Protocol, art 9*quinquies*.
2 See *Patent Office Annual Report 1995–96* p 1.
3 Or who has a 'real and effective industrial or commercial establishment': Paris Convention, art 3.
4 See [1996] OJ C293/11 and C300/11.
5 See [1995] EIPR D-24.

including the UK, and is intended to simplify the formalities involved in applying for registration in other contracting states. However, it will be some years yet before the benefits of the Treaty – in terms of reduced bureaucracy and associated costs – will become apparent to businesses in the UK seeking trade mark protection abroad.

Index